International Business

This new edition of *International Business* examines the impact of globalization on key aspects of the business environment. It offers a comprehensive overview of this phenomenon that is altering corporate strategy fundamentally, critiquing the complexities of globalization and its impact on international business.

International Business offers a holistic examination of the processes that influence the evolution of strategy in the modern global economy. It is divided into three sections:

- Impact of globalization: how globalization has driven the processes of regional integration and the emergence of transnational governance structures
- Environmental drivers: how international strategy is shaped and the emergence of internationalised businesses
- Resource issues: what resources can determine success in the global economy or impede firm evolution
- A companion website provides additional material for lecturers and students alike: www.routledge.com/textbooks/9780415437646

Featuring a wealth of new case studies, updated pedagogy and a fresh new design, this new textbook will prove essential reading for all those studying international business.

Debra Johnson is Senior Lecturer at Hull University, UK.

Colin Turner is Senior Lecturer in International Strategic Management at Heriot-Watt University, UK.

International Business

Themes and issues in the modern global economy

2nd edition

Debra Johnson and Colin Turner

Routledge
Taylor & Francis Group

LONDON AND NEW YORK

First published 2003
by Routledge
2 Park Square, Milton Park, Abingdon, Oxon OX14 4RN

Simultaneously published in the USA and Canada
by Routledge
270 Madison Ave, New York, NY 10016

Second edition published 2010

Routledge is an imprint of the Taylor & Francis Group, an Informa business

© 2010 Debra Johnson and Colin Turner

Typeset in Berling by
Keystroke, Tettenhall, Wolverhampton

British Library Cataloguing in Publication Data
A catalogue record for this book is available from the British Library

Library of Congress Cataloguing in Publication Data
  Johnson, Debra, 1957–
  International business / Debra Johnson and Colin Turner.
      p. cm.
    Includes bibliographical references and index.
  1. International business enterprises. I. Turner, Colin. II. Title.
  HD2755.5.J64 2009
  338.8'8—dc22   2009028261

ISBN 10: 0–415–43763–6 (hbk)
ISBN 10: 0–415–43764–4 (pbk)
ISBN 10: 0–203–86161–2 (ebk)

ISBN 13: 978–0–415–43763–9 (hbk)
ISBN 13: 978–0–415–43764–6 (pbk)
ISBN 13: 978–0–203–86161–5 (ebk)

Contents

Contents Outline

List of Case Studies

List of Boxes

List of Figures

List of Tables

Preface

When the possibility of a second edition of this text was first mooted, the world economy was growing healthily and it was 'business as usual'. However, once work began on the text, it became clear that the world economy, and consequently international business, had entered a period of greater turbulence than had been seen for many decades. This made writing the text particularly interesting and challenging as mainstays of the international business world, such as General Motors and Lehmann Brothers among several others, encountered severe, sometimes terminal, problems. We have incorporated some of the turmoil into the text but, at the time of writing, the long-term implications of the financial and economic crisis are unclear. Recent events have certainly shaken strongly held assumptions but they must also be kept in perspective. When caught in the middle of a storm (real or metaphorical), it is often feared that things will never be the same again. However, in time, the familiar often reasserts itself. This will probably be the case with the current economic crisis, albeit perhaps with some changes to the momentum of globalization, attitudes to regulation and the role of the bigger emerging economies.

In short, the economic upheaval that began towards the end of 2007 has had an impact on the international business environment but international business has always been distinctive because of the additional layer of complexity that arises from conducting commercial transactions on a cross-border basis. This feature creates unique challenges in terms of governance of the business environment and the managing of diversity in culture and business practices, and can have a fundamental impact on the decisions made by firms about whether and how to internationalize. This complexity remains. Recent events have, among other things, merely served to confirm this level of complexity.

In this second edition, although as shown below we have given greater emphasis to some factors, the approach remains essentially the same as in the first edition. As with all authors, our slant on international business is deeply rooted in our own specific academic background and preferences. Although there are certain core aspects of the international business curriculum (such as the emphasis on the multinational firm), there is also a great variation in the range of the curriculum and how the subject is dealt with in international business texts. Some of these texts are re-badged economics books; some are purely descriptive and neglect theory; others are essentially strategy books whereas others adopt a regional or functional approach. We have deliberately done none of these.

Many books also reflect their own particular cultural context in terms of content, presentation or both. Although conscious of the fact that we are all creatures of our own cultures, we have tried to be as culturally neutral as possible and to avoid an overly Eurocentric approach. For example, we have attempted to use examples and case studies from across the world. However, we acknowledge that we cannot totally escape our European roots.

Our approach is also rooted in the fundamental belief that business students need an education that, as well as enabling them to develop functional knowledge, skills and understanding, also broadens their outlook in terms of understanding the political, economic and social context of business. In the contemporary world, their horizons needed to broaden to take international issues into account. All too often, the business curriculum is only internationalized in a desultory way, perhaps by the addition of a couple of 'international' sessions at the end of a finance or marketing module. In our view, this is not enough.

We wanted to develop an integrated text in which, although individual chapters can stand alone, there is a common theme underpinning the volume. Our chosen theme for the first edition was globalization and it remains the overarching theme of the second edition. Although there are opposing views about the degree to which globalization exists or whether the world is globalizing or internationalizing, there is at least some consensus that there has been an increase in the degree of economic interdependence during recent decades. This is a useful starting point for debate and study. It is the extent and implications of such interdependence for business that permeates each of the chapters. Moreover, the financial and economic crises have invited speculation about the future of globalization. In addition to globalization, other themes recur throughout the volume. These include issues surrounding development and business; the role of emerging economies; the use of information and knowledge as a key business resource; and corporate responsibility and pressure for an expanded policy agenda for international institutions.

Our intention is that individual chapters should, as far as possible, provide a mix of theory and practice. Theory is important to give students a framework and context for applications and practice and can deepen their understanding of issues. The body of theory chosen is relevant to the subject matter of each chapter but, where appropriate, is linked back to the core concepts of globalization and international integration.

In order to achieve our objective of drawing out the impact of globalizing or internationally integrating forces on economic governance and business and to highlight common themes and linkages, the book itself has been subdivided into three distinct sections dealing with environmental, enterprise and resource issues. However, a new feature of the second edition is an introductory chapter which discusses some of the strategic challenges and concerns that businesses face in an international context. The purpose of this chapter is to act as a reminder that however wide ranging some of the topics in subsequent chapters, it is always important to return to the interaction of these topics with the international firm.

Part I deals with trends and developments in the international economy that shape the business environment and thus the development of corporate strategies and operations. Chapter 2 explores the major trends, drivers and patterns in the international economy and highlights those factors that have led commentators to talk of globalization. In the process, it highlights the main questions posed by globalization and tentatively identifies indicators of globalization and ways in which international economic integration affects business. Chapter 3 deals with regional integration, the rise in which parallels the rise of globalization and which many commentators argue has become a major consideration in the choice of business location. Key themes like whether regional integration is complementary to globalization or is liable to fragment international markets are discussed. Chapter 4 examines the architecture and role of international institutions, the actions of which have a profound effect on the business environment and whose role is profoundly affected by globalization. The chapter also throws the spotlight on frequently heard criticisms of international institutions. Chapter 5 looks at the thorny problem of development and globalization and at differential regional development patterns, identifying those regions that have managed to integrate themselves into world production and trading systems and those that appear marginalized. In the process, it sets out different theoretical explanations of the development process and links development to the growing integration of production networks. The final chapter in this part, Chapter 6, is new and deals with emerging economies, concentrating particularly on the rapid changes in China and India. So much is written about emerging economies, we decided that separate treatment of them was warranted in order to distinguish what makes them 'special' and also to highlight areas in which change is still required. Emerging economies also make an appearance in other chapters in this volume.

Part II focuses on the enterprise within the international context. Chapter 7 is concerned with international trade in both goods and services. Much of the emphasis of this chapter is on international regulation and its implications for these markets. Chapters 8, 9 and 10 represent a significant change to the first edition, where, one chapter focused on the multinational enterprise. Given the central role of the MNE in international business, it was decided to strengthen this part of the volume. Consequently, Chapter 8 deals with international investment and the risks attached to it. Chapter 9 discusses the process of internationalization, whereas Chapter 10 is about entry modes and the structure and organization of MNEs. Chapter 11 is about the often neglected internationalization of small and medium-sized enterprises, particularly from the perspective of international entrepreneurship. Chapter 12 is also new and discusses individual business functions with a view to determining how internationalization affects them. The two final enterprise chapters, Chapters 13 and 14 respectively, cover the cultural and ethical issues that have to be confronted when conducting business across borders. In the second edition, as opposed to the first, these issues receive their own separate treatment in recognition of the increasing attention given to them.

Part III is based on the premise that as firms become more global, or international (depending on one's view of the growing interdependence that is underway), they will increasingly source their needs from more diverse international factor markets. The following chapters not only analyse traditional factors such as capital and labour but also treat information, the environment and natural resources such as energy and water as key production factors. Key issues raised in these chapters range from the ethical (labour and the exploitation of resources) to concerns about the possibility of 'races to the bottom' (labour and the environment again) and the scarcity of resources (the environment and energy). A common theme in each chapter is how these factors of production are feeding into growing pressure for regulation above the level of the nation state and how some of the issues surrounding these factors are contributing to the reconsideration of the configuration of firms' production systems and value chains.

The final chapter briefly draws together recurrent themes and how they relate to international business.

The reader is the best judge of the extent to which we have achieved our objectives. The project turned out to be more ambitious than anticipated but it also confirmed how important it is to encourage the development of an international perspective and to discourage parochialism in business graduates. While it is certainly true that not all business graduates will end up working for multinationals, we do believe that virtually all businesses and their employees these days are affected by international developments, whether it is international regulations or the entry of foreign actors into their domestic market. An international perspective enables businesses, including those with a primary or sole focus on the domestic market, to anticipate such developments and thus respond to them more effectively.

Debra Johnson and Colin Turner,
Hull and Edinburgh, June 2009

List of Abbreviations

ACP	African Caribbean Pacific
ACSM	Agreement on countervailing duties and subsidies measures
AFTA	Asian Free Trade Area
AGOA	Africa Growth and Opportunity Act
APEC	Asia Pacific Economic Cooperation
ASEAN	Association of Southeast Asian Nations
ATC	Agreement on Textiles and Clothing
bcm	Billion cubic metres
b/d	Barrels per day
BIS	Bank for International Settlements
BOO	Build-own-operate
BOOT	Build-own-operate-transfer
BOT	Build-operate-transfer
BPI	Bribe Payers Index
BRIC economies	Brazil, Russia, India and China
BSE	Bovine spongiform encephalopathy
BTU	British thermal unit
C&W	Cable & Wireless
CACM	Central American Common Market
CARICOM	Caribbean Community and Common Market
CBD	Convention on Biological Diversity
CBTPA	Caribbean Basin Trade Partnership Act
CCL	Contingent Credit Line
CIS	Commonwealth of Independent States
CITES	Convention on International Trade in Endangered Species
CPI	Corruption Perceptions Index
CRTA	Committee on Regional Trade Agreements

CSR	Corporate social responsibility
CTE	Committee on Trade and Environment
CU	Customs union
DDA	Doha Development Agenda
DPW	Dubai Ports World
DRC	Democratic Republic of Congo
DSU	Dispute Settlement Understanding
ECT	Energy Charter Treaty
EEC	European Economic Community
EFF	Extended Fund Facility
EFTA	European Free Trade Area
EICC	Electronic Industry Code of Conduct
EKC	Environmental Kuznets Curve
EMIT	Group on Environmental Measures and International Trade
EMS	Environmental management system
EMU	Economic and Monetary Union
EPA	Economic Partnership Agreement
EPZ	Export processing zone
ESH	Environment, safety and health
ESI	Electricity Supply Industry
EU	European Union
FAO	Food and Agricultural Organization
FCPA	Foreign and Corrupt Practices Act
FDI	Foreign Direct Investment
FII	Foreign Indirect Investment
FLA	Fair Labour Association
FSA	Firm specific advantage
FSU	Former Soviet Union
FTA	Free trade area
FTAA	Free Trade Area of the Americas
GATS	General Agreement on Trade in Services
GATT	General Agreement on Tariffs and Trade
GCC	Gulf Co-operation Council
GDP	Gross Domestic Product
GLOBE	Global Leadership and Organizational Behaviour Effectiveness
GM	Genetically modified
GNP	Gross National Product
GPA	Government Procurement Agreement
GSI	Geographical Spread Index
GSP	Generalized System of Preferences
HIPC	Heavily Indebted Poor Countries
HQ	Headquarters
HRM	Human resource management

IAEA	International Atomic Energy Authority
IBRD	International Bank for Reconstruction and Development
ICSID	International Centre for the Settlement of Investment Disputes
ICT	Information and communication technology
IDA	International Development Agency
IEA	International Energy Agency
IFC	International Finance Corporation
IHRM	Intenational human resource management
II	Internationalization Index
IIA	International Investment Agreements
ILO	International Labour Organization
ILSA	Iran Libya Sanctions Act
IMF	International Monetary Fund
IMO	International Maritime Organization
IMS	International Monetary System
IP	Innovation Process
IPR	Intellectual Property Right
ISO	International Organization for Standardization
ITA	Information Technology Agreement
ITO	International Trade Organization
ITU	International Telecommunication Union
LDC	Least developed country
LNG	Liquefied natural gas
LSE	Large-sized enterprise
M&A	Merger and acquisition
MAI	Multilateral Agreement on Investment
MAV	Management audit verification
MEA	Multilateral environmental agreement
MFA	Multi-fibre Arrangement
MFN	Most favoured nation
MIGA	Multilateral Investment Guarantee Agency
MNE	Multinational enterprise
NAALC	North American Agreement on Labour Co-operation
NAFTA	North American Free Trade Area
NAO	National Audit Office
NGO	Non-governmental organization
NICs	Newly industrialized countries
NSI	Network Spread Index
NTB	Non-tariff barrier
NYSE	New York Stock Exchange
OBM	Original brand manufacturing
OECD	Organization for Economic Co-operation and Development
OEM	Original equipment manufacturing

OPEC	Organization of Petroleum Exporting Countries
PPM	Process and production methods
PPP	Polluter pays principle
PTA	Preferential trade agreement
R&D	Research and development
REACH	Registration, evaluation, authorisation and restriction of chemicals
RO	Rules of origin
RTA	Regional trade agreement
SA	Social accountability
SAA	Stability and Association Agreements
SADC	South African Development Community
SAP	Structural Adjustment Programme
SBU	Strategic business unit
SCM	Supply chain management
SDR	Special drawing right
SEA	Single European Act
SEC	Securities and Exchange Commission
SEM	Single European Market
SFO	Serious Fraud Office
SHAPE	Safety, health, attitude, people and environment
SME	Small and medium-sized enterprise
SPS	Sanitary and phytosanitary measures
SRF	Supplementary Reserve Fund
SWF	Sovereign Wealth Fund
TBT	Technical barriers to trade
TMB	Textiles Monitoring Body
TNI	Transnationality Index
TRIMS	Trade-related investment measures
TRIPS	Trade-related intellectual property
UDHR	Universal Declaration of Human Rights
UN	United Nations
UNCTAD	United Nations Conference for Trade and Development
UNDP	United Nations Development Programme
UNEP	United Nations Environmental Programme
UNFCCC	United Nations Framework Convention on Climate Change
USSR	Union of Soviet Socialist Republics
WAEMU	West Africa Economic and Monetary Union
WTO	World Trade Organization
WWF	World Wildlife Fundxxiv

Chapter 1

The Strategic Context of the Shifting International Business Environment

You may not be interested in strategy, but strategy is interested in you.

Leon Trotsky (1879–1940), Russian revolutionary and Marxist theorist

LEARNING OBJECTIVES

This chapter will help you to:

- understand the key dimensions of international strategy
- identify the major forms of international strategy
- comprehend the core internal and external drivers underpinning international strategy
- appreciate the importance of integrating non-market actions in international strategy

The shift from a purely domestic focus to one with a higher degree of internationalization poses many challenges for firms. These arise from two sources. First, the firm can be a passive recipient of such changes. For firms of all sizes and across all industries, it is increasingly difficult to remain isolated from the impact of globalization on their business environment. Second, the firm can be active in seeking out international markets. The latter is very much the focus of this book and is based on the recognition that international strategy is different from purely domestic actions. The move towards a more spatially diverse business configuration increases the complexity of operations and exposes the firm to a new set of challenges. The aim of this chapter is to set the context for the rest of this volume by outlining the core tenets of international strategy. The main focus is on market-based strategies but the chapter concludes with an examination of non-market actions. This latter theme is important, since it highlights the political aspects of developing international actions.

THE FORM AND NATURE OF INTERNATIONAL STRATEGY

The essence of international strategy is based on a firm undertaking and dealing with the consequences of international diversity. This is driven by:

- the globalization of markets;
- firms following customers;
- the desire to overcome limitations of the home market;
- exploitation of differences between countries and regions based on culture, regulation and specific economic factors.

International strategies can also be based on the firm exploiting its strategic capabilities (see below), the internationalization of its value chains and enhancement of its knowledge base.

The most evident expression of international strategy is the expansion of the spatial dimension of the firm. This comprises three core elements:

1. the extension of the geographic reach of the business;
2. the increasing penetration of the MNE in current host economies;
3. integration of the international activities of the firm.

The first element involves extending the geographic boundaries of the firm thereby giving rise to the need for an international strategy as the firm has to deal with a more diverse spread of competitive conditions than it has encountered previously. This does not merely involve competitive strategy but may also include all aspects of the firm's value chain. As later chapters indicate, there is a thriving academic debate on the form and nature of this geographic spread (see Chapter 10). The inference is that over time the firm will gradually extend its geographic reach to as many countries as is feasible given commercial constraints.

The second aspect, market penetration, alludes to the tendency towards greater involvement in states where the firm has already entered or established a presence. This could involve an increase in the number of value-adding activities undertaken within a location or expansion of the number of segments in which the firm is seeking to establish a presence.

The third element of international strategy is based on the integration and coordination of the firm's overseas activities to enhance its competitive position. As later chapters highlight (see esp. Chapter 9), this may occur through exploiting location-bound factors or through ensuring that knowledge generated locally is transferred throughout the rest of the organization for the mutual benefit of its constituent parts.

Overall, thinking about the development of international business characterizes international strategy from three different but overlapping perspectives.

Standardization-adaptation

From this perspective, strategies are differentiated according to the degree of standardization (or adaptation) pursued by the firm. Frequently the degree of standardization is based on one or more of the mix of the marketing elements (price, place, product, promotion). Thus a standardization strategy is characterized by uniformity across locations of the marketing mix whereas adaptation reflects a higher degree of adjustment to local conditions. This perspective focuses on the market offering aspect of international strategy.

Concentration-dispersion

Linked into Porter's notion of international competition (see p. 7), this perspective is concerned with the spatial design of the firm. The core idea is that the firm needs to achieve the optimal spread of activities as a means of achieving competitive advantage. The objective is to achieve synergies across locations and/or to exploit local competitive advantages for the benefit of the firm. As a result, strategies are differentiated according to the degree of concentration or dispersion of activities across the global economy. This perspective focuses on the structural/organizational aspect of international strategy.

Integration-interdependence

This is concerned with the organization and orchestration of the activities of the firm. The central concern is the extent to which subsidiaries are treated as separate profit centres with a high degree of discretion for local managers. At the other end of the spectrum, there is potential for the centre to regard units as part of a broader, overarching strategic objective. Thus strategies are differentiated

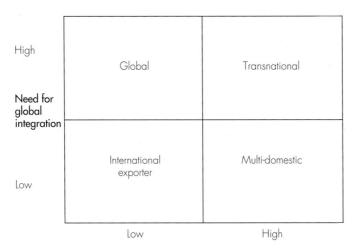

FIGURE 1.1 The Integration/ Responsiveness Framework

Source: Porter (1986).

according to the degree to which integration takes place across multiple locations. This perspective focuses on the competitive aspect of international strategy (see below).

These differing perspectives on the form and nature of international strategy have been used as the basis for the categorization of different strategy types. At the core of the issues underpinning these different categorizations of the form and nature of international strategy is the global–local dilemma which reflects the degree to which products, processes and strategies can be standardized across – or need to be adapted to – local markets. Resolving this dilemma has led to the emergence of a common typology of MNC strategy which is reflected in the integration/responsiveness framework (see Figure 1.1).

The pressure towards global integration highlights the need for – or the desirability of – standardization of the processes and activities across space; and an integrated approach towards strategy and the concentration of activities to support the objectives of the operation. National responsiveness reflects adaptable marketing strategies as well as the need for sufficient discretion to be given to local managers to achieve these objectives. Thus the integration responsiveness framework is entirely consistent with the objectives of the trio of approaches to international strategy outlined above which differ across a number of dimensions (see Figure 1.1).

The International Exporter

Of all the types of strategy and structure, this is mentioned the least, probably because it represents the minimalist international strategy. Indeed, the company may not even think of itself as an international company, as its structure and configuration may be entirely national. Often, the firm will export opportunistically while its domestic customers represent its core market. However, this form of business may be purely transitional: it may move to other forms and structures as it matures and as opportunities for overseas sales and production increase (see Chapter 10).

The Global Company

The global company produces standardized products and a uniform value proposition across multiple markets. The standardization is normally extended to other elements of the marketing mix. Ensuring such uniformity means that these companies are also characterized by integrated structures with only limited discretion afforded to local managers. As a result, most decision making is centralized with strict levels of operational control from the centre. These strategies and structures are common in sectors where economies of scale are available and central to securing competitive positioning. The strategic configuration of the global company is centralized, often upon the home country of the firm (see Case Study 1.1: Ernst and Young).

CASE STUDY 1.1

Ernst & Young

In April 2008, Ernst & Young announced a radical shift in both its structure and strategy by merging its operations in 87 countries into a single unit. This new unit covers Europe, the Middle East, India and Africa, and represents an attempt to overcome the national legal and regulatory hurdles that have hindered its ability to develop a company structure that mirrors the global requirements of their main clients – MNEs. All firms in the professional services industry face a continuing struggle to match the global demand of the industry with the fragmentation created by strict national rules regarding audit and to mitigate the risk that a single catastrophic lawsuit could bring down the entire company.

The unit will be centrally managed and integrated financially with a single profit-sharing scheme and region-wide investment decisions. Thus Ernst & Young will no longer be configured as a series of national partnerships – often difficult to oversee effectively and of differing quality – but will seek to offer a genuine global service. This will mean that strategies will be implemented more effectively and staff moved around more easily.

Traditionally, the large global professional services firms (such as KPMG, PWC and Deloitte as well as Ernst & Young) have operated on a network-based model. Despite a uniform global identity, these networks are based on national partnerships. These partnerships have often struggled to create links between themselves due to the panoply of regulations across the industry. The current structure reflects industry regulation of the ownership of audit firms and a desire by partnerships to limit the liability made by a sister firm. In the past, other audit firms have taken sanctions against rogue partnerships.

However, other professional service firms have found such integration difficult to achieve. It was notable that one of the other 'big four' (KPMG) voted against such a similar move. Indeed many of Ernst & Young's partners had an incentive to vote down the move as they could lose independence and the attractive profit-sharing opportunities creating by the existing arrangements. Partnerships can have strong independent cultures. KPMG tried to merge many of its European operations, only to be voted down by its Dutch partners. However, regulatory changes, most notably within Europe, have facilitated this move. Nevertheless national-based partnerships can be beneficial when problems within a single national operation can be held at arm's length from the other businesses, minimizing the collateral damage to the rest of the group.

CASE STUDY QUESTIONS

1. What are the major advantages of a 'global' structure?

2. Under what circumstances could a global structure be successfully deployed?

3. What other sectors lend themselves to such global structures?

The Multi-domestic Company

This type of structure/strategy formation is characterized by a series of independent subsidiaries within which local managers are given a high degree of discretion over the marketing mix. As a result, strategy is characterized by a high degree of adaptation with operations being country-centred and value propositions determined locally. As a consequence, there is little coordination between strategic business units (SBUs), since there is little overlap between them due to the idiosyncratic nature of the strategy followed within each locality. As a result, most if not all value-adding activities are undertaken within the host economy. This strategy depends upon the firm being able to differentiate the product offering sufficiently on a bespoke basis with few opportunities for economies of scale. This differentiation has to be a sufficient source of competitive advantage to overcome the lack of economies of scale in the production process.

The Transnational Company

The transnational company adopts a form of structure/strategy based on the firm operating as a loose network of businesses. In this approach, the firm moves beyond the conventional trade-off in terms of integration and responsiveness by being locally responsive while allowing for sufficient coordination between SBUs to realize economies of scale and scope. In short, this represents a hybrid strategy between multi-domestic and global strategy. Thus, by capturing knowledge from all parts of the organization network, the transnational company can ensure that it benefits from the experience of others, even if value propositions are not uniform. As a result, the transnational must integrate flows of parts, components, finished goods, funds, skills, intelligence, ideas and knowledge, and other scarce resources. These are shared around the company for the benefit of all subsidiaries.

Much of the literature on international strategy and structure has focused on the extremes of global and multi-domestic strategy. Early advocates of global strategy argued that it would become the dominant form of strategy as globalization created uniformity across markets (see Levitt 1983) and that localized firms would be vulnerable to firms that competed on a global basis. Such views were based on the assumption that the market was characterized by the globalization of consumer preferences and that scale economies were available from production processes. Yip (1989) has argued that there are four major benefits from adopting a global strategy:

1. Economies of scale and replication: these apply not merely to products (which have diminished as s source of advantage over time) but also to the ability to replicate knowledge across units.
2. Economies from international production: these efficiencies are created by integrating operations across space to exploit local competitive advantages that feed into efficiencies in the value chain.
3. Economies of learning: due to the integrated nature of the firm, learning and innovation in one market is transferable to another.
4. Competing strategically: the firm can use its scale to compete more effectively in targeted national markets through, for example, cross-subsidization.

However, pressures still remain for local adaptation, especially as the conditions under which pure globality occurs are rare. Adaptation pressures are created not only by the sustenance of national differences in customer preferences but also by national laws and regulations, location-specific distribution channels and different levels of economic development.

THE ENVIRONMENTAL CONTEXT OF INTERNATIONAL BUSINESS

An assessment of the operating environment of the MNE is core to developing an international strategy. Many of the chapters within this text assess assorted aspects of the political, economic, social and legal considerations that need to be addressed in the development of international strategy. As chapters on the MNE and internationalization indicate, the information sensing undertaken by the MNE to add to its knowledge of markets is central to strategy development. Thus, the starting point for the formation of international strategy is information gathering to improve the firm's knowledge of the international market place.

Turning information gathering into knowledge and into a strategy depends upon assessment of the material gathered. Perhaps the most common framework for analysing such information is Porter's 'Five Forces' framework which facilitates assessment of the competitive environment facing the firm in terms of the following forces:

- The bargaining power of buyers: the firm will need to know how powerful customers are within any market, as this will determine the most appropriate strategy to be followed and will even influence whether entry is desirable. In a global marketplace, buyers have increased choice from an increasingly diverse set of suppliers, thereby eroding further any market power of the enterprise.
- Bargaining power of suppliers: the influence of suppliers will be pivotal, as it will influence not merely the operations of the business but also the extent to which the firm will be able to seek cost advantages from these firms. As suggested above, the power of existing suppliers may be expected to diminish as firms are able to procure from an expanded (and increasingly transparent) supplier base.
- The threat of new entrants: the ability of the targeted segment to attract new entrants is also important, as this will influence longer term sustainability of the chosen position and influence strategy. This reflects the fact that potential competition can influence market positioning and strategy.
- Threat of substitutes: strategy will clearly be influenced by the ability of users to switch between products. In an increasingly transparent, global marketplace it is assumed that consumers have greater awareness of the alternatives to existing offerings and are able to substitute products to minimize customer sacrifice.
- Rivalry: a central tenet of Porterian analysis is that nothing is better for competitiveness than competition itself, though it is evident that entry strategy will be influenced by the intensity of the rivalry within the chosen segment. Again, this stresses that internationalization will increase the population of firms within any given niche, causing adaptation by incumbents in terms of products, pricing and promotion.

While use of the Five Forces is an inexact science, it does highlight the strategic concerns that influence a firm's decision to enter a market and how the firm will try to compete once it is in the market. However, the plethora of concerns that shape the international environment are only indirectly referred to within this framework. For example, political and legal issues often have a direct influence on these forces as they shape the background against which these firms operate. Internationalization increases the rivalry between firms by:

1. lowering seller concentration;
2. increasing the diversity of competition;
3. increasing excess capacity;
4. increasing the bargaining power of suppliers.

The above implies that firms need an initial competitive advantage (see Chapter 9) if they are to mitigate these competitive forces when seeking to enter new locations. Generally, competitive advantages are easier to find in less developed markets where the forces tend to be less intense than in developed states. However, a core weakness of the Five Forces framework when developing international strategy is that it does not directly address cross-border issues.

THE INTERNAL CONTEXT OF STRATEGY

The internal environment for the development of international strategy is shaped by two linked considerations. The first concerns the core tangible and intangible resources that are used to carry out the strategic plan, and the second relates to how the MNE configures and coordinates the value chain to ensure effective operation of the firm across borders. To establish a competitive advantage, resources must be scarce and relevant. To sustain competitive advantage, resources must be characterized by:

- durability;
- lack of transferability;
- lack of replicability.

The simple fact is that physical resources such as capital and finance conform to none of these. As a result, the longer lived source of competitive advantage is based more upon intangible, more especially, human resources. Intangible resources such as technology, reputation and branding can all deliver competitive advantage and can create and sustain a position in the medium to longer term. However, each of these is subject to erosion through assorted processes such as the replication of technology or the erosion of brand. However, a more long-lasting source of advantage are intangible human resources such as embedded skills and know-how.

Organizational capabilities are based on the ability of a firm to undertake a particular activity. These may consist of combining the aforementioned resources to create a source of competitive advantage. However, in order to sustain an advantage, the firm has to possess a distinctive competence that differentiates it from the rest of the marketplace. These core competences make a disproportionate contribution to customer value and operate as the basis for entering new markets. Like resources, these core capabilities are difficult to imitate and are durable sources of advantage for the business.

Many theories of the MNE (see Chapter 9) underline the importance of the internal environment of the firm to yield distinctive resources and competences that enable it to overcome the difficult problem of the liability of foreignness. For many MNEs, the ability to leverage core resources and key capabilities from one market to another forms the basis of international strategy. Thus, great importance is attached to the ability to replicate key capabilities internally in order to make the firm successful within and across host markets.

It is these resources and capabilities and the ability to apply them across multiple markets that is central to a firm creating competitive advantage across international markets. In this context, international markets allow firms to earn a greater return from these resources than would be available if they were limited to the domestic market. However, this element of exploitation of existing resources and capabilities is compounded by the increased capability of the firm to access and develop new resources and capabilities through the market entry process.

THE GLOBALIZATION OF THE VALUE CHAIN

The value chain has been central to assessing the impact of globalization of both industries and firms. The value chain (see Porter 1996) conceptualized the development of products as passing through a chain of activities with each stage increasing the value of the product. Importantly, the accumulation of these sequential activities adds more value to the product than the sum of the added value of the actions. Use of the value chain framework is complementary to the assessment of the internal environment and is based on analysing the operations of the business according to the nine generic primary and supporting activities outlined below.

As suggested, these activities are interdependent: the manner in which one activity is conducted can impact upon the cost and/or effectiveness of another. Thus, for example, higher costs in one part of the value chain may lead to cost reductions elsewhere in the operations of the business as the firm seeks to mitigate such effects through increased efficiency. These linkages are not merely internal to the firm but include connections with third party suppliers and buyers. This reflects the fact that the firm's value chain is part of a larger value system. Porter (1986) argues that the nature of the value chain reflects the chosen competitive scope of the firm which is based on:

- the number of segments served;
- the range of industries served;
- the vertical scope of the firm;
- geographical scope.

The above are important, as they shape the configuration of the value chain; how and where each activity is performed and how and where different units undertake these activities.

Porter (1986) stressed that a core component of international strategy is how the firm decides to spread activities within the value chain across all locations. Generally, downstream activities (i.e.

those that are more related to the end user) are normally focused upon the locality where the buyer is located. Upstream activities, as well as support activities, can usually be divorced from this perceived necessity. Such differentiation between activities is important, as it implies that downstream activities create and rely upon competitive advantages that are normally country specific, whereas upstream activities tend to take place in the entire range of states where the firm competes. Furthermore, multi-domesticity will tend to be more common where downstream activities are central to competitive advantage. If upstream activities are more important, then global strategy is more common. Consequently, Porter (1986) identifies two dimensions of international competition:

1. Configuration: that is, where a firm locates particular value-adding activities across the global economy.
2. Coordination: that is, how geographically dispersed activities are coordinated with each other.

Across both primary (i.e. the main operational aspects of the business) and secondary (i.e. those activities that facilitate the primary actions) activities, the impact of globalization through coordination and coordination can be affected in many ways (see below).

Primary Activities

- Inbound logistics: depending on the dispersal of inputs and where the main operations are undertaken, inbound logistics becomes ever more important. With a more dispersed network of suppliers, coordination is needed to ensure that logistics delivers the appropriate inventory at the right price. The quality of transnational infrastructure and competition in the supply of logistics services also becomes an important determinant of how this activity can shape competitive advantage.
- Operations: in a global economy, firms face decisions regarding where to locate production and may split operations according to the competitive advantage of states. For example, where labour is an important input, the firm may relocate to areas where this resource is abundant. The firm may also segment the operations of the business to exploit local advantages. This creates a need for effective coordination within a network of plants.
- Outbound logistics: the need for partially completed products to be transferred to other plants, as well as the need for completed products to reach increasingly transnational buyers, requires an effective and timely logistical system which needs to reach all markets and to ensure that the inventory of all parts of the firm's operations are met.
- Marketing and sales: the firm must choose what products to sell and where. This requires assessment of the degree of coordination needed in terms of branding, accounts and pricing.
- Service: decisions have to be taken as to where and how customers are serviced. Should they be serviced locally or can the process be centralized? There has been a trend (via outsourcing) to disperse aspects of the service operation to locations such as India. This has been facilitated by new technology.

Supporting Activities

■ Firm infrastructure: with the aid of new technology, activities such as accounting, legal management and so on have become increasingly dispersed throughout the global economy. For example, data inputting has been outsourced to remote locations and the advent of video conferencing allows all managers to undertake coordinated management roles.

■ Human resource management: the pool of resources upon which the enterprise draws to undertake its activities is broadened by the process of globalization. This refers not merely to activities at the local level but to the expansion of the pool of potential top managers. This shift in configuration creates a need for coordination of these labour resources to ensure they are complementary to the firm's objectives.

■ Technology development: the process of research and development becomes more dispersed as the firm seeks to develop a number of centres to undertake this activity to exploit local advantages. This new configuration requires the coordination of such efforts to avoid overlap and to ensure ideas are exchanged between different subsidiary units.

■ Procurement: a major impact of the globalization process has been widening the choice of where to source inputs. As a result, location of the purchasing function is diversified. This requires coordination of purchases common to all units, and to ensure that different suppliers in different locations are managed effectively.

The above underlines that competitive advantage can be sourced from the manner in which activities are configured and coordinated across locations. The firm faces a choice of whether to centralize or

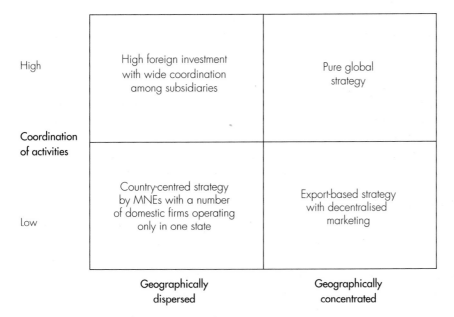

FIGURE 1.2 The Configuration/Coordination Matrix

Source: Porter (1996).

localize these activities as a means of creating competitive advantage. As already mentioned, such choices reflect the activity and whether it is upstream or downstream. The more dispersed the firm becomes and the more sourcing opportunities become available, so the opportunity for cross-border activity increases. Porter (1986) argues that the interaction between coordination and configuration creates the opportunity for the firm to develop its preferred type of strategy (see Figure 1.2). Thus, as mentioned above, global strategy is possible only when a specific set of conditions are in place. In other cases, different degrees of adaptation to local conditions will occur.

NON-MARKET STRATEGIES

The existence of non-market strategies reflects the need for firms to engage with non-market components in the international business environment. The non-market environment comprises the social, political and legal structures that shape interactions both within and outside markets. As such, non-market transactions cover those interactions that the firm undertakes with:

- individuals;
- interest groups;
- government entities.

These actions are guided not by the market but by public and private institutions. Strategy reflects the reality that markets exist within a political and legal context which the firm seeks to influence as a means of supporting and enhancing its competitive positioning.

Non-market strategies may be voluntary or involuntary. Throughout this text, there are numerous references to codes of conduct and regulations with which firms work when establishing their broad strategic direction. A clear implication of the internationalization of business is that the non-market environment has grown increasingly complex as the number of host economies within which an MNE operates grows. However, as later chapters highlight, the non-market environment of international business has not been unaffected by the process of globalization. This is highlighted by the emergence of transnational governance structures and of national and non-governmental bodies that reflect the broad range of issues affected by this process.

According to Baron (2006), the non-market environment is characterized by the following:

- Issues: these are the basis of non-market strategies and tend to be industry specific (e.g. environmental regulations). Issues are specific occurrences that have the potential to impact upon the performance of the business and can operate as a constraint upon managerial discretion and their ability to adapt to shifts in their environment.
- Interests: these are all the parties that have a stake in or a preference about the issue. This includes not merely the firm (and other commercial entities affected by the issue) but also activists, pressure groups and the public.
- Institutions: these exist as the forum within which the issue will be addressed. Typically, this will include governmental and non-governmental entities.
- Information: this relates to what interested parties know or believe about the issues and forces affecting their development.

Across all industries, these components interact to shape the non-market environment. The nature of the interaction between these components varies from issue to issue. In the modern global economy, interaction, interdependence and integration between national economies often create overlap between policy domains (as highlighted most evidently by the environmental debate).

The salience of non-market factors to MNEs has been highlighted by the emergence of issues such as environmental protection, labour policy, trade policy, competition policy, human rights, and corporate social responsibility. This non-exhaustive list highlights issues that are of sufficient importance that their management and control can have significant consequences for managerial discretion and MNE performance. They create a desire for firms to influence the development of such issues to ensure they are compatible with management objectives. The response to particular issues will be proportionate to the effect of the issue upon the firm. This underlines the interrelatedness between market and non-market strategies. Indeed, the existence of externalities indicates that an MNE's market activities can generate non-market issues and change within the non-market environment. This can stimulate a reaction from non-market forces to which the MNE has to react and/or adapt.

Clearly, there exist channels of mutual influence between market and non-market environments. As a result, just like its market equivalent, the non-market is characterized by competition. This competition is characterized by interaction between political entities seeking influence to ensure that their perspective on an issue prevails. Such competition is overseen and managed by public and private institutions such as legislatures, courts, regulatory agencies and public opinion. Thus the non-market environment is responsive to the strategies of firms and other stakeholders.

Shifts within the non-market environment arise from both internal and external sources. Baron (1995) identifies five sources for such changes:

1. Scientific discovery and technological advancement: this can produce fundamental changes within both market and non-market environments. In the latter, awareness of new technologies can spawn legislation and new controls upon business activities. As new technologies evolve, so a series of non-market issues often emerge. For example, globalization has spawned a series of moral and ethical issues (many of which are highlighted within Chapter 14).
2. New understandings: increased public understanding of new issues can result in pressure for change in the corporate sector. For example, pressure for US firms to disinvest from Sudan came from concerted pressure group activity.
3. Institutional change: legal decisions, shifts in government policy, regulation or market pressures can also affect the non-market environment. For example, court decisions regarding promotion or product safety can shape actions undertaken by the firm.
4. Interest group activity: interest groups are involved in lobbying political and public bodies to draw attention either to their members' interests or to specific issues. The effectiveness of such actions is judged in terms of increasing awareness among the public or in generating change in legislation.
5. Moral concerns: public opinion over specific issues (such as privacy or the use of child labour) can generate a moral climate whereby specific corporate actions may be deemed inappropriate or even outlawed.

Given the many and diverse interests inherent within the dynamics of the non-market environment, there is a significant incentive for firms to make this aspect of their activities more predictable. This requires a proactive non-market strategy whereby the firm attempts to manage issues. For some businesses, maintaining a full-time proactive strategy can be prohibitive and reactive strategies may have to be followed.

The more market opportunities are created by government, the more salient non-market strategies become. In a global economy of nation states, host governments are able to exert some degree of control over their own market environment, though, as mentioned, this action has an increased transnational dimension. However, these trends mean that governments can create market opportunities for MNEs. Such opportunities can also be created by private politics and moral concerns (see Chapter 14). This underlines the integrated nature of international strategy and the need for market-driven actions to be complemented and supported by a series of non-market actions.

In terms of the frameworks offered for the market-based international strategy identified above, it is apparent that the market environment can be influenced by the non-market environment. Porter's Five Forces can all be directly and indirectly influenced by the non-market environment via pressure from consumers, suppliers, rivals, substitutes and barriers to entry, as can the value of resources. In addition, the ability to configure and coordinate across borders is also influenced by non-market issues. Indeed, Baron (2006) maintains that non-market strategies can also be delineated along the same lines identified by Bartlett and Ghoshal (1989):

- Global non-market strategies: these involve issues where the firm applies universal principles across all locations, including trade and ethical stances.
- International non-market strategies: this is where parent company experience is transferred and adapted across markets.
- Multi-domestic non-market strategies: this is based on issue-specific actions that are tailored to individual states.

THE INTEGRATED NATURE OF INTERNATIONAL STRATEGY

International strategy reflects a need for market and non-market aspects to be mutually supportive. It is clear that while an effective market strategy is necessary for successful performance, a non-market strategy is rarely sufficient on its own. As much as market strategies respond to opportunities, non-market strategies are needed to monitor and influence the political processes through which such opportunities emerge. Thus performance depends on the mutually supportive nature of market and non-market strategies given there are evident synergies between these two sets of actions, as both are geared to improving enterprise performance.

Exploiting the synergies between the twin planks of strategy is to include both in the process of strategy formation. Thus, when entering host economies, the interaction between market and non-market actions needs to be accounted for in the positioning of the business. This requires a firm to take both market and non-market positions. The latter reflects a deliberate choice of specific issues that influence performance within and across host market economies. Such actions are geared not merely to sustain market position but also to sustain the legitimacy of the MNE in those locations within which it operates. As such, they determine the nature of the relationships that the firm will forge with non-market actors in these locations.

As highlighted in later chapters, non-market positioning can have a direct bearing on market strategies through, for example, an MNE's position on issues such as the environment relating to its corporate social responsibility which will impact on to its mission statement. Differentiation extends into non-market environments and can even be leveraged back in some cases to underpin market positioning. For example, as the environment has become of greater public concern, so many MNEs have placed this issue at the heart of their strategy. A very obvious example of this is General Electric, which is seeking to become the market leader in environmental technology.

As with the resource-based view of international strategy, non-market strategy also reflects the skills and competences possessed by the firm and its ability to secure positioning. Effective non-market strategy depends upon the firm possessing inimitable and difficult-to-replicate skills in areas of non-market interaction. This may include several classes of action:

- expertise in dealing with the media, the public, government, interest and activist groups;
- knowledge of the processes and procedures of the institutions where issues are resolved;
- a reputation for responsible actions.

Where these skills are absent, the firm can outsource this aspect of the work to other parties such as lobbyists. In addition, the MNE may use networks (such as trade bodies) to combine competences to create a more effective and influential non-market body.

CONCLUSION

The internationalization of firms has generated both adaptive and reactive behaviour. The most evident impact has been upon the intensity of competition faced by firms. However, all elements of the value chain have been affected by these broad environmental changes. For firms, this means they have to reconsider the form and nature of their strategic position as well as the sources of competitive advantage and to attain a new fit with the shifting environment within which they operate. This involves both an assessment of the external environment and of those internal drivers that form and shape competitive advantage. There is an increasing sense that in a more complex environment made up of a multitude of political institutions, there is a need to consider the non-market determinants of corporate strategy. This implies that non-market actions need to be integrated into market-based activities to create an integrated, holistic international strategy.

Summary of Key Concepts

- International strategy reflects decisions by MNEs regarding the degree of global integration versus national responsiveness.
- Global, multi-domestic and transnational strategies are the major forms of international strategy.
- The choice of strategy reflects the internal and external drivers faced by the MNE.
- MNEs need to integrate non-market activities into their international strategies.

Activities and Discussion Questions

■ Using a company with which you are familiar, attempt to determine the form and type of international strategy followed.

■ Identify how non-market drivers can influence the form of international strategy.

■ How best do you believe firms can seek to influence the non-market environment?

■ Explore the major debates surrounding the decision by MNEs to geographically disperse their value chains.

References and Suggestions for Further Reading

Baron, D. (1995) 'Integrated strategy: market and non-market components', *California Management Review*, Vol. 37, No. 2, 47–65.

Baron, D. (2006) *Business and Its Environment*, 5th edn, London: Pearson.

Bartlett, C. and Ghoshal, S. (1989) 'Organizing for worldwide effectiveness: the transnational solution, *California Management Review*, Vol. 31, No. 1, 54–74.

Douglas, S. and Wind, Y. (1987) 'The myth of globalization', *Columbia Journal of World Business*, Vol. 22, No. 4, 19–29.

Kogut, B. (1985) 'Designing global strategies: profiting from operational flexibility', *Sloan Management Review*, Vol. 27, No. 1, 27–38.

Levitt, T. (1983) 'The globalization of markets', *Harvard Business Review*, Vol. 61, 92–102.

Porter, M.E. (1986) 'Competition in global industries: a conceptual framework', in Porter, M. E. (ed.), *Competition in Global Industries*, New York: Free Press, pp. 15–60.

Porter, M.E. (1996) 'What is strategy?', *Harvard Business Review*, November–December, 61–78.

Yip, G.S. (1989), 'Global strategy . . . in a world of nations?', *Sloan Management Review*, Vol. 31, No. 1, 29–41.

Part I

Globalization and the Context of International Business

The degree to which business is internationalized is a function of changes and developments in the world economy. Central to these developments in recent years is the process of globalization or increased global interdependence which many allege took place in the closing decades of the twentieth century. The globalization process is pervasive and provides the backdrop for many of the issues and ideas discussed throughout this volume. Not only globalization but also issues of the governance of international business and development, raised initially in this first part, recur in later chapters.

The opening chapter of this section discusses the characteristics of globalization, introduces various arguments about the uniqueness or otherwise of current trends and sets out some preliminary indicators that help assess the degree to which globalization has taken place. The remaining chapters are important in their own right and are also presented in connection with their relationship to globalization. For example, regional integration has accelerated in recent years, a development that has significant implications for the regulation and governance of international business, trade and investment. It is legitimate to ask the question whether the renewed impetus towards regional integration complements the increasing integration at international level or whether it is a reaction to it. Even if the former is the case, it is possible that enhanced regional integration could still facilitate fragmentation of the marketplace if globalization begins to unravel.

Globalization has also provided new challenges for the world's international economic institutions such as the World Trade Organization (WTO), the World Bank and the International Monetary Fund. The establishment of the WTO in 1995 represented a more extensive and legally grounded international trading system. The pressures of globalization imply a need for an even greater shift of regulation and powers to international institutions. Anti-globalization protestors single out international institutions as the servants of international business and the cause of many of the world's ills. Many of these ills are said to reside in the developing world which, according to globalization critics, is excluded from any benefits of greater international integration and, at worst, exploited for the benefit of wealthier countries. Such debates feed into issues on economic development and highlight some of the complexity of the arguments and theories surrounding development, and identify how the development, process interacts with international business activity. In this context, the final chapter of this section looks at the emerging economies of Brazil, Russia, India and China, and highlights how these states have come to challenge the global hegemony and alter international business into the twenty-first century.

Chapter 2

Globalization and the Changing Business Environment

I think he bought his doublet in Italy, his round hose in France, his bonnet in Germany, and his behaviour everywhere.

William Shakespeare, *Merchant of Venice*, 1596–8, Act 1, Scene 2, line 78

LEARNING OBJECTIVES

This chapter will help you to:

- define and distinguish between globalization and internationalization
- identify and appraise the main drivers behind globalization
- describe the extent of and limits to globalization
- assess the controversies surrounding globalization
- identify how the interaction between business and globalization works (you will have a much fuller view by the time you have worked your way through this book)

Towards the end of the twentieth century, it became apparent that fundamental changes were afoot in the world economy that profoundly affected business, politics, society, citizens and the ways in which various stakeholders interacted with each other. This process became known as 'globalization' – a frequently overused and contested term that came to mean all that was good or bad in the world economy. For those who welcomed the supremacy of markets and economic liberalism, globalization offered the possibility of boundless growth and prosperity, not only for developed countries but also for those developing countries brave enough to embrace rather than resist globalization in all its manifestations. For others, globalization threatened rising inequality, economic anarchy and a surrender of political control. In developed countries, job losses and the unravelling of social progress were anticipated as a result of greater competition from low-cost countries whereas developing countries feared that their former colonial subjugation had been replaced by the dominance of market forces and its agents in the form of multinational enterprises (see Chapter 5).

The focus of this volume is on the implications of globalization for international business. The primary purpose of this chapter is to establish a context and platform for subsequent chapters. It begins with an exploration of the concept of globalization and a discussion of some of the key drivers in the process. The analysis then highlights the main debates surrounding globalization, before attempting to measure key indicators of globalization with a view to linking the theoretical debate about globalization with what is actually happening in the world economy and the international business environment. It concludes with preliminary thoughts about how globalization has changed the way business operates before considering whether globalization processes are currently being undermined.

WHAT IS GLOBALIZATION?

Globalization is a complex phenomenon, contested in terms of its definition, extent and implications and therefore in terms of the most appropriate response to it. Economists, political scientists, sociologists, anthropologists and lawyers, among others, have all debated the meaning of the term within the context of their respective academic disciplines.

Definitions of globalization vary and highlight different aspects of the globalization process. Some highlight the compression of space and time resulting from enhanced information and communications technologies. Others speak of the homogenization of markets and cultures or of increased interconnectivity and integration into a single economic unit without barriers to trade. Others focus on the firm, speaking of enterprises that operate on a global scale with manufacturing taking place in several countries or, more precisely, of firms demonstrating a high degree of functional integration across internationally dispersed economic activities. In short, globalization is a multidimensional phenomenon, making it difficult to reach a commonly agreed definition with consensus around the weighting that should be given to specific factors. A useful starting point, however, is a definition which appeared in the IMF's World Economic Outlook in the mid-1990s, which defined globalization as:

> the growing interdependence of countries world-wide through the increasing volume and variety of cross-border transactions in goods and services and of international capital flows, and also through the more rapid and widespread diffusion of technology.

This definition is a useful starting point, highlighting interdependence, the increasing number and range of cross-border transactions and the important role played by technology. In order to understand globalization in terms of its deeper meaning and significance (or at least in terms of its implications for economic governance and business), it is essential to analyse the key, closely linked drivers behind the globalization process.

Globalization Driver One: The Changing Economic Paradigm – from Demand Management to Neo-liberalism

The growing interdependence of economies referred to in the above definition of globalization has only taken place because of the growing acceptance of economic liberalism as the preferred method of 'managing economies'. Indeed, the idea of managing economies is a contradiction in terms in the context of neo-liberalism, an approach based on limiting the role of government to the provision of an environment in which businesses can flourish and which relies heavily on unleashing the forces of competition.

Liberal economic ideas initially took root in external economic policy. The philosophy of the General Agreement on Tariff and Trade (GATT) set up in the aftermath of the Second World War was essentially liberal. GATT's objective was the progressive reduction of tariff barriers, a reaction to the damaging protectionist spiral that had occurred in the 1930s. GATT met with some success: in 1950, the weighted average tariffs in Germany, the UK and the US, for example, were 26 per cent, 23 per cent and 18 per cent respectively. Following the Uruguay Round, the last completed round of multilateral trade talks, the weighted average tariff in advanced industrialized countries was less than 4 per cent. As tariff removal gained ground, the removal of non-tariff barriers to trade became increasingly important within GATT and its successor organization, the WTO.

Composed solely of developed countries upon its formation, membership of the GATT/WTO subsequently expanded to include many countries to which GATT's philosophy had previously been alien. For example, during the 1990s, many former communist countries acknowledged the benefits of free trade by applying for membership. In December 2001, the landmark accession of communist China to this arch neo-liberal international economic organization took place. Ukraine followed suit in May 2008. Algeria, which had long maintained a detached role in the international economic arena and exercised extensive state control over its domestic economy, is also in line for WTO membership. Russian negotiations for membership have been ongoing for many years and, although at times Russian accession seems to move nearer, more often than not there is stalemate between the two sides.

By the end of the 1970s, liberal economic ideas had begun to permeate thinking about domestic economic policy management. During the 1950s and 1960s, the prevailing orthodoxy was based on Keynesian economics, particularly the belief that by managing demand, governments could exercise significant control over their economies. However, the international economics troubles of the 1970s challenged many basic assumptions about economic policy. Not surprisingly, the shift in policy occurred first in the United States, where the idea of competitive capitalism was strongest. Its main proponent was President Ronald Reagan whose primary domestic mission was to roll back the frontiers of the state. Indeed, the term 'Reaganomics' was invented to describe his programme of free market economics. Closely allied to this thinking and practice was the UK government of Margaret Thatcher which came to office in 1979. Thatcherism swept away many economic sacred cows to such an extent that the Labour government elected in 1997 took as given many of the reforms that had been introduced so controversially in the 1980s. Although liberal economic thinking caught on most quickly and extensively in the US and the UK, it also started to influence economic policy in the rest of the developed world, albeit adapted to the specific political and cultural context of individual countries. By the mid-1980s, for example, liberalism had become so pervasive that it formed the basis of the European Union's (EU) transformational single market programme.

Acceptance of free market ideology quickly spread beyond the advanced industrialized world. Countries like Hong Kong, Taiwan, Singapore and South Korea had long accepted the benefits of openness in external economic policy and had followed a development path of export promotion that took advantage of engagement with the global economy (see Chapter 5). However, this development also tended to be accompanied by extensive state direction and guidance of their economies – a grip that began to loosen somewhat towards the end of the twentieth century. Ideas about free trade and the introduction of liberal economic policies in the form of deregulation, privatization and a generally reduced role for the state began to be introduced, to varying degrees, in Latin America, parts of Africa and other parts of Asia (see Chapter 5). Economic liberalism rapidly replaced communism following the fall of the Berlin Wall in 1989 and the disintegration of the Soviet Union in 1991. Most noteworthy of all has been the phased introduction of the market into China, the hitherto 'sleeping economic giant' of Asia: this process began in the early 1980s and has occurred without the dismantling of the state and party apparatus that occurred in the former Soviet Union (see Chapter 6). Since the early 1990s, India, too, has embarked upon the path of reducing the role of the state and liberalizing markets (see Chapter 6).

The extension of competitive liberalism into domestic economic policy has increased the complexity of interdependence and deepened the globalization that has taken place with significant implications for corporate strategies and behaviour (see Chapter 1). At one level, changing regulations and attitudes create additional and more secure investment opportunities, not only through traditional market entry modes like mergers and acquisitions and joint ventures (see Chapter 10) but also increasingly through participation in privatization programmes in developed countries, newly industrialized economies, transitional economies and in many developing countries. At a deeper level, the greater openness arising from the spread of liberal ideas and policies encourages the emergence of a mindset and a strategy that operates beyond traditional national market boundaries.

In 2008, the WTO continued to experience severe difficulties in reaching agreement on the Doha Agenda. The ramifications of this are not yet fully understood. On the one hand, failure to reach agreement on further trade liberalization could be seen as a rejection of years of the opening of markets. On the other hand, this failure is, to a large extent, attributable to the sustained assertion of their interests by emerging economies for the first time. If this turns out to be the case, the stalled talks may represent a reworking or even a relaunch of a liberal international trading system rather than its demise (see Chapter 4).

Globalization Driver Two: The Spread of International Governance and Regulation

As legal barriers to trade and investment fell into line with growing economic liberalism, it became progressively easier and more attractive for companies to trade and invest across borders, and questions were asked about the most appropriate location of policies to regulate the business environment. These questions were levelled not only at conventional matters of external commercial policy, such as trade, but to issues like technical standards, competition policy and labour standards – that is, to topics traditionally regarded as matters for domestic policy. From the perspective of MNEs wishing to operate seamlessly across borders, it is time-consuming and costly to adapt their products and processes to different national regulations and much more efficient to comply with one set of rules agreed at a supranational level – whether regionally or globally.

The shift from what Prakash and Hart (2000) term 'shallow' integration (trade-led integration brought about by tariff reductions) to deep integration (the need to harmonize or at least approximate domestic regulations) has not progressed as far at international as it has at regional level. In the case of the EU, which has experienced the deepest integration of all regional organizations, much of what is perceived as domestic policy, at least in market regulation terms, has already shifted from the nation state to the regional level by way of the Single European Market (SEM). However, as subsequent chapters demonstrate, the pressures for deep integration are present in several policy areas at international level (see Chapter 4).

In part, this upward policy shift is a manifestation of the globalization trend and originated with the progressive reduction of tariff barriers among GATT contracting partners and later among WTO members. As integration through trade developed, other barriers to integration were thrown into the regulatory spotlight, resulting in the emergence of a trade agenda with both a broader (for example, the Uruguay Round incorporated agriculture and services trade) and a deeper scope. Technological developments, particularly developments in ICT and the emergence of e-commerce, have also posed new challenges to traditional governance structures.

Moreover, the spectre of a shift to a higher level of governance on a number of erstwhile domestic issues has strengthened the argument that integrative trends are blurring national boundaries and eroding the sovereignty of nation states. Perspectives on desirable or likely outcomes vary, resulting in a number of complex questions. The answers to these questions are of the utmost importance to business, given that governance structures scope out the regulatory framework in which businesses operate and hence shape their operating environment and the strategic options available to them. These questions, many of which are addressed in Chapter 4 in particular and throughout this volume, include:

- Is there a case, particularly given the emerging international regulatory gap, for greater global self-regulation?

- Is the world moving towards a system of multi-level governance in which national, regional and international interests work together to perform tasks traditionally performed by nation states?
- Does the tendency to shift part of the public policy agenda to an international level represent the deathknell of national sovereignty or a redefinition of sovereignty that will enable greater regulation of the activities of MNEs?
- Is the demise of the nation state exaggerated, given that the emerging multilateral international governance system is not supranational and is based on the nation state?

Globalization Driver Three: Finance and Capital Spread

The additional trade and investment generated by globalization requires parallel movements of capital and finance (see Chapter 17). Deregulation, liberalization and technological change have combined in recent decades to transform the finance sector to support the growing number of transnational transactions. Finance was traditionally always a heavily regulated, and hence fragmented, activity geographically, but change began in the 1960s with the emergence of the Eurodollar markets (markets in dollars held outside the US banking system and control). A series of US reforms in the 1970s made it easier for US banks to operate abroad and for foreign banks to gain access to the US banking market. In 1975, the New York Stock Exchange abolished fixed commissions on dealing in securities, and subsequent reforms of the US financial system have enabled banks to offer a much wider range of financial services. In the UK, the 'Big Bang' of 1986 ended the demarcation between banks and securities houses and allowed foreign firms entry to the stock exchange. Other European exchanges have undergone similar reforms. Within the broader context of the SEM, policies like the Second Banking Directive created the possibility of banks operating throughout the EU on the basis of a so-called 'single banking licence'. A key component of the SEM was the removal of the remaining controls on capital movements within the EU. Without such a measure, the additional trade, investment and industrial restructuring resulting from the creation of the SEM would not have been possible.

On a multilateral level, negotiations on the liberalization of financial services continued after the end of the Uruguay Round, resulting in the 1997 Financial Services Agreement according to which binding commitments were made to provide non-discriminatory national treatment and market access in financial services to firms from other WTO members. Work continues to liberalize trade in financial services further on a multilateral basis.

The combination of more open markets with the adoption of new information and communications technologies (ICTs) has transformed international capital movements. In principle, capital can now be transferred around the world in an instant. In practice, although significantly reduced, regulatory barriers continue to prevent the full collapse of time and space for financial transactions. However, the potential for instantaneous financial transactions spanning the globe remains and is moving nearer to realization.

These developments have also increased both the complexity and volatility of international financial markets (see Chapter 17). A range of new financial instruments, many inherently volatile such as derivatives, has emerged to serve a broader marketplace. Although more mobile capital is clearly needed to support a more integrated international economic system and all parts of the production chain within multinationals, this mobility also brings with it more volatility. Individuals and institutions, for example, are able to transfer vast amounts rapidly around the globe to arbitrage between exchange and interest rates. Such movements can intensify crises and transmit crises from country to country, or even from region to region. The 1997 Asian financial crisis was a prime example of contagion in an interdependent world.

A further consequence of these trends is a weakening of the link between currencies and their traditional locations – the nation state – and the multiplication of forms of money. The former trend is particularly marked for the US dollar, which has become the currency of choice in a number of Latin American countries and elsewhere. Indeed, there are as many dollars in circulation outside as there are inside the United States. The birth of the Euro on 1 January 1999 also reflected a movement away from the strong identification of currency with national territory and heralded the demise of such prominent currencies as the German mark, the French franc, the Italian lira and the Spanish peseta. The possibility of further regional currencies, albeit unlikely in the short term, cannot be ruled out. The link between national territories and means of payment is also further weakened by the cross-border use of credit cards and discussions about digital currencies within the context of the growth of electronic commerce.

Globalization Driver Four: The Diffusion of Information and Communications Technology

Technological innovation and its diffusion have clearly played a significant role in the redefinition and reorganization of commercial and economic space known as 'globalization' by facilitating restructuring of the manufacturing system and transforming the configuration of value chains, and by lowering the cost of and speeding up transportation and communication. Indeed, for companies in many sectors the development of new technology and/or its exploitation makes the difference between success and failure. This is increasingly the case not only in explicitly technological sectors but also, with the advent of e-commerce (see Chapter 18), in traditionally less technologically sensitive sectors such as retailing.

However, technology's precise significance in the globalization process is a subject of some controversy. Technological determinists such as Kevin Kelly (1999) argue that technology is the prime mover of change and that it makes globalization inevitable and irreversible. A more eclectic approach maintains that technological developments, although central to the transformation of intra- and inter-state and enterprise relationships, are not sufficient to bring about such change on their own account. Other social, political and economic factors, such as the spread of neo-liberal economic philosophy with its themes of liberalization, deregulation and open markets, are also needed. In other words, technology is an important facilitator of change rather than its primary mover.

Even without the more extravagant claims for technology, it is possible to identify far-reaching effects of its diffusion. Transportation and telecommunications technologies have transformed space–time distances, reducing the effective economic distance among nations and organizations. Transportation technologies are concerned with the carriage of goods and people and, through progress from horsepower, sail and steam to the internal combustion engine and the jet engine, have significantly reduced the time taken to travel large distances. From 1500 to the mid-nineteenth century, average travel times using horse-drawn carriages and sailing ships were about 10 mph. In the mid-nineteenth century, steam trains and steamships operated at an average of 65 mph and 35 mph respectively. The advent of jet aircraft in the 1960s meant that the transport of people and of high-value, low-volume goods at 500–700 mph became possible. These faster transportation times have lowered a significant barrier to trade and have helped reduce the lead time between placing an order and the delivery of the goods ordered. This is particularly important in relation to just-in-time management and to trade in goods which are reactive to changes in fashion and consumer tastes, and has contributed to trade growth.

Given the fall in tariffs since the formation of the WTO, aggregate transport costs can be several times higher than tariffs. Reductions in transport costs are therefore good for trade. In the second half of the twentieth century, the trend for transport costs in all modes has been down, reinforcing the globalization trend. Higher fuel costs in the early part of the twenty-first century have undermined this trend somewhat (see Chapter 19).

Communications technology, increasingly converging with computer technologies into ICTs, has resulted in the virtually instantaneous transfer of data and information throughout the world. Such technology has resulted in lower transaction and operational costs. In 1930, the cost of a three-minute telephone call between New York and London at 1990 prices was almost $250. By 1990, the equivalent cost was 75 cents. The value of telecommunications has also risen as a result of the increase in the size of the network. Greater diffusion of network services and increasing access to these networks enhances their value and contribution to business, an argument which also applies to the internet and all the technology associated with e-commerce. This relatively new form of business organization is potentially a prime agent of de-territorialization. However, cross-border payments, taxation and consumer protection issues, among others, require resolution before e-commerce fulfils its potential.

Globalization Driver Five: Social and Cultural Convergence

A consequence of greater liberalization and the spread of global communications technology is a degree of social and cultural convergence, in itself a pre-condition for globalization. This does not imply that a global culture has replaced or is replacing the diversity of local and national cultures in the world. The range and deep-rootedness of beliefs, values, experience and symbols is too extensive for that. However, helped by the global consolidation of mass media especially in broadcasting and by the power of the internet, there is growing recognition of common symbols and experience. Such commonality does not need to be deeply embedded, or even much more than superficial, before it becomes useful for the development of a global mindset and hence global marketing. Social and cultural convergence across boundaries is only possible when there is no clash with more profoundly held cultural beliefs specific to a particular place or grouping, such as religion.

The emergence of a global consumer, or at least consumers with common preferences across a significant part of the globe, provides opportunities for the creation of global products – that is, homogeneous products that can be sold throughout the world on the basis of global marketing and advertising campaigns. Truly global products are relatively few and far between but, where their existence is possible, they increase the viability and desirability of developing international production systems and value chains, with all the potential gains in terms of scale economies and utilization of different comparative advantages.

DIVERGENT VIEWS OF GLOBALIZATION

The debate about international economic integration is highly significant, since it frames the business environment and shapes corporate strategies. However, globalization has proved to be a highly controversial process. The controversy centres upon the interpretation of the strength and significance of changes in the world economy and on its impact on different stakeholders. The most fundamental question concerns whether the economy is becoming truly global or simply more international. A global economy implies a borderless economic space in which the integration of operations and markets takes place according to economic and market imperatives as opposed to the fragmentation of production and markets that has traditionally occurred owing to continuing barriers between countries. An international economy implies no fundamental shift in the underlying principles of economic organization but simply more cross-border transactions. Globalization brings fundamental implications for governance and political organization whereas internationalization, although posing governance challenges at national and international level, can be absorbed within existing governance frameworks.

Are the changes to the world economy discussed so far in this chapter to be welcomed or resisted? A different answer would be forthcoming depending on who you asked! Another salient issue considers whether globalization is inevitable and irreversible. If this is the case, the best path for those concerned about the consequences of globalization is to work within the existing framework but to push for incremental improvements in the international business environment. Just how global is the global economy anyway? Hirst and colleagues (2009) argue that the world economy was more global before the First World War (1914–1918) – if this theory is correct, then continuing contemporary international integration might not be inevitable.

Degrees of international economic integration may be located on a globalization/fragmentation continuum (see Figure 2.1). At the globalization end sits what Kenichi Ohmae (1994) calls the 'borderless world', that is, a world in which all obstacles to the movement of the factors of production have been removed. At the other end is a world of individual nation states that are still divided by continuing barriers to trade and commerce. Reality lies somewhere in between: as barriers disappear and the economy becomes more internationalised, the world moves towards the globalization end of the continuum whereas the construction of barriers marks a shift towards fragmentation and reduced

FIGURE 2.1 The Globalization/Fragmentation Continuum

internationalization. The characterization of 'ideal types', although removed from reality, provides a useful benchmark against which to judge the implications of different outcomes.

A borderless world is truly global in the sense that, as a result of policy changes and the rapid development of transport and communications technology, national borders become increasingly irrelevant. This process is facilitated by the emergence of a single, homogenized world culture as the result of globalization of the media, particularly via satellite broadcasting. Divergent policy outcomes are possible in this scenario.

A pure market forces view would argue that greater uncertainty and volatility is a price worth paying for giving free rein to unregulated market forces – the best guarantee of wealth generation through enterprise. From the corporate standpoint, competition is intensified within domestic and export markets, requiring increasingly rapid adjustments to changes in business environments. More profoundly, a borderless world encourages the growth of genuinely stateless enterprises that plan according to the dictates of the market and regard national borders as an irrelevance. This requires a global conception of markets and a striving for critical mass as both a defensive and offensive response to intensified competition. It also undermines the role of the nation state in the organization of economic and political activity.

Not everyone regards market forces, or Adam Smith's 'invisible hand', so positively. In order to overcome the consequences of market failure, others argue not for a retreat to within national boundaries but for a strengthening of international governance. By developing governance structures that correspond with the scope and scale of modern international business, civil society can regain some control over key economic actors. The challenge of achieving this is immense and requires a greater willingness to reconcile conflicting interests and to reach compromises than has hitherto been the case.

To a degree, this characterization of the 'borderless world' is a straw man that can easily be knocked over by numerous examples of the persistence of nation state power and of strong cultural differences between nations. However, this does not exclude the possibility that the world is moving in the direction of fewer borders. The important question is how far it has moved along the continuum. Similarly, the version of the world as a continuing patchwork of fragmented nation states and markets is not sustainable in a world in which regional integration is such a pronounced trend (see Chapter 3) and the role of international organizations like the WTO is expanding (see Chapter 4).

Somewhere in between these two extremes lies the scenario outlined by Hirst and Thompson (Hirst *et al.*, 2009). While they do not deny that there is greater interconnectedness among the world's economies and markets, they are of the view that much of the case for globalization and the ungovernability of world markets is overstated. They claim that the existence of genuine stateless MNEs is almost unknown and that most firms are transnational, based in one member state while trading and operating in a variety of countries and maintaining strong links with the home country.

The world economy itself is also far from global: capital flows and trade and investment are concentrated in the triad of Europe, North America and Japan/East Asia with developing countries marginalized – although trends in the first years of the twenty-first century suggest that this trend is becoming less pronounced (see the following section). The triad itself, particularly if it engages in policy coordination, has the capability of exerting strong governance pressures over a significant portion of the world economy and, even if its members act separately but as trading blocs, they retain strong powers to influence economic events. Again, recently, it appears that contrary to the views of many anti-globalization critics, the triad is far from having its own way: the failure hitherto of the WTO to reach agreement on the Doha Round is, to a large extent, a consequence of developing states asserting themselves. These states may not yet be able to achieve policy outcomes that they perceive to be in their interests but they have managed to block initiatives which they regard as being against their interests.

Rather than describe the growing economic interdependence as globalization, Hirst and Thompson refer to a shift towards a more 'inter-national' economy. In doing so they stress the original meaning of the word 'international' – that is, 'between nations'. Through use of the concept of inter-nationalism, Hirst and Thompson acknowledge the growing interconnection between national economies. Despite these tighter links, Hirst and Thompson argue that domestic and international frameworks remain separate for economic policy-making purposes. They also maintain that international events do not necessarily directly penetrate the national economy but have an indirect effect through national policy and processes or work 'automatically' through market forces. This has very different implications for business: greater interdependence still intensifies competition and companies continue to seek entry to new markets via a variety of different modes, but strategy is developed to take into account regional and national differences.

Box 2.1 Relative Economic Power of Nations and Multinationals

Underpinning much of the debate about globalization is the belief that MNEs are significant economic entities in their own right, and yield greater economic power than many nation states. Table 2.1 compares the 2007 gross domestic product (GDP) of a number of nation states with the turnover of some of the world's biggest companies in the same year. Clearly, the GDPs of G-7 countries, namely China, South Korea, India, Russia, Brazil and a number of European countries, exceed the total sales of Wal-Mart, the world's biggest company in terms of sales, by a significant amount. However, the value of Wal-Mart's 2007 sales fell between the value of Saudi Arabia's and Austria's GDPs, the world's 24th and 25th largest economies respectively. Furthermore, the company ranking fourth in terms of sales, BP, registered sales greater than the GDP of South Africa, a country of almost 50 million people. In 2007, there were also almost 100 companies with sales greater than Bangladesh, a country with a population of 158.6 million, the seventh largest country in the world in terms of population. There were also 500 companies that had sales figures higher than the GDP of Tanzania, the country in 95th place in the World Bank's GDP rankings.

Although the observations arising from Table 2.1 do not, in themselves, reveal anything about the economic and indeed political power yielded by individual companies, it does highlight the fact that, when considered as economic units, the world's biggest companies are of a similar size to all but the world's biggest economies. That is, MNEs are important economic entities in their own right. In addition, MNEs are often criticized for their role in developing countries. The above analysis indicates that when it comes to dealing with MNEs, all but the biggest developing countries are dealing with better-resourced organizations with potentially more economic power and political clout than themselves. Concentration of economic power in the hands of private organizations is not new, as witnessed by the history of the East India Company and the Hudson Bay Company, for example, in previous centuries. The number, range and diverse origin of large MNEs in the contemporary world, however, are unprecedented.

TABLE 2.1 Ranking of Countries and Companies by GDP and Total Sales, 2007 ($ billion)

	GDP or sales	Rank[1]			GDP or sales	Rank[1]	
		GDP	Sales			GDP	Sales
United States (302)[2]	13,811	1		Bangladesh (158.6)	68	59	
Japan (127.7)	4,376	2		Merrill Lynch	64.2		100
Germany (82.3)	3,297	3		Angola (17.0)	59	60	
China (1,320)	3,280	4		Dominican Republic (9.8)	36.7	73	
UK (61)	2,728	5		Motorola	36.6		200
Saudi Arabia (24.2)	382	24		Oman (2.6)	35.7	74	
Wal-Mart	379		1	Latvia (2.3)	27.1	80	
Austria (8.3)	377	25		Cathay Financial Holdings	26.8		300
ExxonMobil	373		2	Costa Rica (4.5)	25.2	81	
Greece (11.2)	360	26					
Royal Dutch Shell	356		3				
Denmark (5.5)	308	27		Cyprus (0.8)	21.3	87	
BP	292		4	Canadian Imperial Bank of Commerce	21.2		400
South Africa (47.6)	278	28		Cameroon (18.5)	20.6	88	
Thailand (63.8)	246	33		Ethiopia (79)	19.4	94	
Toyota Motor	230		5	Fluor	16.7		500
Venezuela (27.5)	228	34		Tanzania (40.4)	16.2	95	
Kuwait (2.7)	102	55					
Nissan Motor	94.8		50				
Slovak Republic (5.4)	75	56					

Notes
[1] Rankings for countries based on World Bank Development Indicators (2007 GDP); rankings for companies derived from Fortune Global 500 (2007 sales).
[2] Figures in brackets refer to population in millions.

Source: World Bank and Fortune Global 500.

MEASUREMENT OF GLOBALIZATION

This section attempts to identify ways of measuring globalization trends. The objective is not to develop highly precise indicators but to investigate some of the claims about globalization such as whether or not it is inclusive. Where possible, the indicators developed quantify linkages between countries and between and within firms. The indicators developed attempt to address the following dimensions of interdependence:

- *Scope*: that is, the extent to which international economic integration is truly global rather than confined to the 'triad' of North America, Europe and Japan/East Asia.
- *Intensity*: the depth, embeddedness and extensiveness of the integration that has taken place, both between countries and within firms.
- *Sensitivity*: the degree to which events in one part of the global system transmit themselves to other parts of the system. The more integrated the system, the more rapid and complete will be the transmission of effects of economic developments and crises throughout the system.

Scope

Given that trends normally associated with globalization relate to the experience of three regions, namely North America, Europe and East Asia (often referred to as 'the triad'), the term 'globalization' has been criticized as a misnomer. The developing countries, so the argument goes, are weakly integrated into the world economy and are effectively excluded from the integration process.

Growth

A common criticism of globalization is that it is not really global and that it favours the already rich advanced industrialized economies. Certainly, as Table 2.2 shows, world income is heavily concentrated in the advanced economies of North America, Europe and Japan. In 2007, although containing only 15.4 per cent of the world's population, the world's most advanced economies accounted for over 56 per cent of world GDP. Conversely emerging and developing countries, which include almost 85 per cent of the world's population, account for only 43.6 per cent of world GDP. No conclusion about the causation of this skewed income can be drawn from these figures alone; indeed, it preceded the current international integration trend; nor is it realistic to expect a direct correlation between share of the world's population and the world's GDP. Nevertheless, the figures do indicate that world economic activity is dominated by relatively few economies. Over time, if the proponents of the market are correct, greater integration should result in a more even spread of economic activity. Despite the rapid growth of the large emerging economies, the share of world GDP accounted for by the advanced economies remained stable between 2000 and 2007.

TABLE 2.2 Share of World GDP, Exports and Population, 2007 (%)

	GDP	Exports	Population
US	21.4	9.6	4.7
Japan	6.6	4.7	2.0
Eurozone	16.1	29.5	4.9
Other advanced	12.3	22.6	3.7
Advanced economies	**56.4**	**66.4**	**15.4**
Africa	3.0	2.5	12.8
sub-Saharan Africa	2.3	1.9	11.6
sub-Saharan Africa (excl. S Africa and Nigeria)	1.2	1.0	8.6
Developing Asia	20.1	13.2	52.6
China	10.8	7.8	20.5
India	4.6	1.3	17.5
Middle East	3.8	4.7	3.7
Western hemisphere	8.3	5.1	8.6
Emerging and developing countries	**43.6**	**33.6**	**84.7**
CEE	4.1	4.6	2.8
Russia	3.2	2.3	2.2

Source: Derived from IMF (2008) *World Economic Outlook* (April 2008).

Goods and Services Exports

Table 2.3 traces the changing regional composition of merchandise trade exports since 1948, the year the GATT officially came into existence. The relative shares of the main trading regions have fluctuated over time. The developed countries dominate world exports but not as much as they used to. During the early post-war period, economic reconstruction in Europe and Japan in particular contributed to an increasing share of world exports for the developed countries, rising from 66 per cent in 1948 to almost 73 per cent in 1963 and peaking at 76.3 per cent in 1973. Since then the trend has been mostly downward, falling below 60 per cent in 2007. The decline in North America's share of world trade has been steady and consistent throughout the period, whereas Japan's share of world trade peaked in the early 1990s before falling back in subsequent years after it lost economic momentum and competitiveness. Although Europe's share of world trade has declined in recent years, at 42.5 per cent in 2007, Europe clearly continues to punch above its weight in trading circles.

For a quarter of a century after the end of the Second World War, the share of developing countries in world exports declined steadily. This was the result of many factors, including government policy and deteriorating terms of trade (see Chapter 5). However, since 1993 the developing countries' share of world trade increased impressively from around a quarter to almost 37 per cent in 2007. Some of this improvement is due to rising commodity prices towards the end of the period and some is due

TABLE 2.3 Changing Regional Composition of Merchandise Trade Exports, 1948–2007 (%)

	1948	1953	1963	1973	1983	1993	2003	2007
North America	28.1	24.8	19.9	17.3	16.8	18.0	15.8	13.7
US	21.7	18.8	14.9	12.3	11.2	12.6	9.8	8.6
South and Central America	11.3	9.7	6.4	4.3	4.4	3.0	3.0	3.7
Europe	35.1	39.4	47.8	50.9	43.5	45.4	46.0	42.5
Africa	7.3	6.5	5.7	4.8	4.5	2.5	2.4	3.1
Middle East	2.0	2.7	3.2	4.1	6.8	3.5	4.1	5.3
Asia	14.0	13.4	12.6	15.2	19.1	26.1	26.1	28.0
Japan	0.4	1.5	3.5	6.4	8.0	9.9	6.4	5.3
China	0.9	1.2	1.3	1.0	1.2	2.5	5.9	9.0
India	2.2	1.3	1.0	0.5	0.5	0.6	0.8	1.1
Developing countries	31.4	28.3	22.6	20.2	26.8	25.2	30.3	36.6
Developed countries	66.4	68.2	72.9	76.3	68.2	73.3	67.1	59.7

Note:
1 difference between developed and developing countries is accounted for by the Soviet Union and latterly by Russia.

Source: WTO, *World Trade Report* (2007and 2008).

to the impressive export growth of the large emerging economies, particularly China, whose share of world exports grew from 2.5 per cent in 1993 to 9 per cent in 2007, representing a major and ongoing shift in the structure of world trade. Not all developing regions have fared so well. Despite slight increases in their share of world exports between 2003 and 2007, Africa's share was much higher several decades ago as was that of South and Central America and other parts of Asia. The Middle East's share of the value of world exports rises and falls in line with the fluctuations in energy prices.

Trade in services has become increasingly important in international transactions. In 2006, the value of world service exports was almost 23 per cent of world merchandise exports compared to 18 per cent in 1980. The growing role for services trade reflects a faster growth rate for service than for goods exports for most of the period and the continuing structural shift in many economies away from agriculture and industry towards services.

As with merchandise trade, the developing countries' share of world services exports is marginal compared to developed countries, especially Europe which in 2007 accounted for over half of world services exports and approximately 11 per cent of the world population. In 2007, for example, the value of European services exports was over six and a half times the combined value of services exports from Latin America, Africa and the Middle East, regions where the combined population total is four times greater than that of Western Europe. The main beneficiary is Asia, whose share of

FIGURE 2.2
Merchandise
Exports by Region,
1948–2007 –
share of world
exports

Source: WTO.

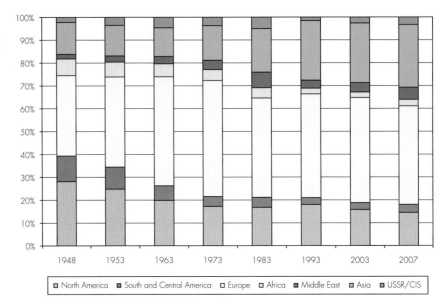

FIGURE 2.2
Merchandise
Exports by Region,
1948–2007 –
share of world
exports

Source: WTO.

world services exports has increased from less than 14 per cent in 1980 to almost 23 per cent in 2007. The Asian increase has been steady over the period whereas the shares of other regions have been more changeable. North America's share, for example, grew between 1980 and 2000 but has subsequently fallen back. Europe's share has also fluctuated but has been around the 50 per cent mark for nearly two decades. The always small share of Africa and South and Central America has fallen since 1980.

TABLE 2.4 Changing Regional Composition of Commercial Services Exports, 1980–2006 (%)

	1980	1990	2000	2007
North America	12.4	19.3	22.2	16.3
South and Central America	4.8	3.8	3.2	2.8
Europe[1]	58.1	53.1	48.5	51.0
Middle East	Not available	Not available	2.3	2.4
Africa	3.5	2.4	2.1	2.6
Asia	13.7	16.8	20.7	22.9

Note:
[1] Figures for Europe for 1980 and 1990 are for Western Europe only. For 2000 onward they include Central and Eastern Europe.

Source: WTO.

FDI

The growing complexity of world economic integration means that it is no longer sufficient to use trade in goods and services as measures of interdependence. Foreign direct investment (FDI) grew even more rapidly than trade in goods and services since 1980. Between 1980 and the mid-2000s, nominal GDP increased four times whereas bilateral trade grew six times and the stock of FDI grew twenty fold. However, the value of world FDI flows is still significantly below the value of world trade: in 2006, world FDI inflows totalled $1.3 trillion compared to $11.8 trillion for world merchandise exports. Nevertheless, FDI is highly significant owing to its interaction with trade and its contribution to the intensity of interdependence.

Over the very long term there have been some significant shifts in the composition of world FDI. According to Dicken, in 1938 two-thirds of world FDI was located in developing countries. Most FDI at the time was composed of investment in colonial possessions by countries like the UK. More recently FDI has become a phenomenon that primarily takes place among developed countries. As Table 2.5 shows, developed countries accounted for almost 80 per cent of FDI inflows and over 90 per cent of FDI outflows in 2000, the year in which world FDI peaked. Between 2000 and 2003, FDI flows slowed steadily but rapid growth has resumed since then. Renewed FDI growth has seen some shift in the pattern of FDI flows with inflows into developed countries falling to two-thirds of all FDI inflows in 2006. Although this remains disproportionately high, it nevertheless reflects a significant decline from the 80 per cent-plus share of global FDI inflows that had prevailed for the previous quarter of a century. Developed country dominance in FDI outflows is also diminishing as developing country MNEs, particularly in India and China, start to look for overseas investment opportunities, but, as yet, the shift is not as marked as it is for inflows.

In 2000, developing countries accounted for less than 20 per cent of world FDI inflows and 11 per cent of world FDI outflows, reflecting the reversal in the status of developing countries as destinations for FDI between the first half of the twentieth century and the final decade of the century. By 2006, the developing country share of FDI inflows had risen to almost 30 per cent and of outflows to almost 15 per cent. Much of the increase in developing country FDI is concentrated in individual countries (see Table 2.5) and regions. For example, 60 per cent of FDI flowing into developing countries ends up in Asia, particularly China and, to an increasing but much lesser degree, India. Within Latin America, over 70 per cent of FDI inflows are directed towards the larger more advanced economies of Mexico, Brazil and Argentina. Africa accounted for less than 8 per cent of FDI going to the developing world in 2006 and less than 3 per cent of total world FDI inflows. Within Africa, the distribution of FDI is heavily concentrated in the more developed North African countries, South Africa and resource-rich Angola and Nigeria. The least developed countries receive very little FDI. Moreover, FDI flows are generally more volatile than trade flows and are potentially vulnerable to crises in individual developing country destinations. For example, flows into East Asia were adversely affected for a couple of years by the backlash from the 1997 to 1998 financial crisis.

TABLE 2.5 FDI by Type of Economy, 1970–2006

1. Inflows	1970		1980		1990		2000		2006	
	$ bn	% total	$ bn	% total	$ bn	% total	$ bn	% total	$ bn	% total
Developed	9.6	71.3	47.6	86.1	165.6	82.2	1,146.2	81.2	857.5	65.7
Developing	3.9	28.7	7.7	13.9	35.9	17.8	256.1	18.2	1,305.8	29.0
Transition	. . .	. . .	0.24	. . .	0.8	. . .	9	0.6	69.3	5.3
World	13.4	100	55.3	100	202.6	100	1,411.4	100	1305.9	100
2. Outflows										
Developed	14.1	99.7	50.7	94.1	217.6	94.8	1,102.7	89.0	1022.7	84.1
Developing	0.5	0.3	3.1	5.9	11.9	5.2	133.3	11.0	174.4	14.3
Transition	. . .	. . .	. . .	. . .	. . .	. . .	. . .	. . .	1.9	1.6
World	14.2	100	53.8	100	229.60	100	1,239.2	100	1216.0	100

Note: Transition economies refer to CIS and S.E. Europe.

Source: Derived from UNCTAD *World Investment Reports.*

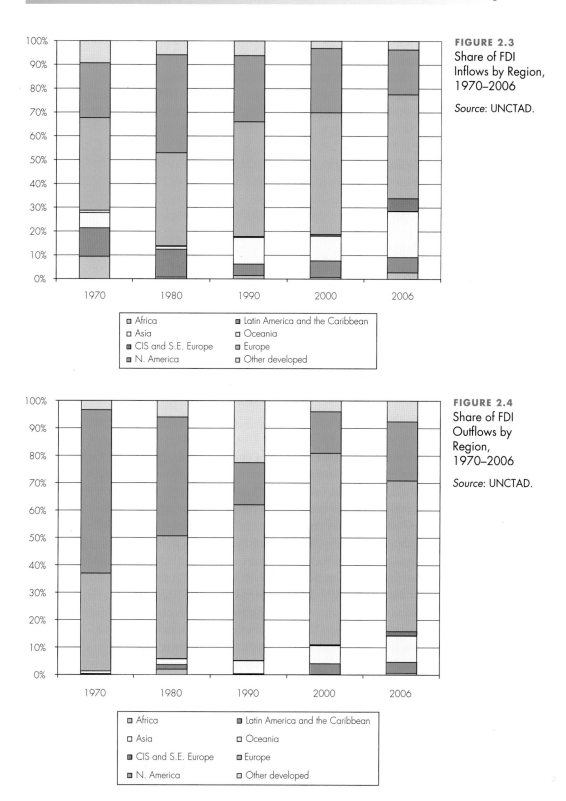

FIGURE 2.3
Share of FDI Inflows by Region, 1970–2006

Source: UNCTAD.

FIGURE 2.4
Share of FDI Outflows by Region, 1970–2006

Source: UNCTAD.

TABLE 2.6 Distribution of FDI Inflows among Developing Countries, 2006

	$bn	% of developing country FDI
Africa	35.2	7.9
North Africa	22.3	5.0
Latin America and the Caribbean	83.8	18.7
Asia and Oceania, of which	259.8	58.1
Asia	259.4	58.0
– West Asia	60.0	13.1
– Central Asia	2.7	0.6
– South, East and South-East Asia	199.5	44.6
South Asia	22.3	5.0
Oceania	0.3	0.1
South-East Europe	26.3	5.9
CIS	42.9	9.6
Total developing countries	447.6	100

Source: UNCTAD, World Investment Report (2007).

Technology Diffusion

Given the emphasis placed on technology as an agent of change and integration, it is appropriate to consider the diffusion rates of broadcast technologies and ICTs throughout both the developed and the developing world. Table 2.7 compares the spread of various technologies by region in 2005. The oldest and cheapest of the technologies in the table, TV, has the greatest global penetration of such technologies but significant regional diversities remain. In the developed world TV ownership is almost universal and in middle-income developing countries as many as 88 per cent of households own televisions. The picture is different in low-income countries: in Africa, only 14 per cent of households own a TV and 32 per cent in South Asia. Even assuming that each television in the developing world is almost certainly watched by a greater number of people than in the developed world, the power of television to make any meaningful transformation of cultural norms is limited, not only by the number and distribution of televisions but also by the material broadcast on them. Cable television, a medium that transcends boundaries, has the greatest potential as a vehicle for cultural convergence. However, the ratio of cable subscribers to the number of TV sets is significantly higher in developed than in developing countries where cable subscriptions are limited to the wealthiest groups, hotels and the expatriate community.

The debate surrounding the new economy revolves to an extent around the power of computer technology, particularly the internet, to transform business-to-business and business-to-consumer relationships. Telecommunications links lie at the heart of this technology. Telecommunications infrastructure is notoriously poor in developing countries: mobile phones can help bypass inadequate

TABLE 2.7 Broadcast Media and ICT Penetration, 2005

	Broadcast media	Telecommunications		Information technology		
	TVs	Fixed mainlines	Mobile subscribers	Personal computers	Internet users	Broadband
	% of households	per 1,000 people		per 1,000 people		
China	89	269	302	41	85	28.7
India	32	45	82	16	55	1.2
US	98	606	680	762	630	166.6
Eurozone	96	531	980	421	439	134.7
UK	99	528	1088	600	473	163.8
Japan	99	460	742	542	668	175
sub-Saharan Africa	14	17	125	15	29	...
East Asia and Pacific	36	214	282	38	89	25.9
Latin America and Caribbean	87	177	439	88	156	16.4
Middle East & North Africa	84	160	229	48	89	0.5
South Asia	32	39	79	16	49	1.0
Low income	**15**	**37**	**77**	**11**	**44**	**0.9**
Middle income	**88**	**211**	**379**	**58**	**115**	**22.6**
High income	**97**	**503**	**835**	**579**	**527**	**163.2**
World	**79**	**180**	**340**	**130**	**137**	**Not available**

Source: Derived from 2007 *World Development Indicators*, World Bank. In turn many of these indicators originated from the International Telecommunication Union (ITU).

line-bound infrastructure but mobile subscribers in developing countries still lag behind those in developed countries.

Ownership of personal computers and internet access itself are extremely uneven across the globe. In the US, for example, there were 762 personal computers per 1,000 population in 2005 compared to 15 in sub-Saharan Africa and 16 in south Asia. Internet usage varies from 29 per 1,000 in sub-Saharan Africa to 668 in Japan. Even in middle-income economies, internet access is only 22 per cent of that in developed economies. Moreover, in some low- and middle-income economies, although internet access is technically available, political factors have limited the access of the general populace to the full power of the worldwide web. The availability of broadband connections is a measure of speed and quality of internet connections and, in this respect, it is clear that the developed world is far ahead of middle- and low-income countries. Less than one person per 1,000 has access to a broadband connection in low-income countries compared to almost 23 in middle-income countries and 163 in high-income countries.

Clearly, the internet is still developing and its expansion is rapid, particularly in the developed world, but, unless there is a major and rapid expansion into both lower and middle-income developing countries, the lag in ICT technology within these countries will inhibit, or in extreme cases prevent their development. MNEs located within a developing country will be able to take advantage of ICTs but their exploitation by other actors, both corporate and consumers, could be limited.

In brief, scope indicators confirm that the interdependence and integration of the world is dominated by the developed economies of North America, Europe, Japan and the Asian Tigers. In terms of trade and investment, the share of developing countries has been increasing. However, much of the increased share has been accounted for by China or by one or two countries within much bigger developing regions. Similarly, with technology diffusion: although penetration of individual technologies in developing regions does increase over time, new technologies change the quality of what is possible (see Chapter 18). For example, personal computer ownership and internet usage has increased in middle-income countries. Meanwhile, the introduction of broadband represents a qualitative difference in internet connections and requires developing countries to begin another round of catch-up with developed countries.

Intensity

The intensity of international economic integration relates to the depth and embeddedness of the integration that has taken place between countries and within firms. The deeper the cross-border corporate linkages and the greater the density of network interconnections, the more difficult it will be to disentangle the integration of recent years. Robert Keohane and Joseph Nye (2000) usefully distinguish between 'thin' and 'thick' globalization. They describe the 'Silk Road' as an example of thin globalization: although an important economic and cultural link between Europe and Asia, the trade itself involved only a small group of traders and the goods reached only a relatively small elite of consumers. Thick globalization encompasses links that are both extensive and intensive. In the modern world, these links involve flows of capital, goods, information, knowledge, people and resources.

Thickening links represent more than simply an increase in the number of links but also a qualitative transformation of connections. For MNEs, this means greater complexity in their cross-border operations including the international integration of production systems and marketing arrangements. In particular, this implies the growth of intra-industry and intra-firm trade. Intra-industry trade refers to transactions in similar but differentiated goods within the same sector whereas intra-firm trade consists of trade between a parent company and its affiliates abroad or between affiliates of the same country. The growth of both intra-industry and intra-firm trade reflects the increasing internationalization of production and a greater intensity of cross-border links.

The changing role and modus operandi of MNEs has caused some speculation that, although the world has previously been as open to trade, the current intensification of networks signifies a major break with the past. The key to this argument is the changing relationship between trade and investment. As the previous section shows, the scope of globalization can be measured by looking at the geographical breakdown of trade and investment. Such indicators are useful, traditional measures of economic interdependence but they do not tell the whole story; nor do they reflect the complex interrelationship between the two indicators.

The 'steps' view of internationalization (see Chapter 9) posits that companies initially trade before investing, enabling them to test the market. Furthermore, exporting can involve small or large quantities whereas overseas production requires a minimum size for it to be worthwhile. Exporting is also easier and less risky than FDI: FDI requires the long-term, direct commitment of assets to a foreign environment and greater knowledge, managerial expertise and experience and organizational restructuring. Even in this relatively straightforward view of the world, FDI is more complex than the simple displacement of exports by investment. In the initial stages of FDI, an overseas affiliate creates demand for capital goods or intermediate goods and services: this demand may be satisfied by the parent company or by other companies. Complex manufacturing operations like car producers, for example, often act as magnets that pull their domestic suppliers abroad. Even in this simple case, therefore, FDI both replaces and creates trade and changes its composition.

The advent of globalization encourages firms to maximize gains from the integration of international production systems and value chains across borders. This change resulted from the continuing liberalization of trade and trade-related activity through the GATT–WTO framework, regional liberalization measures such as the SEM and the North American Free Trade Area (NAFTA) and the unilateral freeing up of FDI rules throughout the world. This process has also been driven along by the technological developments, especially in the realm of ICTs, that have enabled firms to process more information at drastically reduced costs and given them greater ability to manage complex organizational structures, including extended and dispersed production and value chains.

The upshot of these changes is that access to foreign markets and factors of production has improved tremendously, creating more choices about how to serve those markets and organize production. As barriers have fallen, the markets themselves have grown, resulting in both greater opportunities and greater competitive pressures requiring firms to constantly assess their strategies to stay ahead of their competitors. In short, the traditional rationale for FDI (the need to gain access to specific markets) has declined, whereas factors such as cost differences between locations, the quality of infrastructure and the labour force and the ease of conducting business across borders have increased in importance. This results in integrated international production and distribution systems on a global scale and greater intra-firm trade.

Figures on the growth of intra-firm trade are not easy to obtain but those that do exist confirm the increasing complexity of corporate integration in this changed international environment and the intensification of cross-border links. UNCTAD estimates that about one-third of world trade has been internalized within MNE systems and that a further one-third involves exports of MNEs outside their own corporate networks. In 2006, majority-owned US affiliates of foreign-owned companies accounted for 19 per cent and 26 per cent of US exports and imports of goods respectively. Almost 50 per cent of these exports and approximately 80 per cent of imports were the result of intra-firm trade between the affiliates and their overseas parent or with other affiliates in the same group. In other words, 10 per cent of US exports and 20 per cent of US imports were accounted for by intra-firm trade involving foreign affiliates located in the US. This does not tell the whole intra-firm trade story in the US, as the figures do not include trade between US parent companies and their majority-owned foreign affiliates. Such figures probably underestimate the intensity of interdependence because many flows, particularly the provision of intra-firm services, will not necessarily be measured and recorded.

The distinction between traditional multi-domestic FDI and the more complex integrated efficiency-seeking variety can be blurred, as the example of the EU shows. When the SEM was first mooted in the mid-1980s, Europe's trading partners were concerned about the potential for a 'Fortress Europe' in which internal integration was combined with higher barriers to the rest of the world. Therefore US, Japanese and other Asian companies with eyes on the large and lucrative European market increased their FDI in Europe so that they would be firmly established there once the barriers went up. Fortress Europe never happened. Indeed, the SEM increased the access of foreign companies to the European market and the foreign investors quickly appreciated that the SEM offered them opportunities to take advantage of scale economies and to specialize within the framework of a regional strategy. In other words, the initial defensive FDI to Europe was not wasted as firms sought to exploit their comparative advantage within the European market and embarked upon cross-border production within Europe to take advantage of new opportunities.

The implications of intensification of networks within firms are far-reaching. According to traditional economic and trade theory, resource allocation, the core of economics, is undertaken by the market or the state. This function appears to be increasingly taking place within corporate systems, thereby becoming less transparent and more difficult to regulate, and supports the writings of transactions cost and internalisation theorists (see Chapter 9). The increased intensity of cross-border linkages discussed above not only reflects a difference in the quantity of links but also represents a different and more complex relationship between a parent company and its foreign affiliates.

Sensitivity

If assumptions about growing interdependence are correct, the effects of economic events in one part of the global system will transmit themselves to other parts of the system. Indeed, the more integrated the system, the more rapid and complete will be the transmission of effects of economic developments and crises throughout the world, thereby giving rise to more volatility and uncertainty and providing ammunition to those urging a retreat from globalization.

The idea of the transmission of effects throughout the world economic system is not new. For example, the 1973 oil price shock stimulated worldwide inflation and the onset of international recession at a time when the concept of globalization had not emerged. However, globalization, through deregulation, greater market access and assistance from ICTs, has extended the range of channels and items that can be the subject of almost instant transmission of changes in fortune. In 2000, for example, after a period of intense hype in world stock markets about the vast profits to be made from technology stocks, particularly the so-called 'dot com' companies, the bubble burst and technology shares plummeted in value on the world's markets. The early twenty-first-century economic crisis in Argentina, coupled with devaluations in Brazil, its major trading partner, also precipitated a banking and economic crisis in neighbouring Uruguay. By the end of 2008, it had become clear that the credit crunch that began in the US sub-prime mortgage markets during the summer of 2007 had triggered one of the most severe international recessions of recent decades. So far, there have been ramifications in Europe but the impact has been limited in the rest of the world.

In the final two decades of the twentieth century, four crises illustrated the speed at which negative economic factors could transmit themselves from one country to another, ultimately affecting a significant proportion of the world's economy. These were:

1. Debt crisis: in August 1982, Mexico announced it was unable to repay its international debts and suspended payments. Brazil and Argentina shortly followed suit and, by the following spring, about 25 countries had to reschedule their debts.
2. The ERM crises of September 1992 and August 1993: as a result of intolerable strains within the European Monetary System, the pound sterling and the Italian lira left the EMS and ERM in crisis and the bands around which members currencies were allowed to fluctuate was extended from ± 2.25 per cent to ±15 per cent.
3. The 'tequila' crisis: in December 1994, Mexico devalued the peso against the dollar by 14 per cent. Panic selling of pesos resulted in floating of the currency and speculative attacks against other Latin American currencies, especially those of Argentina, Brazil, Peru and Venezuela. Brief speculative attacks also occurred against the currencies of Thailand, Hong Kong, the Philippines and Hungary.
4. The Asian crisis: this crisis began in Thailand in 1997, spread quickly through East Asia and also infected economies in Latin America and eastern Europe (see Case Study 2.1).

The currency crises all occurred within pegged exchange rate systems, systems that are particularly vulnerable to contagion when cross-border assets are highly mobile. Once investors believe, for whatever reason, that the government cannot or will not maintain the fixed rate, they are liable to flee the currency. Such capital flight runs down hard currency reserves and brings about the feared devaluation. In addition to a currency crisis, the tequila and Asian crises also precipitated a crisis in the domestic financial system, resulting in the closure or merger of banks and significant government assistance to the financial sector, and caused real social hardship.

WHAT DOES ALL THIS MEAN FOR BUSINESS?

Globalization and its associated drivers shape the environment in which business operates. The speed of change within this environment and the greater intensity of competition resulting from lower

CASE STUDY 2.1

The 1997 Asian Financial Crisis – The Domino Effect

The 1997 Asian financial crisis began in Thailand. Like others in the region, the Thai economy had been booming for over a decade. Prior to the crisis, the five main affected Asian countries – Thailand, Malaysia, Korea, the Philippines and Indonesia – had experienced enormous inflows of private, foreign capital. This capital was largely liquid portfolio investment in short-term bank loans, securities and high-risk property investments, and represented more volatile and mobile investment than FDI. However, during the most intense six months of the crisis, the private capital that had flowed into these economies to the tune of over $100 billion in 1996 (up from $25 billion two years earlier) had become capital outflows of a magnitude that represented about 10 per cent of GDP.

Early capital movement out of the Thai economy began towards the end of 1996: asset prices fell, thereby increasing the number of non-performing loans and concerns among investors in Thailand about the country's abilities to pay its debts. At the time, and like several Asian currencies, the Thai currency, the baht, was pegged to the dollar – a factor that had begun to cause problems when the dollar started to appreciate against the yen in the mid-1990s. The capital outflows and concern about the economy (a huge foreign debt, trade deficits and a fragile banking system burdened with huge loans) began a rush by both foreign investors and Thai companies to convert their baht to dollars. The Central Bank tried to support the domestic currency by buying baht with its dollar reserves, thereby running foreign reserves down still further, and raising interest rates. Higher interest rates drove down share prices, hit ill-conceived and over-leveraged property and industrial investments, and generally hit economic growth. Before long, the Central Bank had run down its reserves to the extent that it could no longer support the baht and, on 2 July 1997, let it float, whereupon it depreciated by 16 per cent in one day.

Meanwhile, investors and companies in the Philippines, Malaysia, Indonesia and Korea realized they shared similar problems, beginning a headlong rush into the dollar and a repeat of the Thai experience. In the second half of 1997, currencies and stock markets fell steeply across East Asia and many banks and construction and manufacturing companies went bankrupt. By the end of 1998, the crisis had spread to Russia, Brazil and others in Eastern Europe and Latin America.

The transmission of a crisis in one not over-large economy to others in the region and throughout the world, whatever the precise cause of the crisis, demonstrates the heightened sensitivity of events in a more integrated environment. As described above, the crisis had a substantial panic element. Even without this effect, increasingly connected trade and investment means that a downturn in one economy has an effect upon the well-being of another through its effect on exports. Moreover, when one country devalues, other countries feel under pressure to follow suit to prevent their own exports from losing competitiveness. The crisis also demonstrates the downside of greater integration with international capital markets and the speed with which fortunes can be reversed. Small countries in particular, which in world terms the crisis countries were, are particularly vulnerable to volatility in global markets.

By 1999, the countries affected by the crisis, with the exception of Indonesia, had begun to recover, although the following years were not easy owing to the US economic slowdown and increasing competition from China. As a result of the crisis, many East Asian countries tightened their banking and financial sector regulations and introduced corporate sector reforms to improve corporate governance standards. Recovery was also facilitated by a series of IMF rescue packages totalling over $180 billion from the start of the crisis to the end of 1998.

barriers to cross-border transactions and greater interdependence between countries and markets requires firms to constantly monitor its external environment and to adjust to it accordingly.

In broad terms it is useful to distinguish between two forms of globalization in the business context – globalization of production and globalization of markets. Globalization of production involves decisions about where production is most efficiently carried out. Lower barriers to trade and investment mean that production locations that may not previously have been considered may become feasible, enabling firms to take advantage of particular locational advantanges, whether it be land, labour, resources or something else. Globalization of production may take the form of the concentration of production in one location in place of multiple locations, enabling firms to benefit from scale economies, or it may result in extended value chains across several borders with each production stage occurring in the most competitive location. Offshoring and outsourcing are examples of the latter phenomenon which is also partially responsible for the growth of intra-firm trade referred to above. The globalization of markets involves a decision about where to sell products. This requires analysis of whether standards and tastes have converged sufficiently to enable the same product to be sold in several markets or even globally (rare), and whether one or several marketing strategies need to be developed.

Many factors need to be taken into account by firms (see Figure 2.5) when assessing how they need to respond to the external environment. In broad terms, globalization lowers trade and cross-border investment barriers which in turn intensifies competition in both domestic and foreign markets with clear implications for prices, costs, innovation and efficiency. Globalization reduces fragmentation of markets and encourages the emergence of a global or at least multinational perspective of products and markets.

There is no definitive response to the complex interplay of forces facing firms, which vary across industries, regions and time and are open to differing interpretations. Pure globalists would argue that the globalization drivers encourage the growth of the truly stateless enterprise that plans according to the dictates of the market and considers national borders to be an increasing irrelevance. Characteristics of such strategies include a global conception of markets and a striving for critical mass as both a defensive and offensive response to intensified competition in domestic and foreign markets with all the associated pressures on prices, costs, efficiency and the need to innovate. Such

FIGURE 2.5
Pressures and
Opportunities from
Globalization
Shaping the
Operating
Environment of
the Firm

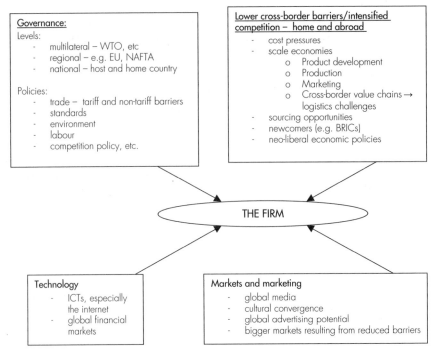

developments, so the argument goes, will ultimately spill over into the transfer of dominant cultures, facilitating the emergence of global products. In this world, market forces come to dominate not only economic but political life as national governments find it increasingly difficult to exercise any real control over what happens within their borders. Others acknowledge increased interdependence and the accompanying intensification of competition but argue that nation states and markets retain their importance, albeit perhaps in a slightly different way. They may argue for a consolidation of operations within a region but continue to see significant differentiation with other regions.

CONCLUSION

It is easy to be carried away by the rhetoric of globalization. There has undoubtedly been a big increase in economic integration and interdependence but it is worth asking the question whether there are trends underway which could undermine this interdependence.

Indeed, while the technological progress that has underpinned globalization developments continues, difficulties within institutions that have hitherto supported greater international integration and signs of economic nationalism in key countries do give cause for concern. The Doha Round of multilateral trade talks under the auspices of the WTO appears to be floundering (see Chapter 4) as divisions between members appear to be hardening at the expense of the multilateral system. One consequence has been a rapid rise in the number of bilateral and regional trade agreements (see Chapter 3). This trend has the potential to be exclusive and discriminatory, resulting in new trade and investment barriers. The development of the EU, a regional organization which has been trying to drive globalization through the creation of multilateral rules, has stalled as a result of its preoccupation with its constitutional affairs and neglect of the economic measures which drove its integration so successfully for a while.

As economic conditions become harder, so protectionism and economic nationalism become more likely. Workers in developed countries are concerned about the impact of Chinese exports on their jobs. The record US trade deficit gives grist to this argument and has contributed, along with security fears, to the blocking of two major tranches of foreign investment in the states – the proposed acquisition of US oil company Unocal by Chinese oil company CNOOC in 2005 and Dubai Ports World's attempt to acquire P&O, a British company that controlled several US ports. Signs of economic nationalism have also emerged within the EU with France and Spain taking action to prevent other member states from taking a stake in their power sectors.

Geopolitical factors also potentially serve to fragment the world once more. The destruction of the World Trade Center in New York in 2001 has potentially created a major schism between two major civilizations. Developments in the CIS, including the assertive nationalism of Russia and the fall-out over Russia's activities in Georgia in the summer of 2008, have caused some commentators to raise the spectre of a new Cold War. Scarce energy resources and the subsequent high prices (Chapter 19) increase international tension and recall some of the conflicts and competition over resources that have occurred in the past.

The above economic and political factors plus the greater heterogeneity resulting from the assertion of their place in the world by the emerging economies (as demonstrated by their leading role in the WTO talks) and conflicts over the movement of people all potentially serve to increase conflict and increase the distance between nations. Harvests of the benign impacts of globalization all depend upon a consensus around its benefits and a recognition of a core at least of common interests from the opening of the world's markets and borders. The above factors do not necessarily mark an end to globalization as we know it but they do endanger it.

Summary of Key Concepts

- There is a general consensus that international economies and markets have become more interdependent with fundamental implications for global governance and corporate behaviour. However, there is nothing but controversy about exactly what these implications are.
- The growth of neo-liberalism and global governance, financial and capital market liberalization, the diffusion of ICTs and social and cultural convergence underpin the move to greater international economic interdependence/globalization.
- The incomes of the largest multinationals are equivalent to those of medium-sized economies.
- The developing country share of world trade in goods and services and of investment has increased in recent years but much of this is down to the performance of China.

- FDI growth has changed the nature of interdependence, resulting in complex, cross-border networks that allocate resources rather than markets. This is represented by high levels of intra-firm and intra-industry trade.
- Globalization and greater integration of markets results in the rapid transmission of crises from one country to another.
- Globalization helps shape the business environment, resulting in greater risks and new opportunities. In some cases, businesses have responded by developing supply chains that cross many borders.

Activities

1. Research an anti-globalization group and critically assess its arguments.

2. Choose two or three of the largest multinational enterprises and determine whether they are truly global in scope and strategy or have a more regional dimension to their activities.

3. 'Globalization is good.' Hold a whole-class debate on this topic. It is likely to be a heated and not necessarily conclusive occasion.

Discussion Questions

1. It is often argued that globalization undermines the role of the nation state. Do you agree and, if the assertion is true, what are its implications?

2. Taking into account indicators of scope, intensity and sensitivity (and any other evidence you deem relevant), assess the extent to which we live in a globalized world.

3. 'Globalization is a fact of life. But I believe we have underestimated its fragility' (Kofi Annan, former UN General Secretary). Explain this statement and identify and assess factors which may have caused Annan to talk about the fragility of globalization.

4. 'It has been said that arguing against globalization is like arguing against the laws of gravity' (Kofi Annan, former UN General Secretary). Explain and assess this statement.

5. Identify and assess how globalization influences the competitive environment of international business. How have these influences changed business behaviour?

References and Suggestions for Further Reading

The literature on globalization is vast and growing. The following books and articles give a representative flavour of what is available.

Abdelal, R. and Segal, A. (2007) 'Has globalization passed its peak?', *Foreign Affairs*, Vol. 86, No. 1, 103–114.

Bhagwati, J. (2004), *In Defence of Globalization*, Oxford: Oxford University Press.

Brakman, S. *et al.* (2006) *Nations and Firms in the Global Economy: An Introduction to International Economics and Business*, Cambridge: Cambridge University Press.

Chanda, N. (2007) *Bound Together: How Traders, Preachers, Adventurers and Warriors Shaped Globalisation*, New Haven, CT: Yale University Press.

Choo, S. (2006) 'Defragmenting world trade', *Northwestern Journal of International Law and Business*, Vol 27, No. 1, 39–88.

Cowling, K. and Tomlinson, P. (2006) 'Globalisation and corporate power', *Contributions to Political Economy*, Vol. 24, No. 1, 33–54.

Dicken, P. (2007), *Global Shift*, 5th edn, London: Sage.

Fatehi, K. and Veliyath, R. (2008) 'Emergent realities of global competition: the changing demands on managers and governments', *International Journal of Commerce and Management*, Vol. 18, No. 1, 77–92.

Friedman, T. (2005) *The World Is Flat: A Brief History of the Globalized World in the 21st Century*, London: Penguin.

Held, D. and McGrew, A. (eds) (2003) *The Global Transformations Reader*, 2nd edn, Cambridge: Polity Press.

Held, D., Barnett, A. and Henderson, C. (eds) (2005) *Debating Globalization*, Cambridge: Polity Press.

Hill, J. (2005) *World Business: Globalization, Analysis and Strategy*, Mason, OH: Thomas South-Western.

Hirst, P., Thompson, G. and Bromley, S. (2009) *Globalization in Question*, 3rd edn, Cambridge: Polity Press.

Holton, R. (2006) *Making Globalization*, Basingstoke: Palgrave Macmillan.

Hopper, P. (2006) *Living with Globalization*, Oxford: Berg.

James, H. (2002) *The End of Globalization*, Boston, MA: Harvard University Press.

Jones, G. (2005) *Multinationals and Global Capitalism: From the Nineteenth to the Twenty First Century*, Oxford: Oxford University Press.

Kelly, K. (1999) *New Rules for the New Economy: 10 Ways the Network Economy is Changing Everything*, London: Fourth Estate.

Keohane, R. and Nye, J. (2000) 'Globalization: what's new? what's not? (and so what?)', *Foreign Policy*, No. 118, 104–119.

Ohmae, K. (1994) *The Borderless World*, London: HarperCollins.

Oppenheimer, M. (2007) 'The end of liberal globalization', *World Policy Journal*, Vol. 24, No. 4, 1–9.

Parker, B. (2005) *Introduction to Globalisation and Business Relationships and Responsibilities*, London: Sage.

Prakash, A. and Hart, J. (eds) (2000) *Coping with Globalisation*, London: Routledge.

Rodrik, D. (1997) *Has Globalization Gone Too Far?* Washington, DC: Institute for International Economics.

Scheve, K. and Slaughter, M. (2007) 'A new deal for globalization', *Foreign Affairs*, Vol. 86, No. 4, 34–47.

Scholte, J. (2005), *Globalization: A Critical Introduction*, 2nd edn, Basingstoke: Palgrave.

Stiglitz, J. (2002) *Globalization and Its Discontents*, London: Penguin.

Stiglitz, J. (2006) *Making Globalization Work*, New York: W.W. Norton.

Wolf, M. (2004) *Why Globalization Works*, New Haven, CT: Yale University Press.

Chapter 3

Regional Integration and Globalization

Throwing sand into the wheels of deeper international economic integration in order to reduce adjustment costs, as contemplated by some, is not an attractive option.

Joaquin Almunia (1948–), European Commissioner

LEARNING OBJECTIVES

This chapter will help you to:

- understand and identify the nature and form of regional economic integration

- comprehend the interface between the motives for regional economic integration and the process of globalization

- identify the diverse number and forms of regional economic groupings across the globe

- appreciate the importance of regional economic integration for international business

- understand the importance of new regionalism

The process of international integration – as reflected in globalization (see Chapter 2) – has bred a response from states both within and beyond the context of the regions within which they are located. Indeed, the trends which stimulate integration on a global level are in evidence in greater intensity at the regional level. Even then, the degree of maturity between regions on the state of regional integration varies markedly among different parts of the global economy. These differences occur for both political and economic reasons. At its heart, regionalism is about preferential trading agreements among a limited group of states. In practice, formal economic integration very often, although not always, follows from such preferential trade agreements – the forms of which are given in Box 3.1. All of these definitions highlight the fact that the basis of regional economic integration is the removal of discrimination among economic actors of participating states. Despite this, regionalization at its core implies discrimination between states that are members of the regional grouping and those that are not.

Initially, this chapter examines the motives for the push towards regional economic integration, highlighting the underpinning objectives of such actions. In assessing the role these moves have had for global trade, the chapter assesses the main regions where integration has risen on the commercial and political agenda. The chapter then moves on to examine the development potential of preferential trading agreements through the emergence of 'new regionalism'. It then examines the implications of these developments for the internationalization of business, before drawing conclusions.

Box 3.1 Levels of Regional Integration

Regional economic integration arrangements can take many different forms, including:

- Preferential trade agreements (PTAs): this is the loosest type of arrangement and is based upon the granting of partial preferences to a set of trading partners. The concessions offered tend to be unidirectional such as those extended by the EU to the African Caribbean and Pacific (ACP) states. If reciprocated, the term preferential trade area is applied.
- *Free trade area (FTA)*: when two or more states eliminate internal barriers to trade – such as tariffs and border restrictions – while sustaining their own independent tariffs vis-à-vis non-member states. Rules of origin are used to prevent trade deflection.
- *Customs union (CU)*: when two or more states not only eliminate internal barriers to trade but also introduce a common external tariff. This avoids trade deflection – where all goods and services imports from non-members enter the area through the state with the lowest tariffs – and implies a common trade policy.

- ■ *Common market*: when member states agree to supplement free trade in goods and services with free movement in factors of production (notably labour, capital and, increasingly, information). The removal of these barriers expands the size of the market available to most if not all enterprises, thereby allowing businesses to expand their operations to other member states.
- ■ *Economic union*: this occurs when countries agree to coordinate core economic policies (such as interest rates and exchange rates). This implies a common stance on inflation and ultimately a single currency. As factors of production move freely between states, so pressure grows for coordinated policies to manage these flows.
- ■ *Political union*: when states agree to common policies in almost every sphere of activity (including foreign and defence policy). Deeper economic integration could stimulate political integration as governments increase interaction among them. Such interactions could legitimize moves towards political union.

THE NATURE OF REGIONAL INTEGRATION

Regional economic integration is influencing an increasing number of states and is becoming ever more prominent in commercial decisions. The World Trade Organization (WTO) has sanctioned an increasing number of preferential trade agreements over recent decades covering all continents (see below). Current moves towards regional integration represent a departure from previous efforts which have been neither as numerous nor as successful. The WTO identified four main trends in the formation of regional trade agreements (RTAs):

1. Most states have placed RTAs at the centre of commercial policy, implying in many cases a shift of resources from multilateral trade objectives towards these preferential agreements.
2. These RTAs are exhibiting a higher degree of sophistication, expanding to include trade in services, trade policy areas not regulated multilaterally, and their approach is becoming both innovative and not guided merely by physical proximity.
3. There is a shift in the geopolitics of these zones as the number of North/South agreements increases, often replacing long-established non-reciprocal systems of preferences.
4. The expansion of RTAs as different blocs are consolidating into single pan-continent wide blocs.

In the past decade or so, there have been qualitative as well as quantitative changes in regional integration schemes. The first such change is a growing recognition that effective integration involves more than the reduction of tariffs and other conventional barriers to trade. Participants have come to recognize that new non-tariff barriers have worked to fragment markets. The second emerging facet is the shift from closed regionalism to a more open model. As mentioned, agreements have shifted from being based upon import substitution towards export-led models. A third development has been the emergence of trade agreements between developed and developing countries such as the North American Free Trade Area. These have been compounded by the following factors:

1. the replacement of national markets by global markets;
2. the perceived success of existing agreements, most notably those in Europe;
3. the decline of the geographical determinants of financial location and the internationalization of the division of labour;
4. the continued strengthening of multinational and private policy-making structures relative to the authority of the state;
5. a concern not to be left out of the growing web of preferential deals by both the US and developing states;
6. a belief in the business community that, as product cycles get shorter and multilateral negotiating cycles get longer, quicker results may be obtained regionally;
7. the desire to use regional liberalization as a catalyst for domestic reform;
8. a concern by the government to use preferential trading deals for political or strategic purposes;
9. the pursuit of non-trade concerns such as the environment or labour issues.

These factors stress how rationalization and neo-liberalism are implicit in moves towards regional integration. The resulting exposure to international markets requires not only domestic policy adjustment but also an increased desire to solve common problems collectively. The result has been convergence between policy makers as to how exactly the challenges of globalization should be met.

It is useful to make a distinction between the twin interrelated forces of regionalism and regionalization. The former is policy-driven regional integration stimulated by formal economic cooperation agreements. The latter is market-driven integration spurred by regional growth dynamics, the emergence of international production networks and related flows of FDI. Regionalism is often identified with preferential trading agreements among neighbouring states. These may take different forms, with the main difference being based on the extent of preference granted to members and the degree of policy coordination among states. Whether such agreements are beneficial or not is often seen as a trade-off between the benefits of liberalization against the increased discrimination that arises as a result. Conventional economic theory dictates that economic welfare is maximized under conditions of global free trade. Thus it is argued that in the absence of the ideal scenario, regional integration represents a second-best option. However, a summary of research seeking to quantify the gains from regional trading blocs tends to be mixed. Indeed, many reach the conclusion that in the absence of clear-cut benefits many have turned to rationales based on political economy.

It is difficult to quantify the rising importance of RTAs. Simply using a count of the number of RTAs signed as an indictor of regionalism is flawed, since many of those that are signed are of limited importance to the global economy. In particular, according to Pomfret (2007), many of these bilateral deals reflect the fall-out from the transformation of Western Europe and the USSR. Using the share of world trade covered by RTAs as an indicator is an alternative measure. It is noted that RTAs cover 55 to 60 per cent of global trade and as much as 90 per cent of total trade of members (2007). However, many RTAs are pre-dated by lower tariffs; thus it cannot be argued that they necessarily caused increased trade, as the aforementioned political factors may be in evidence. Furthermore, many of the new regional blocs reflect deeper integration, since policy measures are included as a means of seeking to harmonize trade conditions. As RTAs extend beyond trade, measuring their importance in terms of trade can overstate their importance in terms of this transaction (as these were already taking place) but may understate their importance in terms of international political power.

The removal of discrimination between states – the *raison d'être* of the process – is a means of increasing the welfare of participating states. Such welfare increases are derived from the potential boost to competitiveness arising from the process of regional economic integration and greater efficiency in resource use. These welfare changes underline the core reasons as to why states form regional agreements, notably that:

- these agreements have the potential to raise economic growth through the economies of scale;
- states can lower trade barriers to partners and increase discrimination against third parties and can increase the welfare of citizens;
- regional specialization allows firms to derive tangible commercial benefits from 'learning by doing' and attracting FDI;
- domestic policy reforms can be sustained, thereby enhancing the credibility and sustainability of the chosen measures;
- there are evident opportunity costs from remaining outside a trading bloc;
- regional economic integration can act as an effective platform for competing within global markets;
- such economic agreements can stimulate regional cohesion and security.

Many of the welfare effects of the creation of PTAs are derived from the relative effects of trade creation and trade diversion. This is based on a recognition that while governments will lose tariff revenue they may gain through efficiencies in terms of the lower cost of alternative sources of supply and on trade policy towards non-member states. The changes in the trade flows also alter the location of production – something that is determined by the comparative advantage of the respective member states. This will be influenced by cluster effects and by the possibility of technology transfer among member states. This process could lead to the convergence of economic development between states as labour-intensive activities switch towards lower wage states, although the opposite forces can also apply if activity focuses upon the wealthiest areas of the regional bloc. In addition to these benefits, there is a perception that the process of regional economic integration and the liberalization that accompanies the process will aid the channelling of resources of partner economies into activities where they are most likely to excel.

The notion of natural trading partners arising from physical proximity has often been called into question. Despite this, geographic proximity seems to be a feature of regional and/or preferential trading agreements. This reflects the fact that there is an unavoidable spatial dimension to these processes. In part this spatial dimension is created by savings in transactions costs, availability of specialized inputs and assorted spill-overs. In addition, there are historical and geographical forces at play which can translate a home bias into a neighbourhood bias. Alongside these forces are those driven by politics. These are integral to regional integration reflecting the fact that political and economic forces are busy coevolving within any integration agreement. The most notable features of the new impetus towards regional integration are that:

- it reflects the move towards liberalization;
- most groupings tend to be outward-looking with the regional agreements as a reason for economic growth;
- it represents attempts by states to benefit from trade creation, economies of scale, product differentiation and efficiency gains;
- the resulting agreements encourage foreign direct investment between participants;
- regional integration is a global phenomenon with a rising number of agreements between North and South becoming evident (e.g. NAFTA and Asia Pacific Economic Cooperation – APEC);
- some states are members of a number of regional groupings (e.g. the US is a member of both APEC and NAFTA).

As Figure 3.1 shows, the majority of RTAs are FTAs, reflecting the fact that this type of agreement best reflects the needs of states in terms of speed, flexibility and selectivity. CUs appear to have become less popular and are perhaps out of tune with the current trading climate. Another key trend is the dominance of bilateral over plurilateral deals. Indeed, over 80 per cent of all RTAs are bilateral. This is caused by the fact that the opportunities for plurilateral deals are fewer and they are technically more complex: though it should be noted that many of these bilateral deals are based around plurilateral agreements, pointing to the consolidation of established trading relationships. The erosion of proximity as a driver of RTAs is underlined by statistics which suggest that while 88 per cent of all RTAs in force are intra-regional, 43 per cent of those that are signed and being negotiated are cross-regional. This figure is even higher for those that are proposed (as of December 2006) where 52 per cent are cross-regional. These figures lead to a questioning of the rationale for RTA formation among natural trading partners and reflect the fact that states will look further afield once regional opportunities have been exhausted.

It has been argued that the process of regionalization exists in opposition to the process of globalization. This viewpoint is based on a perception that the latter is characterized by openness of economies and an emerging global market for enterprises. Enterprises push for regional integration as an anti-competitive device to limit the negative effects of competition. Others, such as Bhagwati (1992) see regional integration as a force that fragments the global economic system and removes the incentives for states to engage in global free trade. The result is that regionalism is at the direct expense of multilateralism. It is clear from basic economic analysis that the process of regional economic integration can be both negative and positive – negative in that it can lead to trade diversion, and positive in that it can lead to trade creation (Robson, 1998). Clearly the relative benefits of trade creation and trade diversion determine the extent to which the moves towards regional economic integration work to the advantage of integrating states.

It can be credibly argued that regionalization is a logical response to globalization. Traditional economic theory perceives regional integration as a second-best scenario compared to the ideal of global free trade. Thus in a situation in which a truly globalized economy is not practical in either political or economic terms, regional

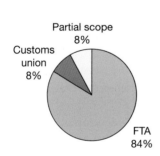

FIGURE 3.1 Notified RTAs in Force by Type of Agreement, December 2006

Source: WTO.

integration is the next best thing. Regionalization is also compatible with the process of globalization, as the former can easily stimulate the latter – acting as a building block for deeper global integration. In a relatively closed environment, an island of free and preferential trade is likely to be detrimental to the efficient functioning of the global economy. However, if regional integration takes place against a background of liberalizing global trade, then concerns are lessened as the benefits from more open markets can potentially offset losses from the absence of global free trade. In any case, increasingly few of these regional agreements emerge as solely protectionist measures.

Regionalism confronts states with a number of broad policy choices. First, they initially have to decide with whom to form an agreement. Broadly, states that are similar in terms of economic and political development as well as being geographically close provide a greater case for regional integration. Second, they are faced with choices regarding the policy to be taken vis-à-vis non-members. States have to decide how discriminatory they will be towards non-members as well as how favourable they will be to key trading partners. Third, they have to decide upon the degree of integration to be pursued. Different states have different motives for the integration process and differ on the salience of political sovereignty. Finally, states have to decide on the extent of the agreement. This depends upon the policy areas covered as well as the number of states bound by the agreement.

The trend towards these agreements is not likely to come without political costs. In particular, there have been concerns expressed over the trade-off between a state's desire to preserve political sovereignty with the desire to enjoy the benefits of economic integration. This could become a salient issue if there is an internal dynamic within the process that moves states towards deeper political unification almost by default (Robson, 1998). Broadly, according to Lawrence (1995), the political implications of the shift towards regional economic integration lie along a continuum of six options:

1. *National autonomy*: almost total freedom over decision making by governments.
2. *Mutual recognition*: again decentralized decision making with market competition guiding moves towards common standards (notably the EU's guiding principle of mutual recognition).
3. *Monitored decentralization*: limited restrictions on policy to secure international harmonization. International bodies such as the IMF may monitor this.
4. *Coordination*: an open recognition of the need to converge policies with jointly agreed adjustments to policies.
5. *Explicit harmonization*: this requires explicit agreement on regional wide standards.
6. *Federalist mutual governance*: centrally enforced rules through supranational institutions.

The position of a state along this continuum would depend upon the extent and intensity of policy spill-overs between separate states within the regional grouping. The more intense these spill-overs, the greater the legitimacy of deeper levels of political integration.

However, there are evidently political motivations pushing states towards developing regional agreements. These are essentially threefold:

1. *Security*: the participating states can use the regional economic agreement as security against non-members as well as enhancing security vis-à-vis other members of the grouping. The integration of states not only makes conflict more expensive but the regular political contact involved also establishes trust and other forms of cross-border cooperation. However, this has to be

counterbalanced by the potential for conflict through commercial tensions between participants, especially where the benefits of the moves towards regional integration are unevenly distributed.

2. *Bargaining power*: this is based on the premise that when states combine their power, they can 'punch' more effectively within the global economy. These benefits, of course, depend upon states being able to reach common agreement on key issues.

3. *'Lock-in'*: the process of political and economic reform can be effectively locked in through membership of a regional integration body. Thus the agreement acts as an effective commitment mechanism.

GLOBAL TRADE AND REGIONAL INTEGRATION

Regional integration agreements are officially sanctioned (subject to conditions) deviations to the GATT's rules on non-discrimination. Generally – under Article 25 of the GATT – three principal restrictions are imposed upon regional agreements.

1. The agreement must not 'on the whole' raise protection against excluded states.
2. Agreements must reduce internal tariffs to zero and remove other restrictive regulations on commerce within the regional agreement area, other than those justified by other GATT articles.
3. Agreements must cover 'substantially all trade'.

These conditions seek to ensure that regional integration agreements do not undermine the access of other countries to the integrating area. The second and third conditions are designed to deter pressure to use tariffs to offer political favouritism towards either domestic industries or partner countries. The conditions imposed by the GATT/WTO can be imposed gradually, although greater leniency is generally extended to developing than to developed economies. Article 5 of the GATS is tighter than Article 24 of the GATT and applies on a sector-by-sector basis rather than 'on the whole'. In addition, it gives businesses from third countries operating within the region before the agreement is signed the same rights as indigenous businesses. Again, developing states get greater flexibility over the rules. The conditions over the coverage of trade allow developing countries to reduce tariffs on mutual trade in any way they wish.

There is a clear overlap between RTAs and the WTO in that both share the common objective of trade liberalization though the former is discriminatory, a facet not shared by the latter. While discrimination was meant to be outlawed by the GATT, the MFN principle has been eroded by successive preferential trade arrangements. Some of these were introduced to account for differing levels of development while others were introduced to allow like-minded members to pursue faster liberalization of trade. Given the difficulties of multilateralism, it should come as no surprise that RTAs are proving increasingly attractive. This has implications for multilateralism as the benefits of RTAs could be extended to a multilateral framework. However, such open regionalism has no precedent in fact. In addition, the lack of a framework over the dos and don'ts of the RTAs give members significant flexibility in their design. As a result these agreements rarely address sensitive sectors. Overall, international policy towards regionalism seeks to:

- allow agreements to realize trade creation and avoid trade diversion and to ensure that the process does not unduly harm non-members;
- permit deep integration among members;
- preserve effects of previous liberalization and ensure that any liberalization within the agreement has credibility;
- support a liberalizing dynamic throughout the global economy.

By 2005, only one of the WTO's 151 members – Mongolia – was not party to a regional trade agreement. Not all agreements notified to the WTO are still in force today – although, in practice, most of the discontinued agreements have been superseded by redesigned accords. Out of a total of 420 (2005) agreements that have been notified to the GATT/WTO, 247 are still in force. In the 1950s, there were very few notifications to the GATT. In the 1960s, notifications averaged two to three a year. In the 1970s, the number of notifications increased, reaching a peak of ten in 1973. During the 1980s and early 1990s, notifications dropped off considerably until 1992 when 11 new regional trade agreements were notified. Since then an average of 11 regional trade arrangements have been notified annually to the GATT/WTO. The result of all these agreements is a complex set of interrelationships. In addition to those that have been notified to the GATT/WTO, the number of regional trade arrangements which have not been notified has also grown.

The number of trade agreements notified to GATT/WTO has increased from 20 in 1990 to 86 in 2000 to 159 in 2007. The agreements concluded over the past two decades have been mainly bilateral in nature and primarily between developed and developing economies. Furthermore, many of these have included provisions aimed at deepening integration through harmonizing elements of national policies in line with agreements to free up market forces between partners. To some, the shift towards agreements between states from different geographical regions constitutes a 'new regionalism' (see below). Although most of these agreements are bilateral, the 'new regionalism' represents a diversion from multilateralism as states grew frustrated with the protracted negotiations involved in multilateral trade negotiations. Overall, it may be seen that multilateralism affects RTAs on three levels:

1. through WTO rules on RTAs;
2. market access commitments;
3. other trade-related rules and disciplines.

There are major difficulties with the rules provided by the GATT/WTO Treaty over regional integration agreements. There are uncertainties over what is actually meant by 'substantially all trade'. Does it refer to the proportion of trade or to all sectors? Similarly, there is a lack of definition over rules of origin and no method of assessing the overall level of trade restrictions. Such uncertainties have resulted in weak enforcement of Article 24. This has resulted from the consensual nature of the enforcement bodies and from an inability to make an adverse comment without the agreement of the offending party. The rise in the number of RTAs created led to an administrative bottleneck as, according to GATT practice, a working committee has to be established to examine the agreement. As a result, the WTO established the Committee on Regional Trade Agreements (CRTA) to verify the compliance of notified RTAs with the WTO provisions and consider the systemic implications of such agreements for the multilateral trading system. However, failure to agree on the provision contained in Article 24 became a major concern of the DDA.

The impact of regional integration arrangements upon the multilateral system revolves around three sets of arguments.

1. *Multilateralism as a response to regionalization.* Some states excluded from the regional integration process may respond by seeking to speed up multilateral liberalization. Some saw the formation of the EEC as a catalyst for the Dillon and Kennedy rounds of GATT. This is simplistic: regional integration may not only be defensive but also offensive within the context of multilateral negotiations and therefore act as a powerful force driving the liberalization process forward.

2. *Regionalization and multilateral negotiation.* If regional blocs aid and simplify the process of negotiation, it is feasible that freeing up trade on a global basis would become easier. While this might appeal intuitively, it does assume that all blocs are able to present a uniform front – something that has often been lacking within trade negotiations. Indeed, the benefits of coordination may be outweighed by the costs of combining different interests. This issue is likely to be made more difficult as the WTO extends its capabilities into areas where the central bodies of regional agreements have little power. Thus combining national and regional responsibilities complicates matters further. There is also a danger that regional integration may result in inward-looking blocs that may be less willing to negotiate multilaterally. The result would be harmful to the credibility and effectiveness of the WTO.

3. *Regional integration and the frontiers of liberalization.* It is claimed that regionalism makes it easier to handle difficult issues. Agreement between like-minded states can aid liberalization, even if only on a limited geographical scale in instances where multilateral progress is simply not possible. But in some areas (such as agriculture), there have still been problems on difficult issues. The impact of regional integration agreements depends upon whether they are liberal and whether they are well suited to the needs of other countries.

The Doha Declaration recognizes that RTAs can play an important role in promoting the liberalization and expansion of trade and development. Indeed, while states have made a renewed commitment to multilateralism within Doha they have also increased their commitment to regional groupings. This gives RTAs the green light, though Doha does seek to clarify and improve the disciplines applying to these agreements. Negotiations within the DDA have focused on two tracks: procedural and systemic/legal issues. There has been progress on the former, as member states agreed to increase transparency in July 2006. The latter is proving more difficult due to the complexity of the issues involved. The improvement in transparency has set a procedure for early announcement, a time frame for notification, the type of information to be submitted and streamlined procedures for notifications and reporting. This should revitalize the CRTA and help overcome the problem related to the 'spaghetti bowl', and enable businesses to unravel the complexity associated with the multitude of agreements.

Some argue that all agreements should be open to outsiders if they meet the necessary requirements. However, this conflicts with the desire of some states to limit access to their grouping for political as well as commercial reasons. A more fundamental concern is the inadequate enforcement of existing rules. In part, this results from the prolonged period some states are given to implement

GATT/WTO rules. The result is that all states lose out through trade diversion effects. Such poor enforcement is symptomatic of the lack of implementation of rules generally – something that potentially undermines the benefit states can gain from the internationalization process.

There is a case to make for an economic system based on regional groupings, especially in terms of the development of the progressive liberalization of the global economy. In an increasingly complex system, any attempt to rationalize the number of parties around the table in trade agreements has the potential to make the liberalization of the trading system easier. In addition, as states exist in groups, they have the power to punch collectively above their weight and avoid any sidelining that may occur had they been negotiating alone. Thus the development of a series of blocs could act as a system of countervailing powers preventing any state from dominating the system. The WTO Report *The Future of the WTO* (2005) criticized the proliferation of bilateral and regional trade agreements on the basis that they had made the MFN clause the exception rather than the rule. The consequence of this is that it had increased discrimination in world trade. Despite this, these agreements continue to progress with the US being especially active in concluding many deals with developing states.

Research from the World Bank (Solaga and Winters, 1997) reaches a negative conclusion on the argument that regional integration works to the benefit of the multilateral system. Indeed, the institution fears that regionalism could dilute the power of those bodies dedicated to multilateral trade liberalization. Frankel (1998a) suggests that if regional trading agreements are to work for and not against the global trading system, then they have to adhere to strict guidelines such as a proper enforcement of GATT rules, an insistence that barriers to exclude third parties are lowered and an assurance that membership to these groups is open. In adhering to these principles these blocs could lead the way in multilateral trade development.

To strengthen the rules governing regional integration agreements (particularly so that they do not reduce overall levels of welfare), many suggest that approval should be subject to a commitment to lower barriers vis-à-vis non-members. Such a commitment should reduce the potential for trade diversion as a result of the instigation of the regional trade agreement. Srinivasan (1998) suggests that regional trade agreements should be merely temporary and contain a commitment by participants to extend the benefits to other states within a given time frame. This would effectively ban regional agreements. Others suggest non-exclusive membership criteria but this – due to geography – is often unrealistic. More feasible is to enforce existing rules more completely. A starting point would be to remove the legal uncertainty regarding key terminology (such as that surrounding 'substantially all trade'). In this sense a benchmark figure needs to be established. The World Bank suggests 98 per cent within 10 years of the initiation of the agreement.

Such changes need the political commitment of the member states and the WTO to take them forward. As yet, the WTO seems unlikely to do this. It lacks credibility and legitimacy as well as the resources to operate an effective scrutiny system of regional trade agreements. In short, the management of regional agreements and their compatibility with the global trading system cannot be ensured without credible regulation, scrutiny and enforcement. Without this, the WTO relies on bilateral relations to ensure that these developments do not turn the mass of regional blocs in on themselves.

Baldwin (2006) argues that the global economy is characterized by a 'spaghetti bowl' of unilateral, bilateral and multilateral deals which no one agrees is the best way to organize trade. This can create too complex a system or a multilateral system to emerge. The spaghetti bowl is based on the following features:

1. Different rules of origin and/or exclusions of different lists of sensitive goods can mean that bilateral agreements can procure trade that is less than free.
2. Bilateral cumulation (where inputs from one state are considered as originating in another) can distort purchase pattern.

The result is a tangled web of uncoordinated and often conflicting rules of origin and bilateral cumulation. In among these trends, which could undermine multilateralism, the WTO – according to Baldwin – has remained largely passive. The spaghetti bowl creates a problem, as they generate the following:

1. *Economic inefficiency*: multiple tariff rates introduce inefficiencies especially within industries that have complex value networks.
2. *Stumbling-blocks*: they can hinder progress towards multilateralism due to tariff differentials.
3. *An absence of hegemony*: the WTO rules tend to mitigate the power of the hegemons this could be subverted by the complexity of the spaghetti bowl.

These problems could be overcome by setting all MFN tariffs to zero and switched to diagonal rules of cumulation (a common set of rules of origin are agreed where, once a product enters the market, the product is determined by common standards). Thus the product will never lose its original status. The complexity of the spaghetti bowl reflects the complexity of the political economic forces that evolved them. The result was a hub-and-spoke system that was highly selective over the form and nature of the deals. The power exists within the hubs while the spokes will each face different rules with regard to access to the hub.

Baldwin (1997) argued for the existence of a domino effect within regionalism, believing that the forces of regionalism, initially working independently of each other, will at a certain point trigger a multiplier effect that would knock down trade barriers like a row of dominoes. This would open up a path to regional and potentially global liberalization. This domino effect is generated by trade and investment diversion created by the process of regionalism leading other states to join existing or establish their own RTAs. These effects are created through a new political economy in non-participating states which pressurizes governments to join RTAs. Firms from excluded states see their performance undermined by exclusion and pressurize government to act to ensure that export costs are not sacrificed for import-competing concerns. According to Baldwin, the key organising principle behind this process is reciprocity which creates a juggernaut once export interests outweigh import-competing interests.

The OECD (2003) highlights the fact that many RTAs go beyond the WTO rules as they contain measures that are more far-reaching across a broader range of sectors. For services, many RTAs adopt a top-down or negative list approach whereby everything is liberalized unless otherwise specified. This is in stark contrast to the 'positive list' approach of the WTO where liberalization only applies to specified sectors. Furthermore, many RTAs eschew anti-dumping measures in favour of coordination in competition policy, allow limited labour mobility, allow freer FDI and allow freer competition in public procurement. Overall across many areas, the OECD highlights the fact that RTAs go beyond the remit of the WTO. This can extend to issues such as the environment.

There is also a concern as to whether RTAs create convergence or divergence over multilateral standards. There is a concern that these agreements can create an à la carte approach in areas such as investment rules and competition that could result in confusion and inconsistency across the global economy. The OECD suggests that the picture is mixed. The RTAs can promote harmonization through applying WTO approaches, using other international agreements or by helping to forge future common standards. This can be complemented by RTAs facilitating cooperation and technical assistance. Alternatively, these RTAs can promote divergence, as convergence at the regional level does not always translate into harmonization at the global level. This has already been evident in the treatment of intellectual property rights (IPRs) and anti-dumping where approaches differ markedly across RTAs. This could raise transaction costs for MNEs and cause trade frictions.

Similarly the issue as to whether RTAs are beneficial or harmful to outsiders has to be handled carefully. While these are clearly discriminatory, there is evidence to suggest that RTAs are willing to extend regional preferences to non-members on a MFN bias especially under GATS. Similarly there is scope for non-discrimination within the domain of competition policy as well as investment. However, there are clearly benign effects, as they can alter investment patterns vulnerable to capture by protectionist interests as well as other areas where politics may play a role.

MOVES TOWARDS REGIONAL INTEGRATION IN THE GLOBAL ECONOMY

Although it is beyond the scope of this chapter to analyse all regional integration agreements, it is worth taking a brief look at their form and nature on a continental basis. It is evident that not only are these agreements – as noted above – becoming more widespread but they are also becoming increasingly complex as states develop deeper relations with others at different levels of economic development. Thus these regional trade agreements are not merely about the formally agreed groupings pursuing an integration plan but are also about preferential trading agreements with more geographically dispersed states.

Europe

Economic integration within Europe revolves around the EU and to a lesser extent the European Free Trade Area (EFTA). The EU was originally conceived of as a political project that sought to promote economic cooperation among states as a strategy to ensure that war between these states became impossible. Membership of the group is open to all European states as long as they conform to basic principles, namely that they are European and are committed to democratic and market processes. The 1957 Treaty of Rome not only committed states to a customs union but also required deeper integration through the development of common policies in a number of areas. The management of such policies was aided by the establishment of a governance structure based around supranational institutions. The gradual enhancement of the power of these supranational bodies has been a salient factor pushing the integration process forward.

Europe has for a long time provided the model for economic integration. While the process was initially a political one, commercial forces have increasingly driven it. This has led to the deepening of integration as the EU has evolved from a customs union to a common market and, for the majority of states, into an economic and monetary union – a reflection of the acceptance by states that deeper integration was in their broad political and commercial interests. This gradual extension has resulted in states ceding sovereignty in an increasing number of areas. Successful deepening depends upon continual commitment by member states to sustained micro-economic reform. A broadening process has accompanied this deepening as the membership has been extended from six to 27.

The cementing political and economic reform is the primary reason why the ex-communist states of Central and Eastern Europe applied to join the EU. On the whole, existing members were agreeable to such an extension. In practice, the deepening of European integration alongside the extension of membership could result in the emergence of a multi-speed Europe or a Europe of 'variable geometry' given the variation in economic readiness and political enthusiasm for deeper integration among European states.

In 1992, the smaller ETFA grouping joined with the EU to form the European Economic Area. This effectively opened up the single European market to small Northern European and Alpine states. In gaining access to the single market, the EFTA states had to implement the same competition and single market laws as the EU. This agreement led the larger EFTA states to seek and obtain full membership of the EU. This highlights how important the Single European Market programme was to the integration process in Europe. The programme, in effect, kick-started an integration process which had lain dormant for two decades.

With the accession of Central and Eastern European states into the EU and with the likely accession of the remaining Balkan states, attention is turning to the limits to the defined European region. Of especial controversy is the proposed accession of Turkey to the EU. Many argue that the Bosphorus is a natural physical barrier to Europe and that as a result most of Turkey is in Asia. Furthermore, there are cultural concerns and issues as to whether the EU would be able to absorb a large state that is at a substantially lower level of economic development. However, political imperatives are pushing the EU towards integrating with Turkey as Western economies seek to build commercial and cultural ties with Muslim economies.

The impact of the deeper integration initiatives upon outsiders is difficult to assess. However, two features are evident. First, deeper integration stimulated the expansion of the EU, as applicants felt that the political and economic benefits of deeper integration outweighed any potential political and economic losses. Second, there is little indication that a deeper Europe resulted in a more protective Europe as many feared – although the EU does remain, at best, a highly discriminatory trading partner. To this end it has signed a number of preferential trading agreements with developing states.

Europe is the region that has signed the highest number of RTAs accounting for over half of the RTAs notified to the WTO and in force. These are based around the EU, EFTA and to a lesser degree, South-Eastern Europe. This latter subregion has concluded the CEFTA-plus agreement. The ties between this region and the EU are being formally enhanced by the planned membership of the latter by the former as both the Croatia and Turkey applications are under negotiation. In addition, the EU has signed a stability and association agreement (SAA) with Serbia and Montenegro. In the Mediterranean basin the EU has signed a FTA which is gradually being deepened. Beyond its neighbourhood the EU has signed RTAs with Mercosur, the GCC, and has signed six economic partnership agreements with the ACP states. More recently it has signalled its intent to develop a new FTA arrangement with Korea, India and states party to the ASEAN, CACM and CAN. Parallel to the EU, EFTA has signed numerous agreements with Mediterranean states, the GCC and some South-East Asian states.

The Americas

The economic turmoil that hit the Americas in the 1980s was a primary catalyst behind the moves towards economic integration in this part of the global economy. The debt crisis and deteriorating trade balances pushed a wave of reform including privatization and a sustained attack on traditional trade and investment barriers. Latin American states became especially vulnerable to US pressure to pursue reform. In the 1990s, virtually all Latin American states instigated reforms aimed at integrating their economies into the global economy. In short, there was a distinct policy shift from import substitution to export promotion.

For Mexico, the NAFTA agreement broke its traditional policy of intervention and was a means of securing access to the US market. The external impact of this agreement has yet to be seen, but the temptation of accessing the US market has led to other Latin American states seeking NAFTA membership and NAFTA has come to be the focus of regional integration in the Americas. It is entirely possible that NAFTA could facilitate a restructuring of the hegemonic positioning of the US with regard to Latin America and ultimately eliminate the numerous Latin American regional trade agreements. However, extension of the agreement concerns non-members, notably the newly industrializing states of Asia, as it could lead to a redirection of US investment away from them. The NAFTA agreement is much shallower in terms of integration than the EU. It seeks to remove all barriers on trade in goods as well as barriers to foreign investment and trade in services. Other states may join as long as all existing members assent but, unlike the EU, there are no explicit longer term political objectives. NAFTA is unique, since it represents an almost free trade agreement between two developed states (US and Canada) and a developing country (Mexico). The agreement has been criticized due to its rules of origin that – according to many – will have large trade diversionary effects. However, evidence seems to suggest that these states are natural trading partners and that the current low tariff barriers will ensure that trade diversion will be limited.

By 2005, NAFTA covered around 30 per cent of US merchandise trade and about 70 per cent of total Canadian and Mexican merchandise trade. About 14 per cent of US FDI stocks are covered by NAFTA and over 60 per cent of FDI stocks for Canada and Mexico. The agreement remains the reference point and template for US trade agreements. Indeed, NAFTA was the direct stimulant for the creation of a proposed FTAA, though such ambitions have been overtaken by events (see Case Study 3.1 on NAFTA).

Efforts towards regional integration in Latin America had little success until their renewal in the 1980s. It is estimated that between 1990 and 1994, 26 bilateral and multilateral trade agreements were signed between Latin American states. These new agreements were primarily export driven and were part of a strategy of integrating with the rest of the global economy. For these reasons, these new efforts have proved more successful than have previous attempts at integration. This export-led stance has led to the growth of manufacturing trade, intra-industry trade and inter-regional specialization in Latin America.

CASE STUDY 3.1

NAFTA

From its beginnings in 1994, NAFTA has proved controversial. In part, this is due to the fact that it is unusually a free trade agreement between three states of differing levels of economic development. In particular, the vast differences between Mexico and the US have given rise to serious concerns. The more extreme critics within the US span the political spectrum and regard the agreement as detrimental on grounds as diverse as environmental standards, lower wages and employment, and lower product health and safety. As such, the criticisms of NAFTA include a mixture of scaremongering and legitimate concerns.

Sufficient time has passed since the birth of the organization to assess whether the dire predictions proved correct or whether the agreement worked as its architects said it would in promoting free trade and aiding the economic performance of its members. During the first 10 years of its existence, the agreement may be said to have been a success in terms of overall trade performance. Trade between the three states doubled, with US exports rising the fastest. However, US-based critics argue that while exports have increased, imports have increased even faster. Moreover, many point to the job losses that have resulted. The US government claims NAFTA created 900,000 jobs in the decade to 2004, but it is estimated that the cost in terms of employment has been roughly the same. In addition, it is argued that NAFTA has resulted in job losses in Mexico which, in turn, has put increased pressure on migration to the US. Ultimately such figures and their interpretation can be disputed.

From an agnostic viewpoint, most trade economists see NAFTA as a success given the increases in both intra-area trade and investment. In the first 10 years of its existence, the US saw trade with its NAFTA partners rise from around 25 per cent to one-third of its total trade.

However, many sceptics feel vindicated, a view shared by some citizens from all states. In part, this is an inevitable result of unrealistic expectations. The agreement was never likely to be a big net creator of jobs but would alter trade patterns. Furthermore, NAFTA was also never going to be a win-win scenario for all stakeholders: there were always going to be losers as well as winners. However, many regard the agreement as a failure. This view comes in part from treating the agreement as the cause of the many economic problems facing the individual economies. To blame NAFTA entirely, or even mainly, for job losses risks understating the structural causes of such employment shifts. Economies have their own dynamics of which NAFTA is but a single factor of change.

Canada feared that exposure to international competition would undermine its welfare system as enterprises flowed to lower tax states. However, this fear was misplaced: the growth increase induced by NAFTA boosted government coffers and Canadians also proved willing to pay higher taxes. The initial impact of NAFTA on Mexico was difficult to assess as its introduction coincided with a peso crisis. However, NAFTA membership was credited with increasing the speed with which the Mexican economy recovered from the crisis. While stronger ties to the US affect Mexico when the US goes into recession, they also protected Mexico from broader turbulence within the financial markets in the late 1990s. However, while Mexico has seen sharp rises in its trade and investment, NAFTA offers no solution to the deeper problems faced by the economy, especially in terms of generating employment and the continuing migration to the US.

Overall, NAFTA is only one in a series of factors that are changing the economies of its members. Greater economic openness generally, globalization, and pressures for more structural and radical economic reforms are all at play. These pressures would exist regardless of the existence of NAFTA.

However, NAFTA serves as an example of an agreement between developed and developing states in which expectations and the economic and political realities of economic integration have not been managed effectively.

CASE STUDY QUESTIONS

1. How and to what extent is NAFTA different from other preferential trading agreements?

2. To what extent was NAFTA a victim of its own success?

3. What can other trade agreements learn from the experience of NAFTA?

- The Central American Common Market (founded in 1960) sought to establish free and fair trade with a common external tariff as a means of fostering the economic development of these states. Internal frictions have left the ambitions of the group largely frustrated after an initial fivefold rise in intra-group trade. Since the 1980s, this project has waxed and waned with political instability. With emerging stability – both in economic and political terms – there has been a renewed push towards economic integration in Central America.

- The Andean Pact (established in 1969) was designed to increase the size of the market of the Andean states (Bolivia, Colombia, Ecuador, Peru and Venezuela) through trade liberalization and the coordination of common policies. However, trade liberalization and industrial planning were not really compatible and resulted in many exceptions to the trade liberalization policies. Thus its trade impact was severely curtailed, although intra-group manufacturing trade did rise sharply. In 1989, the process accelerated rapidly with the decision to create a common market by 1992. This decision resulted in the further liberalization of trade and the dropping of the industrial policy coordination aspects of the agreement. These changes have had a profound impact upon the form and intensity of intra-group trade.

- The Latin American Integration Association (formerly the Latin American Free Trade Association) was formed in 1960 and covered the largest Latin American states. It sought to encourage the growth of members via the agreed removal of collective barriers to trade. This is a broader agreement than the above Latin American agreements which are subsets of this larger group. Increases in intra-group trade result more from these smaller groups and their more liberal leanings than from this broader agreement. The conclusion therefore is that this agreement has had little impact upon intra-group trade.

- The Caribbean Community and Common Market (CARICOM) was established in 1973. It aims to foster economic cooperation and to integrate economies through freer inter-group trade. As the states involved are small, the tangible gains have been slight, but there is evidence of growing inter-group trade in recent years. CARICOM launched the Association of Caribbean states in 1994 to increase the links of the group with Central America but free trade concerns in this initiative are largely secondary to those of closer cooperation.

■ The Common Market of the South (MERCOSUR) was founded in 1991 and emerged as a result of sectoral integration between Argentina and Brazil: other states (Paraguay and Uruguay) have joined and more still are forming associate agreements with the group. MERCOSUR is a customs union and since its formation has witnessed a surge in internal trade. Internal liberalization was accompanied by external liberalization, resulting in a cut in average tariffs from 56 per cent to 15 per cent.

The US has been active in developing RTAs notably with Latin America as well as agreements further afield in Africa and the Middle East. In Asia Pacific, the US has opened discussions with Korea and Malaysia as a precursor to enhancing its ties with ASEAN states. This activism has also extended to the other NAFTA states as well as those in Latin America, where MERCOSUR is pursuing FTAs on an individual basis, though as a group it is aiming to sign up agreements with the GCC and other states in the Middle East.

Asia Pacific

Regional integration within Asia does not appear to have had any great impact upon the trade orientation of members. Indeed, most of the groupings that have emerged have been formed for reasons other than intra-group trade promotion. In terms of regional integration, this region differs from both Europe and the Americas: inter-state relationships tend to be based more on bilateral relationships and are not grouped around common institutions or alliances. Historically, Asian states have been distrustful of regional agreements because:

■ Asia has been successful without such arrangements;
■ smaller states risk domination by bigger states;
■ the cost of exclusion from regional agreements is not prohibitive;
■ they believe trade diversion effects would be greater than trade creation effects at the moment.

However, rising economic pressures for greater integration are removing this initial hesitancy as formal moves to instil integration become common.

The progress of economic development and trade liberalization has accelerated markedly on an inter-regional level. The result is that regionalization is what Gilbert and Mommen (1998) call a *de facto* process – that is, the result of the complementarities (in terms of technological capabilities, factor endowments and wage and income levels) of the constituent states. This underlines that the region's integration is driven by:

■ a tradition of market-led growth;
■ the large stake these states have in the multilateral trading system;
■ the inadequate incentives for states to engage in geographically exclusive regional agreements;
■ The transfer of industries from early starters to latecomers.

Between 1980 and 2005, intra-regional trade as a share of East Asia's trade has risen from 35 per cent to 52 per cent. This has been matched by a sharp increase in investment within this region. This has been driven by a more progressive attitude towards liberalization among these states, the creation of production and supply networks across Europe, improved digital and physical connectivity, and the emergence of China. Thus, despite East Asia having been a relative latecomer to RTAs, the number of agreements has soared since the 1990s. This was driven by a combination of the deepening of market-driven integration, the perceived success of European and North American integration, and the fall-out from the Asian financial crisis.

Generally integration has taken place within two overlapping fora – the Association of Southeast Asian Nations (ASEAN) and APEC.

■   ASEAN was founded in 1967 and sought to foster the peaceful national development of member states through cooperation. The move towards establishing trade arrangements among members only started in 1977 when a limited PTA – the Asian Free Trade Area (AFTA) – was established. At the time of its instigation, this PTA only covered some 2 per cent of intra-ASEAN trade. By 1985, this figure had only risen to 5 per cent. The slow growth was due to the laborious nature of the negotiations (conducted on a product-by-product basis); the lack of credible offers of preferences; high domestic content requirements; the long list of exclusions and the limited nature of the preferences themselves. A free trade area was proposed in 1991. The aim was to reduce tariffs on intra-group trade to between 0 and 5 per cent during the 15 years from 1993. This process was speeded up in 1994 when certain products were fast-tracked towards liberalized markets by 2000. AFTA was a defensive move promoted by regional integration elsewhere across the globe. The ASEAN economic community is one of the three pillars of the ASEAN community and it is envisaged that the area will become a single market by 2020. This requires new mechanisms and measures which are expected to be introduced in areas such as labour mobility. ASEAN has been extended through the ASEAN +3 (Japan, China, Korea) and ASEAN +6 (ASEAN +3 and Australia, New Zealand and India) agreements which have extended the scope of free trade arrangement throughout the region. Such agreements, especially the ASEAN+3, are likely to be the main vehicle for further integration.

There are a growing number of subregional agreements throughout the newly industrializing states in Asia. The ASEAN+3 grouping (essentially all the East Asian members of the APEC group) is becoming increasingly active in the development of regional integration. The agreement is tending to happen much faster in terms of financial integration than trade – an interesting contrast to the case of the EU. These groups have announced measures to closely integrate their financial systems to aid them to cope better with any repeat of the 1997 financial crisis that hit the region. This is being complemented by a series of bilateral and multilateral trade agreements among these states. In turn, these will be complemented by agreements the area is forming with the free trade area of Australia and New Zealand. The reason for this aggressive push towards integration is both positive and negative (the consequences of the 1997 financial crisis, the inspiration of the EU, disenchantment with the WTO and disquiet at the attitude and behaviour of the US and the EU). However, the legacy of the 1997 financial crisis seems to be the paramount driver as states react against the perceived lack of support from the US and Europe.

■   APEC – created in 1989 – provides a useful contrast to the EU in the process of economic integration. APEC is not a formal trade agreement but a 'community' of diverse states from three continents. The agreement stresses its members' commitment to free and open trade. APEC was created under the framework of open regionalism. As such, members are committed to reducing barriers to non-members as they move towards freer trade within the region. Indeed, some members of APEC have conditionally agreed to extend APEC preference to non-members since the agreement has no intention of evolving into customs union. APEC has established a degree of international division of labour with Japan providing essential capital goods, Hong Kong, Taiwan and Singapore finance, and Thailand, China and Indonesia labour-intensive operations. Increased trade and investment links have enhanced these complementarities. APEC's antipathy to becoming an exclusionary block indicates that it can be a powerful force for the liberalization of the global economy. Free trade among APEC states is only expected to be achieved by 2020 and will not be binding. This is further challenged by the fact that there is by no means a universal acceptance of the benefits of free trade between member states. As a result tariff cuts are negotiated on a state-by-state basis. APEC is evolving into an inter-governmental body with a ministerial council and secretariat and is planning to extend liberalization to functional cooperation. In 2005, an evaluation of APEC's achievement concluded that both tariff and NTBs have been reduced to a great extent and that linkages between APEC members and the rest of the world had been strengthened. However, the benefits are not solely created by APEC as it may also reflect the rise of China and of the productivity gains in the US and Canada.

The overlapping nature of many of the RTAs within the Asia-Pacific region is putting consolidation on the agenda, with several individual agreements such as ASEAN+3 being pursued or suggested. Japan has been pursuing an agenda of enhancing its regional RTAs with cross-regional agreements. This pattern is also being followed by Korea. China is also following up by signing RTAs with Chile and Pakistan and launching negotiations with the GCC, Pakistan, Singapore, Australia and New Zealand. As a group ASEAN is negotiating with India, Japan and New Zealand as well as considering an FTA with Korea. The reach of these formal integration blocs is being extended through a network of FTAs singled with other states. There is a concern that the proliferation of overlapping agreements is creating a 'noodle bowl' effect (the Eastern equivalent of Baldwin's spaghetti bowl' – see above) where the complexity works to counter multilateral objectives. The proliferation of agreements has created a complexity through multiple rules of origin and proliferation of standards leading to increased business costs. Thus to some extent there needs to be a hub that can act as a focus of these RTAs to simplify these arrangements.

These processes of integration are increasingly driven by the five largest economies (Singapore, Japan, Korean, China and Thailand) with many of the smaller economies relying on ASEAN to arrange FTAs, though ASEAN has only one FTA in force (with China). This covers 13 per cent to trade and 7 per cent (2007) to FDI stock. Extending it to the rest of the ASEAN three would raise these figures to 37 per cent and 32 per cent respectively.

Since its accession to the WTO in 2001 China has been active in concluding bilateral agreements which it sees more as a tool for diplomacy than as a means of building commerce. This explains the lack of comprehensiveness of such agreements. They highlight a desire to play a leading role in East Asian integration, to promote a North East Asian FTA with Japan and Korea and to secure the supply of natural resources (especially energy) from the Middle East and Australia. Initially, China did deals with culturally and geographically proximate states. This list has expanded as China has sought to increase its influence over world affairs. This pattern is being repeated in Japan where the state has ditched the sole focus of external policy on multilateralism towards concluding a series of bilateral deals in reaction to the Asian financial crises and to deals being concluded elsewhere. Most of Japan's deals are within the ASEAN region.

The Middle East and Africa

For many years, regional economic integration in Africa was limited by political instability and economic decline. The lack of economic development meant that regional economic integration would not yield these states any significant influence or power over the global economic system. The reliance of African states upon bilateral trade and aid deals with developed states renders them subject to external scrutiny of their policy strategies. Increasingly, African leaders are coming around to the view that regional integration is necessary if they are to successfully address their marginal position within the global economy. This is despite the failure of past efforts to deliver much in the way of benefits to the states involved.

Across Africa there are more than 200 regional groupings and agreements covering a wide variety of arrangements and issues. Some of these schemes have become quite mature, especially among West and Central African states. On the whole, the progress of economic integration has been very slow. Furthermore, the efforts that have been made have not been successful in terms of intra-regional trade, economic convergence or policy harmonization. In addition, Africa's share of intra-African trade has fallen continuously. The reasons for these problems highlight a number of potential deficiencies within regional integration schemes, especially when:

- the production structures of member states are not complementary;
- tariff changes cause loss of government revenue;
- the benefits of market integration are not assured to individual states;
- there is unequal distribution of integration benefits;
- long-term integration takes second place to short-term losses;
- there is an absence of central institutions at national and regional level;
- there is a lack of coordination and harmonization of economic policies;
- civil society is hardly involved in the integration process.

Some of the groupings within Africa date back to the colonial era and reflect a shared historical legacy among states having the same colonial power. This has created common institutions, a common language and even a common currency. In others, regional groupings were based on geographical proximity. Most of the African economic integration schemes came into existence during an era marked by inward-looking development based mainly on import substitution. The goal of self-sufficiency was pursued through the creation of subregional markets with the eventual aim of creating a Pan-African Community.

For the Mahgreb states, difficulties in the 1980s pushed these states to work more closely together. The Arab Mahgreb Union, signed in 1989, was heavily shaped by its relations with the EU and its economic dependence upon Europe. The Mahgreb states and the Middle Eastern states (through the Gulf Cooperation Council) tend to be more developed than the sub-Saharan African states. The willingness of the EU to assist the Mahgreb states is limited by the dominance of Maghreb exports by products such as agriculture and textiles in which the EU is very vulnerable to competition. EU aid is focused on helping these states promote intra-regional trade to make them more attractive to outside states and investors.

The Gulf Cooperation Council was established in 1981 and sought to create a customs union involving free trade among members and a common external tariff (CET). Initial phases of the plan were easy to implement (the removal of tariffs) but the establishment of a common external tariff proved more difficult. Generally the desire for the development of such an agreement has ebbed and flowed with the price of oil. Overall, the agreement has had relatively little impact upon the relative share of mutual trade due to similarity in the trade and production structures of member states and the fact that there is already a low level of protection vis-à-vis third countries. Indeed, in the first 20 years the agreement only managed to increase intra-regional trade by 2 per cent. This is due to the low level of intra-industry trade as many of these states rely heavily on oil. It is evident that Saudi Arabia as the largest economy in the region will not be a force for integrating these economies. Instead of operating as a leader it has opted to trade outside the region.

The nature of these regional integration agreements is becoming increasingly diverse and there has been a growing number of trade agreements between states at different stages of economic development (see above). The World Bank suggests that developing states should seek regional trade agreements with developed states rather than with other developing states if they are to benefit commercially. Its research suggests that:

- Agreements among developing countries tend to create divergences between partners with one state benefiting at the expense of others as well as being more likely to lead to trade diversion.
- Developing–developed country agreements are more likely to aid technology transfer and provide lock-in mechanisms for political and economic reform.

For the middle-income states, the benefits of integration will only come with deeper integration, as this is more likely to realize scale and competition benefits. These measures have been complemented by the Agadir agreement between Jordan, Egypt, Tunisia and Morocco. This was signed in February 2004 and was seen as a precursor to the development of a Pan-Arab Free Trade Area. This will be aided by the gradual extension of the Agadir agreement to other members of the region.

Of all the regions in the world, sub-Saharan Africa integration conforms to the conventional concept of integration based on proximity. In many ways, this reflects the dominant role played by regional politics in the design of these RTAs. It also helps explain the ambitious agenda for these agreements despite the relatively low levels of trade between them. Extra-regional agreements have historically been based on non-reciprocal performances under schemes such as the GSP from the EU. Most states continue to benefit from such schemes with the exception of states in North and Southern Africa which have tended to prefer reciprocal agreements. This shift towards reciprocal preferences will soon extend to other states as EPAs replace unilateral preferences. The EPAs are supposed to enhance regional integration, though this does not seem likely in Central and Eastern Africa where asymmetries between members are leading to new configurations based around East and Southern Africa. Such arrangements are likely to clash with existing agreements.

There has been talk of the development of currency unions within Africa. This interest is generated by a desire to counteract the small size of their economies and by the successful launch of the euro. ECOWAS, COMESA and SADC have all talked about creating a common currency among their members. In West Africa this process is complicated by the fact that half of ECOWAS are already part of the West Africa Economic and Monetary Union (WAEMU). However, the non-WAEMU members of ECOWAS do not wish to join this club which they see as largely a relic of French rule. Thus these states have proposed establishing a monetary union of their own. However, as trade between these states is relatively low it is hard to pinpoint the exact benefits of the creation of monetary union for these states despite efforts by these states to increase trade through better investment in infrastructure, lowering political tensions and lowering tariff and non-tariff barriers to trade.

NEW REGIONALISM: A PARADIGM FOR ECONOMIC DEVELOPMENT

The fact that regionalism extends beyond those states that are geographically proximate opens up new forms of cooperation. These new agreements extend beyond trade into investment and other previously sensitive policy areas. What is also marked is that often these agreements can occur between states that would not normally be considered partners due to differences in levels of economic development and performance. These tenets (extension and penetration) are the two central planks of new regionalism: though the term can be misleading, as they are often bilateral deals between states in different regions of the global economy. This trend has arisen out of frustration with multilateralism and a belief that such a framework can provide an alternative method of liberalization and harmonization.

Thus in some ways new regionalism can bypass multilateral institutions and arrangements as well as seeking to develop links between developed and developing states. Much of the rise in the bilateral RTAs over the past decade or so is symptomatic of this new regionalism. Indeed by 2007, 27 per cent of agreements in force were between developed and developing states; compared to 14 per cent in 1995. This rise may be accounted for by several factors such as fragmentation in Central and Eastern Europe and the desire of developed states (especially by the US) to parallel multilateralism with bilateralism.

The incentive for developing states to accept such bilateral deals rests in the prospect of positive discrimination vis-à-vis other states. However, these have to be offset against potential problems where there is inconsistency between the state's stance in multilateral negotiations and its obligations as part of the bilateral deal. This could be especially troublesome where the agreements enforce developing states to undertake liberalization beyond that expected under WTO commitments. Such commitments will limit the room to manoeuvre for these states. The benefits of these agreements are also undermined by the developed states agreeing similar deals with other developing states. As a result, the size and durability of the benefits from such agreements can be highly uncertain. Another by-product of these bilateral deals is that they would tend to weaken existing or evolving regional common markets that may offer long-term gains for these states. This may in fact lead to these agreements being unwound. Furthermore, such a network of deals may pose a new challenge to the coherence of the global trading system. For example, developing a number of diverse deals with a number of separate developed states may impose financial pressure on developing state customs authorities and firms. The former would have to deploy different treatment to the same products from different states; whereas the latter may have to adjust products to different markets. However, the EU and the US (who have both been active in developing such agreement disputes) suggest that these deals are a stepping stone to a coherent multilateral framework.

NAFTA is perhaps the most high-profile example of new regionalism (see Case Study 3.1). Evidence provided by UNCTAD suggests mixed benefits for Mexico from such an agreement. It is evident that Mexico has enjoyed strong export and FDI growth. Its share of world manufactured exports grew by over 100 per cent between 1994 and 2004. However, its value-added in manu-facturing has been low. This highlights the fact that despite economic gains its ability to translate these gains into tangible economic and social progress has been limited, as there is little evidence that the agreement has narrowed per capita income between Mexico and its partners. Thus, overall, these agreements have added little to the prospect of economic development. Indeed, in some areas NAFTA has had negative consequences notably in agriculture and banking. Perhaps the best indicator of the failure of NAFTA to live up to its expectations is that it has failed to stem the tide of migration from Mexico to the US. Such labour flows highlight the fact that the pressure to migrate remains strong despite NAFTA.

Given the absence of any tangible benefits for economic development from such arrangements, an alternative may be for intra-developing state agreements. These agreements have been growing the fastest of all forms of bilateral agreements. As intra-regional trade grows, so the rationale for such agreements grows. In South East Asia regional trade is 40 per cent of total trade and is increasing in other regions albeit from a low base. For example, trans-regional trade in Africa has increased from 5 per cent in the mid-1980s to 10 per cent in 2006. However, the benefits of trade for development depend on:

- links between the export sector and the rest of the economy;
- the amount of employment created;
- the extent of technological spill-overs to the rest of the economy;
- the proportion of domestic value-added in exports;
- the revenue generated;
- the share of revenue generated for domestic sectors.

Evidence offered from UNCTAD (2007) suggests that the composition of trade between develop-ing states can often aid diversification and development more than trade in general. However, while regional agreements among developing states may promote trade and allow for efficiency gains through intra-industry trade, there is a tendency for these benefits to be unevenly spread. The more developed and larger states tend to benefit more than the smaller, less advanced states. Such differences reflect structural differences within the grouping. As a result there may be a need to transfer funds between states to ensure the coherence of the group.

Overall regional blocs enable developing states to find markets more easily than they would with the bilateral deals with developed states. This suggests the possibility of a link between regionalism and industrialization for these states. While not precluding multilateralism, these blocs can provide

TABLE 3.1 Notified RTAs by Type of Partner, December 2006

Type of partner	RTAs in goods	RTAs in services
Developed only	11	16
Developing only	25	33
Developed–developing	27	44
Developing–transition	5	0
Developed–transition	5	7
Transition only	27	0

Source: UNCTAD (2007).

the basis for global competitiveness; this necessitates a strong commitment by states to deepen integration beyond trade liberalization and may even involve regional policies. Table 3.1 indicates the cluster of North–South agreements within both trade and services, accounting for over 50 per cent of all agreements in goods and nearly 80 per cent in services. Within these RTAs there is an in-built agenda to expand the scope of the North–South agreements both in terms of services and the soc-called WTO-plus issues of competition, government procurement, IPR and investment.

REGIONALISM AND THE MNE

Assessment of how industry responds to the strategic challenges posed by regionalization has to be carried out on an ad hoc basis. Each industry differs in terms of its regionalization drivers and the idiosyncrasies of its market segment. At a firm level, enterprises differ over the degree to which they need to have different regional strategies and the extent to which they should integrate operations. A starting point for analysis is to remember that the forces influencing strategy on the regional level also influence strategy on a global level. The core drivers pushing enterprises towards regional-wide strategies are:

- The convergence of customer needs and tastes.
- The existence of customers and channels that purchase on a multi-country basis. The most notable examples of this are multinational companies that buy on a regional basis and the emergence of regional-wide retailers.
- The rise of transferable marketing whereby enterprises use the same marketing approaches in different states.

These pressures towards the regionalization of enterprise strategy are also driven by cost factors such as lower transportation costs, the wider availability of economies of scale and the existence of cost–space and time–space convergence. As integration progresses, it is expected that variations in country costs will converge as industry locates to reflect intra-regional differences in cost. The extent of such cost differences within any regional grouping is a function of the degree of integration within the group. Conventional economic wisdom indicates that the cost advantages tend to increase with the higher degree of commercial freedom and greater degrees of transparency among states.

Furthermore, enterprise strategy is also strongly influenced by governmental actions, especially in areas such as trade policy, technical and related standards and commercial regulations. Strategy may be as much reactive as it is proactive. The former implies that regional strategy could be a response to the actions of an enterprise's competitors. Enterprises may also respond through the development of shared services that increase the interdependence of states and lead to the creation of pan-regional networks. The result could lead to enterprises competing with each other through the framework provided by their respective networks. Within the context of these developing regional networks, there should be a greater transferability of competitive advantage between states. For example, technology advantages have become more transferable in developed economies via the spread of high technology enterprises responding to regional integration.

According to Yip (1998) – within the context of regional integration – the strategic choices available to enterprises revolve around:

- The choice of markets in which to participate (the world economy is moving towards a hierarchical marketplace based on global, regional and then smaller national or subnational niches);
- The choice of products: this is especially pertinent when enterprises move towards standardized products – though marginally differentiated – on both a global and regional basis.
- The choice of location: in locating activities (including shared services), firms are tending to centralize rather than develop on a national basis.
- The choice of marketing: once again standardization is becoming increasingly evident.
- The kinds of competitive moves to make to secure new positions (such as cross-subsidies and linkages).

The nature of the chosen strategy will depend on the nature of the drivers noted above and how they directly impact upon the business concerned. Clearly enterprises need to balance the regionalization of their industry with the regionalization of their strategy. However, 'going regional' could cause the firm to lose its position within indigenous markets to rivals who are more nationalistic in terms of strategy.

The strategic impact of this trend towards regionalism has impacted upon the strategy of the MNEs. Whether this impact is proactive or reactive is a moot point; however, what is above debate is the core focus that for the top MNEs the notion of globality is a myth, as most tend to generate the majority of their sales within their home region (Rugman, 2000, 2005). The regional focus of MNEs suggests that the global market is not becoming homogenized and the psychic distance between regions still remains a significant barrier to trade. The majority of MNEs are based mainly in the triad of the US, Japan and Europe, and it is these regions that are the focus of these enterprises activities. Indeed, in 2008, 375 out of the top 500 MNEs (over 75 per cent) were from the triad.

Rugman's evidence suggests that there are no evident trends towards uniformity within the global economy. Firms neither desire to have a ubiquitous reach nor do they seek to deliver uniformity across those regions within which they operate. In terms of branding, there are very few global brands, with Coke being a notable exception. There is also little evidence to suggest that value chains are being reconfigured and coordinated across regions. Indeed, most manufacturing tends to take place within the region served. This pattern is even more marked within the service sector. Further up the value chain this regional pattern is also evident for R&D. Most R&D has tended to be undertaken by firms within their locality.

However, Rugman concedes that this regional focus of the 'front end' of the value chain may not be replicated at the 'back end'. There is evidence to suggest that while sales tend to be regional, production tends to be more global. However, this should not be overstated – according to Rugman – as a significant amount of this production takes place within regionally based clusters. Indeed, it was only in electronics that there was evidence of a global production network. Often the relative costs of distribution to assembly inhibited the dispersion of the production process. The emphasis by Rugman on sales data is seen as a major weakness of his hypothesis. To many, such a narrow measure risks understating the extension of MNEs beyond their home region. For example, it is noticeable within the modern economy how firms have started to become active seekers of knowledge in pools of value-adding information. This may not show up in sales but it is nonetheless important to globalization. A further criticism is that the definition of what is a 'region' has been fluid. Both formal and informal membership of regional grouping has been flexible with many regions expanding overtime.

This analysis supports conclusions made by Ohmae in 1985 who identified a geographic space based on the triad of Japan, the US and the EU which share a number of common features (such as low macro-economic growth and mature technological infrastructure). To capture innovation costs, large MNEs need to achieve deep penetration within each of these regions. However, MNEs face problems in seeking to enter these other regions which can often only be overcome via the use of networks. This may often be due to the inability of the MNE to transfer home-based advantage into other locations. However, Ohmae understated the degree of regionalism that would become apparent within the global economy.

The fact that MNEs are regionally focused reinforces the desire for governments to develop regional trading blocs. As a result, regional trading blocs should seek to support this activity through the development of the appropriate policy frameworks that enable regional sales and other value-added activities to find the most appropriate location within the specific regional theatre and enable these firms to resist external threats. This policy practice has been supported by Rugman and D'Cruz's (2000) advocacy of regional business networks. These networks create business systems around a 'flagship firm' which collaborates with partners for mutual advantage. The flagship leads the network with the intention of shaping the competitive position of the firms within it. Clearly such cooperative frameworks need the agreement of the regulatory authorities.

CONCLUSION

RTAs have become a common feature of the multilateral trading systems over recent years. It is unlikely that they are going to diminish in influence given the current impasse within the multilateral framework. Indeed, in response to the breakdown of the DDA there has been a flurry of new agreements. These developments should not be overlooked or understated as they will influence the form and nature of international trade relations. The World Bank (Solaga and Winters, 1997) notes that moves towards regional economic integration have been more political than economic. The aim was to enhance security, increase bargaining power and improve cooperation. Inevitably such benefits spread into the economic domain, especially if they lock states into a process of political and economic reform. It is clear that regional agreements can be economically harmful if they result in trade diversion or if they arrest progress towards liberal multilateral outcomes. Despite these dangers, states are committing themselves to regional integration agreements for all manner of reasons. It is probable that these agreements will develop further and prove to be a significant landmark on the international business landscape of the twenty-first century.

Summary of Key Concepts

1. Regional integration agreements are becoming increasingly common within the global trading arena.
2. Tradtionally, agreements were seen as a second-best option in the absence of global free trade and are both offensive and defensive.
3. The benefits of these agreements for the multilateral trading system are ambiguous.
4. Regionalism is emerging as a channel for economic development.
5. MNEs tend to focus on their home regions.

Activities and Discussion Questions

1. To what extent is regional economic integration a logical response to the process of globalization?

2. Using a regional economic grouping of your choice, identify the motives, form and method of integration.

3. Examine a single developing state and assess how it is using preferential trade agreements to its economic development.

4. Using a single MNE, examine how its sales are broken down by region. Does this confirm or refute Rugman's hypothesis?

References and Suggestions for Further Reading

Baldwin, R. (1997) 'The causes of regionalism', *The World Economy*, Vol. 20, No. 7, 865–888.

Baldwin, R. (2006) *Managing the Noodle Bowl: The Fragility of East Asian Regionalism*, CEPR Discussion Paper.

Baldwin, R., Cohen, D., Sapir, A. and Venables, A. (eds) (2008) *Market Integration, Regionalism and the Global Economy*, Cambridge: Cambridge University Press.

Bhagwati J. (1992) 'Regionalism versus multilateralism', *The World Economy*, Vol. 15, No. 5, 535–555.

De Lombaerde, P. and Langenhove, L. (2006) *Multilateralism,Regionalism and Bilateralism in Trade and Investment: World Report on Regional Integration*, New York: Springer-Verlag.

Frankel, J. (1998a) *Regional Trading Blocs in the World Trading System*, Washington, DC: Institute for International Economics.

Frankel, J. (1998b) *The Regionalisation of the World Economy*, Chicago, IL, and London: University of Chicago Press.

Gilberto, A.E.F. and Hommen, A. (1998) *Regionalization and Globalization in the Modern World Economy*, London: Routledge.

Hoekmann, B., Schiff, M. and Winters, L. (1998) 'Regionalism and development', *World Bank Working Paper*, New York: World Bank.

Honninghausen, L. (2004) *Regionalism in the Age of Globalism: Concepts of Regionalism*, Max Cade Institute for German-American Studies, University of Wisconsin.

Lahiri, S. (2001) *Regionalism and Globalization: Theory and Practice*, London: Routledge.

Laird, S. (1995) 'Fostering regional integration', *WTO Working Paper*, Geneva: World Trade Organisation.

Lawrence, R. (1995) *Regionalism, Multilateralism and Deeper Integration*, Washington, DC: Brookings Institution.

OECD (1996) *Regionalism and Its Place in the Multilateral Trading System*, Paris: OECD.

OECD (2003) *Regionalism and the Multilateral Trading System*, Paris: OECD.

Ohmae, K. (1985) *Triad Power*, Boston, MA: Free Press.

Pomfret, R. (2007) 'Is regionalism an increasing feature of the world economy?', *The World Economy*, Vol. 30, No. 6, 923–947.

Porter, M. (1996) *Competition in Global Industries*, Boston, MA: Harvard Business School Press.

Robson, P. (1998) *The Economics of International Integration*, London: Routledge.

Rugman, A. (2000) *The End of Globalization*, McGraw Hill/Amacom.

Rugman, A. (2005) *The Regional Multinationals*, Cambridge: Cambridge University Press.

Rugman, A. and D'Cruz, J. (2000) *Multinationals as Flagship Firms: Regional Business Networks*, Oxford: Oxford University Press.

Shaw, T. and Soderbaum, F. (eds) (2003) *Theories of New Regionalism: A Palgrave Macmillan Reader*, Basingstoke: Palgrave Macmillan.

Solaga, I. And Winters, L. (1997) 'Regionalism in the nineties: what effect on trade?', *World Bank Working Paper*, New York: World Bank.

Srinivasan, T. (1998) 'Regionalism and the WTO', in Krueger, A. (ed.), *The WTO as an International Organisation*, Chicago, IL: University of Chicago Press.

UNCTAD (2007) *World Investment Report 2007*, www.unctad.org.

World Bank (2005) *Global Economic Prospects 2005: Trade, Regionalism and Development*, www.worldbank.org.

WTO (2005) *The Future of the WTO: Report by the Consultative Board to the WTO Director General*, www.wto.org.

Yip, G. (1998) *Global and Regional Integration for Competitive Advantage*, www.gtnews.com/articles2/1265.html.

Websites

The WTO website (www.wto.org) is an excellent first port of call for those seeking statistics of RTAs. The UNCTAD (www.unctad.org) website is also very good.

Chapter 4

Governance Issues in an Integrating World Economy

The nation state is becoming too small for the big problems of life and too big for the small problems of life.

Daniel Bell, US sociologist

LEARNING OBJECTIVES

This chapter will help you to:

- understand the link between globalization and the changing role of international institutions

- describe the functions of the main international institutions

- identify and assess the arguments of critics of international institutions

- assess the crisis in the WTO

- describe how international institutions can have a direct impact upon international business

Increasing international economic integration and the emergence of cross-border, and even globally, integrated networks of production and distribution raise the need for regulation that spreads across the customary regulatory (that is, state) boundaries and beyond the reach of traditional regulatory authorities. This increased difficulty in regulating business is welcomed by arch neo-liberalists: the placing of the activities of the private sector beyond the reach of the state fulfils a basic tenet of neo-liberal philosophy – that is, the removal of the state from as much economic life as possible. For others, globalization, through its bypassing of the state, undermines democracy and excludes non-elite groups, whether they be labour interests in the developed world or developing countries, from decisions that have a significant impact upon their well-being.

Assuming that it is not possible to put the globalization genie back into the bottle, the focus of regulatory attention must shift from the national to the supranational level. The majority of international institutions were established immediately after the Second World War to deal with the problems facing the post-war world. They have since evolved to take account of subsequent international political and economic changes, encountering scathing criticism along the way. According to some, the globalization imperative has superseded the nation state and undermined national sovereignty and democracy. Some critics go further and assert that international institutions have been captured by big business and have driven the globalization agenda to the detriment of the rest of society. Other critics acknowledge the enlargement of market boundaries and the need for regulation to correspond to the world, since it is not the world it once was. Their remedy is not to dismantle international institutions, as urged by some, but to reform existing institutions or establish new international institutions and/or instruments of governance. George Monbiot, a strident critic of globalization, is one example of this: his solution to the problems of globalization as he sees them is not to destroy international institutions, seen by many anti-globalization campaigners as the tools of globalization, but to reform them so that they become more democratic.

The purpose of this chapter is to examine contemporary international institutions that have an impact on the world economy and on business, and to address key questions about their role in a more integrated international economy. The chapter begins by briefly tracing the evolution of contemporary institutions and establishing their scope in relation to business and the challenges facing them. It then outlines the characteristics and functions of the main institutions and considers the criticisms commonly directed at them. In order to pursue these points in more detail, particular emphasis is placed on the case of the World Trade Organization (WTO).

THE EVOLUTION AND SCOPE OF CONTEMPORARY INTERNATIONAL INSTITUTIONS

The major contemporary international organizations were established not to deal with globalization but to contribute to the architecture of the post-1945 world and to prevent a repetition of global conflict. The United Nations (UN) was primarily concerned with the preservation of peace and security, although, as it has evolved, it has taken on a number of economic and business-related functions. In the economic sphere, the victorious allied powers were of the opinion that a totally new system of trade and finance relationships should be established to avoid the currency volatility and trade conflicts that contributed to the pre-war economic instability. Accordingly, the International Monetary Fund (IMF) and the World Bank were created at the 1944 Bretton Woods Conference: the IMF was originally designed to oversee international financial markets and the World Bank to assist with reconstruction. The third leg of the Bretton Woods system was to be the International Trade Organization (ITO). The Havana Charter setting up the ITO was never ratified, partly owing to US concerns about erosion of sovereignty. Instead, the General Agreement on Tariffs and Trade (GATT), never intended to be more than a transitional device preceding the ITO, became the primary, and very successful, instrument of progressive trade liberalization. It was not until the WTO came into being in 1995, 47 years after the GATT came into effect, that construction of the Bretton Woods institutions was complete.

Box 4.1 Milestones in the Development of International Economic Institutions

1865	International Telegraph Union founded (later International Telecommunication Union) – now a UN special agency
1875	Universal Postal Union – now a UN special agency
1919	League of Nations (UN forerunner) established
1919	International Labour Organization (ILO) created
1930	Bank for International Settlements (BIS) established
12.6.41	Inter-Allied Declaration 'to work together with other free peoples, both in war and in peace' – seed of the United Nations
14.8.41	Atlantic Charter: Roosevelt and Churchill propose a set of principles for international collaboration to maintain peace and security
1.1.42	26 allied nations pledge their support for the Atlantic Charter – first official use of term 'United Nations'
Oct, Dec 43	Moscow and Teheran Conferences – leaders of China, UK, US, USSR call for establishment of international organization to maintain peace and security
July 1944	Bretton Woods Conference: articles of agreement negotiated for IMF and World Bank

Sept–Oct 1944   UN – Dumbarton Oaks Conference – blueprint of the UN drawn up

24.10.45   UN: Charter comes into force following conference in April 1945

27.12.45   IMF: articles of agreement enter into force

25.6.46   World Bank: formal commencement of operations with 38 members

1946   ILO becomes first specialized agency of UN

1.3.47   IMF formally begins operations

1.1. 1948   GATT in force with 23 contracting parties; first multilateral round of tariff concessions comes into effect

10.12.48   UN General Assembly adopts Universal Declaration of Human Rights

1949   GATT: Annecy Round of multilateral tariff cuts – 13 countries involved

1951   GATT: Torquay Round of multilateral tariff cuts – 38 countries involved

Aug 52   World Bank: Japan and West Germany become members

1956   Geneva Round of multilateral tariff cuts – 26 countries involved

30.6.56   World Bank: International Finance Corporation established as affiliate of World Bank

Sept 60   UN: 17 newly independent states join UN – biggest membership increase in one year

1960–1   GATT: Dillon Round of multilateral tariff cuts – 26 countries involved

24.9.61   World Bank: International Development Association established as affiliate of World Bank

1964–7   GATT: Kennedy Round of multilateral tariff cuts and anti-dumping measures – 62 countries involved

14.10.66   World Bank: International Centre for Settlement of Investment Disputes established as affiliate of World Bank

1.1.70   IMF: first allocation of special drawing rights (SDRs)

Aug 71   IMF: US informs IMF it will no longer buy and sell gold to settle international transactions – beginning of the end of the Bretton Woods system

Dec 71   IMF: Smithsonian Agreement provides for realignment of industrial country currencies and increase in price of gold. IMF establishes temporary regime of central rates and wider margins

June 72   UN: First UN Environment Conference in Stockholm leads to creation of UN Environment Programme (UNEP)

19.3.73   'Generalized floating' begins as European Community countries introduce joint float for their currencies against the US dollar

13.9.74   IMF: Extended Fund Facility (EFF) set up to give medium-term assistance to members with balance of payments problems resulting from structural economic changes.

1973–9   GATT: Tokyo Round: multilateral tariff cuts, non-tariff measures and 'framework' agreements – 102 countries involved

30.6.79   World Bank: lending for fiscal year 1978–9 exceeds $10 billion for the first time

13.8.82   IMF: Mexico encounters serious debt-servicing problems, marking onset of debt crisis. IMF supports major adjustment programmes in Mexico and other countries facing severe debt servicing difficulties

2.12.85	IMF and World Bank: express broad support for debt initiative proposed by US Treasury Secretary James A. Baker
27.3.86	IMF: Structural Adjustment Facility established to provide balance of payments assistance on concessional terms to low-income developing countries
Sept 87	UN: UNEP's efforts lead to signing of the Montreal Protocol (protection of the ozone layer)
12.4.88	World Bank: convention establishing the Multilateral Investment Guarantee Agency takes effect
28.11.90	World Bank: Global Environment Facility, jointly administered by the World Bank, UNDP and UNEP, launched
Apr–May 92	IMF membership for countries of former Soviet Union approved
June 1992	UN Conference on Environment and Development (the 'Earth Summit') held in Rio attended by leaders from over 100 countries
Jun–Sep 92	World Bank: Russia and former Soviet Republics become Bank members
1986–94	GATT: Uruguay Round – multilateral tariff cuts, non-tariff measures, services, intellectual property, dispute settlement, textiles, agriculture, creation of WTO – 123 countries involved
April 1994	GATT–WTO: Marrakesh Agreement concluding Uruguay Round and establishing the WTO
Jan 1995	WTO: World Trade Organization comes into existence
17.12.97	IMF: in the wake of the Asian financial crisis, the IMF establishes the Supplementary Reserve Facility (SRF) to help members cope with sudden and disruptive loss of market confidence.
8.4.98	IMF: Uganda becomes first member to receive debt relief under the HIPC initiative
6.10.98	IMF: launch of concept of new finance architecture to address world economic problems: its tenets are increased transparency; consolidation of banking super-vision; orderly, cautious progress towards liberalization of capital movements, and partnership with the private sector
1.1.99	Launch of euro by 11 EU countries; European Central Bank granted observer status at IMF
Dec 1999	WTO: Seattle Ministerial attempt to launch new trade round ends in failure
8.1.01	IMF and World Bank: 22 countries (18 in Africa) qualify for debt relief under the HIPC initiative. Relief represents an average two-thirds reduction of the foreign debt of these countries
Nov 2001	WTO: Doha Ministerial establishes framework and agenda for new round of multilateral trade talks
Dec 2001	WTO: China becomes WTO member
4.2.02	IMF: approval of three-year, $16 billion loan for Turkey – the IMF's largest loan to date
25.09.05	IMF: agreement on G-8 proposal to provide 100 per cent debt relief on all debt incurred by the world's heavily indebted countries (HIPC) to IMF, World Bank and African Development Fund
July 2008	Deadlock in latest negotiations within the Doha Round of trade talks

All the major institutions set up in the aftermath of the Second World War have subsequently undergone significant change as unenvisaged political and economic changes have brought about a coordinated international response. The IMF's role, for example, has changed: the first challenge to it was the collapse of the Bretton Woods system of fixed exchange rates in the early 1970s. Moreover, with the expansion of its membership, the IMF's reach has become global and, as well as shouldering the responsibility of international financial stability, the IMF has become a key player in development finance.

The United Nations

Most well known for its role in maintaining international peace and security, the 192-member UN also plays a significant role in fostering international cooperation in international economic, social, cultural and humanitarian problems and in promoting respect for human rights and freedoms. As such, UN activities have significant implications for international business, both in terms of helping to create a safe, stable and favourable environment for business and development, and more directly in terms of specific initiatives like the United Nations Environment Programme (UNEP) (see Chapter 16) and the Global Compact which commits signatories to operate along the line of corporate social responsibility in the areas of human rights, the environment, labour and corruption.

The UN has six main organs – the General Assembly, the Security Council, the Economic and Social Council, the Trusteeship Council, the International Court of Justice and the Secretariat. Most of the economic work of the UN is the responsibility of the Economic and Social Council. This body oversees many of the UN's programmes and funds, including the United Nations Conference for Trade and Development (UNCTAD), UNEP and the United Nations Development Programme (UNDP); consults with NGOs and is the vehicle by which the UN's specialized agencies work with the UN. There are 15 specialized agencies, autonomous organizations that work with the UN and each other through the coordinating mechanism of the Economic and Social Council.

The International Monetary Fund

Established as part of the Bretton Woods institutions in 1944 with 45 members, the IMF was a central part of the framework for economic cooperation that was intended to avoid some of the economic policies that had contributed to the 1930s Depression. The IMF's main objectives are the promotion of international monetary cooperation; facilitation of the balanced growth of international trade; the promotion of exchange rate stability; assistance in the establishment of a multilateral system of payments and making resources available to members encountering balance of payments difficulties. In short, the IMF is responsible for ensuring the stability of the international financial system.

The IMF obtains its resources from the quota or capital subscriptions paid by its 185 members. The quotas are determined according to a member's relative size in the world economy. Accordingly the US pays the largest quota ($61 billion out of total quotas of $357.3 billion – or 17.1 per cent – at the end of March 2008) and Palau, a remote island in the Pacific Ocean, the smallest ($5.1 million or 0.1 per cent of the total quota). Unlike the UN General Assembly and some other international institutions the IMF does not operate a one-member, one-vote system. It is the size of the quota that determines a country's voting power and therefore its say in IMF policy: each member has 250 basic votes plus one extra vote for each SDR 100,000 of quota. This formula yields 371,743 votes for the US and 281 votes for Palau.

The IMF's main activities include:

1. *Lending*: the IMF provides credits and loans to members in balance of payments difficulties and extends financial resources to its members via a range of facilities. The IMF's lending is conditional on countries following appropriate policies to correct balance of payments problems. It is the terms of this conditionality that have brought forward the most intense criticisms of the IMF. Some adjustments have been made to IMF conditionality to address some of the complaints, and the IMF is making greater attempts to tailor policies to individual country needs and to enable countries to retain ownership of their domestic policy programmes.

2. *Technical assistance*: the IMF offers technical assistance and training to help members strengthen their institutional capacity, and design and implement effective macroeconomic and structural policies.

3. *Surveillance*: the IMF engages in a policy dialogue with each of its members and annually appraises the exchange rate policies of each of its members within the context of their overall economic policies. The IMF also conducts multilateral surveillance, the outcome of which is published twice a year in the World Economic Outlook and quarterly in the Financial Stability Report.

The formal role of the IMF has remained unchanged but the institution has had to reform and adapt to major changes in the world's economic and monetary systems. Globalization, particularly advances in technology and communication, has increased the international integration of financial markets and fostered more intense linkages between economies. Consequently, financial crises tend to be more contagious and spread their effects more rapidly among countries than previously when borders were less porous.

Although primarily a monetary and not a development institution, the IMF has increasingly assumed a development role, requiring countries to adopt sound and stable macroeconomic policies. This has become a much greater imperative as its membership has expanded to include many of the world's poorest countries. Accordingly, there is some overlap between the role of the IMF and World Bank as reflected in the joint IMF–World Bank *Initiative for the Heavily Indebted Poor Countries* (the HIPC Initiative).

The World Bank

Also set up at the Bretton Woods Conference in 1944, the World Bank's initial focus was on the reconstruction of post-war Europe. The official title of the institution, the International Bank for Reconstruction and Development (IBRD), which has 185 members, reflects the Bank's role in reconstruction, an imperative that continues in terms of its work in areas like humanitarian emergencies, natural disaster relief and post-conflict rehabilitation in developing and transition economies.

Since the early 1980s, the Bank has become heavily involved in macroeconomic stabilization and debt rescheduling in developing countries, a role that has led to some overlap with the work of the IMF. Social and environmental issues have also increasingly permeated the World Bank's work. All these issues are important for the World Bank but its current overriding objective is to provide technical and financial assistance to reduce poverty and improve living standards in the developing world. The World Bank's approach to development issues has been the target of severe NGO criticism for applying market criteria indiscriminately across developing countries. The Bank's approach, never quite as black and white as its critics asserted, has subsequently become more nuanced with greater emphasis on the institutional and governance structures of the recipients of development assistance as well as the economic context.

These days, it is more accurate to refer to the World Bank Group rather than the World Bank. It consists of five institutions that specialize in different aspects of development. Technically speaking the term 'World Bank' only refers to the IBRD and the IDA whereas the IFC, the MIGA and the ICSID are World Bank affiliates. The five institutions are:

- *The International Bank for Reconstruction and Development (IBRD)*: the original World Bank institution, the IBRD's main role is the provision of loans and development assistance to middle-income countries and creditworthy poorer countries.
- *The International Development Association (IDA)*: the IDA began its operations in 1960 and is the World Bank's concessional lending window, providing long-term loans at zero interest to the poorest developing countries.
- *The International Finance Corporation (IFC)*: the IFC was established in 1956 to promote sustainable private sector development in developing countries and has become the largest multilateral source of loan and equity financing for private sector projects in the developing world.
- *The Multilateral Investment Guarantee Agency (MIGA)*: the MIGA was established in 1988 to promote FDI in emerging economies. It carries out this task mainly by offering political risk insurance (guarantees) to investors and lenders and by helping developing countries attract and retain private investment.
- *The International Centre for the Settlement of Investment Disputes (ICSID)*: the ICSID was set up as an autonomous organization (albeit with very close links to the Bank) in 1966 to provide facilities for the conciliation and arbitration of disputes between member countries and investors. Arbitration within the ICSID framework has become the main mechanism for the settlement of investment disputes under multilateral trade and investment treaties such as NAFTA, the Energy Charter Treaty, the Cartagena Free Trade Agreement and the Colonia Investment Protocol of Mercosur.

The World Trade Organization

Despite its transitory status, during the 47 years in which it operated as the main focus for the regulation of international trade, the GATT was extremely successful in its main task – the liberalization of trade. As a result of the eight multilateral tariff-cutting rounds that have taken place, the weighted world average tariffs on manufacturing goods have fallen from about 40 per cent in 1947 to 3–4 per cent following the Uruguay Round. Nevertheless, despite low average tariffs, tariffs remain substantial on a number of products and tariff reductions remain an important aspect of the GATT agenda, which has been carried forward into the work of the WTO.

The basic objectives and principles of the GATT were also carried forward into the 1994 Marrakesh agreement setting up the WTO – that is, 'in search of . . . rising living standards and full use of the world's resources' (substituted for by 'sustainable development' in the WTO), the WTO will seek 'the substantial reduction of tariffs and other barriers to trade and . . . the elimination of discriminatory treatment in international commerce'.

Notwithstanding this continuity, the role of the GATT/WTO has expanded and developed in the following important ways:

- *Membership*: membership has risen from the original 23 contracting parties in 1947 to 153 by July 2008. Several new members have joined in recent years, including Saudi Arabia in 2005, Vietnam in 2007 and Ukraine in 2008. The most significant addition to WTO membership occurred in December 2001 when, after long and complex negotiations, China became a full WTO member, closely followed by Taiwan. Several other countries are queuing up to join, including Russia. Negotiations with Russia have proved long and tortuous and, in 2008, the Russian authorities have been downplaying the importance of WTO membership to it. As a result of expansion, WTO rules now cover over 95 per cent of world trade.

- *Agenda expansion*: as tariffs reduced and market access became easier, other barriers to entry became more apparent and negotiations to reduce these non-tariff barriers began. The Tokyo Round (1973–9) represented the first occasion when this happened in an extended way with agreements, among others, on anti-dumping, subsidies and countervailing measures, procurement, technical standards and import licensing procedures. The Uruguay Round pushed an expanded agenda even further and included negotiations on previously excluded areas like trade in agricultural products and services. The expansion of GATT/WTO activity also marks a move to deeper integration (see Chapter 2). In other words, as the removal of barriers existing at the border becomes more complete, the emphasis shifts to regulating away differences in domestic policies that may discriminate between domestic and foreign producers.

- *Reduced plurilateralism*: in the pre-Uruguay Round era, many GATT undertakings were plurilateral – that is, contracting parties would choose which of the agreements they would sign up to. As part of the obligation implicit in being a member of the WTO, member states have to commit themselves to comply with all the obligations of GATT, GATS, TRIPs and so on. This redresses the situation in which countries could pick and choose which regulations they wished to adhere to. This requirement is known as the 'single undertaking'. A parallel may be drawn between the single undertaking and the basic EU principle of the acquis communautaire which states that to become a member of the EU, a country must accept all the existing policies of the EU.

- *Strengthened disputes settlements*: one of the most important developments of the Uruguay Round was the transformation of the GATT disputes settlement system from one that was weak and whose decisions could be vetoed by the contracting party against whom a decision has been taken to one in which decisions were enforceable.

The WTO continues to evolve in the same direction of wider membership and with a wider agenda but has encountered serious problems in carrying all its members with it during the current Doha Round, discussed in more depth below.

The above constitute the major international institutions that regulate economic and finance matters that have an impact on business but they are far from being the only organizations playing such a role, either on a regional or a world basis. For example, regional development banks such as the Asia Development Bank, the African Development Bank and the Inter-American Development Bank complement the work of the World Bank. The main objective of the Bank for International Settlements (BIS), created in 1930 to deal with issues of war reparations, is to foster cooperation among central banks and other agencies in pursuit of market and financial stability. New institutions have also emerged in line with changing circumstances. The International Energy Agency (IEA) is itself a case in point: it was established following the 1973 oil crisis for the purpose of coordinating the response of industrialized nations to the sudden tightening of crude oil supplies.

GLOBALIZATION AND GOVERNANCE

The biggest and most challenging changes to global governance have occurred since the end of the Cold War and the collapse of many long-held assumptions about competing power blocs and ideologies. Within this context, Francis Fukuyama in 1989 spoke of the 'End of History', a reference to the ending of the struggle for supremacy between communism and capitalism with victory for the latter. In other words, the neo-liberal revolution that had begun in the early 1980s with Reaganomics and the Thatcherite Revolution in the UK (see Chapter 2) had spread to most corners of the globe. However, as the post-Cold War era unfolded, it became apparent that economic and political issues were as fiercely contested as ever but that the controversies were no longer couched in terms of competing political and economic systems and ideologies. For international institutions, this meant the expansion of membership as former Communist states adopted free market principles and focused their agenda on measures to help the market operate more efficiently.

In addition to these politically driven changes, other factors came to the forefront and challenged the agenda and working of international institutions, including greater capital mobility, more flexible exchange rates, ongoing development issues, the growth of emerging economies, the spread of e-commerce and the proliferation of regional trading arrangements. All these factors, many of which are discussed in more depth in other chapters, have come together to increase interdependence in the international economy and to pose serious questions about how and to what extent these increased international transactions can and should be controlled and regulated. Although the rationale and motivations of participants in contemporary debates vary, many of the arguments are essentially about what is the most appropriate level for regulation in a more interdependent world in which commercial transactions are less and less contained within traditional political (i.e. state) boundaries. These debates are often expressed in terms of concerns about the undermining of national sovereignty and the alleged excessive power of multinational corporations.

In view of the economic, social, political, cultural and technological pressures that have resulted in increased international interdependence, the key question becomes how to compensate for the restricted ability of member states to regulate economic and business activities on their own. Is it appropriate to try to reclaim some of the power of nation states as parts of Civil Society would argue (see below), or is it preferable to seek international responses to regulation challenges, either through greater cooperation among countries or through multilateral arrangements?

The changing and increasing number and roles of international institutions is not accidental but a response to the manifold changes alluded to above. Robert Keohane (1998) explains this enhanced role for international institutions in the following way: 'institutions create the capability of states to co-operate in mutually beneficial ways by reducing the costs of making and enforcing agreements – what economists refer to as "transaction costs"'. In other words, given the increased need for nations to make agreements about cross-border transactions, it is more efficient for them to do so within an established framework of agreed rules and understandings than for them to negotiate multiple (i.e. with many countries) agreements from scratch every time a new cross-border issue requires their attention. In this way, greater transparency and predictability within the international environment is achieved, both for governments and for MNEs working within the international system.

The pressure from increasing cross-border transactions to find new methods and forms of governance is felt in areas of labour market regulation, the environment, investment, intellectual property, finance, competition policy and so on. The optimal solution is not always a supranational one: in some circumstances, governance at a sub-state level (that is, at local, municipal, district, provincial or the equivalent) may be the most appropriate. Indeed, many sub-state organizations and institutions have reacted to new cross-border realities by seeking direct contact with their equivalents in other states, bypassing their own governments, or by seeking direct contact themselves with supranational institutions. For example, many regions within EU countries and individual US states maintain an office in Brussels to facilitate contact with EU institutions. Furthermore, there has been a growing trend for devolution of power from central state institutions to lower levels. Between the state and the international institution, there has also been the emergence of regional arrangements (see Chapter 3), many of which have devised new regulations and ways of dealing with increasing interdependence and integration. In some ways, regionalization may be viewed as an alternative to globalization but in others it is driven by similar forces of cross-border technological penetration and transactions, and provides a less extensive platform for the reaping of scale economies in production, distribution and marketing. In the latter sense, regional trading arrangements may be seen as a stepping stone to globalization rather than a turning away from it.

In short, globalization has profound effects for the governance of economic and commercial flows. However, it is too simplistic to view globalization as merely implying a shift in governance from the national to the supranational level, although the latter is clearly becoming more important. Rather, governance is changing in two important ways. First, as discussed above, the location of governance is shifting to a multitude of different levels, both above and below the state levels. Second, elements of governance are developing not in the public domain, as is traditionally the case, but are increasingly becoming the focus of private sector activity.

The privatization of governance encourages a focus not on international institutions but on international regimes; that is, the norms, rules and decision-making processes that have been created to govern international life within specific issue areas. The broadest definition of privatized governance regimes would include the activities of various NGOs as contributors to the work of international institutions and to the scrutiny of private sector schemes. In a narrower sense, privatized governance is concerned with private or quasi-public sector involvement in regulating the international business environment. The International Organization for Standardization (ISO) is an example of a non-governmental international organization that draws up and oversees international standards in a range of areas, including quality and environmental management (see Case study 16.1), that affect business. In other areas, as well as NGOs, private sector accounting and consultancy firms are frequently used to carry out monitoring of corporate codes of conduct in relation to treatment of the workforce and the environment. In the financial sector, the ratings given by private bond rating agencies such as Standard and Poor's have taken on a quasi-official status that impacts upon official policy at all levels. In collaboration with the UN, banks and insurance companies have adopted a Statement of Environment Commitment and the high-profile 'Responsible Care' Programme has been developed by chemical manufacturers to improve the environmental record of their industry. Inevitably, part of the motivation for this latter initiative is to forestall the implementation of more stringent or more inflexible mandatory regimes but such initiatives only ultimately work if they are underpinned by substance.

THE CRITICS OF INTERNATIONAL INSTITUTIONS

The current role and policies of many international institutions are under attack. The most visible signs of this are the street protests that have dogged the most high-profile meetings of the IMF, World Bank, the WTO and other forums in which international leaders get together. G-8 meetings for several years (especially the meeting in Genoa in 2001 when a protestor was killed), the annual meeting of the IMF in Prague in 2000, the 2000 World Economic Forum in Davos in 2000 and, most famously, the WTO Ministerial in Seattle in 1999 which helped delay the launch of the latest round of multilateral trade talks are just some of the more prominent examples of campaigning against the current global governance system. Demonstrations at G-8 meetings have continued, the latest occurring in Japan in 2008. The WTO continues to be a target for protests: many arrests of protestors, particularly of South Korean farmers, occurred at the 2005 Hong Kong Ministerial. Other international events continue to attract protests but, for the most part, not in such a high-profile way with more demonstrations currently taking place in developing and emerging economies against rising food and energy prices.

The critics of international institutions are often referred to as 'Global Civil Society'. The term 'Civil Society' has a long history, referring to the relationship between the individual and society in general and particularly to the duty of individuals to behave responsibly towards society and of society to take some responsibility for the individuals within it. Civil Society, however, is not a call for a return to efforts to build collectivist societies: indeed, modern usage of the term stems from the emergence of the popular movements in Eastern Europe that were central in bringing down communism. Rather, Civil Society in the contemporary context is a response to the absence of civil and social responsibility from the versions of unfettered markets and capitalism championed by arch neo-liberalists. In short, the idea of Civil Society is a halfway house between excessive state control and no state control whatsoever, and also implies a more active and responsible role for individuals, a role that is absent in both the communistic and extreme neo-liberal view of the world.

In more prosaic terms, global Civil Society refers to the broad range of NGOs that operate across borders. The global dimension is a response to the increased global interconnectedness and the complexity, uncertainty and lack of control experienced by individuals and small groups within this environment. Global Civil Society is an attempt to regain some control. The methods that NGOs advocate to achieve this vary, ranging from efforts to reform the institutions and make them and the activities and organizations they regulate more accountable to the rejection of globalization altogether and a reassertion of individual autonomy and more local organization.

In short, the protestors represent a diversity of views and interests that are only able to come together on the basis of their opposition to the policies of international institutions. There is no unity in terms of what they support or propose. This is unsurprising given the diversity of subject areas, organizational forms and geographical locations from which Civil Society is drawn. Specific issues on which NGOs are campaigning include the environment, health, human rights, labour conditions, education, development, gender issues, food safety and animal welfare. Groups belonging to Civil Society include trade unions, charitable organizations, humanitarian groups, church groups, business associations and organizations and single-issue organizations. Bodies like Amnesty International, Oxfam, Greenpeace, the World Wildlife Fund and Médecins Sans Frontières are high-profile examples of individual NGOs. Some NGOs are global in coverage, in large part thanks to the improved communications and organizational capacity offered by the internet. Others are more strongly associated with a region: although having an international dimension, trade unions, for example, are still organized nationally and represent the interests of their members which can conflict with those of workers elsewhere in the world.

NGOs may be classified along a number of dimensions. The rejectionist–reformist dimension has already been alluded to: that is, rejectionists reject the current international system altogether and reformists seek to work within the system to improve it. Green and Griffith (2002) take this further and break down the rejectionist group into 'statists' and 'alternatives'. The statists maintain globalization has been a disaster and seek to rebuild the role of the state in economic management. They are dominated be sections of the traditional Left, parts of the labour movement and large groups of southern activists. The alternatives tend to be small, decentralized and anti-corporatist in nature. Although not anarchists in the strictest ideological sense, they reject globalization and concentrate on developing small-scale alternatives and resist the intrusion of the market and market power relations into their cultural and political spaces. The reformists account for the majority of formally structured groups and agitate for gradual and peaceful change within existing systems to offset injustice and inequalities. They accept a role for the market but want it to be better regulated and managed to ensure social justice and sustainability. This group includes some trade unions, faith groups, charities, development organizations and most mainstream environmental groups.

Robertson (2000) draws a useful distinction between advocacy and operational NGOs. Advocacy NGOs are essentially political organizations and lobby to influence decisions taken by governments and international organizations. These groups tend to portray themselves as outlets for public participation when national governments are unwilling or unable to act: in other words, they see themselves as making good some of the democratic deficit that has arisen as a result of globalization pressures. As such they belong to the reformist NGO trend.

Operational NGOs are those NGOs that work with and for a variety of international institutions to deliver services, usually in the developing world. The utilization of NGOs in this way by international institutions is an example of the privatization of governance referred to above. These services include humanitarian relief, health care, education and other development-related projects.

Robertson (2000) reports estimates that 15–20 per cent of total official development assistance is currently distributed by NGOs. Scholte (2000) reported that more aid is now distributed by NGOs than by the recipient states themselves. Not only do NGOs provide assistance on the ground but they also play an increasingly important role in terms of proffering expertise and information to feed into the policy formation process. Indeed, many NGOs have long played a technical, operational role but this has been in relation to projects financed by their own fund-raising as is the case with development charities like Oxfam. It is this experience that gives them credibility in delivering programmes on behalf of international organizations such as the World Bank, the World Health Organization and the UN High Commission for Refugees.

The reliance of international institutions on the operational and technical expertise of NGOs reflects the underfunding and underresourcing of many international institutions. UNEP, for example, is heavily reliant on environmental NGOs which have played a central role in pushing forward a number of multilateral environment agreements such as the Montreal and Kyoto Protocols and even have observer status in relation to their implementation.

GENERIC CRITICISMS OF INTERNATIONAL INSTITUTIONS

The criticisms levelled by NGOs at international institutions are many and varied. Some are highly specific to issues and institutions. The WTO often gets criticized, for example, because its trade policies are deemed to be bad for labour or environmental standards (see Chapters 15 and 16 respectively). Others are more general and are aimed at some or all of the main international institutions to varying degrees. These criticisms fall into three overlapping categories: sovereignty concerns, democratic concerns and inclusiveness concerns.

Sovereignty

In the traditional view of sovereignty, nation states exercise complete and exclusive authority over the territory within their borders. Globalization has undermined this. Many issues now spread across borders, especially in view of the lowering of barriers to trade. Technology has reduced the importance of fixed locations and territory in the conduct of commercial transactions. Hence, US and European companies are, for example, increasingly utilizing the back-office and call-centre facilities offered from within the Indian subcontinent. Financial flows, the use of credit cards and pressures towards regional or global currencies have undermined the ability of countries to operate their own monetary and exchange rate policy.

In short, economic interdependence and the need to regulate it have changed the nature of sovereignty itself. Regaining exclusive authority for national governments over what happens within national borders would require a reversal of many of the current globalization trends and a degree of isolation that has resulted in the past in lower levels of economic growth than among more connected countries. The comparative experience of export-promoting countries from Asia compared to import-substituting developing countries and the contrast between the fortunes of Spain and Portugal before and after their accession to the EU (the pre-accession period was marked by high tariff walls and GDP per head significantly below that of other Western European countries whereas integration into a much bigger market has stimulated growth and brought these countries up to European levels) indicates that a return to a less integrated world may not be desirable on a number of grounds. Moreover, it may not be feasible.

The response to sovereignty concerns may be to rethink sovereignty. That is, not to regret the passing of the all-powerful nation state but to reclaim control over events and trends that impact upon the lives of citizens. To some critics, the EU is a major cause of the loss of national sovereignty within Europe. To others, the EU is not a cause of the decline of national power but a response to it: through cooperation and joint decision and policy making, member states are pooling their sovereignty and regaining some of the lost control.

The above argument may also apply at the international level through the creation of effective international institutions that help states regain collective control over transnational issues. The 2008 financial crisis poses serious questions in this area. On the one hand, financial interdependence appears to be exacerbating the weakening of financial institutions across an increasing number of countries. On the other hand, the resolution of the problem, or at least measures to prevent similar events, could lie in the emergence of a global banking or financial institution regulatory authority. This outcome is far from certain but it is a possibility that the consequences of a collapse of the international financial system may concentrate the minds of key decision makers.

Democracy

A common criticism levelled at international institutions is that they are undemocratic and deny the individual citizen a voice in their proceedings. In many, albeit far from all, countries, dissatisfaction with a government's performance will result in their removal from office via the ballot-box. No such accountability confronts international institutions. However, international institutions are largely supranational organizations made up of individual member states that collectively set the agenda and determine policy. In institutions like the UN, the principle is one nation one vote whereas in organizations like the IMF voting weights are determined by relative financial contributions. Whatever the representative process, the institutions are ultimately responsible to the constituent member states that, in turn, are responsible to their electorate, where appropriate.

In the above sense, the international institutions may be regarded as democratic, however imperfectly. However, the democracy in question is indirect and the link between the citizen and the international institutions is so distant and remote that the anti-democratic complaints about international institutions are understandable. Many NGOs argue that this lack of direct representation can be overcome by greater engagement of Civil Society organizations in the activities of international institutions. On the positive side, this offers the possibility of natural coalitions forming across borders around key issues like the environment or human rights, creating communities of interest across national boundaries.

However, this suggestion raises a number of serious questions about the democratic nature of the proposed solution itself to the democratic deficit of international institutions. First, there are thousands of NGOs. How is it to be determined which NGOs should participate in the international institutions? Second, and most importantly, who do the international institutions themselves represent and how are they held accountable? The governance structures of NGOs vary but many of them contain no provision for election of officers or forum for scrutiny of their policies or finances. One potential partial solution to this problem is the development of codes of conduct for NGOs that would commit them to appropriate scrutiny and to respect relevant national laws. In practice, international institutions are becoming more open to NGO participation to varying degrees. However, the optimum solution to problems of democratic deficits within international organizations is to develop proper democratic forms that extend beyond the nation state and to ensure that these institutions are sufficiently powerful to regulate global markets.

Inclusiveness

A key criticism of international institutions is that in practice their policies discriminate against the poor in favour of the rich. This argument reflects the arguments examined in Chapter 2 that globalization is not really global but affects only the triad group of countries. It also reflects concerns about overreliance on neo-liberal policies as the driving force behind the international economy as such policies rely on competition which tends to favour the strongest. However, although sharing the frustrations of NGOs regarding the domination of major international institutions by vested (that is, developed country) interests, developing countries also recognize the benefits of open markets and often choose not to align themselves with NGOs. Moreover, developing countries have asserted themselves more and played a greater role in the Doha Round of multilateral trade talks. However, so far the outcome has been deadlock and an inability to find common ground not only between developed and developing countries but among developing countries themselves.

CASE STUDY 4.1

The WTO at a Crossroads

In July 2008, talks to break the deadlock in the Doha Round of multilateral trade talks under the umbrella of the WTO failed yet again. The Doha Round has been plagued by setbacks: the initial attempts to launch the talks in 1999 in Seattle failed in the context of violent demonstrations and poor preparation. When the talks eventually got underway in 2001 at Doha in Qatar, progress was tortuous: the headline ministerial meetings, intended to confirm the deliberations of officials and make key political decisions, failed, or at best ended inconclusively, and

in 2006, the talks were even suspended for a while.

Press coverage of the failure of the talks so far has understandably focused on key negotiating issues but some of the responsibility must lie in the nature of the organization itself. When it was established in the late 1940s, the GATT had 23 members: these members were largely industrialized countries with common interests. Consequently, the GATT was able to conclude the Dillon Round of talks in 1960 to 1961 in less than a year. By 2008, the WTO had 153 members, the majority of whom were developing countries, and no deal is possible until the agreement of all members is obtained.

There has been a notable change in the dynamics of the trade talks since the Uruguay Round. Previously, the US, the EU and Japan had been able to reach a consensus on negotiating matters and impose it on the rest of the members. This process was facilitated by the 'Green Room' where ministers from the bigger, more influential countries would meet in an attempt to break the deadlock, perhaps inviting one or two developing countries into the process but essentially excluding smaller and developing countries. During the Doha Round under the leadership of Brazil, India and China, developing countries have asserted themselves and developed country domination of the talks has declined. Tension between developed and developing countries has been apparent throughout the negotiations, particularly but not only in the agricultural sphere. However, developing countries are not a homogenous group and they have differing interests which have increased the difficulties in reaching agreement.

The Doha Agenda has also not helped the negotiating process. Launched ostensibly as a 'development round', the Doha Agenda has suffered paradoxically from being both too wide and too narrow. As trade liberalization has developed through the work of both the GATT and then the WTO, tariffs have fallen to an historical low. Further tariff reduction remains an important element of the WTO negotiations, especially in relation to the reduction of tariff peaks (that is, relatively high tariffs, usually on sensitive products) and the reduction of tariff escalation (that is, where there are higher import duties on semi-processed products than on raw materials and even higher tariffs occur on finished products). This practice inhibits the development of processing, which yields value-added, in the developing countries in which raw materials originate.

However, the relative decline of tariffs on industrial goods has highlighted the importance of non-tariff barriers and attention has shifted to the liberalization of new sectors such as agriculture and services. Non-tariff barriers first appeared on the agenda in a minor way during the Tokyo Round (1973–9) in relation to government procurement, technical standards and special and distinctive treatment of developing countries. The Uruguay Round expanded the agenda further, including intellectual property, trade-related investment measures and dispute settlement. The agenda had expanded even further by the Doha Round and included:

* agriculture;
* market access – non-agricultural products;
* services;
* trade-related aspects of intellectual property rights;
* anti-dumping and subsidies;
* regional trade agreements;
* Dispute Settlement Understanding (DSU);
* trade and environment;
* electronic commerce;
* small economies;
* trade, debt and finance;
* trade and technology transfer;
* special and differentiated treatment;
* trade facilitation.

One major change since the Uruguay Round has been the shift from a plurilateral method of determining the outcome of negotiations to a single undertaking. Under the plurilateral system, members were able to choose which parts of the negotiated package they signed up to. As a result of the Uruguay Round, members have to sign up to the whole package. This makes negotiations more complex and should encourage members to seek trade-offs between one part of the overall package and another. In other words, members may agree to something about which they have little enthusiasm if they can get agreement on something in which they have a keen interest. However, for the single undertaking model to work, there must be something for everyone in the overall package.

Although the Doha agenda encompasses a much broader range of issues than ever before, it may be argued that the agenda is too narrow for the single undertaking to work. For example, the EU and Japan were anxious to include the "Singapore issues" (so-called because they were the subject of four working groups set up at the Singapore Ministerial meeting in 1996) – transparency in procurement, trade and investment, trade and competition policy and trade facilitation – on the Doha agenda. The US was lukewarm about this whereas developing countries opposed it. The only one of the Singapore issues to remain on the Doha agenda is trade facilitation, which is essentially about making the bureaucratic side of trade more efficient and which could greatly benefit developing countries. Once these issues disappeared off the agenda and, given the strong focus on liberalizing agricultural trade, there is limited scope for developed countries to trade off any concessions they make on agricultural trade for gains elsewhere.

Agriculture proved to be the sticking point in the July 2008 negotiations as India and the US failed to reach agreement on the terms of a safeguard mechanism that would allow developing countries to increase tariffs temporarily if there was a sudden surge in imports. Agriculture is a key component of the talks. Developing countries want an end to agricultural subsidies in developed markets and greater access to developed markets. This requires deep cuts in support to farmers in developed countries, a policy which it will only be possible for developed country politicians to sell at home if there are real gains to be made elsewhere.

The immediate aftermath of the July 2008 talks was an outbreak of the blame game. The US and India blamed each other for the failure of the talks. China blamed 'the selfish and short-sighted behaviour of wealthy nations': in other words, the EU and the US were not willing to scrap huge subsidies to their farmers. Japan was critical of India and China for not taking more responsibility for the success of the talks and Peter Mandelson, the European Trade Commissioner at the time, spoke of 'a collective failure'. Attempts are likely to be made to recommence the talks, as the consequences of failure would be serious, but they could also be overshadowed by the collapse of the international financial system which seems a real possibility in autumn 2008.

The consequences of the stalling of the talks, and particularly if they ultimately fail, are far-reaching.

Many would celebrate the end of the WTO which they see as a secretive, undemocratic institution which rides over the interests of sovereign states and shows scant regard for the needs of the poor. While the WTO may not be perfect in everything it does, it has established the framework of a transparent, rule-based international trading system which does not allow its members to arbitrarily raise tariffs. The rules for businesses operating in this environment are, for the most part, clear and predictable. Without the trading environment established by the WTO, trading conditions would become infinitely more complex and costly, and would most probably descend into anarchy and trade wars.

Moreover, although a case can be made that developing countries have so far not got a good deal through the WTO, it is far from clear that they would be better off operating on a bilateral rather than a multilateral basis. The limited bargaining power of all but the biggest developing or emerging countries would make it difficult for them to negotiate successfully on an individual basis with more powerful developed countries. They almost certainly stand a better chance of promoting their interests on a multilateral basis.

Although a collapse of the multilateral trading system is a long way off, the current impasse does damage it. An immediate consequence is the acceleration of the growth of bilateralism and preferential trading agreements (see Chapter 3 for a discussion of the relative merits of regionalism and multilateralism). Following the failure of the Cancun Ministerial in 2003, the then US Trade Representative Robert Zoellick said, 'As WTO members ponder the future, the US will not wait: we will move towards free trade with can-do countries.' In other words, if the US cannot achieve its aims multilaterally, it will seek to achieve them bilaterally, and indeed it has negotiated or is in the process of negotiating deals with a number of partners, including Australia, Morocco and South Korea. The European Union has also been exploring its own bilateral deals.

The ideal outcome for the WTO would be reform of the institution to address legitimate concerns of its critics. Some criticisms of the WTO are based on misrepresentation of its role and a misunderstanding of what it can achieve. The fundamental purpose of the WTO is to regulate the international trading environment within a framework of multilateral rules designed to liberalize trade and prevent disputes. However, globalization has thrown the interface between trade and the environment and between trade and labour issues into sharp relief. Many anti-WTO groups have environmental or labour issues as their primary purpose – unlike the WTO – and are looking for the WTO to give the environment/labour angle primacy over trade. The WTO is not in a position to do so: it is essentially a trade body charged with regulating trade. It lacks the expertise and mandate to fulfil the role expected of it by many NGOs in relation to trade and the environment. Unless and until the WTO's role is expanded, these issues are more properly dealt with elsewhere.

Globalization has created many interdependencies apart from trade, many of which interact with trade. These interdependencies need to be addressed either through the WTO or elsewhere. This institution, like other international institutions,

needs to catch up with the rapidly changing international business environment. It also needs to find ways to respond to the needs of all its members and to safeguard its legitimacy in a way which is open and accountable – a challenge which is greater than any it has met before.

CASE STUDY QUESTIONS

1. Research the progress of the Doha talks. In your view what are the main reasons for their failure to date?

2. What does business have to gain from the successful conclusion of the Doha Round?

3. What does business have to lose from the failure of the Doha Round?

4. Should the WTO be reformed and, if so, how?

5. Does the world need the WTO or an organization which establishes the rules for a multilateral trading system? Imagine a world without such an institution – this may give you some ideas.

CONCLUSION

The WTO, other international institutions and their constituent members need to come to terms with the substantial changes that have occurred in the world economy during the final quarter of the twentieth century and beyond. Globalization implies a shift to larger and expanding markets that have moved beyond and no longer correspond to traditional state boundaries. Many anti-globalization protestors argue that this places MNEs beyond the reach of national regulators and above the law. Their response falls into one of two categories – either to reject globalization (an objective that would be difficult if not impossible to achieve) or to reform existing international institutions so that they catch up with the new market realities. Although international institutions have adapted their roles to the changing circumstances over the years, their response to the implications of an increasing borderless environment has been sluggish and lags behind market realities. This relative unresponsiveness is a function of the difficulties of reconciling the divergent interests of nation states and regions, and the jealousy with which nation states guard their increasingly illusory sovereignty. The contemporary problem of global governance is that the globalization process and the need for transnational regulation of this process are occurring at a quicker rate than the international institutions and their constituent national members can respond.

Summary of Key Concepts

■ Globalization has made it more difficult to regulate the activities of business and has created a regulatory gap.

■ International institutions have been strongly criticized by NGOs: some NGOs seek to abolish international institutions and turn their back on globalization whereas others seek to reform them.

■ The role of international institutions has evolved along with changing social, economic, political and technological circumstances. Nevertheless, international institutions are reactive and lag behind economic and market realities.

■ The imperative for increased global governance will strengthen as international economic integration intensifies.

■ It is economically more efficient for states to engage in cross-border governance issues at a multilateral level. However, it may not always be politically expedient for them to do so.

Activities

1. Identify an NGO which has lobbied against one or more of the international institutions. Research and assess its case.

2. You are a consultant to a major multinational (the choice of company is up to you). Report back to the client (either through a presentation or a report) on the implications for them of lack of agreement in the Doha Round.

Discussion Questions

1. From the perspective of international business, which is the most important level of regulation – the national, the regional or the international?

2. Consider reasons why the role of international institutions has changed.

3. Discuss the contention that the NGOs represent no one but themselves and that they are no more democratic than the institutions they criticize.

4. Is the problem with international institutions that they are too powerful or that they are not powerful enough?

5. 'The international institutions are not perfect. The solution is not to abolish them but to reform them to ensure they reflect contemporary reality.' Do you agree with this statement. Justify your answer.

References and Suggestions for Further Reading

Alejandro, J. and Dominguez, M. (2006) 'Liberalisation of trade in services and trade negotiations', *Journal of World Trade*, Vol. 40, No. 1, 113–128.

Anderson, K. (2005) 'On the virtues of multilateral trade negotiations', *Economic Record*, Vol. 81, No. 25, 414–439.

Bardouille, N. (2005) 'Globalisation and the WTO: reconciling "development" in global trade talk', *Journal of Eastern Caribbean Studies*, Vol. 30, No. 1, 108–121.

Barnett, M. and Duvall, R. (eds) (2005) *Power in Global Governance*, Cambridge: Cambridge University Press.

Chimni, B. (2006) 'The World Trade Organization, democracy and development: a view from the South', *Journal of World Trade*, Vol. 40, No. 1, 5–37.

Coffey, P. and Riley, R. (2006) *Reform of the International Institutions: The IMF, World Bank and the WTO*, Cheltenham: Edward Elgar.

Das, D. (2006) 'The Doha Round of multilateral trade negotiations and trade in agriculture', *Journal of World Trade*, Vol. 40, No. 2, 259–290.

Djelic, M. and Quack, S. (eds) (2003) *Globalization and Institutions: Redefining the Rules of the Economic Game*, Cheltenham: Edward Elgar.

Elsig, M. (2007) 'The World Trade Organisation's legitimacy crisis: what does the Beast look like?', *Journal of World Trade*, Vol. 41, No. 1, 75–98.

Evenett, S. (2005) 'Can the WTO rise to the challenge of economic development', *Aussenwirtschaft*, Vol. 60, No. 3, pp. 257–277.

Finger, J. (2005) 'The future of the World Trade Organization: addressing institutional challenges in the new millennium', *Journal of World Trade*, Vol. 30, No. 4, 795–805.

Green, D. and Griffith, M. (2002) 'Globalization and its discontents', *International Affairs*, Vol. 78, No. 1, 49–68.

Heiduk, G. and Wong, K. (2005) *WTO and World Trade: Challenges in a New Era*, Heidelberg: Physica-Verlag.

Hoekman, B. and Vines, D. (2007) 'Multilateral trade cooperation: what next?', *Oxford Review of Economic Policy*, Vol. 23, No. 3, 311–334.

Keohane, R. (1998) 'International institutions: can interdependence work?', *Foreign Policy*, No. 110, 82–96.

Koopmann, G. (2005) 'Doha Development Round perspectives', *Intereconomics*, Vol. 40, No. 4, 235–245.

Kosack, S., Ramis, G. and Vreeland, J. (2006) *Globalization and the Nation State: The Impact of the IMF and the World Bank*, London: Routledge.

Lal, D. (2005) 'The threat to economic liberty from international organizations', *Cato Journal*, Vol. 25, No. 2, 503–521.

Lee, S. and McBride, S. (eds) (2007) *Neoliberalism, State Power and Global Governance*, Dordrecht: Springer.

Lewis, M. (2007) 'WTO winners and losers: the trade and development disconnect', *Georgetown Journal of International Law*, Vol. 39, No. 1, 165–198.

McRae, D. (2005) 'Developing countries and "the future of the WTO"', *Journal of International Economic Law*, Vol. 8, No. 3, 603–610.

Martin, W. and Messerlin, P. (2007) 'Why is it so difficult? Trade liberalisation under the Doha Agenda', *Oxford Review of Economic Policy*, Vol. 23, No. 3, 347–366.

Matsushita, M. et al. (2006) *The World Trade Organisation: Law, Practice and Policy*, 2nd edn, Oxford: Oxford University Press.

Mattoo, A. (2005) 'Services in a development round: three goals and three proposals', *Journal of World Trade*, Vol. 39, No. 6, 1223–1239.

Moore, M. (2003) *A World Without Walls: Freedom, Development, Free Trade and Global Governance*, Cambridge: Cambridge University Press.

Perdikis, N. and Read, R. (2005) *The WTO and the Regulation of International Trade*, Cheltenham: Edward Elgar.

Petersmann, E. (2005) 'Addressing institutional challenges to the WTO in the new millennium: a longer term perspective', *Journal of International Economic Law*, Vol. 8, No. 3, 647–665.

Robertson, D. (2000) 'Civil Society and the WTO', *World Economy*, Vol. 20, No. 9, 1119–1134.

Rodrik, D. (2007) *One Economics, Many Recipes: Globalization, Institutions and Economic Growth*, Princeton, NJ: Princeton University Press.

Sampson, G. and Chambers, W. (2008) *Developing Countries and the WTO*, Tokyo: United Nations University.

Scholte, J. (2000) *Globalization: A Critical Introduction*, Basingstoke: Palgrave.

Singh, R. (2008) 'The World Trade Organization and legitimacy: evolving a framework for bridging the democratic deficit', *Journal of World Trade*, Vol. 42, No. 2, 347–365.

Stephenson, K. (2006) 'World trade policies and restricted market access by developed nations: a cause of marginalisation of sub-Saharan Africa economies in World Trade', *The Business Review*, Vol. 5, No. 1, 334–343.

Stiglitz, J. (2002) *Globalization and Its Discontents*, London: Penguin. (Former World Bank Chief Economist makes a strong critique of the IMF and World Bank.)

Stone, D. and Wright, C. (eds) (2006) *The World Bank and Governance*, London: Routledge.

Sutherland, P. (2008) 'Transforming nations: how the WTO boosts economies and open societies', *Foreign Affairs*, Vol. 87, No. 2.

The Board (2003) 'Globalization through WTO integration: neither friend nor foe', *Legal Issues of Economic Integration*, Vol. 30, No. 2, 95–102.

Trebilcock, M. and Howse, R. (2005) *The Regulation of International Trade*, 3rd edn, London: Routledge.

Vachani, S. (ed.) (2006) *Transformations in Global Governance: Implications for Multinationals and Other Stakeholders*, Cheltenham: Edward Elgar.

Van Den Bossche, P. and Alexovicova, I. (2005) 'Effective global economic governance by the World Trade Organisation', *Journal of International Economic Law*, Vol. 8, No. 3, 667–690.

Weinstock, D. (ed.) (2007) *Global Functions: Global Institutions*, Calgary, Alberta: University of Calgary Press.

Wilkinson, R. (2006) *The WTO: Crisis and the Governance of Global Trade*, London: Routledge.

Chapter 5

Development and International Production

Colonies do not cease to be colonies because they are independent.
Benjamin Disraeli, British Prime Minister, House of Commons, 5 February 1863

LEARNING OBJECTIVES

This chapter will help you to:

- describe and distinguish between major theories of development

- outline the major differences in development in different regions

- highlight how mainstream development thinking has changed

- explain commodity chain analysis and appreciate its relevance for business and development

- understand how progression through higher value-added export activities illustrates the interdependence of business and economic development

The dominant trend in the international business environment in recent decades has been greater openness in trade, investment, finance and technology resulting in increased international integration and interdependence in business and between states. What is also apparent is that large swathes of the world's population are effectively marginalized or excluded from these trends (although there have been some improvements in the first decade of the twenty-first century – see Chapter 2). This exclusion has been a major factor in contemporary anti-globalization campaigns and is frequently used to justify proposals to reform or even abolish international institutions and to reverse policies that have contributed to international integration.

Although aspects of globalization and the policies of the IMF and the World Bank have not always been positive for developing countries, it is an over-simplification to place all or most of the blame for the marginalization of developing countries on to these factors. Development is a complex process but some countries have managed it successfully. Significantly, it is those countries that have engaged most intensively with the outside world (that is, in East Asia) that have been most successful in their development endeavours. Equally significant has been the willingness of each state to take a central role in the development process, a role that varies from country to country depending on its culture and initial circumstances.

Development is an important, and often neglected, issue for international business. Too often, international business and development are only discussed within the context of problems such as child labour or environmental degradation (see Chapters 15 and 16). Undoubtedly, these and similar issues pose serious challenges for MNEs and policy makers but they are ultimately problems that, with sufficient political will, are amenable to solution (admittedly, the political will required is of a much greater magnitude than has hitherto been seen). Successful development, however, creates markets and improves the quality of labour forces and key aspects of infrastructure, thereby creating investment opportunities. Investment in turn is central to the development process.

This chapter explores the development challenge more thoroughly. It begins by tracing the development experience of different groups of countries and tries to identify factors contributing to success and failure within individual countries and regions. It then explores different theoretical approaches and perspectives towards development, highlighting linkages where appropriate with the first section. It then discusses the evolution of production methodologies and how it has an impact on how developing countries engage with the external sector and how international business interfaces with developing countries.

DIFFERENTIAL EXPERIENCES OF DEVELOPMENT

Developing countries are a heterogeneous group and are becoming more so. At the height of decolonization in 1960, African, Asian and Caribbean countries had similar development levels: the

GNP per capita of South Korea was $217 and the equivalent figure for Haiti, the Central African Republic, Uganda, Togo, Egypt, Angola, Nigeria all fell within 10 per cent of the Korean figure. By 2007, in terms of purchasing power parity, Korean GNP per head was 33 times greater than that of the Central African Republic; 31 times greater than Togo; 27 times greater than Uganda; 21 times greater than Haiti and almost five times greater than Egypt. Even in oil-rich countries like Nigeria and Angola, Korea's living standards in terms of GNP per head were 14 and six times greater respectively in 2007. Such widely differing experiences pose questions about why some countries have been able to transform their economic fortunes while others have not. These issues are addressed later in this chapter.

Box 5.1 Categorization of Countries according to Their Level of Development

Countries are often categorized according to their level of development. Although inevitable, such categorizations are value-laden and often misleading, particularly as a country's circumstances can and do change over time. The following terms are in common usage:

- *The Third World*: the term 'Third World' has outlived its usefulness. The term was a creature of the Cold War, essentially an ideological war between two economic systems – capitalism and communism – and two political systems – liberal democracy and the one-party state. The First World referred to the advanced Western industrialized economies. The Second World referred to the Soviet bloc and to other communist countries such as China and North Korea. Countries outside these two systems, that is, countries in the process of development in Africa, Asia, the Middle East, Latin America and the Caribbean, belonged to the Third World. The 'Third World' was a useful unifying concept for the Non-Aligned Movement and for economically weak and underdeveloped countries, but given the end of the Cold War and the diversity of developing countries, the term 'Third World' has become inappropriate.
- *North–South*: the 1980 Brandt Commission Report popularized this terminology. The 'North' includes all advanced economies, namely those of North America, Japan, Europe and, from the southern hemisphere, Australia and New Zealand. The 'South' covers all developing countries. Superficially attractive, this categorization is too broad, failing to recognize the different capitalist models in the North, such as Anglo-American capitalism, the Continental European welfare model of capitalism and the more developmental Japanese model. More to the point, it treated the South as a homogenous group whereas the reality is very different.
- *Developed, developing, less or least developed*: the terminology of developed and developing countries is adopted in this text, not out of a commitment to any particular development theory but because some words have to be chosen and these are words used by the countries themselves and by international institutions such as the World Bank. Again these words have their drawbacks. To describe an economy as 'developed' suggests it has reached the end of a long journey. This is clearly not the case. 'Developed' countries, such as those of North America,

Western Europe and increasingly East Asia, continue to evolve, as the emergence of the Information Economy (see Chapter 18) demonstrates. Their description as 'advanced industrialized economies' belies the fact that they are no longer as industrialized as many developing countries and that the growth of the service sector means that industrialization is no longer synonymous with the highest levels of development. Furthermore, at what point does a country move from the developing to the developed category? For some countries, particularly 'failed states' such as Afghanistan, the Democratic Republic of the Congo and Somalia, to describe them as 'developing' seems overly ambitious.

Many of the world's poorest countries are located in Africa, although some Asian countries (Bangladesh, for example) and some island countries are also classified as least developed countries. From the 1960s to the 1990s, real GNP per head declined in many sub-Saharan African countries. However, in the first decade of the twenty-first century, the fortunes of some, at least, of these countries appeared to improve. Whether this improvement can or will be sustained is discussed below.

The experience of Latin American and Caribbean countries, which started from a higher base, has been more positive, although annual average per capita growth for the region as a whole from the mid-1960s was not particularly high at 1.3 per cent. The most spectacular long-term performer is East Asia where real GNP per head grew at an annual average rate of 5.7 per cent between 1966 and 1998 – a trend which continued into the new millennium with the result that living standards in Hong Kong and Singapore are on a par with those in advanced industrialized economies.

TABLE 5.1 LDCs Real GDP and Real (GDP) per Capita Growth Rates, 1980–1990, 1990–2000, 2000–2006 (Annual Average Growth Rates, %)

	Real GDP growth			Real GDP per capita growth		
	1980– 90	1990– 2000	2000– 06	1980– 90	1990– 2000	2000– 06
LDCs	2.6	4.0	6.5	–0.4	1.3	4.0
African LDCs	1.9	2.0	6.4	–1.0	0.6	3.6
Asian LDCs	2.7	5.1	6.8	0.7	2.6	4.8
Island LDCs	4.6	4.3	4.0	0.5	2.3	4.9
Other developing countries	3.9	5.0	5.7	1.8	3.4	4.3
All developing countries	3.9	5.0	5.7	1.7	3.2	4.2

Source: Derived from UNCTAD (2008) *The Least Developed Countries Report*.

Sub-Saharan Africa

Which ever measure is chosen – trade in goods, trade in services, inward investment (see Chapter 2) – Africa is the world's most marginalized continent. For the vast majority of Africans, poverty and subsistence are the order of the day. Apart from South Africa and the countries along the North African coast, the continent contains no emerging economies. Indeed, the economic reality for most countries has been steady decline. According to UNCTAD and World Bank figures (see Table 5.2), GDP growth per capita in sub-Saharan Africa as a whole from the 1960s through into the 1990s went backwards. There were one or two bright spots like Botswana and Lesotho but these were the exception. In the

TABLE 5.2 Growth in Real GNP per Capita – Selected Countries of sub-Saharan Africa

	Real GDP per capita (average annual % growth)			Gross national income per capita, 2007	
	1980– 1990	1990– 2000	2000– 2006	$ per capita	PPP per capita
Angola	–0.2	–5.9	9.8	2,560	4,400
Benin	–0.1	1.2	0.6	570	1,310
Burkina Faso	–0.1	2.4	2.9	430	1,120
Burundi	0.7	–4.0	–1.0	110	330
Central African Republic	–1.2	–1.3	–2.4	380	740
Chad	3.3	0.1	10.4	540	1,280
Democratic Republic of Congo	–1.4	–7.6	1.8	140	290
Ethiopia	0.1	1.5	3.2	220	780
Madagascar	–1.6	–1.0	–0.2	320	920
Malawi	–1.2	4.9	1.2	250	750
Mali	1.4	2.0	2.6	500	1,040
Mauritania	–1.0	0.2	2.3	840	2,010
Mozambique	–1.0	2.7	5.6	320	690
Niger	–3.1	–0.7	0.5	280	630
Rwanda	–1.9	–0.9	2.4	320	860
Senegal	0.1	0.9	1.9	820	1,640
Sierra Leone	0.2	–8.0	7.4	260	660
Sudan	–2.6	3.5	5.2	960	1,880
Togo	–1.8	–1.7	–0.5	360	880
Zambia	–2.1	–2.0	3.0	800	1,220

Source: World Bank World Development Indicators (2009) and UNCTAD *The Least Developed Countries Report, 2008.*

early to mid-2000s, several countries experienced some growth in their living standards for the first time since independence but, as discussed below, the sustainability of such growth is questionable.

The reasons for the relatively poor performance of Africa in terms of development are varied and contested – and beyond the scope of this chapter – but some continuing problems and challenges may be identified. Many sub-Saharan countries, for example, face continuing structural dependency. During the colonial period, their role was defined for them as exporters of primary commodities to industrialized countries. Commodities still dominate the trade and economies of many sub-Saharan African countries. Commodity prices are notoriously volatile, subject as they are to the vagaries of harvest, to stock levels and supply and demand, but the movement of real primary commodity prices in most years has not favoured developing countries since the beginning of the 1960s.

Figure 5.1, for example, shows that the prices of non-energy commodities (which include agricultural products, fertilizers, metals and minerals) were relatively static in the 1960s; fluctuated within a narrow band during the three decades of the 1970s, 1980s and 1990s; and only really soared during the first years of the 2000s when demand was pushed up by the booming emerging economies. Non-oil commodity prices peaked in mid-2008. For 2008 as a whole, non-energy commodity prices were 20 per cent above 2007 levels but by May 2009 the average commodity price for the year to date, driven by recession, had fallen to 75 per cent of 2008 levels. A similar but more pronounced pattern (see Figure 5.2) was observed for energy commodities (which include coal, crude oil and natural gas): 2008 energy price levels were 40 per cent above those of 2007 but, by May 2009, the average for the year to date was half 2007 levels. This recent experience demonstrates the problems encountered by developing countries reliant on commodity exports. African countries were not alone in their commodity dependence in 1960 but countries like Brazil, Thailand and Malaysia have been able to move away from it.

Overdependence on commodities is only a small part of sub-Saharan Africa's problems. In many cases, there is a wide divergence between the traditional subsistence economy and the limited modern

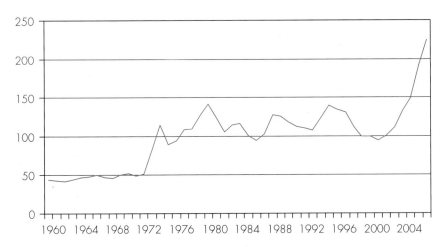

FIGURE 5.1 Non-energy Index of Commodity Prices, 1960–2007 (2000 = 100)

Source: World Bank.

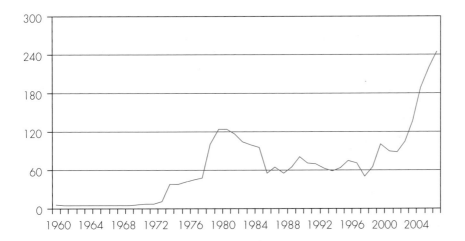

FIGURE 5.2 Energy Price Index, 1960–2007 (2000 = 100)

Source: World Bank.

sector. This makes it difficult for the limited investment that does take place to start a virtuous circle of further development – i.e. there are few opportunities for backward linkages into the rest of the economy. Economic development is also hindered by inadequate and deteriorating infrastructure – a factor which deters inward investment which, as Chapter 2 shows, is concentrated in only a few countries in Africa, and indeed mostly in the oil and mineral sectors. These sectors have increasingly attracted the interest of Chinese investors (see Case Study 5.1).

The geography of colonization resulted in national boundaries that reflect convenient lines on maps rather than territories with common histories and cultures. This has resulted in post-colonial conflict and weak governance systems. The absence or weakness of the traditional apparatus of statehood has also made it difficult for development plans to deliver their objectives, whether domestically or internationally inspired. The neo-liberal agenda and programmes of the IMF and World Bank have been heavily criticized as inappropriate for these countries and many have been held up as failures. As discussed below, some of their shortcomings have been recognized, leading to greater adaptation to the specific circumstances of individual countries rather than the 'one-size-fits-all' model that underpinned earlier programmes.

More than that, the stability of several countries has been precarious and the state has, in cases like Sierra Leone, Rwanda and the Democratic Republic of Congo, virtually imploded. In less extreme cases, internal and civil strife has also deterred investors. In these circumstances, it is hardly surprising that FDI has been limited in sub-Saharan Africa. There is much competition for capital from across the world, and the volatility and instability within Africa translates into too much risk for many potential investors.

Cutting themselves off individually or as small regional groups will almost certainly result in further deterioration of the political, economic and social situations of sub-Saharan states. Yet these countries are not in a position to withstand the competitive pressure that immediate and full exposure to the external economic environment would produce. A more fruitful halfway house might be to

CASE STUDY 5.1

Out of Africa

During the Cold War, Africa was the subject of an ideological stand-off between the West and the Soviet Bloc as both sides sought to gain influence and to protect their interests on that continent. Since the end of the Cold War, despite the occasional initiative such as the African Growth and Opportunities Act during the presidency of George W. Bush, the interest of the rest of the world in Africa waned and the continent threatened to stagnate even further. That is, until China moved in to fill the vacuum.

The scale and growth of trade and investment flows between China and Africa since the mid-1990s has been phenomenal (see Figure 5.3). Following years of negligible interaction, Africa's exports to China increased 36-fold whereas Africa's imports from China increased 18-fold between 1995 and 2007. Both figures are remarkable: the growth in Africa's exports only seem more so because they started from such a low level.

Much of China's activities in Africa were focused on a limited number of countries (see Figure 5.4), especially those engaged in the extractive industries – oil and mining. Indeed, in 2007, three countries –

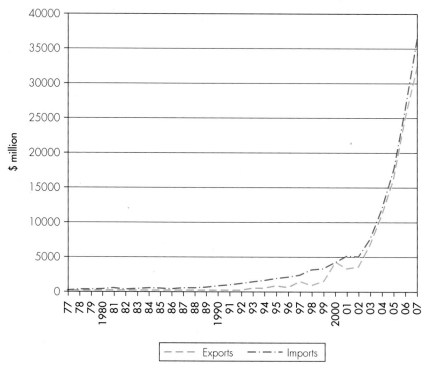

FIGURE 5.3 Africa's Exports to and Imports from China

Source: IMF, *Direction of Trade Statistics*.

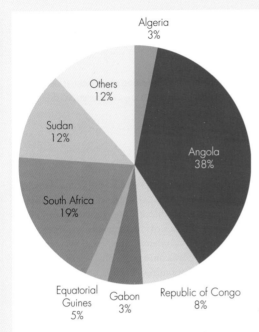

Algeria
3%

Others
12%

Sudan
12%

South Africa
19%

Angola
38%

Equatorial
Guines
5%

Gabon
3%

Republic of Congo
8%

FIGURE 5.4 China's Imports from Africa, 2007

Angola, South Africa and Sudan – accounted for 69 per cent of all African exports to China. Angola and Sudan are major exporters of crude oil to China which imports up to 30 per cent of the former's oil production. Angola is challenging Saudi Arabia as the main foreign supplier of crude oil to China and, in some periods, has actually exported more oil to China than Saudi. China also imports crude oil from other African producers, including Equatorial Guinea, Gabon and the Republic of Congo. Although the quantities exported to China may not be as great as those from Sudan and Angola, they make a significant difference to these relatively small economies. Exports to China, for example, account for half of the Democratic Republic of Congo's crude oil production. China is also involved in exploration and production in Chad, a country hitherto ignored by foreign traders and investors.

China's thirst for oil comes from its rapid growth, limited indigenous resources and the scramble for resources in world markets. Similar factors are at work in the minerals sector, which is important to China as a source of copper, cobalt and so on for its construction industry and of which there are rich reserves to be mined across the African continent. Altogether, manufactured products account for only 8 per cent of Africa's exports to China, a figure which will need to rise if Africa is to break away from its long-term dependence on the export of commodities, raw materials and natural resources.

China's exports to Africa on the other hand are largely composed of manufactured goods, machinery, electronics and medical products, many of which compete with Africa's domestic industries. Chinese capital goods exports to Africa, however, have the potential to facilitate Africa's ability to develop and improve its competitiveness.

China's investment in Africa has also been increasing. About half of this investment has gone to the oil- and mineral-rich countries of Angola, Sudan, Nigeria and Zambia. However, the geographical and sectoral scope of this investment has begun to widen out and is increasingly going to apparel and clothing, food processing, tourism, telecommunications, and particularly transport and power infrastructure projects in countries like Ethiopia, Botswana, Senegal and Uganda.

China's activities in the Democratic Republic of Congo (DRC) are typical of China's policy towards individual countries. The DRC has huge mineral wealth, including the world's biggest reserves of cobalt and tantalum and large reserves of copper, manganese, uranium and zinc, among other metals and minerals, and contains large tropical forests. As such, the DRC should be a wealthy country. Instead, it is one of the world's poorest countries with low life expectancy and living conditions, a judicial system that does not work and virtually no physical infrastructure. It is also renowned for corruption. Because of the difficulties of carrying out business there, the DRC has effectively been abandoned by Western investors.

In 2008, it was announced that Chinese state-owned enterprises would overhaul the DRC's transportation system, build two hydroelectric dams and invest in the country's mining industry at an initial cost equivalent to $9 billion. Infrastructure investment accounts for about two-thirds of the deal and the mining investment the rest. Such investment dwarfs the DRC's budget. In return, China will mine copper and cobalt equivalent to the cost of the investment. The DRC gets much-needed improvements in its infrastructure while China gets the minerals it needs and the means to export copper and cobalt out of the country.

The pattern of Chinese investment in infrastructure, schools, hospitals and prestige projects such as sports stadiums has been repeated in many countries across the continent. The spread of Chinese influence is also demonstrated by the emergence of Chinese SMEs and even Chinatowns in most major African cities as Chinese entrepreneurs (estimated to number at least 300,000 throughout the continent) move to Africa, often preceding the arrival of bigger, often state-run enterprises.

What are Chinese interests in Africa?

In 2006, China issued its *Africa Policy* which set out the core principles to guide its future relations with Africa. At a summit hosted by China for 48 African leaders around the time of the publication of the policy, President Hu Jintao promised, among other things, to increase concessional loans to Africa, to set up investment funds to encourage Chinese investment in Africa and to cancel interest-free loans owed to it by some of the poorest African countries.

In broader terms, Chinese policy towards Africa is driven by a mixture of economic and political factors, leading some commentators to suggest that Chinese companies involved in Africa are agents of Chinese foreign policy. Others point to the commercial aspect of the link which they claim dominates the relationship. China's main motivations in Africa include the following:

* the need to access oil, minerals and agricultural products to allow it to continue its rapid development;
* the wish for good relations with African countries so that China can rely on their political support in international organizations and other forum;

* the end of Taiwan's diplomatic presence on the continent (at the time of writing, four African countries accorded Taiwan official diplomatic recognition);
* to be in a good position to increase its exports to Africa in anticipation of the strengthening of their economies.

The African view

African leaders have almost universally welcomed China's enhanced presence in China which is viewed as an alternative source of financial assistance and support to that of the West. Many countries welcome the lack of conditionality and interference in their internal affairs in their relations with China. Particularly welcome is the absence of the donor–recipient relationship which is present in so many links with western countries.

China's involvement in Africa has proved especially popular with states that have become pariahs in the West, such as Zimbabwe and Sudan: the latter has been condemned roundly in the West for its role in the disaster in Dafur. Without Chinese assistance, Sudan would not have been able to increase its crude oil output from virtually nothing in the mid-1990s to 480,000 b/d in 2008, thereby boosting government revenue and enabling it to overcome US sanctions. Western critics argue that China's policy in Africa serves to support dictators and undermines efforts to foster democracy and curtail corruption. China, however, is not the only country against which this charge could be levelled.

Not all African groups are quite so sanguine about the Chinese presence in Africa. The views of African NGOs, civil society and trade unions are more mixed. Unions have argued that many Chinese companies often import their labour (even unskilled) from China and therefore Chinese investments do not necessarily yield the claimed boost to employment. Given that many Chinese investments in Africa are capital intensive, the net increase in jobs is limited in any case.

Moreover, Chinese companies setting up in Africa are able to rely on Beijing's resources and reap economies of scale. This gives Chinese companies an unfair advantage, so the argument goes, over their African counterparts and can lead to Chinese companies out-competing African companies in their domestic markets, sometimes putting them out of business as has happened in the textiles and apparel sector. Although competition can improve overall efficiency, many African firms are not well equipped to respond positively to this and any casualties in African light manufacturing are to be regretted as they represent the best opportunity for Africa to break the cycle of dependence on commodities.

In countries where Chinese companies are perceived to displace workers, anti-Chinese sentiment has come to the fore. This has been the case in Zambia where a major textile factory, employing over 1,000 people and supporting many cotton growers, was forced to close in 2007 in the face of Chinese competition. An accident in a Chinese-owned Zambian copper mine which killed 49 miners two years earlier resulted in riots and questions about safety conditions. Indeed, the Zambian opposition leader Michael Sata has campaigned in recent elections on an anti-Chinese platform.

Opportunities and challenges in the African–Chinese relationship

In theory, the African–Chinese relationship should be mutually beneficial and complementary given the relative differences in resources, capital and labour. The increasing purchasing power of Chinese households potentially creates a market for Africa's light manufactured goods, processed foods and even back office services. If African countries can take advantage of these opportunities, the continent could move away from its reliance on commodities and rise up the export development ladder (see the final section of this chapter). Indeed, China has already been involved in Nigeria and Uganda in the development of export-processing zones: the second rung on the export development ladder. Chinese businesses are expected to benefit from investing in such zones within Africa.

The emergence of global value chains, in which China is increasingly involved, creates opportunities for African companies to integrate into such chains through their greater involvement with Chinese business. Regional integration also represents a real opportunity for African countries to work together and reap scale economies that have hitherto escaped them. Indeed, Africa has embarked on regional integration with too much gusto, creating a 'spaghetti bowl' of overlapping agreements that are overly complex and deter rather than encourage trade and investment (see Chapter 3). The extent of Chinese commercial operations in Africa integrates China into Africa's regional trade networks across wide geographical areas. In short, Chinese firms have the potential to help lead the practical integration of African economies. This has proven to be an elusive goal when left to formal diplomatic negotiations among African countries.

Trade between China and Africa also needs further liberalization if the full potential of the relationship is to be fulfilled. Although in 2006 to 2007 China unilaterally eliminated tariffs on 440 commodities from Africa's least developed economies, there is still scope for improvement. In particular, African exports face the problem of escalating tariffs in China, an item which in general terms appears on the Doha Development Agenda. Tariff escalation refers to the practice of imposing higher tariffs on products which have undergone higher levels of processing, thereby removing the incentive for many commodity producers to process their products before exporting them and ensuring that they lose out on the higher value added from processed products.

In recent years, several African countries have lowered tariffs on many items and generally liberalized trade. Importers of machinery and transport equipment in particular have benefited from such policies but tariffs tend to remain high on textiles and yarn, a factor which increases costs and constrains competitiveness for African apparel manufacturers.

Conclusion

Assessing the long-term impact of the growing role of China in Africa is complex and multifaceted. Whether China represents the modern face of colonial exploitation or is a boon to Africa's development remains a subject of controversy. However, it is clear that although China can help with some problems (for example, the development of infrastructure), African countries themselves have to grasp the nettle and confront issues which have been holding back their development such as poor governance, corruption, a lack of transparency and the absence of appropriate skills.

Note

An English translation of China's Africa Policy appears on the website of China's Ministry of Foreign Affairs – http://www.fmprc.gov.en/eng/zxxx/t230615.htm (last accessed June 2009).

CASE STUDY QUESTIONS

1. Choose an African country and investigate the full range of activities of Chinese business in that country. Compare your findings with those of classmates who have researched other African countries.

2. Identify the positive and negative factors of China's increasing involvement in Africa from the viewpoint of both Africa and China.

3. Discuss whether China's policy towards Africa is a predatory raid on Africa's resources or will it help sub-Saharan Africa break out of its stop-go development cycle?

4. What are the implications of China's engagement with Africa for countries in the rest of the world?

nurture potentially viable sectors behind short-term protection, possibly within some form of regionally integrative framework to increase the size of the domestic market and then to launch the sector on the international stage in a more phased manner.

Latin America

Latin America is far more developed than sub-Saharan Africa according to all main indicators, but it lags behind the East Asian NICs. Before the Second World War, Latin America was, like other underdeveloped regions, an exporter of primary commodities, most of which were produced on foreign-owned plantations and mines. After the War, most of the continent, under the influence of economist Raoul Prebisch, tried to escape from this traditional relationship by adopting an import substitution policy. This strategy required the state to take a leading role in the development process through state ownership and high tariff walls to protect infant industries. It gradually became apparent that the restricted engagement of Latin American economies with the rest of the world failed to deliver sustainable, stable growth and that prosperity was confined to a small elite.

By the late 1970s, many Latin American governments were under military control and finding it difficult to escape from the heavy debt burden that resulted from extensive external borrowing from private banks. The absence of a significant export sector made it virtually impossible to meet debt-servicing requirements and development was stymied. By the mid-1980s, several Latin American countries were taking large doses of IMF and World Bank medicine and more were to follow suit. Initially, economic progress was stop-start and some countries embraced the abandonment of import substitution with more enthusiasm than others. However, the policy change did herald a return to growth, but it has been less strong than that experienced in East Asia. Moreover, Latin America remains dogged by large income inequalities.

In broad terms, by 2000, or even before, it was possible to talk of a common set of policies within Latin America. However, there is great variation in how far countries have changed policy direction and in the effectiveness of the new policies. The majority of Latin American countries currently place their reliance on the market mechanism and the private sector, in both the domestic and external spheres, to deliver development. This has manifested itself in supply-side reforms focusing on trade liberalization, privatization and regulatory changes such as more FDI-friendly policies. On the macro-side, the emphasis has been on achieving stability, an objective that requires strict budgetary discipline, monetary restraint and realistic exchange rates.

Compared to previous decades, Latin American economies have become much more open and competitive and generally welcoming to international business. Although IMF and World Bank programmes have played their part in this turnaround, as time progressed it has been globalization and the need to integrate with the rest of the world that has driven Latin American policy forward. In addition to the macro and micro policies referred to above, a number of countries have turned to regional integration schemes such as Mercosur (see Chapter 3) to deliver further growth. Tried previously as a way of extending the domestic market in a relatively closed world, the new regionalism in Latin America is an open regionalism intended to provide links for greater integration with the international economy.

East Asian NICs

By the 1990s, the four East Asian NICs of South Korea, Taiwan, Singapore and Hong Kong were more properly described as developed than as developing countries. Behind them are Malaysia and Thailand: these second-generation NICs have also substantially transformed their economies but not yet quite so fundamentally as the 'Big Four'. In all cases, though, the achievements are striking given that in 1960, these countries had more in common in terms of GDP per head and economic structure with many countries who were and who remain among the world's poorest (see above). The big question relating to the East Asian economies is: why have they been able to develop whereas the African story is one of stagnation and/or decline? This question is beyond the scope of this section but it can identify some of the factors in the success of the East Asian NICs.

Whatever the reasons for East Asian success, it is inappropriate to attribute it to full-blooded implementation of neo-liberal policies. Although East Asian countries have shown themselves prepared and able to take advantage of globalization opportunities, particularly in relation to export-led growth, they have frequently followed a strategy of active state involvement in the developmental process, although the exact nature of this involvement varies.

Like Latin America nations, the countries of East Asia also followed an import substitution policy during the 1950s. This allowed them to start the industrialization process without being undermined by imports from developed countries. However, the restricted size of domestic markets and shortages of foreign exchange to pay for the machinery and equipment imports needed for industrialization contributed to the shift to an export promotion strategy that occurred in the early 1960s.

South Korea and Taiwan had two further development advantages over other developing countries. First, they had a privileged role in the post-war foreign policy of the US, which poured substantial sums of money into them to reduce their vulnerability to Communist infiltration and/or take-over. The likely cessation of US financial aid, worth about $100 million per annum to Taiwan alone, encouraged the shift to export promotion. Second, both South Korea and Taiwan began their post-war development with a more developed infrastructure and education system than other countries at a similar level of development.

Since 1960, East Asia has been the world's fastest growing region. East Asian success has threatened to put obstacles to further development in their way. In the 1980s, access to the markets of the developed countries was compromised by a wave of 'new protectionist' measures, including 'voluntary' export restraints, anti-dumping measures and a focus on intellectual property rights. The 1986 US Trade Act identified a range of alleged unfair trading practices: Article 301 of the Act required the US Trade Representative to act against such practices. The East Asian trading position was also made more difficult by the high wage growth that eroded their original cheap labour advantage in labour-intensive sectors. On the other hand, their relatively skilled and educated workforces gave them advantages in the transition to post-Fordist production.

East Asian NICs partially overcame these potential obstacles in their traditionally strong sectors of electronics and textiles by engaging in the process of triangle manufacturing (see below). In other words, the more value-added, labour-intensive and/or the final assembly phases of production are carried out in lower wage countries, usually elsewhere in the region. Local producers meanwhile have moved up the production hierarchy to engage in more technology intensive, higher value-added activities, bringing competition from the South Korean and Taiwanese electronics sectors, for example, to the erstwhile dominant US, European and Japanese producers.

Despite these broad similarities, each of the East Asian NICs has followed its own distinctive development path as discussed below.

South Korea

The South Korean government has played a decisive role in directing the economy to its current advanced state of development. During the key early days of development in the 1960s, a hybrid policy of import substitution and export promotion was followed. The government chose to do this through developing selected strategic industries such as automobiles, shipbuilding and electronics. The chosen companies were granted subsidies and privileges, including protection from foreign competition, in return for establishing capital- and technology-intensive activities and export capacity. The favoured, largely family-owned companies evolved into giant industrial conglomerates (chaebol), several of which (e.g. Samsung, Hyundai and LG) are now among the world's top MNEs. In order to ensure efficiency and competitiveness, despite the isolation from foreign competition, the government encouraged competition among the chaebol.

This strategy met with some success: for example, South Korea dominated the world's ship-building industry by the 1980s. This strategy was not without its problems. It relied heavily on imports of capital goods and technology licensing against the background of a relatively small and, in the early days, a low-income domestic market. Much emphasis is currently placed on the need for developing countries to follow liberal FDI policies to promote development. However, South Korea's development was achieved by building up domestic capacity rather than relying on foreign capital. In order to acquire the necessary technology, Korea relied initially on reverse engineering (that is, Korean firms deconstructed existing technology to understand how it worked and used this understanding to improve the technology) and increasingly on the development of its own research and development capacity: its research and development expenditure as a percentage of GDP is among the highest in the world. Educational spending and university enrolments are also among the highest in the developing world, reinforcing the importance of human capital in development.

Taiwan

The Taiwanese government has also played a major role in economic development. Since 1960, Taiwan has moved away from import substitution towards a strong export promotion policy, including selective inducements to foreign investors and support for indigenous skills and technology development and acquisition. However, unlike South Korea, the Taiwanese government did not encourage the creation of giant private conglomerates or concentrate on the development of heavy industry. Rather, it has focused on developing the SMEs that dominated Taiwan's business sector.

SMEs can find it difficult to engage in the research and development needed for success in sectors like electronics so the government has acted to ensure that Taiwanese companies can compete. Government agencies undertake research that is too costly and risky for private companies in aerospace and advanced metals engineering, for example. Other measures include high levels of investment in education and training, and the development of Taiwan's own Silicon Valley through the construction of the science town at Hsinchu which brings together thousands of university researchers, several national laboratories, a huge technology institute and over 400 high-technology companies involved in the integrated circuit, computing and peripherals, telecommunications, optoelectronics, precision machinery and biotechnology sectors. Programmes to promote sub-contracting, a strategy which strengthens the emergence of backward linkages into the rest of the economy, have also played a key part in Taiwan's development. Initially, such measures included minimum local content requirements for foreign affiliates based in Taiwan. Measures later became more indirect such as offering incentives to local subcontractors.

Hong Kong

Hong Kong has followed the most liberal economic policy of all the East Asian NICs and has not taken on the role of the developmental state like South Korea or Taiwan. During the final decades of British rule (which ended in 1997), official policy was described as 'positive non-interventionism'. In other words, Hong Kong's modernization occurred under a system of 'laissez faire' – an approach which delivered significant economic success. However, Hong Kong's location, unique history and relationship with mainland China and its traditional role as a trading entrepôt make it an unusual NIC and reduce its usefulness as a development role model. A combination of free trade and substantial inward FDI that, together with its indigenous entrepreneurial population, the long-standing presence of large British companies and associated trade and finance infrastructure, made it possible for Hong Kong to develop a dynamic, export-oriented, light manufacturing sector. However, Hong Kong's lack of government-driven or assisted research and development means that, although Hong Kong has seen some industrial deepening, it has not developed the same level of industrial complexity and technological sophistication as other East Asian NICs.

As Hong Kong's wages and other costs rose, much manufacturing activity relocated to mainland China. As the 1997 handover of Hong Kong to China approached, FDI activity became increasingly geared towards servicing the Chinese economy. Although losing a significant proportion of its manufacturing activity at home, Hong Kong has continued to thrive by moving into financial services, becoming the region's and one of the world's leading financial centres.

Singapore

Like Hong Kong, Singapore has a long history as a trading entrepôt. However, the similarity ends there. The Singapore government has been much more interventionist. Import substitution was quickly abandoned in favour of selective industrial targeting and free trade. More than any other East Asian NIC, Singapore's development policy has been based on liberal FDI rules and attracting MNE investment.

Singapore's initial development occurred in the garment and semi-conductor industries but the government intervened early and decisively to upgrade the industrial structure and encourage more higher value-added activity. Like South Korea and Taiwan, Singapore has recognized the importance of a skilled and educated workforce. As a small island with a population of only four million, Singapore has chosen not to spread itself too thinly, specializing in high technology and guiding inward investors to higher value-added investment and technology provision. As a result, Singapore has developed a capacity in complex technologies without the existence of an extensive research and development base. However, the government encourages MNEs to establish laboratories in Singapore and is fostering indigenous research through targeting individual sectors like biotechnology. This process is not helped by a shortage of trained scientists but investment in education is directed towards easing this problem in the longer term. In short, as costs have risen, Singapore's response has been to systematically move up the high-technology production ladder and to identify and remove obstacles that might otherwise inhibit its strategy.

Overall, the East Asian economies have a propensity for export promotion and selective government intervention in common (with Hong Kong the exception in the latter case). In other words, it is not liberal market economics but interventionist policies that underpin their success. Hong Kong, Taiwan and Singapore (less so South Korea) have welcomed FDI but their intervention strategies have varied. Their development has also been marked by less income inequality than in other regions.

Increasingly, as labour and other costs have risen, the East Asian NICs have engaged in outward investment to South East Asia and China, resulting in enhanced intra-regional trade and the emergence of a regional division of labour. This marks reduced dependence of the region on Western capital and technology; the growing role of these NICs as the engine for growth in the wider region, and the emergence of regionally integrated trade and production networks. This integration, both formal and informal, reflects the emergence of greater intra-industry trade on a world level and represents the optimal path for future success, given the relatively limited domestic markets of the East Asian NICs and the potentially lucrative, albeit as yet underdeveloped markets of the rest of the region.

THEORIES OF DEVELOPMENT

Consideration of development theory is important in that it influences the approach of developing countries and international institutions towards development and provides a context for the engagement of international business in developing countries. This section briefly outlines the two main competing development theories. It is far from an exhaustive discussion of all variants of development theory; nor does it purport to critique these theories, but it does outline two of the most influential strands of development policy which continue to shape thinking today.

Dependency Theory

At the heart of dependency theory is the contention that the problems of developing countries stem from their reliance on more developed economies for capital, markets, technology and so on. In colonial times, this dependence was perpetuated by subordination of the interests of the colonized country to those of the colonizing power, namely through the structuring of economic relations so that the colony's sole role was to supply primary commodities and raw materials to the industries of the colonial power (see above). Even after independence, so the theory goes, a dependency relationship persisted, not through political and administrative control as before, but through continuing reliance on foreign capital in the form of MNEs. In other words, the negative effects of colonialism had been replaced by a new form of exploitation termed 'neo-colonialism'.

Ironically, given that most Latin American countries threw off their colonial bonds in the nineteenth century, dependency theory originated in Latin America during the 1950s and 1960s. However, Latin American economies were badly scarred by the 1930s Depression which, within the space of four years, had slashed their export earnings by over two-thirds, creating severe problems in financing the import of manufactures from industrialized countries. This experience was interpreted as demonstrating the dangers of overreliance on external economies. Given that the world's most successful economies had originally industrialized behind tariff walls, Latin American policy makers also concluded that the only way to develop was to do likewise. Thus Latin America's post-war import substitution strategy was born.

Dependency theory quickly spread beyond Latin America and was important in attempts to generate developing world solidarity via the Group of 77 and the New International Economic Order in the 1970s. Such initiatives stressed the importance of self-reliance and the de-linking of developing economies from developed economies and were an (unsuccessful) attempt to shift the balance of power away from the dominant economic and political role of the developed countries and thus to reduce the dependency of the developing countries on them.

Despite its attractiveness to Latin America and other developing countries in their early years of independence, dependency theory had fallen out of favour by the 1980s. Import substitution had not yielded the expected benefits. Indeed, import substitution did nothing to break the unequal relationship between developing and developed countries as the former relied heavily on imports of capital goods and technology from the latter to promote their industrialization. Furthermore, it had proved virtually impossible to forge a common identity for developing countries given their wide diversity of interests and experience. Often, but not solely, used as a means of constructing an alternative model to capitalism, dependency theory became further neglected as the Cold War ended when the only choice available for developing countries appeared to be between competing forms of capitalism rather than between capitalism and something else. In short, the route out of poverty and underdevelopment appeared increasingly to be more not less engagement with the process of globalization. Indeed, more and more countries started to shift their policies towards greater utilization of market forces, both domestically and externally (see Chapters 2 and 6).

In addition, dependency theory has been criticized as too deterministic, too general and lacking in power to explain the divergent development experiences of countries in sub-Saharan Africa and in East Asia. Nevertheless, dependency theory has left an important legacy: it emphasizes the impact of and interaction of the international economic system with development. However, its analysis of the impact tends to run contrary to much contemporary thinking on the matter and it underestimates domestic factors as an explanation of underdevelopment – a shortcoming addressed by modernization theory.

Modernization Theory

Modernization theory is based on entirely different assumptions to dependency theory. Rather than attributing the failures of developing countries to their unequal relationships with developed countries or to their links, or lack of them, with the international economic system, modernization theory focuses on shortcomings inherent in the developing countries themselves and proposes strategies to overcome them. In addition, dependency theory emerged from the developing countries themselves, supported by sympathetic left-leaning Western intellectuals, whereas modernization theory originated within the developed countries and international institutions like the IMF and World Bank.

According to modernization theory, lack of development stems from inadequate technology and cultural factors that inhibit economic growth and, more specifically, industrialization, the process that delivered development to Europe, North America and Japan. In other words, modernization theory in its purist form requires universal application of the Western model of development. Walt W. Rostow in his 1960 work *The Stages of Economic Growth: A Non-Communist Manifesto* identified five stages of growth through which economies must pass in order to modernize (see Box 5.2). This highly prescriptive programme for development has been criticized for failing to take account of the political, economic and cultural diversity of developing economies and of neglecting the relationships between developing countries and the outside world.

Box 5.2 Rostow's Five Stages of Growth

1. *Traditional society*: predominantly agricultural with a rigid, hierarchical social structure and little/no scientific endeavour.
2. *Pre-conditions for take-off*: often triggered by some external factor resulting in the economy becoming less localized, greater trade, improved communications and the creation of an elite group.
3. *Take-off*: an increasing share of investment in national income and changes in social and political institutions to facilitate growth.

---

4. *The drive to maturity*: a period of continuing high levels of investment, political reform and an expanding commitment to science and technology, enabling development to take a firm hold.

5. *The age of mass consumption*: consolidation of the above with diffusion of economic benefits throughout the population.

In *Politics and the Stages of Growth* (1971), Rostow added a sixth stage – the search for greater quality of life.

Given the underlying assumption that development is about convergence with the Western model, modernization theory resulted in a highly technocratic, mechanistic, problem-solving approach to development, culminating in what Hoogvelt described as a 'how to develop manual for less developed countries' (Hoogvelt, 2001). Given the geographical origins of modernization theory, the measures proposed to achieve development are in line with the prevailing economic philosophy of the developed countries – that is, neo-liberalism or a reliance on freeing up the private sector and releasing the power of market forces to bring about this growth. This philosophy is reflected in IMF conditionality and in the World Bank's Structural Adjustment Programmes (SAP).

Modernization theory has attracted much criticism. Particularly powerful are allegations of ethnocentricity – that is, the attempt to parachute inappropriate Western development models into developing countries and a failure to take into account the unique social, cultural, historical and economic backgrounds of individual developing countries. Critics also argue that success of the modernization approach has been limited to parts of East Asia. Even in East Asia, it may be argued that development has not occurred not as a result of convergence to the neo-liberal model but through adaptation and tailoring of development policies to the individual circumstances of South Korea, Taiwan, Singapore and Hong Kong by the governments of those countries (see above). In other words, growth and development are more likely to occur when policies work with rather than against the culture and traditions of individual countries.

CHANGING APPROACHES TO DEVELOPMENT

Approaches to development have become more complex, more nuanced and more sensitive to the specific conditions of individual developing countries. Consideration of the so-called 'Washington Consensus' is a useful starting point for understanding how development thinking changed in the 1980s and 1990s and how it has evolved since. The term entered common usage around 1990 following publication of an article by economist John Williamson which referred to the common features of policy advice proffered by the Washington institutions (that is, the IMF, the World Bank, the US Treasury and mainstream academic economists) about the development process. Box 5.3 lists the main features of the Washington Consensus which essentially represents the neo-liberal SAPs to which developing countries had to adhere in return for financial assistance from international institutions like the World Bank.

Box 5.3 The Washington Consensus

The components of the Washington Consensus identified by John Williamson are:

1. *fiscal discipline*: the restriction of budget deficits to avoid inflation and capital flight;
2. *public expenditure*: the elimination of subsidies and the redirection of government spending towards education, health and infrastructure;
3. *tax reform*: development of a broad tax base with moderate marginal tax rates;
4. *interest rates*: interest rates at a level to discourage capital flight and encourage saving;
5. *exchange rates*: competitive exchange rates to promote exports;
6. *trade liberalization*: reduction of tariffs, especially on primary or intermediate inputs into export production;
7. *foreign direct investment*: encouragement of FDI as a source of capital and skills transfer;
8. *privatization*: privatization of state-owned enterprises as part of a drive to encourage the private sector;
9. *deregulation*: deregulation of the economy to encourage the growth of private enterprise and to discourage bureaucratic corruption;
10. *property rights*: the enforcement of property rights to encourage domestic capital accumulation and FDI.

Williamson himself expressed concern about use of the term 'Washington Consensus'. His original intention was to identify 'which of the policy initiatives that had emanated from Washington during the years of conservative ideology had won inclusion in the intellectual mainstream rather than being cast aside once Ronald Reagan was no longer on the political scene' (Williamson, 2000). However, the phrase soon took on a life of its own. In other words, the 'Washington Consensus' rapidly became shorthand for adherence to a set of policy prescriptions based on the primacy of the market and minimization of the role of the state. In Williamson's view, the phrase 'intended to describe a technocratic policy agenda that survived the demise of Reaganomics came to be used to describe an ideology embracing the most extreme version of Reaganomics' (Williamson, 2000).

Williamson is concerned that this gives the impression that much of the economic liberalization in developing countries in the 1980s and 1990s was imposed by the Washington-based institutions rather than resulting from a wider intellectual consensus he believed underpinned the reforms. Nevertheless, many would argue that the conditionalities attached to IMF loans and World Bank SAPs were imposed on reluctant developing countries. However, this view underestimates the extent to which developing countries themselves have taken on board elements of a less state-centric, more market-oriented approach to economic development. This process accelerated after the end of the Cold War when development ceased to be viewed as a competition between opposing political and economic systems and ideologies. The demise of communism and the bipolar world recast economic policy choices but also, for developing countries, into a question not of whether to accept the market but of how much and whether to accept the market at all.

Bringing a complex range of policies under the umbrella of a simple phrase froze debate at a certain point in time. In reality, the debate was always more complex than this phrase implies and was constantly evolving. Williamson himself later highlighted a number of areas where there were more policy disagreements than his original characterization of the Washington Consensus implied. This was particularly true of interest rate and exchange rate policy.

More fundamentally, it was increasingly recognized that macroeconomic stabilization and supply-side policies such as privatization and liberalization were not in themselves sufficient to deliver development and that the persistence of extremes of poverty and unequal income distribution impaired development and threatened stability and competitiveness. Consequently, poverty alleviation became the primary objective, not only of development NGOs, but also of the international institutions and development agencies. There was also growing awareness that even the most appropriate economic policy initiatives would fail without the existence of efficient and transparent governance systems. Consequently, much greater emphasis was placed in development thinking and policy on achieving impartial legal systems, incorrupt and incorruptible bureaucracies and political systems, transparent regulations and so on.

In short, development policy in the 1990s was more than a device to let market forces rip. Rather it attempted to take on board the implications of the end of the bipolar world and growing international integration and to reflect the increasing concern for sustainable development. Although the operation of the market mechanism is integral to many contemporary development policies, it became more and more apparent that the Washington Consensus would not provide a miracle cure for development shortcomings. Policy proposals also increasingly recognized the importance for the development of health, education and welfare policies of poverty alleviation and of the state more generally. These factors were reflected in the Millennium Development Goals (see Box 5.4), launched in 2000 by the UN, and which set out eight key development goals to be achieved by 2015. Moreover, greater emphasis has been placed on designing policies that address the structural and cultural realities of individual countries and on making public administration and service delivery more efficient and the legal systems more transparent and accountable.

Box 5.4 The Millennium Development Goals

The Millennium Development Goals were launched in September 2000 and represent eight goals and 21 sub-targets that the international community has pledged to achieve by 2015. The goals were drawn up by the UN, endorsed by its members and have the support of 23 international organizations. The individual goals and their associated targets for 2015 are:

1. Eradicate extreme poverty and hunger
   - halve the proportion of people with an income of less than $1 per day;
   - achieve full, productive and decent work for all, including women and young people;
   - halve the proportion of people suffering from hunger.

2. Achieve universal primary education
   - ensure all children everywhere will be able to complete their primary education.

3. Promote gender equality and promote women
   - end gender disparity in primary and secondary levels by 2005 and at all levels by 2015.

4. Reduce child mortality
   - reduce the under-5 mortality rate by two-thirds from 1990 levels.

5. Improve maternal health
   - reduce the maternal mortality rate by three-quarters from 1990 levels;
   - achieve universal access to reproductive health.

6. Combat HIV/AIDS, malaria and other diseases
   - halt and begin to reduce the spread of HIV/AIDS;
   - achieve, by 2010, universal access to HIV/AIDS treatment for all who need it;
   - halt and begin to reduce the spread of malaria and other diseases.

7. Ensure environmental sustainability
   - integrate sustainable development principles into country policies and reverse the loss of environmental resources;
   - achieve a significant reduction in the rate of biodiversity loss by 2010;
   - halve the proportion of people without access to safe drinking water and basic sanitation;
   - significant improvement by 2020 in the lives of at least 100 million slum dwellers.

8. Develop a global partnership for development
   - develop an open trading and financial system that is rules-based, predictable and non-discriminatory, including a commitment to good governance;
   - address the special needs of least developed countries;
   - address the special needs of landlocked and small island developing states;
   - address the debt problems of developing states;
   - provide affordable access to essential drugs in developing countries in cooperation with pharmaceutical companies;
   - make available new technologies, especially ICTS, to developing countries in cooperation with the private sector.

GLOBALIZATION, PRODUCTION AND DEVELOPMENT

Globalization has changed the architecture of international production with significant implications for developing countries. Pessimists argue that the opening up of markets, intensified competition and the growing mobility of firms lowers wages and increases unemployment in the developed countries while enabling the exploitation of developing world labour to continue. Optimists claim that globalization is to be welcomed because it removes distortions in the world economy, enabling firms to specialize and forcing them to maximize efficiency, and in the long term facilitate improvements in the economies of developing countries.

Chapter 2 implies that the international economic integration that has taken place is not truly global in scope and that the intensification of trade flows and FDI affects a minority of developing countries only. However, the link between development and globalization is about more than increases in trade and investment flows between developed and developing countries – important as these are. It incorporates what Dicken describes as the 'functional integration of internationally dispersed activities'. In other words, international economic integration has facilitated the emergence of global manufacturing systems in which different parts of the production process are located in different parts of the world. These changes in production patterns have had a major influence on how developing countries interface with the rest of the world.

For many years, mass production, or 'Fordism' pioneered by Henry Ford in the automobile industry, was the most common form of production organization. Mass production breaks down each part of the production process into basic tasks that are then performed repetitively by unskilled workers. In other words, Fordism relies on standardized, assembly-line techniques with clear demarcation of tasks. It is also a system that requires large amounts of capital, scale economies and mass markets, and was therefore not a viable industrialization model for most developing countries.

Mass production methods have to some extent given way to more flexible production methods, which were also pioneered in the motor industry, by Japanese car manufacturers and by Volvo in Sweden. The development of adaptable dies and tooling, for example, enabled the same equipment and machinery to be used to make a range of products rather than just one product, resulting in batch and customized production. Flexibility was thus applied not only to manufacturing but also to marketing as firms were able to tailor their production to specific niches or to respond more quickly to changes in taste and fashion. This shift in production methodology also required changes in how the workforce was deployed. Rather than simply performing the repetitive task on an assembly line, workers became members of teams responsible for all stages of the production process. This required multi-skilling and empowerment of workers. Lean production and just-in-time management techniques also provided opportunities for cutting down on inventories and hence costs.

What does flexibility mean for developing countries? On the one hand, although flexible production does not require large-scale, homogenous production runs, the start-up costs of flexible production in terms of the generic technology remain high, resulting in the need for large markets, although differentiated markets will do. On the other hand, flexibility has the potential to fragment production into smaller units, making it more suitable for smaller industries and workplaces.

The concept of global commodity chains, developed primarily by Gary Gereffi (Gereffi and Korzeniewicz, 1994; Stallings, 1995) draws on the mass production–flexibility dichotomy and also sheds light on the development process. Global commodity chains refer to transnational production systems that link technological, organizational and institutional networks for the development, production and marketing of products. As such, they represent the emergence of global production systems or world factories, the practical manifestation of Dicken's view of functional integration across borders. In reality, these production systems do not cover the whole world but parts of it, resulting in the reservation by Hoogvelt (2001) of the term 'globalization' for the deepening rather than the widening of capitalist expansion, a process which corresponds to the intensification of the globalization process discussed in Chapter 2.

Each global commodity chain is unique but, according to Gereffi, they have four main dimensions (Stallings, 1995):

1. a value-added chain linked across a range of relevant industries;
2. geographical dispersion of production and marketing networks of different sizes and types spanning national, regional and global levels;
3. authority and power relationships between firms within the chain to determine the allocation and flow of finance, materials and human resources;
4. an institutional framework that identifies how local, national and international conditions and policies shape the globalization process at each stage in the chain.

Gereffi then distinguishes between two main types of global commodity chain:

1. *Producer-driven chains*: producer-driven chains are typical in capital- and technology-intensive industries such as automobiles, heavy machinery, computers and aircraft. MNEs own most of the production system but not necessarily all of it: strategic alliances between rivals and the subcontracting of components are common. Indeed, most automobile producers maintain a complex and extensive network of component suppliers. In producer-driven chains, the MNE's headquarters exercise a large degree of control and coordination over all elements of the production process.
2. *Buyer-driven chains*: buyer-driven chains are typically concerned with the production of consumer goods like footwear, clothing, toys, consumer electronics and other household items – that is, industries that are labour, design and marketing intensive. The companies concerned, which include large retailers and branded marketers such as Benneton, IKEA, Reebok, Nike and The Gap, do not engage directly in production themselves but set up and manage decentralized networks across many, usually developing, countries. Entry barriers in these industries are not production related but arise from product development, advertising and marketing costs. Buyer-driven chains provide excellent examples of flexible production. By use of electronic point-of-sale data, the retailer or branded company is in close touch with the consumer and can closely monitor changes in consumer taste and fashion, thereby enabling production to respond rapidly to shifts in demand and keeping inventory, and therefore costs, to a minimum.

The parent company in the buyer-driven model does not correspond to the traditional idea of a multinational which owns and controls production through a network of subsidiaries and affiliates. Production in this model is almost entirely outsourced, enabling the parent company to avoid the risks of investment in production capacity. The parent company takes on the role of production broker: if part of the network becomes too costly, it can be replaced by other contractors relatively easily.

The competitive and cost pressures are intense for producers in buyer-driven chains. Production in early buyer-driven chains was frequently located in the NICs of Hong Kong, South Korea and Taiwan but, as these countries developed (leading to higher wages) and became subject to import quotas in developed countries, a new form of managing the buyer-driven chains emerged – 'triangle manufacturing'. In this model, overseas buyers continue to place production orders with the manufacturer with whom they have a long-term outsourcing relationship. These manufacturers in turn outsource some or all of the production to affiliated production in low-wage countries like China, Indonesia, Vietnam, Guatemala and the Dominican Republic. The NIC companies retain a foothold in manufacturing but in higher value-added production. As such the role of the NIC manufacturers in buyer-driven commodity chains has shifted from that of direct producer to one of production broker for retailers and branded marketing companies. Higher costs have not cut them out of the network because the contractors have no production experience and rely on the NIC company to take responsibility for compliance with delivery schedules and quality requirements. However, as the countries and companies at the base of the triangle develop, it is probable that the 'middleman' role will disappear and contractors will again deal directly with the producers.

This analysis implies a hierarchy of activities within buyer-driven global commodity chains in which higher levels of development are associated with higher value-added activities. In the fashion industry, for example, exclusive designer products are produced in high-cost developed countries like Italy and France whereas inexpensive, high-volume garments such as T-shirts are produced in low-cost countries like China, Sri Lanka or Bangladesh. However, even this distinction is breaking down as high-end designers like Gucci and Armani source an increasing proportion of their products from China. Gereffi argues that the export role taken on by an individual country signifies their level of development and that development requires an ability to move towards more complex, higher value-added export functions. He identifies five rungs in the export development ladder:

- primary commodity exports;
- export-processing assembly operations;
- component supply subcontracting;
- original equipment manufacturing (OEM);
- original brand manufacturing (OBM).

- *Primary commodity exports:* the least developed countries depended overwhelmingly on the exports of one or two primary commodities, leaving them highly vulnerable to commodity price volatility. Indeed, over time, the terms of trade (the ratio of export prices to import prices – see above) have moved against these countries, requiring them to increase their commodity production to be able to buy the same quantity of imports (see above). The countries of sub-Saharan Africa in particular continue to be overdependent on primary commodities and have barely moved beyond this stage of exporting.
- *Export-processing assembly operations:* this form of exporting involves the assembly of manufactured products from imported components, often within export-processing zones (EPZ) – small areas with high-quality infrastructure allocated by governments for the development of export-oriented industries. Incentives are offered to companies to locate in the zone and to manufacture or assemble products from imported inputs and raw materials (often imported duty-free). EPZs sprang up in the 1960s in parts of Asia and Mexico. Most EPZs are currently located in Latin America, especially Mexico and Central America, the Caribbean and Asia, and involve textiles, clothing and electronic goods assembly. In Asia, the more advanced NICs have moved into higher level manufacturing but other Asian countries have taken up exporting processing assembly. EPZs are part of broader industrialization strategies and offer a quick way to get started.

However, their isolation from the rest of the economy renders linkages into the rest of the economy weak, thereby reducing their potential as motors of development.

■ *Component supply subcontracting:* component supply subcontracting involves the manufacture and export of components in middle-income developing countries and final product assembly taking place in a developed country. This exporting role offers greater development potential than EPZs because it operates at a higher level of industrial sophistication, frequently entails technology transfer and offers greater opportunities for generating links with local suppliers. This production role continues to be particularly important for Latin American countries, many of whom produce parts for US and Japanese motor manufacturers. In East Asia, component supply subcontracting played an important role in the emergence of the electronics industry.

■ *Original equipment manufacturing (OEM):* OEM refers to the production of finished products by manufacturers in developing countries under contract to developed country retailers or branded marketers. In other words, OEM involves the production of products that are sold under another company's brand name. The OEM manufacturer must have the ability to interpret designs (hence the alternative name 'specification contracting') and source and manufacture the product in line with the client's price and quality requirements and according to tight delivery schedules. Given these heavy demands, OEM activity has involved only more advanced developing countries and has been central to the growth of East Asian economies. Constant demands by buyers for higher quality and new products have ensured that industrial and technical upgrading and the creation of a range of supportive industries have taken place, often with government assistance.

■ *Original brand manufacturing (OBM):* the drawbacks of OEM have encouraged a shift to original brand manufacturing. OEM producers face intense low-cost competition but they do not have direct access to markets, the most profitable area of business. In order to overcome this, OBM companies establish and produce their own proprietary brand and some companies engage in a mixture of OEM and OBM manufacturing. Garment manufacturers in Hong Kong, for example, continue to subcontract from developed world retailers while establishing their own brand names and retail outlets. The most successful OBM companies manage the difficult task of establishing a brand beyond their region: Korea's Hyundai, for example, has become a respected brand in North American and European automobile markets and Samsung and Goldstar have developed an international reputation in consumer electronics. Taiwanese companies have concentrated more on ICTs, with Acer, for example, selling their own brand of computer. Not all OBM producers are so successful and some revert to OEM operations.

CONCLUSION

The exclusion of developing countries from the globalization process is frequently regarded as testament to the iniquity of the globalization process by many anti-globalization NGOs and as justification for resisting and protesting against initiatives taken by international institutions to promote development. However, although criticizing the dominance of the agenda of major institutions by developed countries and strongly resisting individual policy initiatives of international institutions, developing countries themselves tend not to join in the anti-globalization rhetoric but rather strive to gain greater access to the globalization process and engage more positively in it.

Summary of Key Concepts

■ Development is often neglected in international business analysis but successful development creates markets and business opportunities.

■ Development policy now recognizes the complexity of the development process and is moving away from a 'one-model-fits-all approach' to one which takes account of good governance and the specific social, political, cultural and economic circumstances of individual countries.

■ The most successful countries in terms of development have tended to be those that have fostered a positive approach to engagement with the rest of the world, initially in terms of trade promotion and latterly in terms of policy to encourage FDI.

■ Commodity chain analysis, especially progression through higher value-added export activities, is a useful indicator of how business and economic development are inter-dependent and of how far a country has developed.

Activities

1. Research a company which maintains a buyer-driven commodity chain (e.g. Nike, Benneton, The Gap) and assess whether and how it makes a contribution to development in the country in which it operates.

2. Research the experience of a sub-Saharan African country and identify the obstacles it faces regarding development. If this exercise is undertaken in preparation for a seminar, students can compare and pool their findings from research into different countries.

3. You are a consultant hired to prepare a report for an African country striving to develop. The government is anxious to attract foreign investment to help in its development strategy but is finding it difficult to do so. Your report should analyse why the government is encountering such problems and offer recommendations as to how it can make itself more attractive to foreign investors. You may tackle this in a number of ways, including identifying sectors on which the government may wish to focus or, conversely, by giving advice on the general attractiveness of the country for investors.

Discussion Questions

1. Many developing countries have not prospered during the current globalization era. Does this require a retreat from the globalization process or greater engagement with it?

2. In your view, which of the major development theories has been the most useful in explaining the development process? Justify your answer.

3. Discuss the usefulness of commodity chain analysis in explaining the link between production and development.

4. Research the Millennium Development Goals with a view to assessing success in achieving them.

References and Suggestions for Further Reading

Brautigam, D. (2009) *The Dragon's Gift: The Real Story of China in Africa*, Oxford: Oxford University Press.

Broadman, H. (2008) 'China and India go to Africa: new deals in the developing world', *Foreign Affairs*, Vol. 87, No. 2, 95–109.

Buckley, P. (2009) 'The impact of the global factory on economic development', *Journal of World Business*, Vol. 44, No. 2, 131–143.

Chari, S. and Corbridge, S. (2008) *The Development Reader*, New York: Routledge.

Gereffi, G. and Korzeniewicz, M. (1994) *Commodity Chains and Global Capitalism*, London and Westport, CT: Praeger.

Haynes, J. (2008) *Development Studies*, London: Routledge.

Henderson, J. (2009) *The Political Economy of East Asian Development*, London: Routledge.

Hoogvelt, A. (2001) *Globalization and the Postcolonial World: The New Political Economy of Development*, Basingstoke: Palgrave.

Luiz, J. (2009) 'Institutions and economic performance: implications for African development', *Journal of International Development*, Vol. 21, No. 1, 58–75.

Oetzel, J. and Doh, J. (2008) 'MNEs and development: a review and reconceptualization', *Journal of World Business*, Vol. 44, No. 2, 108–120.

Padayachee, V. (ed.) (2009) *The Political Economy of Africa*, London: Routledge.

Rostow, W. (1960) *The Stages of Economic Growth: A Non-Communist Manifesto*, Cambridge: Cambridge University Press.

Rostow, W. (1971) *Politics and the Stages of Growth*, Cambridge: Cambridge University Press.

Ross, A., Forsyth, D. and Huq, M. (2008) *Development Economics*, London: McGraw Hill Education.

Special Issue (2008) 'Management in Africa in the global context', *Journal of African Business*, Vol. 9, No. 1.

Stallings, B (ed.) (1995) *Global Change, Regional Response: The New International Context of Development*, Cambridge: Cambridge University Press.

Stiglitz, J. and Charlton, A. (2005) *Fair Trade for All: How Trade Can Promote Development*, Oxford: Oxford University Press.

Todaro, M. (2009) *Economic Development*, 10th edn, Harlow: Addison Wesley/Pearson Education.

UNCTAD (2008) *Least Developed Countries, 2008 Report*, Geneva: UNCTAD.

Williamson, J. (2000) 'What should the World Bank think about the Washington consensus?', *World Bank Research Observer*, Vol. 15, No. 2, 251–264.

Chapter 6

Emerging Economies
The Major Beneficiaries of Globalization

When China wakes it will shake the world.

Napoleon Bonaparte, French military and political leader (1769–1821)

LEARNING OBJECTIVES

This chapter will help you to:

- describe what is meant by the terms 'emerging' and 'transition' economies

- identify key milestones in and characteristics of the transformation of China and India, including similarities and differences between them

- explain the importance of emerging economies for international business

- analyse the impact of the emerging economies, both regionally and globally

By the early 2000s, the emergence of new players in the world economy that could, and most probably would in the longer term, challenge the economic domination of the developed economies became apparent. Suddenly, every commentator became aware of China, and to a lesser extent India, and speculated about their impact on and the potential for change in the world economic order. Much of the debate has been tinged with fear – fear about job losses in developed countries resulting from production relocation and outsourcing, and about the difficulties of competing with economic powerhouses with much lower costs.

Those of a more positive disposition have identified opportunities offered by the integration of these markets into the world economy and by the potential to reconfigure value chains to enhance efficiency and competitiveness. In other words, the rapid development of the emerging economies is seen as an extension and a validation of the globalization process by incorporating a much greater proportion of the world's population and output into the global economy. Given that the emerging economies, to a large extent, owe their success to liberalization of their domestic economies and to a greater opening to the outside world in the form of trade and investment (see below), this view has some justification.

Emerging economies are important because they bring new players into the global economy, opening up new markets and opportunities for business, as well as intensifying competition, which places a greater onus on business to adapt more rapidly to change. As a by-product – as has become clear since late 2007 in particular – their growing success and prosperity has also meant greater competition for resources: namely food, energy, raw materials and commodities in general. The large emerging economies – the BRIC economies of Brazil, Russia, India and China – are important economic powerhouses in their own right with sufficient economic weight in terms of markets and production to have a significant impact not only on neighbouring countries but also increasingly on the world economy. Their status as the world's fastest growing economies and their increasingly prominent role in global economic relations also gives these countries a greater influence in international relations generally and could well lead, in the longer term, to a shift in the balance of power in international institutions and negotiations (see Chapter 4).

This chapter opens with an exploration of what is meant by the terms 'emerging' and 'transition economies'. Although many countries throughout the world may be described as emerging economies, the chapter focuses on the two largest – China and India and how they have reached their present status as two of the most rapidly growing and modernizing economies in the world. In the process, similarities and differences in their development paths are highlighted. We then discuss the emergence of these economies and their implications for business in terms of opportunities, risks and challenges, both from the perspective of enterprises inside and outside the emerging economies. We conclude by discussing the growing contribution of emerging economies in the broader global context.

WHO AND WHAT ARE EMERGING ECONOMIES?

The terms 'emerging' or 'transition' economies imply that some form of change is underway. This change involves the transformation of key aspects of the economy and also reflects an acceleration of the pace of change and development. Emerging economies are usually low or middle economies and may be big or small in size. They exist in Southeast Asia, Eastern Europe, parts of Africa, the Middle East and Latin America. Big emerging economies include Argentina, Brazil, Chile, China, Egypt, India, Indonesia, Mexico, Poland, Russia, South Africa, South Korea and Turkey. Much of the discussion of emerging economies in the media, and in this chapter, focuses on two of the BRIC economies – India and China.

Each emerging economy sits within its own unique historical, social, cultural, political, legal and economic context but they have broad characteristics in common. In general, they are all experiencing the transition from developing to developed country status and/or from state dominated to a freer, more liberal market economy. India and China, for example, may both be described as 'developing countries' but in certain regions/areas of economic activity they are beginning to resemble more developed economies. Although state-owned enterprises remain important in China, their role is declining and China is rapidly transforming itself from a command into a market economy. India has long been a mixed economy but its recent past has seen, if not the elimination, at least the scaling down and limiting of state intervention in the form of ownership and regulation.

These overarching characteristics have given rise to other trends. First, emerging economies are undertaking economic reform to varying degrees in the direction of freeing up the market. This can take various forms from reducing restrictions on business, privatization and tax reform to developing the infrastructure of the market in the form of legislation (e.g. competition law or the establishment of private property rights) and institutions, such as ensuring that a viable and efficient financial system exists. Of particular interest to international business is the greater freedom accorded to inward investors, a reduction in trade barriers and a greater orientation to the rest of the world. In short, emerging economies are engaged in opening up their economies, both domestically internally and externally. In the case of China, this was exemplified by its accession to the World Trade Organization in 2001. Both countries have asserted themselves in international institutions: this has been apparent, for example, in the Doha negotiations in which China and India have taken a leading role and at the April 2009 G-20 Summit when China set out the case for an overhaul of global financial institutions.

As a consequence of the above, and of the ongoing and incomplete nature of reform, emerging economies tend to exhibit common economic and structural performance characteristics. First, compared to developed countries, emerging economies retain relatively large agricultural sectors compared to developed countries (see Table 6.1). Indeed, agriculture in emerging economies accounts for a similar share of GDP as that prevailing in Europe in the mid-1950s. The share of agriculture in most European economies is currently no more that about 2 per cent GDP – and is frequently less. Given the rapid growth of the industrial and service sectors in emerging economies, agriculture's role in emerging economies will see a relative decline. Many emerging economies are already experiencing significant migration from rural to urban areas in line with this trend.

Table 6.1 also throws up an important difference between India and China which reflects differences in their development paths. Well over half of India's economy is composed of the services sector. Although this is not unusual for developed countries where services often account for three-quarters or

TABLE 6.1 Comparative Economic Structures of the US, India and China

(% GDP)	US	India	China
Agriculture	0.8	17.5	11.7
Industry	19.3	27.9	48.9
Services	77.9	54.6	39.4

Source: National statistical offices.

more of GDP, it is unusual for a country at India's stage of development and is a function of its strengths in IT, software, the outsourcing of backroom activities and other service-related activities.

Second, as the constraints on business ease up, investors are seizing opportunities in emerging economies. Foreign investors in particular are taking advantage of the more business-friendly environment, especially in China (see Figure 6.1), where FDI inflows started to soar from the early 1990s. FDI inflows into India have grown steadily in recent years but they remain a fraction of the funds being attracted to China. Such investment is a sign of confidence in the emerging economies but is not without risks (see below and Case Study 19.2).

Third, as a result of the reforms and greater investment, growth in emerging economies has been stronger and more buoyant than in most OECD countries since the 1990s (see Figure 6.2). In the case of China, growth has been at remarkably high levels from the onset of reform in 1978. India's growth has mostly been above 5 per cent since 1980 and has accelerated noticeably since 2000. The Russian economy, however, declined through much of the 1990s as it adjusted to the new post-Soviet

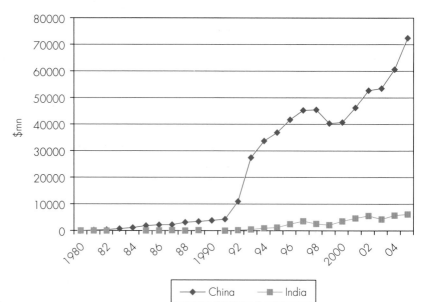

FIGURE 6.1
FDI Inflows into India and China, 1980–2005

Source: UNCTAD, *World Investment Report*.

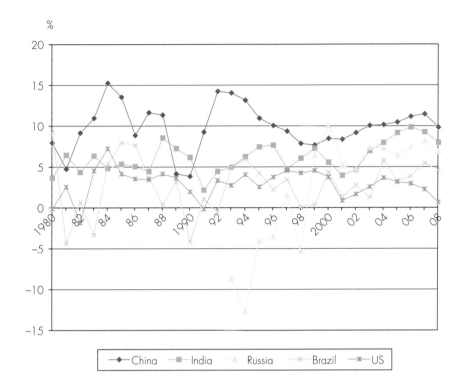

FIGURE 6.2
Real GDP Growth in the BRIC and US Economies, 1980–2008

Source: IMF.

political, economic and social systems. However, Russia has benefited from the increase in energy prices which has resulted in a turnaround in its economic fortunes. Brazil's economic journey has been much more volatile and has been affected by financial crises and problems in commodity markets, but the fluctuation in its fortunes has been less marked in the 2000s. Growth in the world's largest developed economy, the US, has, since the downturn of the early 1990s, largely been within the 2 to 4 per cent range. The impact of the financial crisis that began in 2007 on the long term future of the BRIC economies is unclear. However, early indications suggest that the growth outlook for China is less buoyant in the short term but growth is still likely to be significantly stronger than in the developed economies and to be strongly positive.

THE EMERGENCE OF INDIA AND CHINA

In the early twenty-first century, China and India are modernizing, rapidly growing economies undergoing fundamental change. Although very different in many ways, in broad terms at least they have key features in common. Both have their roots in ancient civilizations with their own rich culture and tradition of learning. Both have known great wealth but by the 1960s and 1970s had, for different reasons, become a byword for overpopulation, poverty, famine and stagnation. Since then, their transformation, although far from complete, has been remarkable.

Key to their success has been a rejection of inward-looking policies intended to generate self-reliance and self-sufficiency in favour of liberalizing domestic markets and opening up trade and investment to the rest of the world. The outcome has been growth of around 10 per cent per annum for nearly three decades in the case of China. In India, growth has been less consistent but average growth levels have risen in recent years (see Figure 6.2). As a result of reform, these growth levels have been achieved with the assistance of foreign capital and expertise, especially in the case of China, a development that would have been unthinkable in the pre-reform era. Both countries have benefited from large diasporas: the early phases of inward FDI into China, for example, were bolstered considerably by capital inflows originating from the millions of individuals of Chinese origin located outside China in particular, but not only in Hong Kong and Taiwan.

Rapid growth has contributed to mass urbanization and led to social and environmental pressure, and placed unprecedented demands on infrastructure which China has been able to respond to more fully than India. Both countries have also experienced widening income disparities and the exacerbation of differences in regional development.

Although reform has been motivated by similar objectives and has created similar problems, the emergence of China and India as important players in world markets has taken place within very specific historical, political, economic and social contexts which have helped shape the progress of reform and its outcomes. China is traditionally a large, stable, centrally run state and, for the most part, has not experienced foreign rule. India has had the opposite experience: it has only been a nation since the mid-nineteenth century; large parts, albeit not all, were under foreign control until independence in 1947 and its diversity has resulted in a federal system, albeit with a relatively strong centre.

The immediate post-Second World War era brought crucial changes to both states: in China, the Communist Party came to power, where it remains, and began the systemic transformation of Chinese life, and India gained its independence. In both cases there was a strong incentive to demonstrate that both countries could succeed independently and on their own terms. Both countries, for a period at last, were inspired by the perceived achievements of planning in the USSR and saw the state as the primary, if not the sole, driver of growth, rejected foreign capital and sought self-sufficiency. Their initial instinct was to pursue industrialization as their prime development objective, notably to focus on heavy industry such as steel and machinery and neglected consumer and light industrial sectors. China used its political monopoly to develop a central control and planning system which relied heavily on bringing industries under state ownership in the form of state-owned enterprises (SOEs). India had a lively democracy but its first Prime Minister, Jawarhal Nehru, also operated a socialist economic planning system.

Neither approach brought long-term success. For ten years from 1966, after the failure of the Great Leap Forward which was intended to modernize and revitalize the Chinese economy, Mao's China underwent the Cultural Revolution which managed to paralyse Chinese society and the economy. India did not undergo such self-induced trauma but its approach to development was far from successful, leading to low growth, increasing poverty and, in some cases, starvation. In the late 1970s, after the death of Chairman Mao in 1976, Deng Xiao Peng gradually asserted greater control over the reins of power and began the reform in China which continues today. India did not have a Deng Xiao Peng but it instituted desultory reform attempts in the 1980s before reform began in earnest in 1991.

The beginning of reform in China and India was motivated by the failure of the post-war approach. The speed, consistency and extent of the reforms varied between the two, but in both cases they have moved away from almost total reliance on the state, which retains an important but different role, and towards integrating into the world economy and markets rather than resisting them. To date, Chinese living standards have risen more quickly than those in India but this should not undermine India's achievements in this respect.

China

Following the Cultural Revolution (1966–1976), which was about ideological purification and the playing out of a power struggle in the upper echelons of the Communist Party, and the death of Mao in 1976, Deng Xiaoping became party leader. He recognized that existing economic policy was condemning China to economic backwardness and from 1978 introduced a series of wide-ranging reforms to modernize China and to transform it into a powerful, modern socialist economy. Initially, the reforms were stop-go but by the end of the 1980s they became more consistent as Deng consolidated his hold on power.

Deng's reforms were guided by the general principles of increasing the role of the market mechanism and of reducing the direct control of the economy by the government and centralized planning. The reforms were phased in gradually and were driven by pragmatism rather than by ideology as in previous years. Nevertheless, they all pointed in the same direction of liberalization of the domestic economy and greater integration with the economy of the rest of the world.

The key reforms in the late 1970s and 1980s were as follows:

■ Introduction of the household responsibility system in agriculture: farmers were allowed to sell surplus crops on the open market. This gave them a strong incentive to reduce costs and increase productivity. As a result food production increased rapidly and the people's communes soon became obsolete. By 1984, approximately 98 per cent of all farm households were on the responsibility system. This new system was important not only for the positive impact it had on farm production but because it clearly demonstrated the potential power of market incentives.

■ The beginning of trade and investment reform: China began to promote inward FDI as a means of acquiring technology and foreign exchange and, as such, joint ventures were particularly encouraged by the government. Trade was also made easier. In pre-reform days when self-sufficiency was one of the abiding principles of economic management, the combined value of imports and exports rarely exceeded 10 per cent of GDP. As early as 1986, trade reached 35 per cent of GDP. The process of trade and investment liberalization continues. China's 2001 entry into the WTO represents a major consolidation of trade reform and a commitment to further liberalization.

■ The creation in 1979 of four coastal special economic zones where foreign investors received special treatment and, in 1984, the creation of economic development zones in 14 of the largest coastal cities, including Dalian, Tianjin, Shanghai and Gunagzhou. These latter zones were intended to create strong links between foreign firms with advanced technology and domestic producers. These initiatives represent an important reversal of decades of deliberate economic isolation from the rest of the world and a recognition that China could benefit from greater contact with the outside world.

- ■ The reduction of the role of government in most sectors: managers were given greater decision-making powers and autonomy, and less emphasis was placed on planned quotas. Enterprises were encouraged to produce outside the plan for profit and sale on the open market, rather similar to the household responsibility system in agriculture.
- ■ Efforts were made to correct the imbalance between light and heavy industry, resulting in the rapid growth of consumer and service sectors.

By the late 1980s, reform was well underway but the state remained dominant, retaining control over the financial system and attempting to redistribute wealth and organizing grain rationing. Private ownership was in its infancy: agricultural land was farmed under lease, for example, but was formally owned by villages, towns and townships, the collective units that replaced the communes. During the next period of reform in the early 1990s, the emphasis was on enhancing the price mechanism, creating market institutions and reducing the role of the state in the allocation of resources. Accordingly, private entrepreneurship and free market activities were legalized and encouraged. A market-based system requires a robust banking system and capital markets to support it. It was during the 1990s that work on banking system reform began in earnest – work that continues in the 2000s.

The move to the market mechanism exposed the deficiencies of the SOEs. Under the pre-reform system, SOEs were faced with fixed input and output prices with the difference being used to fund social services. The introduction of the market mechanism and market prices meant that many SOEs were producing goods that no one wanted and chalking up impressive losses. By the late 1990s and early 2000s, many SOEs were restructured or closed and an independent social security system was set up. By 2005, 70 per cent of China's GDP was in the private sector. The remaining SOEs are located in industries that are regarded as strategically important such as energy, utilities and heavy industry.

At the end of the first decade of the twenty-first century, China is an intriguing mix of old and new. The emergence of the private sector and the role played by foreign investors is attributable to the removal of barriers in many areas. Nevertheless, despite the decline of the state's direct control in the economy, the state retains an important role in terms of the regulation and control of the private sector via the state bureaucracy. As such, the Chinese economy is composed of a mixture of foreign-owned companies, private Chinese companies including former SOEs, foreign–Chinese joint ventures and current state enterprises. The unique Chinese formula of a free market operating within the framework of a totalitarian state has led to questions about the long-term sustainability of the Chinese system (Hutton, 2007). Free market activity and the autonomy and personal choice and freedom it confers upon economic operators, so the argument goes, is inconsistent with continuing control of the Chinese Communist Party and lack of political choice. It is also argued that, while the economy and living standards continue to flourish, any challenges to the political control of the Communist Party will be muted.

India

India's current development push began later than China's. There was some limited reform in the 1980s following the abandonment by Prime Minister Indira Gandhi of the ideology of self-sufficiency.

During this period, India began to borrow from abroad, initially from the IMF, but Indian economic policy remained largely dirigiste and India remained essentially a closed economy with high tariffs on imports and rigid controls on foreign investment. Indian businesses were subject to the 'licence raj' – that is, a regime that required a business to obtain a licence or permit before it could embark upon any type of activity. This highly bureaucratic system was time-consuming, and was susceptible to bribery and corruption.

This situation persisted until 1991 when a financial and balance of payments crisis made wholesale reform inevitable. The architect of the reforms was Manmohan Singh, who became Indian Prime Minister in 2004. The immediate response to the crisis was to take out a $1.8 billion loan from the IMF and to introduce macroeconomic stabilization measures to reduce the budget deficit and to devalue the rupee. It was apparent however that short-term measures were insufficient and that the Indian economy needed root-and-branch reform which would enable it to integrate with and ultimately to compete with the rest of the world. The process has moved slowly and in a stop-go manner owing to the need to build up coalitions and consensus in favour of reforms which have been the subject of much political bargaining. The reversal of policies of regulation and government intervention continues and much remains to be done, but growth has become more sustained and stronger, and Indian business has undergone major restructuring to help it reduce costs, improve quality and meet foreign competition. Key reforms undertaken or in progress in India include the following.

- *Trade reforms*: before 1991, Indian import tariffs were high and other trade barriers were commonplace. Imports of consumer goods were banned and imports of raw materials, intermediate goods and capital goods for which domestic substitutes were available were only possible following a complex licensing procedure. After 1991, India stepped up its commitment to free trade, even before its WTO entry in 1995. Tariffs were slashed on goods; trade in services and technology was liberalized and import licences were eliminated. Scope exists for further reduction in import duties and in costly import and export procedures.
- *Investment reforms*: prior to 1991, foreign ownership and investment was only permitted in some sectors but even then it was subject to many restrictions, including caps on investment. Many of these restrictions have subsequently been lifted and 100 per cent foreign ownership is currently allowed in a majority of industries, excluding banks, insurance, telecommunications, airlines and retail. The fear that inward investment will undermine domestic businesses means that some restrictions remain. The prime example is the retail sector which is dominated by small family businesses known as 'mom-and-pop' shops and which is closed to foreign retailers. There is a potential role for the latter however in distribution and wholesale and the mom-and-pop shops are beginning to feel pressure from Indian-owned retailers such as those set up by Reliance.
- *Fiscal reform*: individual and corporate taxes, excise and custom duties have been lowered; the tax base has been broadened; and the system has been simplified to close loopholes and increase compliance. However, tax revenues are falling as a share of GDP and the budget deficit and public debt remain high, and spending cuts remain politically difficult. Tax evasion remains a problem and greater coordination is needed among different levels of government.
- *Financial sector reforms*: before 1991, lending was restricted to specific sectors and all the funding activities of large manufacturers were controlled by the Controller of Capital Issues, a post which

has since been abolished. Banks were state-owned and subject to political forces. Subsequently, cautious efforts have been made to privatize and introduce competition among banks, but more could be done, especially in terms of access for foreign banks. The functioning of capital markets has been improved by the liberalization of interest rates and the abolition of the complex approval system for financial transactions. Increases in the amounts of venture capital and improvements and deepening of debt markets are still needed.

■ *Privatization and industrial reform*: many government enterprises have been privatized and subject to competition but many small-scale industries remain protected. For over a century, a handful of families dominated the large-scale industrial sector in India. This changed after 1947 when the government increased its role. However, following the retreat of the state, family conglomerates such as the Tata, Birla, Ambani and Moda families (see Case Study 6.1) once more dominate Indian business and wield enormous commercial power. India's success in the knowledge sector has been made possible by government policy and by the work of visionary entrepreneurial leaders such as Narayana Murthy of Infosys and Azim Premji of Wipro. Nevertheless, government-owned and controlled corporations are very significant in the airlines, shipping, railway, post, steel, machine tools, mineral exploration, power, oil and gas sectors.

■ *Dismantling of the licence raj*: although bureaucracy and red tape remains a problem for domestic and foreign firms in India and is high by the standards of many other countries, the worst excesses of the licence raj have been abolished.

CASE STUDY 6.1

The Emergence of an Indian Multinational – The Case of TATA

From the mid-2000s, Indian-owned and controlled businesses became increasingly visible outside India. The extent of internationalization of Indian business remains modest by the standards of companies from triad countries but the rapidity with which Indian businesses have become outward looking is significant and continuing. One measure of this new trend is the involvement of Indian companies in outward cross-border mergers and acquisitions. In 2005, Indian companies made 103 cross-border acquisitions, totalling $2.9 billion and averaging $28 mn. Although small compared to other cross-border deals, the number of deals involving Indian companies had tripled in the three years up to 2005. In 2007, the value of such deals had risen to $32 billion with 90 per cent of the deals by value concentrated in North America (38 per cent) and Europe (52 per cent).

The first forays of Indian companies into the international arena were in the IT, automotive, pharmaceutical and banking sectors but latterly they have also become active in commodities, telecommunications, energy and steel. Their involvement extends beyond mergers and acquisitions with exports and greenfield investments also playing a key role in the internationalization story. Indian companies rapidly gaining a name for themselves as vibrant multinationals include software companies Wipro, Infosys and TCS (Tata Consultancy Services); pharmaceutical giant, Ranbaxy; Reliance Industries and other members of the Tata Group, Tata Motors and Tata Steel.

The Tata Group provides an insight into the internationalization process that is underway in India. The group is one of India's largest business conglomerates: in 2007 to 2008, its revenues, excluding those of its recent acquisition Corus, totalled $55 billion and it had a market capitalization in May 2008 of $65.2 billion. Altogether, the group has operations in 80 countries, exports goods and services to 85 countries and has 350,000 employees. There are 98 operating companies within the Tata Group, each of which is active in one of seven business sectors. These are information systems and communications; engineering; materials; services; energy; consumer products and chemicals (see Figure 6.3).

The Tata Group was founded in 1868 by Jamsetji Tata. One hundred and forty years later, the Chairman of the Group, Ratan Tata, is a descendant of the founder. The Group has always been a broadly based business and in its first 100 years became active in sectors which remain important today. In 1902, the Group began its hotel business; in 1910, the Group entered the electricity market and in 1912,

production began at India's first steel plant, Tata-owned of course. Tata began making consumer products in 1917 and Tata Chemicals followed in 1939. The forerunner of Tata Motors was established in 1945 and what later became Tata Tea was founded in 1962. In 1968, India's first software services company, Tata Consultancy Services (TCS) began operating.

The Tata Group has always exported and been involved in international markets but the extent of its internationalization has intensified since 2000. The landmark action in this process was its 100 per cent acquisition of the UK's Tetley Group for £271 million in 2000. Not only was this Tata's first major acquisition of a well-known international brand but it was also the first such acquisition by an Indian group. Since then, Tata has intensified its acquisitions of well-known international companies and brands, including:

* the purchase by Tata Motors of the heavy vehicles unit of South Korea's Daewoo in 2004;

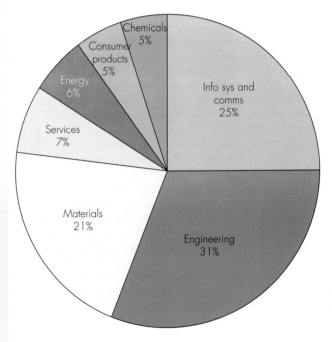

FIGURE 6.3 Tata's Revenues by Business Sector, 2006–2007

* 100 per cent control of the UK's Brunner Mond Group by Tata Chemicals in 2006;
* the acquisition of Corus in 2007 by Tata Steel which became the world's sixth largest steel producer;
* the purchase by Tata Motors of Jaguar and Land Rover from the Ford Motor Company in 2008;
* the acquisition of the US company General Chemical Products Inc in 2008.

As a result, Tata Steel, Tata Consultancy Services (TCS), Tata Motors and Tata Tea have become key players in the Tata empire but the above represent only the headline Tata activities. Members of the Group have made acquisitions and/or acquired stakes in businesses throughout the world, have embarked on greenfield investments overseas and have set up joint ventures with foreign partners, both in developed and developing countries. In the case of the latter, Tata has been active in South Africa and is looking for further involvement in developing Asia, identifying Bangladesh and Vietnam as possible targets.

Tata is also anxious to expand in China where its activities are relatively limited, registering sales of only $300 millionn in 2006 to 2007. It acknowledges the complexity of the Chinese business environment and culture, and its activities there tend to take the form of start-ups and joint ventures owing to corporate governance and regulatory issues. In 2007, for example, TCS began TCS China in collaboration with the Chinese government and Microsoft to develop software and Tata Refractories set up a greenfield plant in China. Tata Steel, however, has gone down the acquisition route with the purchase of two rolling mills in China. Other Tata companies, including Tata Hotels, Tata Tea and Tata Chemicals, are forging their own plans for development in China. In general, the Tata Group sees great potential for China to act as a procurement hub for its myriad businesses across the world.

In 2005, Chairman Ratan Tata set out his vision for the internationalization of the Tata Group. In a short period, some of his expectations have been overtaken by events. First, Tata's internationalization has proceeded more quickly than envisaged. In

the financial year 2003 to 2004, just over 20 per cent of Tata's revenue was generated internationally with Chairman Tata stating: 'Over the next few years, I would like to see more than 30 to 35 per cent of our turnover coming from our overseas operations.' In reality, 65 per cent of Tata's revenues came from international sources in fiscal year 2007 to 2008.

Second, Chairman Tata also stated: 'We believe our presence will be much more substantial in developing countries in Asia, Africa and parts of Eastern Europe. Investments may be more of an exception in the developed countries, except in areas like IT services.' In practice, the Tata Group, as a result of the above major acquisitions, has forged a bigger role in the developed world than this statement suggests. The integration of Corus Steel, Jaguar and Land Rover, Brunner Mond and General Chemicals has increased the weight of Tata's overseas involvement in the developed world and will ultimately make Tata's overseas earnings less reliant on the communications and information sector, which in fiscal year 2006 to 2007 accounted for two-thirds of Tata's overseas earnings (see Figure 6.4).

Tata's increasing internationalization has been based, according to its Chairman, on 'select geographies' – not on trying to establish itself throughout the globe. According to Ratan Tata, 'One of the major drivers of going international is to reduce our vulnerability to a single economy. A broader base in multiple geographies equips us better against a downturn.' He identifies the fact that the current round of internationalization differs from past efforts because 'it goes beyond exports'. The first initiatives in the current internationalization process came from the corporate centre, that is, from the Group level, but as the process and experience develops, the expectation is that internationalization initiatives will increasingly come from the individual companies within the Group. Notably, when making acquisitions, the Tata Group has tended to retain the services of the senior management of the acquired group. This has been the case with Daewoo's commercial vehicle business, with Tetley and with Corus Steel. This helps integration of the companies and enables Tata to maximize the benefits from an acquisition.

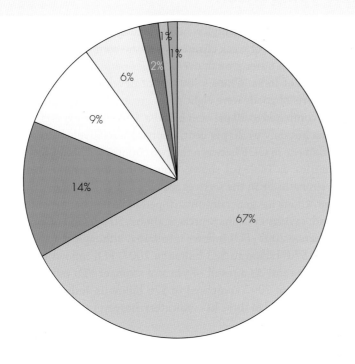

FIGURE 6.4
Tata's International Revenues by Business Sector, 2006–2007

- ☐ Info sys and comms
- ☐ Engineering
- ☐ Materials
- ☐ Services
- ☐ Energy
- ☐ Consumer products
- ☐ Chemicals

CASE STUDY QUESTIONS

1. One of the drivers behind Tata's increasing internationalization is to reduce the vulnerability from over-reliance on one market. To what extent is this a realistic aspiration in an increasingly interdependent world?

2. Tata is a diverse conglomerate with interests in services, heavy industry and consumer products and in many countries. Consider whether such diversity is a strength or a weakness in the contemporary international business environment.

3. Compare and contrast Tata Group's internationalization strategy with that of another emerging Indian multinational such as Reliance Industries, Ranbaxy, Infosys or Wipro.

4. In 2008, Tata Motors has acquired Jaguar and Land Rover and announced the launch of its new, low-cost small car – the Tata Nano. What do these developments tell us about the future direction of Tata Motors and how will they affect the company's position in the Tata Group as a whole?

5. To what extent has the TATA Group invested in products and companies that have been adversely affected by the 2008 to 2009 economic crisis?

China and India: A Comparison

China's reform began much earlier than India's and has been pursued consistently, whereas India's reform has been more stop-start as a result of weak coalitions and the complexity of India's politics. China's political stability has resulted in faster growth over a longer period. China's GDP and GDP per capita are both over twice that of India. China's strategy of developing through exporting is illustrated by the fact that its exports of goods were eight times greater than those of India in 2007, representing 36 per cent of GDP compared to 20 per cent in India. China also exports a greater value of commercial services than India but only by 20 per cent, implying a relatively better performance for services in India given the difference in GDP between the two countries. This reflects the differing structure between the two countries: as Table 6.1 shows, China's development has been driven by manufacturing whereas India's strengths lie in the services sector.

In terms of overall investment, China has generally outstripped India and has benefited from high levels of domestic savings. Indeed, savings in China represent almost 50 per cent of income. Similar trends have existed in FDI but, since 2005, FDI inflows into India, although remaining far below Chinese levels, have tripled from $7.6 billion to $23 billion in 2007. FDI inflows into China over the same period have grown 15 per cent. As a result of years of stronger FDI inflows, inward FDI stocks in China stood at $327 billion in 2007 compared to $76 billion in India (less than China's FDI inflows in the same year). China's lead in these key indicators, however, should not mask India's progress.

The large Chinese and Indian diasporas have both been instrumental in boosting the economies of their countries of origin. The Chinese diaspora made a significant contribution to China's FDI in the 1980s and 1990s when funds from Hong Kong, Singapore and Taiwan, in particular, were directed to small-scale, manufacturing investment and, according to some estimates, accounted for almost 60 per cent of Chinese FDI. Diaspora investment made use of the strong relationships and inter-connected networks that are so central to the concept of guanxi (see Case Study 13.1), the powerful and complex cultural dynamic that operates at the core of China's business environment. The Indian diaspora has played an important but more modest role in India's development: the size of India's diaspora is much smaller than that of China and its influence has been mostly felt in facilitating the emergence of entrepreneurial activity in the IT and IT-enabled services sectors.

BUSINESS AND EMERGING ECONOMIES

The dynamism of emerging economies creates a multitude of opportunities, both for foreign and domestic businesses and also carries certain risks. As discussed in Chapter 9, MNEs have several motivations for embarking upon FDI. One key reason, and one that is highly relevant for emerging markets, is market-seeking investment. The markets of the BRIC economies, in particular, are large and growing rapidly. Ownership of consumer goods that have reached near saturation point in developed markets is low in emerging economies but growing prosperity there means the demand for white goods, mobile phones, cars and so on is extremely attractive for inward investors. Case Study 6.2, for example, shows how foreign auto manufacturers have flocked to China to make cars to sell to the Chinese market.

TABLE 6.2 Comparison of China and India

	India	China
Political system	Democratic, weak coalitions	Authoritarian, one-party rule. Long-term tension between market and state system
Rule of law	'Licence raj' toned down but still overly bureaucratic	Many laws in place but weak and inconsistent enforcement of regulations and contracts
Corruption	Widespread corruption in politics and business.; ranked 85 on Transparency International's Corruption Perception Index	'Red envelope' culture – corruption and bribery in public life – is rife; ranked 72 on Transparency International's Corruption Perception Index
Economic structure	Excellence in services – IT consulting, software, call centres; growing strength in financial analysis, industrial engineering and drug research	Manufacturing workshop of the world – increasingly sophisticated products
Infrastructure	Poor – an obstacle to development: black-outs; much electricity obtained illegally; inadequate transport	Much investment made (more to be done): 10 times more paved roads than India; power costs 10 times lower; phone penetration rates six times higher
External trade	Some trade liberalization but scope for more; FDI opened more recently but caps remain	Well integrated into global economy – dependent on foreign firms (half exports by MNEs); heavy use of FDI
Public sector	Large and loss making – smaller in India	Large and loss making
Banking sector	Weak, underdeveloped	Weak, underdeveloped
Income distribution	Some poverty reduction – but also potentially destabilizing increases in inequality	Many out of poverty – but impact of economic crisis unknown – potentially destabilizing increases in inequality; increasing inequality: rural vs. urban; coastal vs. western provinces
Environment	Deteriorating – could hinder growth	Deteriorating – could hinder growth
Education	Heavy investment in higher education – basic later.	Heavy investment in basic education – higher later
R&D	Majority in public sector	Majority in productive sector

China's Automotive Industry Shows a Good Turn of Speed

The attraction of China's car market for foreign manufacturers is not difficult to understand. The size of the population, low levels of car ownership compared to developed markets and the growing prosperity of the middle classes have made China an attractive option for foreign investors. In 2007, China was the world's third largest producer of cars and the second largest market. By 2009, China had become the world's biggest producer of and market for cars with output and sales exceeding 10 million.

Foreign investors have poured into the Chinese market, especially since China's 2001 entry into the WTO, but they face serious competition among themselves and from domestic producers. The latter fall into two categories:

1. the traditional state-owned controlled producers. Many of the traditional producers are small and play an important regional economic role. However, the majority are too small to compete successfully against bigger domestic and foreign competitors (only a minority have the capacity to produce 50,000 vehicles a year). There are approximately 120 registered auto makers in China and the government has sought consolidation within the domestic industry, encouraging the big three domestic producers – Shanghai Automotive Industries Corporation (SAIC), First Automobile Works (FAW) and Dongfeng Motor – plus other established OEMS such as Guangzhou Automobile to buy smaller manufacturers. So far, some consolidation has taken place but it has been limited.
2. New independent producers that have diversified into car production from other sectors and which have seen the biggest growth in domestic production. The largest Chinese independent is Chery, established as recently as 1997 and which

sold 381,000 vehicles in 2007. Other noteworthy independents include Geely, founded in 1986 as a manufacturer of refrigerators and which shortly afterwards diversified into advanced decorative materials and then motorcycles before producing its first car in 1998; Hafei Motors, a subsidiary of an aircraft manufacturer; and Changfeng, which was initially associated with the People's Liberation Army in the production of military trucks but in 2007 produced 200,000 passenger cars.

Domestic producers face several problems in their domestic market where foreign producers are, on the whole, well established. Consumers are status conscious, making it difficult for domestic producers to compete in the higher value-added end of the market which is dominated by foreign producers. This trend has intensified as institutional buyers (that is, government bodies and other official organizations) have been steadily replaced by private buyers. There are also many local firms, only a few of which are of a sufficient size to compete on a national basis with the major automotive multinationals. Moreover, despite the size of the Chinese market and its rapid growth, competition is intense and, as a consequence of fierce discounting, average car prices fell 5.7 per cent in 2007.

Two characteristics differentiate the independents from other domestic producers in China. First, their market share has grown significantly as a result of their concentration on the lower price end of the market. In 2007, Chinese brand vehicles had an estimated market share of around 40 per cent.

Second, unlike the Big Three and foreign producers in China, the independents see exports as a key part of their strategy. In 2007, for example, Chery sold 120,000 vehicles abroad (that is, 20 per cent of all car exports from China) out of a production of 489,000 vehicles and was China's biggest auto exporter. Chery has increased its production capacity and is striving to meet standards that will enable it to export to Europe and the US. Only SAIC of the Big Three has a serious export strategy which it is developing via its Korean Sangyong brand and its ownership of MG Rover intellectual property. FAW and Dongfeng both export but so far only in marginal quantities. Foreign manufacturers see production in China as primarily giving them access to the large domestic market. For the most part, they do not regard their investments in China as an opportunity to utilize lower costs and to develop China as an export platform to the rest of the world. In 2008, Honda was the only foreign-owned auto maker to have opened an export-only plant in China (see below).This, of course, may change.

The majority of exports are being shipped by Chinese producers to emerging markets in the Middle East, Asia, South America and Africa. Very few Chinese-brand cars have so far been exported to the developed markets of Western Europe and the US where entry is difficult for Chinese producers who still have some way to go before they can meet tough safety and environmental standards there. Indeed, by 2008, only the following Chinese brands had been launched in Western Europe – Landwind, Great Wall's Hover SUV and Wingle pick-up and Brilliance Jinbei. All used independent European distributors for their launch rather than setting up their own infrastructure and offered lower price vehicles in the large sedan and SUV market.

Chinese producers are also developing manufacturing bases in emerging markets. Brilliance, for example, has three overseas manufacturing bases in Egypt, North Korea and Vietnam, and is developing a fourth in Russia. Russia is the biggest overseas market for Chinese cars in terms of exports and overseas manufacturing. Russia is attractive to Chinese auto companies because it is a rapidly growing market, is a potential bridge to markets in Eastern Europe and Central Asia and gives them experience of operating overseas. Chinese cars are also regarded as more reliable than Russian-made cars by Russian consumers and are cheaper than other imports. Chinese auto companies moving into Russia as manufacturers, which must be done via joint venture assembly plants or via a licensing arrangement, include Chery, which has a number of assembly deals in Russia, and Nanjing Automobiles, for which Avtotor assembles light trucks. In 2007, Great Wall announced plans for a factory with a capacity to produce 50,000 cars and SUVs a year in Yelabuga in the Russian republic of Tatarstan. If it gets the go-ahead, this would be Great Wall's sixth overseas manufacturing plant. Geely and BYD Auto also produce in Russia.

Foreign JVs

Most of the world's largest auto manufacturers have targeted China as a potentially lucrative market and have set up one or more joint venture operations there. Growth in their production and sales in China has been phenomenal in the 2000s. By 2008, business had become more difficult in their traditional markets of the US, Western Europe and Japan, and their activities in China helped counteract this downturn to some degree. By 2009, the car industry in the developed world was in the midst of its biggest-ever crisis. Although the opportunities in China are undeniable, foreign investors still have to face significant challenges, including:

* the uncertainties and risks facing all investors in China, not only those in the automotive sector;
* the intense competition in China's automotive market from domestic producers and fellow foreign investors;
* relationships with joint venture partners: joint ventures enhance a foreign investor's understanding of the domestic market but can also result in the usual joint venture problems arising from the clashing of different objectives or level of commitment to the joint venture.

A particular problem encountered by foreign investors in China's auto industry has been that of alleged violation of intellectual property rights. Foreign joint ventures tend to concentrate on medium- to high-end products, with domestic producers meeting the demand for lower priced smaller cars. Increasingly, domestic producers are trying to move up the value-added ladder by producing stylish products without the price premium attached to foreign brands. In several cases, this has resulted in 'look-alike models' which appear similar to foreign marques but lack their quality. A number of foreign manufacturers have taken exception to this and have embarked on litigation. Daimler has taken action against Shuanghuan, claiming that Shuanghuan's Noble is effectively a copy of Daimler's Smart Fortwo. Fiat has lodged complaints in Italy and China to prevent the sale of the Great Wall Peri which resembles the Fiat Panda. BMW has successfully instigated proceedings against the European importer of Shuanghuan Auto's Sceo, which BMW claims is a copy of the BMW X5.

The experiences and strategies of foreign investors in China are varied, and some of them are discussed below.

VW

Volkswagen is involved in two production joint ventures in China – Shanghai VW Auto with SAIC founded in 1985 and FAW-VW established in 1985. As one of the early foreign entrants into China, VW has become the biggest supplier of passenger cars in China. In 2007, VW China sold 910,491 vehicles in mainland China and Hong Kong – a 28 per cent increase on 2007 and a figure which represents almost 15 per cent of VW's total car sales. In the first half of 2008, VW sold 531,612 units, putting it on course to break the one million barrier for the year.

VW's figures include those of Audi and Skoda which introduced the Skoda to the Chinese market in 2007. In an attempt to capture a share of the volume end of the market, the Lavida, the first model completely designed and produced by VW Shanghai, was introduced in 2008. VW investment continues into China: in 2008 work began on the construction of a transmission facility in Dalian and plans are underway to develop further R&D capacity at its Chinese joint ventures.

General Motors (GM)

GM operates seven joint ventures and two wholly owned foreign enterprises and employs over 20,000 people in China where it produces and sells the Buick, Cadillac, Chevrolet, Opel, Saab and Wuling brands. In the mid-2000s, GM has invested $1 billion per annum in China. In total General Motors and its joint ventures sold 1,031,974 vehicles in China in 2007 – more than VW which, however, remains the single biggest supplier of passenger cars to China once GM's mini-vans and mini-trucks are taken out of the statistics.

GM's major interest in China is Shanghai General Motors Co Ltd (Shanghai GM) – a 50–50 joint venture with SAIC. This joint venture was established in 1997 and has an annual production capacity of 480,000 vehicles. Also of note is the SAIC-GM-Wuling Automobile Co.Ltd, a joint venture launched in 2002 involving a 50.1 per cent SAIC stake, a 34 per cent GM stake and a holding of 15.9 per cent for Wuling Automotive. This joint venture manufactures mini-trucks, mini-vans and the Chevrolet Spark mini-car, resulting in total vehicle sales of 548,945 units in 2007. GM has also invested in an engine plant, R&D, and the provision of engineering services including the design, development, testing and validation of components and vehicles.

PSA Peugeot Citroen

PSA Peugeot Citroen is involved in a joint venture with Dongfeng Motors in Wuhan and hopes to open another plant with its partner in 2010 as part of its strategy to achieve sales of one million vehicles in the Chinese market by 2015. In 2007, the group sold 209,000 vehicles, representing a market share of 4 per cent. The company has also embarked upon a feasibility study regarding the formation of a second joint venture with Hafei Automobile Company, the subject of takeover interest by Dongfeng.

Ford

Ford is a relatively late entry to the Chinese market. The first Chinese-built Ford passenger car, the Ford Fiesta, was produced in 2003. Ford and its joint venture partners operate three assembly plants and one engine factory in China. Ford's interests in China also include an automotive finance company, a sourcing and R&D centre, and sales and services operations.

In 2007, Ford Motor China sold 216,324 units in China, representing a 30 per cent increase over 2006. Strong growth continued into 2008 with sales of 172,411 units for the first half of the year. Such a performance helped offset Ford's poor performance in its home US market. Ford's joint venture with ChangAn Automobile Group (ChangAn Ford Mazda Automobile – CFMA), which produces Volvos and Mazdas, saw its wholesale deliveries rise 60 per cent to 217,100 vehicles in 2007. In the first half of 2008, CFMA sold 118,903 vehicles – a 25 per cent increase on the same period of 2007. A key element in Ford's recent success in China has been the Ford Focus, the fast-growing medium-sized car in China as a result of a strategy of aggressive and discounted pricing.

Toyota

Another late entrant to the Chinese market, Toyota is rapidly building its production presence there. In 2007, Toyota sold 499,000 vehicles in China, 62 per cent more than in 2006 with sales of the Camry Sedan proving particularly brisk. Sales for the first half of 2008 reached 285,000 vehicles. Plans are underway to boost production capacity to 830,000 units by 2010 and the company aims to sell one million cars per annum in China early in the second decade of the century. In 2007, an interesting development took place when Toyota set up a three-way logistics joint venture – Tong Fang Global Logistics – involving itself, Guangzhou Toyota and FAW Toyota to increase efficiency and lower costs by consolidating the logistics elements of its joint venture activities.

Honda

In 2007, Honda and its joint venture partners produced 463,998 vehicles, a 32 per cent increase on 2006. Its two partners are Guangzhou Automobile and, since 2004, Dongfeng Motors. Two factors differentiate Honda from other foreign investors in the Chinese automotive market. First, Honda

Automobile (China) Company, is the only foreign-owned company to operate a production plant dedicated exclusively to exports. Since 2005, it has taken advantage of China's lower cost base and exported the Honda Jazz to Europe. Second, a new R&D centre will design and develop a car specifically for the Chinese market which will be differentiated from the Honda brand and sold under the Guangzhou Honda brand. According to Honda's president, 'it will be a low-priced car unlike anything Honda would sell on its own'.

Nissan

In 2003, Nissan embarked upon a 50–50 joint venture with Dongfeng Motors, a company which is also involved in joint ventures with PSA Peugeot Citroen. By 2007, the joint venture had sold 610,000 vehicles in China. Further investment and the introduction of new models are key parts of the strategy to expand sales to one million by 2012. The joint venture also plans to export about 10 per cent of its output to emerging markets in the Middle East and Southeast Asia.

Renault

Renault is unique among the biggest auto multi-nationals in not maintaining a production presence in China. An earlier initiative to set up a joint venture with Dongfeng Motors was abandoned and, although establishing a manufacturing presence in China remains under consideration, for the time being Renault's presence in China comes from imports.

CASE STUDY QUESTIONS

1. To date, foreign investors in China have focused on market-seeking investment and have chosen not to use China as an export base. Why might this be the case? What factors might cause this to change?

2. What risks and challenges do foreign investors experience in China?

3. What difficulties do Chinese producers face in entering the markets of (a) emerging markets and (b) developed economies?

4. Research one of the foreign auto manufacturers active in China and present an analysis of their Chinese strategy.

5. Research either SAIC or Chery and present an analysis of their domestic and overseas strategy.

6. The year 2009 saw the the biggest-ever crisis in the world's car industry. What are the implications for the industry in China?

Although the large emerging economies and their domestic markets are developing rapidly, it is essential to recognize the diverse levels of development existing in the same economy. In China, the greatest levels of wealth are concentrated in the coastal regions where there is well-developed infrastructure, a plentiful labour supply and a good technological base. In the central and western parts of China, the country is less developed, more remote and poorer with a much bigger proportion of the population living in rural areas. India's development is also concentrated, with software and business-processing firms focused on cities like Bangalore and Pune. In both countries, the provinces and states have played an important role in development with the more successful demonstrating a distinct entrepreneurial bent.

Moreover, although there is a growing, increasingly prosperous middle class in both countries, the general level of income is much lower than in developed countries and mass marketing needs to recognize this. New entrants to emerging markets also need to take time to understand how consumer behaviour differs from that in known developed markets. Brand loyalty, for example, is unlikely to be as entrenched as in developed countries and, for many products, given the still relatively low living standards, the focus will be on value for money. However, for some market segments, there will be a demand for luxury items and foreign brands may be prized over domestic brands. In Case Study 6.2, for example, foreign branded cars are dominant at the higher end of the market, whereas domestic producers are stronger in the lower cost end of the markets.

The impact of emerging economies on markets is also felt in other ways. The development process, as well as increasing consumer demand through rising prosperity, also increases demand for capital goods, plant and equipment and raw materials associated with the creation and improvement of infrastructure and construction generally. Development also necessitates the need for deep and efficient capital markets. Accordingly, emerging markets are becoming increasingly open to foreign banks and other financial institutions.

A major attraction of China and India for foreign investors has been the low cost of production, particularly lower labour costs. Labour costs in Germany, for example, have been up to 40 or even 50 times higher then in China, depending on the sector. Manufacturing labour costs in India are even lower than those in China. In software and business-processing operations, Indian costs remain considerably cheaper than in developed countries but the gap has been narrowing. However, China's labour cost advantage, although substantial, is declining. In part, this is an inevitable response to development. It is also the result of labour supply problems: from late 2004, reports emerged in China of labour shortages in some sectors with businesses facing the challenge of finding and retaining good workers. The resulting surge in labour turnover and wages has a number of potential effects. First, if wage cost increases are reflected by productivity increases, any potential impact on investment can be contained. Second, higher wage costs can be absorbed if production of higher value-added goods can be increased. Significantly, China has gradually increased the technology content of its manufactures. Third, higher real wages in China create a larger consumer class and bigger markets for domestic and foreign investors. Fourth, in sectors where, despite the above, China has lost its competitive advantage, production can be outsourced to cheaper locations. These could be in the interior of China, elsewhere in Asia such as Vietnam, or even to Africa.

The potential rewards of doing business in emerging markets are high and the opportunities for investment and trade in these markets are many, but this potential and these opportunities are also accompanied by a level of risk which is greater than in developed markets. This risk comes from many sources, including the rapid rate of transformation and growth. Emerging economies are beginning to resemble developed countries in parts but retain many of the characteristics traditionally used to define developing countries such as large agricultural sectors; big disparities between rural and urban populations with significant migration from the former to the latter; a divide between traditional and modern sectors; and low productivity and underdeveloped infrastructure (more of a problem in India than in China).

The bureaucratic and legal framework also needs development in both countries. The degree of bureaucracy and red tape, although on the decline, is renowned in India. In China, the culture of guanxi (see Case Study 13.1) emphasizes relationships and downplays the notion of contracts – a factor which many foreign investors find confusing and which lacks transparency. This disregard for abiding by the written word also extends to laws and regulations. Although many market laws and regulations have been put in place in China, there are frequent reports of weak and inconsistent implementation and enforcement of laws and regulations. In reality what happens in practice is usually determined by local institutions and officials. This keeps the door open for corruption. Neither China nor India performs well on Transparency International's Corruption Perceptions Index (see Table 14.1). Bribery of officials is reportedly not unusual in both locations, despite, in the case of China, very severe punishments for officials caught engaged in corruption.

Both emerging markets therefore pose major challenges for foreign investors but this has not deterred them. Market-seeking, efficiency-seeking and strategy-seeking investments have all occurred in China and India. In the early years of reform, FDI was primarily about resources as firms sought to take advantage of low-cost factors of production, particularly but not only labour, as a prelude to export. Indeed, China's exports remain dominated by the output of foreign multinationals. The rising income of local populations has resulted in much more market-seeking behaviour. Major multinationals like Coca-Cola, Du Pont, General Motors, Kodak and Motorola, to name but a few consumer goods companies remain active in China and India with an eye on the domestic market.

EMERGING ECONOMIES IN A GLOBAL CONTEXT

Increasingly, MNEs can ill afford to ignore the markets and production possibilities of China and India. In terms of population, they account for about 40 per cent of the world's population – significant both in terms of the number of consumers and the size of the labour force. More to the point, increasing living standards are making their markets more attractive.

China and India's emergence is having a major impact on the rest of the world. China is challenging its neighbours in competitive terms but it is also providing opportunities for them in terms of trade and investment. Indeed, FDI inflows into China from the rest of Asia have certainly been greater than those from Europe and have been of a similar magnitude to those from the US. Resource-rich countries like Australia have also benefited from Chinese investment in natural resources.

The impact of China's development on developing countries has been mixed. On the one hand, they have benefited from the increase in commodity prices that occurred in the face of escalating Chinese demand for crude oil, construction products and agricultural products as a result of sustained high levels of growth. The hunt for commodities has resulted in substantial investment by Chinese companies in African oil, minerals, infrastructure and simple manufacturing, a process helped by China's policy of extending concessional loans for such activities. India has followed suit to a lesser extent. However, the jury is out on whether the impact of such investment is always positive (see Case Study 5.1).

On the other hand, developing countries have at times found it difficult to compete with Chinese light manufacturing. This has been the case with textiles and clothing, for example. After the end of the Multi-fibre Arrangement in 2005, many developing country textile producers were no longer able to hide behind the protection afforded to them by textile quotas and were subject to full competition from Chinese producers in their main overseas markets. Unable to compete, many textile producers from small developing and emerging countries began to struggle. It is not only in their export markets that developing country textile and clothing manufacturers have faced intense competition from Chinese products. Many, particularly in Africa, have been out-competed in their domestic markets. Chinese labour costs are low (although not as low as those of many of their competitors) but Chinese manufacturers have the additional advantage of access to raw materials, economies of scale and higher productivity stemming from advanced equipment supplied by Japanese, Taiwanese, Hong Kong and South Korean investors.

Chinese manufacturing is no longer mostly about the production of lower value-added products. Indeed, this has been the case for some time. Chinese manufacturing and exports have steadily been moving up the value-added ladder towards more sophisticated products with increasing high technology content. This process has been helped by technology-intensive investment from the US, Japan and the Southeast Asian NICs, supported by government policy, the growing number of graduate engineers and technologists, and the attention that has been paid to developing efficient infrastructure to support supply chains and logistics. The outcome of this will be even greater competition for developed countries, both internationally and in their domestic markets. This leads to a scenario of the US in particular running even bigger trade deficits with China, a prospect which raises the possibility of higher trade barriers at US borders.

CONCLUSION

Both China and India have undergone long periods of sustained growth. In 2008 to 2009, the world suffered a major financial and economic crisis. Although sheltered from the first stages of the crisis by virtue of the limited integration of their financial sectors with the afflicted international financial sector, China and India could not avoid the second stage of the crisis – the more traditional economic downturn which resulted from the financial meltdown. China's growth in particular relied on exports, and the collapse of demand in several key markets has taken its toll with factory closures, growing unemployment and the government encouraging workers that had migrated from the country to the town for work purposes to return to their rural roots. Despite this, at the time of writing, the consensus among economists is that China's growth in 2009 will be in the 6 to 7 per cent range. This represents a significant reduction of the double-digit growth of earlier years, but is nevertheless a level of economic performance envied by the majority of countries. However, some commentators argue that China cannot lose too much growth momentum without facing negative social consequences and the resultant social unrest. In short, the world's two largest emerging companies continue to grow at rates significantly above those of most other countries but they have a long way to go before they catch up with more developed countries and achieve their relative stability and sustainability.

Summary of Key Concepts

- Not so long ago, the economies of India and China were moribund and isolated from the rest of the world. Now they are the world's most rapidly growing economies.
- The recent economic and business success of India and China has come from the liberalization of their domestic economies and an opening up of trade and investment to the rest of the world.
- The opportunities for foreign investors in India and China are significant but not without risks.
- The growing economic strength of China and India is having an increasing impact on the rest of the world via increasing competition, the emergence of Indian and Chinese multinationals and the contest for resources.

Activities

1. Research how the 2008 to 2009 financial and economic crises have affected China and India.

2. Chose an Indian or Chinese multinational. How has your chosen company internationalized and what problems has it faced?

3. You are a consultant to a Western manufacturer or retailer considering a major investment in one of the BRIC economies (you choose the industry sector and location). Your role is to advise on whether this is a desirable objective. The CEO requires analysis of the general business environment (in the widest sense) in which the investment will take place. S/he also needs advice on what form the investment should take (if you decide it should proceed) and on possible cultural/institutional obstacles to the investment. Feel free to include any other challenges/opportunities posed by the project.

Your findings can be presented in the form of an oral presentation, a report or both.

Discussion Questions

1. In what ways can the emergence of India and China be regarded as an extension of the process of globalization.

2. Compare and contrast the major obstacles to foreign investment in China and India.

3. The experience of China and India demonstrates the superiority of the market over government intervention in the marketplace. Do you agree? Why?

References and Suggestions for Further Reading

Ceglowski, J. and Golub, S. (2007) 'Just how low are China's labour costs?', *World Economy*, Vol. 30, No.4, 597–617.

Chai, J. and Roy, K. (2006) *Economic Reform in China and India: Development Experience in a Comparative Perspective*, Cheltenham: Edward Elgar.

Dauderstädt, M. and Stetten, J. (2005) 'China and golobalisation', *Intereconomics*, July/August, 226–234.

Enderwick, P. (2007) *Understanding Emerging Markets: China and India*, London: Routledge.

Grainger, R. and Chatterjee, S. (2007) 'Business systems and societal context: comparing Chinese and Indian models', *South Asian Journal of Management*, Vol. 14, No. 3, 7–27.

Hutton, W. (2007) *The Writing on the Wall: China and the West in the 21st Century*, London: Little, Brown.

Panagariya, A. (2007) 'Why India lags behind China and how it can bridge the gap', *World Economy*, Vol. 30, No. 2, 229–248.

Rajadhyaksha, N. (2007) *The Rise of India: Its Transformation from Poverty to Prosperity*, Singapore: John Wiley.

Siebert, H. (2007) 'China: coming to grips with the new global player', *World Economy*, Vol. 30, No. 6, 893–922.

Tseng, W. and Cowen, D. (eds) (2007) *India's and China's Recent Experience with Reform and Growth*, Basingstoke: Palgrave Macmillan.

Part II

Enterprise Issues
in the Global Economy

The enterprise is at the heart of international business. Following on from Part I which establishes the context and environment of contemporary international business, Part II focuses on the enterprise within the international context. The opening chapters of Part II focus on international trade and investment. These two flows lie at the bedrock of enterprise actions within the global economy as they establish the rules of engagement with the international economy determining what, where and how they can sell. Such issues will directly drive international strategy.

Thereafter the chapters move on to examine the nature of the multinational enterprise, tracing the evolution of theory on why firms become international and discussing the various options available to them in deciding how to go international. The globalization and related themes of Part I clearly link into and permeate this section on the international enterprise. However, international business is not only about large companies. Increasingly, the activities of small and medium-sized enterprises are being internationalized – a theme which is also picked up in Part II. Chapter 11 focuses on whether and how globalization offers SMEs opportunities to extend beyond their traditional markets or whether they are threatened by such trends.

Building on these strategic choices, the chapter moves on to examine how the business is operationalized both within and across host markets. This involves a plethora of issues from International HRM through to marketing. Such operational issues are inevitably framed by cultural and ethical issues. Cultural issues have to be confronted on many dimensions when conducting business across borders and enterprises also potentially have to contend with conflicting ethical frameworks. Increasingly, issues of corporate responsibility and ethics are coming to the forefront in relation to a whole raft of issues, including labour, human rights, environmental factors and corporate honesty. This section looks at these issues in a generic sense while specific matters of corporate social responsibility are discussed in Part III.

Chapter 7

International Trade

A Building Block of International Strategy

Free trade is not based on utility but on justice.

Edmund Burke, Irish Statesman (1729–1797)

LEARNING OBJECTIVES

This chapter will help you to:

- understand the theoretical basis for international trade
- comprehend trends in global trade
- identify the causes and forms of protectionism
- understand the rising importance of trade in services

International trade is the motor behind the process of globalization and in both a reactive and proactive fashion is a key driver in the development of international strategy. Conventionally trade was associated with the movement of physical products. However, post-industrialization trade has a strong intangible element as services and – increasingly – digital bits become increasingly prominent in the trading process. This chapter explores this extensive area of study by initially revisiting the major theoretical explanations for international trade. Thereafter, through subdividing the topic into trade in merchandise and services, the chapter explores trends and controversies in the global trading system.

FROM COMPARATIVE TO COMPETITIVE ADVANTAGE

International trade theory has been a pivotal factor underpinning policy actions within the international arena. It provides an explanation of how states interact with each other and has been developed from a free trade perspective. Governments can both distort the benefits resulting from trade and ease the moves towards freer exchange. Trade theory can also be descriptive (describing how trade occurs) or prescriptive (identifying whether governments should intervene in the process).

Historically, trade was based upon the principle of mercantilism according to which each state effectively viewed itself as a public limited company (plc). Thus a state (UK plc, US plc) should seek to export more than it imports. This crude measure of international success (and maybe competitiveness) was pursued in an era when wealth was measured merely in terms of the state's holding of treasure and very much reflected the politico-economic circumstances of an era characterized by colonialism. The strategy of mercantilism was essentially based upon viewing trade as a zero-sum game.

Mercantilism regards exports as a benefit, since they stimulate domestic industry. Imports are seen as a burden because they reduce the demand for the products of domestic industry. Thus, a mercantilist policy seeks to stimulate exports and promote import substitution. Trade theory emerged as an attack on mercantilism which had increasingly become a synonym for economic nationalism. The process of mercantilism had resulted in trade barriers that limited specialization, technological progress and wealth creation. In short, mercantilism restricted the intensity of competition within the global economy. Consequently, the basis of trade theory stems from the view that competition is a socio-economic good for all parties involved.

It is worthwhile noting at this juncture that it is impossible to draw parallels between states and enterprises. While enterprises are motivated by purely commercial motives, states seek to secure competitiveness within the context of a broader socio-economic agenda. In short, the national interest is not the sum of the interests of all enterprises located within it but is the sum of the interests of all stakeholders within the national economy concerned.

Conventional trade theory started to evolve with the development of the theory of absolute advantage, which states that a country's wealth is based upon available goods and services. It stresses that different states produce some goods more efficiently than other states. Thus, states should specialize in these goods and buy other goods from states that produce them more efficiently. This specialization is derived either from natural (such as resources) or acquired (usually derived from process or product technology) advantages. Under this system, trade can work to the benefit of both parties: a state exports those goods in which it has an advantage and imports goods from other states which specialize in producing those goods in which it does not have an advantage.

If a state can produce all goods at an absolute advantage, then gains from trade to both parties may still occur because of the principle of comparative advantage. This principle states that gains in trade are possible when a state specializes in those goods that it produces most efficiently. It will then buy those commodities which it no longer produces from countries with fewer natural or acquired resources. Differences in the supply or production conditions between states are a core source of this comparative advantage.

While traditional theories seek to explain the nature of trade patterns, they do lack an adequate explanation of the source of comparative advantage and do not identify the types of products that will deliver an advantage to states. This gap was partially filled by the factor proportions theory. This theory states that differences in a state's endowments of labour, land and/or capital explain differences in the cost of production factors. Thus, a state would specialize in producing those goods that utilize its most abundant factor of production. Thus, if labour is abundant relative to capital and land, then its relative cost would be lower, allowing a state to excel in the production and export of labour-intensive products.

However, the key weakness in the theory is that it assumes that factors of production are homogenous. There are, of course, wide variations in the quality of skills inherent within the labour market. Wide variations in terms of education and training mean that cost is not the sole factor determining the utilization of labour. Increasingly, states could deploy the international division of labour to ensure competitive advantage in the global economy. The theory is further complicated when technology is added to the equation and the same product can be produced by different methods and at minimal cost, irrespective of relative factor abundance.

Despite research indicating that there is, at best, limited empirical support confirming the factor proportions theory, it remains important as the foundation of conventional thinking on trade. While it cannot explain all trade movements, it can assist in explaining a significant part of it. Thus many find the theory a useful starting point upon which to develop ideas regarding trade.

Alternative theories exist to explain the location of production. The product life cycle theory advocates that the production location for many products evolves over the product's life cycle. As the life cycle unfolds, the location of production shifts from one state to another. The following four phases are said to apply:

1. *Introduction phase*: this involves innovation and usually emerges within industrial and innovating states.
2. *Growth phase*: production remains largely based within industrial and innovating states, though there is some evidence of a limited shift to foreign production.
3. *Maturity*: this starts to involve production across multiple locations in several states, notably within emerging economies.
4. *Decline*: production shifts towards emerging economies.

The product cycle tends to be a more complicated theory than others but it is still based on opportunity cost. It essentially states that as production processes become more standardized, so they become increasingly footloose and can be performed by less skilled labour. This reflects the fact that over time the blend of factor inputs will shift away from highly skilled, engineering and marketing elements towards semi- and unskilled fundamentals. This process reduces the opportunity cost of production in these states – a direct link back to the theory of comparative advantage. Evidence seems to suggest that this explanation, like the others, has only limited validity and applicability. For example, products with very short life cycles that are deemed luxurious and require specialized labour cannot readily be included within the model.

The theories of trade explained thus far are based upon the principle of inter-industry trade where states specialize in the production of one type of good and exchange it for other goods produced elsewhere. However, this is not borne out by reality. Much of global trade involves the import and the export of the same type of good – so-called intra-industry trade. This intra-industry trade may be intra-firm trade or it may involve products from unrelated firms. The extent of intra-industry trade is often difficult to measure due to differences in the definition of industries. Evidence seems to suggest that intra-industry trade is highest within technology sectors where rapid generation of new products and constant variations of old products lead to a greater degree of product differentiation. Intra-industry trade also grows in importance as a nation's income rises.

One of the core features of intra-industry trade is a differentiated product. These goods have unique characteristics that make them distinct. Each of these goods appeals to different consumer tastes and preferences, and each has its own market niche. This underlines one of the core benefits of intra-industry trade: that is, that it allows firms to differentiate their products and increase the variety of options and choices available to consumers. Furthermore, goods traded within intra-industry trade are subject to economies of scale in production. Thus, as trade expands, the price to consumers falls. This is especially true for complex technology goods.

Most trade tends to take place between states at similar levels of economic development. This is due to the growing importance of acquired advantage (product technology) as opposed to natural advantage (agricultural products and raw materials). This reflects a country-similarity theory, which is linked into the process of intra-industry trade. This theory states that once a firm develops a new product in response to perceived needs, it will turn to those markets that it regards as possessing similar characteristics to those of its domestic market. Furthermore, as highlighted above, markets in advanced economies can support different product markets. This explains why many leading industrial states are exporters of automobiles.

While these economies may have similar demands, they may also specialize in order to gain advantages. This is particularly the case in areas of research and development or in sectors where knowledge is more important such as pharmaceuticals or software. This is compounded by the large economies of many of these developed states which provide a solid base for exports. The nature of trading partners is influenced by:

■ *Distance*: the closer states are physically, the more likely they are to trade with each other. In this instance, transport costs are a pivotal factor influencing trade flows.
■ Cultural similarity: this has a direct influence, as trade tends to be easier between states that are seen as similar.

■ *Similarity of political and economic interests*: links in these areas can have a direct influence over trade flows. Better politico-economic relations generally aid the trade process.

(For fuller details see Chapters 9 and 10.)

Much of trade theory has, thus far, focused on why states trade. However, these issues remain largely irrelevant unless there is broad understanding of why companies trade. Clearly states will only be exporters or importers to the extent that the enterprises located within it are willing to undertake international activities. Thus firms will see an incentive to divert resources towards foreign enterprises if they are able to attain a competitive advantage within existing or new markets.

Porter (1990) sought to understand these advantages through attempting to identify the competitive advantages and trade opportunities accruing to businesses. In the process, Porter identified four conditions that are important for competitive superiority:

■ *demand*: competitive firms tend to locate near their market;
■ *factor endowments*: linked to the theories of absolute and comparative advantage;
■ *related and supporting industries*: linked to areas such as transport, business services and other key industries needed to support a firm's activities;
■ *firm strategy, structure and rivalry*: the ability of the firm to develop and sustain competitive advantage.

These issues are directly related to those addressed by other trade theories. What Porter contributes is an understanding of the links between those factors which sustain and enhance the competitive positioning of firms and those which help identify where competitive enterprises can develop. Generally – though not always – all these conditions need to be in place for a sector to sustain competitive advantage. Underpinning Porter's perspective is the view that there is nothing better for competitiveness than the intensity of competition. However, inevitably and like other theories, Porter's contribution does provide a greatly simplified view of the circumstances under which competitive positioning can be developed and sustained.

The theories discussed above seek to provide a rationale as to why and how free trade is regarded as the best framework for economic policy. However, there are exceptions to this belief and these stem from the following:

■ *Optimal tariff theory*: where a big state is able to impose tariffs and thereby exert influence on the world prices of the goods it imports. By raising tariffs, such states can significantly reduce world demand, thereby cutting the world price of the product and tilting the terms of trade in their favour.
■ *Strategic trade policy*: this emerged in the 1980s, where an industry has sufficient economies of scale, the imposition of tariffs allows a firm to cut its costs, thereby undercutting foreign rivals in overseas markets. The use of strategic trade policy has in the past been advocated in sensitive sectors such as automobiles and aerospace.

The flaws in both approaches stem from the inability of the state to have sufficient information and power to predict behaviour. They also exclude the possibility of retaliatory actions that could undermine such strategies.

Box 7.1 Rules of Origin

The proliferation of preferential trade agreements (PTAs) across the world has given rise to a set of rules which help define the relationship between members and non-members of the PTA. Rules of origin (ROs) fall into this category and are embedded in many (if not all) PTAs. ROs are powerful trade instruments that seek to limit access to the PTA by non-members. They are used to determine where a good is made and set out the criteria that establish whether they can be used in a discriminatory or non-discriminatory manner. In the case of the former, RO are used within a generalized system of preferences (GSP) to define the conditions under which the importing state will regard a product originating elsewhere as eligible for the preferential trading regime. In the case of the latter, the device is used to apply other trade policy instruments, such as anti-dumping duties.

A major motivation for the use of ROs is to curb trade deflection whereby a non-member of the PTA can gain preferential access to the group via a low tariff partner or via a state with which the group has a GSP. However, ROs are often used for more strategic ends, such as where a group of states seeks to secure access to and for a partner's inputs into the development of its own intermediate products. This ensures that partners support each others' input markets in the development of their own goods. ROs may also be used to meet the political economy objective of extending protection to intra-PTA final good producers that may not be globally competitive but are intent on exporting.

Both preferential and non-preferential ROs have two dimensions:

1. *Product-specific ROs*
    The Kyoto Convention recognizes that there are two basic criteria to determine origin: wholly obtained or produced and substantial transformation. The former applies to only one member of the PTA and assesses whether the product has been wholly developed within that member or whether a second country has been extensively involved in the process. The substantial transformation procedure is more complex and involves one or more of the following criteria: the degree of transformation arising from extra-PTA inputs; specific prohibition of inputs from third countries; the degree of value added from inside the PTA compared to outside, and technical bans on the use of certain processes in the production of the good.
2. *Regime-wide ROs*
    These are based on three considerations:
    - A de minimis rule which specifies a maximum percentage of non-originating materials to be used without affecting origin.
    - The roll up or absorption principle which allows non-originating materials that have acquired origin via processing requirements.
    - Finally, cumulation which allows a member from one PTA to use inputs from another without losing preferential status.

The impact of ROs on trade comes through two channels. The first is via administration costs: RO compliance costs are likely to be high, as establishing the origin of a good incurs bookkeeping costs.

The second is via production costs. These can emerge from technical criteria imposed by the RO regime or when a firm has to use intra-PTA inputs rather than extra-PTA inputs, even when the latter are cheaper. The result is a rise in trade diversion.

Within a global economy characterized by many different PTAs, there is an increasingly complex set of ROs by which firms have to abide. For the WTO, the most immediate course of action is to increase transparency. In the long term, however, there is a need for a more harmonized set of conditions or preferential ROs. This will be difficult given the political economy which underpins their development.

Activity

Using the example of the automobile sector, investigate how rules of origin shape industry value chains. How significant are such rules of origin in shaping firm advantage?

THE GLOBAL FRAMEWORK FOR TRADE IN PRODUCTS

International trade in goods is covered by the General Agreement on Tariffs and Trade (GATT) (see Chapter 4). The workings of the GATT are the responsibility of the Council for Trade in Goods (or Goods Councils). The Goods Council has 11 committees which deal with specific issues (such as market access and subsidies). The GATT was the only international institution regulating trade from 1948 until the establishment of the WTO in 1995. Successive rounds of multilateral trade negotiations sought to gradually liberalize trade in goods – an aspiration which has been largely met. There has been a progressive reduction in the level of tariffs covering industrial goods as well as a gradual liberalization of access. Nevertheless, there are evident loopholes within the framework, notably with regard to the persistent restrictions on trade in agriculture products (see below).

The core underlying principles of the trading system as represented through the GATT are:

- *Non-discrimination*: a country should not discriminate between its trading partners. This is enshrined within the most favoured nation (MFN) principle and the principle of national treatment.
- *Freer trade*: with barriers coming down via negotiation.
- *Predictability*: all commercial actors should be confident that trading rules will not be arbitrarily changed.
- *Reciprocity*: rights of access and reduced tariffs are reciprocated.
- *Transparency*: all restrictions should be clearly identifiable.
- *Aid economic development*: enables less developed states to integrate themselves into the global trading system.

These core principles underpinning the trading system aim to ensure a level playing field for trade in goods: that is, there should be no discrimination between states and any concessions should be reciprocated. These principles are driven by the logic that states receive benefits primarily from increases in exports rather than through unilateral free trade.

The framework was extended within the WTO agreement of 1994. This agreement spelt out the process of further liberalization and its underlying principles as well as permitted exemptions. It also outlined the commitments of individual countries to lower tariffs and other barriers as well as strengthening procedures for dispute settlement. With regard to goods, the WTO agreement underlined the GATT as the basic instrument of trade regulation. Also included were agreements on specific sectors such as agriculture and textiles and clothing, and a set of schedules outlining the commitments of all states to open up their respective markets to trade.

The GATT has traditionally ignored the politically contentious sectors of agriculture and textiles and clothing (see below). These were areas where the founding principles of non-discrimination as highlighted within the most favoured nation clause were generally ignored (see below). The GATT had an inherent weakness, not merely because of the large number of exemptions but also because of the cumbersome process of negotiation; the lack of effective enforcement and credible sanctions, and an inherent suspicion by some states of non-members who sought to benefit from free trade without offering reciprocal rights.

TRENDS IN MERCHANDISE TRADE

Tariff reductions on merchandise trade (i.e. trade in physical goods) are the greatest success of the eight multilateral rounds of trade negotiations that have taken place since the end of the Second World War. In 1945, the weighted average industrial tariff was 40 per cent: this had fallen to 6 per cent by 1979 and to under 4 per cent as a result of the Uruguay Round which was concluded in 1994. The Doha Round, incomplete at the time of writing, is seeking further tariff cuts. The effects on merchandise trade of tariff cuts have been impressive with it rising to a 20-year high in 2007. Merchandise exports topped $14 trillion in 2007. The world's leading exporters and importers of goods are set out in Table 7.1.

One of the key results of the Uruguay Round was to improve market access for industrial and agricultural products. The resulting implications and challenges for a number of important sectors are highlighted later in this chapter. In broad terms, the Round resulted in a 64 per cent reduction in tariffs. Developed states cut their average tariff on imports by 40 per cent, although these reductions tended to be discriminatory in terms of product groups and partner states. In other areas, the agreement sought to phase out quantitative forms of protection imposed by developed states on textiles and clothing and to reduce levels of protection facing agricultural products entering developed economies (Figure 7.1).

WTO estimates suggest that the level of trade in goods will be between 9 and 24 per cent higher than it would have been without the Uruguay Round agreement and that developing and transition economies will be the major beneficiaries from the liberalization of the products affected. The stimulus to global income was at least $109 billion in the decade up until 2005. This is likely to be an underestimate given that the dynamic effects of trade liberalization are difficult to pin down and that the benefits of a more effectively managed system are not easy to quantify.

With regard to the merchandise trade element within the Doha Round (see Chapter 4), the aim is to focus on those areas where developing states have a stronger competitive edge within export markets. In practice, this has meant a focus on further opening up of the key export market for many

TABLE 7.1 The World's Top Ten Exporters and Importers of Goods, 2007

Rank	Exporters	Share of world exports	Annual % change	Rank	Importers	Share of world imports	Annual % change
1	Germany	9.5	20	1	US	14.2	5
2	China	8.7	26	2	Germany	7.4	17
3	US	8.3	12	3	China	6.7	21
4	Japan	5.1	10	4	Japan	4.4	7
5	France	4.0	12	5	UK	4.4	3
6	Netherlands	4.0	19	6	France	4.3	14
7	Italy	3.5	18	7	Italy	3.5	14
8	UK	3.1	-2	8	Netherlands	3.5	18
9	Belgium	3.1	17	9	Belgium	2.9	17
10	Canada	3.0	8	10	Canada	2.7	9

Source: WTO (2008) *International Trade Statistics.*

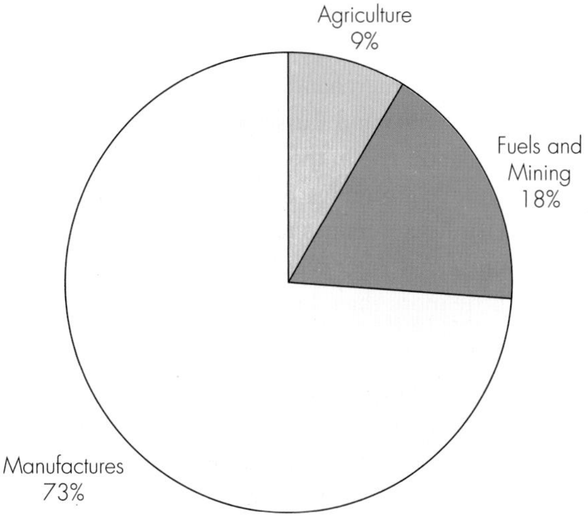

FIGURE 7.1 World Merchandise Trade Exports by Product, 2007 (%)

Source: WTO (2008) *International Trade Statistics.*

Agriculture 9%

Fuels and Mining 18%

Manufactures 73%

developing and emerging states – namely agriculture. The developed states are pushing for a compromise in which they agree to lower agriculture support in return for a sharp reduction in the tariffs applied to manufactures in developing and emerging markets. The OECD estimates that scrapping all tariffs on merchandise trade would boost global welfare by around $170 billion per annum. This would add up to 2 per cent to the GDP of some states.

Backed by strong economic growth since the signing of the Uruguay Round agreement, merchandise trade growth has continued its upward path. In recent years (see Table 7.2), the growth

TABLE 7.2 Growth in Volume of World Merchandise Exports, 2000–2007

	2000–07	2005	2006	2007
World merchandise exports:	5.5	6.5	8.5	6.0
– agriculture	4.0	6.0	6.0	4.5
– fuels and mining products	3.5	3.5	3.5	3.0
– manufactures	6.5	7.5	10.0	7.5

Source: WTO (2008) International Trade Statistics.

in the volume of manufactured exports has exceeded exports of agriculture, fuels and mining products. The growth of iron and steel exports has risen especially quickly, as a result of the demands of the emerging Chinese economy. Indeed, as emerging economies continue to grow, it is expected that they will continue to suck in increasing imports of primary products and food.

As Table 7.2 shows, there has been a noticeable increase in merchandise exports since 2000. Across all major product groups, the growth in exports in the seven years to 2007 has been 5.5 per cent. Geographically the largest exporters in merchandise trade were the CIS, Asia and Latin America. However, the single largest importers and exporters of merchandise trade remained the US and the EU. The states exhibiting the fastest growth were China and Russia as well as countries in the Middle East. In the latter case, this was caused by the sharp rise in the price of oil.

Figure 7.2 indicates the trend across the major product groupings from 1950 to 2005. It is noticeable how the sharp rise in trade in the immediate post-war era has tailed off. As a percentage of GDP, world exports of merchandise trade grew an average of 4.7 per cent between 1950 and 2005. By contrast, between 2000 and 2005, the average was little more than 2 per cent.

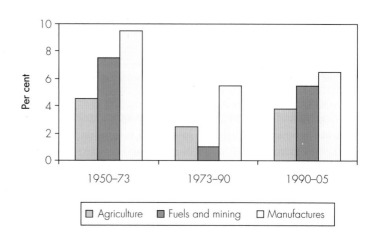

FIGURE 7.2 Change in Merchandise Trade, 1950–2005 (Average Annual % Change)

Source: WTO (2007) International Trade Statistics.

Aside from the generic impact of sustained global growth upon the current upward trend of merchandise trade, there are clearly other trends driving this process. The first of these is the rising price of natural resources, ranging from oil to copper. The rapidly rising demand for these products has boosted their value significantly. Linked to this is the rise of China and India (especially the former) which is driving a rising demand for raw materials. By developing into the workshops of the world economy, these states are becoming resource hungry and consuming large quantities of raw materials and energy to sustain their rapid growth in manufacturing.

The demand for resources by these high-growth economies has also led to sharp increases in exports of oil and primary commodities by the least developed economies. Indeed in 2006, their exports grew by 30 per cent. This was in the face of a fear that their labour intensive sectors (most notably textiles – see below) would be devastated by competition from China. As a result of these trends the share of developing countries of world merchandise reached 36 per cent (2006), an all-time high. This was also true for the least developed states whose 0.9 per cent, (2006) share was the highest level since 1980. The share of world merchandise imports was 31 per cent, the largest share for more than 25 years. Overall, among the 30 leading exporters, the eight most dynamic comprised five oil exporters, one metal exporter and China and India (all had export growth of more than 20 per cent in 2006). The developed world had by comparison a sluggish performance. Interestingly, in the second half of 2006, China's merchandise exports exceeded those of the US for the first time in contemporary business history.

CASE STUDY 7.1

Parallel Imports

A parallel import is a non-counterfeited good that has protected IPR within one state but which is imported into another without the permission of the rights owner. The opportunity for parallel importing is created by the ability of the rights owner to segment markets. This is often achieved through exclusive distribution agreements between the rights holder and its partner within the host economy. In many developed states, such market restrictions are largely without controversy if the producer faces competition from other brands. However, where inter-brand competition is weak, as in many developing states, these agreements can prove controversial.

The fact that price differentials exist between markets allows for a process of simple arbitrage whereby an importer is able to access stocks of a good in lower price states and import them into higher cost states and charge a price between those within the exporting and importing states. While the rights owners and their distributors would argue for the benefits of segmentation, it is apparent that these only occur when a limited set of conditions apply. The benefits of parallel importing are that it can enable a market to be served that may otherwise be neglected and allow for lower prices than would have occurred.

However, these benefits have to be balanced against problems of undersupply and the abuse of dominant positions, problems which constitute the controversial elements of the control of parallel imports. In many developed economies, controversies over attempts to control parallel imports have centred on the extent to which controls limit effective competition. New technologies and improved customer awareness are allowing end users to bypass these controls and have forced rights holders to back down. However, the issue is more controversial where segmentation by rights holders is based on banning parallel imports to keep prices high for medicines and other necessities in locations where price levels prohibit mass consumption of the product.

At the core of the debate surrounding parallel imports is the issue of the control and protection of IPR. Some see the rise of parallel importing as a simple case of arbitrage. Such flows offer obvious benefits to consumers and widen the choice of products available. However, others protest that such uncontrolled flows can damage the rights holder, limit remuneration from their property and, in the longer term, research and development. In other cases, these flows can also encourage copyright infringement and piracy. Such concerns highlight the tension surrounding the rights of the property holder. The choice of price is a reflection of who the rights holder wishes to serve and who it does not. Moreover, the existence of parallel imports is a direct challenge to monopoly control.

CASE STUDY QUESTIONS

1. To what extent is the existence of parallel imports a positive by-product of the globalizing economy?

2. In what circumstances (if any) would the protection afforded by parallel imports be justified?

3. Can you think of any sectors where the issue of parallel imports is especially salient? Why is this the case?

Trade in Agricultural Goods

In the OECD states alone, agricultural policies cost consumers and taxpayers over $300 billion a year (2006). Although food production has increased, it has done so at a substantially higher cost than would have been the case if global markets had been allowed to determine what should be produced and where. The motives for this farm support are political, economic and social. Farmers in many developed states still leverage a great deal of political support and influence, despite representing a small and declining proportion of total production and employment. Ultimately, many of the concerns about agriculture are linked directly to the issue of food security. To many states, food security is not compatible with freer agricultural trade. The ability of each state to meet the needs of its own population is still a salient political issue in the eyes of many, which renders farming an important strategic industry worthy of special treatment. Policy has traditionally recognized that the way to ensure food security is to increase indigenous food production. The result has been assorted forms of protection and other trade-distorting measures. Tables 7.3, 7.4 and 7.5 highlight the key trends in agricultural trade, notably how the importance of trade in this product category varies across space.

Increasingly, however, liberalization of agricultural trade is being advocated as a means of increasing food security through more efficient resource allocation, thereby reducing the cost of food. Global markets provide supplementary sources of food that are important in the case of an economic or political shock which leads to a temporary disruption to domestic supply. The benefits of global trade have been directly fostered by greater political and economic stability within the global

TABLE 7.3 World Trade in Agricultural Products, 1980–2007 (% Change)

1980–1985	–2
1985–1990	9
1990–1995	7
2000–2007	11

Source: WTO (2008) *International Trade Statistics*.

TABLE 7.4 Share of Agricultural Products in Total Traded Goods, 2007

	Exports	Imports
World	8.3	8.3
North America	9.6	6.0
South and Central America	25.1	8.7
Europe	9.0	9.2
CIS	7.6	10.9
Africa	8.1	14.0
Middle East	2.5	10.2
Asia	5.6	7.4

Source: WTO (2008) *International Trade Statistics*.

TABLE 7.5 Share of Agricultural Products in Total Primary Product Exports, 2007

	Exports	Imports
World	29.8	29.8
North America	40.8	23.9
South and Central America	37.9	31.3
Europe	46.2	35.2
CIS	10.3	49.6
Africa	10.4	47.5
Middle East	3.3	47.8
Asia	35.1	21.8

Source: WTO (2008) *International Trade Statistics*.

economic system. Indeed, states with poor agricultural resources rely upon imports in order to achieve food security. Despite this, many states still regard world markets as too volatile and food prices as too politically sensitive to leave to free markets. Furthermore, states regard reliance upon foreign suppliers for a core domestic resource as a suspect strategy. Too much reliance upon imports could leave the state exposed if wars or other forms of political turmoil affect international trade flows. This is further compounded by fears that food sourced from other states may not meet the health, safety or quality requirements of domestic markets.

The original GATT did apply to agricultural trade but a number of escape clauses allowed states to directly protect or distort markets for this product grouping. Notably, the GATT allowed states to use non-tariff barriers (NTBs) such as import quotas and subsidies. The latter have proved especially important in distorting the international market for agricultural products. Consequently, the GATT was limited and ineffective in terms of freeing up trade in agriculture. A large number of exceptions exempt agriculture from many of the provisions applying to manufactured goods. The Uruguay Round marked a genuine attempt to redress these distortions. The agriculture agreement within the Uruguay Round set out to make the sector more market-oriented with the aim of improving predictability and security for both importing and exporting states. The new rules and commitments apply to:

- market access;
- domestic support;
- export subsidies and other methods that make exports artificially attractive.

Despite these commitments, the agreement does allow states to offer support to their rural communities, although it is hoped that such support will not have a knock-on effect in terms of trade. The trend in global trade in agriculture is outlined in Table 7.3.

In terms of market access, the WTO is seeking to ensure that protection – where it is deemed necessary – occurs through the most visible form: tariffs. Thus, subsidies and other forms of support have undergone a process of tariffication in which support was converted into a tariff equivalent. In addition, states agreed to reduce tariff levels. Developed states reduced tariffs by an average of 36 per cent (over six years) whereas developing states were committed to an average cut of 24 per cent over 10 years. The least developed states were under no obligation to reduce their tariffs. Safeguards within the agreement were designed to ensure that the changes did not create commercial turbulence for farmers in the form of sudden falls in prices or increases in imports. This is essentially a form of short-term protectionism offered while farmers adjust to the wider implications of greater exposure to market forces.

The agreement also specified that domestic policies that have a direct effect upon production had to be scaled back while those with minimal impact upon output could be used freely. This was designed to ensure that overproduction was curtailed, thereby removing the incentive for states to distort global markets by allowing overproduction to flood world markets. There was a shift in farm support towards measures that offered direct income support and resulted in cutbacks in production. Export subsidies were prohibited unless included within a state's commitments to the WTO. Where they are listed, there is a commitment to cut them in terms of both the money spent as well as the number of exports that receive support.

The initiative to open markets was complemented by an agreement on food safety and plant and health standards. This aimed to ensure that freer markets in agricultural produce do not lead to deterioration in the quality of produce. The WTO agreement set out basic rules to encourage states to meet quality standards based upon credible scientific research. Clearly the system has to generate sufficient confidence to ensure that health and safety concerns do not re-emerge as a justification for renewed protectionism. Thus, measures are in place to ensure that any changes in safeguards are compatible with the agreed quality concerns.

Despite the above measures, agriculture remains a highly protected sector with tariff levels on average three times higher than those on manufactured goods. In many instances, high tariffs are locked into the system of support and states still intervene heavily in the market. While tariff protection is now more visible (through the process of tariffication), the overall level of protection remains high. Thus there has been little diminution in the overall level of protection. This is compounded by the fact that constraints upon domestic policies have turned out to be rather weak. In practice, many agricultural tariffs remain in the region of 60 per cent compared to the industrial tariffs that rarely exceed 10 per cent and are normally much lower. For some products, notably those that are deemed politically sensitive, protection has actually increased. Furthermore, tariff profiles have become more complicated with several different rates applying to the same products. Tariff variability has also increased, as has the number of tariffs that are higher than the simple average.

The Uruguay negotiations represented a watershed for agricultural trade in the areas of market access, export subsidies and domestic support. In the case of market access, the switch to a tariff-based regime was a major achievement. However, many states bound their tariff rates at high levels. On average (by 2005) agricultural tariffs averaged 60 per cent, with real tariffs (i.e. tariffs accounting for inflation) being around 200 per cent. Many states have made a commitment to reduce the level of export subsidies. Commitments were also made to reduce domestic support with a shift towards more decoupled measures (where support is more targeted than linked to output). Under the Uruguay Round agreement, developed states agreed to reduce tariffs over a five-year period by an average of 36 per cent with a minimum of 15 per cent, while developing states agreed to smaller cuts over a longer time period. However, to pin the blame solely on developed states would be unfair as, on average, tariffs in developing states are 2 per cent higher. This differential reflects the fact that for a large percentage of developing countries agricultural trade is with other developing states. However, the OECD argues for all to move to freer markets while preserving the social aspect of agriculture with income decoupled from output, enhanced support for rural communities, and the promotion of environmental sustainability.

In an evaluation of the WTO's Agriculture Agreement, the OECD (2001) noted that the immediate effect had been moderate due to the weakness of many of the measures as well as to the historically high levels of support offered. The report highlighted that the market remained highly distorted and underlined the points made above: that is, that the agreement was flawed and in some cases actually raised the level of tariffs. Furthermore, much of the domestic support (around 60 per cent) is exempt from the agreement and, despite the best efforts of the WTO, many of these support mechanisms have trade-disrupting effects. This is further compounded by the fact that states have been nimble in circumventing attempts to control export subsidies. Overall, the level of support has fallen since the mid-1980s when it represented 37 per cent of farm receipts to less than 30 per cent (2006). In addition, the level of the most trade-distorting support has declined from 90 per cent of producer support in the mid-1980s to 74 per cent by the end of 2004.

The WTO Agriculture Agreement has a 'built-in' agenda that requires further talks on agricultural reform. For such talks to be successful they must be backed by an explicit political commitment. To many reformers in the developed world, the key to reform lies in creating concrete political reforms for the process. Creating this political awareness depends on effective education of assorted groups to create an understanding of the negative impact of protection. Consumers, for example, need to be aware of the effect upon food prices of sustained protection. Once they understand how this impacts upon them, greater support for reform is expected. In short, there needs to be a separation between agriculture as a commercial activity and its existence as a way of life.

According to the WTO, subsidies are graded according to their harmfulness, and negotiations take place in relation to the various classifications of subsidies:

- *Green box subsidies*: green box subsidies do not distort trade or cause minimal distortion. Such subsidies must not involve price support. Examples of green box subsidies include direct income support, environmental protection measures or regional development measures. These subsidies are permitted but some pressure groups argue that they should be scrutinized more fully to determine whether they are, indeed, non-trade distorting.
- *Blue box subsidies*: blue box subsidies have been described as 'the amber box with conditions': that is, support that would normally be in the amber box belongs in the blue box if the support requires farmers to limit production.
- *Amber box subsidies*: amber box subsidies include all domestic support measures considered to distort production and/or trade (with some exceptions). In addition, there are 'de minimis'

subsidies where payments are limited to a small share of total agricultural production (around 5 per cent). There are currently limits on amber subsidies but not on blue. In the Doha Round, the US proposed cutting its amber box subsidies by 60 per cent, capping blue subsidies and capping de minimis subsidies to 2.5 per cent. However, the US also plans to reclassify some controversial subsidies from the amber to the blue box. However, if the US is willing to cap subsidies at $17 billion, then the EU is willing to cut agricultural tariffs by 54 per cent. However, the EU wants to spare 'sensitive' tariffs from this cut. For many businesses Doha is a 'non-round', since agriculture – according to the *Economist* – accounts for 90 per cent of the debate and only 2 per cent of US and EU economies. However, these priorities need to be understood in term of how an agreement would create a log jam in other areas and generate more far-reaching benefits.

Further reform and increasing the impact of market forces upon agriculture requires the addressing of existing weaknesses and the enforcement of greater discipline on states. Clearly, further effort needs to be made to reduce the high level of tariffs that remain. Reform of the agriculture sector also has to address the issue of multifunctionality: that is, any agricultural trade agreement must recognize and reconcile the various social, economic and political aspects of agricultural activity. In short, states will still want to support rural communities and should be encouraged to do so within the context of freer market forces. Agricultural policy is about more than food production: there are issues related to the environment, rural communities and food security that need to be addressed within any agreement. While these issues may be considered 'non-trade' issues, they certainly affect the process of trade liberalization (Figure 7.3).

The reform of agriculture is a key theme of the Doha Development Round and has been the main stumbling-block to reaching a final agreement. Clearly, the ability to generate export earnings from agriculture is key to the integration of many emerging and developing states into the global economy and to overcoming vicious cycles of underdevelopment. Many developing countries are looking to the developed states to reduce the level of subsidies given to their farmers. In 2005, the OECD estimated that member states gave $225 billion (around 30 per cent of farm receipts) to domestic farmers. Around two-thirds of government support was in the form of price support: the rate of price support varies from 32 per cent in the EU to 5 per cent in Australia. The largest level of support as a percentage of receipts was Japan (56 per cent), Korea (63 per cent), Norway (65 per cent) and Switzerland (68 per cent). Much of this support is not based on need and a large proportion of it goes to unintended beneficiaries (such as suppliers or individuals who own but do not farm the land).

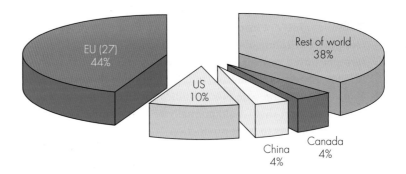

FIGURE 7.3 Agricultural Products as a Share of World Trade, 2007 (%)

Note: Includes intra-EU trade.

Source: WTO (2008) *International Trade Statistics.*

The Doha Round has been plagued by disputes between the US and the EU over farm subsidies. This was compounded by more aggressive tactics by emerging economies and the G20 over this issue. This group – led by Brazil – has sought to act as a counterweight to the US and the EU to deliver the optimal trade deal. Any deal would have to be limited to the least developed states with the larger emerging markets and middle-income developing states excluded unless they were willing to offer compromise on trade in other areas.

The agricultural sector is moving towards new forms of trade based around high-value products and away from bulk homogenous products. Today, this high-value trade accounts for around three-quarters of all trade. Such a trend offers a further commercial rationale for liberalization of the sector. The degree of commercial sophistication is also increasing as IPR becomes a more important issue in the biotechnology trade. This more sophisticated industry based around more complex consumer tastes implies a move away from commodity production and a greater emphasis on providing added value through more effective marketing. These processes cement what has been the implementation of increasingly market-oriented policy at the domestic level.

Since the conclusion of the Uruguay Round, food security has emerged as a salient economic issue within international trade and public health domains. Technological developments such as genetically modified food and health fears such as BSE highlight public concerns over the increased commercialization of the agricultural sector. New rules governing the quality of food imports can enhance trade if they create greater certainty amongst consumers. On the other hand, such regulations can become another technical barrier. Evidence provided by the OECD suggests that such regulations have been employed by developed states to restrict imports from developing economies. These concerns are further heightened by the growing politicization of the agro-environmental issue, particularly in relation to the growing concern that further trade liberalization would have detrimental effects upon the natural environment.

Many argue that the sharp rise in food prices in late 2007/2008 would give governments the opportunity to undertake wholesale reform of the agricultural sector as protection had often been justified on the grounds of low prices. Thus, as prices rise, this should – in theory – free governments from the need to subsidize production and keep prices high. However, the sharp rises in prices have seen a change of direction on food security issues as the rises in prices mean a lessened need to protect farmers to avoid further shortages. High prices are a buffer against falling protection and it seems reasonable that governments take the opportunity to push for further reform when farmers are least likely to feel the consequences.

Trade in Textiles

Textiles were among the earliest manufactured goods and play a persistently prominent role in international trade. This is especially true for developing states where labour-intensive activities play to their natural advantages. Like agriculture, this sector is one of the hardest fought in multilateral trade talks. Prior to the Uruguay Round, international trade in textiles fell under the Multi-Fibre Arrangement (MFA). The MFA allowed states to place highly discriminatory quantitative restrictions upon imports of textiles and clothing. The MFA was introduced in 1974 and provided a framework for a series of bilateral agreements and unilateral actions designed to protect the industry in developed countries. The quotas were the feature of the system that directly conflicted with the principles of GATT.

Under the auspices of the Uruguay Round, states signed up to the Agreement on Textiles and Clothing (ATC) which established multilateral rules and made the sector subject to the basic rules of the GATT. The ATC required the progressive elimination of all quantitative restrictions over a 10-year period. At the end of the period (that is, in 2005) the sector became fully integrated into the multilateral trading system. Despite the clear benefit of the ATC to developing states, there have been accusations that developed states delayed liberalization in sectors of key importance until the last moment.

In practice, the ATC was a mixed blessing for those developing countries that were beneficiaries of preferential agreements with larger developed countries or groupings (such as those developed by the EU with its ex-colonies) as they faced stiffer competition when the MFA was abolished. In addition, China's entry into the WTO meant that any gains were lost given China's ability to unleash large quantities of cheap textiles onto the global marketplace. However, temporary trade restrictions were possible if damage occurred to the sector during the transition process (as indeed happened in the European Union). To oversee the implementation of the agreement, the Textiles Monitoring Body (TMB) was established. The TMB monitors actions under the agreement and deals with disputes under the transitional ATC.

In general, the products integrated into the GATT were lower value-added products, given that the transition was defined in terms of quantity rather than value. Thus the shift towards WTO rules has occurred to date mainly in the least sensitive textile and clothing products with liberalization of only a few quotas on products of export interest to developing states. Even after the agreement came into force, tariffs on textiles and clothing remained higher than those on industrial goods. Indeed, the Uruguay Round increased the gap as tariff reductions on textiles and clothing were only half of those on industrial goods. In developed states, tariffs on textiles and clothing average 12 per cent – three times the average for all industrial goods.

Given these concerns, it is expected that trade negotiations need to focus on:

- speeding up the process of the integration of textiles and clothing into the GATT framework. The process of 'back loading' (that is, delaying as long as possible the opening of sensitive markets) by developed states will only make the process harder;
- achieving further reductions in tariffs on textiles and clothing;
- removing other protective measures, especially those linked to regional trading agreements;
- assisting states to adjust to the changes promoted under the ATC.

However, the 10-year commitment offered under the ATC means that further reform is low on the list of WTO priorities. This also reflects the tariff-free (albeit rule-of-origin-ridden) nature of much textile and clothing trade given that most of it takes place under preferential trading agreements, notably NAFTA and the EU's agreements with Central and Eastern Europe. Pressure for further reform has also been limited by increased conflict between developing states over trade within this sector.

The WTO's main priority is to ensure that existing commitments are met and that the MFA is removed in its entirety. Further reform also has to recognize the increasingly complex nature of textile trade. A split is emerging in terms of the sector's division of labour as design takes place within the developed world and is transmitted electronically to manufacturing facilities in developing countries. Furthermore, technological change is occurring in parts of the industry's value chain, notably in cutting and sewing, which could remove the competitive advantage of low-wage economies. There are also issues to be addressed in terms of barriers to the import of textile equipment.

It was expected that the phasing of the ATC would lead to long-term structural changes as competitive advantage shifts towards production in lower income states, especially China. The short-term impact was negligible, as increased imports from low-cost states were offset by reduced supplies from higher income states as well as new restraints on Chinese imports. Outside the EU, evidence suggests that the end of the ATC did little to accelerate long-term change: employment and production continued to decline at the same rate prior to the end of the ATC. However, trade creation effects were evident as exports to the EU and the US from high-cost areas in East Asia were replaced by increased supplies from China, India, Turkey and Bulgaria. The worst affected areas were sub-Saharan Africa, Morocco and Bangladesh.

As mentioned, in the initial period following the end of the ATC, many developed states saw imports from China rise sharply. Indeed, China's exports rose by 41 per cent in 2005, though this rate of increase fell to around 15 per cent in 2006. Despite this decline, the growth rate of Chinese textile exports was twice the rate of growth of exports from other states. In the US, textile imports have increased and there has been a switch away from NAFTA members and Africa towards China. Those states that have sustained their position within developed markets benefit from preferential trading agreements, and both Pakistan and India have also increased their textiles and clothing exports markedly.

The trends indicated in Table 7.6 suggest that the end of the ATC did not cause any substantial increases in textiles or clothing trade but merely created a shift among exporters. This under-mined estimates that trade would increase by as much as 60 per cent following the abolition of these quotas.

TABLE 7.6 Major Regional Flows of World Textiles and Clothing, 2000–2005 (Annual % Change)

	Textiles	Clothing
Intra-Europe	4	9
Intra-Asia	3	4
Asia to Europe	11	10
Asia to North America	11	6
Intra-North America	–1	–4
Asia to Middle East	8	n/a
Asia to Africa	14	n/a
Asia to CIS	n/a	34

Source: WTO (2007).

TRADE IN SERVICES

Services require interaction among actors before the service can be rendered. Thus, if a service with a cross-border element is offered, the provider must interact with the consumer in another state. In an international context, this interaction or initial meeting may occur in one of the following ways:

■ Through cross-border communications that involve no physical mobility by either party. Such interactions may take place by post or through ICTs. The latter have become especially evident with the emergence of electronic commerce as a method of service delivery.

- Through the consumer moving to the service supplier's state of residence.
- Through the movement of the service provider to the consumer's state of origin.
- Through the movement of a commercial organization to the consumer's state of residence.

These definitions have been adopted by the General Agreement on Trade in Services (GATS) (see below) and emphasize that international commercial transactions in services encompass FDI and the movement of labour as well as conventional cross-border transactions.

With changes in technology, many services previously thought of as untradable have started to be traded internationally. Other services become more tradable through the movement (often temporary) of the producers (such as accountants) and consumers (such as the consumers of medical services). Furthermore, service suppliers seeking to trim costs have transferred some service operations overseas – a move directly facilitated by the emergence of the aforementioned electronic networks. These trends have been prominent in sectors such as airlines where booking functions have been moved to places where labour costs are a fraction of those elsewhere. These trends have also been reinforced by a global network of professionals offering services to multinationals wherever they operate.

The share of services in international transactions is low compared to their economic importance. Trade in services comprised less than 20 per cent of international trade in 2005. The share of the sales of services in foreign affiliates is also likely to be lower than in trade. However, this is changing due to the impact of increased international integration in the service sector and progress in ICTs is increasing the tradability of services. Indeed, the distinction between trade and services becomes blurred in the case of e-commerce (see Chapter 18). Integration is also being aided by the international fragmentation of industry/firm value chains.

A common misconception is that trade in services is almost solely of benefit to developed states. This trade can also benefit developing states insofar as competition allows gains from comparative advantage as well as increasing the degree of competition and reducing monopoly power. This can have benefits in lowering the costs of production for industry and allowing the more efficient development of infrastructure. In addition, this can foster FDI as well as knowledge and technology transfer.

Many of the barriers that restrict trade in services are opaque in nature (Findlay and Warren, 2000) and mostly take the form of non-tariff barriers (NTBs). NTBs can be difficult to identify and measure and pose a severe challenge to removing the more direct forms of protection on either the producer or consumer as they interact across borders. This leads to further problems: the liberalization process becomes difficult to track and gauge, and remaining impediments to service trade can remain undetected. A major barrier to service liberalization remains regulatory fragmentation. In cases where a freer market for services has been sought (as witnessed by the EU's single market programme), efforts have been devoted towards reducing this regulatory fragmentation through moves towards harmonization and/or mutual recognition. Differences in regulation not only increase the cost of market entry but, more often than not, are also directly discriminatory. States have developed these differences for a number of reasons, ranging from cultural justifications to the preservation of public service. In addition, because services encompass a diverse range of economic activities, it is difficult, if not impossible, to develop a uniform method of liberalization.

The persistence of barriers to service trade, as in other sectors, is due to the innate political economy of the state concerned. The role of the state in regulating services, when added to the role of the private sector in their provision, has tended to hamper the process of deregulation of service markets. This highlights a central theme in the globalization of services – that is, that many key services such as communication and postal services have not only been state owned but also state controlled. Indeed, in the liberalization era, many states still seek to retain a degree of control over the free play of market forces to ensure that specified service obligations are met. Even in sectors where there is significant experience of market forces (such as the airline sector), the legacy of state intervention remains. Although this is changing, airlines still tend to follow the series of bilateral deals agreed under the Bermuda agreement established in the 1950s. Actions are focused upon limiting access to domestic markets by foreign suppliers of services. In some cases, entry is directly prohibited. In others, there is implicit or explicit discrimination through, for example, an 'entry fee' or market share restrictions. Through such actions, there appears to be little difference between trade in goods and trade in services, especially when considered in terms of their treatment at the hands of NTBs. Over recent times, the Bermuda agreement has started to look anachronistic, especially as the EU and others seek to establish open sky agreements. Consequently, despite a move towards the progressive liberalization of services, governments (either directly or through intergovernmental bodies) remain an important influence over the evolving market for services.

There is a clear need to remove the discrimination in service trade. These measures will also have to be accompanied by an active process of regulatory reform at the domestic level. This has been evident in a number of cases: for example, WTO measures relating to telecommunication services required reform of the domestic telecommunications sector in many states if WTO commitments were to be met.

The most typical forms of protection utilized by states in terms of service provision are:

- *Quotas, local content and prohibitions*: quotas typically fall upon service providers rather than upon the service itself. Restrictions placed by many authorities upon the slots available to foreign airlines at major domestic airports are examples of this. In other instances the device is cruder, such as a straightforward ban on the provision of services by foreign firms. This was the position for a long time in the telecommunications sector where state-owned or controlled enterprises were granted service monopolies over domestic markets. The issue of local content was especially prevalent among the many francophone states that resisted the flood of services (especially media) that are English-language based. Thus, there was a campaign to place quotas upon US-based English-language films as a means of preserving identity. Linked to these issues was the desire to restrict services regarded as harmful to domestic culture. For example, many Muslim states have sought to limit access to the Internet as a means of restricting the circulation of pornography within their borders.
- *Price-based instruments*: as highlighted above, customs duties or tariffs are difficult to apply to services; their application is feasible to the movement of persons in the form of visas, taxes and so on. Furthermore, tariffs may be applied to core components of service production such as software and TV production facilities. Alternatively, price controls may be utilized by states to ensure that core services are accessible by all persons regardless of income. This is evident where there is a government-sanctioned monopoly and where price controls are linked to quantitative restrictions. These price-based measures are often supported by direct subsidies to supply the provision of services. Such actions have been evident in the provision of rail transport, for example.

- *Standards, licensing and procurement*: it is common to require providers of services to meet a minimum set of standards and to obtain certification as evidence that such standards are being met. Such standards, or minimum legal requirements, are especially evident in areas such as accountancy and medical services. Furthermore, environmental standards can influence service activities such as tourism. These devices have traditionally been used to restrict entry into domestic markets by non-indigenous suppliers, especially in terms of the provision of professional services and the limits imposed on the mutual recognition of qualifications. Such discriminatory measures have been common in many states. Other examples include government procurement and sourcing policies that favour domestic service suppliers (such as management consultants) over their foreign equivalent. This raises important equity concerns given that governments represent such a large percentage of national GDP.

- *Discriminatory access to distribution networks*: in many instances, the provision of services is directly linked to access to distribution and communication infrastructures. Clearly, where there is denial of access to the network or where access is granted on unfair terms, there is clear potential to undermine the competitive process. There is evidence of this in the tele-communications and transport industries. In the latter case, denial of or limited access to landing slots at airports has had a direct influence over the intensity of competition faced by airlines. Limitations to networks can also take the form of limited access to distribution networks (such as in the case of branded cars) and restrictions on the access to marketing channels.

CASE STUDY 7.2

The US and Internet Gambling

Gambling has been and remains tightly controlled within the US. However, a gradual loosening up of regulations at both the federal and state levels has stimulated a rapid growth in the gambling industry. Advances in technology (especially with regard to the internet) have introduced a new medium through which individuals can consume gambling services. However, legislators and regulators are wary of a phenomenon which could become 'the crack cocaine' of gambling. Many of these casinos are perpetually open and allow unlimited access from locations such as Antigua and Belize that lie outside the jurisdiction of US authorities. Much of the concern created by internet gambling has also been linked to the sheer rapidity of its rise.

Within the US, gambling is regulated on a state-by-state basis. The consequent patchwork of regulation reflects the variation in philosophies among the states. However, internet gambling is best seen as regulated at the federal level. Efforts to control internet gambling are based on the 'Wire Act' (1961) which pre-dates the activity and prohibits the use of wire technologies for the purposes of betting. Doubts exist as to the ability of legislation from 1961 to cope with the technological advances now being witnessed, but attempts to update this law have been frustrated. Thus, the Wire Act remains at the core of efforts to control online gambling. Aside from social, moral and ethical issues surrounding the growth of internet gambling, there were concerns that its growth would have negative economic consequences through reductions in state revenue, costs to the consumer credit card industry as well as the broader societal costs related to increased gambling.

By the end of 2006, it was estimated that 23 million US citizens had placed (annually) $7.5 billion in online bets – 50 per cent of the global total. Gambling is an activity that lends itself to the landscape of cyberspace. Not only does it allow people to gamble from the privacy of their own homes, it also increases transparency and competition within the industry. Traditional gambling formats are seen as offering poor odds and come with associated costs such as punitive taxes and hotel rooms. The internet has also removed unnecessary intermediaries and lowered the transaction costs associated with gambling. However, making internet gambling illegal risks forcing players underground where they become more vulnerable.

Despite the popularity of internet gambling, the US has pressed ahead with attempts to criminalize it. This has been driven by politics and the 2006 mid-term elections. There is a belief among certain constituencies that internet gambling sites allow customers to bet on anything, encourage underage gambling and are designed to be as addictive as possible. However, the main concern is criminality.

While legislation has made it more difficult for US gamblers, it has also led to attempts to circumvent the law. A notable trend has been the emergence of new intermediaries that take credit card transfers or payments which are then used for gambling. The payment system has loopholes which make it difficult to locate the user or to identify for what purpose funds are being used. Despite this innovation, legislation to stop banks handling online payments to gambling sites hit the industry hard and many of the major providers left the US segment of the market.

In March 2003, a complaint was registered with the WTO under the GATS agreement by two Caribbean states, Antigua and Barbuda, where many of the gambling sites were hosted. The complaint argued that the act of limiting banks from honouring online gambling transactions was a barrier to free trade in service activity. The complainant pointed out that the law created asymmetry of treatment between domestic and overseas operators as the Wire Act allowed US-based firms to take bets but banned overseas operators from doing the same. A total of 18 states allowed US firms to operate interactive betting activities – a market from which foreign operators were excluded. Antigua alleged that the act had resulted in extensive job losses and that many of its providers had gone out of business. The US insisted that any interactive gambling must be legal both in the jurisdiction of the gambler and the operator.

The WTO initially outlawed the US actions as gambling was not excluded from its GATS commitments and they were thus inconsistent with its obligations under the agreement. Furthermore, as the US failed to negotiate with Antigua in the first place, it could not use public interest as a legitimate defence. This latter point was overturned on appeal but a further decision decreed that the US had to ban all interactive interstate horserace betting or allow access to this service by all GATS members. This still meant, however, that the US had acted illegally in the case of online gambling. Consequently, it either had to ban it outright or allow equal access to its markets.

By late 2006, it became apparent that the US would ignore the final ruling. Antigua felt it had won every battle but had lost the war. The US had shown no desire to comply with the ruling and withdrew its gambling industry from its free trade commitments. As a result, all 151 WTO members (2007) signalled their intent to seek compensation totalling an estimated $100 billion. The US decision to retroactively exclude gambling from its GATS commitments could set an important yet detrimental precedent for the WTO. If other states follow its lead, the WTO system could implode. The credibility of the US as a trading partner has also been undermined by these actions. Moreover, the internet gambling dispute could have long-term implications for the development of e-commerce within the global trading system.

THE GENERAL AGREEMENT ON TRADE IN SERVICES (GATS)

The creation of the GATS was one of the important achievements of the Uruguay Round. The aims of the GATS are essentially the same as those of the GATT; that is:

- the creation of a credible and reliable system of international trade rules;
- fair and equitable treatment of all participants;
- stimulation of economic activity through guaranteed policy commitments;
- promotion of trade and development through progressive liberalization.

The main goal of GATS is to promote more competitive and efficient markets by reducing or removing restrictions on the number of service suppliers; the total value of transactions or assets; the total number of service operations or total quantity of services output; the total number of natural persons who may be employed in any given sector and the specific type of legal entity through which services can be supplied.

All WTO members have signed up to the agreement and apply it across the service sector with the exception of those services 'supplied in the exercise of government authority' and aspects of air traffic services. It applies to 12 main sectors – within which there are 150 subsectors:

1. business services
2. communication services
3. construction and related services
4. distribution services
5. educational services
6. environmental services
7. health related and social services
8. financial services
9. tourism and related travel services
10. transport services
11. recreational, cultural and sporting services
12. other services not included elsewhere.

As with the typology highlighted above, the agreements distinguish between four modes of supplying services:

- *Mode 1*: cross-border supply: this covers service flows from one state into another;
- *Mode 2*: consumption abroad: where a consumer moves to another country for the purpose of consuming a service (e.g. tourism or health care);
- *Mode 3*: commercial presence: where a service supplier from one state establishes a presence in another for the purposes of supply;
- *Mode 4*: the presence of natural persons: where one person moves to another state to supply a service.

Obligations under GATS are twofold. General obligations apply automatically to all states and services sectors. These include aspects such as MFN treatment and transparency. Specific obligations apply to market access and to national treatment commitments for dedicated sectors and are designed to end the process of discrimination in trade in services. Each member has a schedule that identifies the services for which the state guarantees market access and national treatment and any limitations that may be attached. Under national treatment, the state is only required to treat services equally if it has made a specific commitment to do so. This contrasts with goods where national treatment is applied once a product has crossed the border irrespective of whether the state has made a commitment to that sector. The sector-specific commitments are addressed in terms not only of the sector itself but also in terms of each mode of delivery and concern issues of market access and national treatment limitations. Market access commitments are made by reducing restrictions on the number of allowable service suppliers; the participation of foreign capital or the total value of foreign investment. These commitments should help ensure that foreign enterprises are treated no differently from indigenous firms.

In recognition of the differences between international trade in services and trade in goods, the GATS include a number of annexes that reflect the characteristics of services trade in specific sectors. The movement of natural persons does not apply to those seeking permanent employment or migration; the measures for financial services may be curtailed if states fear instability within their financial systems; the telecom measures seek to sustain the social aspects of the services and, as mentioned, air traffic rights are completely excluded from the agreements.

The GATS represents the beginning of the process of the liberalization of services. Indeed, the signing of the GATS agreement in the mid-1990s itself did not immediately result in a sharp push towards the liberalization of these sectors as the framework did little to extend liberalization beyond commitments already made by many states. In short, in many respects, the GATS reflected the status quo. However, states had given a commitment to proceed with the process of liberalization, both in agreed areas and in areas not covered (such as subsidies and public procurement), and to expand commitments in existing sectoral undertakings. Initial progress in market access was quite disappointing, merely reflecting the status quo and not pushing a liberal agenda. Developing countries were especially reluctant to commit themselves to anything other than standstill commitments.

The GATS rules are modest when placed alongside the GATT framework. The GATS is a framework agreement with special provisions negotiated for each sector with few attempts made to develop cross-sector rules or trade-offs. However, a generic approach has been attempted in several sectors. Overall, generic rather than sector-specific attempts are preferred where possible as they reduce negotiating effort; lead to the creation of discipline for all services rather than only the politically important ones, and reduce the potential for regulatory capture by special interest groups. Furthermore, a generic approach helps to ensure that the same criteria and policies are applied to different products and industries to address the same policy objective, thereby reducing the potential for distortions within resource allocation. Indeed, where there are objectives that relate to both goods and services, there is a case for developing generic rules that apply to both.

The impact of GATS depends upon the content of the specific commitments made by states. It is evident that states have only agreed to liberalize part of their services and that they maintain numerous measures that violate the principle of national treatment or market access. According to the World Bank, developed states have commitments covering 47.3 per cent of the total possible as compared to 16.2 per cent in less developed states (2007). This reflects the fact that the latter have made only limited commitments to liberalize their service sectors. Indeed, 25 per cent of developing states have agreed to liberalize only 3 per cent of their service sectors. This highlights the limited commitments within GATS and how much needs to be done in terms of liberalizing global trade in services. Enterprises seeking to sell services abroad, for example, have encountered numerous problems such as classification issues where some sectors may be too narrowly defined or dispersed among a host of sectors. Such uncertainty clearly limits the ability to trade in services.

Many of the more liberal states feel that the GATS is too vague and that the reach of the commitments within it fall short of their expectations. While the agreement is a step forward, it offers no indication of how these rules might evolve. Thus, it runs the risk of locking in protectionism and of failing to reflect the trend towards liberalization. Many states are concerned about 'maximizing' their own economic welfare in the short run with the result that many states are less liberal than hoped and few genuine concessions have been granted. The result is that regulatory fragmentation remains unresolved and states still have too much flexibility over their degree of and commitment to liberalization of services as well as discretion over the timing of these changes. The main impact of the GATS is that it includes a standstill promise in terms of protectionist policies towards services – that is, it contains a commitment not to introduce new distortions. When compared to regional integration agreements, the scope of the GATS agreement on services liberalization tends to be more limited. This suggests that these regional agreements can be a platform to push the liberalization process further forward.

The GATS has generally been successful in promoting trade in services as well as creating a healthier service environment within states. For both developed and developing states, services represent an increasing proportion of GDP. For OECD states, services exports accounted for over a quarter of all exports. In 2005, total services exports reached $1.9 trillion (compared to $6.6 trillion for merchandise exports). Thus services represent less than one-third of all exports. However, nearly three-quarters of all exports in services were from OECD states. The relatively minor role that services play in trade is in contrast to the contribution that services make within domestic economies. On average across OECD states, services contribute 70 per cent of value added. This reflects the aforementioned problems in trading services across borders. However, since 2000, trade in services has been growing at around 10 per cent per annum. The fastest growing service sectors of all were computer and information services and financial and insurance services. The slowest growers over the period were travel and construction.

Services are also growing in importance in developing states where they account for over 35 per cent of employment (compared to 70 per cent in developed states) with their share of GDP rising from 45 to 52 per cent. In addition, the share of services in developing countries trade has risen from 18 to 24 per cent between 1990 and 2005 with services exports growing at an annual growth rate of 8 per cent (2007). However, six states are responsible for over half of this trade (China, Hong Kong, India, Singapore, Korea and Turkey). Indeed, the top 15 developing country service exporters account for 80 per cent of all developing country services exports. Among the tradable service sectors, transport and other commercial services are both the largest and fastest growing categories. The growth in travel services has also halved over the period. This has been driven by shifts in the North American travel market. The major traders in services are the US, the UK and Germany. This reflects that services are the major source of growth within OECD states (see Table 7.7).

THE FUTURE OF THE GATS

The GATS contains a 'built-in' agenda with a work programme which reflects the fact that not all service-related negotiations could be concluded within the time frame established by the Uruguay Round. Under Article XIX of the GATS, states committed themselves to a new round of service liberalization by 2000 with the stated objective of pushing for further liberalization of services. Consequently, the GATS negotiations were only the first step in the liberalization process. Much of the need for a further round of trade liberalization within the service sector is based on the widely held belief that the commercial effects of the last round were in effect very modest. To many, the previous round amounted to little more than establishing the principal structure of future agreements. Many of the commitments within the GATS (excepting telecommunications and financial services) did little more than reaffirm the existing status quo in a limited a number of sectors. This may be explained by the novelty of the agreement and by the lack of experience of some states in the process of liberalizing services. Many states needed time to establish and develop the necessary regulations and to ensure that external liberalization is compatible with nationally defined objectives.

TABLE 7.7 World Exports of Commercial Services by Major Category, 2006

	Value (bn dollars)	Annual percentage change			
	2006	2000–06	2004	2005	2006
Commercial Services	2710	10	20	11	11
Transport	626	10	25	12	9
Travel	737	7	18	8	7
Other	1347	12	19	12	13

Source: WTO (2007).

Any new agreement requires states to press each other to increase the scope of the agreement in terms of depth of commitment and coverage. The aim is, as far as possible, to reduce discrimination within services trade. A further key challenge lies in encouraging developing states to expand their commitments within the GATS. Under the current system, only 25 per cent of all service activities have no limitations on market access or national treatment. For developing states as a whole, the figure is only 15 per cent and is even lower in some smaller developing states. In some areas, the commitment is less than the status quo, as many states have refrained from making the current situation binding. Efforts to expand coverage should be directed to those areas where there is the most evidence of efficiency gains and where economic growth can be bolstered. There is no a priori reason why there should not be specific commitments to cover all services and all modes of supply. Once this has been agreed, states need to concur on the nature of the binding agreement and the degree of liberalization and sectoral coverage.

A key theme for the Doha Round is to lock in reforms – a situation which is quite limited under the current regime. This will involve binding the status quo which, when coupled with reform, will provide a platform for significant expansion of national treatment and market access commitments. To encourage the participation of developing states and their integration into the global economy, there need to be efforts to liberalize those services essential to economic development. These include telecommunications, trade services, financial services and transport. If states can see tangible benefits from liberalization it will happen, and there will be reduced resistance to the expansion of the scope of policy. The experience of individual states in liberalizing and agreeing multilateral rules for the telecommunications sector bodes well for the possibility of further liberalization and more ambitious and successful negotiations next time around. With the liberalization of these sectors, states are able to see the economy-wide benefits derived from more efficient services and from greater market contestability. Furthermore, states have developed a sounder understanding of the GATS rules.

For the new GATS rounds to be credible and sustainable, they must be coupled with unilateral action at the member state or regional level. Member states need to recognize the strategic importance of key services to economic development and how the efficient and effective delivery of these services can enhance economic growth. Once this is realized, unilateral liberalization can be justified and used as a basis for increasing the liberalism of the domestic environment as a precursor to the opening up of the sectors to foreign enterprises. Along similar lines Low and Matoo (1999) argue that the new GATS round has to make specific improvements to the framework if it is to become a more effective method of liberalization. Recommended improvements centre around four themes:

- greater clarity in the agreement: existing ambiguities within the framework can stall the liberalization process;
- use of the existing structure to generate more effective liberalization: that is, shifting the emphasis towards more direct competition and dissuading the use of controlled foreign equity participation which may do little to increase the intensity of indigenous rivalry;
- deepening deregulation as a precursor to deeper international deregulation;
- improving the dynamics of negotiation through, for example, standardizing the commitments made by states.

These improvements seek to sustain the commitment to achieve a gradual deepening of the liberalization process and the development of new rules.

Negotiations on services are based on bilateral requests and on offers of specific commitments. These allow any state to choose what sectors and modes to open to competition. One result of this was that offers tended to be very poor and concentrated on mode three where states are trying to attract FDI but were weak in modes one and four. Thus the request-offer approach may need to be re-examined. Indeed, some developed states are calling for benchmarking to gauge levels of liberalization and to establish minimum levels. Some states support a plurilateral approach with groups of interested countries seeking to negotiate deeper agreements. These proposals have met resistance from developing states who fear they would shoulder the burden of adjustment.

The GATS is a flexible agreement that allows states to pick and choose the range and pace of liberalization. While this can be an impediment to success, it can also be a useful device for consensus building. The most pressing priority is to reduce the difference between applied policy and commitment.

The first phase of negotiations under the Doha Development Agenda was concluded in 2001 and sought to cover liberalization and rule making. However, progress has been slow, with member states disagreeing on whether liberalization is in fact desirable. This has been compounded by the difficulties arising from the complex nature of services transactions, and of distinguishing between the different modes and disputes between developed and developing states. A lot of requests have focused on mode one, especially within telecommunications and financial services. However, mode four which touches on migration has still proved controversial. Most states are seeking commitments in areas where they have a comparative advantage and not in those areas which are politically and economically sensitive.

A big challenge is to increase the transparency in prevailing policies. Progress has been slow in this area and there is uncertainty regarding how far the policy has developed. If the negotiations are surrounded by such vagueness, then reaching agreement will be difficult. This is not helped by the extensive coverage of the GATS and the fact that barriers to trade in services are difficult to identify.

THE 'CREDIT CRUNCH' AND GLOBAL TRADE

One of the more immediate side effects of the economic collapse of the early twenty-first century was a sharp reduction in global trade. The WTO estimated that in 2009, global trade fell by 9 per cent: the steepest drop since the Second World War and the first fall since 1982. This fall was caused by a combination of a collapse in global demand and an estimated shortfall of $100 billion in trade finance – a key facilitator of 90 per cent of global trade. These effects have not been confined to the larger, more open economies: the rise of 'vertical specialization' created by global supply chains (which means states specialize in particular steps in the production process rather than in particular products) has meant that the downturn has had a widespread impact.

The immediate policy response by the leading industrial states has been to seek to mitigate the national effects of the downturn by ratcheting up protectionist measures. By mid-2009, 17 of the G-20 had increased protectionism, usually in a covert fashion. In contrast to the 1930s, where protectionism was characterized by a rise in highly visible tariffs, only a few tariffs have been increased: many states have preferred to use tighter licensing requirements, import bans, anti-dumping duties and discriminatory procurement provisions. Global agreements are unlikely to be strong in limiting tariff growth, as applied rates within these agreements are often below the maximum allowed by WTO. This allows for increased tariffs with legal impunity.

However (and in a reflection of the aforementioned vertical specialization), some states (such as Brazil) have rejected protectionism: increased tariffs would raise their own domestic prices, making such measures self-defeating. The interest that states have in supply chains may also offer some insurance against protectionism. Manufacturers that rely upon imported inputs are likely to resist increases in tariffs that make domestic industry less competitive. This makes the benefits of tariff increases less easy to anticipate. Evidence suggests that it would not take a substantial increase in tariffs to cause the disintegration of these supply chains. However, this may be mitigated by falls in other costs and by management commitment to maintaining these arrangements.

The fact that economies are turning to the use of subsidies is reflective of the changing political economy of protectionism created by vertical specialization. For example, within the car industry, subsidies were estimated to amount to $48 billion in 2008/09 – 90 per cent of which was in developed economies. There is a danger that these forms of assistance will reduce the incentives for efficiency within global supply chains. This implies that states need to give a renewed emphasis to concluding the Doha Round to counteract these pressures. Some suggest that the world economy – given its difficulties – is not ready for the ambitions of this round. Thus as other chapters suggest, the appetite for further liberalization is likely to be limited in the short term.

CASE STUDY 7.3

South–South Trade

Historically, developing country trade was based on the export of primary commodities to developed states in exchange for imports of manufactures. This pattern of trade offered developing states little opportunity to achieve sustained economic growth. Commodity export sectors tend to be characterized by limited productivity potential and a comparatively low-income elasticity of demand. This was compounded by slackening growth in demand for primary products as developed economies shift towards service sectors. Limited market access has curtailed the ability of this export strategy to act as a source of growth for developing states.

Given these trends, many are looking towards south–south trade (i.e. trade between developing states) as an alternative to shield these states from increasingly erratic demand for commodity exports and to offer an opportunity for export diversifica-

tion. Much of the rise in south–south trade in the 1970s was driven by rising commodity prices which fell back in the 1980s. Any increases in intra-regional trade in manufactures during these decades were damaged by economic and financial crises.

The rise of the 'Asian Tigers' has given new hope that trade between developing states could offer fresh impetus to economic development. Indeed, since the mid-1980s three trends have become evident. First, there has been a dramatic rise in the value of manufactured exports from developing states. Second, developing states account for a rising proportion of global trade. Third, there has been a strong increase in intra-developing country trade, mainly among upper-middle- and lower-middle-income states. The level of intra-developing state trade involving low-income states remains low and is largely based on the exchange of raw materials and less on processed or financial goods. This position is compounded by the relatively high protectionist barriers imposed by the poorest developing economies.

In the 30 years to 2005, south–south exports rose from 25 per cent to 43 per cent of developing country trade and share of north–south trade fell from 69 per cent to 54 per cent. Much of this rise in south–south imports was driven by the rise of Southeast Asia and China as trading powers. These states now account for nearly two-thirds of global imports (up from 20 per cent in the mid-1960s). There is a similar pattern with exports where these states now account for almost half of global exports (up from 8 per cent in the mid-1960s). This trend has been especially evident within manufacturers and has been accompanied by an increase in the developing countries' share of world trade which – by 2005 – accounted for around one-third.

As suggested, the major driver of the rising export performance of developing states has varied across these economies. For example, in East Asia, manufactures rather than primary products have been a [...] formance. Furthermore, [...] a percentage of total [...] have risen to 40 per cent [...] r in the 1970s). This has [...] ors:

[...] between these states [...] n in the 1980s;
[...] these states follow more [...] relopment strategies.

[...] ost important reason for [...] –south trade has been a [...] rs:

[...] h differential between [...] ing states: for example, in [...] ne new millennium the [...] ing states were more than [...] ped economies.

[...] pidly growing developing countries: the newly industrializing economies, India and China, account for 20 per cent of world income and 40 per cent of total world population.

* The increasing importance of intra-regional specialization and production sharing: firms are exploiting inter-regional differences to develop more effective production systems.

A notable trend has been the sharp rise in exports from Korea and Malaysia to China, fuelled by an increase of Chinese exports to the US generating a demand for goods from their near neighbours. This highlights the fact that the level of south–south trade is dependent on the level of demand for developing country goods by major developed economies and that, as China reduces its reliance on inputs from other developing states, so the level of south–south trade will fall. This reflects potential limits to south–south trade as eight of the top ten exporters of manufactured exports to other developing states are based in Asia.

There is a vast difference in the reliance of developing countries on other developing states for exports. This figure tends to be highest for land-locked states (for example, 80 per cent for Paraguay). Other states export a low level of goods to other developing states: for example, only 5 per cent of Mexico's exports go to other developing states. South–south trade tends to be lower where there is preferential trade access to developed states (for example, Mexico's membership of NAFTA) or where there is reliance on a single export item. Export trends can vary markedly. There are also marked differences over trends: states such as Nigeria have seen their exports to other developing states more than triple over the past decade whereas others (such as Mexico) have seen exports to developing states fall by almost a half. Overall, south–south trade is of more importance to states in Africa and Latin and Central American than it is for those in Asia.

While south–south trade has reduced dependency upon primary exports, the rise of the Asian powerhouses has increased commodity prices and may offer the poorest performing developing states opportunities to diversify their economic base. Trade between developing states is also a means of overcoming the limited growth potential of developed states and of spreading risk across many trading partners. Developing countries therefore need to put policy measures into place that tap into fast-growing emerging markets. However, many developing states still rely on selling commodities and primary products to these states and there are thus limited opportunities to reduce exposure to the price volatility of commodities. Moreover, the OECD suggests that trade barriers remain more important for south–south trade than for other intra-group flows. Indeed, the average tariffs on merchandise imports into developing states are estimated to be three times higher than for north–north trade.

CASES STUDY QUESTIONS

1. How do you account for the rise of south–south trade?

2. To what extent is south–south trade a credible route for economic development?

3. How might south–south trade be encouraged?

CONCLUSION

The past decade has seen a material shift in the form and nature of international trade. One of the most evident changes has been the increased importance of trade in services which, however, remains stifled by trade restrictions. There has also been a persistent loosening up of merchandise trade as states have lowered tariff barriers in this domain. However, persistent problems remain within merchandise trade given the ongoing protection offered to 'sensitive' sectors such as agriculture.

Summary of Key Concepts

■ The post-war environment has been characterized by a sharp rise in merchandise trade.
■ In more recent times this has been coupled with a sharp rise in trade in services.
■ Some sectors are immune from these trends as they remain heavily protected.
■ Shifts in technology and the source of value (especially with regard to knowledge) have created new challenges to the global trading regime.

Activity

Using the example of a sector with which you are familiar, identify the major challenges to free and fair trade within it.

Discussion Questions

1. How relevant is the concept of comparative advantage to the modern economy?

2. Is protectionism ever justified?

3. Why has the liberalization of textiles and clothing been so difficult?

4. Should trade in agriculture be fully liberalized?

References and Suggestions for Further Reading

Alemanno, A. (2007) *Trade in Food: Regulatory and Judicial Approaches in the EC and the WTO*, London: Cameron May.

Barton, J., Goldstein, J., Josling, T. and Steinberg, R. (2008) *Evolution of the Trade Regime: Politics, Law and Economics of the GATT and the WTO*, Princeton, NJ: Princeton University Press.

Deardorff, A. (2001) 'International provision of trade services, trade and fragmentation', *Review of International Economics*, Vol. 9, No. 2, 233–248.

Findlay, C. and Warren, T. (eds) (2000) *Impediments to Trade in Services*, London: Routledge.

Hoda, A. and Gulati, A. (2007) *WTO Negotiations on Agriculture and Developing Countries*, Baltimore, MD: Johns Hopkins University Press.

Krajewski, M. (2003) *National Regulation and Trade Liberalization in Services*, The Hague, London and New York: Kluwer Law International.

Langhammer, R. (2000) *Developing Countries as Exporters of Services*, Kiel: Kiel Institute of World Economics, Working Paper No. 992.

Low, P. and Matoo, A. (1999) 'Is there a better way? Alternative approaches to liberalization under the GATS', Discussion Paper presented at Brookings Institute 'Services 2000' Conference.

Marrewijk, C. (2002) *International Trade and the World Economy*, Oxford: Oxford University Press.

Maskus, K. (2000) 'Intellectual property issues for the new round', in Schott, J. (ed.), *The WTO after Seattle*, Washington, DC: The Peterson Institute for International Economics.

OECD (1998) *Food Security and Agricultural Trade*, Working Paper, TD/TC/WS (98)105, Paris: OECD.

OECD (2001a) *The Uruguay Round Agreement on Agriculture*, Working Paper, Paris: OECD.

OECD (2001b) *Open Services Markets Matter*, Working Paper, TD/TC/WP(2001)24, Paris: OECD.

Pohl, N., Sauvé, P. and Panizzon, M. (eds) (2008) *GATS and the Regulation of International Trade in Services*, Cambridge: Cambridge University Press.

Porter, M. (1990) *The Competitive Advantage of Nations*, Basingstoke: Macmillan.

Stewart, T. (2002) *Rules in a Rules-based WTO*, Ardsley, NY: Transnational Publishers.

Thongpakde, N. and Pupphavesa, W. (2003) 'Returning textiles and clothing to GATT disciplines', in Martin, W. and Pangestu, M. (eds), *Options for Global Trade Reform: A View from the Asia Pacific*, Cambridge: Cambridge University Press.

Tucker, K. and Sundberg, M. (1988) *International Trade in Services*, London: Routledge.

UNCTAD (2000) *GATS 2000: Options for Developing States*, Working Paper, Geneva: UNCTAD.

World Trade Organization – www.wto.org.

Chapter 8

International Investment

If GE's strategy of investment in China is wrong, it represents a loss of a billion dollars, perhaps a couple of billion dollars. If it is right, it is the future of this company for the next century.

Jack Welch (1935–), Chairman and CEO of General Electric, 1981–2001

LEARNING OBJECTIVES

This chapter will help you to:

- differentiate between foreign direct and indirect investment
- identify the major drivers of FDI
- understand the impact of FDI on host and home economies
- comprehend the risks associated with FDI
- identify the main policy challenges posed by international investment

A core driver of the globalization of economies is international investment. While earlier chapters have already noted the flows of assets across borders, investment represents a stock of international assets over which the firm has some degree of control. Thus investment is based on the acquisition of an asset in a non-domestic location which an economic agent holds in expectation of an anticipated return. Central to these actions is the assessment by the agent of the risk attached to the acquisition of such an asset. Convention stresses that investors will seek to strike a trade-off between risks and return within investment holdings. Thus riskier investments require higher returns to mitigate for the extra risk undertaken. This chapter divides international investment into two subcategories:

- Foreign portfolio (or indirect) investment (i.e. investment in non-domestic financial instruments).
- Foreign direct investment (i.e. direct investment in the productive capacity of a foreign country).

This chapter will examine both of these investments but the focus is overwhelmingly on the latter owing to its role in internationalization, MNE activity and trade patterns.

FOREIGN INDIRECT INVESTMENT (FII)

FII is undertaken by individuals, firms or public bodies in the form of investments in overseas foreign financial instruments such as government/corporate bonds, foreign stocks which are denominated in the host country's national currency. Unlike FDI, FII does not imply control by the investor over the assets. Such investments are also likely to be only one component of a portfolio of overseas assets held by an investor. Portfolio theory suggests that the composition of the portfolio is driven by a desire to acquire the highest possible risk-adjusted return. This implies that the firm will hold assets with more stable returns than assets yielding higher but more unstable returns. Integral to portfolio investment is the financial risk undertaken by the firm. The role of the investor is to manage the portfolio so that its variability is less than the sum of its parts.

As the financial performance of assets across markets starts to become increasingly correlated, the central premise of international portfolio investment starts to unravel (i.e. the firm will spread risk/return across space). Thus, in seeking to balance risk and return within the portfolio, investors are increasingly turning towards diversification of portfolios based less on geography and more on sectoral or industrial preferences. However, as economic growth patterns differ between states, investment funds and other investors seek to buy assets where returns (subject to risk) are likely to be greatest.

The scope for FII has increased as financial integration has increased (see Chapter 11). Changes in regulatory regimes as well as improvements in technology have not only increased the flow of finance across borders but have also increased the stock of financial assets held by overseas investors. Thus the ability to invest aligned with increased competition for funds has resulted in rapid growth in flows as well as in stocks of assets, especially in emerging markets. Investment patterns are also driven by the demographic differences between the more developed economies which seek private capital accumulation and the developing states' needs for higher levels of investment. Consequently, FII is driven by the perceived advantages of engaging in this form of international investment, namely:

- *Participation in growth markets*: this allows investors to take a stake in fast-growing economies via the purchase of securities in foreign capital markets. This has been especially true of emerging markets where investors have been rewarded with substantial growth. However, these markets (as experience has shown) can be risky – both politically and economically, though much of this risk is already reflected within asset prices. This caveat is compounded by the persistence of barriers to investment in some high-growth locations.
- *Hedging of the consumption basket*: investors are also consumers of real goods and services and they can use international investment to hedge price swings by owning overseas assets.
- *International portfolio diversification*: firms use investment to lower overall risk exposure and to ensure that risks are diversified across the chosen sectors.
- *Market segmentation*: investors are able to segment the market in order to mitigate risk and/or increase returns.

However, the ability to realize these benefits has to be set against the unique risks and institutional constraints faced by FII in the form of exchange and political risks. In the former case, fluctuations in currency can completely erode the value of the financial investment made. The precise degree of risk across the portfolio of assets depends upon its composition. Linked with this are country risks, including transfer risks (restrictions on capital flows); operational risks (constraints on management and corporate activity); and ownership control risks (where constraints are imposed by government policies on management discretion). Either singularly or in combination, these factors have the potential to affect the return on investments. Political risks also include a default risk according to which government actions and broad socioeconomic uncertainty can lead to uncertain returns on government-based bonds. This confers heightened importance on the quality of information available to an investor prior to making the financial commitment.

Institutional constraints are generally government-imposed and include taxes, foreign exchange controls and capital market controls. These constraints are compounded in some countries by weak or non-existent laws protecting the rights of minority stockholders, lack of regulation of insider trading or simply inadequate rules regarding the disclosure of information. However, these constraints can be an incentive to invest for those able to overcome them, as they segment the market. Tax rates and methods differ markedly between states and these also offer direct incentives for FII. For example, tax is only paid on overseas assets in the UK when the profits are repatriated, thereby creating an incentive to ensure wealth is kept 'offshore'. Indeed, the creation and lure of tax havens (see Case Study 8.1) is often made more attractive by confidentiality rules that protect the identity of investors – a factor which not only encourages tax avoidance but which can also run counter to effective control of criminal activities. In addition, withholding tax can act as a prominent barrier where tax is levied on investors in other states. These are imposed in lieu of income taxes and can often be reclaimed against income within their home state. Other investment barriers include the transaction costs of buying overseas assets (which tend to be higher than for domestic assets) and the degree of familiarity with foreign markets.

CASE STUDY 8.1

Dubai Ports World (DPW) and US Ports

In early 2006, DPW acquired P&O (a UK-based ports operator). DPW was owned by the government of Dubai and already had substantial ports operations, mainly within the Middle East. Indeed, by 2005, DPW was the sixth largest port operator globally, a position secured by an aggressive acquisition spree. P&O was attractive to DPW as its acquisition would strengthen its competitive position and would add port operations to its portfolio to complement existing assets, notably by adding terminal facilities in China and the US. The five US ports (Baltimore, Miami, New Jersey/New York, New Orleans and Philadelphia) were not a significant part of the P&O portfolio but they were important to DPW, as they represented its first foray into the strategically important US market.

However, this part of the acquisition proved to be politically controversial. The deal was brought to the attention of Congress by representatives of Eller and Company, a Florida-based partner of P&O which felt that the acquisition would make it an involuntary partner of DPW. This alerted politicians who honed in on the ownership of DPW. As soon as the deal was approved, concerns were raised by US politicians who felt that foreign ownership of ports was incompatible with issues of homeland security. Many believed that the UAE had too many links to radical Islam to be trusted with the operation of critical infrastructure. Throughout the first quarter of 2006, these concerns spread as security issues rang bells with an increasingly diverse set of stakeholders, despite the fact that the deal had presidential approval. In order to allay any concerns, DPW itself asked for a 45-day investigation by US regulators.

Defenders of the deal argued that the opposition to it failed to differentiate between Dubai/UAE and other Arab states that were more hostile to the US. Many blamed this naive categorization on the Bush government which – by declaring war in Iraq – had lumped all Arabs together in the mind of the public. However, by March 2006, DWP had backed down

and agreed to transfer US-based assets to a US entity – AIG. However, the longer-term damage created by the affair is difficult to assess. Many in the UAE felt offended by their categorization as terrorists or terrorist sympathizers. This belied a very moderate stance towards Western economies and influence and, indeed, the UAE remains a key ally in the US government's 'War on Terror'. However, in the 12 months after the crisis, UAE investment into the US fell by over $1 billion.

This resistance to foreign ownership runs counter to prevailing trends within the US where foreign ownership of terminal facilities is common. By 2006, 66 per cent of US international trade flowed through foreign-owned US ports. However, post-2001, ports were seen as a weak spot in homeland security as only 5 per cent of all containers entering the US were searched. Furthermore, any attempts to secure funding for port security had always met political resistance. By March 2006, lawmakers had introduced 21 bills which sought (in differing ways) to limit the acquisition of US-based assets. Most were broadly based attempts to limit the potential for foreign ownership, leasing, management or operation of US ports. These were broadly based attempts by the US to protect its critical infrastructure and to remove any vulnerability caused by foreign ownership. As a result of this pressure, a bill was eventually passed to give increased power of scrutiny of acquisitions of critical infrastructure.

DPW felt it was the victim of the political cycle. It alluded to the fact that, paradoxically, it is a major partner of the US government's Secure Freight Initiative and that DPW is protecting the US from the very threat it was said to pose. In addition, it felt that the outcry ignored the increasingly global nature of the maritime industry and that is was operations (not outright ownership) that were being exchanged. Furthermore, it is the port owner, the coast guard and the Department of Homeland Security, not the operator, which is responsible for security and also for the location where containers are loaded on to the ship.

CASE STUDY QUESTIONS

1. Why has the acquisition of P&O by Dubai Ports proved so controversial?

2. What are the long-term implications of this case?

CASE STUDY 8.2

Tax Havens

Tax havens have proved one of the more controversial aspects of MNE activity and of globalization generally. While the details of the definition of tax havens vary, all definitions speak of locations where certain tax rates are low or non-existent. These favourable tax regimes are often accompanied by secrecy. According to the OECD, tax havens are characterized by three factors:

1. No or only nominal taxes are levied on non-residents to enable them to escape high taxes within their country of residence.
2. The protection of personal financial information to prevent scrutiny from overseas tax authorities.
3. A lack of transparency in relation to legal, legislative or administrative provisions to prevent other tax authorities from applying their rules effectively.

Despite imperfections, the above is the best working definition, as it captures all the small tax havens, although it excludes larger states such as the US and UK which have some tax haven features.

Tax havens have been heavily criticized as they are often used as a home for the proceeds of criminal activity. They also allow the wealthy to hide the true extent of their wealth from the communities in which they reside. These locations are also contrary to the underpinning principles of taxation, namely equity, fairness, transparency and proportionality. Global tax revenues lost to tax havens can be as high as $225 billion per year and the collective holdings of tax havens are between $5–7 trillion, around 7 per cent of the total wealth under management (2007). Between 1982 and 2003, tax havens enjoyed growth double the global average between 1982 and 2003 and some did even better; Bermuda has become the richest state in the world based on GDP per capita (2007).

While tax havens are nothing new, their prominence has increased as globalization has matured. Many states have become increasingly concerned about issues of equity and fairness as well as seeking to avoid unfair tax competition, something which has concerned the OECD. Tax havens are especially attractive for MNEs which do not require a specific geographical location or an extensive labour set-up within these locations. These locations are also attractive for financial intermediaries (such as mutual funds, banking) which collect funds within the low tax location and lend the money back into the high tax state.

To counter the tax competition effects of these locations (and to mitigate any losses in revenue), many high-tax states have established legislation to counteract tax shelters by:

- attributing income and gains of the company (or trust) in the tax haven to a taxpayer in the high-tax location on a case-by-case basis;
- the standardization of transfer pricing rules;
- reductions on deductibility or the imposition of a withholding tax when payments are made to offshore recipients;
- the taxation of receipts from the entity within the tax haven;
- the use of exit charges or the taxing of unrealized capital gains when an individual or trust emigrates.

Despite these methods and the risk of acquiring pariah status, many states have large incentives to use tax haven status to increase local budgets and encourage investment within their territory. These measures have been supported by Tax Information Exchange Agreements between tax havens and large states. These are bilateral agreements that allow for cooperation on tax matters.

The early years of the new millennium have seen a renewed effort by many leading industrial states to clamp down more aggressively on tax avoidance via tax havens. It is estimated that EU states lost £77 billion tax revenue to tax havens in 2007. Consequently, European countries are more actively pursuing tax havens. The German pursuit of its residents using Lichtenstein as a tax haven demonstrates that large governments are going to make life increasingly difficult for these states. Tax havens regarded as 'uncooperative' are coming under intense political pressure from large states. The UK and Germany have used the case of Lichtenstein to start a broader crackdown on tax havens, especially in relation to secrecy where the issues are tax avoidance and criminal activities. These large states want increased cooperation with tax havens to open their systems to scrutiny by overseas tax authorities. Pressure is also coming from the US which has introduced the 'Stop Tax Haven Abuse' Act. Overall, political pressure is pushing the less transparent states to open up their activities.

Many tax havens are small states (often once part of Britain) which are attracted to the sophisticated businesses that emerge from a favourable tax system.

This process often suited the UK (as these protectorates became independent) as well as the states themselves which were able to find a more stable source of income than tourism or primary products. Aside from their often small size, tax havens are also characterized by good governance with sound legal systems, low corruption and effective checks and balances on governments. This may explain why so many ex-UK colonies are tax havens. However, being a tax haven has become increasingly difficult: not only has competition increased but so have the costs of regulatory compliance and political pressure from high-tax states.

Alongside tax avoidance, the other major concern regarding tax havens is tax competition. Tax competition compels states to lower tax rates to either encourage resource inflows or to inhibit resource outflows. However, high-tax states have extensive welfare systems to support which inhibits their ability to freely adjust tax rates to mitigate any flows. Thus, the ability of small states to use tax haven status to attract funds potentially not only erodes revenue bases but also undermines welfare systems. This suggests that there is a limit to tax competition. High-tax states see tax havens as distorting and without sound economic justification. Others, however, see tax havens as positive because they push states to undertake tax reform. The big risk is that open competition would create a 'race to the bottom', but many large states are able to resist tax competition and there is little evidence of such a race taking place.

It has been argued that tax havens can have indirect benefits for non-havens. These can occur through two channels. First, through value-adding inputs into the production process via their activities in the haven. Second, nearby tax havens can lower domestic tax bills and thus make the high-tax state more attractive to investment. Thus tax havens and non-havens can be mutually supportive. This may explain why many governments do little to close these havens. The existence of such tax havens deters flight but keeps high-spending, high-value-adding businesses within these locations.

A big problem in trying to control the use of tax havens by companies is that tax systems are based on national boundaries whereas MNEs are not. MNEs seek to maximize profits so they will base themselves in the lowest cost/tax location. To MNEs, this is a natural response to the threat of global competition. The logical course of action is to harmonize national tax systems but this is unlikely. The best option is containment of the negative aspects of tax havens through less secrecy and the targeting of criminal activity. Tax reform within developed states may also remove the attraction of tax havens.

CASES STUDY QUESTIONS

1. To what extent is tax competition harmful to the global economy?

2. What are the major problems posed by the existence of tax havens?

3. Is it fair to argue that the existence of tax havens runs contrary to the basic tenets of a fair taxation system?

Table 8.1 differentiates between direct and indirect channels for FII. Direct channels, as implied, involve the investor dealing directly with a broker to purchase specific assets. This may be done either in the host country or within the investor's country of domicile. Indirect channels reflect the complexity of the process of purchase as well as information concerns. This means that investors may decide to invest in overseas markets by buying assets issued or traded within their home state. This could involve purchase of MNE assets which offer a foreign portfolio by virtue of the firm's strategies. International mutual funds will be attractive to smaller investors.

Table 8.2 sets out the major holders of international assets and liabilities across the global economy. There is a high degree of continuity across both elements, with the US and UK the leading holders

TABLE 8.1 The Major Channels for FII

Direct
- purchase of foreign securities in foreign markets
- purchase of foreign securities in the domestic market

Indirect
- equity-linked Eurobonds
- purchase of shares of MNEs
- international mutual funds

TABLE 8.2 Global FII – Portfolio Investment: Top Ten Economies by Size of Holdings (end of 2005)

Assets	Liabilities
1. United States	1. United States
2. United Kingdom	2. United Kingdom
3. Japan	3. Germany
4. France	4. France
5. Luxembourg	5. Netherlands
6. Germany	6. Japan
7. Ireland	7. Luxembourg
8. Netherlands	8. Italy
9. Italy	9. Cayman Islands
10. Switzerland	10. Spain

Source: IMF (2006).

of both assets and liabilities. By the end of 2005, the total value of investment assets/liabilities held by these states was nearly $26 billion. The only apparent aberration in this table are Switzerland, Luxembourg and the Cayman Islands, but their appearance is due to the special tax and other institutional arrangements available in these locations (see Case Study 8.1).

FOREIGN DIRECT INVESTMENT (FDI)

FDI is where the MNE invests directly in production or other facilities over which it has effective control in a host economy. The modal choice made by the MNE represents the degree of control desired by the firm relative to the cost and risk of undertaking such a measure (see Chapters 9 and 10). Whereas exporting – as a form of market entry, for example – is seen as a low-risk, low-control option, FDI is the polar opposite. However, as the steps model suggests (see Chapter 9), FDI exists across a spectrum of entry modes. Thus FDI may not always result in effective control, depending on the nature of the joint venture or strategic alliance. Control is total only when the investment takes the form of an acquisition, a stand-alone, wholly owned subsidiary or a greenfield project.

It is useful to distinguish between the flow of FDI and the stock of FDI. The flow of FDI refers to the amount of FDI undertaken over a specific time period and represents flows in or out of a country, whereas the stock of FDI refers to the total accumulated value of non-domestically owned assets at a given point in time in a particular country. Furthermore, FDI can be categorized according to its motives. Horizontal FDI is where the firm invests in an overseas location to produce the same product it produces in other markets. This form of FDI is driven by a desire to serve the local market better and often involves the duplication of resources across multiple markets as a means of reducing the cost of market supply. This assumes that the cost of horizontal FDI is lower than the cost of exporting as a market strategy. Thus horizontal FDI is more common in larger markets where economies of scale are greater. Vertical FDI is where the firm invests in a foreign market to reconfigure its value chain as a means of injecting new inputs and greater efficiency into the production process. This form of FDI is normally export orientated, often to the MNE's home market, and is often unresponsive to the size of the host market. Thus, where different parts of the value chain require inputs which vary in price across states, vertical FDI will be stimulated.

The Determinants of FDI

Many of the theories explaining why FDI occurs are addressed elsewhere (see Chapters 9 and 10). Early perspectives stressed the existence of relative factor endowments (Mundell, 1957) as a core driver of FDI, especially where there is a division between capital-rich and capital-poor states. In the presence of limited barriers to trade and migration, FDI is attracted towards low GDP and low-wage economies. However, this approach offers only a limited perspective on the motives for FDI.

At the microeconomic level, many determinants of FDI are linked into process models of internationalization. Alongside the Uppsala model (described in detail in Chapters 9 and 10), microeconomic explanations have centred on the product life cycle and industrial organization-based theories. The former explains the shift in production in terms of the maturity of the product concerned. This assumes that FDI becomes more common when the product is at a mature stage of its life cycle and goes into decline. This is symptomatic of domestic market saturation and of commoditization of the product. Industrial organization theories stress that FDI (notably horizontal FDI) is driven by the existence of firm-specific advantages (see Chapter 9). Vertical FDI is driven more by the avoidance of oligopolistic uncertainty.

At the macroeconomic level, the following variables are seen as important:

- *Exchange rates*: there is assumed to be a negative relationship between FDI and the value of the exchange rate. Currency shifts reflect directly upon the earning capacity of overseas assets. As the exchange rate of a host economy rises, so the stock of FDI within that economy diminishes. Alongside the absolute value of the exchange rate, variability will also be an important determinant of FDI.
- *Economic growth*: the rate of growth within the host economy is also important and generally has a positive relationship with the level of FDI. Relative growth rates rather than growth rates per se are key when determining how resources are to be deployed globally.
- *Market size*: the size of the host economy has a generally positive effect on the level of FDI. Indeed, many studies have indicated that market size is the most influential factor on FDI. Market size influences exploitation of scale economies and standard factor specialization, allowing for cost minimization and market growth.
- *Stage of economic development*: the more developed a state, the better the level of infrastructure and the more able the state will be to generate wider agglomeration effects.
- *Human capital*: for labour-intensive and export-orientated FDI, the quality and quantity of human capital is pivotal. Thus, as more capital is employed and more labour is trained, the attractiveness of FDI is sustained.
- *Agglomeration economies*; the presence of other firms, industries and labour acts as an incentive to invest.
- *Governmental policies (see below)*: many governments consider FDI an important antidote to rising and high unemployment and introduce policies to encourage FDI. These can take the form of tax incentives, subsidies, regulation and privatization. Tax is especially important when subsidiary revenues are subject to both host and home country taxes. Linked to these concerns is the quality of the institutions (especially in developing states) which provide legal protection, transaction costs and the supporting infrastructure.
- *Liberality of the trade regime*: there is assumed to be a positive relationship between FDI and a liberal trade regime. This is related to factors such as liberalization of foreign ownership, privatization and financial deregulation. The more open a market, the less the MNE has to use horizontal FDI to circumvent trade barriers.

In addition to the above, there are other FDI determinants such as the degree of openness, labour costs, privatization, trade linkages and borders, risk and macroeconomic stability and so on. Table 8.3 offers an extensive list of the major host country determinants across three major categories.

It is becoming increasingly evident that the major conventional determinant of FDI (the size of national markets) has decreased in importance as globalization has matured. At the same time, cost differentials between locations, the quality of infrastructure, the ease of doing business and the

TABLE 8.3 Host Country Determinants of FDI

Economic conditions	■ *Markets*: size, income, income distribution and levels and growth prospects; access to regional markets; distribution and demand patterns.
	■ *Resources*: natural resources; location.
	■ *Competitiveness*: labour availability, costs, skills, trainability; managerial technical skills, access to inputs, physical infrastructure; supplier base; technology support.
Host country policies	■ *Macro policies*: management of crucial macro variables; ease of remittance; access to foreign exchange.
	■ *Private sector*: promotion of private ownership; clear and stable policies; easy entry/exit policies; efficient financial markets; other support.
	■ *Trade and industry*: trade strategy; regional integration and access to markets; ownership controls; competition policies; support for SMEs.
	■ *FDI policies*: ease of entry; ownership incentives; access to inputs; transparent and stable policies.
MNE strategies	■ *Risk perception*: perceptions of country risk based on political factors; macro management, labour markets, policy stability.
	■ Location sourcing, integration transfer: company strategies on location, sourcing of products/inputs, integration of affiliates, strategic alliances, training, technology.

Source: Lall (1997).

availability of skills have become increasingly important. Traditional economic determinants such as natural resources, low labour costs and the size of the market protected from export competition also remain important but the relative importance of location determinants for competitiveness enhancing FDI is shifting. Firms are seeking a competitive advantage based on a combination of wages, skills and productivity when deciding on the location of FDI. The emergence of regional markets is also important and, in some cases, these are superseding national markets as important FDI determinants. This depends on how well the state is integrated into the regional bloc in terms of policy harmonization and physical accessibility.

The Impact of FDI

The conventional assumption is that the main beneficiaries of the increase in the level of FDI are the recipient/host economies. However, this understates the extent to which home economies can also benefit from outward flows of FDI. This is especially true for developing states where investment is in states with higher levels of economic development. The major impacts upon home and host economies are outlined below.

Impact upon Home Economies

The impact upon the home economy of FDI is manifold but perhaps the most important relates to competitiveness benefits. The positive impact depends largely on the consequent improved performance of the outward investing firm and on whether the FDI leads to improved competitiveness across other industries and throughout the economy as a whole. The latter clearly depends on ripple effects from MNEs to other businesses. This can translate into broader benefits for the home economy if improvements in the performance of the capital-exporting sectors feed through into industrial transformation, the upgrading of value-added activities, improved export performance, higher national income and improved employment opportunities.

Alternatively, outward FDI represents risks for the home economy. These outflows can reduce domestic investment, create balance of payments problems and lower additions to home capital stock, a 'hollowing-out' of parts of the economy and loss of jobs. The net effect of these benefits and costs of outward FDI depends on the underlying motives for the investment strategies followed by the investor and the characteristics of the home economy.

Impact upon the Host Economies

No matter from where it is sourced, FDI impacts upon the host economy's welfare, development and growth in a number of ways. First, the investment increases the productive capability of the economy through investment in capital and labour. Second, the MNE will invest in the development of local networks within the host to supply inputs and offer distribution channels for outputs. These have the potential to stimulate production in supplier and distribution firms within the host and can operate as a channel for technology transfer. Third, affiliates of the MNE can create local spillover (albeit indirect) effects on local firms through stimulating an improvement in the performance of local firms. Finally, there are potential increases in employment and income driven by FDI, which can be further enhanced by multiplier effects. However, employment effects and other benefits can be offset if the FDI results in the crowding out of domestic industry. Overall, the extent and nature of these effects directly derives from the scale of the initial FDI; the technology used; the number of people employed; the training and wages offered; the market organization of affiliates; the extent to which affiliates buy goods and services locally, and the ratio of profits reinvested. All of these factors are compounded by the state of the host economy.

The form and nature of these benefits is a reflection of the state of the development of both host and home economies. Many of these benefits are clearly of more relevance to developing economies but this is not to deny that developed economies can benefit from being both FDI recipients and investors. If the benefits are real, they undermine the traditional notion of restricting trade and limiting the intensity of competition as a motive of economic policy. Protection, even if it results in no reciprocal measures, can still harm an economy by denying its actors access to resources that can aid its competitiveness.

Trends in FDI

As might be expected with the progressive onset of globalization, FDI stocks and flows have risen markedly over the past two decades, a trend which is common to all major groups of countries (developed, developing and transition: see Table 8.4). This persistent rise in FDI reflects strong economic growth and performance across the global economy, leading to rising corporate profits (and rising share prices) that have boosted FDI levels, especially mergers and acquisitions. There has also been a sharp rise in the number of greenfield investment projects. This has been especially notable within developing states where, by 2007, FDI inflows accounted for half of all net capital flows (Figure 8.1).

After peaking in the late 1990s, FDI (as measured by the number of cross-border M&As and total global inflows) started to rise again. The rise in FDI was driven by rising investor confidence on the back of lower operational risks across major investor markets. For example, the number of cross-border M&As valued at over $1 billion reached a peak of 175 in 2000 (up from 14 in 1987): this fell back to 56 in 2003 before rising to 172 in 2006. This rise has been driven by improving financing conditions. One notable trend has been a switch towards cash-based investment away from acquisitions based on the exchange of shares. This has been enabled by the petro-cash available to West Asian states and to the high rates of foreign exchange available to states such as China.

Outward FDI stocks have been on an upward trajectory for the past 25 years. By 2006, it was estimated that 73 million workers globally were employed within foreign affiliates, representing a threefold increase since 1990 and 3 per cent of the total global workforce. By 2006, overseas affiliates of MNEs accounted for 10 per cent of world GDP. Between 1982 and 2006, the level of employment within subsidiaries rose at a slower rate which suggests that FDI stocks and the gross product of foreign affiliates are shifting towards more capital- and knowledge-intensive production (see Table 8.4).

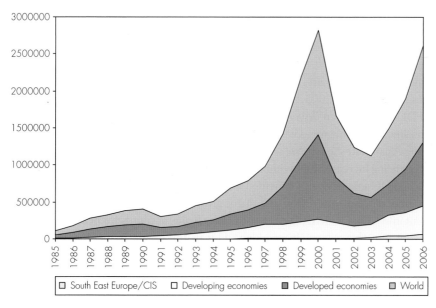

FIGURE 8.1
FDI, 1985–2006
($mn)

Source: UNCTAD
(2007).

TABLE 8.4 FDI Stock (Measured by Value at Current Prices) ($bn)

	1982	1990	2005	2006
Inward FDI stock	637	1779	10 048	11 999
Outward FDI stock	627	1815	10 579	12 474

Source: UNCTAD (2007).

The geographic pattern of FDI has changed in various ways over the past decade. Most evident has been the emergence of new states, especially from the developing world, as both host and home economies. Nevertheless, in 2005, two of the three largest bilateral FDI relationships were between two states – the US and the UK: the UK has a FDI stock worth $282 billion in the US whereas the US maintained FDI stock valued at $234 billion within the UK. The second largest relationship was between Hong Kong and China. Of the top 50 bilateral FDI relationships, 41 were between developed countries only. The rest mainly involved either China and/or Hong Kong. These figures suggest that there is a strong correlation between proximity and bilateral FDI relations.

The most important trend in the sectoral and industrial distribution of FDI has been the shift towards services. This has been accompanied by a decline in the share of FDI in natural resources and manufacturing. By 2005, investment stock in the primary sector was less than 10 per cent of the total while manufacturing accounted for around 30 per cent of FDI stock. This represented an 11 per cent drop since 1990 whereas the figure for the primary sector was only marginally lower in 2005 than in 1990. In 2005, services represented 61 per cent of global FDI stock – up from 49 per cent in 1990. Under the direct influence of China, the flow of FDI into the primary sector has increased and accounted for 12 per cent of FDI flows in 2005. The sectoral breakdown of investment varies between developed and developing states. In developing and transition states, there tends to be a higher total of inward FDI stock than in developed economies. This has been especially high, and is rising in the mining and petroleum industries.

A notable trend, especially over the past decade, has been the emergence of developing states as host and home locations for FDI. Since 2005, Africa, for example, has managed to attract historically high levels of inward FDI. This has been driven by a number of factors, particularly high and rising commodity prices. In no small part, this trend has increased south–south FDI, most notably the rising levels of FDI by emerging Asian states in Africa (see Case Study 5.1). Consequently Africa is bucking the global trend by experiencing increased FDI within the primary sector. For different reasons, south, east and Southeast Asia and Oceania have also benefited from substantial inflows of FDI. This process has been driven by the emergence of this region as a major growth pole. Inflows into the region are dominated by investment into China which, together with Hong Kong, accounts for nearly two-thirds of the investment flowing into this region. Increasingly, FDI in the region is moving away from manufacturing and towards services and high technology. Certainly in terms of FDI via acquisitions, investment in service activity is dominant. However, many manufacturing investments are greenfield investments. Trends in the Middle East have been dominated by shifts in oil and gas prices: as these have risen, FDI into and out of this region has followed. These strong growth trends have not been as evident in Latin or Central America.

While developed countries continue to account for the majority of FDI, an ongoing trend over the past two decades has been the rise in FDI from developing states. In 1982, less than 3 per cent of FDI outflows came from developing and transition states. By 2005, this figure had risen to almost 18 per cent, representing 13 per cent of total FDI stock. These figures are likely to continue to rise further in the foreseeable future. This rising trend is further evidenced by the rise in cross-border mergers and acquisitions involving developing and transition states. The share in terms of value of cross-border M&A involving MNEs from these states has risen from 4 per cent to 13 per cent between 1987 and 2005. In terms of the number of deals, their share has risen from 5 per cent to 17 per cent over the same period. Tellingly, developing and transition economy MNEs are also making more and more mega deals (over $1 billion) up from one in 1990 to 19 in 2005 (many of these deals are with MNEs from developed states). Similarly there has been a rise in greenfield investment by MNEs from developing and transition economies which currently account for 15 per cent of the total.

The composition of this FDI has altered over time, notably as Asia has grown in importance as an economic powerhouse. Throughout the 1980s and much of the 1990s, Brazil was the developing state with the highest stock of FDI. By 1990, it had been replaced by Hong Kong. Services accounted for 81 per cent of outward FDI by developing and transition states. The majority of this investment goes to other developing and transition states with intra-Asian investment especially strong.

Risks and FDI

Core to the FDI decision is an assessment of the risks faced by the MNE in entering a particular market. As Chapters 9 and 10 highlight, the market entry decision is a reflection of the trade-off between risk and control. Convention states that there is a negative relationship between these two variables. FDI as a form of market entry and of an ongoing commitment to a host economy represents a relatively high control mode of operation. This suggests that FDI is characterized by a higher degree of risk than other modes of market entry/involvement. Consequently, FDI depends upon effective country risk analysis to identify the imbalances that increase the risk of a shortfall in the expected return.

Cross-border risks typically emerge from national differences in economic structures, policies, sociopolitical institutions, geography and currencies. The major categories of country risk are identified below.

1. *Economic risk*: this is the major shift in the economic circumstances of structure or growth rate of a host that could generate a major change in the anticipated returns from FDI. These could arise from policy shifts or from the erosion of the host economy's comparative advantage (for example, major shifts in the price of natural resource endowments). Clearly these risks overlap the political system.
2. *Transfer risk*: this arises from a decision by the host government to restrict capital movements. This makes it difficult to repatriate profits, dividends or capital. The degree of transfer risk is negatively related to the ability of the state to generate foreign exchange.

3. *Exchange rate risk*: this is driven by unexpected adverse movements in the exchange rate. This includes an unanticipated shift in the currency regime from a fixed to a float, for example.
4. *Location or neighbourhood risk*: this includes spillover effects created by problems in a region, a host country's major trading partner or in countries with similar characteristics. The latter, for example, can make the host state subject to problems of contagion.
5. *Sovereign risk*: this is based on the ability and/or willingness of the host government to meet its loan obligations and the likelihood of it reneging on loans. This can occur when the state runs low on foreign exchange in a balance of payments crisis or when a government decides not to honour its commitments for political expediency.
6. *Political risk*: this involves the risk created by political changes stemming from change in government control, social fabric or some other non-economic factor. This form of risk includes the potential for internal and external conflicts, expropriation risk and more conventional forms of political risk (see Case Study 8.1).

FDI involves different risks from those faced by a bank lending to a government. The MNE must consider a longer time horizon and is at risk from a broader set of country characteristics. The nature of sunk costs involved in FDI opens the firm to higher degrees of risk: an MNE has to commit to the state and suffers a consequence from higher barriers to entry than other less substantive and more flexible investments. Across the spectrum of risks identified above (Meldrum, 2000), FDI faces a different set of risks compared to FII. These are reflected in Table 8.5.

These risks are assumed to be made in the local currency and their perceived impact across these forms of foreign investment is subjective. Clearly these risks would differ if the investments were held in reserve currency. However, the table does indicate the relatively high degree of risk faced by FDI compared to FII. Much of this is accounted for by the longer term time horizon of FDI. Transfer risk is less of an issue for FDI as capital restrictions are unlikely to last for the entire period of the investment, since they are often used as a temporary measure to counteract short-term difficulties.

TABLE 8.5 Risks to FII and FDI in Major Risk Categories

Risk category	FDI	Short-term finance to private sector	Short-term loan to government	Long-term loan to government
Economic	high	low	low	low to moderate
Transfer	moderate	high	high	moderate
Exchange	high	none to high	none to high	high
Location	high	moderate	Low	moderate
Sovereign	low	low	high	high
Political	high	low	moderate	high

Source: Meldrum (2000).

Based on a ranking of 150 states, Table 8.6 indicates the most and least risky places to undertake FDI across the global economy. The degree of risk is based on the following criteria: security, political stability, government effectiveness, legal and regulatory risk, macroeconomics, foreign trade and payments, financial tax policy, labour markets and infrastructure. As Table 8.6 indicates, the least risky places to undertake business are mainly European whereas, unsurprisingly, the most risky states are concentrated in the world's trouble spots. Interestingly, neither Japan nor the US appears among the least risky places to do business.

TABLE 8.6 Operational Risk, 2007

Least risky		Most risky	
1.	Switzerland	150.	Iraq
2.	Denmark	149.	Guinea
3.	Finland	148.	Myanmar
	Sweden	147	Turkmenistan
5.	Singapore		Uzbekistan
6.	UK		Zimbabwe
7.	Netherlands	144	Venezuela
8.	Austria	143.	Tajikistan
	Luxembourg	142	Eritrea
	Norway	141	Ecuador
11.	Canada		Nigeria
12.	Australia	139	Chad
	France		Iran
	Hong Kong	137.	Kenya
15.	Germany	136.	Cote d'Ivoire
	Ireland		
	New Zealand		

Source: *Economist* (2007).

TRADE-RELATED INVESTMENT MEASURES (TRIMS)

The TRIMS Agreement came into force at the beginning of 1995 and represented an attempt by the WTO to eliminate investment measures that were trade related and which violated provisions on national treatment and quantitative restrictions. TRIMS are prohibited on the grounds that they extend more favourable treatment to domestic products compared to imports. The aim of TRIMS was to prohibit WTO members from inward investment conditional on their compliance with laws, policies and/or regulations that favoured domestic products. While the agreement did not define TRIMS, it did offer an illustrative list which included:

- local content requirements where the host government insists on MNEs using domestically sourced inputs;
- trade-balancing measures where governments impose limits on the amount an MNE can import or links its imports to the amount it exports;
- foreign exchange-balancing requirements where host governments limit imports as a means of maintaining net foreign exchange earnings;
- exchange restrictions where access to foreign exchange is limited.

However, the lack of a formal definition has led to ambiguity over the application of TRIMS.

Under the agreement, WTO members had 90 days to notify the WTO of any TRIMS. This was followed by a transition period during which such measures were to be eliminated. The length of time was dependent on the level of economic development of the offending member. TRIMS were, in fact, used mainly by developing states to promote development objectives. Indeed, in the notification period, the WTO was made aware of 43 TRIMS by developing states, including 19 related to the auto industry and 10 to the agri-food industry. In their defence, TRIMS were established by states to counteract what they regarded as the restrictive business practices and anti-competitive behaviour of MNEs.

Evidence shows that these measures tend to be applied within specific industries, especially the automotive, chemical, petrochemical and ICT sectors. The most common form is local content rules which tend to be applied within the automotive sector. However, the TRIMS agreement is limited in scope as it identifies only five TRIMS that are inconsistent with the rules and gives states a prolonged transition time to remove them,. Furthermore, it does not prevent states from using other TRIMS. For example, states are free to impose export performance requirements that stipulate the export of a certain proportion of outputs; the holding of a certain given percentage of equity by local investors; the use of the most up-to-date technology by the investor, and/or the conduct of a minimum amount of R&D locally by the MNE.

Many developing states still use TRIMS, particularly local content rules. Many of these states argue that the abolition of such requirements would be detrimental to ancillary industries and to the overall development process of these states. However, many states are reviewing the role of TRIMS in the light of more open trade policies and the goal of securing more FDI. Indeed, many have come to realize that TRIMS impose costs which can inhibit many of the benefits of FDI.

INTERNATIONAL ECONOMIC AGREEMENTS AND FDI

The emergence of international investment agreements (IIAs) has coincided with the development of bilateral and regional trade agreements. By the end of 2006, there were over 2,500 IIAs in the world, constituting a web of overlapping and mutually supportive commitments by states. The rise in the number of IIAs was stimulated by the decision not to pursue investment issues as part of the work programme of the Doha Development Round. The IIAs include rules and, in effect, provide an international framework for FDI. Together with investment provisions in at least five WTO agreements (GATS, TRIMs, TRIPS, the GPA and the ASCM), the IIAs are contributing to the development of an increasingly complex setting for international investment which requires governments to ensure consistency between different sets of obligations.

The rise in the number of IIAs has gone hand in hand with the rise in RTAs noted in Chapter 3. They also mirror the pattern in RTAs in that there is an increased number of IIAs signed between states at different levels of economic development. By 2005, 99 per cent of all states were party to at least one IIA. The development of these agreements has followed two paths. First, since 1945, 61 per cent of IIAs were linked to the formation of a new regional grouping. Over 60 per cent of these were between the group and a third party. The rest were bilateral in nature. Countries in the Americas have signed the largest number of intra-regional IIAs with European states close behind. However, most inter-regional IIAs have been concluded between Asia and Europe.

Differences between IIAs reflect the underlying motive behind such agreements. IIAs are often signed as part of a broader push towards economic integration. In such cases, IIAs are about protecting and liberalizing investment, including the regulation of anti-competitive behaviour. In addition, these

IIAs tend to have a broader scope and more tightly embedded commitments. Bilateral deals have a broader agenda, which often includes development, and means that such agreements are less restrictive in their application.

From their inception, the major focus of IIAs has been on the protection of investments against nationalization or expropriations and on the transfer of funds. However, they are being extended to other areas. IIAs are important in creating a level playing field for investment across a limited range of states where they help change pre-existing legal and policy structures and create important habits and patterns of expectations at the transnational level. In terms of their substance, IIAs are concerned with two types of issues:

- *The process of liberalization*: this involves the gradual decrease or elimination of measures and restrictions on the entry and operations of MNEs; the application of positive standards of treatment with a view to ending discrimination against non-native operators, and the implementation of measures that aid the proper operation of markets. Over time, states are reducing their influence over the FDI process..
- *Protection of existing FDI*: these are measures to protect overseas investors against discriminatory acts of host country governments. There is also provision for the settlement of disputes within IIAs.

The OECD has identified two broad types of IIAs: the European model and the North American model. The main difference between the two is that the European model tends to apply only to investment after establishment whereas the North American model extends coverage to the pre-establishment phase. The North American model also controls the imposition of performance requirements on investment. However, there is strong overlap between the two models in terms of their conceptual base and use of dispute settlement mechanisms.

Many developing country states have signed IIAs as part of their plans to embed inward FDI into their development strategies. However, the extent to which such measures are effective is questionable as discretion may be limited. To counter any limits on discretion, many IIAs are characterized by flexibility in terms of their adaptation to the needs and realities of particular states and the asymmetries between developed and developing states. This often means that developing states face less onerous obligations on a non-reciprocal basis. In practice, this can mean allowing these states more time to transform to the new regime or offering limited exemptions from specific aspects of the agreement.

The most important element of IIAs is the national treatment standard. This standard stresses that a host country extends to foreign investors the same rights and treatment that are applied to home-based investors. The aim is to ensure competitive equality between investors. This can raise difficult issues regarding the relevant benchmarks by which this comparison takes place. National treatment applies mainly to post-entry investment but an increasing number of IIAs are extending the principle to pre-entry situations. Nevertheless, many states still impose limits on national treatment by issuing a list of exempt activities in areas such as public heath, national security or broadly defined strategic concerns. Such exemptions are often applied to the infant industries argument where equal treatment with non-indigenous investors may harm emergent businesses.

POLICY TO STIMULATE FDI

Increasingly, policy frameworks to stimulate FDI have taken on a more liberal slant in both developed and developing states. As a means of stimulating FDI, policy makers are liberalizing core FDI policies by reducing barriers to FDI; enhancing the standard of treatment of overseas investors; creating a level playing field for all investors, and ensuring the proper functioning of domestic markets. However, the market for FDI is becoming increasingly competitive and, as a result, many states need to extend and enhance their efforts to attract overseas investment, particularly as FDI is seen by many states as a main contributor to long-term growth.

Policy measures to entice FDI act as a direct influence over the aforementioned determinants of FDI. However, FDI policy measures extend beyond simply attracting investment via actions on determinants. The objectives of FDI policy also include:

- deepening and broadening the economic base;
- generation of employment opportunities;
- promotion of linkages;
- export generation and performance;
- trade balancing;
- regional development promotion;
- avoidance of restrictive business practices;
- technology transfer.

These objectives reflect a strong mutual interest between foreign affiliates and domestic firms. This is most evident in agglomeration economies where the cluster attracts investment but also benefits the network which then benefits the investor.

Investment incentives have been a major device to attract FDI. These have proliferated across the global economy, with many states engaging in competition with one another to offer the most favourable terms to the MNE. Despite this, it is widely believed that these measures play little direct role in location decisions and many of the measures used by states to affect FDI have become subject to new international rules, most notably TRIMs.

States have shifted to newer investment promotion policies based on the aggressive marketing of their states, often through dedicated national investment promotion agencies. Such aggressive marketing has evolved into promotion policies that target specific investors at the level of the firm or that meet specific developmental goals. The success of such measures is based on both understanding the needs of the MNE in terms of the location and on targeting specific economic determinants of FDI (often pools of skilled labour or the competitiveness of the domestic sector). However, such targeted strategies are risky: resources can be wasted on investment that may not be realized; the wrong type of firm may be targeted or the incentives may be taken up by a firm that would have invested in any case.

All this underlines that, in an intensely competitive environment for FDI, states need to develop an investment product that differentiates the location in terms of its advantages. Eventually, the location will become a brand name recognizable for its ability to deliver specific advantages to the foreign investor. However, such policies are time consuming and costly to develop. Furthermore, this policy needs to develop within a coherent and coordinated institutional framework so that different localities in the same state and region do not compete for the same funds.

There is increasing recognition that policy needs to go beyond simply liberalizing investment measures. The best magnet for future investment is often the success of past FDI. This can sometimes mean offering post-investment services. Policy has not only to attract investment but also to ensure that the commitments by MNEs to states are reciprocated by governments to ensure the investment process is beneficial for all parties. Policy measures need to ensure that once an investment is made, agencies continue to liaise with the foreign affiliate to ensure that the investment realizes its potential.

To guide the evolution of the necessary supporting policy for FDI and to make a location attractive to inward investment, the OECD has devised a *Policy Framework for Investment*. This encompasses the following 10 policy areas that are important to both small and large business:

1. investment policy, including non-discrimination, transparency and property protection;
2. investment promotion and facilitation, including incentives that correct market failures and enhance the strong points of a host economy;
3. trade policy, that is, policies that secure a more open environment for trade in goods and services;
4. competition policy – aggressively implemented anti-trust and cartel busting measures;
5. a tax policy that does not penalize inward investment excessively while maintaining the necessary revenues to meet obligations;
6. corporate governance – the obligations upon non-indigenous business should not be overly onerous or discriminatory;
7. responsible business conduct: policy measures to secure responsible business need to be applied in a coordinated manner;
8. human resources – the necessary investment in human capital is required to make the host economy attractive;
9. infrastructure and financial sector development to secure mobility and the raising of capital;
10. public governance: public policy needs to be transparent, certain and predictable, and applied in a non-discriminatory manner.

Common to all these diverse topics is an underpinning logic of ensuring that policy is, first, coherent (i.e. that all policy works towards the same objective of making the location attractive for FDI); second, transparent and accountable (i.e. ensuring that policy is clearly and openly explained and implemented in a responsible manner), and finally, subject to regular evaluation (i.e. that policies are regularly evaluated to ensure their compatibility with the overriding objective).

Where there is increased interest for economic development based on FDI, the process of policy reform must also extend to home countries. This implies that if developing states are to realize the benefits of FDI, developed states need to commit to further trade liberalization and remove barriers to investment in non-domicile locations. In addition, home-based policy needs to ensure that technology policies allow the rapid transfer and diffusion of technologies and know-how where appropriate especially when intellectual property rights are not under threat. Finally, developed states also need to increase the synergy between FDI flows and official development assistance.

Policy within all states needs to highlight that openness to exports and imports is key to making FDI a success. Subsidiaries within hosts also need access to international networks of related enterprises – both within and external to the MNE. Thus measures that seek to secure development by deliberately limiting trade and by denying access to these networks will inhibit the benefits from FDI flows. This implies that policies have to be guided by a pro-market perspective with direct action focusing on market failure considerations.

Policy within home states also needs to reflect that there are advantages from outward FDI. Many developing states fear repercussions from outward FDI flows. Policies to lower outward FDI have been used by developing states to lower the risk of capital flight and was mainly accomplished through foreign exchange restrictions and capital controls. According to UNCTAD, only a few states completely ban outward FDI (notably Nepal and Sierra Leone) but over 40 states place constraints on investment abroad. However, as these states develop, so their economies – as sources of capital – are beginning to grow and, as policy makers recognize the need for domestic firms to internationalize, so the policy stance is changing. Policy to support outward FDI can be set within the context of broader competitiveness policies (such as seeking access to technology) or more specific actions.

A number of policy options are available to actively promote outward FDI, including:

- the provision of information for investment opportunities for domestic firms;
- 'matchmaking' services whereby official bodies search for links for domestic firms in target markets;
- training services:
- the creation of 'comfort zones' where the state can create a home country environment in a host economy;
- financial incentives such as preferential loans, equity finance;
- investment insurance to mitigate the risks of FDI.

These measures can be supported by institutions such as investment promotion agencies or trade promotion organizations designed to promote outward FDI. These bodies can provide information and financial support to open up target markets. Where the effects of outward FDI have to be mitigated, states will seek to create as favourable a business environment as possible to generate reciprocal flows or to undermine the motives for outward flows in the first place.

CONCLUSION

The rising flows of foreign investment across the global economy have been central to the process of globalization. Such investment broadly consists of two types of flows. The first is portfolio investment (based on investment in overseas financial assets); the second is direct investment which is a direct purchase of assets within the host country. The latter is the major focus of study within international business. However, while such actions can have a positive impact on host economies, they are subject to risk associated with a high commitment to these economies.

Summary of Key Concepts

- Overseas investment can be either direct or indirect.
- Direct investment in a host economy is driven by a wide variety of factors.
- Direct investment in host economies is subject to many political and economic risks.
- Attracting FDI is a major policy objective of many states.

Activities

1. Using a country with which you are familiar, identify those factors that will attract and/or limit the level of investment within that location.

2. What sort of policy measure makes an economy attractive for investment? Why?

3. How does politics influence FDI? Give examples.

Discussion Questions

1. What do you believe are the most important factors driving international portfolio investment?

2. How do you believe the international financial crisis is likely to affect flows of international investment?

3. How has the degree of risk attached to foreign investment (both direct and indirect) been affected by the international financial crisis?

References and Suggestions for Further Reading

Axarloglou, K. and Pournarakis, M. (2007) 'Do all foreign direct investment inflows benefit the local economy?', *The World Economy*, Vol. 30, No. 3, 424–445.

Bora, B., Lloyd, P. and Pengestu, M. (2000) 'Industrial policy and the WTO', *The World Economy*, Vol. 23, No. 4, 543–559.

Enderwick, P. (2005) 'Attracting "desirable" FDI: theory and evidence', *Transnational Corporations*, Vol. 14, No. 2, 93–119.

Ghauri, P. and Oxelheim, L. (eds) (2004) *European Union and the Race for Foreign Direct Investment in Europe*, Oxford: Elsevier.

Jensen, N. (2006) *Nation States and the Multinational Corporation: A Political Economy of Foreign Direct Investment,* Princeton, NJ: Princeton University Press.

Lall, S. (1997) *Attracting Foreign Investment: New Trends, Sources and Policies*, Economic Paper 31, Commonwealth Secretariat.

Meldrum, D. (2000) 'Country risk and foreign direct investment', *Business Economics*, Vol. 35, No. 1, 33–40.

Mody, A. (2004) 'Is FDI integrating the world economy?', *The World Economy*, Vol. 27, No. 8, 1195–1222.

Moosa, I. (2002) *Foreign Direct Investment: Theory, Evidence and Practice*, Basingstoke: Palgrave Macmillan.

Mundell, R. (1957) 'International trade and factor mobility', *American Economic Review*, Vol. 47, 321–335.

Websites

www.unctad.org/wir/ – *World Investment Report.*

www.oecd.org/ – survey work on international investment.

www. FDI.net – foreign direct investment information portal of the World Bank Group.

Chapter 9

Multinational Enterprises
The Conduits of Globalization

Globalization has gone wrong, as it has no rules. Multinationals are almost above the law. They are so huge they are bigger than governments.

Dick Smith, Australian Entrepreneur, (1944–)

LEARNING OBJECTIVES

This chapter will help you to:

- distinguish between different motives for engaging in foreign direct investment
- understand the form and nature of the spread of MNEs
- examine the different explanations of multinationality
- demonstrate an understanding of network and alliance capitalism and why they are increasing in importance
- comprehend the knowledge-based view of the MNE

Multinational enterprises (MNEs) lie at the heart of international economic integration and international production. According to UNCTAD (2007), in 2006 over 78,000 MNEs owned more than 780,000 foreign affiliates. Most MNEs have a home base in the triad countries of North America, Europe or Japan. In 2005, for example, 91 per cent of UNCTAD's list of top 100 MNEs were based in the triad, the home base of 58,000 MNEs. As a rule of thumb, MNEs account for two-thirds of world trade. About half the share of MNEs, or one-third of total trade, is intra-firm trade: that is, cross-border transactions within the boundaries of a single firm. The purpose of this chapter is not to make the case for or against MNEs but to explore their nature and role as well as accounting for their emergence. It begins by addressing the issue of what exactly constitutes a multinational enterprise. This is followed by analysis of how multinational MNEs are in practice. The concluding section introduces major theories regarding the evolution of MNEs.

THE NATURE OF THE MULTINATIONAL ENTERPRISE

There are several definitions of what precisely constitutes a multinational firm. A useful starting point is to consider what constitutes a non-multinational firm. Clearly, firms that are headquartered in one country and produce and market all their goods and/or services in that one country are not multinational. Such domestically oriented firms have a lesser exposure to international risk than other firms, although they are not immune from it altogether. For example, they usually import raw materials and other inputs and are subject to the impact of the international economy upon their own domestic market. In addition, firms that are headquartered and produce in the same country but export some of their output are not multinationals. However, their exposure to international risk will be greater than that of purely domestic firms because of their exposure to foreign markets and their need to take cultural differences into account in their marketing.

Once a firm invests in value-adding activities outside its domestic market or starts to exercise control over such activities outside its domestic market, then the description 'multinational' becomes appropriate. Commonly cited definitions of MNEs include:

- 'an enterprise that controls and manages production establishments located in at least two countries' (Caves, 1996);
- 'enterprises which own or control production or service facilities outside the country in which they are based' (the United Nations);
- 'an enterprise that engages in foreign direct investment and owns or controls value-adding activities in more than one country' (Dunning, 1993);
- 'a firm which has the power to co-ordinate and control operations in more than one country, even if it does not own them' (Dicken, 1998);

■ 'the means of co-ordinating production from one centre of strategic decision making when this co-ordination takes a firm across national boundaries' (Cowling and Sugden, 1987).

Several characteristics of these definitions are worthy of note. First, size does not figure in any of them. Provided a firm exercises ownership or control in more than one country, it is regarded as multinational. This sits at odds with the popular view of multinational firms as giant corporations. In practice, the world's biggest firms are multinational but it is also the case that small and medium-sized enterprises (SMEs) are regarded as multinational firms according to the above definitions. Chapter 11 discusses the specific challenges confronting SMEs attempting to reach beyond their traditional local markets.

Second, the definitions include not only ownership but also control. In view of the blurring of the boundaries of the firm discussed below, this enables a wide range of business organizations to be regarded as multinational, including the buyer-driven commodity chains that make up the multinational organizing strategy of firms like Nike and The Gap. Although these companies do not own all, or sometimes any part, of their production facilities, they nevertheless exercise a significant degree of control over the production chain and should be regarded as multinationals.

Third, the definitions are framework definitions. They are wide-ranging and general but do not capture the diversity of ownership, structures, geographical and organizational forms that constitute contemporary MNEs, nor could they reasonably be expected to do so. Indeed, it is this diversity that has made it difficult to develop a single theory or model of internationalization (see Chapter 10).

In terms of ranking by financial assets, there has, in the five years to 2005, been little change in the composition of the top 100 non-financial MNEs (see Table 9.1 for the top 20). The only really major difference has been the rise of foreign activities by MNEs from developing countries. In 2005, the top 100 non-financial MNEs accounted for 10 per cent of foreign assets, 17 per cent of sales and 13 per cent of employment among the total population of MNEs. The top 10 MNEs have almost $1.7 trillion (nearly 40 per cent) of the total foreign assets of the top 100 MNEs. They include three MNEs in the automobile and four in the petroleum sector. As highlighted within the introduction, the majority of the top 100 MNEs are from the triad of the EU, Japan and the US. Indeed, five of the states within the triad (the US, UK, Germany, France and Japan) account for 72 of the top 100 MNEs. The top 100 MNEs currently include seven from developing states. Furthermore, of the top 100 firms, 58 belong to six industries: motor vehicles (11) petroleum (10), electrical and electronic equipment (10), pharmaceuticals (9), telecommunications (9) and electricity, gas and water (9).

If these enterprises were ranked by alternative criteria then the ranking would change significantly. Ranking by sales places the petroleum MNEs in the top four positions and moves another four motor vehicle manufacturers into the top 10. The largest MNE by sales is ExxonMobil which is ten times larger than the firm ranked fifty-fifth in the list. Ranking by employment would put three retail MNEs into the top 10. On average, MNEs had affiliates in 39 countries with Deutsche Post having the largest number of affiliates with a presence in 103 states and Royal Dutch Shell following up with a presence in 96 states.

TABLE 9.1 Top 20 Non-financial MNEs Ranked by Foreign Assets

1.	General Electric (US)	11.	France Telecom (France)
2.	Vodafone (UK)	12.	Volkswagen (Germany)
3.	General Motors (US)	13.	RWE Group (Germany)
4.	BP (UK)	14.	Chevron Group (US)
5.	Royal Dutch /Shell (UK/Netherlands)	15.	E.On (Germany)
		16.	Suez (France)
6.	ExxonMobil (US)	17.	Deutsche Telekom (Germany)
7.	Toyota (Japan)	18.	Siemens (Germany)
8.	Ford (US)	19.	Honda (Japan)
9.	Total (France)	20.	Hutchinson Whampoa (Hong Kong, China)
10.	EdF (France)		

Source: UNCTAD (2007).

MOTIVATING FACTORS FOR MNES

The major motivating factors for MNEs may be subdivided into the following broad categories. These groupings are not mutually exclusive, as FDI will often be influenced by a multitude of concerns, although one often tends to predominate.

Resource-seeking Investment

Resource seekers invest abroad to acquire resources that are either unobtainable or only available at much higher cost in the home country. Typically such investment involves primary products, especially agricultural goods, minerals and raw materials. Usually, most of the output from these investments is exported. Oil production in developing countries, for example, frequently involves inward FDI (although the terms on which MNEs engage in hydrocarbon production depend on host country policies regarding exploitation of natural resources by non-nationals). FDI enables oil companies to secure inputs for their downstream activities (refineries and ultimately retail outlets) located outside the country where the oil is extracted. From the perspective of the host country, multinational oil companies bring technical expertise, expertise that is particularly useful in exploration and production in difficult terrain or in enhancing recovery rates from existing fields.

Other resources sought by foreign investors include cheap unskilled, semi-skilled and, increasingly with the development of software exports from developing countries, skilled labour. Such investors come from countries with high real labour costs: initially they invested in the more advanced developing countries of East Asia or Latin America but, as wage costs have risen there, they are increasingly casting their net wider. Other location-bound resource-seeking investments (corresponding to Dunning's 'L' factor – see below) include tourism and construction – that is, investments that can only take place in a particular location because they utilize resources or attributes that are immobile.

Resource-seeking investment dominated FDI in the nineteenth century and into the twentieth century, representing the basis of the colonial relationship between Europe and Japan and their respective overseas possessions. It survived the end of empire, and remains significant, but has been overtaken in importance by other types of FDI.

Market-seeking Investment

Market seekers invest in a country, not as an export platform, but to supply goods and services to it (see Case Study 9.1). Advantages of locating production directly in a market rather than exporting to it (which the market seeker may have done at an earlier stage of the establishment chain – see Chapter 10) include the following:

- Greater proximity to the consumer: this facilitates the adaptation of products to local custom, tastes and needs (polycentric firms).
- Market size: the presence of a sizeable emerging market as in the Far East, China, India, Russia or parts of Latin America.
- Continuation of existing relationships with major customers: for example, when Japanese car producers began to invest overseas, many of their suppliers followed them. The internationalization of business services such as accountancy, legal services and consultancy is also a response to the movement of clients into an increasing number of markets.
- Government policy: government policy in the form of investment incentives can stimulate inward FDI. Government policy can also spark defensive FDI. For example, much of the FDI in Europe towards the end of the 1980s was driven by investors' fears that construction of the Single European Market (SEM) would lead to a 'Fortress Europe' which would reduce, if not eliminate, their access to the EU market. In practice these fears proved unfounded.
- the belief that it is necessary to maintain a physical presence in a foreign market because one's competitors do so.

CASE STUDY 9.1

Unilever and Emerging Markets

Given the high and sustained growth rates of emerging markets (see Chapter 6), it is no surprise that many consumer goods companies are looking to them as a source of revenue and growth. Given its head start, its diverse product portfolio and in-depth local knowledge, Unilever should have been number one in these markets. However, when rivals began to challenge its leading position, Unilever ceded market share quickly, forcing the company to re-examine its strategy in these locations.

In part, these changes stemmed from the aggressiveness of Unilever's main competitor – Procter and Gamble (P&G) – which extended its product and brand reach across the consumer goods segment rapidly from the late 1990s. Unilever's response to this challenge was very 'top down' and was characterized by the removal of unnecessary complexity and administration, including a move from being run by a committee and two chairmen towards consolidation under a single chief executive. However, while structural issues were resolved, the company's ability to compete successfully in the leading emerging economies was still under severe threat. In part, this reflects Unilever's history according to which it emerged as a vertically integrated consumer goods company that allowed its subsidiaries a great deal of discretion. In addition, unlike its major rivals (P&G and Nestlé), Unilever evolved a diverse product portfolio ranging from food to personal care products.

In order to turn around its business, Unilever looked at all its brands, product categories and its location of operations and concluded that its problem lay not in brands but in the execution of strategy. This problem originated from what was historically its greatest strength – its strong position in local markets. The power granted to local managers meant that there was much duplication of activities, overcomplex structures and a consequent inability to exploit its size or its extensive reach. However, the desire for greater uniformity had to be reconciled with Unilever's strength in tailoring offerings to local markets. In some cases, the geographic segmentation of local markets went too far as synergies across markets were ignored and complexity was allowed to flourish. This complexity was apparent both at the marketing and at the operational level where single countries were sometimes served by multiple businesses.

The most high-profile effect of this reduction in complexity was a sharp reduction in head count which fell by over 40,000 in the five years to 2008, with further rationalization planned as factories are shut, units combined and a further 10,000 jobs

culled. It is anticipated that these reductions will save the company over $1.5 billion per annum. However, these savings have to be set against a backdrop of high commodity prices that have eaten into sales from emerging economies where nearly 44 per cent (2008) of its sales are generated. Defending its position in these locations has eaten into the profits of what is increasingly Unilever's core market. The untapped market potential is evident, and as prosperity grows, so the demand for consumer goods will increase accordingly. This is especially true in those locations with an emerging and aspiring middle class such as China and India.

By 2008, it was evident that the job was only part finished as there were challenges to be met in food, marketing and mergers. In terms of food, Unilever's high profile at the processed end of the market goes against current market trends for health foods. However, pushing too far towards this emerging end of the market may compromise the desire for local products. Marketing has been a mixed bag for Unilever: as much as some campaigns have been successful (such as the Dove brand's use of ordinary woman as opposed to supermodels), others have backfired by being too aggressive. Finally, while consolidation is likely, it is expected to be on a small scale: acquisition will be of small companies rather than large-scale takeovers that are more difficult to undertake in this difficult financial environment.

CASE STUDY QUESTIONS AND ACTIVITIES

1. Given the experience of Unilever, what are the major challenges of operating in emerging economies?

2. Why are emerging markets becoming increasingly core to MNEs that produce consumer goods?

3. Compare Unilever with either Nestlé or P&G in terms of the strategies of these businesses when entering and operating within emerging markets.

Efficiency-seeking Investment

Efficiency seekers strive to rationalize their value chains. They focus and concentrate different parts of their value chain in diverse locations, seeking to maximize the benefits from each location by arbitraging costs and specialisms. On a global scale, efficiency seekers attempt to take advantage of traditional differences in factor endowments. This helps explain the concentration of labour-intensive activities in developing countries and of capital and technology-extensive activities in developed countries.

Efficiency-seeking FDI is also prominent in regionally integrated markets: these markets are frequently similar in economic structure and income levels, enabling producers to exploit economies of scale and scope to serve a number of markets. Efficiency-seeking investment requires coordinated communication, production and inbound and outbound logistical networks, and a business environment in which there are few or no barriers to cross-border activity. The emergence of the SEM was intended to yield such efficiency gains for producers within Europe, and the introduction of the euro, which entered its final stage in 2002, is anticipated to extend these possibilities. Indeed, there has been significant rationalization in several European sectors as a result of the SEM.

Strategic Asset Investment

Strategic asset seekers engage in FDI to achieve long-term strategic objectives. These objectives vary. An acquisition may be motivated, for example, by a wish to make life more difficult for a rival in a specific market or to reduce competition in a particular market (provided the local competition authorities do not object). International conglomerates may collect acquisitions to spread risk across a wider range of markets and locations.

Other Motivations for Investment

In some cases, FDI occurs because firms wish to escape restrictive legislation in the domestic market. Chapter 16 discusses the emergence of so-called pollution havens as firms seek to avoid expensive environmental legislation by locating in countries with less strict laws. Chapter 15 discusses a similar phenomenon in relation to labour laws. Some firms invest abroad buoyed by success at home and to overcome limited growth prospects at home. Others invest because they feel that their competitors may gain an advantage over them by investing in a particular country or because they fear exclusion in the long run.

Box 9.1 Perlmutter's Classification of MNEs

MNEs can be categorized along dimensions other than those relating to their reasons for internationalization. The value of these classifications lies in the way in which they highlight different characteristics of multinational firms. By distinguishing between ethnocentric, polycentric, regiocentric and geocentric MNEs, Perlmutter (1969), for example, draws attention to the extent to which MNEs are domestically or internationally oriented.

1. *Ethnocentric firms*: the parent firm and the domestic market are the dominant factor in ethnocentric firms: the needs of domestic consumers determine product development and the parent company headquarters, located in the home country, exercise significant control over foreign affiliates, either through highly centralized decision making and/or the utilization of expatriate senior management from the home country in the overseas operations. These firms are at stages one or two of Vernon's product life cycle.
2. *Polycentric firms*: polycentric firms are more oriented to foreign markets. They are market seeking, closely attuned to the needs and cultures of the countries in which they operate, and act as a series of domestic firms, loosely linked to the parent company. Such firms are likely to operate in a less centralized and hierarchical way than ethnocentric firms, although some core decisions may be taken centrally.
3. *Regiocentric firms*: regiocentric MNEs develop their strategy and organization along regional lines. Regional offices are responsible to the parent company headquarters but have some autonomy. There is integration of links of the value chain within regions but little integration across regions. This approach tailors output to regional needs and is particularly suitable within the context of regional integration (see Chapter 3). Many Japanese and American firms, for example, adopted a regiocentric, or European, approach to the EU market as a result of the campaign to develop the SEM rather than separate strategies for each national market.
4. *Geocentric firms*: a geocentric firm views its value chain from a global perspective: it aims to integrate its activities across regions and the most geocentric firms will develop global products, while remaining sensitive to local or regional cultures and market peculiarities where necessary.

THE MULTINATIONALITY OF MULTINATIONAL ENTEPRISES

Pure globalists expect MNEs to become increasingly detached from their home country and that the configuration of assets, management, employees and sales will reflect global market forces and not be dominated by the home country. However, the truly geocentric firm is rare: management practices, for example, tend to remain embedded in home country traditions. Research and development in overseas subsidiaries, although gradually changing, still tends to focus on adaptation of new products to local markets, whereas higher level research functions and basic product design and development remain in the home country.

Production and related activities are more multinational in nature. Some overseas investment is market seeking and facilitates the adaptation of production to local demands and tastes or the evasion of trade barriers. Other MNEs engage in specialized production to serve larger integrated markets like the EU, NAFTA or even the world market. Although this type of overseas production practice requires more complex and costly logistics and distribution, the additional costs are offset by economies of scale arising from the concentration of production facilities. The most globally oriented form of production entails the vertical integration of production across borders. In other words, successive parts of the production process will be carried out in different locations according to relative costs and the availability of appropriate resources and skills. Unlike the previous examples, there is no particular relationship between the host country and its market: that is, production is not intended for the local market, although some sales may, of course, occur there.

UNCTAD uses two main indicators to measure the degree of multinationality of MNEs. First, there is the Transnationality Index (TNI) which comprises the average of three ratios: foreign assets/foreign sales; foreign sales/total sales and foreign employment to total employment. The second measure is the more recently devised Internationalization Index (II). This comprises the number of foreign affiliates divided by the total number of wholly or majority-owned affiliates. This indicates the physical spread of assets compared to the source of value created by the network of affiliates. These different indices can offer contrasting perspectives on the degree of multinationality across MNEs. As highlighted across a number of key sectors, II and TNI values can vary markedly (see Table 9.2). This is further reflected in Tables 9.3 and 9.4 on a company basis.

The degree of transanationality as measured by the TNI (2005) throws up some interesting facts (see Table 9.4). First, the under-representation of US firms from the list despite US companies representing a quarter of the top 100 (see Table 9.5). Although the leading US firm (AES) falls just outside the top 10 a great many US-based MNEs are a long way down the list. Second, it also reiterates the pattern of MNEs from smaller states, being more spread out. Notable, for example, is the number of Canadian firms within the top 10. Table 9.3 also confirms the high spread of pharmaceuticals enterprises.

Generally these results are supported by MNEs ranked by the II (see Table 9.3). However, this ranking does throw up some interesting anomalies. For example, Wal Mart is the 28th ranked MNE as measured by the II but 97th as measured by the TNI, or IBM is 15th in the II ranking but 54th as measured by the TNI. What this seems to show is that these companies have a high physical presence but the majority of revenues and assets are geographically concentrated. There are other noticeable

TABLE 9.2 Comparison of II and TNI Values for the Top 100 MNEs (by Industry, 2005)

	Largest TNCs	
	II	TNI
Motor vehicles	62.1	55.5
Electrical/electronics	76.2	53.9
Petroleum	60.5	55.5
Pharmaceuticals	81.9	60.2
Telecommunications	71.6	61.6
Utilties	53.1	52.3
Metals and metal products	77.7	62
Food and beverages	77.8	73.3
Transport and storage	62.9	73.3
All industries	69.5	59.9

Source: UNCTAD (2007).

TABLE 9.3 Top 20 Non-financial MNEs as Measured by the Internationalization Index (Home Country/Industry)

1. Inbev (Belgium/brewers,consumer goods)	11. LG Corp (Korea/electrical,electronic)
2. Mittal (Netherlands-UK/steel)	12. Alcan (Canada/metal)
3. Cemex (Mexico/non-metals)	13. Nokia (Finland/telecoms)
4. Singapore Telecom (Singapore/telecoms)	14. Hewlett Packard (US/electrical/electronic)
5. GSK (UK/pharmaceuticals)	15. IBM (US/electrical/electronic)
6. Holcim (Switzerland/non-metals)	16. Liberty Global (US/telecoms)
7. Thomson Corporation (Canada/media)	17. Hutchison Whampoa (China, Hong Kong/telecoms)
8. Nestle(Switzerland/food and beverages)	18. Sabmiller (UK/consumer goods)
9. CRH (Eire/timber products)	19. Samsung (Korea/electrical/electronic)
10. Novaratis (Switzerland/pharmaceuticals)	20. Roche Group (Switzerland/pharmaceuticals)

Source: UNCTAD (2007).

TABLE 9.4 Top 20 MNEs as Measured by the TNI, 2005

1. Thomson Corporation (Canada/media)	11. Hutchison Whampoa (Hong Kong (China, telecoms)
2. Liberty Global (US/media)	12. Honda (Japan/motor vehicles)
3. Roche (Switzerland/pharmaceuticals)	13. Alcan (Canada/metals)
4. WPP (UK/business services)	14. AES Corp (US/utilities)
5. Philips (Netherlands/electronics)	15. Cemex (Mexico/cement)
6. Nestle (Switzerland/food & beverages)	16. BP (UK/petroleum)
7. Cadbury Schweppes (UK/food and beverages)	17. L'Air Liquide (France/chemicals)
8. Vodafone (UK/telecoms)	18. CRH (Eire/timber products)
9. LaFarge (France/non-metals)	19. Ahold Koniklijke (Netherlands/retail)
10. Sabmiller (UK/consumer goods, brewers)	20. Inbev (Belgium/consumer goods, brewers)

Source: UNCTAD (2007).

differences between indices scores for the II and TNI when the major MNEs are assessed. For example, Inbev tops II rankings but barely makes the top 20 for the TNI. Similarly, Mittal which is number two in the II rankings barely makes the top 50 in the TNI. Vodafone (number eight in the TNI index) comes in at 94 in the II rankings, while WPP comes in at number four in the TNI rankings but a lowly 75 in the II rankings. This reflects that a high number of overseas assets do not always translate into value creation which may be more highly connected.

Comparing the top 20 MNEs as measured by TNI with those measured by II does show some overlap with nine MNEs appearing on both lists and with each index highlighting the high spread of pharmaceuticals. However, there are notable differences between the two measures, the most notable of which is the II which suggests that US firms are more dispersed as measured by affiliates. The low measures on the TNI probably reflect the strong effects of the home market. The II also has not a single, solely owned UK representative and shows the rise of the larger, more well-known MNEs such as IBM, Walmart and Sony as more important when measured through the Internationalization Index.

The Network Spread Index (NSI) reflects the pattern of the TNI index. The NSI has been developed to capture the extent to which companies locate their activities in foreign locations. It is calculated as a ratio of the number of foreign countries in which an MNE is active as a percentage of the number of countries in which it could have located. The latter figure is taken as the number of countries that have inward FDI stocks minus one (that is, the home country of the MNE in question) in the year in which the calculations take place. According to UNCTAD's World Investment Report, on a country dimension, those companies in the top 100 MNEs with the largest index are from smaller countries with a history of FDI – Switzerland (25.8 per cent), Netherlands (21.8 per cent) and the UK (19.6 per cent). Larger countries like the US and Japan, on the other hand, have bigger home markets on which to concentrate their expansion efforts and so the average NSI of US and Japanese MNEs comes in lower at 13.2 per cent and 14.3 per cent respectively.

Analysing the spread of MNEs across the global economy, it is evident that there are large discrepancies between states and regional groupings. Among the largest MNEs it is apparent that those from the US, Latin America and South Africa tend to be the least transnationalized. Table 9.5 offers an indication of the TNI for the leading MNEs by states in 2004. This shows that despite its dominance of the largest MNEs, US-based MNEs are not as multinational as those from European states. The table also indicates that of these states with the largest number of top MNEs, it is the UK and France that have the highest degree of transnationality. However, these figures are even higher

TABLE 9.5 Top 100 MNEs Spread by TNI, 2004

Region/Economy	Average TNI		Number of entries
	2003	2004	
The top 100 Largest MNEs Of which	55.8	56.8	100
US	45.8	56.8	25
France	59.5	62.3	15
Germany	49.0	52.2	13
UK	69.2	70.5	11
Japan	42.8	52.2	9

Source: UNCTAD (2007).

for smaller states such as Finland (70.35), Switzerland (80.3) and Ireland (94.5). Altough these cover a smaller sample, they do reflect the strong outward-looking nature of these economies.

As a measure of the spread of MNEs, UNCTAD uses the Geographical Spread Index (GSI) which is defined as the square root of the II multiplied by the number of host countries. While the US has the largest number of firms with the highest spread (22) this is underrepresentation of their dominance when MNCs are ranked by foreign sales. The US is then followed by Germany (14), France (13) and the UK (11). The pattern among the top 20 firms as measured by the GSI shows that there is a strong representation of German firms. The relatively low number of US firms by spread when compared to their pre-eminence when measured by sales highlights that the these firms tend to gain revenues from a more limited range of states.

Table 9.6 indicates that there is a broad correlation between the GSI and the number of hosts across which the MNE operates. However, Deutsche Post, which has the most extensive reach, is outranked by Nestlé in terms of the GSI.

TABLE 9.6 Top 20 MNEs as Measured by Number of Host Countries and GSI

	Company	No. of hosts	GSI
1.	Deutsche Post (Germany)	103	93.1
2.	Royal Dutch Shell (UK/Netherlands)	96	71.1
3.	Nestle (Switzerland)	94	93.9
4.	Siemens (Germany)	85	79.5
5.	BASF (Germany)	84	80.8
6.	Bayer (Germany)	76	75.0
7.	Proctor & Gamble (US)	72	74.9
8.	IBM (US)	66	77.3
9.	Philips (Netherlands)	62	67.7
10.	Total (France)	62	66.2
11.	BP (UK)	62	65.3
12.	WPP (UK)	59	58.1
13.	Abbott Laboratories (US)	57	68.9
14.	Nokia (Finland)	56	71.3
15.	Altria (US)	56	68.6
16.	Novaratis (Switzerland)	55	71.0
17.	GE (US)	55	65.3
18.	Mitsui (Japan)	55	55.2
19.	Mitsubishi (Japan)	55	49.6
20.	Roche Group (Switzerland)	53	67.8

Source: UNCTAD (2007).

THE EVOLUTION OF INTERNATIONAL PRODUCTION THEORY

A burgeoning literature on why and how firms decide to internationalize only developed in the second half of the twentieth century despite the fact that MNEs have existed in one form or another for centuries. It required the post-war increase in FDI among industrialized nations and the subsequent increase in the scale of international production to prompt a theoretical focus on the multinational firm. Until that point, explanations of activities of firms outside their national boundaries relied heavily on neo-classical trade theory and the neo-classical theory of capital arbitrage. There were also contributions from writers like Edith Penrose who, through her work on the theory of the growth of the firm, explored the idea that cross-border production represented not only an alternative to international cartels but was also a rational extension of the benefits of horizontal and vertical integration.

The real breakthrough in theorizing about multinationals occurred in 1960 with the work of Stephen Hymer. Hymer overturned the prevailing orthodoxy by focusing on the firm and on international production rather than on international trade and investment theory. His first step was to emphasize the distinction between portfolio investment and FDI. Portfolio investment theory was based on assumptions of efficient, perfectly competitive markets, costless transactions and perfect information, and explained international capital flows in terms of firms taking advantage of differential interest rates. For Hymer, the key difference between portfolio investment and FDI was control. In the former case, the transaction involves the transfer of assets from the seller to the buyer via the market mechanism. In the case of FDI, the transfer of assets across borders is made within the investing company and the control of the transferred resources remains with the investing company.

According to Hymer, the rationale for FDI is not to take advantage of higher interest rates but to finance international production through the transfer of resources, including equipment, technology, skills and know-how. This option became feasible owing to the existence of firm-specific advantages (FSAs). Hymer reasoned that domestic firms have a number of crucial advantages over foreign firms given their greater understanding of the local market, culture and legislation. Domestic firms may also have advantages in terms of preferential access to natural resources. In order for foreign firms to produce successfully in overseas locations, they need strong FSAs of their own to counteract the advantages of indigenous firms. These advantages could come from economies of scale, size, market power, brand ownership, know-how or technological prowess, for example.

FSAs are notable in the evolution of thinking about international production for two reasons. First, they are central to the theoretical literature about the internationalization of the firm, feeding into the 'O' factor of Dunning's eclectic paradigm (see p. 225). Second, FSAs and their exploitation can only exist as a result of market failure – a distinctive move away from the assumptions of functioning markets in the cases of neo-classical trade and capital arbitrage theories. In other words, MNEs must have an advantage over competitors, including indigenous producers, to invest in another country. This implies the existence of an imperfectly competitive market structure and barriers to entry. FSAs are therefore tied up with oligopoly power. According to this view, the MNE is the result of market failure and exists to exploit market imperfections.

Although reliance on market imperfections remains a key dimension of multinational theory, another factor is emerging to challenge the oligopolistic-monopolistic view of the multinational firm. International economic integration and globalization represent the reverse of market failure: they are essentially about the reduction or removal rather than the erection of entry barriers. As such globalization represents a move towards greater perfectability of markets. This is not to say that the market imperfection view of the internationalization of the firm is no longer relevant but that some adaptation is required to accommodate globalization and the implication that the multinational-ization of the firm may occur when no obvious FSAs are present. This development goes some way, perhaps, towards explaining the resurgence of interest in the work of Edith Penrose. While Stephen Hymer was interested in the expansion of firms as a means of exploiting or advancing monopoly power, Edith Penrose was interested in growth and expansion as a way of reducing costs.

Internalization

Internalization theory implies that an MNE internalizes its international transactions to overcome market imperfections. Work on internalization and the firm generally derives from the writings of Ronald Coase and Oliver Williamson. The international dimension originated with the work of scholars like Peter Buckley and Mark Casson, Alan Rugman and John Dunning. Although drawing heavily on Hymer, the international version of internalization theory also evolved from a critique of Hymer that his version of market failure emphasized the role of MNEs as monopolistic/oligopolistic profit maximizers and neglected efficiency considerations. The market failure concerning internal-ization theorists arises not from market structure but from a failure to carry out transactions in the marketplace at a lower cost than within a firm or hierarchy. Such market failure arises from imperfect information, giving rise to opportunism and bounded rationality, and is more likely to be present in the case of cross-border than purely domestic transactions. In other words, firms seek to overcome market imperfections by performing the functions of the market within its own boundaries – that is, by internalizing economic activity to reduce transaction costs. The greater the market imperfections and general uncertainties, the greater is the incentive to internalize transactions.

Internalization potentially offers the international firm, indeed all firms, certain advantages. It provides opportunities for exploitation of internal economies of scope and scale, perhaps through vertical integration of production processes across borders with coordination and control exercised by the parent company. Such organization of value-adding activities within the firm enables it to secure guaranteed and reliable sources of inputs for its production facilities and to secure outlets for primary products such as crude petroleum or metals.

Internalization is also attractive to firms because of the control it offers them over their FSAs. This is especially appropriate when it comes to advantages arising from knowledge and technology. MNEs can exploit these advantages via franchising and licensing, for example, (see below) but internalization enables them to retain direct control of this asset and avoid a dilution of their property rights.

Internalization theory is therefore primarily aimed at explaining why cross-border transactions of intermediate products are organized within the boundaries of firms rather than within markets. While the net cost of market transactions exceeds the net cost of internalization, MNEs will continue to flourish.

The Eclectic Paradigm

The dominant explanation for the growth of multinational activity since the 1980s has been Dunning's eclectic paradigm. The eclectic paradigm is not so much a theory of international production as a framework for investigation and analysis. It represents a synthesis and integration of different theories and draws upon various approaches such as the theory of the firm, organization theory and trade and location theory. As such, the eclectic paradigm represents John Dunning's view that

> it is not possible to formulate a single operationally testable theory that can explain all forms of foreign-owned production. . . . At the same time . . . we believe that it is possible to formulate a general paradigm of MNE activity, which sets out a conceptual framework and seeks to identify clusters of variables relevant to an explanation of all kinds of foreign-owned output. . . . Within this framework, we believe that most of the partial micro- and macro-theories of international production can be accommodated.
>
> (Dunning, 1993, p. 68)

In crude terms, the eclectic paradigm rejects an 'either/or' approach to international production and, as its names suggests, takes the most useful parts of apparently competing approaches to explain the internationalization phenomenon.

The starting point of the eclectic paradigm is the Heckscher-Ohlin factor endowment explanation of international trade according to which countries specialize in the production of goods that require inputs of resources in which they are well endowed and trade them for goods in which they are not. It was the limiting assumptions of Heckscher-Ohlin such as factor immobility, identical production functions and perfect competition that stimulated the search for further explanation. These assumptions imply that all markets operate efficiently, that there are no economies of scale and that there is perfect and costless information. Once these restrictive assumptions are relaxed, in addition to relative factor endowments, variables such as market structure, transaction costs and corporate strategy become key factors in determining international economic activity, thereby opening out the debate about international production to a range of theoretical traditions.

The eclectic paradigm uses three sets of factors to explain the 'why', the 'where' and the 'how' respectively of the internationalization of production (see Case Study 9.2). These are as follows:

1. *Ownership factors*: a firm needs ownership advantages over other firms in the markets in which it is located or in which it is considering locating. These advantages can include technology and general innovative capabilities, information, and managerial and entrepreneurial skills. These factors link both to Hymer's FSAs and to the core competences or resource-based school of corporate strategy.
2. *Location factors*: these advantages are specific to a particular country but are available to all firms and include the availability of natural resources, labour (either in terms of quantity or of skills) and the general social, legal, political environment.
3. *Internalization factors*: internalization relates to the extent of ownership and control. Transactions made through the market, such as exporting, are arm's-length transactions. Internalized transactions take place within the boundary of the firm and enable multinational firms to overcome examples of market failure or imperfection (see above).

CASE STUDY 9.2

The Eclectic Paradigm in Practice – The Case of Guinness in Nigeria

In practice, the eclectic paradigm may be used to explain how ownership, location and internalization advantages can shape an MNE's entry into and subsequent operations in a specific market. The example of Guinness (a UK-based brewer renowned for its distinctive beverage) in Nigeria illustrates this point well. By 2007, Nigeria had become (behind the UK) the second biggest consumer of this distinctive alcoholic beverage, a process driven by demand from the local populace and not merely by expatriate consumers. The ascendancy of Guinness in the Nigerian market may be directly contextualized by the use of the OLI framework. By analysing each element of the framework in turn, it is evident that – while some elements have been more important than others – each has contributed to the firm's success within this distinctive market.

- *Ownership advantages:* in the case of Guinness, differentiating what can be a commoditized product rested upon ownership advantages in marketing and more especially branding. Historically, Guinness has strong competence in marketing which it has leveraged across those markets in which it operates. In Nigeria, these brand-based advantages were tailored to the market through the 'Michael Power' branding programme. This offered a James Bond-like character who not only represented the brand but also appeared in a Guinness-financed film. This local branding was so successful that many Nigerians view Guinness Nigeria as a domestic brand.
- *Location advantages:* the Nigerian market proved itself to be especially open to the central 'muscular/macho' image at the core of Guinness's value proposition. The aggressive marketing strategy stressed the macho elements of Guinness, a factor which found notable currency with Nigerian consumers. This advantage was com-

pounded by an absence of local competition and by Guinness's ability to adapt products to the local marketplace and colonial-era history associated with the brand. These conditions have benefited from enhanced political and economic stability which has made the national beer market less volatile. However, when the market was especially volatile in the mid-1990s, many smaller brewers disappeared, also creating benign conditions for Guinness.

- *Internalization:* due to its bulky nature, the product is manufactured locally where the parent company – Diageo – has a controlling interest in a subsidiary in which its partners are a range of local investors. For quality reasons, Guinness Nigeria invested in its own brewing facilities and does not – as other brewers do – allow third parties to brew under licence. This position was aided by the aforementioned market volatility which led to many breweries lying idle, some of which Guinness was able to acquire on favourable terms.

Guinness's experience in Nigeria demonstrates that, despite the difficulties of operating within Africa (especially with regard to logistics), there is potential for considerable MNE success within these markets. Indeed, the Nigerian market has become dominated by Guinness Nigeria and Nigerian Breweries (part-owned by Heineken). However, Guinness faces a number of challenges given the rise of religious fundamentalism and the emergence of new competing businesses. This underlines that the dynamics of the OLI framework continue to work to shape and reshape MNE configurations.

CASE STUDY ACTIVITIES

Chose an MNE with which you are familiar and analyse the extent to which its entry into a particular market can be explained by the eclectic paradigm framework.

According to Dunning, an MNE's degree of foreign value-added activities depends on the satisfaction of the following four conditions:

1. The degree to which a firm possess ownership advantages over other firms in a particular market.
2. The degree to which an MNE believes it is in its best interests to exploit its ownership advantages rather than sell them to another firm, perhaps in the form of technology licensing or franchising (the internalization factor).
3. The degree to which there are location-specific advantages of a particular country which raise the value of ownership advantages relative to elsewhere.
4. The degree to which foreign production is consistent with the long-term strategy of the firm.

The Evolution of Network and Alliance Capitalism

Dunning's eclectic paradigm has become the dominant tool in the analysis of the internationalization of production and allows for a number of theoretical approaches to nest within its framework. However, significant changes in the international business environment, brought about by globalization and its main drivers, have necessitated a reassessment, or at least a modification, of thinking about international production.

The original eclectic paradigm is set within the framework of hierarchical capitalism: that is, given that market failures have become larger and more commonplace with the growing specialization and complexity of economic activity and technological and political changes, large, hierarchical firms have developed to compensate for these failures. However, the nature of challenges to the firm is changing and, with it, their response to market failure. Rather than rein in their value-adding activities within the confines of a single hierarchical organization, firms are increasingly acting to reduce the transaction and coordinating costs of arm's-length market transactions by constructing complex networks of relationships and developing strategic and collaborative alliances.

Such networks and alliances take many forms and include cooperative and strategic alliances, various types of joint ventures and the networks developed by clothing and sportswear companies in which most, if not all, production is outsourced. The role of the MNE therefore varies, depending on the rationale for and type of network involved. When extensive outsourcing takes place, the MNE acts as the coordinator of a complex network of interdependent, value-added activities across borders and long distances. When collaborating, perhaps over development of complementary or joint technologies, cooperation and relationship building will become more important.

Cooperation and alliances have become commonplace for a number of reasons. The high cost of technological development has encouraged firms to collaborate to share both the costs and the risks of this activity. In other cases, collaboration may take the form of interaction between assemblers and component suppliers – a common situation in the automotive and electronic appliance sectors. Clustering and agglomeration of related activities is another development that, although not new, is intensifying. It also accentuates the role of networking and collaboration and reflects the growing international role of SMEs (see Chapter 11) which are steadily becoming embedded in many cross-border networks. Overall, alliances and collaborations enable companies to leverage the assets, skills and experiences of their partners for the purpose of enhancing competitive advantage.

By blurring the boundaries between firms, cooperative and alliance capitalism challenge conventional thinking about the internationalization of the firm. This is particularly apparent for the internalization school of thinking and for the 'I' factor of the eclectic paradigm which specifically claims that firms deal with the market failure represented by transaction costs by carrying out transactions within the firm rather than at arm's length. It is clearly possible to argue that alliance capitalism significantly weakens internalization explanations of the internationalization of the firm. However, Dunning argues (1995) that 'the internalisation paradigm still remains a powerful tool of analysis' provided it is widened and adapted to the new environment. He argues that external alliances and networks can be incorporated into internalization if it is acknowledged that inter-firm agreements achieve the same objective as internalization, albeit more effectively, and/or spread the capital and other risks among participating firms. In other words, Dunning recommends that an inter-firm alliance or network be either treated as an extension of intra-firm transactions or as a distinctive organizational mode in its own right – a mode that is complementary rather than an alternative to a hierarchy.

Alliance capitalism also requires broadening of both the 'O' and the 'L' factors of the eclectic paradigm. Indeed, the ability of firms to develop and manage networks, alliances and other forms of inter-firm relationships to enhance product quality, to integrate knowledge and learning and to externalize risk may be regarded as an ownership-specific advantage in its own right. Location factors, for their part, need to incorporate the concept of agglomeration and clustering: that is, there are certain geographical locations that have become centres of interaction and innovation within global networks. Such areas offer a concentration of contacts, knowledge, infrastructure and institutions that attract economic activity. Examples include the City of London for financial services, Silicon Valley in California or Silicon Glen in Scotland for information technology, or general areas of concentrated economic activity like southern China or Northwest Europe.

Although some would argue that the elasticity of the eclectic paradigm demonstrates that its generality enables it to fit all circumstances, others argue that its adaptability is its strength. The international business environment is evolving rapidly and its organizational diversity is expanding along with it. The eclectic paradigm is not itself a theory of international production but is rather a framework to help analysts make sense of it. As such, its expansion to incorporate alliance capitalism does not appear unreasonable. In the early twenty-first century, the large-scale, single multinational firm remains the dominant player in the global marketplace and, as such, the focus of research on the internationalization of the firm. However, this does not preclude a growing body of research and literature on networks, cooperation and alliances to complement and sit alongside such research and, in some respects, perhaps even to replace it.

Box 9.2 International Strategy and the Eclectic Paradigm

One of the main criticisms of the eclectic paradigm it that it is simply not dynamic enough to account for changes in strategy by MNEs. Dunning (1993) attempted to build into the eclectic paradigm differences in the strategic response to any given configuration for OLI variables. Dunning argues that at any given point in time the activity of an MNE represents a point on a set of trajectories towards their internationalization path. This trajectory is determined by the interaction between the OLI configuration over successive time periods and the strategy of firms. Thus the OLI configuration is only static at a given point in time. This configuration reflects the strategic choices made by the firm in previous time periods.

The strategic choice made by a firm is one of many of the endogenous variables that will affect the OLI configuration (mainly through O and L advantages). Other variables may include innovation (technological or organizational), change in management and mergers/acquisitions. Also important are exogenous variables such as economic growth and exchange rates. Thus shifts in both endogenous and exogenous variables from one period to the next will alter strategy in the current period and so amend the chosen configuration of OLI to meet its strategic objectives in the next period.

THE KNOWLEDGE-BASED VIEW OF THE MNE

The evolutionary view of the MNE (Kogut and Zander, 1993) was seen by many as the end of the prevailing transaction-based perspective of the MNE. This novel perspective was informed by behavioural (Cyert and March, 1963) and evolutionary (Nelson and Winter, 1982) theories of the firm. The theory seeks to address three alleged weaknesses within internalization theory:

- the focus on minimizing transaction costs understates the potential value created by foreign entry;
- the internalization perspective is overdetermined through neglecting the development of new firm-specific advantages;
- the internalization perspective focuses on individual transactions and ignores (or at least underplays) the firm's past, future and social context of these transactions.

Kogut and Zander conceptualize the MNE as a repository of knowledge. First, they suggest that the more tacit the knowledge, the more likely it is that knowledge transference will be internal. Second, they claim that the boundary of the firm is defined more by knowledge resources than by internalization. Consequently, they conceptualize the MNE as a social community that serves as an efficient mechanism for the creation and transformation of knowledge into products. Thus the key criteria for whether a firm will transfer knowledge internally is its efficiency relative to third parties. Thus market failure concerns are not required. As a result, MNEs exist because they are efficient means of creating and transmitting knowledge. Through repeated interaction, agents develop a common understanding by which to transfer knowledge from ideas into production and markets.

The central tenet is that firms grow by their ability to create new knowledge and to replicate this knowledge so as to expand their market. Their competitive advantage rests on being able to understand and undertake this transfer more effectively than other firms and the inability of rivals to duplicate and imitate this core resource. As a result, horizontal FDI is conceptualized as the transfer of knowledge within the firm and across borders. Such transfers are the primary expression of growth of the firm. Thus modal choice is a reflection of the likely revenues to be generated from that mode given the experiential knowledge that would result. Thus the lower the expectation of extra knowledge, the more devolved the mode will be (e.g. licensing). If the reverse applies, the firm will seek higher control modes.

This marks a break from market failure towards efficiency of the firm in transformation of knowledge relative to other firms as a key explanation of the development of MNEs. As a result, the firm boundary is determined by the difference between knowledge and the embedded capabilities between the creator and users. The more tacit the knowledge and the more experience agents have of sharing this tacit knowledge, the greater the incentive for the firm to internalize this knowledge. Thus firms specialize in transferring knowledge that is difficult to understand and codify. MNEs are able to lower the cost of this transfer internally more than they would be able to do so via third parties. Furthermore, knowledge as a firm-specific advantage is something that will aid expansion.

Kogut and Zander also stress that the dynamic nature of this process underlines that these capabilities and knowledge do not stand still. MNEs seek to combine existing knowledge with new information to constantly evolve their stock of valuable knowledge. There is thus a key advantage in the combinative capability of the firm. This is also linked into the high absorptive capacity of the firm: that is, the ability to absorb, spread, utilize and transform information into new knowledge stock.

The above is typical of an emerging research theme which stresses the knowledge component of the MNE. It seems logical that if the firm is a repository of knowledge, then central to this is the ability of knowledge to flow within the MNE among headquarters and subsidiaries as well as among subsidiary units themselves. This characterizes the MNE as a differentiated network in which each subsidiary (as well as the headquarters) has access to different resources and the ability to generate its own valuable knowledge that can be useful to other parts of the MNE network.

Gupta and Govindarajan (1991) offered a typology of the role of subsidiaries in the knowledge development process. This is part of a long line of literature that has sought to explore headquarter–subsidiary relations as a means of control and coordination. Gutpa and Govindarajan have examined knowledge flows within MNEs, which they see as the most important of all the flows between the constituent units of the network, and have identified two aspects to these flows:

- the magnitude of transactions (i.e. the extent to which subsidiaries engage in knowledge transfer);
- the direction of transfer (i.e. whether a subsidiary is a recipient or a provider of knowledge).

Using these two dimensions they have defined four generic subsidiary roles:

1. *Global innovator (high outflow, low inflow)*: as the firm moves towards a transnational model, so the subsidiary becomes more important and acts as a centre of excellence for specific product lines.
2. *Integrated player (high outflow, high inflow)*: these engage in knowledge transfer but are also simultaneously receiving knowledge from other units. This makes it an important mode within the MNE network.
3. *Implementor (low outflow, high inflow)*: these do not engage in extensive knowledge creation and offer little to other units. Consequently, they are heavily dependent upon knowledge flows from either the headquarters or other subsidiaries.

4. *Local innovator (low outflow, low inflow)*: these are self-standing subsidiaries that engage in knowledge creation but do not seek to transfer this knowledge across the rest of the network. In addition, the firm also sees little value in knowledge being created elsewhere within the MNE network.

The above suggests that knowledge within the firm needs to be studied at the nodal (i.e. individual units), dyadic (i.e. focus on the behaviour of pairs) and systemic (i.e. the focus on the network) levels. According to this model, the causes of knowledge flows in and out of a subsidiary are a function of the value of the source unit's knowledge stock, the motivational disposition of the source unit, existence of richness of transmission channels, the motivational disposition of target units and the absorptive capacity of the target unit.

The value of a unit's knowledge stock to the MNE network is seen as directly related to the type of entry mode utilized. It is understood that acquired units tend to exhibit greater outflows to the rest of the group than greenfield operations as acquisitions tend to be motivated by the unique resources within the acquired unit. Furthermore, the value of a unit is also positively linked to the size of the unit relative to other units and to the level of economic development relative to the home state.

These actions have to be supported by an open-minded attitude by managers within the units and may have to be linked to remuneration schemes. Units need to be open both as sources and as recipients of knowledge and to rely on incentives within the firm to offer and accept knowledge as well as similar economic levels that allow such information to be transmitted and understood between units. These strategies will be supported by the ability of transmission channels (both formal and informal) to aid the flow of knowledge. Formal mechanisms include direct interaction between personnel and so on. Informal channels include corporate socialization mechanizations. Finally, absorptive capacity is key, as the unit has to be familiar with incoming knowledge, and be able to diffuse and use the information for competitive advantage. Again, the entry mode is an important determinant as acquired firms will be less obvious recipients of knowledge than greenfield operations.

THE MNE AS A NETWORK

This analysis has opened up a field of research on the role of the subsidiary within the network of firms. A subsidiary is a wholly owned unit of the MNE which exists outside the MNE's home. The role of the subsidiary is key to understanding the form and nature of the MNE. Birkinshaw (2000) claims that many MNEs are attempting to reduce the discretion available to local managers by seeking to integrate subsidiaries within the whole. Thus there is a move towards a more defined global structure. This research has highlighted the different roles that subsidiaries take within the network and defines the MNE as a differentiated network comprising a number of specified subsidiaries that contribute value to the network in some fashion. The role of these subsidiaries is driven by a mixture of central discretion but also, more importantly, by the ability of local managers to act in an entrepreneurial manner.

The MNE develops as a network of businesses that comprises capital, product and knowledge flows. A core current debate within international business is the nature of the links between these businesses, in particular the configuration between subsidiaries and between them and the headquarters. Such debates link the structure of the firm to the form and nature of the strategy followed and help define the intensity of the links between the separate components of the firm and the nature of knowledge and resource flows that exists between these units.

The notion of the MNE as a network was advocated by Hedlund (1986) in his extension of Perlmutter's categorization of MNEs (above). Hedlund argued that MNEs were heterarchical, consisting of many centres where subsidiary managers are given a strategic role both for their own unit and for the MNE as a whole. Hedlund's concept implies different kinds of centres based on a division of labour across locations with each of the units comprising a loosely coupled system. This can often mean that integration is achieved through normative control. What Hedlund identified was the emergence of a particular type of MNE composed of a loosely coalesced set of businesses.

Bartlett and Ghoshal (1989) have highlighted how strategy and structure interact within the context of the network-based MNE. These authors offered a typology of four organizations, based on two key criteria, operating within the international business environment. The first determinant involves matching the firm's capabilities to the demands of the businesses and the second is the company's organizational heritage. Using these criteria, the following typology (reflecting the strategy typology identified in Chapter 1) of MNEs was offered.

- *Multinational*: these are MNEs that follow conventional multi-domestic strategies. These build a strong local presence through sensitivity and responsiveness to local differences in a decentralized federation of resources and delegated responsibilities. These are likely to rely on local knowledge and networks which are often tacit. The national subsidiaries solve all operative and some strategic tasks.
- *Global*: these are MNEs that seek to attain cost advantages through scale and involve a network based around a strong central hub. Behaviour will be group oriented requiring intensive communication and a complex internal network. National subsidiaries are primarily seen as distribution centres and many strategic and operational decisions are centralized.
- *International*: these MNEs exploit parent company knowledge through worldwide diffusion and adaptation in a coordinated federation and suit companies with a reputation for professional management. Although overall control is maintained centrally, some control is ceded to subsidiaries. Thus some strategic areas are naturalized to the subsidiary while others are retained within the centre.
- *Transnational*: these companies seek global competitiveness through multinational flexibility and worldwide learning capability. These MNEs are dispersed, interdependent and specialized with differential contributions made by different units. Knowledge is developed jointly and distributed worldwide.

While all of these conform to network-based approaches, the transnational is seen by Bartlett and Ghoshal as the most efficient and effective. This allows the MNE to benefit from flexibility while maintaining some elements of centrality which would also be advantageous to the network. This typology is useful, as it can reduce the complexity of MNEs into manageable groups which may be used in a predictive manner.

As identified in Chapter 1, Porter (1986) defined the nature of the relationships within the MNE as one in which an enterprise looks to configure the firm value chain across the locations in which it operates. This configuration/coordination approach underlines the integrated nature of the centre and subsidiaries, and represents the source of competitive advantage for the MNE. The chosen configuration reflects a desire by the firm to divide activities according to where that activity is best performed to meet specific needs. This may be open-ended, as it implies that in some instances global configurations may be superior to multi-domestic and vice versa. Thus these advantages can be country specific. In other areas, especially in downstream areas, configuration will take place according to where the group is best able to benefit from key facets of that location. This underlines the benefits of coordination of mutual learning between units. Thus units can be self-supporting if necessary. Thus coordination can run from total to nothing just as configuration can be dispersed to concentrated. The choice of strategy will depend on environmental factors and facets of the market concerned and the firm's ability to match these needs. Overall, Porter concludes that the interface between structure and strategy is the degree of relationship among competitive environments. If this interrelationship is high, global industries will dominate, whereas when links are low, multi-domesticity will prevail. The difference between Porter's and Bartlett and Ghoshal's approaches is that the former is focused on the industry level while the latter is based on the firm level. The latter superseded the former as it was recognized that strategy could differ between subsidiaries.

Using the independent dimensions of geographic location of activities and the degree of integration activities, Jarillo and Martinez (1990) offer another typology of subsidiary strategy.

- *Autonomous subsidiary*: this type of subsidiary undertakes most of the functions of the value chain in a manner that is independent of its parent organization or other subsidiaries. This strategy will typically be followed by units within multinational firms competing in multi-domestic industries.
- *Receptive subsidiary*: receptive subsidiaries exist when a few of the functions of the value chain are performed in the host state and are highly integrated with the rest of the firm. These subsidiaries typically exist where the MNE is following a global strategy.
- *Active subsidiary*: many activities within the host are done in coordination with the rest of the firm as is the norm within transnational strategies. These units have strong mandates from the centre. However, not all subsidiaries will allow such strategies, as only important units will be given this degree of discretion.

For many, the emergence of the transnational was seen as the end-point of MNE evolution as it represented the best configuration. In part, this occurred because the analysis was no longer dealing with an internationalization process but with a large internationalized enterprise. With this development, a greater emphasis of academic endeavour has focused on subsidiary roles.

CONCLUSION

MNEs are central to the process of globalization. As in earlier chapters, they remain a controversial but important feature of the international business environment. However, it would be misleading to call them global in terms of reach, as many MNEs tend to limit their multinational endeavours.

What is apparent is that there has been a shift in the conceptualization of the MNE. Increasingly, the MNE is seen as a differentiated network of subsidiaries where value is created by the knowledge flows within them.

Summary of Key Concepts

- MNEs are at the core of the process of globalization.
- Multinationality is motivated by a number of factors such as resource-, market- and/or efficiency-seeking investment.
- The geographic spread of MNEs tends to be very uneven.
- The issue of why MNEs exist has often been based on internalization factors.
- Increasingly, evolutionary perspectives are coming to the fore.

Activities

1. Using an MNE of your choice, seek to identify the major drivers and motivations underpinning its multinationality.

2. Why do many MNEs have a very limited geographic spread?

3. Compare and contrast the major theories explaining the MNE.

Discussion Questions

1. How do you explain the existence of MNEs?

2. How does 'knowledge' shape and form the MNE?

3. Using an MNE with which you are familiar, seek to identify the major components of its OLI configuration.

References and Suggestions for Further Reading

Bartlett, C. and Ghoshal, S. (1989) *Managing across Borders: The Transnational Solution*, London: Hutchinson Business Books.

Birkinshaw, J. (2000) *Entrepreneurship in the Global Firm: Enterprise and Renewal*, London: Sage.

Birkinshaw, J. (2003) *Multinational Corporate Evolution and Subsidiary Development*, London: St Martin's Press.

Buckley, P. and Casson, M. (1991) *The Future of the Multinational Enterprise*, Basingstoke: Palgrave Macmillan.

Caves, R.E. (1996) *Multinational Enterprise and Economic Analysis*, 2nd edn, Cambridge: Cambridge University Press.

Cowling, K. and Sugden, R. (1987) *Transnational Monopoly Capitalism*, Brighton: Wheatsheaf.

Cyert, R.M. and March, J.G. (1963) *A Behavioral Theory of the Firm*, Englewood Cliffs, NJ: Prentice Hall.

Dicken, P. (1998) *Global Shift : Transforming the World Economy*, 3rd edn, New York and London: Guilford Press.

Dunning, J.H. (1993) *The Globalization of Business*, Wokingham: Thomson Learning.

Dunning, J.H. (1995) 'Reappraising the eclectic paradigm, in an age of alliance capitalism', *Journal of International Business Studies*, Vol. 26, No. 3, 461–491.

Dunning, J.H. (1997) *Alliance Capitalism and Global Business*, London: Routledge.

Dunning, J.H. and Lundan, S.M. (2008) *Multinational Enterprises and the Global Economy*, Cheltenham: Edward Elgar.

Gupta, A.K. and Govindarajan, V. (1991) 'Knowledge flows and the structure of control within multinational firms', *Academy of Management Review*, Vol. 16, 768–792.

Hedlund, G., (1986) 'The hypermodern MNE: a heterarchy?', *Human Resource Management*, spring, Vol. 25, 9–26.

Jarillo, J.C. and Martinez, J. (1990) 'Different roles for subsidiaries: the case of multinational corporations', *Strategic Management Journal*, Vol. 11, No. 7, 501–512.

Kogut, B. and Zander, U. (1993) 'Knowledge of the firm and the evolutionary theory of the multinational corporation', *Journal of International Business Studies*, Vol. 24, No. 4, 625–645.

Markensen, J.R. (2001) *Multinational Firms and the Theory of International Trade*, Boston, MA: MIT Press.

Navaretti, G. and Venables, A.J. (2006*) Multinational Firms in the World Economy*, Princeton, NJ: Princeton University Press.

Nelson, R.R. and Winter, S.G. (1982) *An Evolutionary Theory of Economic Change*, Cambridge, MA: Belknap Press of Harvard University Press.

Perlmutter, H.V. (1969) 'The tortuous evolution of the multinational corporation', *Columbia Journal of World Business*, Vol. 4 (January/February), 9–18.

Porter, M.E. (1986) *Competition in Global Industries*, Boston, MA: Free Press.

UNCTAD (2007) *World Investment Report*, www.unctad.org.

Chapter 10

The Internationalization of MNEs

Globalization offers short-term opportunities: economies of scale, efficiencies from larger markets, and cost savings from cheaper production or services. But with the 'quick buck' comes greater vulnerability. As the business chain lengthens, the risk of failure from one weak link increases. Risks – structural and reputational – are compounded as business extends around the world.

(Willem Brocker (2006), Partner – PWC)

LEARNING OBJECTIVES

This chapter will help you to:

- understand the major process models of internationalization
- identify contingency and network-based models of internationalization
- comprehend the major entry modes used to internationalize
- assess the link between multinationality and performance

A conventional weakness of MNE theory was a perceived failure to offer an adequate explanation of internationalization. Thus while there were theories to explain why MNEs existed, there were no credible explanations of why these firms were multinational in the first place. To some degree, this conceptual gap has been filled by emerging theories of internationalization. Internationalization is the process by which the MNE expands its geographic/spatial boundaries and consists of three interlinked processes:

1. geographical extension of the firm as it expands into new host markets;
2. extension of the MNE as its increases its market penetration within economies where it already has a presence;
3. improved coordination between those locations where the MNE has a presence.

Theories to explain the process of internationalization may be broken down into four major perspectives: the steps models, process models, contingency models and network-based frameworks. This chapter initially explores each of these perspectives. However, contingency models are explored less intensely as they are covered in more detail elsewhere (see Chapter 11). Building on these increasingly overlapping perspectives, the chapter moves on to examine the differing modes of market entry and presence which are the practical and operational expressions of the preceding theoretical models.

THE STEPS MODELS

Rather than constituting a theory, the steps models basically outline operational aspects of the internationalization models. These operational perspectives may be subdivided into two behavioural models:

■ the Uppsala model;
■ Innovation Process (IP) models.

The Uppsala Model

A study (referred to as the Uppsala model) by Johanson and Weidersheim-Paul (1975) of how four Swedish firms had internationalized provides a framework that has proved useful on a wider stage. The authors argue that many firms begin the internationalization process when they are relatively small and develop their overseas presence gradually. They establish themselves in their domestic market first and then start to move abroad via a series of incremental steps. This movement abroad tends to occur earlier in the case of companies established in small domestic markets like the firms in the Uppsala model. Linked into process-based approaches (see below), the Uppsala model reflects observations of the operational activities of business as opposed to forming a theory per se.

The Uppsala model identifies four steps in the establishment and extension of a firm's operations, a process referred to by its authors as 'the establishment chain':

1.   no regular export activities;
2.   export via independent representatives or agents;
3.   the establishment of sales subsidiaries;
4.   foreign production and manufacturing.

Firms are expected to follow this pattern of internationalization as they move from low to high commitment modes of operation (see below).

According to this model, initial movement abroad is carried out by independent exporting agents or representatives. This entails a limited resource commitment and a lesser risk than immediately setting up a wholly owned sales subsidiary (stage three) in a market of which the incumbent has little knowledge. Indeed, underpinning this model is the general assumption that moving through the different phases of development depends on the acquisition of the expertise and knowledge that enables the firm to move onto the next internationalization stage. Firms only move to the final stage of the establishment chain (foreign production and manufacturing) when they have gained international expertise through other activities and specific knowledge of a particular location.

The authors do not claim that the model applies in all circumstances. They point out that there may be good reasons why firms do not follow the establishment chain exactly. For example, firms with extensive experience in other foreign markets may well jump stages in the establishment chain and invest in production facilities in a particular location without prior knowledge of it. However, the model is useful. First, it points out that firms are more likely to seek international opportunities when their founders or senior management already have international business experience or are internationally minded in some way. Second, and more importantly, it establishes the principle that firms engage in international activity in a way that gradually commits them to more intensive and extensive involvement. The model sets out a four-stage process. In a sense, the precise details of each stage of the process do not matter as they vary from case to case. What does distinguish each stage of the process though is the degree of involvement as highlighted by the commitment offered to the host.

Innovation Process Models

These models, while also seeing internationalization as a series of stages, regard exporting as an innovation for the firm. In this context, the expansion of internationalization in terms of depth and reach can be explained by the diffusion of innovation. Cavusgil's (1980) model was the forerunner of these models and based internationalization on the following stages:

Stage 1: domestic marketing only;
Stage 2: pre-export phase;

Stage 3: experimental involvement with psychologically close countries;
Stage 4: active involvement;
Stage 5: committed involvement.

Internationalization is thus driven by a change in the economic or social potential of an enterprise. This suggests that innovation models stress the internal and external factors that create and stimulate internationalization. Thus, innovation stimulates the firm to enter new markets. This innovation is driven by increased knowledge which in turn increases the commitment by the firm to international markets. IP models focus on the learning linked with the innovation created by the process. The IP model is similar to the Uppsala model in that it is dynamic, incremental and based on knowledge.

PROCESS MODELS

The theoretical underpinnings of the process models are the interrelated concepts of learning and experience. Process models regard experience as the main explanatory construct of the internationalization process, reflecting a belief that the process is driven by 'learning by doing'. This ongoing experience removes uncertainties surrounding the process of internationalization generated by lack of knowledge. The role of experience is to lower the risk associated within the internationalization process by increasing the firm's knowledge of operating in international markets.

Johanson and Weidersheim-Paul (1975) assume that the biggest obstacles to internationalization are lack of knowledge and resources. Incremental learning reduces the perceived risk of overseas investment and continuing internationalization is encouraged by presence in a foreign market. This perspective is underpinned by the importance of psychic distance to the process of internationalization. Linking to culture (see Chapter 13), the concept of psychic distance has been defined as both internal and external factors preventing or disturbing the flow of information between the firm and the market. The theory assumes that a firm's reach and depth are extended as psychic distance is narrowed and the firms get better at the process of internationalization. Familiarity comes from language, culture, education levels, political systems, levels of industrial development and so on. Psychic distance will often be closely linked to physical distance (that is, internationalization may start close to home) but it will not always be the case. The UK and Australia, for example, are physically far apart but the psychic distance between them is much closer.

In terms of the internationalization process, market knowledge is subdivided into objective and experiential knowledge. Whereas objective knowledge can be taught, experiential knowledge is unique and acquired through personal experience. Experiential knowledge is inversely related to uncertainty and derives from the size of the investment in resources and the degree of commitment offered to international markets. Variation in commitment implies that investments are idiosyncratic. Commitment decisions are made by managers to commit resources to target markets and are made in the knowledge that the MNE has of the market and conditions within it. Thus lack of knowledge is inversely related to the commitment to the market. Missing knowledge may take the following forms:

- *Internationalization knowledge*: this is knowledge of the firm's capability and resources for undertaking actions in international markets. This is a reflection of historical actions, is firm specific and combines all past experience of the process to inform current and future activities.
- *Institutional knowledge*: this is knowledge of government and institutional frameworks, rules, norms and values within the host markets.
- *Business knowledge*: this is knowledge of the customers, suppliers and market conditions within the host economies where the firm operates.

The above are interrelated and over time have the capability to inform objective knowledge as experience is taught to other parts of the organization (see Figure 10.1). These will depend upon the depth and reach of the international activities followed by the operation.

Process models have attracted criticism most notably for their simplicity. This reflects the fact that they understate the complexity of the internationalization process. Clearly the conception of the model is highly deterministic, suggesting that feedback loops exist that push the firm towards ever-increasing commitment. This may not be the case. Unidirectionality is not inevitable as strategies do vary in their intensity of physical commitment over time. There is also a need to consider intangible commitment alongside tangible commitment or else the degree of commitment offered to markets could be underestimated. In addition, the choice of market is likely to be determined by more than knowledge alone. The model ignores issues of market size, total resources, bandwagon effects and so on that could determine the choice of market.

CONTINGENCY MODELS

Contingency-based views of the internationalization process initially grew out of rejection of the determinism and gradualism of the process views (discussed more fully in Chapter 11). The central tenet of this perspective is that firms have very uneven internationalization trajectories and that incrementalism is no longer relevant for many firms (Oviatt and McDougall, 1994). The shifts in the environment highlighted by the rise of international entrepreneurship (through Born Globals) means firms can be international from their inception (Rialp *et al.*, 2005). This is especially true where firms possess unique resources. This approach disputes the relevance of the stages model to increasingly service intensive and high-technology-based economies. The main source of competitive advantage is a more sophisticated knowledge base that does not require the evolving features of process-based approaches. The evolution of this perspective has in part curtailed its ability to explore inter-

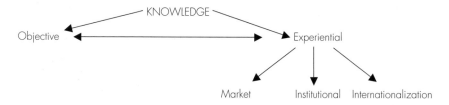

FIGURE 10.1 Knowledge and the Internationalization Process

nationalization beyond the formative period. Authors have attempted to move beyond this limitation by building network views into international entrepreneurship to offer a framework to explore how strategies evolve (Johanson and Vahlne, 2003).

Network-based Internationalization

The network view of internationalization emerged from reflection on the deficiencies of the process models (Johansson and Vahlne, 1990). This perspective is based on empirical observations that networks are important to the internationalization process through social exchange and resource dependency. Networks are defined as 'connections between firms and individuals in an industrial system built as relationships are established and maintained and linked through a variety of formal and informal mechanisms, resources and activities' (Johansson and Mattsson, 1988). Internationalization occurs by using networks to extend reach, increase penetration and connect and integrate different national networks. The network perspective identifies the difficulties in formulating and developing market entry strategy. It highlights how social and cognitive ties between actors shape ongoing interactions that in turn shape the network structure. Network theory stresses how agents interact to influence the form and nature of the internationalization process. Johanson and Mattsson (1988) argue that in the network view, internationalization is based on the gradual learning and the development of market knowledge through networks which allows the firm to establish and develop positions in a foreign network. Thus networks may be used to enhance strategic positioning through access to new resources, skills and flexibility.

Internationalization through networks (defined as long-term relationships) occurs through one or more of the following methods:

- the establishment of relationships within country networks that are new to the firm;
- the development of relationships within these networks by increased penetration;
- connecting existing networks.

These patterns of internationalization suggest that networks are used to extend reach, enhance market penetration and are mutually supportive. Unlike the process models, the network view focuses on the context of the business and the relationships that form the platform of the internationalization process. Furthermore, the degree of internationalization of the firm is a reflection of the network, not of the firm itself. As a result, a highly internationalized firm may have all of its assets within its home market. The network perspective also has implications for the nature of commitment where firms are committed to the internationalization process through their participation in networks and not solely via host market presence.

Bell (1995) argues that network theory explains internationalization better than process models as they were more influential on the market entry choices than conventional notions of psychic distance. More recent times have seen networks become a powerful framework for international entrepreneurship research. Andersen and Buvik (2002) suggest that relationships are a more effective guide to international market selection than that offered by process models.

THE LINK BETWEEN MULTINATIONALITY AND PERFORMANCE: THE S-SHAPE MODEL

The impact of internationalization upon the performance of MNEs has also been a prominent research theme. Prevailing thinking has highlighted an s-shaped relationship between performance and the degree of internationalization (see Figure 10.2). Generally, a positive relationship is assumed between the degree of international diversity and performance. However, this relationship is not straightforward, as it tends to ignore the costs involved in the internationalization process, especially in the formative and mature stages. In these stages the costs of the process may outweigh any benefits.

It is apparent that there are direct benefits to the firm from internationalization through processes of exploration and exploitation, enabling firms to realize economies of scale and to spread risks over a number of states. However, the major immediate benefits are derived from the ability of the firm to exploit market imperfections in the cross-border use of its intangible assets. These benefits are enhanced by exploration benefits derived from the firm's use of the internationalization process to improve the quantity and quality of its knowledge base. These are compounded by the benefits that the MNE gains from being able to access location-specific resources.

The costs of geographic diversification are highlighted by liabilities of newness and of foreignness. The former relates to the challenges facing the firm in terms of adjusting to the demands of new operations such as the purchasing and installation of facilities. This imposes high upfront costs and can place the new subsidiary in a disadvantageous position compared to incumbents. Over time, these liabilities of newness tend to decrease. However, these issues are compounded by liabilities of foreignness that can lead to higher costs compared to indigenous/incumbent firms. These derive from the firm making mistakes in the new market as a result of its lack of knowledge and experience. Again, these costs and liabilities should diminish over time.

However, even within an experienced MNE, costs can also increase. This results from the hypothesis that there is only so much diversity a firm can undertake before the cost of moving into a state erodes any benefits from such a move. Generally, as the firm becomes more diversified, so

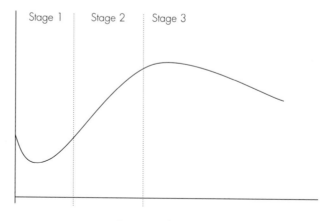

FIGURE 10.2 Multinationality and Performance

transaction and coordination costs increase. As the firm becomes more spread, so information can become distorted or lost and governance becomes more difficult. This may also be compounded as incentives between intra-MNC managers become misaligned as the firm moves into ever more diverse environments. As a result, the link between internationalization and performance may be broken down into three stages (see Figure 10.1).

- *Stage 1: Early internationalization*: in this phase, the firm encounters increased costs from liabilities of newness and foreignness. This means that entry costs are greater than the initial benefits with high up-front expenditure spread over a limited number of operations. Thus, the impact on performance is negative.
- *Stage 2: Later internationalization*: after a while, experience means that benefits from internationalization begin to accrue to the firm. This stems from enhanced knowledge from overseas, accessing cheaper inputs, market power, exploiting firm-specific advantages, scale and so on. The length of time between stage 1 and stage 2 is a function of the sector, market and domestic characteristics. Thus, context makes a difference. Thus, despite continued expansion increasing costs, these would be outweighed by the aforementioned benefits.
- *Stage 3: Excessive internationalization*: after a while, too much diversity begins to reduce profits. Research suggests that the first 40/60 nations are the most rewarding. After this the firm can only extend reach by moving into peripheral and less promising markets. This is compounded by a sharp rise in managerial costs and firms becoming subject to information overload (Glaum and Oesterle, 2007).

Evidence suggests that few firms stray into stage 3. If they do, such actions tend to be followed by divestment of assets within these locations. As a result, stage 3 tends to be short. However, this should not discount the possibility that some firms may take a longer term perspective and deliberately over-internationalize for purposes of market share or to gain a foothold in an emerging market. The Case Study (10.1) of Cable & Wireless highlights how internationalization can vary over time.

CASE STUDY 10.1

Cable & Wireless (C&W)

Cable & Wireless (C&W) highlights how over the history of an MNC the degree of internationalization can ebb and flow. Throughout its history, the international boundaries of C&W have both expanded and contracted as the firm has adjusted its strategy to cope with shifts in its environmental context. C&W is a UK telecommunications enterprise that has its roots in the 1860s. As a means of understanding how C&W's internationalization has evolved throughout its history, four phases are identified.

Phase 1: 1860s to 1950s: The Internationalization of C&W

C&W's political role makes it unique among the population of MNCs. Unlike other MNCs, C&W was a British company with no domestic operations. The enterprise was charged with managing the external communication networks that supported the British Empire. This role was the same for all parts of the Empire where it had minimal internal service but handled most (if not all) overseas traffic. Thus C&W was global from the start and did not follow the normal domestic-to-foreign trajectory common to most other multinationals.

The mid- to late nineteenth century was characterized by the aggressive building of international telegraph systems. Entrepreneurs moved into the building of extensive undersea (as well as overland) cable systems to support what was believed to be an increasing demand for international traffic driven by government and increased trade. The result was a plethora of medium and small-sized cable companies. Under the guidance of John Pender, the Eastern Telegraph Company emerged as perhaps the largest of the operators as it consolidated the fragmented market structure by acquiring many of the smaller companies. By 1887, Eastern owned 22,400 miles of cable.

New wireless technologies were – by the formative years of the twentieth century – proving to be a major threat to these extensive cable systems. In 1928, the Imperial Wireless and Cable Conference worked to integrate these cable and wireless systems under a new operating company: Imperial and International Communications Ltd (which included the assets of Eastern, Pacific Cable and Marconi). This name was changed in 1934 to C&W. The extensive reach and penetration of these cable and wireless systems were pivotal to the management of the 1939 to 1945 war effort where traffic increased 400 per cent.

This protracted initial phase of internationalization was driven by the needs of Empire and the role of government in promoting consolidation. The initial period was characterized by a land grab which led over time to a single network of cable and wireless emerging to support these needs. This underlines the strong political subtext that was driving this phase of internationalization.

Phase 2: 1950s to 1970s: the End of Empire and Its Legacy

This second phase was characterized by a further shift in the environment of C&W. In 1947, the company was nationalized as the government sought to take control and directly influence the repair of those parts of the network damaged during the Second World War. In many ways, this did not materially affect the operations of the business. However, a more far-reaching impact was the gradual dismantling of the British Empire which led to C&W undergoing some degree of de-internationalization.

An immediate consequence of the emerging independence of the colonies was that many states, especially the larger dominions (Canada, Australia and India) sought to nationalize and gain control of external communications systems. For C&W, this meant a shift in position where it had to hand over assets and concessions to these governments. In some cases, the business was kept on to manage overseas networks. In other places, it moved out of the concession market towards offering specialized network services. Yet, by the end of the 1950s, C&W was still the world's largest international telecommunications company representing the single largest component of the global system. Furthermore, as it had lost key markets it had moved into managing concessions within smaller markets. However, what was seen as tele-colonialism was a negative facet which limited C&W to some degree and its ability to sustain its position within key markets.

However, this did not stop the loss of concessions in ex-colonies continuing throughout the 1960s. Despite this, C&W was able to preserve its strong international position through partnerships with host governments, good relations with ministers and making politically expedient concessions where necessary. Often many of the old concessions were still staffed by ex-C&W people while in other cases C&W formed joint ventures with host governments for the operation of networks. The company was proving especially successful in winning concessions in the Middle and Far East. However, international strategy was being influenced by the emergence of more powerful user groups who were likely to generate more traffic for its network. The collective power of these user groups (such as airlines and Banks) was attractive for C&W which wanted to generate traffic for its network.

As more commercial markets matured, C&W's knowledge of international markets (especially developing states) was a competitive strength for the business. By the early 1970s, C&W was starting to explore new opportunities. Using its strong base in Hong Kong, it was moving into the Far East and also made limited forays into Europe and the US. The move into these non-traditional markets highlights how C&W was changing as it moved away from a focus on geographic markets to ones where trans-nationalism was more evident. This dual-faceted nature of C&W would continue for many years to come, as it comprised a series of legacy and high-growth businesses.

Phase 3:1980 to 2000: The Globalization of Markets

In 1979, C&W was privatized. This coincided with a period of rapid change in telecommunications markets as national markets were opened up to competition. Given its extensive experience, this trend should have put C&W in a very strong position to extend its international reach and market penetration. In the 1980s C&W was a company that relied on the cash cow of Hong Kong to support its operations. By 1985, it contributed 75 per cent of the group's revenues. On the back of this revenue, C&W pursued two strategic objectives throughout the 1980s. First, the group expanded its geographic reach, gaining increasing share of small state concessions. Second, the group continued to build up a presence across global segments such as managing increased flows that emerged from the international-ization of business. To support these businesses, the group created a 'Global Digital Highway' (GDH) to connect global financial centres together. The year

1984 was a watershed for C&W, as it established a credible presence in the UK market for the first time with its Mercury subsidiary.

The desire to target global segments pushed C&W into unfamiliar markets such as the US, Japan and Europe where competition was intense. The GDH was at the centre of its strategy with core value proposition behind its business model based on generating traffic for its business model. However, flaws were becoming evident within its strategy. First, despite a presence in around 50 states, there was little synergy between these businesses. C&W was more like a holding company consisting of a series of interlinked businesses. There was, for example, little overlap between corporate and legacy businesses. Second, the concession in the core cash cow of Hong Kong was due to expire in 1995.

By 1992, despite a presence in over 50 states, it was evident that only three states really mattered: Hong Kong, the UK and Jamaica. Thus despite a push into corporate markets it was the older businesses that still mattered the most. C&W tried to present a more coherent image by marketing itself as a federation of businesses bound together by the GDH. However, this did little to overcome criti-cisms from investors that C&W was worth less than the sum of its parts. Indeed, by 1997, C&W had a presence in over 70 states with very little power in key markets. In 1998, C&W attempted to rid itself of the federative 'flags on a map' structure for one that stressed 'globality' by putting its global business as core to its future development.

As a result, C&W repositioned itself towards the global end of the market, divesting itself of non-core assets and using the resulting revenues to build up its corporate business, especially within the triad of the US, Japan and Europe. Throughout the late 1990s, C&W sold off its old businesses and bought new businesses based on internet technology. The aim was to use the mature legacy business to support this repositioning. However, by the late 1990s/early 2000s, it was evident that this repositioning was simply not working. C&W had attempted to enter a very competitive sector just as a glut of capacity was forcing prices down. Its acquisitions in the US, Japan and Europe were proving difficult to turn around. The result was that once again C&W had to alter its positioning.

Phase 4: 2001 to the Present: Back to the UK

Since the formative years of the millennium, C&W has scaled back its international operations substantially. The firm has stopped trying to explain linkages between its two core sets of business: corporate and regional. C&W has gone through period of reducing its organizational reach. It has sold off a substantial array of overseas assets. The Hong Kong assets as well as those in the US, Japan and Australia have all been sold off, and any expansion in geographic reach has been limited to small-scale operations. This retreat from global markets has been compounded by increases in competition within the key remaining legacy businesses in the Caribbean. These states are making a play to liberalize their markets in the very near future.

The consequence is that paradoxically C&W has decided to concentrate on the one market where it was historically banned or had a weak position: the UK. The firm has gone on an acquisition spree within this market to expand the range of segments it serves as well as the range of services offered. By 2006, over 60 per cent of C&W turnover was from the UK (compared to less than 1 per cent 20 years earlier). The remaining international business (mainly in the Caribbean) contributed a declining percentage of total revenue. At the time of writing (2008), C&W is mooting the final disposal of its remaining regional businesses. This would mark a

complete turnaround in the international strategy of C&W.

Throughout its history as a result of shifting priorities, strategic mistakes and the ebb and flow of opportunity, C&W's internationalization has been a core differentiator. In the pre-competitive era, C&W stood more or less alone as the world's major international carrier. Over time, shifts in technology and competition have seen this advantage eroded. Now C&W finds itself in a paradoxical situation where its core market is now the one market from which it was initially forbidden. Over time C&W has slimmed down as it has sought to define a credible value proposition. As it has attempted to do so it has narrowed its scope both in terms of markets and segments. Its experience indicates that internationalization has to be accompanied by a clear strategic rationale for the constituent component to ensure that its parts deliver a coherent strategic message.

CASE STUDY QUESTIONS

1. What does the experience of C&W indicate about the nature of the internationalization process?

2. Identify C&W's main strategic strengths and problems throughout this period.

3. What were the major environmental drivers causing the shift in C&W's international position over its history?

FOREIGN MARKET ENTRY MODES

Once a company moves beyond exporting (stages 2 and 3 of the establishment chain) and into foreign production and manufacturing (stage 4), a wide range of choices opens up regarding how this is achieved. Figure 10.3 sets out two general categories of market entry which reflect different levels of engagement with foreign markets. Types of market entry are divided into equity and non-equity-based modes. Each method has its own strengths and weaknesses (outlined below) and is a response to the specific circumstances of a company. Contractual methods, for example, tend to be for specific

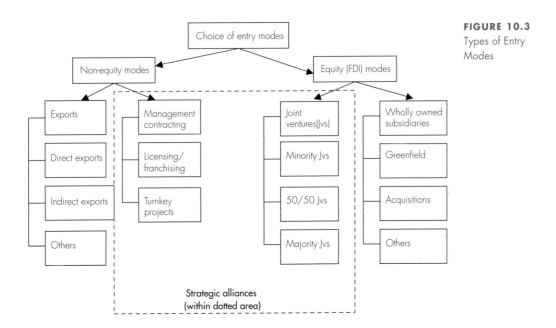

FIGURE 10.3
Types of Entry
Modes

periods of time, although these can be quite long. Equity-based methods on the other hand do not always entail specific time restrictions, although equity stakes can be sold, and offer the company more control and a much more direct engagement in a foreign market than many contractual modes.

Non-equity Entry Modes

Non-equity entry modes are based upon market involvement with no direct physical or financial involvement within the target markets. These methods often involve entry from a distance (exporting) or via the use of intermediaries on either a contract or non-contract basis. The major forms of non-equity modes of entry are given below.

Exporting

Foreign market entry via exporting is traditionally, and according to the Uppsala model, one of the first methods firms use to internationalize their activities. Exporting is relatively straightforward and less risky than other forms of internationalization and offers a relatively cheap and simple exit strategy if required. Exporting is not entirely risk-free, however: exporters still have to contend with exchange rate volatility, for example, but exposure to political shocks and risks is less extensive than for firms that have physically invested in foreign countries.

Exporting is conventionally divided into two categories – indirect and direct exporting. In the former, responsibility for carrying out the export function, including completion of export documentation and distribution, is delegated to third parties. The third parties, or intermediaries, take various forms, including:

■ *Export houses*: export houses buy products and sell them abroad on their own account and the producer may not even be aware that its products have been sold abroad.

■ *Confirming and buying houses*: confirming and buying houses are paid on a commission basis by foreign buyers to bring them into contact with sellers.

■ *Piggybacking*: piggybacking occurs when the exporter (the rider) pays to export its product through a distribution system that has already been set up by an established firm (the carrier) in the chosen foreign market. It can be difficult for piggybackers to find appropriate partners: the ideal combination is for complementary rather than competing products as there is a danger that the carrier may not give the same priority to the rider's product as its own.

The advantages of indirect exporting are that the whole export process is handled by a third party. It requires no international experience or knowledge and avoids many of the costs of setting up an in-house direct exporting operation. On the downside, indirect exporting reduces the producer's control over the export process and yields little or no knowledge about local markets, a factor that is normally instrumental in increasing sales to particular markets in the longer term. This is particularly so for exports conducted through export houses and holds to a lesser extent for other forms of indirect exporting. Indirect exporting also implies the absence of after-sales service, a factor that can have a negative impact on a firm's reputation or on future sales. In view of all these factors, indirect exporting is a technique most commonly used by smaller, inexperienced or occasional exporters.

Direct exporting, as its name suggests, is more proactive and hands-on than indirect exporting and involves an enterprise distributing and selling its own products into a foreign market. This requires greater in-house expertise regarding markets and exporting technicalities. As with indirect exporting, direct exporting may be done in various ways. Direct selling involves sales representatives directly employed by the exporting company, either from the home country (typically used to sell high-value items such as ships or aeroplanes) or domestic representatives based in the target market. In the former case, representatives may lack local knowledge or language skills.

Direct exporters also use agents as direct representatives in foreign markets. Such agents are paid on commission and may be employed on an exclusive, semi-exclusive or non-exclusive basis. This is frequently a successful strategy but, in the latter two cases, care needs to be taken that freedom to sell the products of other companies does not result in a conflict of interests for the agent.

The most developed approach to direct exporting involves the establishment of a local sales office or affiliate in a particular market. This is the most expensive option and requires the greatest degree of local knowledge. Ideally such affiliates are staffed by both home and host country personnel: the former bring knowledge of the company and the latter contribute in terms of local and market knowledge. This exporting strategy marks a bigger and longer term commitment to a specific market: it is able to accommodate growth and makes contact with the customer and the development of an effective after- sales service much easier.

Licensing

Licensing involves the granting of permission in the form of a licence by the owner (the licensor) of a proprietary product or process to the licensee to exploit the licensor's intellectual property in a particular region and/or over a specific time period. The intellectual property in question includes patents, copyrights, trademarks, and increasingly management and technical assistance and product upgrades and improvements. In return the licensor receives payment, usually an up-front payment and royalties, from the licensee.

Licensing is an attractive, albeit limited form of market entry and is most common in high-technology and R&D-intensive sectors such as pharmaceuticals, chemicals and industrial and defence equipment. It requires little or no commitment of resources by licensors while enabling them to exploit their research and development achievements through the generation of royalty income. Licensing also enables firms to avoid restrictive host country regulations regarding their entry into foreign markets. The licensor benefits from the licensee's local knowledge and gains a presence in a foreign market more quickly than through the establishment of subsidiaries or via equity joint ventures.

However, licensing does not provide a basis for further expansion into a market. Indeed, it is possible that licensing can create competitors for the licensor by handing over core competences to potential competitors. Japanese companies, for example, became market leaders in the colour television field by licensing the technology when it was new in the 1960s. They were then able to adapt the technology and overtake its originators within a relatively short space of time. In addition, the sale of a technology licence to a lower cost producer creates the possibility that the licensee becomes a serious competitor in markets in which the licensor is currently strong.

Franchising

Licensing and franchising are conceptually similar: in franchising, rather than buying access to patented technology, the franchisee buys the right to use the franchiser's name or trademark. Broadly speaking, there are two types of franchising. The first, often referred to as 'first-generation franchising', is the more arm's-length approach of the two and involves activities such as soft drink bottling and automobile and petrol retailing.

The second approach, known either as 'second-generation franchising' or 'business-format franchising', involves the purchase and transfer of a more comprehensive business package in which the franchisee not only gains access to brand names and trademarks but also receives extensive instructions on how to operate the franchise, management training and, occasionally, financial support. Second-generation franchises are common in service industries such as the hotel, fast food and vehicle rental sectors. Well-known examples with international scope include Avis, Baskin Robbins, Body Shop International, Burger King, Coca-Cola, Domino's Pizza, Hertz, Holiday Inn, Howard Johnson's, KFC, McDonald's, Pizza Hut, Pronuptia, TGI Fridays, Wendy's and Wimpy's.

The establishment of franchises in foreign locations can pose significant challenges given the requirement that, as a result of the utilization of the brand, the franchised product should be as indistinguishable as possible from the product sold in the home base. For example, when Pizza Hut established its first outlet in Moscow during glasnost, it encountered severe problems sourcing the appropriate type and quality of cheese within Russia. In order to solve supply problems in Thailand, McDonald's itself engaged in potato production there.

Franchising is an attractive internationalization option for service-based industries. It enables them to establish a presence in a new market quickly without significant direct investment and it uses a standard marketing approach to help create a global image. Franchising also yields the usual benefits of market entry with a local partner – that is, local knowledge, especially in relation to dealing with local and national-level public officials and authorities. Although the degree of control varies from operation to operation, the franchiser in business-format franchises exerts much more control over its franchisees than in first-generation franchises: it must do so to protect and promote its global image. With over 70 per cent of its restaurants operated on a franchise basis, McDonald's has followed this strategy successfully for over 40 years. A key component of its success has been the Hamburger University, which has its main campus in Illinois and branches in the UK, Germany, Japan and Australia, and which trains its own employees and those of its franchisees in its philosophy and standards.

From the franchisee's perspective, franchising enables them to tap into the franchiser's goodwill, reputation, merchandising, centralized advertising and promotion, and provides support in the actual operation of the franchise, including central purchasing. Above all, the franchisee avoids many of the risks of start-up businesses by buying into a proven business idea.

Management Contracting

Contractual agreements (or management contracting) are popular in the hotel sector, public utilities, health care, transportation, agriculture and mining. In the international context, it entails the supply of management functions to a client in another country. A wide range of such functions, including general, financial, personnel and production management, can be traded in this way. After the 1979 oil price shock, when oil revenues boosted economic development, management contracts were common in the Middle East, a region which at that time lacked indigenous management skills and capabilities to manage this development. A related category of foreign market entry concerns the provision of technical services across borders, a practice that has become increasingly popular in the maintenance and management of computer and telecommunication networks and has proved a fruitful vehicle for the development of India's call centre and software industries.

Management contracting maximizes the value of the management skills of its service sector and increases the organization's reputation and experience with limited risk and expenditure. The major benefit for the client comes not only from access to proven skills and expertise but also from the transfer of skills and learning resulting from the contract. Indeed, a central part of many contracts involves management training of the local workforce with a view to localization of management at some future date and the avoidance of long-term reliance on third parties for key functions. The danger for contractors is that they are potentially training up their future rivals and competitors.

BAA demonstrates management contracting in action, albeit with mixed fortunes. BAA has expanded its activities outside the UK via a mixture of equity stakes (for example, it holds a 65 per cent stake in Naples Airport and held a stake in six Australian airports until their sale in 2007) and management contracts. BAA has three retail management contracts at US airports – Baltimore-Washington International, Pittsburgh International and Boston Logan Airports. From 1995 to 2007, BAA had a contract with Indianapolis Airport which covered management of all aspects of the airport's operations, including environmental policy, airport information, the food-beverage concession, expansion plans, parking, retail operations and policy regarding the provision of policing and fire-fighting services. It also ran the main airport in Mauritius for five years and embarked upon a 25-year management contract in 2001 to run and manage two airports – Seeb and Salalah – in

Oman. This contract was terminated after only three years following failure to agree financial aspects relating to the development of Seeb in particular.

Turnkey Operations

A turnkey operation entails the construction of an operating facility under contract that is then transferred to the owner who only has to 'turn the key' to enter the facility and begin operations when the facility is complete. Turnkey contracts are used in the construction of large infrastructure or industrial development projects such as power plants, dams, airports, oil refineries, roads, railways, seaports and telecommunication systems. Given their size, only relatively few companies are able to undertake such projects: companies like Bechtel, Fluor, ABB, Brown and Root and the Hyundai Group, for example, have signed many turnkey contracts, although smaller companies do get opportunities to participate as part of consortia or as subcontractors.

Many turnkey projects are set in developing economies that have urgent infrastructure and industrialization needs. The client is usually the government or a government agency, and contracts are often awarded not only on a commercial but also on a political basis: French companies, for example, tend to do well in francophone Africa. Increasingly, given their demands on the public purse, such large-scale projects are increasingly being built according to one of three variants of the turnkey model – BOOs (build-own-operate), BOTs (build-operate-transfer) and BOOTs (build-own-operate-transfer). The names of these models are self-explanatory. For example, in the case of BOTs, the contractor will build the facility, operate it for a period of time (usually 15 to 30 years) during which the contractor hopes to reap a return on the investment, before handing the facility over to the client. Such contracts frequently benefit from low-cost project finance from national or international agencies like the European Investment Bank, the Asian Development Bank or the World Bank and benefit from home government export credit agencies such as the US's Export-Import Bank.

BOOs, BOTs and BOOTs have two major advantages for the host country:

1. A reduced burden on public finances – payment for a project comes in part from its revenues in the initial years of operation.
2. Access to high-quality engineering and management skills, a factor that contributes to efficient operation of the power stations, oil refineries and so on. However, there is a danger that, as the handover date approaches, incentives for the operator to maintain the facility are reduced.

These projects pose major challenges for the contractor, including:

1. The type of project involved means that they are often located in inhospitable or remote regions and are frequently subject to cost overruns.
2. BOOs, BOTs and BOOTs are uncharted territory: these contracts only became commonplace in the 1990s and as yet there are few examples of the transfer of BOTs and BOOTs back to the original client.
3. Given the notoriously difficult task of forecasting revenue on large-scale infrastructure projects over the long run, there is clearly a risk that returns will not live up to expectations.

4. There is a danger that participation in consortia or close cooperation with local companies will create future competitors for the contractor.

Equity Entry Modes

Compared to the above, these forms of market entry are based on the firm taking a direct equity/financial stake within the target market. The major forms of equity modes of market entry are as follows.

Joint Ventures

A joint venture is a long-term alliance in which each member has an equity stake and exercises control and influence over decision making. Many joint ventures involve the establishment of a separate legal entity for a specific purpose, thereby creating a new identity. In other cases, joint ventures involve a degree of asset swapping. However, a joint venture falls short of a merger as these involve the combination of all assets of the partners involved. The organizational structure, membership and control mechanisms within joint ventures vary according to the objectives and circumstances of each case. For example, joint venture partners may be private firms or public sector organizations. In some cases, the partnership may be equal in terms of equity participation and control, whereas in others one party may have a majority share. What each party brings to the joint venture also varies: for example, some partners will be strong in technology, others in resources and others in market knowledge.

In general, joint ventures enable partners to achieve objectives that are difficult to achieve independently. Joint ventures can offer more rapid and successful entry into a new location than trying to enter it alone. These benefits may spring from a partner's local knowledge, the presence of existing distribution channels or the increased likelihood of a successful tender owing to the presence of a local partner. In some instances, joint ventures have been formed because of restrictions on FDI. Although such instances are declining as restrictions on FDI are increasingly lifted, joint ventures remain popular. The involvement of a foreign partner or partners in joint ventures can bring access to proprietary technology or accelerate the process of management learning for the local partner.

Joint ventures also bring together different and complementary resources and skills: this may involve the marriage of one or two technologies or the coming together of an innovative technology with the appropriate capital or production facilities to exploit it. Joint ventures can also yield economies of scale and scope, and enable partners to share costs and risks – an important factor in capital and technology-intensive industries.

Joint ventures are more likely to be successful when there is agreement about long-term objectives and strategic direction. Within this framework, joint venture members must be clear about the type and quantity of resources each brings to the project; the organization and breakdown of responsibilities, and the distribution of benefits. Many joint ventures fail because one or more of the above conditions are not met or because differences in management style and culture make the smooth running of the operation difficult or impossible.

Mergers and Acquisitions (M&As)

Merger with or the acquisition of a company located overseas provides a rapid way of engaging fully in a foreign market. Potential benefits of M&As include immediate access to plant, equipment, personnel, goodwill, brand names, distribution channels and established networks of suppliers and customers – key assets that need to be painstakingly built up in the case of greenfield investment. In addition, unlike greenfield investment, M&As do not require the development of new capacity. Nor do they create new competition, an important factor for sectors already operating at or near full capacity.

On the less positive side, the success rate for M&As is not high. For example, equipment inherited in an acquisition may be obsolete, or at least in need of attention, whereas greenfield investment offers opportunities to begin operations with the latest technology. The industrial relations situation in an acquired firm may be troubled, a probable scenario given the uncertainty created within firms that are the subject of an acquisition. However, even if the acquired assets are in good condition, M&As still require major efforts to integrate both operations, including systems and personnel. The merger of two firms always involves the integration of two different corporate cultures but the challenges are so much greater in the case of international M&As that are also heavily influenced by divergent national cultures.

Two forces underpin the general trend towards more and bigger cross-border mergers and acquisitions:

1. *Globalization*: the removal of barriers to trade and production encourages firms to reconfigure their patterns of production, marketing and other functions to promote greater efficiency. For example, why maintain five separate production sites when one bigger production unit could service all five markets?
2. *Regional integration*: regional integration (see Chapter 3) gives rise to similar considerations as globalization but on a regional scale. Significantly, the EU, the world's most deeply integrated region, experienced a significant increase in cross-border mergers following the launch of the SEM programme.

CASE STUDY 10.2

Tesco Enters the US

In 2007, UK supermarket giant Tesco entered the West Coast market of the US. Funded through an initial capital outlay of up to £250 million, the business will develop organically with break-even expected by mid-2009. Entry was through a new brand, 'Fresh & Easy', which targets the convenience segment of the US market. The choice of segment reflects the past success that Tesco has had in five states with its Express format. The group is aiming for the discount end of the market and seeks to undercut its main rivals (Trader Joe's and Vons) by 10 to 25 per cent. This is to be achieved by minimizing product ranges and creating identical store formats. To reinforce its cost-cutting approach, it has launched its own brand products and out-sourced back office functions to India.

The choice of Fresh & Easy was to tempt users back towards local shopping and away from the larger stores, and is based on competences that Tesco has developed in other markets where it has applied similar formats. Over time, Tesco seeks to expand its format to other locations in San Diego, Las Vegas and Los Angeles. By the beginning of 2008, 120 locations had been identified for its convenience stores. Overall, Tesco plans to spend £1.25 billion over the next five years from 2007 on its US strategy and by 2012 it could have 1,000 stores.

Despite having a presence in 10 other states, the US strategy is most ambitious as it is moving into the territory of Wal-Mart (the world's biggest retailer). The west coast was chosen as Wal-Mart has less of a presence there due to political and trade union resistance. Furthermore, Wal-Mart has not really developed its convenience store format. Tesco's market entry represents the outcome of 20 years of market research and has been partly assisted by an agreement with the US supermarket chain Safeway to provide IT for its 'at home' service. Given the high start-up costs of the distribution centre and head office and the need to gain critical mass quickly, Tesco has taken a big gamble on the US and opened lots of stores quickly in a relatively short space of time.

UK retailers have found it difficult to 'break' into the US market for reasons ranging from naivety to over-confidence. Many underestimate the regional nature of the US where each state has a distinct culture. Some enterprises appeared to decide upon market entry by 'sticking pins in a map'. Opening stores thousands of miles apart made logistics difficult for some retailers. In other cases, parent companies failed to invest to enable the subsidiary to break out of its initial market position or were treated at arm's length by the parent. Anecdotal evidence suggested that Tesco's US operations also suffered from teething problems with sales not meeting initial expectations and the Fresh & Easy format not proving as popular as anticipated.

CASE STUDY ACTIVITY

Compare and contrast Tesco's entry into the US market with its entry into China. How do you account for the differences between these two markets?

Greenfield Investment

Along with mergers and acquisitions, greenfield investment represents the final link of the establishment chain. Greenfield investment, namely the construction of an overseas subsidiary or production facility from scratch, entails the greatest degree of commitment and involvement in a foreign location. The choice of greenfield investment over an acquisition in a particular location may be made owing to the inherent benefits of the former or simply because there is no purchase candidate available. In the transition economies of Central and Eastern Europe, for example, privatization provided opportunities for investment in a wide range of existing companies, but for some investors, there was no suitable candidate available. Motor manufacturers viewed the region, given its relatively cheap but skilled labour, as a potentially fruitful investment location. Although Volkswagen was able to link up with Skoda in the Czech Republic, General Motors, interested in Poland as an investment location, had no alternative but to engage in greenfield investment there owing to the lack of domestic auto producers.

Unlike M&As, greenfield investment provides a clean slate with no inherited debts or other problems from the acquired partner and allows for the introduction of the most modern and up-to-date building, plants, equipment and technology as opposed to the obsolete or substandard equipment that a freshly acquired partner can bring. The workforce of an acquired company is often demoralized and has to be introduced to new working practices. Nissan's greenfield investment in its UK plant in Sunderland occurred in a region with a large labour surplus and an engineering tradition, albeit not in the motor industry. It was thus possible for Nissan to recruit suitable staff and introduce them to its own corporate culture. Greenfield investment also often attracts investment incentives from the host country government anxious to attract new jobs.

On the downside, building a new operation from scratch can be time consuming and require extensive and often frustrating engagement with the local planning authorities. Indeed, the company needs to familiarize itself with many new laws and regulations, ranging from employment to taxation law and from environment to import and export regulations. Even though a greenfield investor does not have to overcome resistance to changes in corporate culture (as can happen in an acquired firm), it may still encounter major national cultural hurdles. For example, when Disney established its theme park near Paris, it initially reportedly found it difficult to bridge the gap between its American culture and philosophy (in large part, what Disney was selling) and the local French culture of its employees and customers.

Strategic Alliances

As highlighted in Figure 10.3, strategic alliances can cross the boundaries between equity and non-equity modes of market entry. Thus alliances can be contractual (including co-marketing, R&D) which require relatively low levels of commitment and may be of limited scope and duration. Equity-based alliances involve a higher level of commitment and can include strategic investment (where one firm takes a stake in another firm) or a joint venture (where a new independent entity is formed whose equity is owned by a minimum of two partners). It is important to stress that not all strategic alliances are joint ventures, as alliances can involve two firms hitching up without creating a separate corporate entity.

A strategic alliance is an agreement between two or more independent firms to increase their level of interdependency via a cooperative agreement. The alliance is based on partners pooling part of their activities as a means of enhancing their market positioning while sustaining separate corporate identities. These alliances may be driven either by the desire for organizational learning or by skill substitutions. Thus, these function as a form of market entry where the alliance acts as a learning device for the entrant, especially where the partners have better skills or resources regarding operations within the target market. While strategic alliances should enhance knowledge, they are not a risk-free mode of market entry: partners have to be carefully chosen as their actions could simultaneously be both cooperative and competitive. Generally, for an alliance to be stable, the former needs to be stronger than the latter. This underlies the conclusion that gaining complementary knowledge is key to making an alliance work to the advantage of the firm.

Strategic alliances have been a common form of market entry within the networks sectors where a combination of institutional control, high entry costs and a desire to exploit network externalities has facilitated such arrangements. Within telecommunications, a desire to offer uniform network coverage across all major places drove a sharp rise in telecommunication alliances throughout the early 1990s. However, such alliances proved unstable and their need was mitigated when markets were fully liberalized. The use of alliances within airlines was also driven by a desire to extend the reach of the network without having to directly enter a marketplace. The alliances were often marketing based and allowed for the development of a seamless service across multiple networks. Such agreements were in lieu of consolidation amongst service providers.

Underpinning alliance formation is the anticipation that such agreements create value for both partners. Value creation within an alliance may be derived from a number of sources such as enhanced efficiency, risk reduction, access to assets/capabilities and the aforementioned learning benefits. However, these have to be balanced against the possibility that these agreements can create problems through the possibility of choosing the incorrect partner, transaction costs involved in alliance formation, risk of partner opportunism and opening up opportunities for competitors to emerge. Overall, the formation of alliances as a form of market entry will depend on the underlying motives of partners. Thereafter, decisions made have to reflect whether to make the cooperation equity or non-equity based and how to position the relationship. Although alliances may be attractive in theory, they are prone to risks associated with trust and relationship management.

CONCLUSION

The heterogeneity of MNEs in terms of their motivations for internationalization, their structures and the variety of international entry modes adopted by them make it difficult to generalize about them. Indeed, the emergence of cooperative networks and alliances in recent decades has added to the complexity of multinational theory and has necessitated some reinterpretation and adaptation of the dominant thinking about multinational firms.

MNEs are major beneficiaries of globalization. However, globalization also threatens MNEs, especially those that are not so responsive to the competitive pressures in a more open, globalized world. Moreover, the shift towards a more globalized world has not necessarily resulted in global firms. Although many firms operate in a wide range of countries across the globe, their production and marketing approach in these countries is often national or regional rather than truly indifferent to national borders. Furthermore, many MNEs remain deeply influenced by and embedded in their home location.

Summary of Key Concepts

- Internationalization is conventionally conceived of as an incremental process based on a series of steps.
- This gradual perspective has been increasingly challenged by contingency and network-based views.
- There are limits to multinationality as excessive reach will eventually cause a decline in performance.
- The choice of entry mode differs according to sensitivity to risk and desire for asset control.

Activities and Discussion Questions

1. How valid is the conceptualization of internationalization as an incremental process?

2. What are the implications of the network-based view of internationalization for the process models?

3. Choose a multinational enterprise and examine the different types of entry modes used. Why do you think such methods were preferred?

4. Are there any limits to the internationalization process?

5. Investigate why so many fast food MNCs prefer the franchise method of market entry. What are the main advantages for this sector of such a strategy?

References and Suggestions for Further Reading

Andersen, O. and Buvik, A. (2002) 'Firms' internationalization and alternative approaches to the international customer/market selection', *International Business Review*, Vol. 11, No. 3, 347–363.

Axelsson, B. and Johanson, J. (1992) 'Foreign market entry: the textbook vs. the network view', in Axelsson, B. and Easton, G. (eds), *Industrial Networks. A New View of Reality,* London: Routledge, pp. 218–234.

Bell, J.D. (1995) 'The internationalisation of small computer software firms', *European Journal of Marketing*, Vol. 29, No. 8, 60–75.

Björkman, I. and Forsgren, M., (2000) 'Nordic international business research: a review of its development', *International Studies of Management and Organization*, Vol. 30, No. 1, 6–25.

Buckley, P.J. and Ghauri, P. (eds) (1998) *Internationalization of the Firm: A Reader*, 2nd edn, London: Thomson Learning.

Cavusgil, S. T. (1980) 'On the internationalization process of firms', *European Research*, Vol. 8, No. 6, 273–281.

Chetty, S. and Campbell-Hunt, C. (2004) 'A strategic approach to internationalization: a traditional versus "born global" approach', *Journal of International Marketing*, Vol. 12, No. 1, 57–81.

Glaum, M. and Oesterle, M-J. (2007) '40 years of research on internationalization and firm performance', *Management International Review*, Vol. 47, No. 3, 307–350.

Johanson, J. and Weidersheim-Paul, F. (1975) 'The internationalisation of the firm: four Swedish cases', *Journal of Management Studies*, Vol. 12, No. 3, 305–322.

Johanson, J. and Vahlne, J. (1977) 'The internationalisation process of the firm – a model of knowledge development and increasing foreign market commitments', *Journal of International Business Studies*, Vol. 8 (spring/summer), 23–32.

Johanson, J. and Mattsson, L. (1988) '*Internationalisation in industrial systems: a network approach*', in Hood, N. and Vahlne, J. (eds), *Strategies in Global Competition*, New York: Croom Helm, pp. 287–314.

Johanson, J. and Vahlne, J.E. (1990) 'The mechanism of internationalization', *International Marketing Review*, Vol. 7, No. 4, 11–24.

Johanson, J. and Vahlne, J-E. (2003) 'Business relationship commitment and learning in the internationalization process', *Journal of International Entrepreneurship*, Vol. 1, 83–101.

Oviatt, B. and McDougall, P. (1994) 'Toward a theory of international new ventures', *Journal of International Business Studies*, Vol. 25, No. 1, 45–64.

Rialp, A., Rialp, J. and Knight, G. (2005) 'The phenomenon of early internationalizing firms: what do we know after a decade (1993–2003) of scientific inquiry?', *International Business Review*, Vol. 14, No. 2, 147–166.

Chapter 11

International Entrepreneurship and the Internationalization of Small and Medium-sized Businesses

Most people think small businesses are not involved in international trade and that's just not true. It's growing.

Willard Workman, US Chamber of Commerce Vice President (2003)

LEARNING OBJECTIVES

This chapter will help you to:

- identify the form and nature of small and medium-sized enterprises (SMEs)
- assess the importance of SMEs to the global economy
- comprehend the impact of globalization upon SMEs
- understand the process of internationalization of SMEs and of the policy measures to support this trend
- comprehend the rise and importance of international entrepreneurship

SMEs are defined by the OECD (2005) as non-subsidiary, independent firms that employ less than a given number of employees. The exact number varies across states but the most frequent upper limit is 250. In other cases, financial criteria such as turnover or balance sheet valuations are used. Within the OECD, it is estimated that SMEs account for 95 per cent of all businesses and 60 to 70 per cent of employment. Albeit crude, these figures underline the importance of SMEs to modern developed economies. A more salient feature – and a characteristic explored within this chapter – is the growing internationalization of these enterprises. After initially exploring the commercial importance of SMEs, the chapter examines forces pushing the internationalization of these businesses. It then examines policy measures to stimulate their development through internationalization.

THE ROLE OF SMES AND ENTREPRENEURSHIP IN THE MODERN ECONOMY

Conventionally SMEs were regarded as organizations that were less efficient, paid their employees less and offered lower innovative potential than LSEs (large-scale enterprises). As a consequence, SMEs were widely seen as on the decline in all major states and as marginal businesses that were a luxury and a drag on efficiency. This view assumed that many factors in the global economy (such as access to capital, knowledge development, internationalization) favoured LSEs. Traditional theory suggested that the more fragmented a country's economic base, the more growth would be retarded. Thus, post-war economic success was linked to scale; a factor that was reflected in policy.

The ability of entrepreneurs to generate renewal and sustain change is an increasingly important factor in competitiveness. Since the 1970s, the bias towards scale has shifted as the interaction of technological, commercial and political change has created an environment in which SMEs could begin to emerge and grow. Audretsch (2002) accounted for the rising significance of SMEs by increasing globalization which has increased the importance of knowledge-based economic activity and placed an increased emphasis on marketing and technological innovation. Although it may be argued that such forces work to the detriment of SMEs, when knowledge starts to become increasingly valuable in its own right, individuals have the incentive to use it to their own advantage and establish their own businesses. This assumes that the entrepreneur (through the business) has the ability to stimulate change through innovation and to offer a unique value proposition that differentiates the firm in the global market.

Markets are fluid: firms constantly enter and leave markets, and new products and methods are always emerging. Most research adopts an evolutionary perspective of SME development based on a process of gradual growth. Generally, the impact of SMEs is felt in the following key areas:

- knowledge: through knowledge spill-overs, SMEs can extend growth throughout the socio-economic body;
- effect on competition: increased competition generated by SMEs stimulates innovation and the spread of new ideas;
- effect on variety: as each business creates a new approach, it can aid the process of growth.

- contribution to employment: the labour-intensive nature of many SMEs and their comparatively rapid growth underlines the importance of SMEs to job generation;
- role in the restructuring and streamlining of large state-owned businesses: SMEs help in the sale of non-core production activities and by absorbing redundant employees;
- innovatory capacity: there is a school of thought that SMEs need to be more innovative to survive, especially in knowledge-intensive sectors such as IT and biotechnology;
- capability to export: although many SMEs do not engage in international activities, this is a key issue in this chapter;
- greater flexibility in the provision of services and the manufacture of a variety of consumer goods;
- contribution to competitiveness and their challenge to the monopolistic positions of large enterprises;
- potential role as seedbeds for the development of entrepreneurial skills and innovation;
- role in the provision of services in the community and in regional development programmes.

These phenomena demonstrate that the impact of SMEs is not restricted to the SME sector. Their effects can be felt throughout the economy, including on larger businesses. Other contributions include increasing consumer choice through the production of a greater diversity of specialized goods and services and their greater agility resulting from flatter management structures. Table 11.2 offers a full SWOT analysis of the issues facing SMEs in the internationalizing environment.

The significance of SMEs is evident across all parts of the global economy. In Western Europe, more than 16 million SMEs comprise 99 per cent of all businesses and provide 66 per cent of employment. SMEs are also the backbone of the Asia-Pacific region, accounting for 90 per cent of enterprises, around 40 per cent of employment and representing an average of 70 per cent of gross domestic product. SMEs also accounted for much of the strong economic growth and 43 per cent of the jobs created in the US in the late twentieth/early twenty-first century. Elsewhere, the importance in terms of employment varies markedly from as high as 100 per cent of employment in Jamaica, to as low as 4 per cent within the Kyrgyz Republic. In the G-8 states, SMEs account for nearly 40 per cent of UK employment, 64 per cent of Canadian, 88 per cent of Japanese, 51 per cent of Russian and 51 per cent of American employment (2004). In other major states, SMEs represent 78 per cent of employment in China and 67 per cent in India. The importance of SMEs to the global economy has risen in line with the shift away from the idea that competitiveness is directly related to the size of an enterprise. This reverses the situation in the 1970s when the share of SMEs in the global economy fell: in the US, for example, the share of SMEs in GNP fell to 39 per cent from 44 per cent in the late 1950s/early 1960s.

Since the oil crises in the 1970s, policy makers sought to enhance the impact of SMEs upon economic growth. It became increasingly evident during this period that larger businesses were failing to adjust adequately to sudden changes in the economic environment. The flexibility and innovative nature of many SMEs were seen as important to the restoration of growth in and regeneration of industrialized economies, leading to the emergence of enterprise policy as an important strand of economic policy. Increasingly, those economies where SMEs account for a high share of economic activity (such as South Korea) have tended to be more successful since the 1970s.

There is a distinct difference between SMEs in developed economies and those in developing states. In developed economies, SMEs derive their strength and competitive advantage, either from specializing in niche markets or from linking up with large – frequently transnational – companies via integration into their supply chain. In developing states (though less so in NICs), SMEs tend to compete head-on with LSEs in the same markets with the same types of products. Predictably many SMEs fail in developing states.

Most SME employment tends to be within the service sector. This is especially evident in the wholesale and retail trade, the hotel and restaurant business, communications and business services and construction. Significantly, SMEs are becoming increasingly prominent in knowledge-intensive sectors and are dominant within the strategic business services subsector (including software, HR development, marketing). The process of outsourcing by larger companies has driven this trend and has allowed smaller businesses to establish successful market niches. SMEs also account for a high percentage of manufacturing firms in many OECD states and provide around half of employment within this sector.

Evidence from the OECD (2005) suggests that some 30 to 60 per cent of SMEs within the OECD area may be broadly categorized as innovative. Despite this, SMEs are less likely to engage in research and development than larger companies. Consequently innovation in SMEs occurs in other ways – through the creation of new products or processes to meet new demands, through the development of new organizational approaches to enhance productivity or new sales techniques.

As mentioned above, the perceived link between size and economic growth led to the neglect of SMEs in the policy process. However, this link broke down as knowledge became more important to commercial success. Thus, entrepreneurs with superior knowledge have an incentive to leave the employment of an incumbent firm and to utilize this knowledge for their own commercial benefit. SMEs are seen as important not only to job creation and competitiveness but also to unlocking personal potential and enhancing the social well-being of national/regional economies. Thus, there was a need for policy to support the growth and development of SMEs and to maximize their contribution to economic growth and development. Fostering an enhanced enterprise culture, a long-term process that has to begin with education is key to achieving this objective.

The impact of entrepreneurship depends upon the context of the business. If entrepreneurship occurs out of necessity – as in many developing states – its effects tend to be negligible. If it is done out of choice, entrepreneurship offers great possibilities for growth. In many developed economies, entrepreneurship is opportunistic as firms seek to create new niches, giving rise to growth and new forms of employment. Overall, entrepreneurship involves the following key elements:

- Exploitation of creativity and/or innovation: a firm has to be based around innovation or creativity to change, create and compete in a new market. Entrepreneurship is a mindset that enables an individual to spot an opportunity and exploit it. These traits need to be supported by sound management.
- Entrepreneurs: in order to build new businesses, there has to be a capability to undertake and understand risk. These entrepreneurs value independence and self-realization.
- Applications of entrepreneurship: this may occur in any sector or type of business and applies to all self-employed and to firms of any size.

The above underlines that the function of enterprise is to change the nature and pattern of the modern economy by promoting change through technology, innovation or new practices. The key is change and how change is linked to the creation of a new commercial agenda by new enterprises.

THE INTERNATIONALIZATION OF SMES AND THE RISE OF INTERNATIONAL ENTREPRENEURSHIP

Conventional thinking states that, as economies of scale become ever more important determinants of competitiveness, larger, more global markets increase the dominance of LSEs and reduce the power of SMEs. Thus, over the long run, it is to be expected that the average firm size will increase. Despite this, the openness of economies has gone hand in hand with increased levels of SME activity. LSEs have been successful in the global economy through exploiting core competencies and ICTs; the ability to use and form alliances, and the capacity to promote inter-firm collaboration. However, the synergy between LSEs and SMEs is important, including the role of SMEs in technological change; the strategic attachment of SMEs to local economies as well as the contribution of SMEs to the growth and evolution of industries. The relationship between SMEs and LSEs in the inter-nationalization process is reinforced by the fact that, as global competition increases, LSEs pay more attention to innovation. This places a greater compulsion upon them to develop stronger links with innovative SMEs.

As suggested by the 'steps models' (see Chapter 10), the internationalization of SMEs is both incremental and lengthy. The traditional focus of SMEs upon local markets means that the change in emphasis towards international markets has to be planned and based on a protracted learning process. However, there are important differences between conventional SMEs (e.g. newsagents) which see themselves as meeting primarily local needs and which will only undertake a protracted process of internationalization, and innovative SMEs which tend to be more global and focus upon narrow product/service segments within this context.

Innovative SMEs highlight the importance of knowledge, of accessing and utilizing networks effectively and of accessing MNCs to support internationalization. Much learning and knowledge is internally focused and based on trial and error. This implies that public policy needs to support this

---

TABLE 11.1 Contributors to the Internationalization of SMEs

Macro level	Micro level
■ The emergence of common or open markets and the reduction of protectionist barriers ■ The increased globalization of large firms ■ Increased levels of foreign investment and world trade ■ Increased mobility of capital, technology and management ■ Increased currency movements that have changed the relative competitiveness of different states	■ Changing technology, communications and organizational forms ■ Increased opportunities for SMEs to extend their value chains across borders as a result of cost differentials and so on. ■ Changing attitudes and managerial skills

TABLE 11.2 Types of Internationalization for SMEs

	Conventional SMEs	Knowledge-intensive SMEs
Motivations	Reactive	Proactive
Patterns	Incremental, psychic markets	Concurrent lead markets
Pace	Gradual	Rapid
Method of distribution/entry	Use of agents/distributors and direct to customers	Agents/distributors plus licensing, joint ventures, overseas production.
Subsequent Internationalization	Ad hoc, continued reactive behaviour, unrelated new customers	Structured/planned approach to international expansion; expansion of networks

Source: Young (2007).

learning process. However, the pattern of internationalization tends to vary between types of firm (see Table 11.2).

The pressures of globalization upon SMEs are transmitted via a variety of mechanisms (see Table 11.1). The salience of each depends upon the socioeconomic context, notably:

- imports and import competition;
- competition from other more internationalized firms;
- customer requirements;
- large firm requirements;
- alliances, joint ventures;
- international conventions and standards.

As the push-and-pull issues (see below) highlight, SME internationalization can often occur in a reactive and passive manner, underlining the fact that the process is not always a deliberate strategic choice by enterprises but occurs by default as more open economies expose their domestic markets to intense competition from external sources. Within international trade, SMEs have a variety of roles, including:

- domestic suppliers of inputs to products exported by larger enterprises;
- exporters of specialized niche products;
- importers/distributors of goods from foreign SMEs;
- providers of support services to international trade transactions (e.g., inland transport, freight forwarding).

In this context, the success of an SME in international markets is determined by an awareness of market imperfections to enable it to create a successful niche for itself. In practice, most actions by

SMEs in international markets tend to be horizontally based as they strive to occupy the same position in different geographical markets and to develop a 'deep niche' strategy. This results in high market shares across a number of core markets within their chosen segment. Plietner *et al.* argue that finding a niche, and therefore achieving success in international markets, is heavily influenced by:

- product quality;
- reliability of delivery;
- quality of management;
- quality of sales staff;
- ability to solve technical problems;
- customer relations.

Welch and Luostarinen (1988) (quoted in Su and Poisson, 1998) identify a number of factors that create a gradual approach to the internationalization process such as the level of acquaintance with foreign markets; the importance of communication networks; perceived risks and/or uncertainty, and the willingness of the manager to enter foreign markets. This implies that variations observed in relation to the internationalization model could be the consequence of environmental changes. Etemad (Etemad and Wright, 2003) suggests that three forces are at play in the process of internationalization of SMEs:

1. *Push forces*: these are a set of drivers that (usually internal to the firm) impel the firm to move into international markets. They are entrepreneurial in nature based on a desire to explore new opportunities. They may be the effect of managers, maturity of local markets and so on.
2. *Pull forces*: these are external to the firm which enhance the firm's competitiveness and signify the benefits of a move into international markets.
3. *Mediating forces*: these are firm-specific factors that facilitate the acting of push-and-pull forces upon strategy and represent the internal dynamics of the firm. Within the firm, there are deterrents and enablers influencing the ability of the firm to develop international strategy.

Recent evidence suggests that there is a group of (mainly small) firms that eschew this evolutionary approach by undertaking rapid and dedicated internationalization. This has resulted from the emergence of international entrepreneurship. According to Zahra and George (2002), these are businesses that seek to derive competitive advantage by operating across multiple locations from their inception. The issue of international entrepreneur though has evolved from merely stressing new ventures to include corporate intrepreneurship (i.e. entrepreneurship within an LSE), though it is the former that will concern us here. These rapidly internationalizing firms are created by one or more of the following factors:

- new market conditions in many sectors, especially the rise of niche markets for SMEs globally;
- technological developments in production, transportation and communication;
- the increased importance of global networks and alliances;
- the more elaborate capabilities of people.

These trends may be expected to strengthen in years to come. Research (see Rialp *et al.*, 2005) has demonstrated that many SMEs are able to compete within their respective niches without any of the disadvantages that are assumed to arise from the absence of scale.

Oviatt and McDougall (1994) argue that there are three types of international new ventures:

1. *New international market makers*: either through selling into new markets in which they previously had no presence or with minimal direct investment in target markets. These may be import/export start-ups (focusing on a few states with which the entrepreneur is familiar) or multinational traders (which focus on an array of states and are always scanning for new opportunities).
2. *Geographically focused start-ups*: these service the specialized needs of a defined region through the use of foreign resources. Unlike the multinational trader, these firms are geographically restricted to the location of need and involve more than just the coordination of inward and outward logistics.
3. *Global start-ups*: these seek to coordinate offerings across multiple markets with an unlimited geographical reach. They both respond to and create new opportunities in globalizing markets.

It is evident from past research (for a review see Rialp *et al.*, 2005) that many of these 'Born Globals' have emerged within high-technology sectors where the process of rapid change has allowed for the emergence of targeted niches. However, further research is indicating the evolution of early internationalizers beyond hi-tech segments into other sectors (Young, 2007). According to Bell *et al.* (2003), these firms tend to be in either knowledge and/or service-intensive or knowledge-based sectors. The latter tend to rely on hi-tech to create a niche in new technology markets. The former tend to base their internationalization on applying knowledge to develop new value propositions but are not inherently knowledge-based firms. Thus, across both types of firms, knowledge is a pivotal factor shaping the process of internationalization, confirming that Born Global firms tend to be knowledge intensive or knowledge based.

Overall, Rialp *et al.* (2005) conclude that the following factors drive the emergence of Born Globals/early internationalizers:

1. a managerial global mindset from inception;
2. a high degree of previous experience in international markets by managers;
3. management commitment to international markets;
4. strong use of personal and business networks;
5. managers with a higher risk tolerance;
6. market knowledge and market commitment;
7. unique intangible assets based on knowledge management;
8. high value creation through product differentiation, leading-edge technology products and innovativeness;
9. a niche-focused, proactive strategy within geographically spread markets;
10. narrowly defined user groups with strong customer relationships;
11. flexibility to adapt to rapidly changing external conditions.

These factors imply that the firm must own valuable assets and use networks to create sustainable advantage within their chosen niche.

Networks are seen as key to the internationalization process: SMEs use these structures to gain access to resources, to improve strategic positions, to control transaction costs, to learn new skills, to gain legitimacy and to cope positively with rapid technological changes. They require trust within personal relationships with the network representing social capital that is intangible and idiosyncratic (see Case Study 11.1). According to Oviatt and McDougall (1994), this implies that new internationalized ventures rely on alternative governance structures due to the lack of sufficient resources. Networks offer the resource-constrained firm a critical leverage opportunity to access resources without high capital cost. The learning process for small firms is also critical to achieving competitive advantage. The Born Global has to build knowledge stocks. In some cases, it may be argued that newness allows firms to learn more rapidly than older firms that develop barriers to learning. This runs counter to the idea that in knowledge development regarding international markets, there is a liability attached to newness.

CASE STUDY 11.1

Immigrant Entrepreneurship

Successive waves of immigration into developed economies from developing states have created more cosmopolitan populations, especially within larger cities. In many ways, these immigrants are just another symptom of the increased pervasiveness of the globalization process as they move country in pursuit of new economic opportunities. An important side effect of these migrant flows has been the increased prominence of business formation by immigrants who choose to become self-employed within their country of settlement. In fact, this group is likely to be more entrepreneurial than native workers. Across the developed economies, the percentage of immigrant labour in self-employment varies markedly. In 2004, nearly a quarter of all immigrants in Denmark were self-employed. In the UK and the Czech Republic, the figures were around 15 per cent, whereas in the US immigrant self-employment was around 10 per cent. The comparative figures for the indigenous workforce are – in each case – considerably lower.

In practice, most immigrant entrepreneurs tend to focus on the lower end of the retail and catering sectors but their involvement in other aspects of the service sector is increasing. This emphasis is caused by an absence of funding and frequently by a lack of formal educational qualifications, resulting in many moving to those parts of the market with low barriers to entry but also intense competition. This pushes many to cut costs, often by cutting corners, maybe via illicit transactions, or by bypassing regulations. The form of such activities is often determined by the attitude of the host state to migrants themselves and whether their status is legitimate or not.

Immigrant entrepreneurship means migrants are not restricted to filling job vacancies which are unattractive to native workers. With self-employment, these workers are able to shape their own destinies; to create their own jobs (and maybe to create jobs for others) and trade with their country of origin. In part, immigrant self-employment is driven by a desire to overcome some of the barriers they find in seeking employment within their state of settlement. In addition, such strategies may deliver implicit social benefits through building bridges to networks outside the ethnic group, thereby enabling social mobility and encouraging social cohesion. The new firms often offer something different from indigenous entrepreneurs; possess expert knowledge of specific demands or sources of supply; may be involved in innovative marketing, and can help in the revitalization of poorer neighbourhoods.

Most studies suggest that first-generation immigrants build businesses based on serving their own ethnic community and thereby develop their own 'ethnic markets'. As migrant entrepreneurships mature, so these businesses rely less on the 'protected' ethnic market. Second-generation migrants adapt to the mainstream and to the changing population. This also means that the niche model of enterprise development is of limited usage: as these businesses integrate into the host economy, links with native suppliers and customers are established. Second and third generations do not exhibit the same entrepreneurial desires or characteristics: as they become economically active, entrepreneurship declines to the same level as the native population.

It is evident that the social embeddedness of the entrepreneur is a key factor in the sustainability of the business in the longer term and that the ability to build social networks is key to survival. This long-term outlook is essential. Entrepreneurship is important for many in establishing an economic building block for future generations within the host economy and, for many, especially in the US, entrepreneurship is key to social and economic progression.

The rise of immigrant entrepreneurship is underpinned by the higher tolerance to risk within this group compared to the indigenous population and by the cohesiveness of extended families and the community generally, which can provide access to low-cost inputs as well as to cheaper credit. Such ties can also create dominance within specific segments of the economy and help overcome the main impediments to the establishment of these businesses within host states. The above factors reflect both positive and negative aspects of migrant entrepreneurship. In a negative sense, these start-ups often emerge as a direct consequence of limited opportunities within the host labour market. Thus, this type of employment may have detrimental consequences in the form of long working hours, unpaid family labour and low incomes.

The stereotypical image of an immigrant entrepreneur as one of low skills and limited financial capital is changing. Recent years have seen the rise of the skilled migrant from China and India in sectors such as IT that have been important sources of entrepreneurship within the US and Germany especially. Realizing the benefits from immigrant entrepreneurship, many governments are taking an increasingly proactive view on business start-ups within this segment of the community. Increasingly many states are offering assistance to members of migrant groups to enable them to start up businesses to free them from welfare dependency and to increase self-determination.

CASE STUDY QUESTIONS

1. How do you account for the relatively high rate of immigrant entrepreneurship?

2. Would you expect such a trend to continue in successive generations?

3. What are the main problems of immigrant entrepreneurship?

4. How can governments best promote immigrant entrepreneurship?

Alongside the Born Global firms are the 'Born Again' globals. These are firms which, after a long period with a domestic focus, suddenly change to a strong international focus. This may be based on a sudden infusion of new human and/or financial resources, access to new networks, acquisition of product knowledge or some other event. These are reactive strategies as opposed to the proactive strategies followed by the Born Global. Ultimately, it is the shift in knowledge that creates scope for a rapid move into international markets after years of a home focus. Understanding and offering theoretical guidance to SMEs facing the internationalization of their markets is important, as few of these businesses can afford to absorb the risk and costs of failure. SMEs in international markets face the double jeopardy of the risk of proactivism and the risk of reactivism from larger firms. Experience suggests therefore that SMEs cannot merely follow MNE strategies: their strategies must have their own drivers based on occupying their own niche and using their own unique resources and competences.

ENTREPRENEURSHIP AND ECONOMIC GROWTH

SMEs are an important contributor to economic growth within the modern global economy. As a source of innovation and change, international entrepreneurship and SMEs are an important source of rising productivity and economic competitiveness in developed, emerging and developing economies. This is driven in part by the perceived link between knowledge and flexibility and aggressive entrepreneurship, and reflects the risk-seeking, innovative and opportunistic nature of entrepreneurship.

Generally, developing economies grow through a process of human and physical capital. However, more mature economies' growth is driven more by technological advances and knowledge accumulation created by a process of research and development. Empirical research supports the idea of the strong link between economic growth and entrepreneurship. In many developed economies, a growing number of SMEs are emerging due to increased outsourcing and the micro-segmentation of markets.

Within many developed economies, SMEs tended to be characterized by lower efficiency than big businesses; lower levels of employee compensation; limited innovative potential, and were of declining importance. However, this trend within developed economies has been reversed since the 1980s as a result of:

- a reduction in economies of scale stemming from technological change;
- increasing globalization;
- changes in the labour force (i.e. increased female participation rates, flexible employment) that were more compatible with the needs of small business;
- deregulation which allowed easier market entry for smaller businesses;
- the increased importance of innovation.

In many developed economies, the shift towards knowledge-based activities is widely recognized as a key driver contributing to the increased salience of knowledge-based economic activity. This, combined with globalization, changed the role of SMEs within the global economy. This is supported by extensive evidence in developed economies of the employment-generating effects of SMEs.

To capitalize on this shift, the G-8 countries developed a strategy whereby remittances could be channelled through the financial systems of developing states to offer easier access to finance; to offer guidance in the creation of the necessary supporting business environment and to expand access to micro-finance for local entrepreneurs (see Case Study 11.2). As a result, aid programmes are increasingly emphasizing the support of entrepreneurship. However, some are sceptical regarding the impact of such programmes. These sceptics, who believe that larger firms offer more advantages, doubt whether SMEs are better at creating jobs in a developing country context and are generally dubious about their benefits. However, a decisive response to these concerns is hindered by the size of the informal sector which makes policy effects difficult to measure and predict.

CASE STUDY 11.2

Micro-finance

By aiming to give the population better access to high-quality financial services, micro-finance is proving to be an increasingly important driver of enterprise growth in developing states. The emergence of micro-finance reflects market failure whereby many financial institutions neglected poorer states on the grounds of lack of profitability. Financing problems in developing countries are compounded by a lack of collateral against which to borrow by the impoverished segment of the population. Without micro-financing or something similar, developing states will be stuck in a cycle of underdevelopment exacerbated by the absence of a financial system able to provide loans in an efficient and financially sustainable way. In order for micro-financing to be sustainable, there has to be a critical mass of customers estimated to be between 10–20,000 borrowers.

In developing states, especially in rural areas, many activities are simply not monetized. However, the rural poor still require money to meet needs related to life cycle, personal emergencies, disasters and investment opportunities. The latter is proving especially salient for developing states as many impoverished people attempt to escape poverty by developing micro-enterprises. Entrepreneurship as a

tool of economic development often encounters the following problems:

1. limited opportunities for profit;
2. poorly developed capital markets;
3. poorly developed infrastructure limiting the development of new niches;
4. social, cultural and religious beliefs which attach little importance to monetary gains;
5. an unfavourable economic and political climate.

By 2005, there were an estimated 10,000 micro-finance institutions lending an average of $300 to 40 million borrowers. The core of the industry is based on around three dozen multinational networks of micro-finance providers and has enabled many lenders to break free from the initial support offered by international financial intuitions. In general, the loss rate for these loans is only 1 to 3 per cent, considerably lower than in developed economies.

Micro-finance has a history going back to the 1950s. By the 1970s, programmes in South Asia were being extended to allow for the development of micro-enterprises based on groups of poor women. The 1980s and 1990s saw further expansion, demonstrating the viability of such schemes both in terms of repayment and the ability of lenders to cover costs. The spread of micro-finance has also been assisted by new technologies, even in the remotest areas. The spread of mobile banking in sub-Saharan Africa, for example, has allowed for the electronic transfer of money.

The World Bank has estimated that making credit available to 500 million micro-entrepreneurs will open up a market worth over $100 billion. The attractiveness of micro-finance is that it addresses two core aspects of international business. First, it reconciles the potentially conflicting needs of globality and locality given that micro-finance emerges from within local communities and cultures to develop a mutual interest with large, global banks. Second, it reconciles profit and development by allowing investment in small businesses in developing economies.

The key element is that financial inclusion is becoming profitable. For micro-finance to be sustainable, the loans must be matched by effective repayment. Generally, micro-finance is effective when:

* there are strong social connections between group members as this aids repayment;;
* repayment is based on strong social trust between partners. However, if social connections are too strong (for example, family), repayment performance can actually decrease;
* individual-based micro-finance institutions, which tend to perform better than group-based institutions, are involved. However, they tend to focus less on poorer clients.

Micro-finance is seen as central to attaining the UN's Millennium Development Goals by creating an ability to diversify incomes and to build human and social capital. Inevitably, the impact of building micro-enterprises spreads beyond increased incomes and offers indirect health and education benefits as that income is spent. It is also notable that many micro-finance programmes target women: they are regarded as more reliable in terms of repayment than men as well as showing a greater tendency to re-invest the income.

Despite strong social rhetoric, micro-finance providers argue fiercely over many issues. The most notable disagreements are whether the needs of the poor are best served by group or individual loans; by market or capped loans; by catering for the poor or the very poorest; by offering credit only or by also offering savings accounts.

The biggest networks are Opportunity International, Procredit and Women's World Banking. These multinational networks are supported by national, regional and even networks of networks. Some of these networks operate at that part of the spectrum where the objective is 'sustainability' rather than profit for its own sake and offer generous repayment terms and interest rates that do little more than cover costs. However, this has resulted in the demand for funds exceeding supply. Consequently, at the other end of the spectrum, institutions based on banking rules akin to those in developed economies have emerged. These institutions argue that it is only through the profit motive that sufficient funds will be forthcoming to meet the needs of developing economies.

As a result of this commercialization of micro-finance, larger international banks are becoming interested in this segment of the market. This reflects a 'bottom of the pyramid' strategy whereby a large number of customers with little money, when combined, create a credible market. Big banks are moving cautiously within this segment and couch their work within the domain of CSR, fearing that the naked pursuit of profit would constitute bad public relations for the firm.

However, the micro-finance industry has come under criticism. Some see it as an unsuitable vehicle for those in abject poverty. There is also controversy over the high rate of return expected by some of the lending institutions. In addition, there are limited opportunities for the development of an entrepreneurial culture within developing states and not everyone in poverty can become entrepreneurs. In addition, if every informal form of self-employment is defined as entrepreneurship, then every small business does not mean economic growth. This reflects the difference between opportunity-driven and necessity- or survival-driven entrepreneurship. Moreover, entrepreneurship for growth means little if there is no effective demand for the products offered.

CASE STUDY QUESTIONS

1. What are the main problems in creating routine banking systems in many developing states?

2. How does the emergence of micro-finance fit into the United Nations Millennium Development Goals?

3. What are the main problems in utilizing micro-finance as a tool of economic development?

In seeking to assist entrepreneurship, policy has traditionally viewed SMEs as inefficient, and has therefore sought to protect them from rather than expose them to competition. Exploiting the opportunities afforded by the internationalization of markets requires that policy and governments facilitate a more entrepreneurial culture within states. In particular, entrepreneurship policy is needed in relation to three market failures:

■ *Network externalities*: where the value of a firm's resources is dependent upon the existence of complementary firms. When firms are excluded from these clusters, they are at a disadvantage.
■ *Knowledge externalities*: knowledge can spill over into the public domain, thereby eroding the uniqueness of a firm's resources.
■ *Learning externalities*: when firms fail, other firms can learn from this experience. This lowers the incentive for a firm to be a first mover.

The role of public policy is to mitigate these market failures by encouraging interaction between firms. As a result, governments will help in the reduction of costs and risks and in the provision of information. The aim is to create networks and a greater openness to the risk taking associated with entrepreneurship. To support the realization of this aim, there is a shift towards enabling policy to be undertaken at the level closest to the enterprise. Consequently, many argue that in developing SME policy, direct stimulation through export promotion policies and the provision of general export market information are of limited use. Policy needs to be targeted at specific types of firm. For 'Born Globals', for example, there is likely to be a more evident resource constraint than for the 'Born Again Globals'. Support is best suited to helping these firms develop network relationships.

The link between economic growth and entrepreneurship has become an increasingly prominent theme in the development agenda. To this end, policy initiatives have emerged from the international arena to use entrepreneurship as a tool to alleviate poverty. As such, the private sector has to be encouraged to support poverty reduction programmes. This requires the development of an interface between domestic and international policy actors that creates the right conditions for these businesses to emerge. This initially relies upon the openness of developing countries to this path of development and the undertaking of the necessary domestic reforms. In many cases, the entrepreneurs are situated in the poorest segments of the economy, recognizing that the poor are consumers and also the partial solution to their problems.

In many developing economies, women are a majority of micro-entrepreneurs in both the formal and informal sectors, confirming that there is a will to undertake start-up. However, three major challenges face SMEs in developing economies:

- *The informal economy*: many firms operate outside the legal system (see Figure 11.1). This limits their ability to raise finance as well as limiting access to other aspects of the formal economy that could help their development. Similarly, formal businesses are harmed by the implicit subsidies received by informal firms. It can be costly to operate in the formal economy. Firms in this sector face taxes, registration costs and complex government regulations. This is compounded by high compliance costs and issues related to bribery and corruption. Thus, there is often little incentive to go formal.
- *SMEs face considerable (often financial) barriers to growth*: despite their importance many SMEs within developing states are marginal in the business ecosystem with few growing to become larger businesses. They are often limited by the unevenness of the playing field against small firms which reinforces the pressure to remain informal. This is compounded by low productivity and an absence of skills exacerbated by the use of outdated technologies, human/knowledge capital and an inability to afford the business services to rectify such problems. However, the major constraining factor is lack of access to capital. The high risks associated with these businesses and the absence of trustworthy information all raise interest rates for SMEs.
- *The absence of competitive pressure upon larger firms*: in many developing states, larger firms inhibit entrepreneurial activity by using weak institutional environments to stifle competitive pressure. This can inhibit the development of a mature financial system that offers cheaper finance to smaller firms. This is compounded by corruption and weak law enforcement.

As a result, the foundations for entrepreneurship are simply not in place in many developing states. There is an absence of a level playing field with entry, operating and credit rules applied in an asymmetric fashion. Access to finance and skills/knowledge compounds these difficulties.

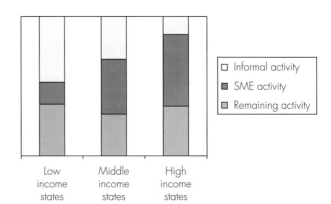

FIGURE 11.1 The Structure of Formal and Informal Activity, 2004 (%)

Source: UN (2007).

CLUSTERS AND THE GLOBALIZATION OF SMES

The impact of SMEs upon the economy depends upon the prevalence of an entrepreneurial culture. This varies across space: some regions or localities are well known for generating 'clusters' of dynamic firms that benefit from information spill-overs as well as other intangible factors (see below). Notable local pockets of activity include Silicon Valley in the US or Valencia in Spain. The development of clusters can be of special importance to SMEs, allowing them to bypass financial and other practical problems that they would otherwise face. Clustering can generate benefits that progressively increase the competitive advantage of a group of firms and enable them to use this base to compete globally. Clusters tend to be characterized by a constant turnover of new entrepreneurial firms and contain a small or large number of firms in a related industry, and can vary in size.

An important factor shaping competitiveness in the global economy is the tendency for firms in the same business to locate and operate in close physical proximity. As the OECD (2005) notes, this is an oxymoron in the globalization process as the phenomenon is compatible with the localization of competitive advantage in various industries and activities, whereas the trend towards globalization should in theory reduce the importance of subnational regions.

Across much of the developed world, clusters are becoming increasingly common. In areas such as northern Italy and Spain as well as Silicon Valley, clusters have become a powerful force in shaping the competitiveness within particular sectors. The development of these clusters is not uniform geographically and does not occur across all industries. The OECD estimates that the US has 380 clusters that employ 57 per cent of the workforce and produce 61 per cent of output.

The attractiveness of clusters to SMEs lies in the ability of these networks to enhance productivity, to stimulate innovation and thereby enhance competitiveness. They allow SMEs to combine the advantages of small-scale with the benefits of large-scale production. For these reasons, clusters have become a primary focus of public policy towards SME development in the global economy (see below). These networks (with firms that are both proximate and geographically distant) hold the promise of allowing smaller firms to compete with larger firms on a global basis and to overcome the obstacles to performance that derive from their lack of scale. Both clusters and networks can aid firm specialization and offer scope for efficiency through collective action, thereby creating openings for economies of scale and scope. Thus while all networks will be geographically concentrated, SMEs will have to engage in networking with different enterprises over a broader geographical reach if the competitive benefits of a cluster are to be realized.

There are a plethora of reasons for the emergence of clusters. The most frequently cited include the presence of a unique natural resource, economies of scale in production, proximity to markets, labour pooling, the presence of local input or equipment suppliers, shared infrastructure, reduced transaction costs and other localized externalities (OECD, 2000). Different clusters have evolved for different reasons. For example, the large labour pools in the Los Angeles area are associated with the global competitiveness of its motion picture industry.

The factors that sustain the growth of a cluster may not be the same as those that caused the cluster to emerge in the first place. The creation of industry-specific knowledge, the development of supplier and buyer networks and local competitive pressures can spur the innovation that generates sustained growth within the cluster. These apply after the cluster's initial advantages have been superseded. In addition, the structure of some clusters allows for high rates of enterprise start-up as a high degree of specialization between firms leads to concentration in a small phase of production and a consequent low degree of vertical integration that can lower barriers to entry. Furthermore, the large number of buyers and sellers in the cluster creates a greater incentive to innovate. Thus innovation and enterprise start-up help to sustain the growth of the cluster.

Clusters allow competitive advantage to be localized. Thus, while globalization can spread activities, it can also allow firms and locations with a competitive advantage to exploit their position over ever-wider geographical areas. The impact of globalization upon clusters is felt not only through increased international competition but also by the response of the cluster to these forces and how enterprises within the cluster choose to go global. Different clusters have assorted strategies. For example, Japanese component enterprises have sought to reproduce clusters by supporting foreign production by Japanese MNEs.

POLICY MEASURES TO SUPPORT THE INTERNATIONALIZATION OF SMES

SMEs face larger barriers to internationalization than LSEs. The full list is reflected in Table 11.3. The main barriers are internal and external. Internal barriers reflect how internationalization of the SME is constrained by inadequacies within the firm, including lack of information, lack of capital and inadequate management skills. External barriers include technical trade restrictions, bureaucratic procedures and marketing/distribution problems. Policy towards the internationalization of SMEs should be based on enhancing internal strengths and external opportunities, and mitigating the internal weaknesses and external threats.

The ability of SMEs to enter international markets is constrained by considerable barriers to entry arising from:

- the higher interest rates facing these firms because they are perceived as a bigger risk than LSEs;
- imperfect information, especially regarding new entrants and access to new materials, labour and so on;
- barriers created by incumbents;
- barriers created by government actions;
- intellectual property rights and innovation.

These barriers to entry are reinforced by the transaction costs of engaging in international trade as well as the costs of transforming an SME into an LSE. Government policy objectives should therefore revolve around lowering barriers to entry; reducing lowering threats and weaknesses, and enhancing the strengths of and opportunities facing these enterprises. SMEs – in internationalizing – face the traditional problems of financing to expand their international presence. Over time, the expansion of private equity markets and the enhanced access to venture capital for SMEs – though there are considerable differences across states – have improved the situation. Venture capitalists can also provide management support to these fledgling companies (see Table 11.4).

Programmes to aid SME internationalization may be subdivided into internal and external policies. Export promotion programmes focus on financial support to and assistance for knowledge

TABLE 11.3 A SWOT Analysis for SMEs Seeking to Internationalize

Strengths	Weaknesses	Opportunities	Threats
■ Flexible cost structure	■ Difficulties in recruiting qualified employees	■ More efficient production process	■ High information costs
■ Flexible decision making	■ Centralized decision making may be inappropriate for an internationalized enterprise	■ Utilization of standardization/differentiation	■ Long decision making processes caused by lack of knowledge
■ Spontaneous ability to adapt to changing market conditions	■ Competitive disadvantage through weak position to negotiate	■ Optimal resource usage	■ New legal and cultural frameworks
■ Ability to avoid over-powering ideology and bureaucracy through personalized communication	■ Limited market influence and lack of knowledge of target markets	■ Realization of price, cost and time advantages	■ Market insecurity facilitated by economic insecurity and exchange rate risks
■ High-quality standards and individualized product and service offering	■ Shortage of financing opportunities and increased risk potential with small equity base		■ Uncollectables because of unknown payment ethics
	■ Mostly involved with day-to-day activities with limited time for strategic management and focus on marketing		■ Increase in transport costs incurred by centralized production, tariff and other trade barriers
			■ Cost of reorganizing
			■ Need for capital

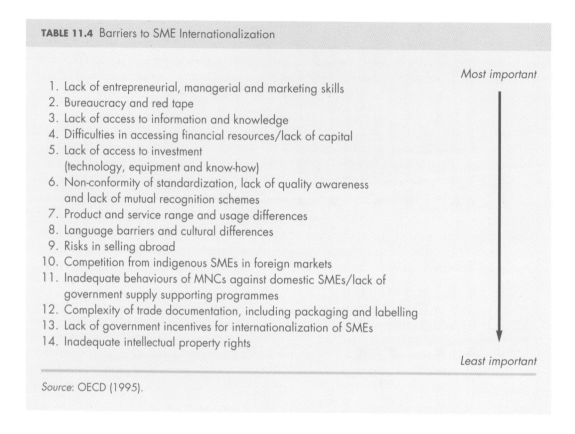

TABLE 11.4 Barriers to SME Internationalization

Most important

1. Lack of entrepreneurial, managerial and marketing skills
2. Bureaucracy and red tape
3. Lack of access to information and knowledge
4. Difficulties in accessing financial resources/lack of capital
5. Lack of access to investment
   (technology, equipment and know-how)
6. Non-conformity of standardization, lack of quality awareness
   and lack of mutual recognition schemes
7. Product and service range and usage differences
8. Language barriers and cultural differences
9. Risks in selling abroad
10. Competition from indigenous SMEs in foreign markets
11. Inadequate behaviours of MNCs against domestic SMEs/lack of
    government supply supporting programmes
12. Complexity of trade documentation, including packaging and labelling
13. Lack of government incentives for internationalization of SMEs
14. Inadequate intellectual property rights

Least important

Source: OECD (1995).

development in SMEs. These are supported by external programmes that seek to aid SME internationalization by removing trade barriers facing SMEs. Five types of intervention appear to be most effective in aiding SMEs:

1. Policy reforms to establish a stable, liberal, low-cost business environment. This is especially noticeable in terms of regulatory reform and the removal of obligations and bureaucracy upon these enterprises that weaken their position internationally.
2. Actions that lower the cost of loans for SMEs.
3. 'Light touch' technical and marketing support.
4. Policies that motivate and facilitate demand-driven access to training and technology. Training needs to be offered in a market failure context to firms that otherwise can ill afford to undertake such activities. Similarly technology policy has to direct SMEs towards those technologies that are useful for their own circumstances and not for its own sake. These need to be supported through networks to share best practice and to create a sound technological infrastructure.
5. Institutions and policies that enhance SME networks and clusters. These aid training, technology access and skill development as well as the organization of finance. Public finance provides support services and helps connect SMEs.

These broad environmental measures need to be complemented by efforts to improve the access of SMEs to technical and managerial skills, to sources of information and knowledge and to research and development. In many instances, a key constraint upon SMEs is not always finance but access to and absorption of technology-related learning that allows these enterprises to produce specialized products of the quality demanded by modern markets. This is especially true in developing states (see Case Study 11.2).

Perhaps most important of all are policies directed towards stimulating entrepreneurship. These policies need to aid start-ups, not only through the above measures, but also by developing innovative methods of finance such as access to venture capital and the development of secondary stock markets. Other policies include business angel networks where public bodies seek to bring together financiers and SMEs. One of the best forms of public policy assistance is reducing the administrative burden on SMEs through concerted regulatory reform. Regulatory systems have often evolved to serve the needs of large enterprises – rewarding economies of scale and stability rather than flexibility. SMEs face high compliance costs, extensive and complicated paperwork and economic regulations that prohibit certain activities. SMEs have a lower capacity to absorb unproductive expenditures because they have less capital as well as fewer managerial resources than LSEs and regard these burdens as directly inhibiting their competitiveness in international markets. Most states try to reduce this burden, not only through reform but also by offering assistance to address these regulatory issues. Alternatively, SMEs rely upon regulation to secure their positions, as their weak bargaining position and their poor liquidity make them vulnerable. In short, these enterprises need a credible, but light, regulatory framework to secure their competitive position, notably with regard to their interactions with large businesses.

In line with the analysis offered above, many policy makers are working towards stimulating clusters. Policy bodies generally play a passive role by offering supporting infrastructures and freeing up resources as well as by facilitating interactions. Thus actions are based around developing an effective framework for clusters. This – as is suggested above – is especially evident with reference to the globalization process. The strategy of policy makers should underline a core principle of modern industrial strategy – working with markets, not against them.

For innovative SMEs, their attainment of commercial success may be assisted through the development of know-how agreements and of effective partnerships. Thus in many instances, innovation within a SME's strategy has to be viewed within the context of the cluster strategy mentioned above. The heterogeneous nature of SMEs also dictates the nature of policy. For example, for the more innovative SMEs, policy will need to enable them to access the finance needed to support their development. For others – technology followers – policy strategy should revolve around offering advice, awareness creation and improving collaboration.

As globalization becomes more advanced and the less SMEs are insulated from its effects, policy makers have to assess the nature and form of the support as well as the increasingly complex and varied forces acting upon an economy's SME base. In many instances, supporting the internationalization of SMEs will seemingly achieve little beyond redefining the scope of existing policies to account for changes in the environment. Supply capability policies need to be geared to enable SMEs to access the information and knowledge required to operate successfully within these markets.

In developing states, the policy issues differ as actions need to be based on developing the following prerequisites for cultivating an entrepreneurial culture:

1. enhancement of the rule of law, ensuring that it is transparent, open and understood;
2. enforcement of property rights with effective policing;
3. creation of a level playing field through domestic reforms;
4. the reform of financial markets through enhancing competition within the sector and increasing the freedom of financing bodies;
5. the development of human skills and knowledge through building networks and public–private partnerships.

Clearly giving small firms access to networks will be central to any policy measures.. This may help alleviate many of the difficulties these businesses encounter when seeking to grow. However, to date there has been limited use of networks beyond the Far East. Where networks do exist, they are often informal. Despite the obvious difficulties with such informality, these networks have proved to be powerful forces (for example, Chinese entrepreneurs overseas).

CONCLUSION

The internationalization of SMEs represents perhaps the most salient impact of the globalization process underlining how far it has penetrated economic structures. SMEs were traditionally exempt from globalization trends, concentrating as they did upon local markets. Changes in the nature of the market and of SMEs have altered this conventional perspective. A new group of SMEs has emerged to deliberately exploit international markets while others are being affected as their traditional markets are opened. This poses a number of policy challenges for authorities as they seek to be both reactive and proactive to these changes to ensure that the SMEs based within their territory are able to respond to the opportunities and challenges posed by globalization.

Summary of Key Concepts

- SMEs are increasingly central to the competitive performance of modern economies.
- The process of globalization is increasingly affecting SMEs.
- There is no homogenous pattern of SME internationalization.
- The more technologically developed SMEs tend to be the more globalized.
- International entrepreneurship is becoming increasingly important.

Activities

1. As a role-playing exercise in a group, seek to identify and surmount the major strategic and marketing challenges posed by internationalization process.

2. Identify the major push-and-pull factors as well as barriers driving SME internationalization.

Discussion Questions

1. How do you account for the rise of international entrepreneurship?

2. In your view, what are the most effective ways for policy makers to assist in the performance of SMEs?

3. What are the core strategic issues that SMEs face in the internationalization process?

References and Suggestions for Further Reading

Acs, Z. and Audretsch, D. (eds) (2006) *Handbook of Entrepreneurship Research: An Interdisciplinary Survey and Introduction*, New York: Springer-Verlag.

Acs, Z. and Yeung, B. (1999) *Small and Medium Sized Enterprises in the Global Economy*, Ann Arbor: University of Michigan Press.

Alvarez, S., Agarwal, R. and Sorenson, O. (eds) (2005) *Handbook of Entrepreneurship Research: Disciplinary Perspectives*, New York: Springer-Verlag.

Audretsch, D. (2002) *Entrepreneurship: A Survey of the Literature*, Prepared for the European Commission, Enterprise Directorate General.

Bell, J., McNaughton, R., Young, S. and Crick, D. (2003) 'Towards an integrative model of small firm internationalisation', *Journal of International Entrepreneurship*, Vol. 1, No. 4, 339–362.

Chappell, C. and Feindt, S. (1999) *Analysis of E-Commerce Practice in SMEs*, Working Paper, Brussels: KITE Project.

Czinkota, M. and Johnsson, W. (1981) 'Segmenting US firms for export development', *Journal of Business Review*, Vol. 9, No. 4, 353–365.

Dana, L. (2006) *Handbook of Research on International Entrepreneurship*, Cheltenham: Edward Elgar.

Etemad, H. and Wright, R. (eds) (2003) *Globalization and Entrepreneurship: Policy and Strategy Perspectives*, Cheltenham: Edward Elgar.

Fujita, M. (1995) 'Small and medium sized transnational corporations: trends and patterns of foreign direct investment', *Small Business Economics*, Vol. 7, No. 3, 183–204.

Haahti, A., Hall, G. and Donckels, R. (1998) *The Internationalisation of SMEs: The Interstratos Project*, London: Routledge.

Jones, G. and Wadhwani, R. (eds) (2007) *Entrepreneurship and Global Capitalism*, Cheltenham: Edward Elgar.

Jones, M. and Dimitratos, P. (eds) (2004) *Emerging Paradigms in International Entrepreneurship*, Cheltenham: Edward Elgar.

Julien P-A. (1996) *Globalization of Markets and Behaviour of Manufacturing SMEs*, Working Paper, Statistics Canada, http://www.statcan.ca/english/freepub/61-532-XIE/05-julien.html.

Luostarinen, R. and Hellman, H. (1993) *Internationalisation Process and Strategies of Finnish Family Enterprises*, Proceedings of the Conference on the Development of Strategies of SMEs in the 1990s, Mikkeli, Vol. 1, 17–35.

OECD (1995) *Globalisation of Small and Medium Sized Enterprises*, Vol. 1, Synthesis Report, Paris: OECD.

OECD (2000) *SMEs: Local Strength, Global Reach*, Policy Briefing, Paris: OECD.

OECD (2005) *OECD SME and Entrepreneurship Outlook*, Paris: OECD.

Oviatt, B. and McDougall, P. (1994) 'Toward a theory of international new ventures', *Journal of International Business Studies*, Vol. 25, No. 1, 45–64.

Phatak, A. (1983) *International Dimensions of Management*, Belmont, CA: Wadsworth.

Plietner, H., Brunner, J. and Habersat, M. (1998) 'Forms and extent of success factors: the case of Switzerland' in Haahti, A. *et al.* (eds), *The Internationalization of SMEs: The Interstratos Project*, London: Routledge, pp. 43–61.

Rialp, A., Rialp, J. and Knight, G. (2005) 'The phenomenon of early internationalizing firms: what do we know after a decade (1993–2003) of scientific inquiry?', *International Business Review*, Vol. 14, No. 2, 147–166.

Shepherd, D. and Katz, J. (eds) (2005) *International Entrepreneurship*, Greenwich, CT: JAI Press.

Su, Z. and Poisson, R. (1998) *Processes of Internationalization*, Working Paper, Faculty of Administrative Studies Laval University, Canada, http://www.sbaer.uca.edu/docs/98icsb/r003.htm.

United Nations (2007) *Statistical Yearbook*, unstats.org.

Wind, Y., Douglas, S. and Perlmutter, H. (1973) 'Guidelines for developing international marketing strategies', *Journal of Marketing*, Vol. 37, No. 2, 14–23.

Young, S. (2007) *Helping SMEs Go Global: Evidence from the World*, http://www.gla.ac.uk/media/media_86949_en.pdf.

Zahra, S. and George, G. (2002) 'Absorptive capacity: a review of reconceptualization and extension', *Academy of Management Review*, Vol. 27, No. 2, 185–203.

Zucchella, A. and Scabini P. (2007) *International Entrepreneurship: Theoretical Foundations and Empirical Analysis*, Basingstoke: Palgrave Macmillan.

Chapter 12

Business Functions within the International Firm

Viewed unemotionally, the offshore outsourcing of IT and call-center work to India is merely the most recent step in a 100-year-old trend in which large corporations farm out pieces of their value chains, through which raw material becomes finished products to be marketed, sold, and delivered.

Michael Treacy, Business Consultant

LEARNING OBJECTIVES

This chapter will help you to:

- comprehend the importance of international human resource and financial management to international business and strategy

- appreciate the importance of corporate governance in international business

- understand the importance of global logistics and knowledge management within the MNE

Chapter 1 outlined the concept of the value chain according to which the MNE is conceptualized as a series of value-adding activities. In essence, it outlined a process whereby firms turn inputs into outputs. While this principle applies to all businesses, the value chain within the MNE is especially complex as inputs may be sourced from a diversity of locations and outputs are marketed and sold to a wide range of markets. The aim of this chapter is to examine the major inputs into the MNE at various points of the value chain to identify how each contributes to the strategy of the business. An exhaustive examination of these topics is beyond the scope of this chapter but identification of salient topics in the international context is possible.

INTERNATIONAL HRM

Chapter 15 deals with the issue of labour from an external dimension. Alongside this external dimension is the internal aspect of labour covered by international human resource management (IHRM). Generally, IHRM relates to the human resource issues and problems created by the growth of the MNE. This encompasses the human resource policies, strategies and practices that MNEs follow in response to their increased internationalization. As a firm extends its geographic reach and market penetration, it needs the support of human resource management (HRM) to help shape financial, marketing and operating decisions. On a generic level, HRM activities include:

■ human resource planning;
■ staffing;
■ performance management;
■ training and development;
■ compensation and benefits;
■ labour relations.

Although non-exhaustive, the above list does highlight the core HRM concerns that need to be addressed as an organization grows more complex, especially when the labour resource is characterized by expatriation. However, IHRM extends beyond the management of expatriates. As knowledge becomes increasingly core to competitive positioning, there is a need for the MNE to manage its human resources in a manner that enables the firm to administer its geographically dispersed labour force to create both local and global competitive advantage.

This means that IHRM is not simply about replicating practices from one location to another. It does not follow that because a management practice works in one location it will transfer successfully to another. Furthermore, IHRM is not simply about managers learning the cultures of all countries where the MNE operates and modifying behaviour accordingly. This overstates both the degree to which cultures may be understood and the ability of the MNE to adapt.

IHRM is distinct from generic HRM on two grounds. First, there is the complexity of operating across multiple national environments (and cultures), and second, of employing different national categories of workers. Thus, IHRM involves the management (defined as the procurement, allocation and utilization) of three groups of workers (host country nationals, parent country nationals and third party nationals) across three types of countries (home, host and 'other'). The above demonstrates the complexity of IHRM in the modern global economy: locating in the host or home economy does not mean that the approach to that workforce will be monocultural. The mobility of the modern workforce has created multinational and multicultural environments within both home and host economies.

Convention identifies the seven 'Cs' of international HRM as:

1. *Cosmopolitan*: IHRM involves employees that spend at least part of their employment overseas. This includes workers whose career path necessitates working in non-domiciled locations. Some workers may move for short periods to work with partners while others may work overseas for a short time on a specific project. Finally, some workers actively seek employment overseas independent of an MNE (see Chapter 15).
2. *Culture*: this theme is dealt with in Chapter 13. In terms of IHRM, the internationalization of business creates interactions between different cultures which require adaptation by the MNE.
3. *Compensation*: once employees have moved out of their home environment, a range of complex remuneration issues need to be addressed. These include incentives to work overseas, tax status, pension issues and treatment of staff.
4. *Communication*: inter-firm communication needs to account for culture, geography and rivalry.
5. *Consultancy*: there is often a need within foreign environments to buy in expertise that the parent company does not possess. Thus, IHRM needs to deal with the contracts of these consultants and their interaction with existing human resources.
6. *Competence*: the MNE will always need to develop its wide variety of human resources to ensure it has the necessary skills to cope with the complexity of the modern global economy.
7. *Coordination*: IHRM has to ensure that different parts of the MNE work together for mutual advantage.

Understanding this complexity is a core strategic issue for business. Organizational failure within host markets is often attributed to poor management of human resources. This has frequently stemmed from a mistaken belief that domestic HRM policies, strategies and so on can readily be transferred to a host environment. This complexity also extends to the interaction between home and host economies where interplay between human resources can lead to shifts in home country HRM.

A number of variables moderate differences between domestic and IHRM. These differences are characterized by more than simple increases in complexity. These variables are the cultural environment; the industry in which the MNE is involved; the degree of reliance of the MNE upon its home economy, and the attitudes of senior management. It is worthwhile looking at each of these variables in more depth.

The Cultural Environment

Chapter 13 highlights the importance of culture as a core feature of the competitive environment and defines and identifies its key attributes. The most immediate impact of culture derives from the shock of moving across cultures as the mobility of labour requires cultural assimilation over a relatively short period of time. Such adjustments can be a major challenge for the MNE and HRM professionals. There is often both a process of convergence and divergence occurring between cultures. The former tends to occur at the macro level (e.g. structure, technology) whereas the latter is more common at the micro level (e.g. behaviour within firms). Although firms from different states are becoming more alike, the behaviour of people within them maintains its cultural specificity. Understanding such trends is important to the support of IHRM for corporate strategy. Failure to understand these trends and differences often contributes to a failure of strategy. As a result, while an expatriate may head up an overseas subsidiary, the MNE often relies on a local HR manager who is familiar with local practices. Such a system is open to abuse if it results in recruitment based on patronage and/or nepotism.

Industry Type

The extent to which competition is characterized by multi-domesticity (at one extreme) or globality (at the other) (see Chapter 1) influences the form and nature of IHRM. Within Porter's value chain, HRM is a support function that cuts across the entire value chain. If the firm is in a multi-domestic industry, the supporting function of HRM will be determined more by the features of the host on a stand-alone basis. The role of HRM in this context is to support the competitive positioning of the business within these locations by enabling primary activities. If the industry is characterized by globality, then there is an increased imperative for coordination to support the activities of the firm on an international/transnational basis. This suggests that the HRM function should be centralized.

Reliance of the MNE on Its Home Market

Generally the more important the home market is for the MNE, the less likely is the firm to seek to adapt to local circumstances. This is in contrast to firms from smaller states with a higher degree of multinationality which generally tend to adapt more to local conditions. A large domestic market influences a manager's need to adapt and the commercial imperative to do so. It also generates a larger number of managers with a solely domestic market focus. This parochialism can be a challenge for businesses from larger states such as the US.

Attitudes of Senior Managers

If senior management does not have a strong international orientation, the importance of international operations will be underemphasized in terms of the broad strategic aims and objectives of the business. As a result managers tend to focus on home country issues and downplay and minimize differences between home and host economies. This behaviour is based on an assumption that there is a high degree of transferability between home and foreign environments – this may not be the case and difficulties for overseas operations often result.

Within MNEs, HRM is not always well understood by senior managers as HRM professionals tend only to be involved in strategic decisions when there is a critical mass of expatriates involved, when staff transfers are of strategic value and when there is a time lag between the making of decisions and their impact on HRM. Approaches to IHRM reflect the typology of MNEs identified by Perlmutter in relation to the following categories: ethnocentric, polycentric, regiocentric and geocentric approaches (see Box 9.1). The implications of Perlmutter's typology for IHRM are as follows:

■ *ethnocentric*: subsidiaries are managed by expatriates;
■ *polycentric*: subsidiaries are managed by locals who are rarely transferred to the parent company;
■ *geocentric*: the pool for managers is global and therefore there is no nationalistic preference for any particular role;
■ *regiocentric*: managers are appointed from a wider pool based on the local region.

These approaches reflect the attitude of top management and the nature of an international business.

IHRM is also shaped by the status of the firm's internationalization process. Generally, at the lower commitment forms of internationalization (such as exporting), there is a higher degree of involvement by local nationals who have better information regarding the host market. Sales subsidiaries tend to use parent country nationals in key positions and this pattern is repeated in international divisions. Thus, the firm needs to consider HRM issues within international expansion strategies as the importance of HRM matures with the process of internationalization. In the formative stages of internationalization, IHRM is usually not an issue as involvement with overseas staff is minimal. As internationalization matures, and as managers are assigned to overseas locations, so IHRM increases in importance. As integration, cost and coordination benefits become more evident, the firm will become more concerned with recruiting the best international managers irrespective of nationality. As issues of global integration and national responsiveness become more apparent, so IHRM becomes a major issue as a firm takes decisions regarding the extent that cultural diversity is necessary for competitive positioning. There are two logics shaping HRM policy. The first is the product-market logic which states that each phase of the product life cycle requires a different type of manager. The second is sociocultural logic which (as mentioned) reflects the different contexts within which the MNE operates. This is reflected within Perlmutter's multiple approaches to overseas markets. Overall, the strategic role of HRM is illustrated in Figure 12.1.

This underlines the mediating role of IHRM. The choice of structure, the stage of the life cycle, interaction with host/regional specifics affect all aspects of HRM policy. The ability of the MNE to attract, retain and train staff is key to the attainment of MNE goals, as the human capital within the MNE is pivotal to successful implementation of its strategy.

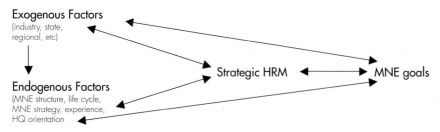

FIGURE 12.1   An Integrated Framework for Strategic HRM

Source: DeCieri and Dowling (1999).

CORPORATE GOVERNANCE WITHIN THE INTERNATIONAL FIRM

A consequence of increased international competition is growing concern about the competitiveness of a state's institutions. Corporate governance ranks high among these institutional concerns. Corporate governance refers to the way in which company boards oversee the running of the corporation by its managers and how board members are accountable to shareholders and the company generally. These relationships have implications for the company's behaviour towards the broader set of stakeholders, such as employees, shareholders, customers and banks. Good corporate governance is essential for the integrity and efficiency of financial markets. On the other hand, poor corporate governance hinders a company's potential and may, in extreme cases, create financial difficulties and/or lead to fraud. Well-governed companies usually outperform rivals and attract investors to finance future growth. Box 12.1 underlines the core facets of the corporate governance environment for MNEs.

Box 12.1 The Corporate Governance Environment

The corporate governance environment is shaped by stock exchange listing rules and a host of rules and regulations covering:

- company formation;
- the issue and sale of securities;
- disclosure requirements and accounting standards;
- shareholder rights and proxy voting;
- fiduciary duties of directors, officers and controlling shareholders;
- contract enforcement;
- bankruptcy and creditors' rights;
- labour relations;
- financial sector practices;

■ tax and pension policy;
■ mergers and acquisitions.

This environment is also supported by:

■ the quality and availability of judicial and regulatory enforcement of laws and regulations;
■ a general understanding of corporate citizenship;
■ societal expectations about the corporate objective;
■ competition within product, service and capital markets;
■ open markets for management, labour and corporate control.

Nations permit corporations to form for many reasons: some focus on the satisfaction of societal expectations while others emphasize profit. Despite these differences, corporate governance in all states aims to:

■ promote the efficient use of resources, both within the company and the economy in general;
■ ensure corporate compliance with the laws, regulations and expectations of society;
■ offer managers oversight of their use of corporate resources;
■ support efforts to reduce corruption in business dealings;
■ facilitate access to lower cost capital by improving investor confidence.

Thus, while managers have some degree of discretion over their actions, this freedom needs to be supported by independent monitoring of their acts; transparency over performance, control and ownership, and to allow participation by shareholders in specific acts. In turn, this requires a supporting legal and regulatory framework, which would normally include the factors identified in Box 12.2.

Box 12.2 Core Legal and Regulatory Requirements for Effective Corporate Governance

■ well-developed and regulated securities markets;
■ laws that identify shareholders as legitimate owners;
■ equitable treatment of minority and foreign shareholders;
■ enforcement mechanisms to protect shareholder rights;
■ strong corporate disclosure requirements;
■ securities, corporate and bankruptcy laws that enable businesses to adjust, transform or fail;
■ anti-corruption laws;
■ sophisticated courts and regulators;
■ an experienced accounting and auditing sector.

These frameworks tend to feature more in developed economies. Before these legal and regulatory frameworks can emerge in developing economies, the creation of key institutions (such as a stock exchange and a credible financial press) and laws (such as shareholder protection, improvement of accounting standards) are needed. These issues are reflected within the OECD's *Principles of Corporate Governance* (first published in 1999) which stress the protection of shareholders' rights through principles of fairness, accountability, transparency and responsibility. The *Principles*, the first international code on good corporate governance approved by governments, stress the primacy of shareholder value added. They are non-binding and should be viewed as recommendations for best practice. Following the Enron and WorldCom scandals, the 2004 revision of the *Principles* broadened their scope to increase the accountability of boards to shareholders and to remove any damaging conflicts of interest.

Economic globalization raises the question of whether there is a 'best' system of corporate governance and whether interaction will push all states towards this 'best' type. Current differences between states over governance systems centre on three issues:

1. The identities of the owners of the corporation and the size and distribution of their ownership stakes. There are three main types of ownership: private ownership (which may be concentrated or dispersed among groups of shareholders), family ownership, and state ownership.
2. The governance structure of the corporation – the number, size and composition of monitoring boards.
3. The legal and political institutions that shape managerial behaviour.

The 'Insider' System of Corporate Governance

When ownership stakes are concentrated, the firm is characterized by 'insider' governance systems. These insider systems are characterized by the direct representation of major shareholders on monitoring boards and/or even by their direct involvement in management. Insider systems of governance are common in Europe and Japan. In Europe, the Germanic system of control is frequently unidirectional, based on a corporate pyramid where the absence of cross-shareholdings means that those in the lower level exert no control over those above them in the hierarchy. Thus, company A may own shares in company B which may own shares in company C which in turn may control companies D and E. Under the Germanic system, companies B, C, D and E do not possess any degree of ownership or control over firms above them in the hierarchy. The Japanese form of insider governance is characterized by interlinkages among several companies based on interlocking directorships and supported by cross-shareholdings. Within these keiretsu, there is also a main bank which holds shares in the respective companies within the group. As a result, control is multi-directional with each company able to exert some control over companies that control it.

The 'Outsider' System of Corporate Governance

By contrast, 'outsider' governance systems are characterized by dispersed ownership with owners exerting indirect control by electing representatives to the board or by voting on specific proposals from management. The US and the UK are the most important examples of outsider systems. Although allowing for dispersed management, concentrated ownership is not unusual in the Anglo-Saxon system. The most often cited criticism of this system is that its preoccupation with ownership creates a tendency to ignore other stakeholders.

Understanding these differences is important for understanding the management of MNEs. Within many MNEs, ownership and control are separate. Under modern capitalism, owners delegate authority to managers. This creates conflicts where there is incomplete overlap between managers and owners. Within insider systems, the potential for such conflict is limited as the overlap is assumed to be greater. Furthermore, insider systems have managers as owners where they can own large shareholdings. 'Outsider' systems are assumed to be characterized by increased conflict as dispersion of ownership creates little incentive to monitor managers closely. Managers have little by way of shareholdings within the company and thus their financial motivations differ from those of shareholders. Alongside these principal–agent issues are conflicts between owners (so-called principal–principal conflicts) where rival major shareholders clash over strategy and so on.

To argue that one system of governance is better than another is to miss the point. These systems have evolved to serve their own needs. Indeed, if the key barometer of whether a system works is the wealth generated by its business, then all the leading states can claim success for their own system. However, such successes often emerged in an environment of limited global competition. In a more globalized era, there is an emerging consensus that outsider systems are better, as insider systems often hide weaknesses. It is also believed that the Anglo-Saxon system is better at protecting shareholders and leads to better macroeconomic performance. This implies that pressures exist on states to converge on the 'superior' Anglo-Saxon system.

There is some evidence of convergence across the global economy. In the US, scandals such as Enron and WorldCom have enhanced the power of institutional investors. This has pushed the US towards an even purer form of outsider corporate governance. There has also been partial movement of insider systems towards the Anglo-Saxon system. While the shift has not been dramatic, the trend is unmistakable. Furthermore, a trend towards continental firms raising capital on UK and US capital markets has subjected them to Anglo-Saxon governance systems. These developments have also been mirrored in Japan. Whether this trend will lead to a full convergence is uncertain, as path-dependent pressures can resist such change. The ultimate driver will be whether states that fail to adopt the 'superior system' suffer a flight of capital and business as a result.

INTERNATIONAL MARKETING MANAGEMENT

Other chapters within this volume discuss issues related to international marketing. However, in addition to the contextual issues that shape the environment for international marketing are those related to the management of marketing in an international context.

In an international context, the primary role of the marketing manager is to understand customer needs both within and across markets. In many developed economies, market segments have become increasingly subdivided. This trend is not yet established within many developing and emerging economies where segments remain much broader in their nature. The trend towards micro-segmentation in developed economies has been driven by the increased sophistication of consumers and their desire and power to minimize customer sacrifice within their purchase decisions. This has created trends towards increased differentiation through customer services and understanding, and has its most obvious expressions within solutions-based value propositions. In other words, micro-segmentation leads to the need for firms to define their value proposition according to the nature of the niche in which they are seeking to compete.

The ability to offer a standardized product within this context depends upon the extent to which customer needs are similar across the world and upon the minimum economic size of production: that is, the greater the volume required for efficiency, the more standardized the product is likely to be. Thus, global standardization only occurs where uniform needs created by a global segment coincide with a high minimum-efficient scale. At the other extreme, where the segment is highly specialized and the minimum economic size is low, the product offered will be highly adaptable to customer requirements. In between these extremes of global standardization and locally defined products lies the hybrid option of modifying the product to meet specific needs based on different modular components.

Typically, globalization implies increased homogeneity characterized by a trend towards standardization. However, in international marketing, this relies upon a set of conditions related to scale and uniformity of customer requirements which are suggestive of commoditization where differentiation based on anything other than price becomes difficult. Clearly, most businesses will want to avoid this part of the market. In many cases, it is widely accepted that the process of standardization is limited in practice. Counterbalancing commoditizing pressures may occur through customer intimacy and solutions. Standardization is also only common where there is a common brand and minimal product knowledge is required for usage. Consumer goods generally require more adaptation due to their higher degree of cultural grounding. As suggested above, the degree of adaptation is also driven by economic conditions. In developing economies, there is often a trend towards uniformity to make the product more affordable.

International marketing also involves product branding issues. Global brands are marketed under a single name across multiple markets and tend to be characterized by:

- persistent strength within the home market;
- consistency in product positioning;
- a geographically balanced presence across regions;
- a consistent value proposition across markets;
- ease of pronunciation with neutral cultural implications.

What is clearly important in establishing global branding are issues related to uniformity of the value proposition across space. In short, the brand should offer a uniform message to the same group of people via a standard product. This extreme form of brand globality can be tempered by hybrid forms of global branding where the message/segment may be consistent but the product is adaptable to local markets. Alternatively, a standardized product may have its message/segment adapted to local conditions. At the other extreme to the pure global brand is the situation where both the brand message/targeted segment and product are fully adapted to specific countries. It is generally accepted that global branding offers three main advantages:

- *Strategic*: the global brand can reinforce market power by enabling spill-over effects across countries and can offer efficiencies in product launches.
- *Economic*: the uniformity of branding creates efficiencies in terms of marketing communications as well as lowering internal costs through reducing product administration.
- *Organizational*: global brands reinforce corporate identity and aid the mobility of personnel around the organization.

Such benefits have to be assessed in the light of any disadvantages created through underplaying national differences.

Pricing issues are an important component of the overall marketing mix. In some cases, firms are attracted to consistent pricing policies where differences between states can only be explained by local taxation or regulatory issues. Attempts to achieve consistent pricing are motivated by attempts to:

- avoid arbitrage where there are limited barriers to trade and to overcome any incentives for consumers to purchase the good in non-domestic but geographically close locations;
- protect the integrity of the brand;
- aid the servicing of local customers.

However, attempts to implement some degree of uniformity can run counter to the value the customer attaches to specific attributes linked to consistent pricing. For example, not all consumers may value the brand highly in the purchasing decision. As a consequence, such pricing strategies only work in a limited number of circumstances, such as when customer profiles are similar or where there is a strong global brand. Given these conditions, a policy of price discrimination tends to be more common within an MNE's marketing strategy. In other words, the MNE charges different prices in different markets for essentially the same product. Generally, a firm charges what the market will bear, thereby enabling it to maximize profits. However, for this pricing strategy to be viable, the following two conditions have to be fulfilled:

1. The MNE has to be able to keep national markets separate. If this is not possible, consumers can engage in arbitrage and undermine price discrimination.
2. The responsiveness of demand to changes in price (so-called price elasticity) has to differ between the markets. If the elasticities are uniform, the firm will move towards more consistent pricing. However, where markets behave differently, the firm can actively discriminate between them.

Inevitably, the decision over pricing reflects the broader strategy followed by the MNE. Thus discrimination between markets may be undertaken for reasons other than simple short-term profit objectives. Price differentials between markets may be motivated by longer term strategic objectives such as undermining host market competitors. As such, the firm can engage in alternative pricing principles that sacrifice short-term profit for longer term objectives. Such pricing policies include:

- *Predatory pricing*: as the name suggests, this is where the firm uses an aggressive pricing strategy to undercut rivals and/or to drive them out of the business. This strategy has the longer term objective of allowing the firm to attain a pre-eminent or even dominant position within its target market.

- *Multipoint pricing*: this occurs when two or more MNEs compete across two or more markets. Reflecting interdependence between markets, this pricing strategy seeks to influence the pricing strategy of a rival through influencing its actions in another market.
- *Market-building pricing*: pricing strategy may reflect an MNE's international experience and the position of their products in their life cycle. Thus, where the firm is experienced, has large-scale economies or where the market is mature, pricing will tend to be lower. In other cases, a firm may seek to build market share by pricing low.

Such pricing strategies are constrained by both domestic and transnational frameworks. These seek to mitigate any potential conflict between the strategic objectives of the business and those of the host or home economy. Thus there are measures to constrain pricing policy through anti-dumping and competition policies.

GLOBAL LOGISTICS

Mobility underpins international business as it involves the movement of tangibles and intangibles across political borders. The issue of the mobility of intangibles has been dealt with elsewhere (for example, see Chapters 7 and 18). The movement of tangibles generates another set of issues for international business and reflects a need for effective supply and distribution channels to allow the effective sourcing of inputs and the servicing of customers and other partners. Unlike intangibles where the cost of digital bits is all but costless, the movement of physical matter is a costly activity and of strategic importance to the business.

The importance of international logistics has grown as a result of the increased demand for these services created by global sourcing and trade. While the trade issue has been discussed elsewhere (see Chapter 7), it is worthwhile examining further the rising importance of global sourcing. In short, this is the process whereby the source of inputs into the business has grown increasingly diverse as a result of the globalization process, a development arising from firms' desires for more reliable, cheaper and/or better quality inputs. These sourcing issues have been compounded by rising international trade flows and changes in the supply side of industry where a combination of liberalization, technological change and increased investment has increased the capacity of global logistical systems.

International logistics is the design and management of a system that controls the flow of materials into, through and out of the MNE. Thus international logistics is concerned with both inter- and intra-firm mobility. In short, the firm is a network of interrelationships based on the flow of physical resources both within and external to the firm. There are two important stages in the movement of materials to the MNE:

- *materials management*: that is, the movement of raw materials or semi-finished products into and throughout the firm;
- *physical distribution*: that is, the movement of the MNE's final product to its customers.

The aim of logistics is to ensure that these two stages are coordinated to minimize stationary periods (i.e. storage and inventory) and to ensure cost-effectiveness while maintaining a broader set of strategic priorities.

Evidently (as indicated in Chapter 8), logistical issues have a direct bearing upon FDI decisions. The state of overseas infrastructure has a direct bearing upon the costs and logistical issues encountered by the business. Logistics requires a transport and communications network that has sufficient capacity combined with the necessary access points to ensure the flow of material within and between firms. This means that access to physical infrastructure must be able to meet the needs and expectations of MNEs.

The process of internationalization has a number of implications for the logistical process:

1. *Inventory*: this is a function of whether the firm is following a global or a multi-domestic strategy. There are clearly advantages to holding all stock centrally especially for high-value products. For more localized strategies, product proliferation requires more dispersed storage.
2. *Handling*: as services practices and regulations regarding storage and transport differ across economies, the MNE may adjust handling processes accordingly.
3. *Transport*: the quality of infrastructure differs across states. Where time to market is a core issue, this may drive localization of production. Alternatively, the existence of good-quality transnational and internal transport links may drive the centralization of production.

Time to market has become an increasingly important issue within international logistics where product obsolescence and the costs of holding inventory are salient costs. The former highlights a risk that long transit times can lead to obsolescence while the product is still in transit. The latter occurs where the infrastructure does not have the capacity to handle the flow. The result is that the firm's outputs are held in storage for longer while waiting to be moved on to the next stage.

The internationalization of firm or industry value chains increases the need for effective supply chain management (SCM). SCM is based on the series of value-adding activities that connect the firm's supply side with its demand side. This requires that the supply chain of the extended enterprise is viewed in its entirety from the suppliers through to the end customer. Such a holistic perspective reflects interdependence and the multifaceted interaction between all parties based on both tangible and intangible (especially knowledge) flows, and allows for the identification of efficiencies and stresses the strategic nature of the extended enterprise. The rise of SCM has been made possible by advances in ICTs that allow firms to monitor their inventories and those of their partners. In short, the overall goal of a logistical system is to get products to the final consumer at the lowest possible cost. This reflects the core strategic role of logistics and the important part it plays in the competitive positioning of the business (see Case Study 12.1).

Logistics therefore represents a source of value. It can be core to the service dimension of products, ensuring that products are up to date, fresh and meet any other criteria where speed, quicker times to market and the volume of flows can be important differentiators. Logistics costs account for an estimated 10 to 30 per cent of the total landed costs of an international order. Given that many firms have looked in other places for efficiency, they are beginning to look at logistics as a source of competitive advantage. This explains the increased usage of ICTs within logistical systems. Part of the means of achieving these efficiencies is through global consolidation where the firm sources

CASE STUDY 12.1

Aviation Supply Chains

As in any industry, aviation companies rely upon effective supply chains to support their competitive position. In an industry characterized by intense price competition, there is a clear advantage in managing the supply chain to squeeze out extra efficiencies through, for example, minimizing the size of the inventory required. Conversely, an inefficient or failing supply chain is problematic for these businesses. Poor customer satisfaction and a failure to meet delivery deadlines can erode the ability of the firm to compete. This is typical of the challenges facing the world's two largest aviation firms: Airbus and Boeing.

Both of these businesses continually face problems within their supply chains and production systems as they seek to cope with a shifting competitive environment. For these giants, their problems became especially evident in late 2007 when the issues raised by the declining dollar (see below) were compounded by the over-complexity of Airbus's value network. Airbus had thousands of suppliers, many of which did not have the critical mass to work on new products.

Driven by the weak dollar, increased competitive pressure and delays to the Airbus A380, Airbus launched its Power8 restructuring programme in early 2007. The aim of Power8 was to turn Airbus into a transnational (see Chapter 1). In order to compete with Boeing, who priced in dollars, Airbus planned cost savings of €5 billion by 2010. A large percentage of the savings were to be generated by a substantial reduction in employment (10,000 job losses). Alongside these measures were efforts to streamline the production process to facilitate faster product development (to reduce development time from 7.5 to six years); lean manufacturing (integrating manufacturing and associated engineering) and smart buying (to lower procurement costs). The firm was seeking to make €2.1 billion savings annually from 2010.

However, the Power8 initiative assumed that the euro was worth $1.38 but a decline in the value of the dollar to $1.47 began to undermine the cost savings sought by the scheme. It was estimated that for every 10 per cent rise in the value of the euro, an extra €1 billion was added to Airbus's costs. The latest rise in the euro forced Airbus to look again at its programme and to send production to low-cost countries or to states that price in dollars. In 2007, Airbus procured over three-quarters of its inputs within Europe but sold 60 per cent of its output overseas. This simple ratio forced a reconsideration of the firm's value chain. The firm has since opened up an assembly line in China with more plants to follow in both China and Russia. Airbus has stated its intention to increase the number of suppliers who price in dollars. By 2013, 70 per cent of the A350 and 50 per cent of the A380 will be purchased from firms that price in dollars, compared to an average of 24 per cent at the onset of the plan. Some aircraft could be made entirely outside the eurozone. The exchange rate is not the only reason for this shift, as the firm is keen to tap into expertise wherever it exists.

Airbus was keen not to repeat the mistakes of Boeing when outsourcing its production. Boeing outsourced around 80 per cent of the manufacture of its new 787 Dreamliner aircraft. However, increased production delays occurred as some suppliers proved unreliable. Boeing was not only critical of supplier capabilities but was also deterred by the need for these firms to fly components and semi-finished parts of the plane substantial distances to the main assembly operation. As a result, the firm is pressurizing suppliers to locate closer to the main assembly plant.

These two cases offer contrasting examples of the pros and cons of globalizing supply chains. As Airbus is increasing its reliance upon overseas suppliers, so Boeing is reducing its dependence upon such structures. While the drivers behind these contradictory strategies are different, this case does highlight key pressures within the global value chain. However, given cost pressures and the potential for exchange rates to alter, these two firms will tend to converge rather than diverge on supply chain issues in the long term.

CASE STUDY ACTIVITY

Using the example of the Airbus A-380, outline how the supply chain can affect competitive position in both a negative and positive fashion.

commodity items from low-wage economies, concentrates activities at specific sites and undertakes bulk transportation.

Methods to improve the efficiency and effectiveness of supply chains include:

- *Focused factories:* these represent a sea change whereby the MNE moves from basing its production system on a limited segment of a geographical market towards one where production of specific products is focused on specific factories. Thus each 'focused factory' supplies its products internationally to a wide range of markets and focuses on a limited assortment of products. While this should deliver efficiencies in terms of production, the same cannot necessarily be said of inventory holding or transport costs.
- *Centralized inventories:* just as the consolidation of production can generate efficiencies, so can the consolidation of inventory. Rather than maintaining a network of warehouses and distribution centres across a region, the firm utilizes a smaller number of locations. This allows for cost savings via reducing duplications and lowering inventories. This has to be balanced against the fact that many products will have longer distribution legs. However, the cost savings from lower inventories can be significant. This is especially true of product (especially high-value) environments where such costs are more significant than distribution costs.

KNOWLEDGE MANAGEMENT, INNOVATION AND THE MNE

Chapter 10 highlights the importance of knowledge to the evolution of the MNE. Knowledge management refers to the structures, processes and systems that actively develop, leverage and transfer knowledge. As indicated, this knowledge may be both tacit (i.e. non-codifiable) and explicit (i.e. codifiable). Operating across multiple environments can present substantial barriers to knowledge flows. These barriers to the free flow of knowledge between the different units of the firm include linguistics, cultural differences, local managerial mindsets and lack of trust. However, there are advantages from transnational knowledge flows through allowing the diversity of contexts and experiences to be utilized for the advantages of the rest of the MNC, allowing for economies of scale and scope within the MNE.

An important subset of the knowledge flows within an MNE relates to the process of innovation. Innovation is the result of or is supported by knowledge flows within the MNE, especially between subsidiaries and the HQ as well as inter-subsidiary. MNEs engage in innovation to refresh their product portfolio. However, there is an increasing trend within MNEs to disperse R&D operations across the global economy. This globalized system of R&D is based on a coordinated integrated system to leverage location-specific advantages to enhance competitive positioning (see Case Study 12.2).

CASE STUDY 12.2

The Rise of the Metanational

Chapter 1 identified the broad generic types of strategy that can be followed by MNEs. A new and emergent structure – the metanational – may be added to the simple three-part typology (global, multi-domestic and transnational). The essence of metanationality is the premise that innovation within increasingly internationalized markets is based less on home-based competences and more on learning from the world by tapping into geographically dispersed unexploited (or underexploited) pockets of technology and market intelligence. This is symptomatic of an environment in which innovative capability is based on the following trends where:

* competitive advantage is fuelled by knowledge;
* key knowledge resources are geographically scattered;
* time/space and cost/space convergence allows these resources to be more widely accessible.

Such practices are not new, as many MNEs have used globally dispersed value networks to tap into dispersed knowledge for some time. However, what is novel is the extent to which such trends have proliferated. As knowledge becomes core to success, so MNEs will free themselves from any home country bias in innovation. The emergence of a dispersed innovation process relies on the creation of competences that know how to seek and utilize such pockets of knowledge. MNEs will need to develop competences that transcend national borders as a means of shaping competitive advantage. Competitive advantage will be based on being able to identify, access, utilize and operationalize 'valuable' knowledge. The competences needed to create

advantage for the metanational lie in three distinct capabilities.

- *Sensing*: the MNE needs to identify new technologies, skills and lead market knowledge. The firm needs to build a sensing network that can locate new knowledge that rivals have not used or accessed.
- *Mobilizing*: the firm has to be able to translate new knowledge into new products and/or processes and thus requires structures that are able to mobilize knowledge. They may need to create designated 'magnets' that attract dispersed and potentially relevant knowledge and then aid its transfer into the rest of the MNE network.
- *Operationalizing*: the final aspect is to turn innovation into enhanced profit potential for the firm. This means spreading the innovation throughout the network to improve efficiencies and to create local adaptations.

While the notion of metanationality does provide a new structure and strategy for the MNE, it is not without its problems. For example, it risks under-playing the role of the home state in the innovation process. Many MNEs rely heavily on their domestic market for innovation – a process that can be shaped by government industrial policies. Indeed, there is little incentive to tap into networks where strategic defence is the priority of the firm. There is also a gap in understanding how sensing actually takes place. Thus, while metanationality may appear at face value to be an attractive strategy for innovation within the MNE, it can treat the process simplistically and ignore the political economy surrounding the activities of MNEs.

The imperative to seek out and utilize location-specific assets highlights the nature of the modern economy and how certain assets that shape competitiveness are immobile and geographically dispersed. Moreover, as a network of businesses, the MNE has to create channels through which these immobile factors of production can enhance the competitive position of all parts of the enterprises.

There are key benefits to be obtained from internationalizing R&D.

- First, R&D may provide a method of accessing and exploiting a host economy's local talent and resources. This may be driven by the quality of local education systems or via a cluster of local, highly innovative firms.
- Second, the process can aid a firm's international competitive positioning. Key resources are dispersed throughout the global economy and these resources are not always mobile. Thus the MNE has to be able to tap into local knowledge to aid its development. This aids competitiveness if, for example, the knowledge embedded within the host economy is important in customizing products to local needs and increases its responsiveness within this context.
- Third, the firm can adapt or create products to meet local needs by locating R&D facilities in close proximity to its target market.
- Fourth, the firm learns about local R&D resources and leverages this knowledge to cross-fertilize and to create new knowledge elsewhere within the MNE network.
- Fifth, the firm can access low-cost and good-quality researchers.
- Finally, it can enable the firm to exploit the international division of labour. Clearly states are diverse in terms of their resources, and firms can divide activities across borders to ensure that the best location to undertake R&D plays that role.

However, these benefits have to be counterbalanced by potential problems. For example, attaining a sufficient scale to make overseas R&D worthwhile is not always possible, plus there is the threat that valuable research is leaked to rivals and the possibility of increased coordination and communication costs. Critical mass issues are important: research is a capital-intensive activity and needs to be well networked in order to be effective. If research units remain small, researchers may be denied access to the necessary complementary skills. The need for face-to-face informal communication is vital to R&D. Dispersing R&D throughout the global economy removes this core advantage.

In knowledge creation and retention, firms face a number of problems. The first is related to employee turnover. Outflows of staff inevitably create knowledge leakage from the firm. Second, some managers may be suspicious of outbound knowledge if it erodes their local power base or diverts local personnel from key tasks. When information can be shared by meeting, the transmission of ideas can come up against linguistic and cultural issues. This can be compounded by issues of causal ambiguity and absorptive capacity. The former suggests that when knowledge is tacit, it may be difficult to identify precise causes and effects. The latter implies that the ability of innovation to aid the business is a function of the ability of the firm to create, understand and deploy knowledge. Often the firm may not recognize the value of information.

Perhaps the greatest risk comes from the inherent risks of innovation. There is no guarantee that research will generate successful products. For this reason, knowledge management has to cross functional teams to ensure that marketing, production and R&D interact so that:

- the products respond to customer needs;
- the products can be easily manufactured;
- development costs are kept in check;
- the time to market is minimized.

Thus the sharing of knowledge across functions and the avoidance of a silo mentality can aid the potential for product success. This becomes more complex for the MNE where the product needs to be adapted for local markets. For this reason, knowledge management systems must ensure that local needs are transmitted to what can be dispersed research centres.

INTERNATIONAL FINANCIAL MANAGEMENT

Financial management is important to all firms. As with other functions, international financial management is more complex than its domestic equivalent as management has to address different financial environments. While the coverage of international financial management can encompass a long list of operational issues, the domain may be broken down into four broadly defined but overlapping issues:

- the finance of international trade;
- the finance of international operations;
- managing currency risk;
- managing the MNE's financial resources.

Understanding these issues is pivotal for MNEs: first, by enabling them to comprehend how turbulence within the international environment (transmitted through devices such as the exchange rate) can have negative or positive impacts upon the firm, and second, by enabling management to anticipate events and to profit from them. As such, it is worthwhile to explore the above four domains in more depth.

The Finance of International Trade

International trade depends upon the credibility of the underpinning financial system and is subject to risk when financing depends upon an unknown entity for payment. If international trade is to overcome credibility issues related to this lack of trust, financial devices need to evolve to cope with this problem. Generally this problem is solved via the use of a mutually trusted intermediary. The most common methods of trade finance are:

1. *Advance payment*: this method avoids the use of an intermediary by the parties agreeing that the importer pays either in advance or upon the goods' arrival.
2. *Documentary credit*: this is provided by the intermediary on behalf of the buyer and promises to honour the payment once goods have been delivered.
3. *Credit facilities*: these are offered by export credit agencies and are based on the intermediary offering credits to cover the political and commercial risks of trade.
4. *Documentary collection*: this allows exporters to retain ownership of the product until payment is made or is perceived as imminent. The intermediary holds the title documents and exchanges them once payment has been accepted.
5. *Open account*: this involves shipping the goods now and billing the importer later.

While this is not an exhaustive list of payment methods, it does indicate assorted means through which the firm can mitigate the degree of risk encountered by the exporter when faced with issues of trust and information asymmetry. Clearly, the persistence and growth of trade depends upon the success of these devices and upon gaining and sustaining the confidence of traders.

The Finance of International Operations

When examining the options for internationalization, the firm has to consider how the investment is to be financed. The choice often comes down to the following:

■ *Intra-company financing*: this is based on internal resource flows, either from the parent or from other subsidiaries. This need not be through a transfer of funds as firms can use inter-company loans, equity or credit to finance new operations. Support can also be generated by allowing the subsidiary to retain a higher percentage of earnings.
■ *Equity financing*: this may be attained either within the host, home or third party economy where the firm either cross-lists existing stock across multiple markets or offers new equity to overseas investors.
■ *Debt financing*: this is attained via international bank loans, the euronote market (i.e. loans issued in countries not using the national currency denomination) and the international bond market.
■ *Local currency financing*: this involves seeking finance for operations within the host economy.

The chosen financing method will reflect a desire to lower the cost of capital needed for the MNE's international expansion. This means configuring resources to minimize tax liability, to limit currency and political risk to exploit uncertainty and information asymmetries within the financial system to raise capital at the lowest possible cost.

Managing Currency Risk

As highlighted in Chapters 10 and 17, a major source of risk facing MNEs is exchange rate instability. A core concern for business is the impact of localized inflation on the value of foreign exchange. Inflation differentials between states erode the value of investments and make returns uncertain. Firms can mitigate such risks by minimizing holding of the depreciating currency by transferring assets into more stable currencies. They can also slow down payments to those who accept payment in the depreciating currency in anticipation of further declines in value. In short, the firm will transfer assets out of this currency or seek to pass the risk on to others. Other risks related to the exchange rate stem from:

- *Translation exposure*: translating overseas financial statements into the home currency undermines earning statements and hinders the ability of the subsidiary to purchase assets from states with stronger currencies.
- *Transaction exposure*: the erosion in earnings created when they are collected in a local currency and converted into the currency of the parent company.
- *Economic exposure*: the exposure of the overseas competitive position, sourcing or investments to sudden swings in the local exchange rate.

Strategies to mitigate these risks may either be reactive (e.g. divestment) or adaptive. Adaptive strategies reflect the underlying desirability of international transactions in a potentially risky environment. Firms protect themselves against these currency risks by hedging against adverse movements. Typically, hedging comprises one of the following methods:

- collecting monies before they are due if the currency is expected to weaken, or early payment if the currency is expected to strengthen;
- delaying collection of money until a currency has regained value or deferring payment if the currency is expected to weaken.

These operational financial strategies can be supported by more formal methods such as:

- *forward exchange contracts*: these legally oblige the payer to deliver the currency at a pre-determined exchange rate on a specified date;
- *currency options*: this device gives the owner the right to buy and sell a specific amount of a given currency at a predetermined rate within a given period of time.

Again, this is not an exhaustive list of devices that are used. Generally, strategies to overcome currency risk are coordinated to allow for economies of scale in the purchase of the relevant financial instruments.

Managing the MNE's Financial Resources

This involves the firm seeking to manage its cash resources as efficiently as possible. In effect, this means minimizing cash balances and lowering transaction costs. While a firm needs a level of cash for day-to-day transactions, it does not suit the firm to hold too much cash due to opportunity costs. Thus the firm will seek to deploy cash balances to maximize returns while maintaining some degree of liquidity. Minimizing transaction costs requires the firm to minimize the number of transactions involving a transfer fee (i.e. the fee charged by the bank to convert money from one currency to another). To some degree, this can be mitigated by multinational netting whereby cross-border cash flows are coordinated among subsidiaries so that only net cash is transferred. Efficiency of cash handling is also aided by centralizing deposits of cash, thereby allowing the pooling of cash and enabling the deposit of larger sums, allowing for the better use of these funds *en masse* and by lowering the amount held to meet liquidity concerns. Cash management also seeks to mitigate tax liabilities through the use of devices such as tax havens (see Case Study 8.2) and methods to avoid double taxation through utilizing tax credits and inter-state tax treaties. In order to enjoy such benefits, the firm must be able to transfer cash between subsidiaries and the parent company. This may be done through dividend remittances or royalty payments. The firm can also reposition funds through transfer pricing. The transfer price is the price at which goods and services are transferred between different parts of the MNE. Thus by pricing accordingly (setting a high transfer price for low-tax states and a low transfer price for high-tax states), the firm can lower its tax liabilities. However, it is often unclear whether such actions undermine the spirit of the law.

CONCLUSION

It is beyond the scope of this chapter to do justice to the diverse issues related to international business operations. However, each of these functions is important in underpinning a firm's activities within the international arena. Indeed, all aspects of an MNE's value-creating activities are important (in both a reactive and a proactive manner) in international strategy. The firm not only needs to understand its customer base but also to ensure that it has sufficient financial resources and the necessary and appropriate human resources to ensure that the strategy is effectively executed.

Summary of Key Concepts

- Successful development of international strategy requires a number of supporting functions.
- These functions are largely a derivative of the overarching strategy pursued by the business.
- This requires that the firm has the necessary personnel, financial resources and marketing capabilities.
- International strategy development also requires appropriate corporate governance and must ensure that knowledge can flow freely around the MNE to support all parts of its network.

Activities

1. Outline how international HRM is core to the firm's achievement of its broader strategic objectives.

2. How does corporate governance need to adjust to a firm's international operations?

3. Examine and explain the interface between logistics and international marketing management.

Discussion Questions

1. Using an example with which you are familiar, demonstrate how the different elements of marketing can differ from state to state.

2. How do you explain the preponderance of foreign chief executives of many leading MNCs?

3. How will the ongoing evolution of the internet affect the development of international logistics?

References and Suggestions for Further Reading

Clarke, T. (2007) *International Corporate Governance: A Comparative Approach*, London: Routledge.

De Cieri, H. and Dowling, P. (1999) 'Strategic human resource management in multinational enterprises: theoretical and empirical developments', in Wright, P., Dyer, L., Boudreau, J. and Milkovich, G. (eds), *Research in Personnel and Human Resources Management: Strategic Human Resources Management in the Twenty-first Century*, Stamford, CT: JAI Press.

De Cieri, H., Cox, W. and Fenwick, M. (2007) 'A review of international human resource management: integration, interrogation, imitation', *International Journal of Management Reviews*, Vol. 9, No. 4, 281–302.

Dornier, P., Ernst, R., Fender, M. and Kouvelis, P. (1998) *Global Operations: Management and Logistics*, New York: John Wiley.

Eun, C. and Resnick, B. (2009) *International Financial Management*, 5th edn, New York: McGraw-Hill Higher Education.

Flaherty, M. (1996) *Global Operations Management*, New York: McGraw-Hill Higher Education.

Harvard Business Review (2000) *Harvard Business Review on Corporate Governance*, Cambridge, MA: Harvard Business School Press.

Hunt, S. and Lambe, C. (2000) 'Marketing's contribution to business strategy: market orientation, relationship marketing and resource-advantage theory', *International Journal of Management Reviews*, Vol. 2, No. 1, 17–43.

Jackson, T. (2002) *International HRM: A Cross-cultural Approach*, London: Sage.

Madura, J. and Fox, R. (2007) *International Financial Management*, London: Thomson Learning.

Norton, J., Rickford, J. and Kleinmann, J. (eds) (2006) *Corporate Governance Post-Enron – Comparative and International Perspectives*, London: British Institute of International and Comparative Law.

OECD (2004) *Principles of Corporate Governance*, Paris: OECD http://www.oecd.org/DATAOECD/32/18/31557724.pdf.

Schuiling, I. and Kapferer, S. (2004) 'Real differences between local and international brands: strategic implications for international marketers', *Journal of International Marketing*, Vol. 12, No. 4, 97–112.

Schuler, R., Budhwar, P. and Florkowski, G. (2002) 'International human resource management: review and critique', *International Journal of Management Reviews*, Vol. 4, No. 1, 41–70.

Sparrow, P., Brewster, C. and Harris, H. (2004) *Globalizing Human Resource Management: Tracking the Business Role of International HR Specialists*, London: Routledge.

Usunier, J. and Lee, J. (2009) *Marketing across Cultures*, 3rd edn, Harlow: Financial Times/Prentice Hall.

Young, S. and Winter, N. (1996) *Managing Global Operations: Cultural and Technical Success Factors*, London and Westport, CT: Greenwood Press.

Chapter 13

Culture

In Paris they simply stared when I spoke to them in French; I never did succeed in making those idiots understand their language.

Mark Twain, US writer, 1835–1910

LEARNING OBJECTIVES

This chapter will help you to:

- define culture and explain its main characteristics
- identify and assess the main determinants of culture
- demonstrate how and why an understanding of culture is important to international business
- understand and assess the usefulness of theories of national cultural dimensions to international business
- appreciate how firms can manage culture and use it to their advantage

Globalization and internationalization increasingly bring firms from different cultures into contact with each other, thereby not only creating opportunities for cross-cultural contact that have potential for mutual benefit but which also contain scope for serious cross-cultural misunderstandings. The increased cross-border reach of business requires an enhanced awareness of and sensitivity to differences in languages, values and behavioural norms. The alternative is less effective or even failed negotiations, marketing drives and investment plans. In a positive light, although it is far from easy, companies can attempt to manage culture to their advantage.

It is important to note the link between cultural and ethical issues. There is an absolutist dimension to some ethical issues but many are perceived through a relativist lens: that is, the presumption of what is right or wrong can be greatly influenced by specific cultural contexts. In short, although some practices are clearly unacceptable in all cultures, there are grey areas where practices that are commonplace in some countries are regarded as unethical in others. These issues are explored more fully in Chapter 14.

This chapter begins by exploring the definition of culture and its key aspects. It then discusses some of the key determinants of culture and how they can impact upon business. The chapter then examines individual business functions and tasks and how they are affected by culture in an international context. It concludes by considering the main theoretical approaches to culture, their implications for business and criticisms of these approaches.

WHAT IS CULTURE?

Culture is a complex concept, open to a variety of definitions and difficult to pin down precisely. Terpstra and David (1991) refer to 'a learned, shared, compelling, inter-related set of symbols whose meanings provide a set of orientations for members of a society' whereas Komin (1994) writes of 'total patterns of values, ideas, beliefs, customs, practices, techniques, institutions, objects and artefacts'. Hofstede (1991) brings this array of symbols, beliefs, values and ideas together and talks of 'a collective mental programming'. In other words, culture is the combination of acquired experience and values that feed into and influence behaviour and responses of distinct groups.

Cultural analysis may take place at various levels and across various dimensions. There are two important distinctions to be made when talking about culture from a business perspective – national and organization culture. National (or country) culture is external to the firm but provides the context in which the firm sits and influences the culture within the firm. The theoretical approaches discussed later in this chapter are examples of national culture.

Organization (or corporate) culture is internal to the firm. Firms may try to shape their corporate culture to help them attain key objectives. The two concepts are linked. Clearly, national culture will help determine corporate culture. Several corporate cultures may exist within the same national culture – that is, the components of national culture may come together in a variety of ways, resulting in different outcomes. Moreover, corporate culture can be a useful way of unifying multinational firms with cross-cultural operations or operations in a number of different countries.

By definition, culture is a learned phenomenon, the outcome of shared experience over many years that is passed down the generations. In other words, individuals and their beliefs and behaviour are to a large extent conditioned by their history and passed on by families and institutions such as schools. Some cultural influences may be traced back through the centuries: claims have been made, for example, that the roots of British individualism go back over one thousand years or that the more competitive and unfettered forms of capitalism and social organization favoured by the US are a result of its early frontier and nation-building experiences.

An essential part of culture is the sense of belonging or identity. This can originate from several sources that may or may not correspond with national boundaries. Language, for example, is often an important symbol of belonging to a group and frequently coincides with national boundaries, but, when it does not, it can be a divisive factor as in Canada, Belgium, Switzerland and several African countries where tribal allegiances coincide with language. Tribes, ethnic groups, religion may thus be a source of cohesiveness or divisiveness, depending on the presence or absence of competition within a territory.

Nevertheless, despite the relative newness and fragility of the concept of the nation state in many locations and the surprising frequency of changes in national boundaries, a sense of belonging to a nation can be a key element of cultural identity and generates strong feelings. For example, a fear of those reluctant to engage in further integration within the EU is the potential erosion of national identity. Although not the only reason for opposition to adoption of the euro in the UK and Denmark, the fear of identity loss is an important element in it, especially as currencies are often regarded as symbols of national identity and independence. The EU denies it is engaging in nation building but is anxious to promote the use of key symbols such as the European flag and the European anthem to create a sense of European identity. European representatives are also anxious to point out that being European does not undermine or replace national cultural identities. An individual French or Italian citizen, for example, is still as French or Italian as before the launch of the euro. In short, individuals have multiple or layered cultural identities.

Culture is not static and non-adaptive: the cultural mix changes through experience, usually gradually, but it is occasionally subject to sudden change through traumatic events such as the collapse of the Soviet system in 1989 and 1990 which affected both the republics of the Soviet Union and its satellite states in Central and Eastern Europe. The sudden collapse of a whole political, economic and social system called into question long-held views, values and practices underpinning political, economic and commercial life. In particular, the undermining of social safety nets and employment guarantees as a result of systemic change overturned expectations and destroyed value systems. The outcome has varied in different countries, depending on their previous experience of the workings of the market and the path chosen for reform by the authorities.

The Soviet experience is an example of a wholesale transformation of the social, political and economic system but cultural transformation may also occur as a result of significant change within a system. The utility privatizations that occurred in the UK towards the end of the 1980s demonstrate this. Pre-privatization, the UK's gas and electricity utilities were dominated by engineers and operated as state monopolies. The emphasis was on production to meet the total demands of domestic, commercial and industrial consumers. Privatization and the subsequent opening up of the markets changed all that, bringing with it new commercial risks and a greater emphasis on marketing. This shifted the demands on the managers in the industry, requiring the emergence of a culture which was much more responsive to market needs, innovative and open to new opportunities.

The challenge for business when deciding upon modes of market entry is to read and correctly interpret the various cultural signs. Failure to do this can result in serious problems for specific initiatives or even failure of joint ventures or mergers. In order to work with rather than against cultural factors, it is necessary to recognize that we all view the world through a cultural prism and that, although our cultural preconceptions may be shared by others within our organization and to an extent by those with the same nationality, they may be alien to those to whom we are trying to export or with whom we are trying to set up a joint venture. Those who see the world solely in terms of their own culture have an ethnocentric disposition and may encounter serious problems when trying to carry out activities with an international dimension. On the other hand, those with a polycentric outlook are open to other cultures, attempting to see beyond their own cultural assumptions and develop an understanding of other cultures. This greater sensitivity to cultural divergence, while not guaranteeing success of joint ventures, acquisitions or other forms of involvement in non-domestic business ventures, does enhance the possibility of success.

WHERE DOES CULTURE COME FROM?

Hofstede (1991) speaks of the 'collective programming of the mind' but what is the source of the inputs into this programming? The common values, beliefs, customs and norms of behaviour that constitute culture are acquired from social institutions such as families and schools. These in turn are shaped by common or shared experiences, history and religions which determine factors like the relationship of the individual to the group (see below for the individualistic–collectivist cultural dimension), gender roles, communication rituals and even details and norms associated with eating, drinking and dress. Figure 13.1 sets out the key determinants and expressions of culture. Although

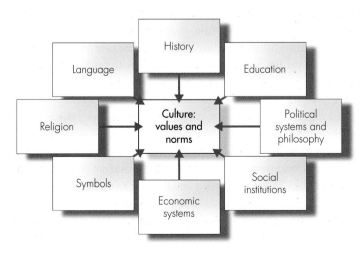

FIGURE 13.1 Determinants of Culture

listed as separate items for the purposes of exposition, in practice these determinants interact with each other, and their combination produces the unique national and subnational cultures that exist today.

Businesses are interested in culture to the extent to which it shapes behaviour and attitudes. A helpful distinction may be drawn between values and norms. Values are ideas and beliefs about what is good, morally correct and desirable. Values are often shaped by religion but there is also often an important input from social institutions such as the family and education (both of which may or may not themselves be influenced by religion). Some values, albeit relatively few, are universal (for example, murder is prohibited everywhere). Other values are uniquely shaped by individual cultures and can lead to difficult ambiguities for international business. The link between culture and ethics is picked up in more detail in Chapter 14.

Norms are the social rules, guidelines and patterns of behaviour that predominate in a particular society. There is no value or moral content attached to norms but transgression of norms within a particular culture can lead to exclusion or to difficulties in conducting a business relationship. For example, displaying the soles of one's feet is a serious breach of etiquette in Arab culture. In some cultures, nodding one's head signifies agreement whereas in others it means 'no' – a phenomenon that can lead to confusion unless these differences are grasped. Attitudes to timekeeping and punctuality vary considerably: to be late in some cultures is impolite and shows lack of respect for those one is meeting, whereas in other cultures being late is the norm. It is important to understand the degree of formality required in different cultures. Underestimation of the formality required (in how one addresses a potential customer or client or in the dress code followed) can also denote a lack of respect and offend. Such miscalculations may take place within a national culture but are even more likely to occur across national cultures.

Religion

Religion is one of the most important factors shaping culture, both in terms of values and norms. At its core, religion lays down a set of fundamental principles and values which govern the behaviour and life of its adherents. The influence of religion may be obvious in some nations or regions where the dominant religion has a strong presence. In states which appear more secular, the role of religion often remains strong, albeit in a less obvious manner. For example, in countries like the UK, this has manifested itself in the reduction of restrictions on Sunday trading. However, the country's Christian heritage means that Christian principles and values continue to underpin British laws and culture, even though the explicit role of Christianity in British life is less pervasive than it used to be. The persistence of religion has been demonstrated in countries like Russia where religion was banned for many decades under communism. A striking feature of the post-communist era has been the revival, indeed thriving, of the Russian Orthodox church.

From a business perspective, religion has to be taken into account in a number of ways. The most obvious is overt religious practices, laws and traditions. These include the observance of religious holidays and the ban on alcohol and certain foods. These are explicit and difficult to misinterpret. More difficult to take into account are norms and practices that are rooted in religion and influence social behaviour. Different practices can abound under the same religion and the impact of the same religion can vary as a result of national and other competing cultural factors. Catholics, for example, are subject to similar influences whether they are Mexican, Italian, Irish or Filipino but the impact or expression of factors varies. Similarly, the stereotypical view of Islam is that women are restricted in and indeed often excluded from the workplace. Although women may find themselves highly restricted in some Islamic societies, in others they have many more opportunities than those recognized by the stereotype.

Language

Language is the main medium of communication and a common language often defines a group within a society. It can therefore act as a great unifier or as a way of delineating groups when there are divisions within a nation. Language at its most basic is important to business as a way of conveying and collecting information, whether in negotiations, within a company or in the interface with customers. In particular, language helps unlock local societies, giving an insight into local culture and mores in a way which is not possible when an interpreter is needed. The consequences of poor verbal communication can seriously undermine what a business is trying to achieve in its overseas investments or when seeking to enter foreign markets (see Box 13.1).

With globalization and the growing internationalization of business, the need to communicate in multiple languages increases. Ideally international managers are bi- or multilingual. In reality, particularly given the number of countries and languages with which contemporary MNEs come into contact, this is often not practically possible. Consequently, since the latter stages of the twentieth century, English has emerged as the international business *lingua franca* (that is, a language used for communication purposes among individuals with different mother tongues). The result is that when Japanese, German and Spanish business people meet, their common point of communication is likely to be English. The use of English has developed to the extent that numerous multinationals with headquarters in non-English-speaking countries but with operations across numerous countries have adopted English for all internal and external communications. Examples include Aventis, ABB, Alcatel, Novartis, Vivendi, Ericsson and Volvo. This appears to give an advantage to native English speakers, and in one sense it does. However, the lack of incentive to speak other languages can leave them at a disadvantage because a rudimentary knowledge of a language (even if it is not the language in which communication is ultimately carried out) shows a willingness to try to understand the other party and can create a significant element of goodwill.

Even use of a common language is not always sufficient for effective communication. The same words may be used in different ways in different regions and countries. The differences between British and American English are well documented. Indeed, the writer George Bernard Shaw allegedly said, 'England and America are two countries divided by a common language'. Similar differences also exist between Spanish, Portuguese and French-speaking nations, for example. Differences arise not only because of different meanings attached to the same words (an inevitability given that languages are constantly evolving and that countries that use the same language can be situated thousands of miles away from each other) but because of cultural differences that can shape the use and interpretation of language. Communication in the US, for example, is usually very direct and literal (as befits a low-context culture – see below) and positive, whereas, in the UK, which is a low-context culture compared to many Asian countries but less so than the US, communication is less direct and literal and often understated. These differences in language use reflect cultural differences between the two countries.

Box 13.1 Lost in Translation

An ideal situation for a business with international aspirations is the ability to seamlessly market a product in multiple national markets. In practice, cultural differences, particularly those of a linguistic nature, often make this impractical. One of the linguistic challenges for international business is to avoid product names that are entirely appropriate in one language but are inappropriate or even offensive in another. Companies also come unstuck through the mistranslation of slogans. Although this should not happen, the fact that slogans often involve the use of the vernacular, or informal language, which is not easy to translate or should not be translated literally, perhaps goes some way towards explaining why it does occur. The following examples illustrate how this has happened or how it could happen (some of the examples are so widely quoted that it is difficult to ascertain whether they actually occurred but have simply become part of business folklore).

Mishaps, or potential mishaps, with product names are numerous. A German chocolate bar called 'Zit' would not sell well in English-speaking countries where zit is a slang term denoting a particularly unpleasant spot, usually associated with acne. The word 'mist' in English has no unfortunate connotations, conjuring up images of freshness and the outdoors. However, in German 'mist' means 'dung' or 'manure' – a fact of which Clairol cannot have been aware when it tried to market the 'Mist Stick', a hair-care product, in Germany. Until the name of the product was changed in the German market, sales unsurprisingly failed to live up to expectations. 'Mist' also occurs in other product names and is especially used in the names of whiskies such as 'Irish Mist' and 'Highland Mist'. In Poland, 'Oil of Olay' became 'Oil of Olaz' as the original was uncomfortably close to a slang term for urine and to the Polish words for cooking oil – neither of which were particularly suitable for marketing a beauty product. In Italy, a linguistic mishap meant that on one occasion a marketing campaign for Schweppes tonic water became one for Schweppes toilet water.

The motor industry, in particular, has faced particular constraints when trying to find model names which work equally well across different national markets. 'Nova' was the name of a General Motors car. Unfortunately, although this name has positive connotations of 'new', it also sounds like 'no va' in Spanish, which means 'it does not go', which is hardly attractive to potential buyers. Toyota's attempts to market its MR2 in French-speaking countries were hampered by the fact that it was pronounced 'emm err deu' – a near homonym (a word that shares its pronunciation with another word but which has a different meaning) for emmerde – a word with scatological connections in French. Once this was realized, the car was marketed as the Toyota MR in French-speaking markets. Other motor mishaps include Ford's Fiera, Caliente and Pinto which respectively mean 'ugly old woman' in Spanish, 'prostitute' in Mexican slang and 'small male genitals' in Brazilian Portuguese slang. Mitsubishi developed a four-wheel drive called the Montero but which was marketed in non-US markets under the name 'Pajero', including Australia where the large number of South Americans living there were bemused by the marketing of a vehicle which meant to them 'one who masturbates'.

Some translation negatives can be turned into positives. Initial attempts to render the name 'Coca-Cola' into its Chinese equivalent came out as 'ke-kou-ke-la' which to the Chinese ear sounds like 'bite the wax tadpole' or 'a female horse stuffed with wax'. Further research led to 'ke-kou-ko-le' which has the more serendipitous meaning of 'happiness in the mouth'. Similarly, the brand name of the Australian beer, Foster's, was initially translated in such a way when it was first marketed in Hong Kong that it sounded like 'disasters have just arrived' in Mandarin.

Company as well as product names can cause confusion. Japan's second-largest tourist agency received several requests from English-speaking countries for unusual sex tours. The realization that 'kinky' in English is an informal name for unusual or idiosyncratic sexual practices led to a rapid change of name for the Kinki Nippon Tourist Company.

Names can also cause problems not because of their meaning but also because of their pronunciation. This was the case with the cleaning product formerly known as 'Jif' which subsequently became universally known as 'Cif' – a name which it was felt would be much easier to pronounce in Spanish markets.

Slogans in particular can easily go astray. A slogan for Braniff, 'fly in leather', denoting luxury, was translated as 'vuelo en cuero' in Spanish, which means 'fly naked' – an invitation which does not have broad market appeal. The translation of the Coors beer slogan 'turn it loose' also came unstuck when it was rendered into Spanish in a way which could be taken to mean to suffer from diarrhoea. Another Spanish *faux pas* was committed when Parker Pen's slogan 'it won't leak in your pocket and embarrass you' was translated into Spanish in preparation for a marketing campaign in Mexico. The word used to translate 'embarrass' was 'embarazar' which means to become pregnant, resulting in a rather bizarre slogan which to the target audience meant 'it won't leak in your pocket and make you pregnant'. Slogan problems have also arisen in Asia. In Taiwan, the Pepsi slogan 'come alive with the Pepsi generation' was translated into 'Pepsi will bring your ancestors back from the dead'. Similarly, in China, KFC's 'finger-lickin' good' became 'eat your fingers off'.

History

As individuals, we are the product of our prior history and experience. The same is true of countries. History shapes national culture in a number of ways, including the development of the political and economic system. Russia, for example, is evolving a form of capitalism which is rooted in the acquisition of wealth for a limited number of the elite and the denial of meaningful democracy. Although not inevitable, this outcome was always probable in a nation where large inequalities in wealth and the centralized concentration of power have been the norm for centuries. History also shapes attitudes to other countries: long periods of distrust or violent conflict between nations can colour contemporary relations between countries.

A foreign investor must also respect the culture and heritage of the host country or encounter potentially severe problems. Following a successful internet campaign led by Chinese TV personality Rui Chenggang, Starbucks, the Seattle-based coffee chain, closed its outlet in Beijing's Forbidden City in July 2007. The campaign claimed it had no objection to the presence of Starbucks in China, which has over 250 outlets there, but alleged that the firm's presence in the Forbidden City, home to generations of Chinese emperors and the location of important events in Chinese history, was inappropriate. Similarly, when developing its northern Moscow store, Scandinavian furniture retailer

IKEA encountered serious resistance to its plans. The company wanted to build a link road between the store and the ring road. This would have required the relocation of an important Second World War monument – a series of anti-tank spikes which marks the spot on the outskirts of Moscow where the Russians halted the German advance. Given the loss of life and the suffering endured by the Russians during this war, IKEA's original plans were rejected. The store was built but with different access arrangements and, the monument remains a place for Russians to visit on Victory Day (9 May) and other important occasions.

Education

Education is an important conduit of culture. Moreover, the culture of education is often also an important consideration for foreign investors. Literacy levels and the percentage of populations educated to secondary or tertiary level can be important determinants of investment decisions. It was the existence of a large number of highly educated individuals with English-language proficiency which facilitated the growth of the call centre and back office outsourcing boom in India. Different education systems stress the acquisition of different skills. Germany, for example, has a long tradition of apprenticeships and vocational training which has provided generations of technicians, mechanics and engineers who have played an important role in Germany's manufacturing success. Other countries emphasize and perform well in mathematics and the sciences: Finland, Hong Kong, South Korea and Japan, for example, consistently rank highly in OECD league tables of attainment in these key disciplines.

Social Systems and Organization

The way society is organized is important for business on a number of levels. The average size of families, for example, affects consumption patterns: the larger the family, the bigger demand will be for grocery items sold in larger packs. There has been a trend in some developed countries for smaller households, including a major growth in one-person households. In societies where this is the case, products need to be sold in smaller quantities and demand will be for smaller houses and apartments. Ageing populations, a situation facing many developed countries, boost demand for health-related products and services and for leisure-related services and activities which appeal to older age groups. Moreover, family obligations sometimes need to be taken into account by HRM departments. In some countries, policies around parental leave are well developed – in other countries, such policies are less developed or non-existent.

The degree and type of social stratification can also have implications for business. If a society is highly stratified, then social mobility is likely to be limited and certain groups will be favoured in recruitment, whereas other groups will find it much more difficult to develop their careers. India is well known for its rigid caste system which traditionally fixed individuals into specific places in the social hierarchy and restricted the ability of individuals to move up the professional level. The caste system still exists in Indian society but is reportedly diminishing in strength in urban areas while remaining strong in rural areas. In more stratified societies, the relationship within firms is generally going to be more hierarchical with communication between managers and workers taking place on a formal basis (see below for power distance).

In societies with a very skewed income distribution system (for example, a few very rich people and many very poor with few in the middle), as is the case in some Latin American and African societies, the absence of a skilled, educated middle class could deter foreign investors. MNEs looking to establish themselves in a new location frequently seek local mangers to ensure that the company adjusts to their new business environment and culture and often to take over the management of the local operation of their enterprise in the longer term. The shortage of such personnel and the absence of the entrepreneurial culture implied by this social structure make these objectives difficult to attain.

Symbols

A symbol is something which represents something else by virtue of association, resemblance or convention. The meanings attached to symbols vary across the world and are shaped by and help shape different cultures. An understanding of the different interpretations and meanings attached to objects, colours, numbers and gestures can be an important element of communication in international business.

The design of logos, websites and advertisements can be undermined by the use of inappropriate colours. Black is the colour of mourning in Europe and the United States. White plays this role in China and Japan whereas in Western cultures white implies peace, purity, goodness and brides. Mourning is signified by red in South Africa, by blue in Iran, by purple in Thailand and by yellow in Egypt and Burma. In general terms, red implies good luck and prosperity in China, purity in India and conjures up strong emotions like excitement, danger, passion and anger in many Western cultures. Similarly, green is the colour of Islam. Green is regarded as a symbol for Ireland, also known as the 'Emerald Isle'. In many Western countries, green is also symbolic of nature, newness and spring. In China on the other hand, a green hat implies that the wife of the man wearing it has committed adultery.

Numbers too have their own symbolic meaning. In China, this has been taken quite far. The luck, good or bad associated with a number in China comes for the most part from homonyms – words that sound the same as the number in question. Number 4, for example, is one of the most inauspicious numbers in China because its pronunciation is similar to the word for 'death'. In East Asia some buildings do not have a fourth floor and in Hong Kong some high-rise residential buildings miss out all floor numbers with '4' in them. Therefore, a building with a 50th floor may, in reality, only have 36 floors as names for the 4th, 14th, 24th, 34th and all the floors from 40 to 49 have been missed out. In some regions of China, where dialects and accents lead to different pronunciations, 4 does not have such a bad press. Two of the luckiest numbers in China are '6' and '8'. The homonyms for 6 are 'flowing' and 'smooth'. Whereas '666' is regarded as the sign of the devil in Western cultures, in China individuals seek to have the 666 combination in their phone numbers and car registrations. Similarly, the homonyms for 8 are 'prosper' and 'wealth'. It is no coincidence that the opening date and time for the Beijing Olympics was at 8 o'clock on the 8th day of the 8th month of 2008. The Chinese culture is not the only culture which attaches particular meaning to certain numbers. In Western culture, 7 is generally regarded as lucky whereas 13 is unlucky. The roots of the distrust of

13 lie in the Christian religion: there were 13 present at the Last Supper before Christ was arrested and crucified, and one of those present at the table betrayed Him.

Economic Systems

An economic system is the way a society organizes the ownership and allocation of economic resources. In broad terms, economic systems differ from each other in the degree to which there is government involvement in the economy. A pure market economy maximizes the role of private enterprise and public sector intervention is limited to the provision of public goods such as defence. The US represents the nearest approximation of this model, although, even there, the state plays more than the minimal role outlined above. At the other extreme, there are economic systems in which it is the state that takes on the role of resource allocator, deciding what and how much to produce. These state or command economies have become fewer and far between since the demise of the Soviet Union and the launch of Chinese economic reforms. In practice, most contemporary economies are mixed economies which strike a balance between the incorporation of aspects of the market system and a continuing role for the state.

In practice, the economic system is shaped by and helps shape the business culture. The more collective the economic system, for example, the more likely it is that group performance and team work are the predominant form of work organization (see below for Hofstede's collectivist/individualistic cultural dimension). Conversely, those economic systems which rely more on private enterprise are more likely to foster individualism. These are important considerations for foreign investors seeking to establish appropriate incentives for their employees in new overseas operations.

Political Systems

An understanding of political systems is invaluable for international business in identifying where key influences reside and in getting to grips with the local culture. Political systems refer to systems of politics and government, comprising sets of institutions, political organizations, interest groups and so on. As with economic systems, political systems are often hybrid: it is possible to have, for example, monarchies, in which the monarch is essentially a figurehead and the system is overwhelmingly democratic, or in which the monarch is an autocrat and democracy is underdeveloped.

Economic and political systems are often linked. Command economies and socialist/communist political systems go together whereas a liberal economic system fits most naturally with a democratic political system. The current situation in China confounds this, however: the Chinese government has been freeing up the economy for several years while maintaining strong control over the political system. Many commentators (see Will Hutton, for example) argue that this situation is unsustainable in the long run because private enterprise creates a new class of entrepreneurs and professionals who enjoy freedom in their economic life and who will eventually wish to see similar freedoms in other aspects of their life. Parallels are drawn with other market-based economies in which the spread of economic prosperity ultimately resulted in greater democracy.

WHY DOES CULTURE MATTER?

Culture, more particularly the need to manage cultural diversity, is important in many stages of the internationalization of business and in all forms of market entry. The following examples seek to demonstrate culture's general importance.

Marketing

Use of inappropriate advertising language or images, for example, can completely undermine attempts to enter new markets (see Box 13.1). Entry into new markets also needs adaptation to specific consumer tastes. Even fast food outlets like McDonald's, which attempts to deliver the same product throughout the world, must adapt their offerings in some countries. For religious reasons, beef is not a suitable ingredient for hamburgers sold in India, for example, and in order to enter the Indian market, McDonald's has had to localize its products. For reasons of taste and of reference to the local culture, McDonald's has also developed products with a regional flavour in particular markets. These include the Teriyaki Burger (a chicken cutlet patty marinated in teriyaki sauce with sweet mayonnaise and lettuce on sesame seed buns) in Japan; the Kiwi Burger (a hamburger with a fried egg and pickled beet) in New Zealand; a McKielbasa in Poland (a Kielbasa – Polish sausage – patty with ketchup, mustard and onion on a sesame seed bun) and the Greek Mac – a pitta bread sandwich with two beef patties and yoghurt.

Cultural diversity can also require a radically different approach to all aspects of a new market. In March 2002, the giant US retailer Wal-Mart acquired a two-thirds share in Japan's fourth largest supermarket chain. Wal-Mart cannot directly transfer its low-cost, high-bulk model, hugely successful in the US, to Japan. The Japanese retail sector is notoriously difficult for foreign companies to enter and thrive in as a result of the intricate distribution system and distinctive Japanese tastes and shopping culture. In the early 1990s, Wal-Mart had its first difficult experience of Japanese retailing: it found, for example, that its own-label biscuits did not sell well because they were too sweet for Japanese tastes. Furthermore, Japanese consumers set much greater store by presentation, with most products in Japan, including individual items of fruit such as oranges, individually wrapped in attractive packaging. As the result of a preference for fresh produce and smaller living spaces which cuts down the space for grocery storage, Japanese shoppers also still tend to visit the supermarket on a daily basis whereas large weekly shopping expeditions are the norm in the US.

Entry Modes: International Mergers, Acquisitions and Joint Ventures

Globalization provides opportunities for firms to enter and invest in new markets. As Chapter 10 shows, firms face a wide choice of how they go about this but there is a cultural dimension to all entry modes in one way or another. Greenfield investment, which involves entering a new market without a partner from the host country, requires the acquisition of knowledge of the local culture and ways of doing things. Mergers, acquisitions and joint ventures, however, bring together employees of at least two different enterprises, each of which has its own distinctive corporate culture. The way in which these various cultures are brought together can have a significant bearing on the success or otherwise of each initiative.

The 1998 Daimler-Chrysler merger (which quickly turned into a takeover by Daimler of Chrysler) is frequently cited as an uneasy match between two very different corporate cultures. The German partner's approach to resolution of the merged companies' problems was based on its traditional preference for engineering solutions and for seeking synergy via shared components and engines, whereas Chrysler's approach was deeply rooted in a tradition of using marketing promotions and price discounting. The former was more formal and dominated by managers with a background in engineering and the latter by managers with a more informal approach and steeped in finance and marketing. The early years of the new company were rocky. Although the merged company's problems had several roots, the cultural dissonance between the two companies did not help and the early years of the merged company were marked by large-scale departures of Chrysler's senior managers. Within ten years, the decision was taken to sell off the Chrysler arm of the company, a transaction that was completed in 2007.

Human Resource Management (HRM)

HRM managers clearly have to consider the challenges posed by the integration of two or more companies involved in international mergers, acquisitions, alliances and joint ventures but they also have to become involved in decisions and strategies that are not relevant to purely domestic operations. In particular, decisions need to be taken regarding the extent to which foreign operations are managed by personnel from the home or the host country and the type and range of opportunities to be given to host country personnel. Care also needs to be taken to manage the relationship between managers and staff from the home country and managers and staff from the host country in terms of working practices. For example, when Nissan in the early 1980s, later followed by Toyota and Honda, chose to locate their initial European manufacturing plants in the UK, there was widespread incredulity. The UK motor industry was notorious at that time for a poor industrial relations record and there was scepticism about whether Japanese companies could transfer their highly successful flexible working methods into an industrial culture that at that time was highly rigid and dogged by demarcation disputes. In the end, the Japanese investment was located in regions outside the traditional car-producing areas of the UK and Japanese working practices were adapted, not exported wholesale, to the British environment. The UK business and working culture was itself changing as a result of the election of the Thatcher government which reduced trade union powers and stepped back from granting heavy subsidies to failing industries. In fact, despite the reservations at the outset, the Japanese-owned car factories located in the UK proved to be the most productive in Europe – at least until the current concentration of automotive investment in Eastern Europe.

CULTURAL THEORIES

Much of the work on trying to understand different cultures is concerned with the classification and categorization of different cultural attributes and may be described as atheoretical in the sense that it attempts to describe rather than explain cultural determination and differences. This section deals with the major cultural distinctions drawn by commentators, beginning with Edward Hall's high- and low-context cultures and followed by the cultural dimensions of Geert Hofstede, Fons Trompenaars and the more recent GLOBE project.

Low- and High-context Cultures

In his work on cultural differences, Edward Hall (1977) drew a useful distinction between 'low-' and 'high-context cultures.' In low-context cultures, communication is explicit, clear and unambiguous. Individuals from such cultures come directly to the point and say precisely what they mean. The US is a good example of a low-context culture. In a high-context culture, much important information is conveyed beyond and outside the words actually spoken. In order to understand fully what is going on in a high-context cultural setting, an individual needs to be able to interpret body language and have a high degree of sensitivity to ambiguity, an ability to read between the lines and a knowledge of the unwritten or unspoken rules of communication. Many Asian countries count as high-context cultures.

Problems can occur when individuals from low- and high-context cultures come into contact within a business setting or between individuals from different high-context cultures with different unwritten rules. For example, what is regarded as directness and openness by individuals from low-context cultures may be regarded as abruptness or even rudeness by individuals from high-context cultures. Similarly, in certain high-context cultures, it is virtually taboo to say 'no' to a request: in the course of negotiations, individuals from such cultures will adopt a variety of strategies to avoid a direct rebuttal of a request. Unless an individual's opposite number in the negotiation process understands the cultural incapability of saying 'no' and that a commitment to consider a request or consult further may not be a 'perhaps' but an outright negative response, the outcome for the individual from a low-context culture will be confusion and frustration.

Hofstede's Cultural Dimensions

The most widely discussed and influential work on business cultures is that of Geert Hofstede (1980, 1991). Following the administration of attitude surveys to over 100,000 IBM employees in more than 50 countries, Hofstede theorized that cultural and sociological differences between nations may be categorized and quantified, thereby allowing comparison of national cultures to take place. Initially, he identified four cultural dimensions to which he later added a fifth – short- versus long-term orientation. These dimensions are:

- **Power distance**: the power distance dimension refers to the extent to which power structures are hierarchical and reflect significant inequalities in power. Countries with large power distances exhibit wide inequalities in power, power that is often concentrated in relatively few hands in heavily centralized and hierarchical organizations. Individuals within such cultures view themselves as inherently unequal: subordinates are dependent on those higher up the hierarchy and accept the power of their superiors by virtue of their position in the hierarchy. All participants in the hierarchy expect their position within it to be clearly demarcated. Hofstede identified Latin American, Asian, African and Southern European countries as large power distance countries.

In small power distance countries, individuals are more inclined to regard themselves as equals: rather than presuming to be told what to do, subordinates expect to be consulted and will argue a case with those higher up in the organization. Respect for individuals within the organization comes from their proven capacity to perform a role rather than from the possession of a particular job title or their place in an organization. Shorter small power distances coincide with flatter organization structures. Anglo-Saxon countries and countries of Northern Europe were classified as small power distance countries.

Concluding a joint venture agreement or a merger or acquisition that brings together partners from large and small power distance countries poses important challenges for businesses. The imposition of a hierarchical structure on employees from a short power distance country could lead to a feeling of disempowerment and frustration whereas individuals from a large power distance culture could feel disoriented and unclear about their role in a flatter structure.

- **Uncertainty avoidance**: uncertainty avoidance measures the lack of tolerance for uncertainty and ambiguity. This manifests itself in high levels of anxiety and emotion. This in turn translates into a preference for highly structured formal rules and limited tolerance for groups and individuals demonstrating deviant ideas or behaviours. Hofstede identified the cultures of Latin America, Latin European and Mediterranean cultures plus Japan and South Korea as exhibiting high anxiety and uncertainty avoidance. Low uncertainty avoidance countries include other Asian and other European countries. In these cultures, business is conducted in a less formal manner, with fewer standardized rules, and individuals are expected to take greater risks and exert greater independence in the performance of their roles. Both large power distance and high uncertainty avoidance countries demonstrate a strong preference for structured hierarchies in which the individual's role is clearly defined and strong leadership is regarded as an antidote to anxiety and stress.

- **Individualism vs. collectivism**: the individualist–collectivist dimension measures the degree to which the interests of individuals or of the group take priority. The social framework in an individualistic society is looser than that of a more collectivist society and individuals take responsibility for themselves and their immediate as opposed to extended families. Individualist societies demonstrate a greater regard for individual rights and freedoms and tend to be characterized by assertiveness and competitiveness rather than by team work and cooperation. The most individualistic societies are to be found in Anglo-Saxon countries.

In more collectivist societies, it is the group (which could be the extended family, the employer or society as a whole) that looks after the interest of individuals and gives them their sense of identity. In return for this protection, individuals offer the group loyalty and work towards the attainment of goals determined by and for the good of the group, organization, tribe or society. Hofstede categorizes Japan, Latin American and other Asian countries as being low on individualism. In such societies group and team work are more common and greater store is set by the cultivation of relationships than the completion of particular tasks.

An understanding of this dimension is useful when developing an incentive strategy for an organization: instituting an individual reward system in a collectivist context is unlikely to be as effective as if it were introduced in an individualistic culture. However, such incentive schemes could be useful in trying to shift the culture of an organization in a slightly different direction.

■ **Masculinity–femininity**: societies that place a high premium on assertiveness, achievement and the acquisition of material possessions are exhibiting aggressive or 'masculine' goal behaviour. Masculine environments also favour conflict and competition in the workplace. Cultures that place a high value on social relationships, quality of life and sensitivity demonstrate passive or 'feminine' goal behaviour. Cultures and workplaces scoring high on the femininity dimension exhibit high degrees of cooperation, negotiation and compromise.

There is some correlation between masculinity/femininity scores and gender roles in individual societies. Japan, for example, scores high on masculinity and, among developed countries, has a low rate of women working outside the home and a dearth of women working in senior positions. Nordic countries and the Netherlands, on the other hand, with their well-developed welfare states, score very low on the masculine continuum. Care should be taken however not to regard the masculine–feminine dimension as a proxy for gender roles in specific societies, as there are too many counter-examples. Iran, for example, since the 1979 Revolution, has increased constraints on the activities of its female population but has a much lower masculinity score than many European countries where women engage much more widely in employment and society in general.

■ **Short- vs. long-term orientation**: this cultural dimension was not included in Hofstede's original analysis but was added at a later stage. In countries with a short-term orientation, which is more characteristic of Western societies and of some Asian countries such as Pakistan and the Philippines, the emphasis is on the immediate gratification of needs, a focus on the present and the attainment of short-term goals. In cultures with a more long-term orientation, which include the cultures of Japan, China, South Korea and Taiwan, the satisfaction of needs is deferred for the sake of long-term benefits and growth. Associated characteristics include persistence and thrift.

Trompenaars's Cultural Dimensions

Fons Trompenaars (1997) has also tried to identify key cultural dimensions. His research involved the administration of questionnaires to over 15,000 managers in 28 countries and identified the five key 'relationship' dimensions plus two dealing with perceptions of time and the engagement with nature respectively:

■ **Universalism vs. particularism**: this dimension measures the relative weight placed on rules versus relationships. In universal cultures, emphasis is placed on the use of formal rules to govern organizations and transactions, whereas in more particularistic cultures there is a concentration on the cultivation of relationships, 'face', paternalism and other types of social control and networks (see Case Study 13.1). In negotiations or joint projects between parties from the universal and particularist tendencies, unless this fundamental difference is recognized, serious problems will arise. For example, representatives from a universal culture will focus immediately on the legal form of a contract or agreement, whereas representatives from a particularist culture will place a premium on developing trust and cultivating a relationship before determining the finer details of a contract. In these cases, the universalist emphasis on rules may seem rushed and rude to the particularist negotiators, whereas the particularist emphasis on relationship building can seem frustrating and a waste of time to individuals from a particularist culture. Western cultures like the US, UK, Australia and Canada place emphasis on formal rules, whereas Middle Eastern countries and some Asian countries like China place more emphasis on relationships.

■ **Individualism vs. collectivism**: Trompenaars's definition and discussion of this dimension is similar to that of Hofstede but there is some disparity in the classification of countries. For example, Trompenaars found Mexico and the Czech Republic to be more individualistic than Hofstede did. This possibly reflects the fact that the research of Trompenaars is more recent than that of Hofstede. Between the two surveys, Mexico moved towards a greater acceptance of market economics, with its implied greater individualism, a trend that has continued. Similarly, in relation to the Czech Republic, although the introduction of the market economy was only in its infancy when Trompenaars's research was conducted, the old collectivist systems had already been challenged and had effectively disintegrated, whereas Hofstede carried out his survey when the Cold War was at its height.

■ **Neutral vs. affective or emotional culture**: in a neutral culture individuals are reluctant to show their feelings, whereas in affective or emotional cultures there is much greater openness about showing feelings and emotions. Japan is regarded as one of the most neutral cultures, whereas Mexico is among the most emotional. The conduct of negotiations or the implementation of projects involving parties from both neutral and affective cultures can be disconcerting for the participants, as both sides are unused to interpreting and dealing with the verbal signals and body language of their opposite number in an appropriate manner. Negotiators from an affective/ emotional culture will have difficulty relating to the reactions, or lack of reactions, of their counterparts from a neutral background, whereas neutral/culture negotiators may well interpret an overtly emotional reaction as being much more significant than it actually is. In short, unless there is a great deal of cultural literacy between both parties, there is a danger of negotiations/ projects going awry owing to mutual misunderstandings.

■ **Achievement vs. ascription oriented culture**: in achievement-oriented cultures like the US and the UK, achievement is what matters and the standing of an individual is related to that. In ascriptive cultures, more common in Asia, status is derived from the job title or general characteristics such as age or birth. Ascription-oriented cultures tend to correspond with Hofstede's high power distance dimension. Care needs to be taken regarding who represents an organization in negotiations between achievement and ascriptive-oriented cultures. Representation of an organization in negotiations by young high fliers from an achievement-oriented culture is often regarded by an ascriptive organization as an indication that the talks are not taken very seriously or even as a sign of disrespect. The size of the team may also be an issue: if the lead negotiator/company representative is not accompanied by a suitably large team of assistants, then an ascriptive-oriented organization can reach similar conclusions about its counterparts.

■ **Specific vs. diffuse culture**: in specific cultures there is a clear distinction between work and private life, whereas in diffuse cultures the distinction between work and private life is blurred. Similarly, in the development of business links and relationships, in a specific culture it is the function or role that is the focus of negotiations, whereas in a more diffuse culture the successful conclusion of a deal depends not only on the precise details of the deal but also on the construction of a relationship between the parties. The US, UK and Australia are cultures at the specific end of the specific–diffuse continuum and China and Japan are at the diffuse end (see Case Study 13.1).

The GLOBE Project

In the 2000s, publication began of the results of a major transnational research project, GLOBE (Global Leadership and Organizational Behaviour Effectiveness). GLOBE was established in 1992 and involved 150 researchers collecting data from 18,000 managers working in the tele-communications services, food processing and financial services industries in 62 countries. Hofstede's work served as the model and framework for GLOBE. Not only did GLOBE utilize the cultural dimensions approach, but it expanded the number of dimensions studied up to nine. The study began with Hofstede's five dimensions. Hofstede's collectivism dimension was split into institutional collectivism (the active promotion of participation in social institutions) and in-group collectivism (an emphasis on family and friendship groups). His masculine–feminine dimension was split into an assertiveness (i.e. masculine) dimension and gender egalitarianism dimension (that is, gender roles). Long-term orientation was relabelled 'future orientation' and two new dimensions – performance orientation (similar to achievement orientation) and humane orientation which involves generosity, fairness and altruism – were introduced.

CRITIQUES OF CULTURAL DIMENSIONS

Hofstede, Trompenaars and latterly the GLOBE project have conducted the most extensive and commented-upon research in the field of business culture. However, their conclusions have been subject to intense scrutiny and criticism. Concerns about the work cluster around methodological issues and conceptual matters.

Hofstede's work in particular has been criticized on methodological grounds, particularly the fact that his survey was limited to IBM employees, a highly specific and self-selecting group of individuals within a country's population. These individuals tend to be white collar and middle class and have been socialized into IBM's strong organizational culture that itself could override aspects of national culture. In addition, the fact that individuals are IBM employees probably means that they intrinsically possess characteristics that are compatible with IBM's culture. However, it is also the case that since Hofstede first carried out his pioneering study, other work using similar survey methodology and employees from a range of companies has been conducted and confirms Hofstede's approach. The work of Trompenaars, for example, falls into this category.

The above criticisms have some validity but the more serious concerns deal with the conceptual underpinning of the work. Culture is an enormously complex phenomenon and it is overly simplistic to characterise in terms of four to five dimensions that hide as many differences as they reveal, making it difficult, or even potentially dangerous, to draw conclusions about the appropriate management style from scores on a particular cultural dimension. High collectivist scores, for example, can reflect and act as a proxy for a range of different cultural characteristics: collectivism in the Japanese context can be different from collectivism in the Latin American context with different organizational and management implications.

The unit of analysis in the work is the nation, itself an artificial and relatively recent construct that contains many subcultures. Large industrialized countries like the US are a case in point: the US has a population of over 250 million, spanning the high-tech world of Silicon Valley in California to the farming hinterlands of the mid-West and from the oil-producing region of Texas to the more cosmopolitan world of the East Coast. Smaller countries like Belgium and Canada are divided by cultural differences: in the case of Belgium, the Flemish speakers of the north probably have as much, if not more, in common with the Dutch population across the border as with the French-speaking Walloons in the south and east of the country. The divide in Canada is also highlighted by linguistic differences, in this case between English and French speakers. In other countries, the cultural differences within nations may be tribal and ethnic, as witnessed by several African countries such as Nigeria and the Cameroon.

Similarly, national cultural differences do not necessarily coincide with other cultural signifiers such as occupation. An Indian software engineer based in Bangalore, for example, although sharing many cultural experiences with his compatriots, will also find many common reference points with a software engineer based in the US, perhaps more so than with a hill farmer from Kashmir.

Large-scale studies like those of Hofstede and Trompenaars are also subject to the charge that they are static, reflecting a snapshot of a particular point in time. In reality, cultures are not set in stone: cultural shifts do occur, usually, although not always, over a lengthy period of time. Fixed-point studies like those of Hofstede and Trompenaars are unable to detect these cultural shifts.

Notwithstanding these critiques of the work of Hofstede and Trompenaars, their studies do contain valuable insights and emphasize the importance of sensitivity to cultural differences across nations and within businesses. The more recent GLOBE project uses more recent data and, in broad terms, develops and confirms their approach. There are however differences between Hofstede and GLOBE in terms of their methodology and conceptual approach (see Journal of International Business Studies, 2006), and the resulting debate will help shape the future cultural research agenda.

CONCLUSION

Globalization adds an extra dimension to cultural issues within the firm. All organizations have their own culture based on common language and terminology, behavioural norms, dominant values, informality/formality and so on. This inevitably becomes more complex when an organization has a presence in more than one country. Some companies believe a strong corporate culture is a means of overcoming diverse national cultures, whereas others evolve different cultures in different organizations and incorporate cultural diversity in their management strategy.

Culture also operates in markets as well as within organizations. The development of a global culture, although undesirable in many ways, would facilitate the development of global products, enabling companies to reap economies of scale at all stages of the value chain. Many organizations like Coca-Cola and McDonald's use core brands but still adapt their products for local markets, either out of necessity or to maximize returns. Although it is fair to say that there is a degree of cultural convergence, global culture is more ephemeral and less deeply embedded than national cultures and localization of output is likely to remain the norm for many years.

Summary of Key Concepts

■ Globalization brings divergent cultures into contact with each other, posing challenges to international managers and presenting them with opportunities.

■ Cultural factors represent a complex interplay of values, ideas, beliefs, history, custom and practice, and are powerful shapers of the business environment.

■ Culture is an important dimension in most aspects of international business, including marketing, human resource management, entry modes and negotiations.

■ Hofstede pioneered cultural theory in international business. His approach of identifying key cultural dimensions which distinguish national cultures has continued to dominate work in this field.

■ Cultural literacy is essential for the successful management of international business ventures.

Activities

1. You work for a multinational cosmetics company seeking to sell your products to China for the first time. Prepare a short presentation for the board that alerts it to the cultural issues of which it needs to be aware.

2. You work for an international bank that wants to establish a branch in the Arabian Gulf. Prepare a short report outlining key cultural issues in such a venture (*note*: ideally, your report should take account of cultural differences between Gulf countries).

3. Find examples of how cultural differences have undermined cross-border business activity (for example, in advertising, marketing, mergers and acquisitions, joint ventures).

4. Find examples of how businesses have successfully adapted to differences in national cultures.

Discussion Questions

1. Discuss the main determinants of national culture. Is it possible to say which determinants have the biggest influence on international business or does it vary between cultures?

2. Discuss the main implications for international business of differences in national cultures.

3. How useful are Hofstede's cultural dimensions?

4. Explain which of and how the theoretical cultural dimensions discussed above may be linked to the concept of 'guanxi' (see Case Study 13.1).

5. Discuss ways in which companies can 'manage' differences in national culture.

6. Is cultural convergence taking place? If so, discuss whether it is taking the form of the 'Americanization' of culture or is there a merging of different cultures?

CASE STUDY 13.1

Guanxi – An Essential Tool for Doing Business in China or an Outdated Concept?

The acquisition of good 'guanxi' is often cited as a necessary condition for a foreign company attempting to enter the Chinese business community. At its most basic 'guanxi' means relationships and, allied with the concept of 'xinyong' (or 'personal trust'), guanxi underpins business transactions in China. An in-depth analysis of guanxi reveals a much more complex, nuanced and distinctive concept. However, relationships and the importance of relationships capture the essence of guanxi. At one level, relationships and trust are essential to business throughout the world and are not unique to China. The key questions therefore are how does guanxi differ from business relationships elsewhere in the world and what are the main implications of guanxi for investors in China?

Guanxi refers to an informal network of interpersonal relationships maintained by an individual. These relationships confer a status of mutual obliga-tion upon those in the network and are maintained by a strong sense of reciprocity. Scholars have traced the roots of guanxi back to Confucius and, as such, place guanxi firmly in the Chinese cultural context. A basic Confucian assumption is that individuals exist in relation to each other and that the five most important relationships are ruler–subject, father–son, husband–wife, elder–younger brother and friend–friend. Over time, the salience of certain relationships has changed but Chinese society continues to be highly relationship oriented in all its dimensions, including business.

In order for guanxi to work, it needs to be based on trust, dependability, reliability, shared expectations and reciprocity. In practical terms, guanxi in China is built on institutional bases, including family, a shared birthplace, a common school or university, and employment by the same organization. None of these bases need be contemporaneous. As China and its companies engage more and more with the outside world the possibility of finding common guanxi bases for non-Chinese individuals with their Chinese counterparts increases through shared alma mater or involvement with the same company, profession or trade association.

A number of interpretations of guanxi are possible. On the one hand, some authors argue that guanxi is unique to China and has grown out of and is an essential part of Chinese culture which has developed over the centuries. On the other hand, some authors claim that guanxi is merely a Chinese word for social capital and networks that exist in all economies. Although connections, relationships, 'the old boy network' are clearly important in all cultures, the concept of guanxi does appear to be more complex and underwritten with more informal rules and expectations than many other relationship systems – a reflection, in part, of China as a high-context culture. For example, much more time has to be spent in establishing a relationship prior to conducting business in a Chinese than in a Western context and in maintaining the relationship once it has been established. This may seem frustrating to Western business which tends to base its business dealings on contracts and legal agreements, whereas Chinese firms and individuals prefer to get to know and trust future customers or partners before working with them and are not so concerned with merely concluding deals.

There is also a view that guanxi is important owing to deficiencies in the Chinese business environment. That is, informal networks are important given the inefficiencies and delays inherent in the communist administrative system and the absence of a stable and predictable legal and regulatory environment, which itself is the outcome of ongoing and incomplete reform. The informal networks, so the argument goes, allow businesses to circumvent the problems inherent in the contemporary situation. In the long term, the implication is that as the market economy institutions and environment are fully implemented in China, so the need for quanxi, which is incompatible with a modernized economy, will disappear. This interpretation, although having some appeal, ignores the deep-rootedness of guanxi in Chinese society where individuals do not exist in isolation but in relation to each other. This cultural predisposition goes back centuries and is not merely a phenomenon of post-revolutionary China. Therefore, forecasts of the death of guanxi are probably premature.

Some authors regard guanxi as unethical. This stems from the view that guanxi is all about exchanging favours and gaining 'special treatment' from those in power and, as such, discriminates against those outside the guanxi network. At worst, guanxi networks in this view are seen as sources of bribery and corruption, and at best stifle competition by allocating resources according to relationships rather than on market-led grounds. This latter interpretation is at odds with the above view that guanxi is necessary to compensate for institutional and regulatory inadequacies.

The practical benefits of guanxi for business are widespread. For foreign investors in China, being able to enter and link into established guanxi networks eases entry into the Chinese business arena by providing good local knowledge about key players and regulations, and by facilitating the development of markets and distribution networks. Such benefits potentially apply to a variety of entry modes (see Chapter 10). Indeed, it is good practice to tap into local knowledge and practices when entering any new market, especially, but not only, when there may be significant differences in the business environment and expectations to those at home. This is inherently sensible and by no means corrupt. Problems may arise when relationships are utilized to gain an unfair advantage (for example, access to inside or confidential information or the granting of trading licences in exchange for favours or generally bypassing laws). Such transactions are clearly corrupt and occur to a degree in all economic systems. Undoubtedly, the potential for and actual examples of corruption exist in the guanxi system but the effects emanating from the utilization of guanxi can also be positive and in effect oil the wheels of business in China.

Another potential drawback of guanxi is that it is intensely personal and particularistic. In other words, guanxi exists between individuals and does not operate between organizations. This acts as a constraint. Once an individual leaves an organization, guanxi is lost unless multiple guanxi points have been made. The latter can be time consuming and costly to develop and maintain. Guanxi may therefore limit the scope of operations and is non-transferable. Therefore, a company entering China with pan-Chinese ambitions, or even ambitions beyond one province, will need to develop extensive guanxi. The regions are important in China in many aspects and help fragment the Chinese market: for example, although national laws are operational in China, their interpretation and implementation is often left to local and regional administrations. Local and regional guanxi is therefore important for companies aiming to extend their geographical scope within China.

CASE STUDY QUESTIONS

1. Identify and analyse potential benefits and costs of guanxi.

2. 'Criticism of guanxi is based on a Western ethnocentric view of the world.' Discuss.

3. Research other relationship systems in Asia (for example, in South Korea or Japan), in Russia or in the Middle East and identify similarities and differences with guanxi.

4. Is guanxi doomed in view of China's continuing modernization?

5. Chinese outward investment is growing. What role does or might guanxi play in this?

References and Suggestions for Further Reading

Alas, R. (2006) 'Ethics in countries with different cultural dimensions', *Journal of Business Ethics*, Vol. 69, No. 3, 237–247.

Badrtalei, J. and Bates, D. (2007) 'Effect of organizational culture on mergers and acquisitions: the case of Daimler Chrysler', *International Journal of Management*, Vol. 24, No. 2, 303–317.

Bartlett, C. and Ghoshal, S. (1998) *Managing Across Borders: A Transnational Solution*, 2nd edn, London: Random House.

Begley, T. and Boyd, D. (2003) 'The need for a corporate global mindset', *MIT Sloan Management Review*, Vol. 44, No. 2.

Chen, X. and Chen, C. (2004) 'On the intricacies of the Chinese *guanxi*: a process model of *guanxi* development', *Asia Pacific Journal of Management*, Vol. 21, 305–324.

Chung, M. and Smith, W. (2007) 'The importance of overcoming cultural barriers in establishing brand names: an Australian company in China', *Innovative Marketing*, Vol. 3, No. 2, 31–41.

Foster, M. and Minkes, A. (1999) 'East and West: business culture as divergence and convergence', *Journal of General Management*, Vol. 25, No. 1, 50–72.

Gold, T., Guthrie, D. and Wank, D. (2002) *Social Connections in China: Institutions, Culture and the Changing Nature of Guanxi*, Cambridge: Cambridge University Press.

Hall, E.T. (1977) *Beyond Culture*, Garden City, NY: Anchor Press/Doubleday.

Hatcher, M. (2003), 'New corporate agenda', *Journal of Public Affairs*, Vol. 3, No. 2.

Held, D. (2000) *A Globalising World: Culture, Economics, Politics*, London: Routledge.

Hoffman, R. (2007) 'The strategic planning process and performance relationship: does culture matter?,' *Journal of Business Strategies*, Vol. 24, No. 1, 27–48.

Hofstede, G. (1980) *Culture's Consequences: International Differences in Work-related Values*, Beverley Hills, CA: Sage.

Hofstede, G. (1991) *Cultures and Organisations: Softwares of the Mind*, New York: McGraw Hill.

House, R., Hanges, P., Javidan, M. and Dorfman, P. (2002) 'Understanding culture and implicit leadership theories across the GLOBE: an introduction to project GLOBE', *Journal of World Business*, Vol. 37, No. 1, 3–10.

House, R., Hanges, P., Javidan, M., Dorfman, P. and Gupta, V. (eds) (2004) *Culture, Leadership and Organizations: The GLOBE Study of 62 Societies*, Thousand Oaks, CA: Sage.

Howes, C. and Chiu, T. (2007) 'Foreign strategic investors in the Chinese market: cultural shift or business as usual?', *Banking and Finance Law Review*, Vol. 22, No. 2, 203–237.

Hutton, W. (2007) *The Writing on the Wall: China and the West in the 21st Century*, London: Little, Brown.

Journal of International Business Studies (2006) 'An exchange between Hofstede and Global Leadership and Organizational Behaviour Effectiveness', Vol. 37, No. 6, 882–931. A debate between Hofstede and leaders of GLOBE regarding methodological and conceptual differences between their approaches and commentaries on where this leaves the future for cultural research.

Kirkman, B., Lowe, K. and Gibson, C. (2006) 'A quarter of a century of culture's consequences: a review of empirical research incorporating Hofstede's cultural values framework', *Journal of International Business Studies*, Vol. 37, No. 3, 285–320.

Leung, K., Bhagat, S., Buchan, N., Erwz, M. and Gibson, C. (2005) 'Culture and international business: recent advances and their implications for future research', *Journal of International Business Studies*, Vol. 36, No. 4, 357–378.

Lung-Tan, L. (2007) 'The effect of cultural similarities in international joint ventures: an empirical study', *International Journal of Management*, Vol. 24, No. 2, 230–241.

Matviuk, S. (2007) 'Cross cultural leadership: behaviour expectations: a comparison between United States managers and Mexican managers', *Journal of American Academy of Business*, Vol. 11, No. 1, 253–260.

Morgan, G., Kristennsen P. and Whitley, R. (eds) (2003) *The Multinational Firm: Organizing Across Institutional and National Divides*, Oxford: Oxford University Press.

Sennett, R. (2006) *The Culture of the New Capitalism*, New Haven, CT: Yale University Press.

So, Y. (2006) *Explaining Guanxi: The Chinese Business Network*, London: Routledge.

Tang, J. and Ward, A. (2003) *The Changing Face of Chinese Management*, London: Routledge.

Terpstra, V. and David, K. (1991) *The Cultural Environment of International Business*, 3rd edn, Cincinnati, OH: South Western Publishers.

Terranova, C. (2007) 'Assessing culture during an acquisition', *Organization Development Journal*, Vol. 25, No. 2, 43–48.

Trompenaars, F. (1997) *Riding the Waves of Culture*, 2nd edn, London: Nicholas Brearley.

Trompenaars, F. and Woolliams, P. (2004) *Marketing across Cultures*, Chichester: Capstone.

Zhu, Z. and Huang, H. (2007) 'The cultural integration in the process of cross-border mergers and acquisitions', *International Management Review*, Vol. 3, No. 2, 40–44.

Websites

GLOBE web-site:
http://www.thunderbird.edu/wwwfiles/ms/globe.

Chapter 14

Corporate Social Responsibility and Business Ethics

The International Dimension

Glass, china and reputation are easily crack'd and never well mended.

Benjamin Franklin (1706–1790), statesman, scientist and writer

LEARNING OBJECTIVES

This chapter will help you to:

- understand the range and complexity of CSR and ethical issues facing MNEs

- explain why CSR and ethics have become mainstream issues for MNEs

- compare and contrast the view that the only responsibility that a business has is to its shareholders with stakeholder theory

- assess the usefulness of codes of conduct in shaping ethical and responsible behaviour

Issues of corporate social responsibility (CSR) and business ethics are engaging business more and more – both domestically and internationally. This trend has been accentuated by high-profile breaches of accepted standards of ethical behaviour such as the Enron case where inadequate checks and balances within the firm enabled unethical behaviour to occur, a development made easier by the failure of the external auditor to fulfil its role properly. The quickening of the globalization process has also highlighted CSR issues. For example, there is a time lag between rapid liberalization and the development and implementation of the appropriate regulatory framework. Moreover, international governance in social and environmental areas, both key CSR issues, is underdeveloped and contested, and there is often inadequate or even a complete absence of governance in these areas facing MNEs in developing countries. These examples highlight how rapid globalization can outpace the development of a legal framework to regulate the changing business environment. CSR initiatives can help fill this governance gap.

This chapter builds on Chapter 13 which dealt with culture. Cultural and ethical issues are separate but related concerns. Business practices are the product of their own specific cultural environment. Although some practices are clearly unacceptable in all cultures, there are some grey areas where practices that are commonplace in some countries are regarded as unethical in others and it is these grey areas that present international businesses with some of their greatest dilemmas. This chapter also underpins subsequent chapters on labour and the environment (see Chapters 15 and 16) which have both an economic and CSR theme to them.

The chapter opens with a discussion of what constitutes business ethics and CSR, and why these concepts matter. It then briefly discusses varying perspectives on business ethics. In practice, business ethics draw on a vast array of philosophical literature which ranges far beyond the boundaries of this chapter. It then discusses the specific international dimensions of CSR and business ethics, and some of the ethical challenges facing MNEs when confronted with different standards and practices and with defending the consequences of their actions in farflung corners of the world. It concludes by attempting to provide ethical guidance to businesses.

WHAT ARE CSR AND BUSINESS ETHICS?

It is relatively straightforward to define business ethics and corporate social responsibility. Business ethics refers to the moral principles and standards that guide business behaviour and highlights what is regarded as right, wrong or otherwise unacceptable behaviour. CSR refers to the obligations of a business towards society. In particular, the firm should (as a minimum) limit the negative impact of its activities on society and ideally maximize the benefits. The motives for adopting a CSR policy can vary but underpinning the idea of these obligations is a moral and philosophical perspective about the relationship between business and society.

The above definitions of business ethics and CSR are general and tell us nothing about what these moral principles and standards are or indeed should be. This is where problems begin to arise for international business. Although there are some very clear ethical principles which prevail in all societies (such as the prohibition of murder), there are other aspects of behaviour where it is not always clear which is the morally correct path to follow. These grey areas may also exist within societies. Once the complexities of international business (with the addition of different cultures, religious and other traditions to the mix) are taken into account, determination of appropriate behaviour can become even more problematic. These issues are teased out throughout this chapter and to a certain extent in subsequent chapters on labour and the environment, subjects which raise many ethical and CSR as well as economic issues.

WHY DO BUSINESS ETHICS AND CSR MATTER AND WHY SHOULD FIRMS BEHAVE ETHICALLY?

It has become the norm for companies to develop their own corporate codes of ethics (see below) and to commit themselves to behave in a socially acceptable manner. Admittedly, firms have never declared their intentions to behave unethically or irresponsibly, but recognition of the requirement to behave responsibly has not always been high on the corporate agenda. What has changed? Apart from fact that ethical behaviour is an appropriate end in itself (that is, firms should behave ethically because it is the right thing to do), why do corporations currently place a much greater emphasis on business ethics and CSR than in the past?

First, reputation is an important asset for a firm as an employer, as a supplier, as a purchaser and in marketing terms. Nike, Gap, Nestlé, Monsanto, McDonald's and Shell have famously been the subject of focused campaigns against various aspects of their activities. Such campaigns may take the form of publicity campaigns or even extend as far as consumer boycotts. Popular issues for such boycotts in the late 2000s include the environment, animal testing, the fur trade, the repression of trade union activity; and sweatshop labour and overtly political boycotts such as those against firms active in Burma or against Altria (formerly Philip Morris), Esso, Lucozade (owned by GlaxoSmithKline), MBNA and Microsoft for making donations to the Republican Party and George W. Bush's electoral campaigns.

There are mixed views on the efficacy of boycotts: some work and others do not. Some campaigners oppose boycotts on the grounds that they can harm the very people the boycott is designed to help: for example, boycotting a firm because of sweatshop conditions in a foreign supplier is as likely to lead to workers in those suppliers losing their jobs as to improvements in conditions. This is because MNEs are likely to terminate their contract with suppliers, claiming that they, the MNE, knew nothing about the conditions. Nevertheless, bad publicity and boycotts can be damaging to a firm. Unless a proactive damage limitation exercise is undertaken, harm to a company's reputation from bad publicity can have a serious long-term effect on the bottom line. It is much better from a reputation point of view to behave responsibly in the first place and not incur the bad publicity resulting from exposure of bad practice.

Second, it has become a commonly held view that those firms that behave ethically and responsibly tend to make bigger profits. In other words, as Anita Roddick, the founder of The Body

Shop once said, 'being good is good for business'. Although far from conclusive, research tends to confirm that there is a correlation between profitability and firms that have a strong commitment to CSR. However, it is unclear whether it is the CSR commitment that contributes to higher levels of profitability or whether it is the higher levels of profitability that yield the surplus that enables firms to adopt more responsible policies. Research into specific aspects of CSR is more conclusive. The Porter Hypothesis, for example, posits a positive relationship between profitability and the adoption of green policies as a result of research into the printed circuit board industry (see Chapter 16).

Third is the rise of the 'ethical consumer' and the 'ethical investor' who reward those firms regarded as 'good' by buying and investing in their products and punish those regarded as 'bad' through the withholding of custom. Positive buying is directed, for example, towards products that are cruelty-free, organic, recycled, do not exploit humans or animals, and cause minimal damage to the environment.

In order to exercise ethical choices, consumers and investors need to have information about the companies themselves and about the impact of their activities. The latter can often be difficult to gauge, as estimates of environmental impacts are often contested and measures to improve a situation may often have unintended and negative consequences. Despite these problems, an expanding array of standards and labels has emerged to guide consumer choices in an ethical direction. These include Fairtrade, Social Accountability 8000 (see Chapter 15), the Fair Labor Association, organic food, Co-op America, Product Red and Rainforest Alliance.

Fairtrade is one of the fastest growing of such initiatives. Its aim is to ensure that producers get a guaranteed minimum price for their product. Products covered by the Fairtrade mark include bananas, cocoa, coffee, cotton, dried fruit, fresh fruit and vegetables, honey, juices, nuts, oils, seeds and purees, quinoa, rice, spices, sugar, tea, wine, cut flowers, ornamental plants and sports balls. The Fairtrade minimum price is set at a level that ensures producers receive a price that covers the cost of sustainable production for their product. This is particularly valuable for farmers when prices for their commodities fall. Conversely, when market prices are above the Fairtrade minimum, the buyer must pay the market price. Products certified by Fairtrade must also meet a range of other standards relating to social, economic and environmental criteria. As such, a consumer buying a Fairtrade certified product should be able to do so safe in the knowledge that workers engaged in its production have enjoyed decent conditions, that the money s/he pays for a product is not swallowed up by the rest of the value chain and that the producer receives a reasonable share of the final sales price.

Fairtrade was established in 1988 in the Netherlands under the Max Havelaar label. The initiative spread swiftly to other markets, including Belgium, Switzerland, Denmark, Norway, France, Germany, Austria, Luxembourg, Italy, the US, Canada, Japan, the UK and Ireland. Fairtrade has subsequently spread to Mexico, Australia and New Zealand. In 2007, the sale of Fairtrade products reached €2.4 billion worldwide, a 47 per cent increase on the previous year.

Figure 14.1 shows that the Fairtrade market is the largest in absolute terms in the US and the UK but, in terms of Fairtrade sales per head, Fairtrade products have made the biggest inroads in Switzerland. Notably, Fairtrade sales are made in higher income countries. As individual wealth increases, survival is less of an issue and factors other than price enter the consumption decision.

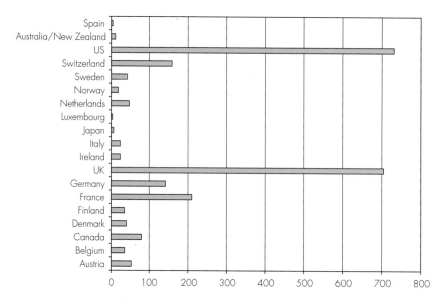

FIGURE 14.1 Retail Value of Fairtrade Products by Country, 2007 (€mn)

Source: The Fairtrade Foundation.

Ethical investors are increasingly offered external assistance in determining which companies represent ethical investments. The Dow Jones and FTSE monitor the performance of companies on the New York and London stock exchanges in particular. Both organizations have launched their own index relating to the ethical behaviour of firms. The Dow Jones Sustainability Index is based on questionnaires and external assurance relating to economic, environmental and social development criteria that determine eligibility for inclusion in the Index. The FTSE4Good index excludes tobacco, arms and nuclear power sectors, and is intended to 'reflect the performance of socially responsible equities and facilitate investment in these companies'. Eligible companies are then selected for the index in accordance with social and environmental criteria in five categories: environmental sustainability; human rights; countering bribery; supply chain labour standards, and climate change.

Overall, the impact of the growth of ethical consumerism and investment is unclear. Firms are certainly paying more attention to ethical issues and may lose a great deal of money if they encounter bad publicity about their activities. Shell claimed it had lost millions following the consumer boycott resulting from Green Peace's campaign against its plans for disposal of the Brent Spar oil platform in the 1990s. However, there is little evidence to suggest that firms reap much reward for 'good behaviour'.

Moreover, the international economic downturn that picked up speed towards the end of 2008 could well challenge the commitment of consumers to ethical purchasing in even the richest countries, given that there is often a price premium entailed in purchasing 'ethical' products. Analysts frequently report a gap between consumers' views on ethical purchases and their actual propensity to purchase ethical goods. The behaviour of consumers during this difficult economic period will indicate how deeply rooted ethical consumption and investment have become.

THE INTERNATIONAL DIMENSION OF BUSINESS ETHICS AND CSR

Ethics and corporate responsibility are matters for all firms whether they operate internationally or not. However, once the international dimension enters the equation, the complexity of ethical and CSR issues increases. A major concern for international business is the universal versus relativist debate. Universal values are those that have been adopted everywhere, or almost everywhere. There have been attempts to identify and codify such values in the UN-inspired Universal Declaration of Human Rights (UDHR) and in the Caux principles (see below), one of several attempts to develop a set of ethical principles which can be utilized by MNEs across the globe. The UDHR was adopted by the UN General Assembly and covered an array of political and civil rights and economic, social and cultural rights that pertain to all UN members. The rights most directly concerning business include the right to equality before law (that is, non-discrimination); the right to an adequate standard of living; the right to work in just and favourable conditions; the right to equal pay for equal work; and the right to rest and leisure and to paid holidays. In reality, despite its underpinning by the UN, it is not difficult to uncover many areas in which these principles are not respected.

Relativism reflects the extent to which different societies have different values and ethical standards to guide behaviour. These values are determined to a large extent by the many influences that have their impact on culture (see Chapter 13) and can lead to different principles of behaviour between societies. The problem for international business is which code of behaviour should be adopted when operating in another country. Should they adopt the 'when in Rome principle' which requires them to comply with host country values or should they be guided by their own values? Both positions can create problems. The former case can create severe ethical dilemmas. For example, in South Africa during the days of apartheid, MNEs were required to comply with employment policies of racial segregation that the rest of the world considered abhorrent. Nevertheless, MNEs continued to invest in South Africa. Many argued that such behaviour was unethical and essentially propped up an immoral regime, whereas others argued that such investment represented a constructive engagement with the regime and this, rather than isolation, would bring about change. On the other hand, if firms are guided by their own values, they may be accused of 'cultural imperialism' and of imposing their own values on other societies.

Two further concepts also need to be taken into account when studying business ethics: that is, the difference between descriptive ethics and normative ethics. Descriptive ethics are about studying, describing and characterizing morality and ethical behaviour. It is this process which draws out the differences in belief systems between societies. A country like India, for example, contains a complex web of influences which have shaped values there: Hinduism is the main religion and influence in India but Islam, Sikhism, Zoroastrianism and Jainism also play their part. In the business field, the influence of Western management traditions can also be thrown into the mix. In reality, the values of many societies are subject to a wide range of influences and can be difficult to unravel for an outsider.

In practice, descriptive ethics is the starting point for an expatriate manager trying to come to terms with a new culture. For many purposes differences in values and norms need not cause a problem for the international manager. However, understanding the ethical system of a society does not provide guidance on how to behave in a specific set of circumstances. This is where normative ethics – the determination not of 'what is' but of 'what should be' – takes on importance. Given the existence of different cultural and ethical traditions, the international manager has to decide on the right thing to do when faced with conflicting values and complex issues.

VARYING PERSPECTIVES ON ETHICS

Perceptions of what is right and wrong are derived from a number of sources, including religion, family and society in general. In democracies, law reflects the values of the society in which it is located. Observance of the law may be necessary for an individual or a firm to behave ethically but it may not be sufficient in itself, as legal behaviour may only comply with the ethical minimum. Conversely, especially in non-democratic societies, legal obligations may be out of kilter with what is regarded as ethical in society at large and could require unethical behaviour of citizens and corporations.

In addition to religion, philosophical traditions also influence views of what is right and wrong. Business literature on ethics tends to be dominated by Western philosophical traditions such as Aristotelean philosophy, utilitarianism and Kantian philosophy. The rise of Asian business will see greater attention paid to Eastern philosophical traditions. The influence of religion and philosophy on business ethics is beyond the scope of this chapter but an awareness that business ethics is rooted in something that ranges far beyond and deeper is important.

In more practical terms, assumptions about ethics and business are influenced inevitably by fundamental beliefs about the role of business in society. On the one hand, there are those who believe that the sole social responsibility of business is to generate profit. The writings of Milton Friedman embody this view. For example, in 1962, in *Capitalism and Freedom*, he wrote:

> There is one and only one social responsibility of business – to use its resources and engage in activities designed to increase its profits so long as it . . . engages in open and free competition without deception or fraud.

For some proponents of this view, profit generation itself takes on a moral dimension, whereas others see profits as the key to wealth generation – the main way of addressing social issues.

On the other hand, some believe that the role of business is much broader than that of wealth generation and that all those who are affected by the way a company operates – shareholders, employees, customers, suppliers, the local community, future generations (especially in relation to environmental issues) – have a legitimate interest and stake in the way a company conducts itself. Figure 14.2 highlights some of the typical stakeholders in a firm. Stakeholders may vary from firm to firm: in some circumstances the impact of a firm upon the local community may be greater than in others. In some cases, the relative impact of a firm upon stakeholders may vary within a firm, depending on the activity or product in question.

Stakeholder theory acknowledges the responsibility of the firm towards its shareholders but also claims that the firm has obligations to others. In terms of employees, the firm must pay due regard to health and safety matters, pay a fair wage and follow a policy of non-discrimination. The stake that customers have in a firm entitles them to expect that they should be dealt with fairly and honestly; that they should not be subject to misleading claims or advertising, and that the products they

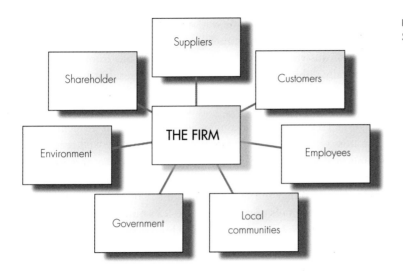

FIGURE 14.2 Typical Stakeholders in a Firm

consume should be safe, healthy and clearly labelled. Suppliers have a right to be fairly treated in terms of prices and the general conditions of their contracts. Late payment of bills, for example, can frequently undermine the day-to-day operations of small suppliers. The activities of a company can impact on a community, both negatively and positively. The environmental impact of firms on local communities can often be a bone of contention, for example. On the other hand, MNEs also provide jobs for the local community. Moreover, it is often at the local level that firms engage in corporate philanthropy in the form of educational projects in the developing world or improvements to local amenities. Firms are also under an obligation to pay local and national taxes and to respect the laws and regulations passed by the government.

Stakeholder theory, developed most notably by Edward Freeman in the 1980s, holds that companies are under an obligation not to violate the rights of others and are responsible for the effects of their actions on others. As such, companies are seen as responsible members of the community with all the accompanying obligations and privileges this entails. Operationalizing the stakeholder concept can be complex: who exactly constitutes a stakeholder and to what the existence of a stake entitles any individual or organization in any given situation is far from straightforward. It is possible that competing stakeholder claims may clash: how can and should these differences be reconciled?

INTERNATIONAL ETHICAL AND CSR ISSUES

The above concerns are relevant to business whether it is domestic or international in nature. However, international business poses particular challenges and questions over and above those facing purely domestic business. The following, far from exhaustive list, includes some of the international ethical challenges facing MNEs:

■ *Human rights*: it is a generally accepted principle that MNEs should not engage in direct infringement of human rights – the UN Universal Declaration of Human Rights (UDHR) is commonly taken as the appropriate benchmark. However, some people would go further, preferring companies to refrain from doing business in countries known to infringe human rights on a systematic basis. Opponents of this view argue that if an MNE abstains from conducting business in a country with an ethically dubious regime, the only concrete result is to hand over business opportunities to companies without such reservations.

On coming to office in 1992, for example, President Clinton proposed to withdraw most favoured nation status from China as a result of the Tiananmen Square massacre in 1989 in which many pro-democracy demonstrators were killed. Such action would have provoked retaliation against US companies operating in China, and US businesses lobbied hard to persuade the President to change his mind. They argued that US business interests would be irrevocably damaged in a rapidly growing market and that the outcome would not be an improvement in human rights in China but a boost to the business prospects of America's business rivals in China. The lobbying campaign was successful: the link between trade and human rights was broken and replaced by the doctrine that the possibility of bringing about change is greater if business and other links and contacts are maintained. Although there is some support for this view, there are also those who believe that it is a convoluted justification for 'business as usual'.

In an uncanny parallel act, in her first visit to China as US Secretary of State in February 2009, Mrs Hillary Clinton refused to raise the issue of human rights on the grounds that economic, environmental and security issues were more pressing. This stance drew criticism from a range of NGOs who maintain that human rights itself is one of the most pressing problems and should not be subject to the vagaries of geopolitics.

■ *Labour issues*: international labour issues can be linked with human rights, especially regarding matters of forced labour and child labour (see Chapter 15). Ethical labour issues also occur outside the framework of the UDHR in circumstances where certain labour practices may be legal and commonplace in the host country but do not necessarily represent fair and equitable treatment of the workforce. The issue facing the MNE is: does it maximize its competitive advantage by locating in a low-cost-low-regulation country and adopt local practices, or does it refrain from reaping all the labour cost benefits by adopting higher standards and more ethical practices than strict compliance with local legal norms requires? A firm may choose to take the latter path and still experience significant competitiveness gains.

■ *Bribery/corruption*: this is not as clear-cut an issue as it may first appear; indeed, it can be rather a grey area. In some cultures, it is regarded as perfectly normal to give an official or host a gift. In others, only minimal value token gifts or no gifts at all are allowed. A problem arises when it is the norm for a contract to be signed only after the payment of a 'commission' to a key official or officials. Such circumstances place MNEs in a difficult position: without payment of these commissions the contract will not materialize and, if they do not make the payment, many other companies will (although that is not an ethical justification for going ahead with the commission). The position of the US is unequivocal about this: it regards all such payments as bribes and, as such, they are both unethical and illegal. The Foreign Corrupt Practices Act (FCPA), enacted in 1977, forbids US companies and companies linked to the US (perhaps through being quoted on the New York Stock Exchange – NYSE) from making improper payments to foreign governments, politicians or political parties to obtain or retain business. Case Study 14.1 looks at these issues in more detail.

By its very nature, the extent of corruption can be difficult to quantify. Transparency International, the world's most influential NGO concerned with combating corruption, has attmpted to do this by surveying business perceptions about the degree of corruption in 180 countries. Table 14.1 sets out

TABLE 14.1 Corruption Perceptions Index for Selected Countries, 2008

Rank	Country	Score	Rank	Country	Score
1	Denmark	9.3	54	South Africa	4.9
1	New Zealand	9.3	57	Greece	4.7
1	Sweden	9.3	58	Poland	4.6
4	Singapore	9.2	58	Turkey	4.6
5	Finland	9.0	61	Namibia	4.5
5	Switzerland	9.0	65	Kuwait	4.3
7	Iceland	8.9	67	Georgia	3.9
7	Netherlands	8.9	67	Ghana	3.9
9	Australia	8.7	70	Romania	3.8
9	Canada	8.7	72	Bulgaria	3.6
11	Luxembourg	8.3	72	China	3.6
12	Austria	8.1	72	Mexico	3.6
12	Hong Kong	8.1	80	Brazil	3.5
14	Germany	7.9	80	Morocco	3.5
14	Norway	7.9	80	Saudi Arabia	3.5
16	Ireland	7.7	80	Thailand	3.5
16	UK	7.7	85	India	3.4
18	Belgium	7.3	92	Algeria	3.2
18	Japan	7.3	96	Jamaica	3.1
18	US	7.3	102	Lebanon	3.0
23	France	6.9	115	Egypt	2.8
28	Qatar	6.5	121	Nigeria	2.7
28	Spain	6.5	126	Indonesia	2.6
35	UAE	5.9	134	Pakistan	2.5
36	Botswana	5.8	134	Ukraine	2.5
39	Taiwan	5.7	147	Kenya	2.1
40	South Korea	5.6	147	Russia	2.1
41	Oman	5.5	147	Syria	2.1
45	Czech Republic	5.2	178	Iraq	1.3
47	Hungary	5.1	178	Myanmar	1.3
47	Jordan	5.1	180	Somalia	1.0
47	Malaysia	5.1			

Note: The scores are based on surveys of business people and risk analysts regarding their perceptions of the degree of corruption among government officials. The lower the score, the greater is the perception that officials are corrupt, and vice versa.

Source: Transparency International – www.transparency.org.

the outcome of the 2008 survey in the form of the Corruption Perceptions Index (CPI). The countries with the highest scores are percived to be the most free from corruption. The world's most developed economies register the highest score.

The CPI does reveal that no region is free from corruption problems. As Table 14.1 shows, European countries dominate the top 20 places in the CPI, indicating relative freedom from corruption. However, Bulgaria and Romania, the newest EU members, perform poorly on this measure, demonstrating that parts of Europe, at least, have endemic corruption problems. The highest-scoring BRIC economy is China where the level of corruption is perceived to be on a similar level to that of Bulgaria. It is not surprising that the BRICs have a corruption problem: they are in the process of major transformation, involving the construction of new institutions and governance systems. In a period of rapid change, it can take time for governance to catch up with the reality of what is actually happening in the marketplace. However, it is important for the BRICs, if they are to sustain their rapid development into the long term and continue to attract foreign investors, that they pursue a strong anti-corruption line.

CASE STUDY 14.1

Bribery – An International Language?

Given the illicit nature of bribery and corruption, it has always been difficult to estimate the extent of such illegitimate practices in the business world. However, in 2004, the World Bank Institute made what it described as a 'conservative' estimate that $1 trillion was paid annually in bribes worldwide. Despite efforts by the OECD to develop measures to combat corruption, these estimates suggest that bribery is not a rare practice in the international business context. Indeed, as the examples below show, many mainstream and respected MNEs have been caught up in bribery scandals in recent years.

The case against bribery is both an ethical and a pragmatic one. Its effects are damaging not only to those directly involved in the transaction but also to other businesses and to society in general. It distorts decision making and undermines democratic institutions and proper governance. Economic decision making is also suboptimal as resource allocation is made according to inappropriate criteria

and income disparities can increase significantly as a result of graft. A reputation for corruption can also discourage investors and thus threaten long-term sustainable economic development. In 2005, in a report commissioned by the Russian government, the OECD reportedly claimed that 'the weakness, inefficiency and corruption of all branches of government are the most important obstacles to further reform in Russia'.

Combating bribery and corruption is far from easy. The first is to determine what type of transaction is illegitimate. In some countries, the giving of gifts, for example, is standard practice and a normal part of the culture: such gifts are regarded as an expression of friendship and good faith. Refusal of the gift could cause offence. On the other hand, a policy of refusing any gift removes any suspicion that the recipient may feel under an obligation as a result of the gift. In practice, many companies have a policy of allowing the acceptance of gifts up to a minimal level.

The situation is not always so clear-cut with other forms of payments. For example, commissions are often large payments to individuals acting as a go-between to set up and/or facilitate a deal. The commission could be a legitimate payment for professional services but the third party may also act as a conduit for paying bribes. A bribe is a straightforward payment to influence officials and/or induce them to do things which they should not do.

A common defence by those accused of bribery is that bribery is the norm where they are trying to do business, and if they did not offer inducements their competitors would. Such claims are frequently true. Notwithstanding this, bribery remains an unethical practice. However, these claims do demonstrate the pressures facing MNEs and their employees if they wish to succeed in certain markets. These pressures were undoubtedly felt by the companies in the examples below.

Table 14.2 sets out the Bribe Payers Index (BPI) for 2008. This Index, drawn up by Transparency International, ranks 22 of the world's most influential economies according to the likelihood of their firms to bribe abroad. The Index is based on questions to nearly 3,000 senior executives and it is their perceptions that form the basis of the BPI. Scores potentially range from 0–10. A score of 10 indicates a zero propensity to bribe. Therefore countries with a lower score have a higher perceived propensity to bribe.

The index reveals that firms from Belgium and Canada, closely followed by those from Switzerland and the Netherlands, are widely perceived to be the least likely to offer bribes. At the other end of the scale, Mexican, Chinese and Russian firms are regarded as the most likely to engage in bribery, at least among the larger, more influential economies.

A further analysis of the BPI data reveals those sectors most likely to wield influence on government rules, regulations and decisions as a result of private payments to public officials. The sectors most likely to make such payments to influence the state were public works contracts and construction, oil and gas, mining, and real estate and property development. Companies least likely to try to exert undue pressure on public policy were in agriculture, fisheries and light manufacturing.

TABLE 14.2 Bribe Payers Index, 2008

Country	Score	Country	Score
Belgium	8.8	Spain	7.9
Canada	8.8	Hong Kong	7.6
Switzerland	8.7	South Africa	7.5
Netherlands	8.7	South Korea	7.5
Germany	8.6	Taiwan	7.5
Japan	8.6	Brazil	7.4
United Kingdom	8.6	Italy	7.4
Australia	8.5	India	6.8
France	8.1	Mexico	6.6
Singapore	8.1	China	6.5
United States	8.1	Russia	5.9

Source: Transparency International – www.transparency.org.

Examples of Bribery Cases

Even firms from countries scoring well on the BPI index have been embroiled in bribery scandals as the following examples, chosen at random, show. What is notable about these examples is that the companies involved are large and generally respected MNEs. This begs the question of how representative are these examples of MNE behaviour. The final example concerning BAE Systems is spelled out in more detail to highlight a number of key issues in the bribery debate.

1. Investigations have been carried out by the Costa Rican authorities and the US Security and Exchange Commission (SEC) (involved because Alcatel shares are quoted on the New York Stock Exchange and therefore come under the auspices of the FCPA) into allegations that the French telecommunications giant, Alcatel, made illicit payments to senior politicians and officials in Costa Rica to secure contracts. The company was also accused of violating a ban on foreign contributions to political campaigns. As a consequence, one former president of Costa Rica spent time in jail in the mid-2000s and latterly under house arrest. Alcatel activities have also been investigated in Taiwan, Kenya, Tanzania and Nigeria.
2. In 2004, Norway's Statoil paid a $3 million fine to settle criminal charges that a consulting firm had acted improperly on its behalf to secure contracts in Iran.
3. In 2005, US agrochemical company, Monsanto, was fined $1.5 million by US authorities for bribing an Indonesian official to avoid the required environmental impact study on its cotton.
4. In December 2008, following a series of investigations by German authorities and the US SEC (involved because Siemens is quoted on the NYSE) into alleged bribery by Siemens, the German MNE received a fine from the US of $800 million – the largest fine in corporate history for bribery. This brought the total cost to

Siemens of bribery investigations to €2.5 billion, approximately one-third of which was lawyers' and accountants' fees. Costs could have been higher had the company not cooperated with the US authorities. The damage to the company was also limited in the US because the company was allowed to plead accountancy violations rather than bribery. Otherwise the FCPA would have prevented Siemens from bidding on government contracts in the US.

The investigations focused on Siemens's activities into telecommunications and, to a lesser extent into power generation, and suggested that between 2001 and 2007 Siemens made $1.4 billion in illegal payments around the world. Indeed, bribery appears to have been endemic to the company. Examples uncovered by the investigations included $5 million in bribes in Bangladesh to win a mobile phone contract; almost $13 million in bribes to senior officials in Nigeria; $40 million in bribes to Argentinian officials to win a $1 billion contract to produce identity cards; and $14 million in bribes in China in relation to medical equipment.

5. In February 2009, Kellogg, Brown and Root (until recently a subsidiary of Halliburton) agreed to pay $579 million in fines for their role in a decade-long scheme to bribe Nigerian officials in exchange for contruction contracts. This represents the largest-ever fine for a US company under the FCPA: the previous largest was the $44 million fine on Baker Hughes in 2007.

BAE Systems and the Al-Yamamah Deal

The first phase of the Al-Yamamah deal between the UK and Saudi Arabia was signed in 1985. Reputed to be not only the single biggest arms sale made by the UK, the Al-Yamamah deal is also said to be Britain's largest-ever export agreement. The main beneficiary of the deal, presumed to be worth an initial £43 billion, is BAE Systems (formerly British Aerospace). At the time the deal was concluded, the company had not long been privatized and Prime

Minister Thatcher was involved in the negotiations – an indication of the strategic and political as well as the commercial dimensions of the deal. At the time, the UK was concerned about securing oil supplies and ensuring that such a big contract went to a British firm and not to France, a major rival in the sale of arms and defence equipment.

Details of the contract have never been fully revealed and there has, from the beginning, been speculation about whether the contract could withstand full scrutiny from a corruption perspective. The first investigation into Al-Yamamah was undertaken by the National Audit Office (NAO) in 1992 but its conclusions were never released, an unprecedented situation for an NAO report, giving rise to suspicions that it had been suppressed by John Major's government.

Allegations about the contracts never went away and in 2004, triggered by stories in the *Guardian* newspaper, the Serious Fraud Office (SFO) launched an investigation into Al-Yamamah, particularly into claims that large bribes or sweeteners had been made to members of the Saudi royal family and to government officials to secure the deal. However, the SFO abandoned its investigations in December 2006 on 'national security' grounds. This was in line with a 2002 UK law which implemented a 1997 OECD anti-corruption agreement. This law banned the suspension of bribery probes unless justified in the name of national security. Speculation has been rife that the British government gave into threats from Prince Bandar bin Sultan (a former Saudi ambassador to Washington and the alleged recipient of more than £1 billion from BAE who, along with other Saudi officials, has consistently denied any wrongdoing) to reduce Saudi cooperation with the UK in the battle against terrorism, especially in regard to intelligence cooperation. The need to retain Saudi Arabia as a military ally and as an arms customer was allegedly enough for the British government to put pressure on the SFO to pull out of its investigation.

The matter did not end there. A judicial review of the SFO's actions concluded in April 2008 that the SFO had 'acted unlawfully' and condemned the decision to abandon the investigation as a consequence of Saudi threats as an attempt to pervert the course of justice by a foreign power. Any requirement for the SFO to reopen the case diappeared in July 2008 when it won its appeal in the House of Lords which overturned the April decision that the SFO had acted illegally. Meanwhile the SFO has continued its investigations into bribery allegations against BAE in Romania, the Czech Republic, South Africa and Tanzania.

The decision in the House of Lords ended official probes into al-Yamamah by the British authorities but the deal remains under investigation by the US Department of Justice under the jurisdiction of the FCPA. It is alleged that BAE Systems used the US banking system to channel funds into Saudi accounts thus have brought the Al-Yamamah case within the scope of the FCPA. Penalties under the FCPA are stringent: fines can reach millions of dollars; executives can be jailed; companies can be forced to bay back profits from corrupt deals, and companies can be excluded from US government contracts. The latter penalty would seriously damage BAE Systems which conducts a significant part of its business in the US.

In order to head off the continuing assault on its reputation by the al-Yamamah affair, in 2007 BAE Systems commissioned an independent report with the remit of making recommendations, not into the specific allegations of corruption, but on the principles and procedures that the company should follow in the future. The resulting Woolf Report, published in May 2008, contained 23 recommendations intended to bring about a serious change of culture within BAE Systems. The company committed itself to implementing all of the recommendations within three years, and by July 2008 had set up a committee of senior executives and six teams of senior managers to look at key areas.

The most important recommendations of the Woolf Report called for the following:

* An independent audit of BAE's business processes to ensure they meet the highest ethical standards. The first audit should be published

within three years and at regular intervals there-after. BAE has committed itself to publishing the first report in 2009.

* New legislation on bribery with the government becoming a champion of ethical behaviour.
* New standards for the use of external advisers and an end to facilitation payments.
* The board to take an explicit role in assessing the ethical and reputational risk of all business decisions made by it.
* Adherence to ethical behaviour should be part of senior executive remuneration.
* BAE Systems to take the lead in developing an international code of conduct for the defence industry.
* Adoption of a global code of ethics.

CASE STUDY QUESTIONS

1. Why is bribery considered so damaging to:

   a) business
   b) the host country?

2. The defence industry is notorious for making irregular payments to its clients, particularly but not only to those in the Middle East. Does this shed any new light on the allegations made against BAE Systems?

3. What issues are raised by the British government's intervention leading to the premature end of the Serious Fraud Office's investigation into bribery?

4. Research the US Foreign Corrupt Practices Act. How does it relate to the activities of non-US firms? Is the FCPA a legitimate attempt to clean up business or does it represent unwarranted interference into the business affairs of other countries?

5. Discuss the main challenges in overcoming the problem of bribery in the international business context. Is the goal of eradicating bribery a pipedream?

■ Environmental protection: firms may encounter damaging publicity as a result of the environmental outcome of their activities (see Chapter 16) as pollution attracts more and more media attention. For many, environmental protection and corporate responsibility in this field has a clear ethical dimension. This debate is couched in terms of the 'global commons' in which all human beings have both a stake and a responsibility to ensure the well-being of the environment for future generations.

■ Miscellaneous issues: international business frequently throws up issues that pose ethical issues in specific sectors. For example, the sale of formula milk in the developing world put Nestlé's activities under the microscope. The emergence of GM food has proved controversial on many fronts; particularly concerning for some is the control it will give to firms like Monsanto over the range of seeds available to developing country farmers. The pharmaceuticals industry is also under attack for pricing many of its products way beyond the reach of developing countries, thereby resulting in the unnecessary loss of life.

INITIATIVES TO ENCOURAGE ETHICAL BEHAVIOUR

Businesses have responded to the increased emphasis on CSR and ethics by drawing up their own codes of conduct and ethics to the extent that they have become the norm in MNEs. Codes of ethics exist at a number of levels, including:

- *the organizational or corporate level*: that is, relating to a single organization;
- *the professional level*: for example, medicine, law and accountancy;
- *the industry level*: these are perhaps more commonplace in relation to specific CSR issues like the 'Responsible Care' Initiative in the chemical industry or the Forest Stewardship Council;
- *programme or group codes*: that is, a code to which companies sign up. These codes may be related to single initiatives such as Fair Trade or they can provide general guidance to ethical behaviour in business. One such example is the Caux Principles (see below) drawn up by business leaders from Europe, the US and Japan in an attempt to establish a global code of ethics for business.

Organizational and group codes of ethics are discussed in more detail below. Both corporate codes and group codes of conduct face the difficult task of developing policies that can be enacted across borders. That is, these codes have to grapple with the grey areas or relativist issues that have been alluded to throughout this chapter. Such issues include gifts, hospitality and bribes (see Case Study 14.1); conflicts of interest; equal opportunities, and discrimination and environmental protection.

Corporate Ethical Codes

MNEs are increasingly developing codes of ethics to protect their reputation, not only in terms of their treatment of labour and the environment (see Chapters 15 and 16) but also in terms of the requirement of ethical conduct. The format of codes vary but they tend to contain words like 'trust', 'integrity' and 'honesty', and deal with specific issues like the environment, bribery, treatment of employees, relationships with the community, and health and safety. Indeed, codes stand a better chance of being effective if they combine general principles to guide behaviour with specific guidance on how to behave in certain circumstances.

The Norwegian oil company, Statoil, for example, has made a clear commitment to socially responsible and ethical behaviour. This includes a commitment to the values and principles of the UN Global Compact and the Global Sullivan Principles, and to 'show respect for local cultures and traditions and cooperate with people affected by our operations'. The company has also made commitments to train its employees in commercial ethics and how to tackle ethical dilemmas, to carry out ethical audits of its own operations and to seek cooperation on best practice and to support efforts by international organizations to fight corruption.

The UK's Cooperative Bank has taken its ethical commitment a stage further by polling its customers on a range of ethical issues such as genetic modification, animal welfare, the environment, human rights, factory farming, hunting, tobacco manufacture, currency speculation and the arms trade. This practice began in the early 1990s and the surveys are used to shape the bank's ethical investment policy, a policy that is unusually detailed and specific. On the one hand, this policy has the benefit of being responsive to what consumers actually want. On the other hand, the bank runs the risk that its investment decisions are based on what is ethically fashionable and that the policies emanating from such a survey do not take into account the ethical complexities and ambiguities of many situations.

In trying to act ethically, corporations need to ensure that their policy is real, that it has substance and is not just a public relations exercise – otherwise ethical initiatives can backfire. In other words, the adoption of a code of ethics alone is not sufficient to ensure ethical behaviour. Firms need to communicate the code to their employees, and to take great care in how their policies are implemented and to ensure the involvement, commitment and training of all their employees. They need to ensure that the code is consistently applied and to demonstrate that breaches of the code may result in disciplinary procedures, procedures that are applied evenly to those in both senior and junior positions within the organization. One route followed by some companies is to regard NGOs not as 'the enemy' but as a potential ally in their search for a socially and environmentally responsible policy by engaging them to monitor and audit the observation of their codes.

Group Codes of Conduct

The heightened concern about CSR has resulted in the adoption by many MNEs of their own codes of ethical behaviour. Accompanying this trend has been the emergence of a number of voluntary international sets of principles that provide a framework and foundation for the development of individual company codes. Three of the most prominent set of international group codes of conduct are outlined below.

The Sullivan Principles

The original Sullivan Principles were developed in 1977 by the Reverend Leon Sullivan, a director of General Motors, to provide guidelines for US companies operating in South Africa under the apartheid regime. The Principles required US firms adopting them to use US rather than South African workplace practices and to promote programmes that had a significant positive impact on the living conditions and quality of life of non-whites in South Africa.

At their peak, the Sullivan Principles involved 178 subsidiaries of signatory firms employing 62,400 workers. By 1986, the US Congress had passed a comprehensive Anti-apartheid Act that required US government agencies and US firms employing more than 25 people in South Africa to adhere to a code of conduct based on the Sullivan Principles. Penalties for non-compliance ranged from a $10,000 fine to ten years' imprisonment for individuals or a $1 million fine in the case of companies. By 1987, Reverend Sullivan had himself withdrawn support for the Principles bearing his name and recommended a policy of disinvestment and embargo.

In 1999, the Global Sullivan Principles were launched. Their purpose is to establish a set of ethical principles to which companies and organizations of all sizes, in all cultures and all sectors could adhere. The eight Principles, concerned primarily with the advancement of human rights and social justice, are:

1. support for the human rights of employees, suppliers and the community in which the firm operates;
2. promotion of equal opportunities in relation to colour, race, gender, age, ethnicity and religion;
3. respect for the freedom of association of their employees;
4. provision of training opportunities and minimum basic remuneration;
5. provision of a safe and healthy workplace and a commitment to environmental protection and sustainability;
6. respect for fair competition, including intellectual and other property rights and a commitment not to pay or accept bribes;
7. commitment to work with governments and communities to improve the quality of life;
8. promotion of these Principles to business partners.

Companies endorsing these Principles also make a commitment to the implementation of internal policies, procedures, training and reporting structures to ensure the Principles are applied. Companies endorsing the Principles include the following MNEs: American Airlines, Avon Products, British Airways, Chevron Texaco, Coca-Cola, Colgate-Palmolive, Ford Motors, General Motors, Hershey Foods, Occidental Petroleum, Pepsi Co, Pfizer, Procter & Gamble, Quaker Oats, Rio Tinto, Statoil and the Tata Group.

The Caux Principles

The Caux Roundtable is composed of business leaders from Europe, Japan and the US. It was founded in 1986 by Frederik Philips, the former president of Philips Electronics, and Olivier Giscard d'Estaing, vice-chairman of INSEAD, as a forum for reducing general trade tensions. However, the organization quickly became focused on issues of corporate social responsibility. Its fundamental belief is that the world business community should play an important role in improving economic and social conditions, and aims to establish a world benchmark against which to measure corporate behaviour. Contrary to the Friedmanite view referred to elsewhere, 'law and market forces are necessary but insufficient guides for conduct' (Preamble to Caux Principles).

The Principles are in two parts. The first part established general principles based on *kyosei* and human dignity. *Kyosei* is a Japanese concept that means living and working together for the common good, enabling cooperation and prosperity to co-exist with healthy and fair competition. Human dignity refers to the value of each individual as an end in themselves, not merely as a means to the fulfilment of another's goals. The general Principles themselves state that:

1. the responsibilities of business go beyond the interests of shareholders: not only does business have a responsibility for wealth creation but it is also responsible for respecting principles of honesty and integrity to customers, employers, suppliers and competitors.
2. MNEs should contribute to social and economic progress, human rights, education and welfare in the host country.
3. Compliance with the law is important, but not enough: companies should nurture the principles of honesty and integrity and develop a spirit of trust.

4. MNEs should respect domestic and international trade rules and be aware that, even if an action is legal, it can still have adverse consequences.
5. Businesses should support the WTO's multilateral trade system and similar agreements, cooperate to promote further trade liberalization and work to relax domestic measures that hinder global commerce.
6. Businesses should protect and, where possible, improve the environment, promote sustainability and prevent the wasteful use of natural resources.
7. Businesses should not engage in bribery, money laundering or other corrupt practices, nor trade in arms, materials used for terrorist activities, drug trafficking or other organized crime.

The Global Compact

The UN Global Compact is a UN initiative intended to encourage businesses around the world to follow socially and environmentally responsible policies. First proposed by the then UN Secretary-General Kofi Annan at the World Economic Forum in Davos in 1999, the Compact requires businesses to embrace ten principles (see Box 14.1 for further details) regarding human rights, labour, the environment and corruption to help sustain the global economy and to spread the benefits of globalization more widely.

Companies aspiring to membership must send a letter of their intent to the Secretary-General and submit annual details of efforts taken to implement the Principles. They must also inform employees,

---

Box 14.1 The Ten Principles of the Global Compact

Human rights – businesses should:
1. support and respect the protection of human rights;
2. ensure they are not complicit in human rights abuses.

Labour – businesses should uphold:
3. freedom of association and recognize the right to collective bargaining;
4. the elimination of all forms of forced and compulsory labour;
5. the effective abolition of child labour;
6. the elimination of discrimination in employment.

Environment – businesses should:
7. support a precautionary approach to the environment (see Chapter 14);
8. promote greater environmental responsibility;
9. encourage the development and diffusion of environmental technologies.

Anti-corruption – businesses should:
10. work against all forms of corruption, including extortion and bribery.

shareholders, customers and suppliers that they have done so and integrate the Ten Principles into the corporate development programme, the company's mission statement and the Annual Report. By 2008, over 4,600 companies had signed up to the Compact, including over 20 per cent of the Fortune 500. NGOs, trade unions, business associations, UN agencies and academic institutions take the membership to almost 6,000.

Strictly speaking, the Global Compact is not a code of conduct; nor are there any penalties for failure to comply with the Principles. Companies, however, do get classified as 'inactive' and are removed from membership if they fail to comply with the above obligations to report annually on progress in fulfilling the Principles. This does not, however, prevent the Global Compact from encountering criticism about the lack of sanctions for non-compliance; about the absence of a requirement to demonstrate progress and the admission to membership of companies that have a dubious record on one or more of the Ten Principles.

CONCLUSION

Globalization adds an extra dimension to ethical issues for the firm. CSR and ethical issues inevitably become more complex when an organization has a presence in more than one country: a factor which results from the link between culture and ethics. Senior managers in overseas subsidiaries may face ethical dilemmas when trying to determine the best course of action to follow. Should they, for example, follow local practice, which may be at odds with the values of the headquarters and home country? Should they act according to the principles of the home country and risk accusations of ethical imperialism? Are there universally applicable ethical principles to which they can appeal?

Corporate codes of conduct can help managers address these issues but the process of drawing up the codes themselves is fraught with the issues raised by moral relativism. Moreover, while codes often set out general principles for employees to follow, they often require interpretation to fit particular circumstances and employees are not necessarily any further forward.

Summary of Key Concepts

- In some cases, what constitutes ethical behaviour is clear-cut but there are grey areas in which cultural factors influence ethical positions, thereby creating difficult areas of decision making for managers of multinational firms.
- Corporate social responsibility is closely related to business ethics. Corporate social responsibility has traditionally incorporated human rights, labour and the environment, but it is increasingly also concerned with issues of corporate governance and corruption.
- Companies increasingly consider themselves responsible not only to shareholders but to a much wider range of stakeholders.
- Ethical business behaviour is an appropriate end in itself but it is also good for business. Unethical or irresponsible corporate behaviour can significantly damage a firm's reputation and hence profitability. MNEs also need to consider the ethical consumer and investor.

Activities

1. Research a recent corporate scandal (there are plenty to choose from) and identify the main issues raised by it.

2. Research and compare and contrast the ethical codes of conduct of two MNEs. To what extent do the codes you have chosen provide a useful guide to ethically and responsible behaviour?

3. Write an ethical code of behaviour for students. Reflect on the difficulties of doing this and be prepared to justify all aspects of your code.

4. 'Corporate concern for ethically and responsible behaviour is no more than a public relations smokescreen to preserve a good public image. Despite this concern, it is business as usual for the MNE.' Use this quotation as a topic for debate.

Discussion Questions

1. What are the implications for international business of differences in dominant ethical values and religious beliefs? Choose two culturally diverse countries to illustrate your argument.

2. Is it ever appropriate for a company to engage in activities abroad that are regarded as unethical at home (for example, the payment of a 'commission' to a key official as the price of gaining a contract)?

3. Identify and assess the practical problems of putting stakeholder theory into practice.

4. Assess the utility of codes of practice in achieving ethical and responsible corporate behaviour.

References and Suggestions for Further Reading

Blowfield, M. and Murray, A. (2008) *Corporate Social Responsibility: A Critical Introduction*, Oxford: Oxford University Press.

Burchell, J. (ed.) (2007) *The Corporate Social Responsibility Reader: Context and Perspectives*, London: Routledge.

Cramer, J. (2006) *Corporate Social Responsibility and Globalisation: An Action Plan for Business*, Sheffield: Greenleaf Publishing.

Crane, A. and Matten, D. (2006) *Business Ethics: Managing Corporate Citizenship and Sustainability in the Age of Globalisation*, 2nd edn, Oxford: Oxford University Press.

Crane, A., Matten, D. and Spence, L. (eds) (2008) *Corporate Social Responsibility: Readings and Cases in a Global Context*, London: Routledge.

Ferrell, O., Fraedrich, J. and Ferrell, L. (2007) *Business Ethics: Ethical Decision Making and Cases*, Boston, MA: Houghton Mifflin.

Fisher, C. and Lovell, A. (2008) *Business Ethics and Values: Individual, Corporate and International Perspectives*, 3rd edn, Harlow: Prentice Hall.

Freeman, R.E. (1984) *Strategic Management: A Stakeholder Approach*, Boston, MA: Pitman.

Friedman, M. (1962) *Capitalism and Freedom*, Chicago, IL: Chicago University Press.

Journal of Business Ethics – the leading journal on business ethics.

Keinert, C. (2008) *Corporate Social Responsibility as an International Strategy*, Heidelberg: Physica Verlag.

Trevino, L. (2007) *Managing Business Ethics: Straight Talk about How to Do It Right*, Hoboken, NJ: Wiley.

Werther, W. and Chandler, D. (2006) *Strategic Corporate Social Responsibility: Stakeholders in a Global Environment*, Thousand Oaks, CA: Sage.

Part III

Challenges for the Global Resource Base

Part III is based on the premise that as firms internationalize and production chains and markets grow more integrated across borders, enterprises will increasingly source their inputs from more diverse international factor markets. The chapters in Part III not only analyse traditional factors of production such as capital and labour from the perspective of globalization and international business but also treat information, the environment and natural resources such as energy as crucial factors. Issues raised in Part III range from the ethical (labour and the exploitation of resources) to concerns about the possibility of 'races to the bottom' (labour and the environment again) and the scarcity of resources (the environment and energy). A common theme in each chapter is how globalization and internationalization of the firm contributes to a reconsideration of the configuration of a firm's production and value chains and feeds into growing pressure for regulation above the level of the nation state.

Chapter 15

Labour Issues in the Global Economy

Most memorable . . . was the discovery (made by all the rich men in England at once) that women and children could work 25 hours a day in factories without many of them dying or becoming deformed. This was known as the Industrial Revolution.

W.C. Sellars and R.J. Yeatman *1066 and all That* (1930), ch. 49

LEARNING OBJECTIVES

This chapter will help you to:

■ demonstrate why and how labour market issues have become more controversial in a globally integrating market

■ identify the potential impact of international migration upon home and recipient countries

■ describe contrasting approaches to labour markets and their differing implications for policy

■ understand the concept of 'social dumping' and its implications

■ distinguish between voluntary and compulsory methods for dealing with labour standards issues in a global marketplace and assess their respective advantages and disadvantages

Issues affecting labour markets in both the developed and the developing world are at the heart of the backlash against globalization. Workers in developed countries and their union representatives allege that low-wage competition from developing countries reduces their real wages and pushes them out of jobs. There are two sources of this low wage competition. First, globalization, which is essentially about freer movement of the factors of production, should, in theory at least, increase the migration of labour, one of the main factors of production. An influx of labour in sufficient quantities will reduce or eliminate problems of labour and skills shortages and restrain wage increases.

Second, if labour does not move to where the jobs are, then jobs can, and frequently do, move to where the labour is. In relation to the second scenario, concerns were initially expressed about competition for developed country business in lower value-added industries like textiles but, with intensification of competition from the developing world across a wider range of sectors, these concerns have spread across the economy. Workers' and human rights groups in developed countries have also become energized about 'unfair' developing country labour standards relating to health and safety, working hours and other workplace rights such as non-discrimination and rights to form and join free trade unions. NGOs have also joined the debate as a result of the utilization of child and forced labour in certain countries and sectors. Not only are such standards and practices portrayed as threatening job security and wages in developed countries but they are also frequently presented as being ethically indefensible.

The addition of a potent moral dimension to what was already a lively economic debate and the growing clamour regarding corporate social responsibility (see Chapter 14) demand a response from companies that are unwittingly or otherwise seen to benefit from divergent labour standards. Developing countries themselves have responded vigorously to these complaints, accusing developed country interests of failing to understand the stark economic realities facing them and their population, of trying to impose values on them in a new form of imperialism – 'cultural imperialism' – and of trying to use concern about labour standards to impose restrictions on them in a form of 'disguised protectionism'.

This chapter highlights the interaction between globalization and labour. It begins by examining the issue of international labour migration in terms of its extent and of its impact upon both the origin and the destination countries. The chapter then discusses some of the issues that arise when it is jobs rather than workers which move. It concludes with a survey of how both the corporate sector and governments have responded to the concerns about labour standards.

MIGRATION OF LABOUR OR MIGRATION OF JOBS?

Globalization is essentially about the removal of barriers to the free movement of the factors of production. In recent decades, barriers to the movement of goods, services and capital have tumbled and cross-border movements of these factors have risen accordingly. However, the same cannot be said of labour. In 2005, about 3 per cent of the world's population were living in a country other than the one they were born in. This does not exceed migration rates of a century ago when immigration was positively encouraged by some receiving countries, nor is it particularly high.

The relative immobility of labour may be explained in part by cultural inertia (that is, the challenge of uprooting and relocating one's family great distances and to a location where the culture may seem alien or unwelcoming can act as an insurmountable obstacle to migration) and/or by the restrictions imposed by recipient states reluctant to welcome large numbers of foreign workers who, in their view, may destabilize the social and labour market status quo.

Notwithstanding the above, there are some signs that labour mobility, helped by lower travel and ICT costs, is increasing. However, it would be overstating it as yet to name this century 'the century of migration', as some have done. Table 15.1 sets out the importance of migration in different world regions. Europe contains the most migrants in absolute terms: much of this migration is intra-European migration resulting from the process of Europe integration and, most recently, from the European Union's eastward enlargement which, eventually, will result in free movement among its current 27 members. Europe is also the destination for migrants from outside the EU. Member states maintain tight restrictions against immigrants from outside the EU but the looming pressure on European labour markets from an ageing population could force a reconsideration of such policies and an easing of restrictions on both skilled and unskilled workers.

Asia is the second-largest area for migration in absolute terms but the migrant share of that region's population is relatively low. However, there are signs that migration in Asia is becoming more common (see Table 15.1). North America and Oceania (primarily Australia and New Zealand) are traditional migrant destinations, hence the relatively large share of migrants in their population. Indeed, in the mid-2000s, Australia, after a long period of relatively tight migration limits by its standards, has been actively seeking to increase its number of migrants to fill gaps in its labour markets. Both Africa and Latin America have seen their already low share of international migration fall further in the 2000s.

TABLE 15.1 Migrant Population by Region, 2005

	Number of migrants (millions)	Percentage of the area's population
Europe	64.1	8.8
Asia	53.3	1.4
North America	44.5	13.5
Africa	17.1	1.9
Latin America	6.7	1.2
Oceania	5.0	15.2

Source: International OM – *World Migration 2005.*

In short, international migrants are concentrated in relatively few countries and 60 percent of them live in the developed world. In 2005, the top 11 countries hosting international migrants were, in descending order, the US, Russia, Germany, Ukraine, France, Saudi Arabia, Canada, India, the UK, Spain and Australia. The attraction of these destinations in most cases was the perception that the host offered opportunities of a better life. However, in the case of Russia and Ukraine, their relativity high position on the list is the result of the redefinition of borders. Traditional countries of migration like Australia, Canada, New Zealand and the US continue to exercise an attraction for migrants but countries like Ireland, Italy, Norway and Portugal have also increased their attraction for migrants. Ireland is an interesting case in point. For many years, in view of the undynamic and depressed Irish economy, young Irish workers left their birthplace to seek their fortunes abroad. Given the transformation of Ireland into a fast-growing, prosperous economy, these labour flows were not only reversed but many non-Irish workers also began to see Ireland as a place of opportunity. This process has been halted somewhat by the financial and economic crisis: it remains to be seen whether Ireland will resume its headlong growth once the crisis is over.

What are the effects of international migration in general and more specifically on the country of origin and the recipient country? Overall, freer labour markets should increase global efficiency as labour in surplus areas moves to regions where labour is in short supply. However, the global economy is a long way from the perfectly functioning market that this would suggest. The impact of international labour migration on individual countries varies and can have both positive and negative effects.

In countries of origin, there could well be improvements in labour markets for those remaining. For a start, the reduction in the size of the labour force could increase real wages, thereby raising living standards. Migrant workers tend to retain strong ties with their country of origin and often remit a significant part of their earnings to their families remaining at home. In 2005, migrant remittances worldwide totalled $276 billion, three-quarters of which were destined for developing countries. In some countries, such as Jamaica, Jordan, Nicaragua and the Philippines, remittances can account for over 10 per cent of GDP. On the other hand, it has been argued that dependency on remittances and the loss of skilled personnel can act as a brake on countries' development prospects by reducing growth, productivity and tax revenue. Moreover, the quality of essential services can be hit as health service workers tend to figure largely in those migrating. The 'brain drain' effect can also make a country a less attractive destination for FDI. Some argue that international migration contributes to a 'brain gain' as well as a 'brain drain' in places like sub-Saharan Africa. The former arises because the prospect of migration and the improved living standards it promises provides an incentive to workers to improve their skills, thereby boosting the stock of human capital. Moreover, a proportion of migrants do return home, particularly if the conditions at home have improved, and in the process can further stimulate the economy by using knowledge, skills, technology and capital acquired abroad. The example of Ireland has already been referred to above but Ireland is not alone. Taiwan, for example, also benefited from returning nationals in the latter stages of the twentieth century and in the early stages of the twenty-first century.

In destination countries, migrant workers fulfil multiple roles: they provide skills where there have been shortages. Examples of this include the migration of IT experts to the US and, to a lesser extent, Europe, and of doctors and nurses trained in developing countries to developed countries generally. Migrant workers also take on jobs in agriculture or in low-paid service industries which citizens of the host country are reluctant to do. However, workers in destination countries are frequently suspicious of migrants: even if they retain their jobs, the fear is that the influx of new workers acts as a restraint on the growth of wages and salaries. A large influx of migrant workers can also place strain on the social infrastructure and increase social tensions resulting from cultural diversity. On the other hand, migrant workers generate additional wealth and tax revenue for their host country.

GLOBALIZATION AND LABOUR STANDARDS

Although, as the previous section shows, international labour migration is increasing, its still relatively low levels mean that it is the movement of jobs more than the movement of people that has so far attracted the most attention from anti-globalization protestors and has been a greater priority for MNEs. This has thrust the issue of differing national labour standards into the limelight: in a globalizing world, it is argued, companies can gain an unfair advantage by locating in countries with no or very low labour standards. This is known as 'social dumping' (see below) and has been a major contributor to the endeavours of almost all MNEs to demonstrate their commitment to socially responsible behaviour (see Chapter 14).

Concern about the international dimension of labour standards is not new. Indeed, the International Labour Organisation (ILO) was set up in 1919 to deal with these issues (see Box 15.1). However, driven by globalization and changing production patterns, the debate has become fiercer since the mid-1980s. Globalization has intensified competition within the corporate sector by reducing national and/or regional barriers to trade and by 'shrinking' the world through more efficient and rapid communications. Consequently, those differences that remain, including differences in labour price (wages) and quality in terms of levels of education and skill, take on a greater relative importance as a factor in competitiveness. Add the apparent ability of companies to relocate almost anywhere in the world and it is not difficult to understand why developed world workers feel vulnerable. However, interpretation of what has been happening with respect to labour standards is controversial and reflects a fundamental theoretical divide regarding approaches to the labour market. These opposing theoretical views also result in different policy prescriptions regarding labour standards and the interaction between trade and labour standards (see below).

Opposing Views of Labour Markets

The neo-classical view of labour markets, given a boost by the resurgence of neo-liberal economic thinking (see Chapter 2), reflects a preference for highly deregulated labour markets in which competition is based on low wage costs and highly mobile global capital. Neo-classicists regard labour market regulation as an unjustifiable interference in the operation of the market, although they do tend to make exceptions regarding the prohibition of forced labour, the worst excesses of child labour and basic health and safety regulation. Non-intervention, they argue, facilitates efficiency and enables employers to pay a market-clearing wage and to compete with low-cost suppliers, particularly from developing Asia, that are placing severe competitive pressures on developed world businesses. Neo-classicists also tend to argue for roll-back of the welfare state and social security benefits which they claim raise the 'reservation wage' – that is, the wage below which the unemployed will not seek employment.

It is important to note that neo-classicists are not arguing necessarily for low standards and wages (although this is often the outcome of their approach) but for the market to regulate these issues. In times of labour surplus, wages will be low. However, if people are in jobs and generating wealth, surplus labour will be absorbed and growth will deliver improvements in wages and living and working conditions. They point to the East Asian examples of Singapore, South Korea and Taiwan where this has occurred.

The neo-classical model gives employers a high degree of flexibility in terms of hiring, firing and wages. It also tends to result in adversarial industrial relations in developed economies and a denial of rights to join unions in developing countries. The neo-classical approach also discourages internal organizational flexibility based on multi-skilling, goodwill and the higher levels of productivity resulting from greater investment in the workforce.

In contrast, neo-Keynesians and neo-institutionalists view labour standards as key devices in securing economic and social progress. This ties in with the 'flexible specialization' view of the world. The phrase 'flexible specialization' was coined by Piore and Sabel (1984) as a reaction to the shift away from 'Fordist' mass production methods and 'Taylorist' traditions of work organization which were too inflexible in the face of new demands for customized and high-quality products. The intensification of competition arising from globalization also encouraged rapid changes in consumer tastes, necessitating more frequent product adaptations and shorter production runs leading to leaner production and greater emphasis on team work, multi-skilling, flexible deployment of labour and closer links between production and marketing. In other words, the new production techniques require a cooperative, skilled labour force that is both prepared and able to respond to rapidly changing consumer demands.

Failure to respect labour standards and a 'sweatshop mentality', according to this view, damages long-term competitiveness and economic efficiency prospects in developing countries. For example, child labour, employment discrimination and exceedingly long working hours hold back productivity gains and have a long-term negative impact on the development of human capital – one of the key factors in contemporary economic success.

This view of the workplace implies a variant of labour market flexibility in which regulation does not inhibit adjustment to changing markets but provides opportunities to reconcile legitimate claims of labour with efficiency. Labour market regulation exists to protect the workforce in terms of health and safety, job security and working conditions. Respect for workers' rights and welfare generates greater workplace flexibility by reducing the alienation frequently present in the neo-classical approach and by encouraging worker identification with the long-term well-being of the firm and generating trust between employer and employee. An emphasis on worker information and consultation and ongoing workplace training also accompanies this approach. Any rigidities in the model, it is claimed, are outweighed by long-run gains in terms of greater technical and organizational innovation. This approach has been criticized on the grounds that it is out of touch with the economic and social reality that persists in many developing countries.

Social Dumping

Central to the rise of labour market issues up the policy agenda is the issue of 'social dumping'. Social dumping occurs when companies relocate to regions with lower wage costs and less stringent labour regulations. This results in downward pressure on wages and standards in high-wage, high-standard countries as these countries strive to retain their businesses. Even the threat of the relocation of firms can lead to lower labour standards, so the argument goes. Furthermore, social security and welfare provision will also decline if it helps improve the ability of companies in higher cost countries to compete. This process is commonly referred to as a 'race to the bottom' – an argument that finds parallels in the debate about the alleged flight of companies to countries with a lower level, and hence lower associated cost burden, of environmental regulation (see Chapter 16).

At the heart of the social dumping debate is the assumption that lower wages and standards are somehow 'unfair'. Although there are several telling arguments against low wages and standards, it is fallacious to label all such differences as unfair. MNEs pay much lower wages in developing countries than they pay in their home country. However, this is not an appropriate benchmark. In practice, in many cases wages paid by MNEs in developing countries are frequently above the average for the host region.

At a fundamental level, wage variations reflect a number of factors, including local labour market conditions and relative levels of productivity and development. Many developing countries, for example, have surpluses of unskilled labour and levels of labour productivity that lag far behind those in developed countries. Once productivity is taken into account, it can be the case that unit wage costs are higher than those in developed countries, making differences in wages perfectly tenable (Golub, 1997). In other words, actual wage levels (including fringe benefits) are only part of the story concerning labour costs. Higher wage levels are perfectly sustainable in a competitive environment provided that they are offset by similarly high levels of labour productivity. The way out of the low-wage trap for workers in developing countries is therefore is higher levels of productivity.

Furthermore, at one level, labour is only one factor of production, albeit an important one, among several. From the developing country perspective, low labour costs constitute a key and legitimate part of their comparative advantage. Any effort to neutralize this advantage through trade sanctions or harmonization of standards is in itself unfair and a negation of the basic principles of free trade, principles promoted vigorously by the developed countries themselves.

Labour cost variations are only one of many reasons for relocation. The lower the share of labour costs in overall costs, for example, the less likely it is that social dumping will occur. In addition, as intimated above, wages and labour costs are only one part of the competitive equation. Among industrialized countries, those European countries with high levels of social protection and high labour standards, such as Germany and the Nordic states, are generally associated with high per capita income as a result of high productivity and other competitive advantages.

Issues for Developing Countries

Campaigns for higher labour standards are ostensibly directed towards improving the lot of workers in developing countries. Developing countries themselves have strongly opposed efforts by some developed countries and NGOs to link labour standards and trade through the introduction of a 'social clause' into trade agreements: that is, provisions within trade agreements requiring them to comply with a minimum level of standards.

Developing countries have marshalled various arguments to support their case. First, they argue that such initiatives are an unwarranted intrusion into their national sovereignty and that regulation of labour markets is purely a domestic issue. However, a key feature of globalization is greater international coordination or harmonization of traditionally domestic policies – that is, the shift from shallow to deep integration (see Chapter 1) – to keep pace with the realities of the marketplace. This does not necessarily imply total harmonization of labour standards but does point towards some minimum agreement on labour standards. In reality an international consensus has already been established in the form of the so-called 'core' ILO standards (see below) relating to freedom of association, the right to collective bargaining, minimum age of employment and equality of treatment and non-discrimination in the workplace. These standards have been signed, although not always ratified, by many developing countries.

Second, developing countries frequently argue that attempts by developed countries and NGOs to impose higher labour standards on them are inappropriate in terms of their level of development. In relation to child labour, for example, developing countries and their supporters often argue that child labour is not a response to low standards but to poverty, and that depriving children of the right to work threatens the survival prospects of these children and their families. According to this view, child labour will gradually disappear as prosperity rises and the most useful contribution of developed economies is to keep their markets open to goods from developing countries to enable this prosperity to occur. Opponents of this argument state that child labour perpetuates economic efficiency by standing in the way of the development of human capital and by depressing productivity, and that the most successful countries in terms of economic development (that is, the countries of East Asia) demonstrated a preference for sending their children to school rather than out to work.

Third, many of the arguments for higher labour standards are couched in moral terms. Developing countries argue that the developed countries are attempting to impose their own cultural and ethical values on them. However, in reality, it is only around issues like slavery that there is universal recognition about the undesirability of a particular practice. Apart from this exception there are a range of attitudes, opinions and values regarding the economy and the workplace that make the attainment of universal attitudes difficult if not impossible to achieve. Some argue, however, that there is a consensus around core ILO standards which has existed for some time.

Fourth, developing countries argue that the case for a social clause, although presented in high moral terms, is merely an attempt at 'disguised protectionism' by developed countries and their workers unable to compete in a more open marketplace. Differences in labour costs are not unfair and represent a perfectly legitimate trading advantage for developing countries. Attempts to deprive developing country producers of these advantages represent efforts to deprive them of their legitimate comparative advantage.

Issues for Business

Global commodity chain analysis (see Chapter 5) provides a useful way of thinking about the relationship between multinational enterprises and production operations in developing countries. In producer-driven chains, production is controlled by the MNE itself. Some of the production outside the home country will take place in wholly owned subsidiaries. The company will also be dependent on joint venture partners and component suppliers. Although these networks of suppliers are often complex, the relationship between the MNE and its partners and/or suppliers is usually close and subject to strict quality controls in view of the interdependence of the quality of components with the quality of the finished product, whether it be a computer, an aircraft or an item of heavy machinery.

Producer-driven chains are not immune from criticism about labour standards in developing countries. However, it is primarily buyer-driven chains (located predominantly in the textiles, clothing, footwear, toy and other relatively low-technology sectors) that have been the object of fierce criticism of the exploitation of the labour that is used to produce the final product. In this model, the production role of the multinational is limited (or non-existent) with production outsourced to subcontractors, sub-subcontractors or even sub-sub-subcontractors. This model, although not conforming to the stereotypical view of a multinational that owns and controls production through a cross-border network of subsidiaries and affiliates, does enhance the ability of such firms to exhibit footloose behaviour and change suppliers regularly and quickly, especially when price is the prime factor. Thus, according to their critics, such firms condone, indeed implicitly encourage, the continued exploitation of labour in terms of wages and working conditions by their suppliers.

The bad publicity arising from campaigns about their labour practices and the rise of the 'ethical consumer' with the threat of consumer boycotts has made it a priority for firms like Nike and The Gap, among many others, to make efforts to ensure that their outsourcing practices survive external scrutiny (see Case Study 15.2). The following section examines both voluntary responses to these concerns and more official efforts to ensure minimum standards and to make a link between labour standards and trade.

RESPONSES TO LABOUR STANDARD CONCERNS

The arguments for and against international labour standards are complex and controversial. Various options, each with their own benefits and drawbacks, exist for introducing international labour standards. In broad terms, these policies fall into two categories:

1. *Unofficial/voluntary standards*: that is, standards arising from corporate sector initiatives like product labelling and corporate conducts of conduct.
2. *Official/compulsory standards*: that is, laws and regulations introduced by nations, regional organizations or international institutions and which involve some form of sanction for non-compliance.

Voluntary Standards

Voluntary international labour standards are the result of corporate, industry and occasionally NGO initiatives. The attraction of voluntary standards for companies is that, provided the standards have sufficient credibility, they can help forestall tougher legislative standards. Even without the immediate threat of compulsory standards, voluntary standards are attractive for businesses striving to overcome bad publicity from the exposure of unsafe working conditions, sub-subsistence wages or the employment of child workers in their own overseas plants or the plants of their suppliers. Of course, there is a danger that measures taken to rectify the issues raised by such publicity will be widely seen as a cynical public relations attempt to convince the consumer that a particular company follows best practice without any change in substantive practice.

Product or Social Labelling

Product labels indicate that the production of a particular product complies with a declared set of standards relating, for example, to the environment or employment. Entitlement to such a label may come from government-organized schemes, through schemes organized by a coalition of interests including NGOs and industry interests (see Case Study 15.1) or may be the result of self-labelling by MNEs. Social labelling is particularly appropriate for final products where consumers have the practical option of engaging in ethical consumption rather than for intermediate products. Industries using social labelling include carpets, textiles, apparel, sporting goods and toys.

Schemes operate in a number of ways but the most credible ones entail adherence to specific standards, often standards resulting from ILO Conventions, and require external verification of compliance with the declared standards to ensure that claims about the product are not fraudulent. In this respect, product labelling has much in common with corporate codes of conduct.

Product labels are not problem-free. They are selective and rely on consumers' negative reactions to more emotive issues like child labour but are of less value in enforcing other core standards like freedom of association or collective bargaining. In practice, product labels also tend to apply only to conditions in export companies. This is unproblematic for those who support international labour standards on competitive grounds – that is, to ensure a more level playing field for companies. However, for proponents of international standards on ethical grounds, product labelling will do little for workers producing goods for domestic consumption. Indeed, product labels could indirectly result in a deterioration of the situation of affected groups, such as children who will be restricted to companies producing goods for the domestic market. In theory, if consumers in the domestic market oppose certain work practices, product labelling can be effective for non-export products. However, it is usually pressure from outside the producing country in question that results in the establishment of a product-labelling scheme. For the ethical supporter of product labels, implementation of ILO Conventions is a better option as they apply without discrimination both to exports and to goods sold domestically.

RUGMARK – Social Labelling in Action

RUGMARK was established in 1994 by Indian NGOs and international aid organizations to eliminate the use of child labour in the hand-knotted carpet industry. At the time of RUGMARK's foundation, an estimated almost one million children were employed in the industry worldwide, usually in poor conditions, for long hours and sometimes under terms of bondage. In its first ten years RUGMARK claims to have helped reduce child labour in the South Asian carpet industry by two-thirds, an achievement helped by Nepal joining the scheme in 1996 and Pakistan in 1998.

Membership of the RUGMARK scheme and the right to display the RUGMARK label on their product is open to carpet producers and exporters who undertake:

* not to employee children under 14 years of age;
* to pay a fair wage to adult weavers (that is, at least the minimum adult wage);
* to allow unannounced inspections of looms (all of which should be registered with RUGMARK) by RUGMARK;
* to notify RUGMARK of all sales of labelled carpets. Each labelled carpet is individually numbered and traceable back to the originating loom to protect against counterfeiting and fraudulent use of the label.

The costs of inspection and labelling are covered by the payment of a levy of 0.25 per cent of the export value of the carpet. In addition, importers of RUGMARK carpets pay at least 1 per cent of the import value of the carpets to RUGMARK to finance education and welfare programmes for former child workers and their families. These programmes are intended to deal with the potential problems of removing children from the workplace and placing them in the education system without addressing the issues of need which pushed them into the labour market in the first place.

Since 1995, RUGMARK has certified over four million carpets exported to North America and Europe. RUGMARK India is considering extending its scheme to the domestic market. In India, 269 exporters, representing 15 per cent of all registered carpet looms, are licensed and inspected by RUGMARK which carries out over 16,000 loom inspections per annum. In Nepal, over 500 manufacturers, accounting for 70 per cent of all Nepalese carpet exports, are inspected by RUGMARK and in Pakistan over 21,000 looms are registered with RUGMARK. If underage children are found working on the looms, the loom owner loses the right to use the RUGMARK label and the children are offered the opportunity to attend school. In total, RUGMARK runs 13 schools and rehabilitation centres and is in partnership with other organizations to support children's education.

For carpet manufacturers, the RUGMARK scheme and its independent verification of working conditions gives them credibility with consumers about claims that their products were made without the use of child labour. RUGMARK also lowers the cost of inspections: without a collective scheme, carpet manufacturers would have to engage their own inspectors to carry out inspections of looms – at higher cost and with lower credibility in the eyes of consumers.

In the importing countries, most of which are in North America and Europe, RUGMARK's activities are directed towards raising public awareness of RUGMARK and the meaning of the RUGMARK label. From the perspective of consumers, RUGMARK gives them the confidence that they can purchase carpets made without the exploitation of child labour.

Like most schemes, RUGMARK is not without its critics.* There are practical concerns that, even though RUGMARK makes every effort to ensure the random nature of its inspections, the structure of the industry, which ranges from single looms in isolated rural villages to small to medium-scale factories, makes the process of inspection hit and miss. Indeed, critics claim that this makes it impossible to give child-free guarantees. Moreover, carpet manufacturers outside the RUGMARK scheme who claim that they operate without child labour argue that RUGMARK discriminates against them.

Note: * In *India in Slow Motion* (2002, Penguin Books), one of the subjects investigated by the journalist Mark Tully is RUGMARK and India's carpet industry. The chapter in question has an open-minded approach to the problems of the eradication of child labour in this industry and highlights practical difficulties encountered by RUGMARK in achieving its objectives.

CASE STUDY QUESTIONS

1. Identify and evaluate the strong and weak points of RUGMARK's approach.

2. Find other examples of product or social labelling and critically assess them.

3. RUGMARK is essentially a voluntary approach involving NGOs and the industry to eradicate an employment practice which is widely considered undesirable. Should governments be taking a more active role? What are the relative benefits and disadvantages of voluntary initiatives and of government-led schemes and/or laws?

Corporate Codes of Conduct

Globalization and the emergence of global supply chains have provided opportunities for MNEs to rationalize their production and raise their efficiency levels but MNEs have also been left open to allegations about child labour, unsafe working conditions and low wages. Firms that outsource much of their production to lower cost locations in the developing countries are particularly vulnerable to such allegations. The initial response to the controversy over labour standards was to establish corporate and supplier compliance with national laws and regulations. However, by the 1990s, in response to rising concerns about corporate social responsibility and socially responsible investment, almost all multinational enterprises have developed their own codes of conduct governing general corporate behaviour and treatment of the workforce in particular. Some critics argue that corporate codes of conduct serve to prevent more thorough official intervention at a national, regional or multinational level. Others suggest that, rather than bypassing the state, corporate codes of conduct offer a possibility of higher labour standards in developing countries which may not have sufficient capacity themselves to enforce their own labour laws.

Corporate codes of conduct take many forms and have generated many heated debates about their function and effectiveness. Case Study 15.2 discusses the campaigns fought against NIKE about the conditions in its suppliers' factories and, in particular, Nike's response in terms of its own code of conduct. Whatever the specific details of a code, they need to satisfy a number of conditions in order to be considered equitable and credible. Notably:

■ The contents of the code must be clearly worded and, at a minimum, comply with core ILO standards.

- The company adopting the code must be committed to it and provide the resources to ensure its implementation, including training, information systems for monitoring and compliance and staff to implement the procedures.
- Knowledge of the code throughout the organization is essential to its implementation: in particular employees of the firm and its subcontractors and suppliers must know the contents of the code and a reporting system must be established that enables workers to report infringements without fear of reprisals.
- The code should ideally be subject to verification by independent assessors who have access to the site unannounced at any time – however, this has caused problems in some cases (see Case Study 15.2).

CASE STUDY 15.2

Nike – Villain or CSR Leader?

In the early 1990s, Nike faced allegations of low wages, poor working conditions and infringements of basic human rights from a variety of sources. Although not the only company to be the subject of such campaigns (The Gap, Puma, Adidas and Benetton are only some of the other companies targeted by NGOs), Nike bore the brunt of the criticisms and appeared to become the symbol of all that was bad in the area of the treatment of labour.

Nike was founded in 1964 and operated initially as a distributor for a Japanese shoe manufacturer. In fiscal year 2007, Nike's turnover reached $16.3 billion and the company was a leading player, not only in the global sports footwear market but also in sports apparel and equipment. Nike operates a business model in which virtually all its products are manufactured by independent contractors, most of whom are located in emerging markets. The company directly employs only about 25,000 people but its products are made by almost 700 contract companies employing almost 800,000 people in 52 countries worldwide. It is this business model, shared with many other labour-intensive, low-technology manufacturing companies based in the developed world, which gives it only indirect control in the factories manufacturing its products that

makes Nike vulnerable to allegations over the treatment of the workers (the majority of whom are women between the ages of 18 and 24) who make its products (Table 15.2).

Initially, Nike refused to accept any responsibility for the labour standards in companies making its products, arguing that the workers in question were not Nike employees. However, the pressure on it intensified and by 1992 Nike had drawn up a code of conduct that required its suppliers to observe basic labour and environmental standards. Potential suppliers were required to sign the code and to display it in its factories. This action was considered inadequate by campaigners who maintained that the code reflected minimal standards only, was not properly enforced and that, given the low literacy levels among the employees of Nike's contractors, the efficacy of informing workers of their rights by displaying them in factories was seriously undermined.

Individual cases of alleged abuses of labour standards continued to dog Nike throughout the 1990s. High-profile cases included, among others, the use of child labour in Pakistan to produce footballs, child labour in Cambodia, underpaid workers in Indonesia, poor working conditions and wages in China and environmental hazards in contracted factories in Vietnam. Confronted with

TABLE 15.2 Nike Contract Factories by Region and Number of Employees, May 2006

Region	Number of contract factories	Number of contract employees
Americas	126	49,734
Europe, Middle East Africa	81	29,858
North Asia	285	422,255
South Asia	195	270,254
Total	687	772,101

Source: FY 05–06 Nike Corporate Responsibility Report.

this bad publicity and the threat of and actual consumer boycotts of its products, Nike has, down the years, developed a complex and comprehensive system of monitoring to try to ensure that its contracting factories comply with minimum standards. Nike continues to be scrutinized by activists and campaigners who view the ongoing problems in Nike contract factories as evidence that Nike's policies serve public relations purposes only. An alternative view of labour standards issues is that, although corporate codes of conduct have a role to play, their effectiveness can be restrained by many other factors.

Early examples of Nike measures to improve conditions in its contracted factories include the raising of the minimum age in 1998 for footwear factory workers to 18 and for all other workers in apparel and equipment to 16. Nike also insists that all footwear suppliers adopt the US Occupational Safety and Health Administration (OHSA) standards for indoor air quality. Despite these regulations, Nike has acknowledged that breaches of its code occur and enforcement is made difficult in some countries where records of birth are inadequate or can be forged and sold for minimal amounts.

Nike now has a well-developed set of tools to monitor conditions in its contracted factories. Its two main tools include:

* Management Audit Verification (MAV) which audits performance in the areas of working hours; wages, benefits, grievance systems and freedom of association. Code Leadership Standards (CLS) or local labour laws and regulations, whichever are the strictest, act as benchmarks. CLS expands on Nike's Code of Conduct and cover 13 management standards and 38 environment, health and safety standards.
* Environment, Safety and Health (ESH) audits, the focus of which is clear from its name and which uses CLS as its benchmark.

Nike staff conduct detailed MAV and ESH audits while the contract manufacturers themselves carry out Safety, Health, Attitude, People and Environment (SHAPE) assessments. The MAV, ESH and SHAPE audit tools have also been published for the purpose of encouraging debate and transparency. Collaboration with the Fair Labour Association (FLA) is also under development. Following completion of the various audits, a factory is allocated a grade A–D in relation to its performance on environment, health and safety and management issues. Grade A, for example, denotes full ESH compliance and demonstration of leadership and best practice and only isolated and minor infringements of management standards, whereas Grade D indicates non-compliance with both ESH and management standards, deliberate misleading of auditors and a general unwillingness or inability to comply.

As Nike's experience of monitoring develops, so it enters new phases. Nike itself describes its first phase from 1996 to 2000 as establishing a presence in which the initial standards were set and the CSR function was established both within the company and with major business partners. At this stage, much of the activity was 'fire-fighting' – that is, responding to specific and damaging allegations about conditions in Nike contracted factories. The second phase which, according to Nike, ran from 2001 to 2006, was essentially about developing the tools to monitor the standards (that is, MAV and ESH), creating transparency and the rating system and applying its tools more systematically. The third stage, which runs from 2006 to 2010, is about 'transformation'. Nike maintains that its monitoring tools help it identify issues and problems but do not shed light on how to resolve them. The emphasis in this third phase of measures is to shift to a focus on the root cause of problems and on how to deliver systemic change. This involves a change from policing and fire-fighting to coaching and increasing the capacity of partners to deal with corporate responsibility issues and to engage its partners in the process. Overall, the intention is to 'drive systemic change across the supply chain'.

Nike maintains that the key to achieving success in its corporate responsibility strategy is to understand and acknowledge the role of each of the key stakeholders – the government, industry, civil society, the consumer, factory management and the buyer (Nike). The company maintains, and with some justification, that where the rule of law is weak, transparency is poor and civil society is limited, contract factories are less likely to comply with its standards. Given that many Nike factories, and those of its competitors, are located in such countries, some campaigners argue that Nike should not contract in such countries. Others argue that by sourcing in such countries, companies like Nike can influence conditions and possibly even promote

change. Nike itself argues that its capacity to instil change varies depending on the conditions in a particular country and usually occurs as a result of a mixture of factors, including industry collaborations, multi-stakeholder initiatives, strong national and international civil society and consumer interest.

A key part of Nike's strategy is the switch to a lean manufacturing system. Traditionally, workers in the apparel and related industries focus on one task only and the emphasis is on reaping economies of scale through the production of large batches on long assembly lines. Increasingly, customers are demanding more choice and variety and more frequent and smaller deliveries, ideally at the same or lower cost. This shift requires a different way of working (see above section on opposing view of labour markets) in which workers are trained for multiple tasks, operate in teams and are empowered/trusted to manage the production process and respond to issues of quality. Nike's aim is to have 90 per cent of its footwear produced on lean production lines by 2011 (it had achieved 40 per cent by 2007) and began implementing lean production techniques in half its contract apparel factories by 2007.

In addition to its ongoing systemic development of its CSR capabilities in the labour standards field, Nike has also taken the lead in presenting new measures. In its 2005 Corporate Responsibility Report, Nike became the first big company in the industry to disclose the names and locations of its suppliers, a list which is updated at least once a year. Under pressure to do so for many years, Nike had resisted the temptation to disclose the identity of its suppliers on the grounds that it could undermine commercial secrecy and would be used by NGOs and other campaigners as an opportunity to make further attacks on the company. Although still concerned about issues of competitive risk, Nike declared itself willing to do so to 'move the industry forward in addressing some of these endemic issues' – that is, the wide range of sweatshop allegations levelled at it and its competitors.

Overall, Nike has been proactive in developing its CSR policy, which remains a work in progress. Critics say that Nike has only done so because it has been forced to, and this may indeed be the case, and many infringements of its Code of Conduct occur. Both claims may indeed be true and at times Nike may have been guilty of a concern more with public relations than with the fundamental issues of conditions in its suppliers. However, Nike does acknowledge that these infringements occur. The important point is what it does about them when they are exposed, and most disclosures in the mid-2000s onward have occurred as a resulted of reporting under Nike's CSR policies.

CASE STUDY QUESTIONS

1. What are the problems endemic for companies using a business model like Nike's in ensuring that basic labour standards are respected?

2. Nike and others are often accused of paying unfair wages. What factors would you consider in determining what constitutes a fair wage in a factory located in China or Vietnam?

3. Nike sees a shift to lean manufacturing as bringing benefits both to itself and to employees in its contracted factories. Why does Nike make these claims and are these claims justified?

4. Discuss whether Nike's actions address the allegations made against it in relation to its labour standards or merely take the sting out of them.

The application of such codes can enhance internal governance and facilitate internal management across geographically dispersed sites. There is some evidence to show that real commercial benefits can be gained from the proper application of fair and equitable labour standards, although more widespread research needs to be done on this. Provided the code of conduct adopted by a firm has external credibility, it can both protect and enhance a firm's reputation. In October 2007, The Gap withdrew a line of children's clothing following allegations of forced child labour by Indian subcontractors. This follows The Gap's policy of stopping working with 23 factories in 2006 after its own monitoring efforts had uncovered infringements of its child labour policy. Although embarrassing for The Gap, the company's immediate response to the revelations and its own proactive stance to monitoring child labour served to minimize the damage to its reputation.

Some industries have developed their own codes. An important example of such a code is the Electronic Industry Code of Conduct (EICC) which was launched in 2004. The code covers labour standards, health and safety, environmental issues and business ethics, and was heavily influenced by the Universal Declaration of Human Rights, Social Accountability International (see below) and the Ethical Trading Initiative. EICC membership includes some of the world's biggest electronics and related companies such as Adobe, Apple, Cisco, Dell, Flextronics, Hewlett Packard, IBM, Intel, Lenovo, Kodak, Lexmark, Microsoft, Philips, Seagate, Sony, Sun Microsystems and Xerox. The code itself is intended as a total supply chain initiative and all participants must, as a minimum, require their next-tier suppliers to implement it. The code's key provisions are:

- no forced, bonded or involuntary prison labour;
- no person to be employed under the age of 15 (or 14 where the law of the country permits) or under the age of compulsory education – which ever is the greatest;
- working hours not to exceed those in national law and should not exceed 60 hours a week, including overtime, unless emergency or unusual situations prevail;
- workers to receive at least one day off in seven.
- wages to comply with all laws relating to the minimum wage, overtime and legally mandated benefit;
- no wage deductions on disciplinary grounds permitted;
- no harsh and inhumane treatment or threat of such treatment;
- no discrimination on the grounds of race, colour, age, gender, sexual orientation, ethnicity, disability, pregnancy, religion, political affiliation, union membership or marital status;
- workers' rights to join unions and to communicate with management about working conditions to be respected.

In addition, a range of health and safety standards are included in the code and were developed using OHSAS 18001 (an international occupational health and safety management system) and ILO Guidelines on Occupational Health and Safety as a reference point.

Framework codes have also been developed by NGOs and charitable organizations and applied by MNEs. For example, Social Accountability International, founded in New York in 1997, is a charitable human rights organization with a mission to work for the improvement of workplace conditions by developing and implementing socially responsible standards. To this end, it has developed SA8000, a uniform auditable standard intended to ensure ethical conditions in the workplace throughout global supply chains. SA8000 employs a third party verification system to provide clarity, consistency and guidance to the multitude of individual corporate codes of conduct springing up. SA8000 is based on international norms defined in ILO Conventions, the UN Convention on the Rights of the Child and the Universal Declaration of Human Rights. It uses proven ISO auditing techniques, specifies corrective and preventive actions and encourages continuous improvement, setting specific performance requirements with minimum requirements. It also contains a complaints and appeals mechanism to bring forward issues of non-compliance at certified facilities. By 2007, there were 1,038 facilities certified as complying with SA8000 in 55 countries and industries. Its signatories include cosmetics company Avon Products, Dole Food, Otto Versand (the largest catalogue retailer in the world) and Toys R Us.

Official/Compulsory Standards

Much of the debate about labour standards is focused on the increasing practice of including 'social clauses' in trade agreements: that is, the provision within trade agreements for the withdrawal of trade preferences or the imposition of trade sanctions if specified labour standards are not respected. The most high-profile debate has been controversy about the inclusion of a social clause within WTO agreements (see below). However, there are various examples of individual countries including social clauses within bilateral trade agreements or unilaterally.

Social clauses potentially satisfy both main sets of advocates of international trade standards. Social clauses provide those advocating their introduction on competitiveness grounds with a mechanism whereby they can offset what they perceive as 'unfair' competitive advantages. However, as indicated above, what constitutes a legitimate competitive advantage and what is an unfair advantage is open to interpretation. Social clauses also enable those favouring their introduction on moral grounds to impose a specific set of ethical values. Debate also rages about whether there are moral values around which a consensus can develop to form the basis of social clauses within international trade agreements. Some of these controversies are aired above. However, practical outcomes in terms of bilateral, regional and multilateral agreements are discussed below.

Regional Standards

Regional economic integration is well underway in many parts of the world (see Chapter 3): regional integration, as with globalization, is essentially about reducing barriers to trade and unifying markets. Inevitably, remaining barriers take on much greater relative importance in the eyes of group members, giving rise to fears and charges of social dumping from members with higher labour market standards. Given the more ambitious and advanced stage of integration within the EU, it is not surprising that the issue of differential labour standards arose early within the EU and that it has developed its own solutions. Other regional integration initiatives like NAFTA (see below), Mercosur and the South African Development Community (SADC) have adopted their own social provisions that incorporate the ILO's core labour standards.

The labour standards issue in the EU manifested itself around competitiveness and social dumping concerns. These concerns were voiced most loudly at the end of the 1980s at the height of the construction of the Single European Market (SEM). In order to implement the SEM, the EU amended its Treaties by means of the Single European Act (SEA). Article 118A of the SEA required member states to pay particular attention to the harmonization of workplace health and safety standards while maintaining improvements already made. In other words, Article 118A, reinforced by 100A, tried to ensure that the SEM would not result in a choice between general lowering of workplace health and safety standards (the race to the bottom) and loss of jobs.

Nevertheless, the SEA did not dispel fears of social dumping. The European Commission chose to combat these fears via the Community Charter of the Fundamental Social Rights of Workers, signed by 11 out of the then 12 member states (the exception being the United Kingdom) in December 1989. The Social Charter rights included freedom of movement; employment and remuneration; improvement of living and working conditions; social protection; freedom of association and collective bargaining; training; equal treatment for men and women; worker participation, information and consultation; workplace health and safety; protection of children and adolescents; and the elderly and the disabled. The Charter was not a legally binding document but a 'solemn declaration' that established basic minimum rights in the workplace. These minimum rights served both as a defence against alleged social dumping and responded to concerns about an over-preoccupation within the SEM programme with the priorities of business. The election of the Labour government in the UK in 1997 ended the EU schism on labour standards. Almost the first act of the new government was to sign the Social Charter, an act that facilitated the incorporation of this Social

Charter, as expressed in the Social Protocol in the Maastricht Treaty, into the main body of the EU Treaties at the Amsterdam Council in June 1997.

The debate over the Social Charter generated a lot of hot air over very little. It has resulted in relatively little change in labour market standards within Europe, even within the UK, where several labour standards were lower than in other member states. In practice, differences in labour standards among EU states were not great compared to differences in standards between EU members and non-members and there was no systematic evidence of sustained social dumping occurring within Europe.

Given the much wider differences in labour standards among Canada, Mexico and the US than in the EU, the North American Free Trade Area (NAFTA), although much less ambitious than the EU in terms of its integration objectives, posed greater labour standards challenges. US and Canadian workers were concerned that companies would migrate to Mexico to take advantage of cheaper labour whose basic rights were not respected. This fear was succinctly expressed by one-time US presidential candidate Ross Perot when he declared, 'that sucking sound you hear is the sound of US jobs going to Mexico'. Freedom of movement of firms (not mirrored by freedom of movement of workers) in combination with the maquiladora system in which multinational firms are given additional investment incentives would, it was feared, destroy US and Canadian jobs, depress wages and perpetuate substandard employment conditions and the denial of basic rights for Mexican workers.

NAFTA came into force on 1 January 1993. Labour issues were not originally included but, after President Clinton succeeded President Bush, the US negotiated the North American Agreement on Labour Cooperation (NAALC), often referred to as NAFTA's 'labour side agreement'. The NAALC does not propose any specific labour standards or harmonization of standards: each signatory retains the right to establish its own domestic labour standards and is obliged to comply with and enforce them. There is an obligation to 'provide for high labour standards, consistent with high quality and high productivity workplaces' but there is no definition of what constitutes these high standards.

Under the terms of the NAALC, the US, Mexico and Canada have committed themselves to promoting the following 11 labour principles:

1. freedom of association and the right to organize
2. the right to collective bargaining
3. the right to strike
4. prohibition of forced labour
5. workplace protection for children and young people
6. minimum employment standards
7. elimination of employment discrimination
8. equal pay for men and women
9. prevention of occupational injuries
10. compensation in the event of occupational injuries and illnesses
11. protection of migrant workers.

At first sight, the NAALC offers substantial promise for upholding basic labour principles and standards within a diverse trading area. However, the agreement's operation has left many hopes for improvements unfulfilled, not only in Mexico but in Canada and the US where there are alleged infringements of the basic right to organize. The major problems with NAALC are:

- A lack of agreement or compulsion regarding core labour standards. The NAALC talks of the provision of high standards but does not define them.
- The weak response to non-compliance with NAALC principles. For most infringements, recourse to ministerial consultation is the only course of action available. It is only violations of the child labour, minimum employment standards and health and safety principles that can lead to arbitration and sanctions.
- The complexity, cost and protractedness of the submission of a complaint. Critics contrast the NAALC process with the speedier processes, which also offer redress for violations, available to investors and defenders of intellectual property rights within NAFTA's dispute settlement procedure.

Bilateral Standards

Since their first tentative use in the 1980s, social clauses have become the norm in many regional and trade agreements. The European Union and the US currently routinely include social clauses in their bilateral trade agreements. In part, the popularity of these clauses is a response to the failure to include such provisions in multilateral negotiations (see below). Social clauses in bilateral agreements subject developing countries to the type of external pressure on labour standards that they have consistently resisted at a multilateral level. Indeed, it has proved more difficult for them to resist this pressure bilaterally than multilaterally.

As far back as 1984, the US incorporated a social clause in its Generalized System of Preferences (GSP), a scheme run by many developed countries whereby developing countries are granted trade preferences. This clause made compliance with certain criteria mandatory before developing countries were granted eligibility for GSP membership. For example, the US administration had to determine whether a country 'has taken or is taking steps to afford workers in that country (including in the free trade zones) internationally recognized worker rights'. The 1988 Trade Act, for example, defined the denial of internationally recognized workers' rights as an unreasonable trade practice and therefore potentially subject to trade sanctions, thereby giving the US government a generic right to act against alleged infringements of basic labour rights by any of its trading partners. The US, for example, excluded Swaziland from benefits under the African Growth and Opportunities Act (AGOA) and threatened to exclude it from the GSP unless it removed labour regulations that the US regarded as oppressive, which Swaziland duly did.

From 1993, a period in which US involvement in bilateral trade agreements increased in scope, social clauses have been included in all bilateral and regional trade agreements negotiated by the US. Completed agreements include NAFTA (see above), Chile, Jordan, Morocco, Singapore and Bahrain. The 2000 US Trade and Development Act encompassed AGOA and the US–Caribbean Trade Partnership Act (CBTPA), both of which contained clauses not only requiring the agreement's beneficiaries to respect core ILO standards regarding rights to organize and collective bargaining but also to establish minimum wage and maximum working hours and to ban the use of forced labour. This Act developed the provisions of the earlier Caribbean Basin Initiative that contained eligibility criteria relating to working conditions. The troubled multilateral WTO talks have also encouraged the US to look more towards bilateral trade agreements. After the relatively unsuccessful Cancun Ministerial in 2003, the US Trade Representative Robert Zoellick reportedly said, 'As WTO members ponder the future, the US will not wait: we will move towards free trade with can-do countries'. As such, the US is exploring possible agreements with Australia, South Korea, countries in Central America and with Latin American countries within the context of the Free Trade Area of the Americas.

The EU has also embraced social clauses in its trade agreements. Unlike the US, whose approach is based more on sanctions or the threat of sanctions, the EU's approach is to give incentives to partner countries to respect internationally recognized standards. Since 1998, the EU's GSP scheme has granted additional preferences to countries applying the ILO's core labour standards (see Box 15.1). In 2004, for example, the European Commission granted additional benefits to Sri Lanka under its GSP scheme on the grounds that it was making good progress towards full compliance with ILO core standards. However, on two occasions, the EU has withdrawn trade preferences owing to violations of these standards. In 1997, it removed Myanmar's access to its GSP schemes owing to the persistence of forced labour practices, and in June 2007 the EU suspended GSP preferences that had been extended to Belarus on the basis that Belarus flouted core standards on the freedom of association. In both cases in which it has taken sanctions against a trading partner for infringement of core labour standards, the EU has been embroiled in broader debates with the countries in question – Myanmar and Belarus – about democracy, the rule of law, fair elections and other related issues.

In 2001, the European Commission adopted a strategy proposing action at European and international levels to support the effective application of core labour standards globally. The strategy requires that the EU integrates core labour standards into its development policy and includes them in its bilateral agreements with third countries. Since then, the EU has systematically included a social clause in its bilateral agreements. Indeed, the EU's 1999 Agreement with South Africa included a commitment to ILO core standards and pre-dated the systematic policy change. Subsequently, the Cotonou partnership agreements with the African, Pacific and Caribbean and the Association Agreement with Chile have incorporated a social clause. The EU has also signalled its intent to make social clauses an integral part of ongoing and future bilateral or regional negotiations.

Multilateral Standards

The prospect of developing a multilateral framework to protect labour standards within the context of international trade goes back many years and has always been controversial. The 1948 Havana Charter (see Chapter 3) contained an explicit link between labour and trade, requiring members to take measures against 'unfair labour conditions'. This was too much for the US which refused to ratify the Charter, leaving the transition measure, the GATT, as the main regulator of international trade for almost 50 years. GATT was much weaker on this issue but Article XX, the general exception clause, did allow for the introduction of restrictions relating to the products of prison labour.

The issue has not made much progress at the multilateral level, a factor which helps explain the enthusiasm for 'social clauses' in bilateral trade agreements. Given its enhanced enforcement mechanisms, the WTO has become a preferred institution for many countries and NGOs lobbying to develop the trade–labour standards link. Accordingly, at the 1996 Singapore WTO Ministerial, the

US, France and a number of other developed countries were keen to push the link but the inclusion of labour standards within the WTO's mandate was opposed by the developing countries and other developed countries, including the UK. The Singapore Declaration therefore supported the continuation of the status quo:

> We renew our commitment to the observance of internationally recognised core labour standards. The International Labour Organisation (ILO) is the competent body to set and deal with these standards, and we affirm our support for its work in promoting them. . . . We reject the use of labour standards for protectionist purposes, and agree that the comparative advantages of countries, particularly low-wage developing countries, must in no way be put into question. In this regard, we note that the WTO and ILO Secretariat will continue their existing collaboration.

Nevertheless, the issue of trade and labour continued to dog the WTO. Indeed, it was President Clinton's championing of the trade–labour standard link immediately prior to the 1999 Seattle Ministerial that had been intended to launch the next round of multilateral talks that made a major contribution to the failure of the Ministerial. However, in the two years between the failure at Seattle and the Doha Ministerial which belatedly did what Seattle had intended, the heat appeared to have been taken out of the labour standards debate from the WTO viewpoint and the Doha Declaration took no new initiatives in this area, merely reaffirming the above declaration made on this issue at Singapore.

The lack of any push to place labour rights on the agenda is partially a function of the more business-friendly orientation of the Bush administration which came to power between the two Singapore and Doha Ministerials and partially a reflection of a negotiating strategy that wishes to give more weight to the concerns of developing countries. Developing countries generally oppose the introduction of labour issues into the WTO, a move that they regard as 'disguised protectionism' and delay improvements in economic growth, which they argue increases labour standards in the longer term. In the absence of the WTO taking on a bigger role in labour matters, the ILO remains the main focus for multilateral action on labour standards (see Box 15.1).

Box 15.1 The International Labour Organisation (ILO)

The International Labour Organisation (ILO) was created as long ago as 1919. As such, it is one of the world's oldest international organizations and is the only surviving major creation of the First World War peace settlement and the associated League of Nations machinery. Motivations underpinning the founding of the ILO continue to be relevant, including:

- ■ *Humanitarian*: the Preamble to the ILO's Constitution notes that 'conditions of labour exist involving . . . injustice, hardship and privation to large numbers of people' and speaks of 'sentiments of justice and humanity' as part of the rationale behind the foundation of the organization. Given contemporary reports of substandard health, safety and general working conditions and the widespread existence of child and forced labour, this reason for the foundation of the ILO remains current.

■ *Political*: the Preamble notes that injustice produces 'unrest so great that the peace and harmony of the world are imperilled', implying that without improvement in working conditions for workers serious social unrest would result. Although, at the beginning of the twenty-first century, there have so far been no upheavals like the 1917 Russian Revolution which gave rise to the above fears of social unrest, persistent social injustice is commonly regarded as a source of political instability with potential to spill over into regional instability.

■ *Economic*: the ILO Preamble notes that 'the failure of any nation to adopt humane conditions is an obstacle in the way of other nations which desire to improve the conditions in their countries'. In other words, low labour standards elsewhere place countries adopting social reform at a competitive disadvantage because of the effects on their cost of production. In short, the concepts of the 'race to the bottom' and 'social dumping' were not unknown in 1919.

■ *Development*: this motivation reflects a view that the retention of low labour standards locks a country into reliance on low costs and productivity and hence into a cycle of poverty. A country's development needs are best served, according to this view, by upgrading the quality of labour input through higher standards rather than by suppressing it through lower standards.

In 1944, 41 countries met in Philadelphia and agreed the Philadelphia Declaration which still comprises the Organisation's main aims and objectives. The Declaration confirms the ILO's original general principles while both spelling them out in more detail and broadening standard setting to cover more general but related social policy and human and civil rights issues. In 1946, the ILO became the first specialized agency of the United Nations, and by 2007 it had 181 members.

The Role of the ILO

The ILO has three main roles:

1. The formulation of minimum standards of basic labour rights: these cover freedom of association, the right to organize, collective bargaining, the abolition of forced labour, equality of opportunity, non-discrimination at the workplace, health and safety and basic working conditions.
2. Technical assistance for vocational training and rehabilitation, employment policy, labour administration, labour law and industrial relations, working conditions, management development, cooperatives, social security, labour statistics and occupational health and safety.
3. Promotion of the development of independent employers' and workers' organizations and the provision of training and advisory services to these organizations.

Core ILO Standards

Corporate codes of conduct, codes of conduct developed by NGOs, trade agreements and so on often include the requirement to comply with core ILO standards, of which there are four:

1. freedom of association and the effective recognition of the right to collective bargaining;
2. elimination of all forms of forced or compulsory labour;
3. effective abolition of child labour;
4. elimination of discrimination in employment.

In order to operationalize these core standards, the following eight ILO conventions have been declared fundamental to the rights of human beings at work and should be implemented and ratified by all ILO members:

1. Freedom of Association and Protection of the Right to Organise Convention, 1948 (No 87) – gives workers the absolute right to form and join independent trade unions;
2. Right to Organise and Collective Bargaining Convention, 1949 (No 98) – allows workers to organize union activities without threat of dismissal or action short of dismissal and protects their right to promote their interests via collective bargaining;
3. Forced Labour Convention, 1930 (No 29) – not allowed under any circumstances;
4. Abolition of Forced Labour Convention, 1957 (No 105);
5. Discrimination (Employment and Occupation) Convention, 1958 (No 111) – requires states to introduce policies to eliminate workplace discrimination on the grounds of race, colour, sex, religion, political opinion, nationality or social origin;
6. Equal Remuneration Convention, 1951 (No 100) – establishes the principle of equal pay for men and women for work of equal value;
7. Minimum Age Convention, 1973 (No 138) – the minimum age for employment must not be below the age for compulsory schooling and should not be below the age of 15;
8. Worst Forms of Child Labour Convention, 1999 (No 182) – designed to eliminate bonded and other forms of slavery; the recruitment of children for armed conflict, prostitution, illicit activities and any other activity that could harm the health, safety or morals of a child.

CONCLUSION

Globalization and labour are closely linked. In an increasingly interdependent world with reducing barriers to cross-border transaction, labour migration, although showing signs of increase, is relatively limited. Indeed, it is often easier for firms to move production to workers in new locations rather than to seek to attract workers to their existing operations. This has created its own controversies and challenges with allegations of 'unfair' competition and sweatshop labour being levelled at many multinationals operating in developing countries.

There is no lobby for low labour standards worldwide but low labour standards are frequently the outcome of the current business environment. However, there is a great deal of controversy about what, if anything, should be done about them. Supporters of higher standards argue that even the threat of investment in a country with lower standards gives rise to lower standards in higher standard countries. Developing countries argue that they are not in favour of child labour and other examples of low labour standards but that economic reality means that preventing children from working can condemn them and their families to starvation. The best way to end these poor standards is, so the argument goes, through higher growth levels.

In the interim, corporations are developing codes of conduct for themselves and their suppliers and participating in product and social labelling schemes. Social clauses are being introduced in bilateral trade agreements in an attempt to ensure a minimum level of standards but their inclusion in multilateral trade negotiations has so far failed to materialize.

Summary of Key Concepts

- Normally, globalization should boost the movement of labour, but, although international migration is increasing, labour is considerably less mobile than other factors of production.
- Work moves to labour more than workers move to work. This creates concerns over employment in developed countries and social dumping in developing countries.
- Efforts to develop minimum labour standards fall into voluntary (product/social labelling and corporate codes of conduct) and compulsory measures ('social clauses').
- Developing countries often oppose efforts to introduce international labour standards, claiming that they damage those they are intended to protect and that they represent 'disguised protectionism'.
- Virtually all MNEs have developed their own codes of conduct which cover, among other issues, minimum conditions in their operations and those of their suppliers.
- 'Social clauses' are becoming the norm in regional and bilateral trade agreements but efforts to give the WTO greater responsibility in this field have stalled.

Activities

1. Compare and contrast the corporate codes of conduct of two multinational companies and assess whether they will meet the objective of attaining a minimum level of labour standards.

2. Find examples of firms relocating to take advantage of lower labour costs.

3. Make the case for and against including labour issues within the WTO. This may be used as the basis for a class debate.

4. You are adviser to the Labour Minister of a developing country. Write a brief for the Minister that may be used as the basis of a speech on child labour to be given at an international forum.

5. You are adviser to the Chief Executive Officer of a multinational enterprise that has been exposed as tolerating very poor conditions in the overseas factories of its main suppliers. What strategy would you advise to enable the company to counter its critics?

Discussion Questions

1. Workers can move to jobs or jobs can move to workers. What are the arguments for and against each alternative?

2. Discuss the implications of social dumping for workers in developed countries and for workers in developing countries.

3. Discuss the opposing views that corporate codes of conduct:

    •   are intended to reduce calls for more stringent and widespread labour standards measures by states, regional organizations and/or international institutions;

    •   serve to increase labour standards in developing countries where the government may have limited capacity to enforce labour laws.

4. What are the costs and benefits to key stakeholders of including social clauses in bilateral trade agreements?

5. Should the trade–labour standards link become an item on the WTO agenda?

References and Suggestions for Further Reading

Athukorala, P. (2006) 'International labour migration in East Asia: trends, patterns and policy issues', *Asia-Pacific Economic Literature*, Vol. 20, No. 1, 18–39.

Auer, P. (2006) 'Perspectives: the internationalisation of employment: a challenge to fair globalisation', *International Labour Review*, Vol. 145, Nos 1–2, 119–134.

Bhagwati, J. (1997) 'Trade liberalization and "fair trade" demands: addressing the environmental and labour standards issues', in *Writings on International Economics*, Oxford: Oxford University Press.

Brewster, C., Sparrow, P. and Vernon, G. (2007) *International Human Resource Management*, 2nd edn, London: Chartered Institute of Personnel and Development.

Cohen, R. (2006) *Migration and its Enemies: Global Capital, Migrant Labour and the Nation State*, Aldershot: Ashgate.

Craig, J. and Lynk, S. (eds) (2006) *Globalization and the Future of Labour Law*, Cambridge: Cambridge University Press.

Cranger, C. and Siroen, J. (2006) 'Core labour standards in trade agreements: from multilateralism to bilateralism', *Journal of World Trade*, Vol. 40, No. 5, 813–836.

DeTienne, K. and Lewis, L. (2005) 'The practical and ethical barriers to corporate social responsibility disclosure: the Nike case', *Journal of Business Ethics*, Vol. 60, 359–376.

Dine, J. (2005) *Companies, International Trade and Human Rights*, Cambridge: Cambridge University Press.

Doumbia-Henry, C. and Gravel, E. (2006) 'Free trade agreements and labour rights: recent developments', *International Labour Review*, Vol. 145, No. 3, 185–206.

Edwards, T. and Reece, C. (2006) *International Human Resource Management: Globalization, National Systems and Multinational Companies*, Harlow: FT Prentice Hall.

Golub, S. (1997) 'Are international labour standards needed to prevent social dumping?', *Finance and Development*, Vol. 34, No. 4, 20–23.

Granger, C. and Siroen, J-M. (2006) 'Core labour standards in trade agreements: from multilateralism to bilateralism', *Journal of World Trade Law*, Vol. 40, No. 5, 813–826.

Grynberg, R. and Qalo, V. (2006) 'Labour standards in US and EU preferential trading arrangements', *Journal of World Trade*, Vol. 40, No. 4, 619–653.

Hatton, T. and Williamson, J. (2006) *Global Migration and the World Economy: Two Centuries of Policy and Performance*, Cambridge, MA: MIT Press.

Hepple, B. (ed.) (2002) *Social and Labour Rights in a Global Context: International and Competitive Perspectives*, Cambridge: Cambridge University Press.

Hepple, B. (2005) *Labour Laws and Global Trade*, Oxford: Hart.

Lee, E. and Vivarelli, M. (2006) 'The social impact of globalization in the developing countries', *International Labour Review*, Vol. 145, No. 3, 167–184.

Locke, R., Kochan, T., Romis, M. and Qin, F. (2007) 'Beyond corporate codes of conduct: work organisation and labour standards at Nike's suppliers', *International Labour Review*, Vol. 46, Nos 1–2, 21–37.

Massey, D. and Taylor, E. (eds) (2004) *International Migration: Prospects and Policies in a Global Market*, Oxford: Oxford University Press.

Moses, J. (2006) *International Migration: Globalization's Last Frontier*, London: Zed Books.

Muchlinski, P.T. (2001) 'Human rights and multinationals: is there a problem?', *International Affairs*, Vol. 77, No. 1, 31–48.

Piore, M.J. and Sabel, C.F. (1984) *The Second Industrial Divide*, New York: Basic Books.

Trebilcock, M.J. and Howse, R. (2004) *The Regulation of International Trade*, 3rd edn, London: Routledge.

Zimmermann, K. (2005) 'European labour mobility: challenges and potentials', *De Economist*, Vol. 153, No. 4, 425–450.

Chapter 16

The Environment

The Greening of International Business

The rose has thorns only for those who gather it.

Chinese proverb

LEARNING OBJECTIVES

This chapter will help you to:

- explain the principles of ecological modernization

- outline the link between globalization and the environment

- describe and critique the 'pollution havens' and 'race to the bottom' hypotheses

- demonstrate an understanding of the key principles of contemporary environmental policy

- describe the role of multilateral environmental agreements and the WTO in the development of international environmental policy

- assess the response of international business to environmental issues

By the 1990s, environmental factors had become an issue for governments, business and society in a way that was unheard of only a few years previously. The common perception is that the environment has been deteriorating for many years, that it continues to do so and that human beings bear the primary responsibility for this. The reasons for this view are not difficult to understand. The world's population has expanded from an estimated 2.5 billion in 1950 to 6.7 billion in 2008 with forecasts of a global population of 9 billion by 2050 as the norm. The increase in economic activity that has accompanied this population growth places additional demands and strains on the world's resources. World energy demand, for example, has risen inexorably, promoting additional emissions of greenhouse gases such as carbon dioxide. Pressure on water resources is also increasing (see Chapter 19); deforestation continues; world fish stocks are under pressure, and biodiversity generally is threatened as a result of the threat to habitats and of pollution.

The challenge of combating environmental degradation and of reconciling the views and interests of the multitude of stakeholders occupies increasing amounts of the time of businesses, politicians, international institutions, NGOs and civil society generally. Unsurprisingly, given the relative lateness with which environmental concerns became the subject of mainstream scientific endeavour, the complex issues involved are frequently fiercely contested. There is, for example, a general consensus that climate change is occurring. However, the causes of climate change are not universally accepted: the majority view at present is that much of climate change is anthropogenic (that is, man-made). However, there is a significant minority view that climate change has always occurred and that the human input is relatively unimportant. The outcome of this debate has major implications for policy: if the minority are correct, for example, policy initiatives to reduce greenhouse gases are not only irrelevant but represent a serious diversion of resources away from other pressing issues. If the majority view is correct, initiatives to reduce greenhouse gas emissions are urgent. Bjørn Lomborg's controversial and challenging book *The Skeptical Environmentalist* (Lomborg, 2001) summarizes some of the problems involved in establishing 'environmental facts' and thus in formulating environmental policy. Lomborg's core argument is that the conventional portrayal of a constantly deteriorating environment is not supported by hard evidence. Lomborg is not, however, against environmental protection. He argues: 'by far the majority of indicators show that mankind's lot has *vastly improved*. This does not, however, mean that everything is *good enough*.' He concludes that considered evaluation of environmental data will 'allow us to make the most informed decision as to where we need to place most of our efforts'.

This chapter begins by discussing the evolution of thinking about the environment before focusing on the increasingly dominant ecological modernization paradigm which reverses the traditional view that economic growth and environmental activity are incompatible. This is followed by exploration of the interface between globalization and the environment, particularly in relation to 'race to the bottom' and 'pollution haven' arguments. The chapter then discusses international policy responses to environmental problems, especially the proliferation of multilateral environmental agreements

(MEAs) and the emerging, but still limited, environmental role of the WTO. It concludes with discussion of the corporate options and response to environmental challenges.

EVOLVING VIEWS OF THE ENVIRONMENT: THE EMERGENCE OF ECOLOGICAL MODERNIZATION

Contemporary environmental concerns have their roots in the 1960s. In those days, many proponents of greater environmental protection were on the margins of politics and society and proposed radical action, arguing that only a profound transformation of the political, social and economic systems would protect the planet. By the early 1970s, environmental issues had become more mainstream and were debated by international think-tanks and conferences. At that time, two environmental battle lines were drawn that remain important to this day.

The first relates to the view that economic growth and environmental protection are incompatible. The title of the Club of Rome's noted report, *Limits to Growth*, published in 1972, sums up this assumption. Another 1972 publication, *Blueprint for Survival*, reinforced this view, arguing that continuation of existing trends of production and consumption would lead to 'the breakdown of society and the irreversible disruption of life-support systems on this planet'.

The second line relates to the divergent environmental interests of developed and developing countries. This became apparent at the landmark UN Conference on the Human Environment in Stockholm in 1972. The developed countries argued for collective action to address environmental issues, thereby avoiding the unilateral action they believed would disadvantage their own industries. The developing countries, on the other hand, regarded development as their priority and were unwilling to sacrifice it to correct pollution problems caused by developed nations. They also argued that developed countries had developed without environmental constraints and that it was only fair that they should be allowed to do the same. Significant polarization between developed and developing countries on environmental issues continues to this day.

However, a rethink of the supposed incompatibility between growth and environmental protection has occurred. The change began in the early 1980s and initially took root most strongly in Europe, where countries with a strong commitment to environmental protection, like the Netherlands and Germany, were able to exercise a strong influence on EC policy. By the 1990s, the perceived positive correlation between economic growth and environmental protection had become the dominant strand in environmental thinking, requiring a reconsideration of attitudes towards environmental policy.

This new mode of thinking is termed 'ecological modernization'. Initially, ecological modernization ideas were merely implicit in policy debates – explicit articulation was rare. Indeed in 1992, Albert Weale wrote, 'there is no one canonical statement of the ideology of ecological modernisation'. However, since the mid-1990s ecological modernisation, which was already having a significant influence on policy and stakeholders, has also figured centrally in academic discourse. The implications of ecological modernization for business can be narrowed down to the following:

■ *The reconciliation of environmental and economic objectives*: in other words, economic growth and environmental protection are mutually beneficial. Economic growth is qualitatively different from the past given the incorporation of environmental features into technology. This integration of growth and environmental objectives results in a 'win-win-win' situation for the environment, the economy and business.

■ *Technocentricism*: that is, the emphasis on innovation and technology (modernism) to deliver both growth and environmental benefits. This is reflected in the so-called 'Porter hypothesis' which states that not only are growth and environmentalism compatible but also that competitiveness depends on this link. Accordingly, stricter environmental regulations and policies act not as a cost burden for industry but as an incentive to innovate and compete. In other words, profitability and the observance of high environmental standards go together. Moreover, there is the potential for environmental activity to go hand-in-hand with job creation.

■ *The primacy of the market* (albeit a market modified by state intervention to correct for market failures). This is marked by a movement away from the command-and-control regulations and standards used to regulate and constrain business activities in the early days of environmental policy activism. Such instruments proved to be inflexible and relatively ineffective. Instead, policy makers are increasingly seeking to use policy instruments that tap into market dynamics such as taxation, eco-labelling and emission trading schemes. This reliance on the market makes ecological modernization entirely compatible with the dominant neo-liberal economic philosophy (see Chapter 2) that has driven globalization and is the complete antithesis of the radical ecologist view that environmental protection requires systemic transformation. Indeed, 'ecological modernisation can best be understood as a late twentieth century strategy to adapt capitalism to the environmental challenge, thus strengthening it' (Young, 2000).

These characteristics of ecological modernization make it attractive to several stakeholders. In the political sphere, ecological modernization has transformed the environmental debate from one of confrontation to one of consensus and cooperation and has been captured by, or adapted to, the market economy and capitalism. Ecological modernization thus holds out the possibility of resolving environmental problems within existing social, political and economic systems. As such it has marginalized the more extreme critics of the status quo and co-opted its more moderate critics who see opportunities to bring pragmatic, technical solutions to bear on environmental problems and to bring environmental issues into the political mainstream. Ecological modernization has not only made environmental protection much less threatening to business, it has also encouraged companies to regard the search for greater environmental protection as a positive factor in competitiveness.

Ecological modernization not only promises greater competitiveness but also job creation, whereas pollution haven concerns point to job losses in higher standard countries (however, the total number of jobs worldwide may well increase, if firms relocate to areas of lower labour productivity). The biggest environmentally induced positive impact on the job market originates from the creation of 'green jobs' in waste management, noise abatement, recycling, the rehabilitation of soil and groundwater, resource management, renewable energy, renovation of urban areas, and nature and landscape protection and conservation. The growth of these eco-industries has been rapid in recent years. Demand for environmental equipment and services has traditionally been limited to the advanced industrialized countries of the US, Japan and Europe but greater interest is anticipated from the rapidly developing countries of south and east Asia and Latin America.

Despite the benefits claimed for it, ecological modernization is not accepted wholesale – far from it. Many ecologists continue to regard reductions in consumption and the cultivation of self-sufficiency as the only long-term sustainable option. These and other less radical critics argue that ecological modernization is effectively a 'business as usual' ploy used to head off legitimate environmental concerns and to ignore demands for a fundamental reassessment of approaches to environmental degradation. Many businesses also continue to lobby against environmental measures on cost grounds.

Developing countries are also suspicious of ecological modernization. They continue to argue that development remains their overriding priority, that they cannot afford to embrace costly environmental measures and that, given the responsibility of the developed countries for much of the world's environmental degradation, it is the developed world that should take and pay for the necessary corrective measures.

However, a concept closely related to ecological modernization, the Environmental Kuznets Curve (EKC), would appear to support the view that growth will ultimately also contribute to the solution for environmental problems in the developing world. The EKC derives its name from the original Kuznets U-shaped curve which posited that as growth increases, income distribution becomes more uneven, stabilizes at middle-income levels and then starts to even out again. In the case of the EKC, as growth gets underway, environmental degradation and pollution grow. It then stabilizes at middle-income levels and starts to decline with prosperity. Once basic needs are met, so the explanation goes, priorities shift towards improvement of the quality of life. If this hypothesis is correct, the emphasis of developing countries on attaining growth is compatible with environmental protection and in line with the philosophy of ecological modernization.

The, albeit limited, available evidence suggests that the EKC applies more to local pollution issues such as urban air quality and freshwater pollutants than to degradation resulting from global phenomena like greenhouse gases (Vaughan and Nordström, 1999). It is also conceivable that the EKC effect may not be attainable for the least developed countries, especially if the EKC effect already experienced by developed countries occurred as a result of migration of polluting industries to developing countries (see below). For the least developed countries, there will not necessarily be any countries to which they can pass on their own polluting industries. However, evidence supporting the pollution havens hypothesis is not strong. On the other hand, the EKC effect may occur if developing countries can utilize technologies that were not available to developed countries when they were at a similar stage of development. In short it is likely that economic growth is a necessary but not sufficient condition for pollution to decline with higher levels of growth. The downward turn of the U-shaped curve also requires the implementation of appropriate policies and has occurred more readily in democratic countries according to the WTO (Vaughan and Nordström, 1999) which has claimed that in countries with similar income levels, environmental degradation tends to be worse where income inequity is greatest, literacy levels are lower and there are few political and civil liberties.

GLOBALIZATION AND THE ENVIRONMENT

Through its elimination of economic borders and the subsequent emergence of MNEs as networks of global integrated production, globalization clearly alters the context in which environmental regulation occurs. Deregulation and liberalization, major globalization drivers, by favouring competition imperatives, are widely held to increase pressure to lower environmental standards. In addition to the trans-border nature of much pollution, globalization critics point to the diminished ability of local and national regulators to implement environmental regulations given the mobility of MNEs and the alleged priority of economic and trade matters over environmental concerns by policy makers generally. As such, globalization raises issues related to links between trade and the environment, technology, corporate competitiveness and governance and institutions.

Some, albeit not all, environmental NGOs have demonized globalization, blaming it for many of the world's ecological ills. To the extent that globalization increases production, consumption and trade flows, it is held responsible for an accelerated rundown of the earth's natural resources and a general increase in environmental degradation. Trade flows, for example, involve more journeys over longer distances, thereby increasing fuel consumption and the greenhouse gas problem. The primacy of market forces fostered by globalization, it is argued, has also intensified competition. The resulting competitiveness concerns make attention to environmental issues an unaffordable luxury. This potential stepping back from environmental responsibility applies to all levels of government and to MNEs themselves. In reality, notwithstanding the dictates of globalization and competition, large and small companies and rule-making bodies at local, regional, national and international level pay much more attention to environmental concerns than previously.

The Pollution Havens Hypothesis and the 'Race to the Bottom'

The pollution havens hypothesis and the so-called 'race to the bottom' constitute two of the alleged environmental negatives of globalization. Both are concerned with the impact of differential environmental standards in a world of globalization-driven factor mobility. These arguments find parallels in social dumping, the argument that globalization lowers labour standards as a result of the enhanced potential for firms to move to countries where lower standards prevail (see Chapter 15).

More specifically, the pollution havens hypothesis states that in order to avoid the costs of complying with high environmental standards, firms will relocate to countries (pollution havens) where standards and hence costs are lower, resulting in the loss of jobs and investment in the higher standard country. In this scenario, higher standards, ironically, lead to greater environmental damage as firms liberate themselves from environmental constraints in their new location. Pollution havens also trigger off a 'race to the bottom' by increasing pressure to lower standards to prevent such migration from occurring. In essence, so the argument goes, open markets undermine national environmental policies and create intense pressure to weaken regulations in order to retain investment, to maintain competitiveness and to remove the incentive to relocate in countries with lower standards. The outcome is a downward spiral of environmental standards.

The pollution haven hypothesis ignores the increasing tendency of MNEs to standardize their technology across all plants: this strategy increases compatibility between different parts of the production chain, yielding cost benefits in the process. According to the US International Trade Commission, 'much research indicates that multinational firms tend to replicate the technologies employed in their home markets when operating in developing countries. Indeed the ability to duplicate technology in a number of countries is deemed central to the competitive strategy of most multinationals' (Vaughan and Nordström, 1999). Furthermore, if the home market has stricter environmental regulations than the host country, thereby requiring integration of pollution control into its technology, FDI will be less polluting than domestic plants in the host country.

Both the pollution havens and the race to the bottom hypotheses depend on the assumption that environmental regulations impose compliance costs that are sufficiently high to become a determining factor in business location. The limited evidence that exists indicates that environmental compliance costs are no more than 2 per cent of total costs, even for the most polluting industries. US Bureau of Census data published in 1996 indicate that on average US industry spent no more than 0.6 per cent of its revenue on pollution abatement. For the vast majority of sectors, the figures were lower than this as the average was pulled up by higher figures for the most polluting industries (petroleum and coal products, chemicals, primary metal industries and paper and pulp products). This phenomenon has also been noted by the OECD, the WTO, and by US NGO, the Worldwatch Institute (Renner, 2000).

However, the additional costs incurred as a result of environmental regulation can be a determining factor in relocation, especially when profit margins are tight and the economic environment is generally unfavourable. Furthermore, it is possible that it is not actual increased costs or job losses that result in governments backing off from higher standards or lowering of standards, but the threat or fear of such effects. Again, there is some, albeit limited evidence that fears of job losses arising from environmental regulations are much bigger than actual job losses and that the cost burden imposed by regulation turns out to be less onerous than originally envisaged. Nevertheless, it can be difficult to gather support for new regulations if the general perception is that the cost of proposed regulations will bear down heavily on domestic industry. It is certainly the case that business often appeals to competitiveness concerns in its lobbying efforts against proposed new regulations.

Trade and the Environment

Trade and the environment are frequently portrayed as being in conflict with each other. The main thrust of international trade policy in past decades has been liberal and non-interventionist whereas environmental policy intervention is needed precisely because, without full internalization of external costs, the market fails to deliver the optimum outcome. The result is intervention to correct for market failure.

Although examples of companies moving to 'benefit' from lower environmental compliance costs exist, there is scant evidence that this occurs in any systematic and sustained way. Analysis of trade and FDI patterns does not reveal a relative shift of 'dirty' industries from developed to developing industries. Indeed, such a move would go against the Heckscher-Ohlin principle that it is differences in factor endowments, namely capital and labour, that determine trade patterns. Accordingly, capital-intensive industries should be attracted to developed countries and labour-intensive industries to developing countries. Trade encourages specialization, implying an increase rather than a decrease in pollution in developed countries given their specialization in more polluting, capital-intensive industries. This effect has been offset to some extent by the introduction of new technology and the relative increase in the role of services in developed economies.

Free traders anticipate environmental benefits from trade and the growth flowing from it (see earlier section on ecological modernization). For example, liberalized trade facilitates the spread of environmental services and clean technology. Indeed, one of the objectives of the Doha Development Agenda is the elimination of tariffs and other trade barriers on environmental goods and services. If the EKC effect holds, the increased income generated by trade will foster demands for cleaner environments. Trade encourages specialization and restructuring according to comparative advantage, resulting in greater efficiency and economies of scale. This will reduce global environmental problems if improved efficiency entails the use of cleaner technology, which is plausible although by no means certain. The impact on the local environment will depend on the net environmental impact of sectors that are expanding and contracting as a result of trade.

The interaction of trade and environment in a policy context is far from straightforward. Given the cross-border nature of many environmental problems, increasing convergence and harmonization of environmental policy would appear to be the most promising environmental approach to tackling these problems. However, given differences in environmental conditions between, and even within, countries, it is perfectly plausible that in order to achieve a common objective, it is appropriate for different jurisdictions to adopt different policies or for international environmental regimes to adopt common but differentiated responsibilities (see Box 16.2).

Furthermore, what seems like a sensible policy can have unforeseen and undesired effects. For example, in order to halt the process of deforestation, a ban on trade in forestry products might appear to be a good idea. However, by depressing returns from forestry activity, such an initiative can accelerate rather than halt deforestation by increasing incentives to look for other sources of income from the land. This has already happened in Latin America where forests were destroyed so that more land could go over to biofuel production. Trade restrictions are also often proposed as ways of dealing with environmental problems but are often suspect in the eyes of free traders who believe (often, albeit not always, with good cause) that such measures are trade rather than environmental protectionist.

The most appropriate relationship between trade and environmental policy is one of trade liberalization carried out against a background of environmental policy that provides for full internalization of external costs (see Box 16.1). This is in line with the current trend towards greater use of market-based instruments such as eco-taxes. Market-based environment and trade policy working together could make a positive contribution to both the economy and the environment by bringing about a more efficient allocation of resources.

INTERNATIONAL ENVIRONMENTAL POLICY

Globalization has played an important role in the appearance of environmental policy on the international agenda but, given the lack of respect of pollution for national borders, the incentive to formulate international environmental policy would exist, even in the absence of globalization. The development of multilateral trade policy preceded the emergence of environmental issues and policy on the international stage but environmental issues in turn got their first international airing ahead of other globalization-driven issues such as competition policy and labour market regulation.

The crucial event in the evolution of contemporary international environmental policy was the 1972 Stockholm Conference on the Human Environment. The conference was held to consider 'problems of the human environment . . . and also to identify those aspects of it that can only, or best be solved through international co-operation' and was attended by delegations from 114 countries. Stockholm's long-term importance lies in its hitherto unique focus on environmental issues, which both aroused public interest and stirred national governments to become involved. More specifically, the Stockholm Conference resulted in the creation of the UN Environment Programme (UNEP), an organization which, in addition to organizing environmental information and monitoring networks, has been instrumental in providing the support for key MEAs. Although the most important, UNEP is not the only international organization involved in the creation of MEAs. Other UN bodies like the International Maritime Organization (IMO) and the Food and Agriculture Organization (FAO) and non-UN institutions like the OECD and the International Atomic Energy Authority (IAEA) also play a key role in their development and operation.

Over 500 international treaties and other agreements relating to the environment are in force. Of these, over 300 are regional. Furthermore, there are believed to be over 1,000 bilateral environmental agreements in existence. Although the first MEAs were negotiated in the nineteenth century, the biggest increase in the incidence of MEAs has occurred since the Stockholm Conference. They may be approximately classified into the following areas:

- Biodiversity – e.g. the Convention on Biological Diversity (CBD) and the Convention on International Trade in Endangered Species (CITES).
- Atmosphere – e.g. the United Nations Framework Convention on Climate Change (UNFCCC) and the Montreal Protocol.
- Land – e.g. the UN Convention to combat desertification.
- Chemical and hazardous waste – e.g. the Basel Convention on the Control of the Transboundary Movements of Hazardous Wastes and their Disposal, and the draft Stockholm Conventions on Persistent Organic Pollutants.
- Regional seas and related matters – e.g. the Protection of the Arctic Marine Environment and other regional marine initiatives.

Many MEAs effectively limit the way businesses carry out their activities and use trade as an instrument in environmental protection – a development that potentially brings them into conflict with the WTO. Indeed, the main objective of CITES is to control trade in endangered species of animals and plants and products made from them. The Montreal Protocol, for example, banned the production and use of several categories of industrial chemicals known to contribute to the depletion of the stratospheric ozone layer and imposed restrictions on others.

The action which business had to take as a result of the Montreal Protocol was immediately clear but the requirements emanating from the UN Framework Convention on Climate Change and subsequent related initiatives like the 1997 Kyoto Protocol are more extensive but less homogenous. The UNFCCC and Kyoto attempt to deal with the complex issue of climate change via a range of strategies, most of which are designed to restructure economic development so that it is less dependent on greenhouse gases. It is left up to signatories to determine how they develop strategies to meet their emissions targets under Kyoto.

In addition, although MEAs have often thrown up deep differences between developed and developing countries (the Basel Convention, for example, was essentially a response to divergent interests over the disposal of hazardous wastes), MEAs have not attracted the same negative publicity from NGOs as have other multilateral instruments such as the failed Multilateral Agreement on Investment. This may be partly explained by the tendency to involve rather than exclude NGOs and other aspects of civil society, either as observers, advisers or sometimes as full participants, in the deliberations of MEAs. This is certainly true of CITES and the Basel Convention, among others.

Box 16.1 Key Principles of Contemporary Environmental Policy

A degree of consensus has merged around the need to encompass the following underlying principles in environmental policy enacted at local, national, regional and international levels.

- **The 'polluter pays' principle** (PPP) stipulates that polluters should pay the full cost of the environmental damage they cause. Environmental costs are often referred to as 'externalities' (for example, damage to health, rivers, the air, arising from economic activity) that are not incorporated into the costs of a product but are borne by society as a whole. By making the polluter pay the full cost of its activities, including externalities, the PPP provides an incentive to make products less polluting and/or to reduce the consumption of polluting goods. This internalization of external costs can be met through the use of market-based, policy instruments.

- **The prevention principle** involves changes to products and processes to prevent environmental damage from occurring rather than relying on remedial action to repair damage after it has taken place. This implies the development of 'clean technologies'; minimal use of natural resources; minimal releases into the atmosphere, water and soil; and maximization of the recyclability and lifespan of products.

- **The precautionary principle** acknowledges that our understanding of ecology and environmental processes is, at best, incomplete. Policy is therefore formulated against a background of uncertainty. However, lack of scientific knowledge should not be used to justify failure to introduce environmental policy. Indeed, even without conclusive scientific evidence about outcomes, precautionary action should be taken if the potential consequences of inaction are particularly serious or if the cost of action is not high.

- **Subsidiarity**: environmental policy is formulated at a number of different levels – local, national, regional and international. The subsidiarity principle requires action to be taken at the lowest possible level of government at which it can be effectively taken. This poses interesting challenges for environmental policy given the lack of respect of pollution for borders. In many instances, regional or international action will therefore be suitable but, in some cases of cross-border pollution, a more local policy approach may be appropriate given differences in environmental conditions.

- **Common but differentiated responsibility**: environmental regimes that deal with environmental problems with international implications often distinguish between countries when formulating policy. For example, all countries have a responsibility for global warming but the contribution of richer countries to the problem has been greater and the poorer countries have more urgent calls on their resources in terms of basic development needs. Therefore, international regimes, while acknowledging common responsibility for the global environment, will allocate differential policies for dealing with the problem.

- *Openness*: the representation of all stakeholders in the formulation of environmental policy is important for good environmental management. Many MEAs are noteworthy for their openness and transparency, encouraging participation from business and environmental NGOs and utilizing modern technology to communicate their activities to the public. A recurring criticism of the WTO, on the other hand, is its lack of openness and transparency when dealing with environmental, and indeed other matters.

The WTO and the Environment

The WTO has attracted more than its fair share of NGO opposition (see Chapter 4), and no more so than in relation to its environmental approach. Given the heterogeneity of anti-globalization groups and environmental NGOs, it is easiest to characterize them as existing along a continuum: at one end sit groups that regard trade and sustainability as incompatible and lobby for the latter. In their eyes, trade liberalization and the WTO are the environment's main enemies. At the other end of the continuum sit groups that believe the best way of tipping the trade–environment balance towards the environment side of the scales is by working to influence and to 'green' organizations. Indeed, an increasing number of NGOs are working with companies, governments and international institutions to do just that.

The most common criticisms levelled at the WTO on environmental matters are that business interests always override those of the environment and that the WTO is essentially undemocratic in nature, failing to take into account arguments that originate from non-business interests or smaller member states. In its defence, the WTO and its predecessor organization, the GATT, were established to uphold a rule-based trading system, not to protect the environment.

In 1947, when the GATT came into existence, environmental considerations were not regarded as important. However, it did incorporate an exception clause, Article XX, which allows countries, under strict guidelines, to set aside normal trading rules if it is deemed necessary to protect human, animal or plant life or health, or to conserve exhaustible natural resources. Such departures from the rules were allowed provided that they did not discriminate between imports or act as a 'disguised restriction on international trade'. In other words, environmental claims should not be used as a pretext for protectionism.

Environmental issues hardly troubled GATT during the first three decades of its existence. This gradually began to change from the 1970s. In 1971, the GATT Council established a Group on Environmental Measures and International Trade (EMIT) 'to examine upon request any specific measures relevant to the trade policy aspects of measures to control pollution and protect the human environment'. The Group was to be activated upon the request of a contracting party, something that did not occur until 1991.

Even though environmentalism had become more prominent by the mid-1980s, the environment was not explicitly included in the Uruguay Round of multilateral talks. However, the 1995 Marrakesh Agreement that ended the Uruguay Round and established the WTO firmly secured the importance of the environment to the work of the WTO by:

1. Including a reference to the objective of sustainable development and the need 'to protect and preserve the environment' in the preamble of the WTO Treaty. In other words, the traditional economic objectives of the WTO must be balanced against environmental considerations.
2. Requiring the WTO's General Council to establish a successor to EMIT, the Committee on Trade and the Environment (CTE). CTE has a broad mandate, requiring it to identify the link between trade and environmental measures and to recommend modifications to the multilateral trading system to bring it into line with sustainability.

The Doha WTO Ministerial Declaration of November 2001, which launched the next round of multilateral trade talks, expressed the conviction 'that the aims of upholding and safeguarding an open and non-discriminatory multilateral trading system, and acting for the protection of the environment and sustainable development can and must be mutually supportive'. In particular, the Declaration registered a continuing commitment to avoid the use of environmental measures as a form of disguised protection and welcomed cooperation with UNEP and other intergovernmental environmental organizations. The Declaration also contained a commitment to the presentation of a report on technical assistance and capacity building in developing countries issues for the Fifth Ministerial Session in 2005. Such declarations were intended to calm developing country fears that environmental concerns could be given higher priority over trade issues and that 'green' conditionality could become attached to conditions of market access.

More specifically, trade negotiators are considering:

■ the relationship between WTO rules and the trade obligations of MEAs;
■ the reduction and elimination of tariff and non-tariff barriers to environmental goods and services.

In addition, the Doha Declaration instructed the CTE to consider whether there is a need to clarify rules regarding:

■ the effect of environmental measures on market access, especially in relation to developing countries;
■ the environmental dimension of the Agreement on Trade-related Aspects of Intellectual Property Rights (TRIPS);
■ eco-labelling.

A handful of high-profile trade disputes have caused the greatest outcry about WTO and the environment. This is despite the fact that relatively few trade–environment disputes have used the disputes procedure, although their incidence is increasing. From 1947 to 1995, only six out of 115 GATT panel reports (i.e. 5 per cent of the total) were concerned with human and animal health or

Box 16.2 The Environmental Dimension of WTO Instruments

In general, WTO rules allow members to adopt their own environmental protection policies provided that they observe key WTO principles: that is, there is no discrimination between imports and domestically produced products (national treatment) or between similar products imported from different trading partners (the most favoured nation principle). In addition to general WTO principles, the Preamble to the WTO agreement, Article XX and the work of the CTE, environmental protection is also a factor in the following WTO instruments:

- *The Agreement on Technical Barriers to Trade (TBT)*: the TBT Agreement concerns the preparation, adoption and application of product technical requirements and compliance procedures for industrial and agricultural products. While recognizing the right of countries to take measures to protect health and the environment at levels they deem appropriate, the Agreement attempts to prevent the misuse of standards for protectionist purposes, a practice that is both subtle and widespread. For example, standards can be written in such a way to match the characteristics of domestic products, effectively excluding imports.

  The TBT Agreement encourages countries to use international standards to limit standards proliferation, but does allow digression from them if there are specific fundamental climatic, geographical or technological factors that make an international standard inappropriate.

- *Agreement on Sanitary and Phytosanitary Measures (SPS)*: the SPS Agreement was negotiated during the Uruguay Round to guard against risks from additives, contaminants, toxins or disease in food. Food safety has become a contentious issue following the controversies over BSE, beef in hormones and the resistance to genetically modified (GM) food.

  The principles and provisions of the SPS Agreement parallel those of the TBT Agreement in that governments have a legitimate right to maintain their preferred level of health protection provided that they respect non-discriminatory principles and notification obligations. In addition, countries intending to impose more stringent standards than international norms must do so on the basis of scientific evidence and/or an assessment of the risks to human, animal or plant life and health. The Agreement allows governments the right to take precautionary provisional measures (see Box 16.1) in the absence of scientific evidence while they seek further information.

- *General Agreement on Trade in Services (GATS)*: Article XIV of the GATS parallels GATT Article XX by listing general exceptions to its provisions. In short, measures can be exempt from GATS regulations provided that they are deemed necessary, among other things, 'to protect human, animal or plant life or health.' As with the GATT, GATS exemptions should not be discriminatory or operate as disguised forms of protectionism.

  The environmental services sector within GATS includes sewage services, refuse disposal services, sanitation and other services (i.e. noise abatement, nature and landscape protection), many of which face obstacles to market access such as discriminatory taxes, subsidies, non-recognition of foreign qualifications, inadequate intellectual property protection and restrictions on investment. Removal of these obstacles is on the Doha agenda and will reduce the costs faced by companies when attempting to operate in a sustainable manner.

the environment. In the first four years of the WTO, six out of 38 panels, or 16 per cent of all cases, dealt with such issues. This increase reflects the movement of environmental issues to centre stage generally and the strengthening of the dispute settlement procedure under the WTO. Key cases include the following.

Tuna-Dolphin I and II

The 1991 tuna-dolphin decision (known as tuna-dolphin I) resulted from the US government's import ban on tuna caught in the East Tropical Pacific Ocean that did not meet the standards for dolphin protection applied to US fishermen. The embargo was aimed specifically at discouraging the practice of using purse-seine nets which, in addition to catching tuna, also encircle and drown the dolphins that swim above them. The case raised important, general issues, namely:

- Whether one country should effectively be able to determine the environmental policies of another country (the issue of extraterritoriality). In this instance, the GATT panel ruled that GATT rules did not allow one country to impose its own domestic rules on another, even in cases of conservation. The concern was that the extraterritoriality principle condoned import restrictions simply because the exporting country had different health, safety or environmental standards, thereby potentially opening the floodgates to protectionist abuses.
- Whether GATT rules allow action against the method of producing the goods rather than the intrinsic quality of the goods themselves (the process versus product argument). The Panel found that the embargo violated core GATT principles, including the national treatment provisions which prohibit discrimination against imported products on the basis of process and production methods (PPMs) – in this case the use of purse-seine nets.
- The scope of exception Article XX. By ruling that Article XX did not apply, the GATT Panel effectively adopted a narrow interpretation of Article XX, arguing that the US action was not necessary to achieve its conservation objectives and that the US had not exhausted all other less trade-restricting means prior to imposing the embargo. GATT Panels in this and subsequent cases have rejected the principle of extraterritoriality in favour of encouraging countries to seek multilateral solutions to trans-border environmental problems through international cooperation.

Tuna-dolphin I was never formally adopted and thus never became legally binding. Mexico (the original complainant) and the US decided to resolve the dispute diplomatically, leading to a multilateral agreement involving nine parties on the protection of dolphins in the Eastern Tropical Pacific Ocean.

Tuna-dolphin II developed because the EU chose in 1994 to continue with the formal complaint in view of the use by the US of secondary embargoes, supposedly to deal with transhipment of dolphin-unfriendly tuna but used in practice against countries that did not operate primary embargoes themselves. As such, tuna-dolphin II also dealt centrally with extraterritorial issues, namely in this case the attempt by the US to impose its environmental policy unilaterally on other countries.

Despite the absence of legal compulsion, the tuna-dolphin cases fuelled the view of many environmental NGOs that GATT was a threat to environmental policy, especially to the use of trade measures to achieve environmental gains. In the same way as the GATT Panel had rebuffed the principle of extraterritoriality, so many environmentalists feared that the tuna-dolphin cases would create the possibility for countries to challenge the environmental policies of others on the grounds that such policies interfered with their trade rights.

Gasoline Standards

In 1995, in one of the first cases to come under the WTO disputes settlement procedure, Venezuela complained that the US was illegally blocking imports of Venezuelan gasoline. Brazil lodged a similar complaint in 1996. The disputes panel and the Appellate Body that considered the US appeal against the original decision both ruled that the US action had violated WTO rules.

The decision hinged on the infringement of the principle of national treatment – more specifically, the use by the US of its Clean Air Act to subject foreign gasoline suppliers to tougher standards than those applying to domestic suppliers. The rulings did not undermine the basic principles or objectives of the Clean Air Act: rather the decision was aimed against the application of the law in a way that discriminated against foreign suppliers. The solution was therefore to correct how the law was applied rather than the law itself. This was subsequently done.

Shrimp-turtles

In 1998, a WTO dispute panel ruled that the US was wrongfully blocking imports of shrimp from countries that did not require its fishing fleets to use 'turtle excluder devices' (TEDs), devices that were designed to prevent endangered sea turtles from becoming entangled in nets trawling for shrimp. The US's 1973 Endangered Species Act required US shrimp trawlers to use TEDs in their nets when operating in regions frequented by sea turtles. In 1989, Section 609 of US Public Law 101–102 was enacted, requiring the US government to certify all shrimp imports and to allow imports only from countries that can prove their trawlers use TEDs.

The US implemented Section 609 by requiring Latin American and Caribbean countries to bring their shrimp-catching methods into line with US regulations within three years. Technical and financial assistance was granted to fishermen from these countries to help them introduce TEDs. Meanwhile, the environmental NGO the Earth Island Institute mounted a successful domestic legal challenge to the US government on the grounds that limiting implementation to certain countries was contrary to Section 609. The government was therefore required to implement 609 provisions worldwide which it subsequently did.

The extended application of Section 609 drew forth a complaint at the WTO from India, Malaysia, Pakistan and Thailand. In 1998, the WTO panel ruled against the US on the grounds that its action represented a unilateral imposition of US legislation on other countries and, by granting technical and financial assistance only to Latin American and Caribbean countries, was discriminatory. Furthermore, the US measure did not accept sea turtle protection by other countries that was equivalent to the US programme and banned imports of shrimp even when harvested in line with US regulations if the exporting country had not been certified under the US regulation. The US subsequently amended the implementation of Section 609 to ensure equal treatment of US and foreign companies. As in the tuna-dolphin cases, the US government was criticized for failing to make sufficient efforts to negotiate conservation agreements with the countries filing the complaint. In

2000, Malaysia challenged the revised regulations but on this occasion the WTO panel found in favour of the US government, stating that 'sustainable development is one of the objectives of the WTO agreement'.

In all three cases, the GATT/WTO bodies accepted the environmental objectives of US policy but questioned the procedures used to achieve these objectives. There was no requirement for the US government to amend its Clean Air Act, for example, in light of the WTO panel decision but rather to change the way it was implemented so that it did not discriminate against imports. Similarly in the shrimp-turtle case, as emphasized in the Appellate Body's report following the US appeal against the original decision, the issue was not the legitimacy of the US law but the measures used to implement it.

In general, the WTO's response to criticisms that it is anti-environment is that it is not anti-environment but pro-trade. Its prime remit is primarily one of trade and its regulations, procedures and objectives are all designed for trade-related objectives. It is therefore inappropriate to criticize it for not allowing environmental concerns to override trade considerations. Certainly, although its preamble acknowledges the importance of sustainability and individual WTO instruments contain environmental provisions, the WTO is essentially not equipped to perform the task that an increasing number of individuals and organizations are asking of it in environmental terms. This raises the question of what is the best way of promoting environmentalism on a world scale. Can it be done via more extensive use of MEAs, an increasingly popular device, or is there a case for a global environmental forum dedicated to the task of coordinating and promoting international cooperation on environmental issues with a trans-border dimension? Possibly, but there is little sign of it happening as yet.

THE CORPORATE SECTOR AND ENVIRONMENTAL POLICY

The pressure for companies to abide by principles of corporate responsibility, which include respect for the environment, has increased and business must and does take the environmental issue into account in its planning. It is now the norm for both large and small companies to integrate environmental planning into their strategic planning and to appoint a senior manager or board member to take responsibility for the environment. This is regarded as essential for a host of reasons, not least because a bad environmental record or bad environmental publicity can inflict serious damage on a company.

Moreover, and most importantly, companies have to be aware of and respect the myriad environmental regulations that are being established at a number of levels, ranging from the local, municipal level, through the state/provincial level to the national, regional and international level. The Montreal Protocol, for example, stopped the production of certain chemicals, forcing companies to look for alternatives. The implementation of the Kyoto and subsequent agreements falls on the shoulders of companies as governments pass down framework strategies to enable their country to reach individual targets.

In addition to compliance with regulation, businesses are also pressing for greater use of voluntary environmental measures which they argue give them more flexibility in achieving environmental objectives than more rigid traditional approaches and, they hope, reduce the likelihood of the introduction of more restrictive mandatory schemes at a later stage. These voluntary methods can take a number of forms. Case Study 16.1 outlines the provisions of ISO 14000, a voluntary international standard for environmental management that has been accepted remarkably quickly since its introduction in 1996. Industrial sectors, usually through trade associations, are also developing schemes to promote the environmental credentials of their members. The 'Responsible Care' initiative by the US chemical industry, which is also becoming increasingly adopted in Europe, is a good example of this. Eco-labelling schemes, both voluntary and mandatory, are also becoming more commonplace.

CASE STUDY 16.1

Voluntary Measures – ISO 14000

The move towards international standards has been accelerated by globalization, driven by the possibility that the persistence of different standards and regulations will act as non-tariff barriers or market fragmenting mechanisms that regulate and limit access to particular markets. This applies to environmental standards and regulations as much as to other types of standards. The adoption of international standards by companies both facilitates access to markets across the globe and the global integration of production networks, and contributes towards successful international tendering.

What?

The International Organization for Standardization (commonly known as ISO) is a non-governmental international organization which draws up international standards and whose membership is composed of national standards bodies. The ISO 14000 family of standards has been available since 1996 and provides guidance on establishing environmental management systems (EMS) aimed at controlling and improving a company's impact on the environment. ISO 14001 is the only standard in the 14000 series that can be certified and sets out the generic requirements for an EMS. Other standards in the series cover environmental audit, environ-

mental performance evaluation, life cycle assessment and eco-labelling and communications.

ISO 14001 is a voluntary standard that commits registered companies to introduce a systematic approach to the improvement of environmental management with a view to minimizing the corporate impact on the environment. Like ISO 9000, ISO's family of general quality management standards, ISO 14001 incorporates the principle of continuous improvement and has similar requirements in terms of a policy statement, document control, management review, internal audit, record keeping and training. Companies registering under ISO 14001 must also make a commitment to comply with environmental regulation, the prevention of pollution and a formal process of planning environmental improvement and control. Many companies have expressed fears about the cost of adopting ISO 14001 but the introduction of an ISO 14001-type EMS into companies that have already adopted a total quality management approach should not be too problematic. Moreover, the costs of adoption have to be offset by the cost savings arising from the operation of the scheme.

Why?

During the first six years of its existence between 1996 and 2002, 36,000 ISO 14001 schemes were certified. By the end of 2006, almost 130,000 certificates had been issued, of which slightly more than 30 per cent were to companies in the service sector. But precisely why have companies chosen to register? In broad terms, environmentally responsible behaviour is increasingly seen as a requirement (and not a luxury) of doing business. As such, companies are scrutinizing their own processes and products, and the processes and products of their suppliers, to ensure they deliver environmentally responsible goods and services in a way which enhances their reputation and their cost and production efficiency. This approach fits in with the EMS approach promoted by ISO 14001 and is suitable for a strategic, proactive approach to environmental issues rather than a series of unconnected reactions to individual and disparate regulatory requirements.

More specifically, companies increasingly recognize that pollution represents an inefficient and incomplete use of resources, requiring firms to carry out tasks like waste disposal that create no added value. Effective environmental management systems are therefore seen as a way of boosting the bottom line and of yielding competitive advantage, a view very much in line with the philosophy of ecological modernization discussed above. Examples of how an EMS, backed up by ISO 14001 certification can help businesses include the following:

* Facilitation of the integration of global business and supply chains through the adoption of common standards and practices. This allows for greater consistency and certainty in environmental strategy and is particularly useful for new market entrants. The process of integration also helps identify poorly performing plants.
* Reduced costs from increased energy efficiency and lower water consumption.
* Waste reduction from improved process yields of raw materials, including lower costs for material storage, handling and waste disposal, and the potential for new income streams from improved utilization of by-products and the conversion of waste into commercial products such as energy.
* Higher quality and more consistent products resulting from changes in the production process.

* Lower packaging costs.
* Less downtime as a result of the greater attention paid to process monitoring and maintenance.
* A safer working environment leading to lower accident rates and costs in the long term.
* Enhanced corporate reputation.
* Reduction in the number of environmental audits required.
* Reduced liability for environmental damage: given the growing tendency for companies to be held responsible for their contribution to environmental degradation, the financial and legal risks associated with poor environmental practices have increased over the years. An effective EMS reduces exposure to this risk. In some cases, insurance companies may even consider reduced environmental risk premiums for companies that adopt such systems and ISO 14001 registration indicates that this has been done.
* Adoption of a recognized standard like ISO 14001 can reduce the burden of surveillance and inspections by local environmental authorities.

Who?

ISO 14001 has rapidly gained acceptance, particularly in Japan with the highest number of certificates for an individual country (17.5 per cent of the total) and the EU (40 per cent of the total). Given the size of its economy and with less that 5 per cent of certificates, the US is underrepresented in terms of ISO 14000 certifications. This is one-third of the number of ISO 14001 certificates in China and 95 per cent of the number of ISO 14001 certificates in South Korea. Certification growth has, however, been strong in many developing and emerging economies as many of them strive to develop their own environmental standards and as a result of the increasingly common trend for large MNEs to require their suppliers to obtain ISO 14001 certification.

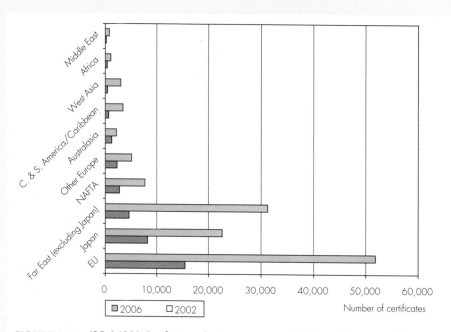

FIGURE 16.1 ISO 14001 Certifications by Region, January 2002 and December 2006

Note: The figures for 2002 refer to the EU(15), whereas the figures for 2006 refer to the EU(27).

Source: Derived from the Federal Environmental Agency, Germany, and the *ISO Survey* (2006).

CASE STUDY QUESTIONS

1. A senior executive of a major multinational chemical company said, 'It's like a windfall profit having ISO 14000.' Consider why this statement may have been made. Explain whether and how the statement is an endorsement of the principles of ecological modernization.

2. Explain how the adoption of ISO 14000 can help companies meet the challenges of globalization.

3. ISO 14001 is an example of a voluntary environmental standard. Why can it be in the interests of companies to adopt voluntary standards?

4. It has become commonplace for MNEs to require suppliers to attain 14001 certification. Find examples of this policy and consider benefits for (a) the environment; (b) the MNE; and (c) the supplier.

Traditionally, businesses have complained about the cost and other burdens placed upon them by environmental regulation. Although the cost argument is still heard, and indeed can be justified in some cases, latterly, the business response has become more complex and responsive to environmental pressures and much less prone to resistance almost as a matter of principle. This change has occurred as companies realize the damage that a bad environmental reputation can do to them and the benefits that can accrue from a positive environmental reputation and green marketing. Shrewd firms also realize that their green claims must have substance behind them.

More positively, increasing numbers of companies are recognizing the benefits to their bottom line by incorporating environmental considerations into their planning – that is, there is a growing acceptance of ecological modernization ideas and of the Porter hypothesis that environmentalism stimulates innovation generally, which in turn has a positive impact on competitiveness, an essential ingredient in globalized marketplaces. Porter and Van der Linde's study (1995) found that of major process changes at ten manufacturers of printed circuit boards, environmental staff were behind 13 out of 33 major changes. Of these 13 changes, 12 contributed to cost reduction, eight to improvements in quality and five in extended product capabilities. Case Study 16.2 also shows that integrating environmental improvements into products is not an add-on but requires fundamental reconsideration of product and process developing and design. This in turn helps reduce costs and promotes innovation, both crucial elements in competitiveness. Sony also applies its environmental targets and strategy throughout its domestic and overseas operations, although some differences are necessary as a result of diverse local and national regulations. However, it is rational for companies that have invested in environmental innovation to try to seek the benefits of this throughout the company, thereby weakening the pollution havens hypothesis.

CASE STUDY 16.2

Environmental Policy of Sony Corporation

Sony Corporation is a Japanese MNE that is the world's fifth largest manufacturer of electronics and electronics equipment and the world's 69th largest company by revenue. Sony has strong international credentials with 163,000 employees worldwide and 83 overseas affiliates. Approximately half of its manufacturing takes place in Japan; a further 10 per cent in China; 10 per cent in the rest of Asia excluding Japan and China and 25 per cent in Europe and the Americas. Sales are fairly evenly spread with 25.6 per cent occurring in Japan in fiscal 2006; 24.6 per cent in Europe; and 26.9 per cent in the US. Its main strengths lie in consumer electronics, including audio equipment; digital cameras and video cameras; DVD-video players and recorders; televisions; ICT equipment, including personal computers and printers; and semiconductors and electronic components. Sony is also active in the entertainments industry and financial services.

Sony, like many multinationals, has developed its own complex environmental policy which has its roots in the following environmental vision:

Sony recognises the importance of preserving the natural environment that sustains life on earth for future generations and helps humanity to attain the dream of a healthy and happy life. Sony is committed to achieving this goal by seeking to combine ongoing innovation in environmental technology with environmentally sound business practices.

Sony aims for greater eco-efficiency in its business activities through maximising the efficiency of non-renewable energy and resource use and providing products and services with greater added value. Efforts will focus on reducing harmful effects on the environment by ensuring compliance with all applicable environmental regulations and reducing the impact of energy and resource use on a continuing basis.

It is the extent to which companies introduce concrete measures and targets to make such feel-good statements meaningful that establishes a company's environmental credentials. Sony's first environmental initiatives go back to the 1970s but the forerunner of current policy was the Sony Environmental Policy and the Environmental Action Plan which was enacted in 1993. This was superseded by updated plans and in 2001 by Green Management 2005, itself superseded in 2006 by Green Management 2010 which sets out environmental policy and targets until 2010. Augmenting this approach was the gradual acquisition of 14001 certification (see Case Study 16.1) by members of the Sony Group. The first Sony company to achieve this in Japan was the Sony Kohda Corporation in 1995. By 1999, all 38 manufacturing sites in Japan had achieved ISO 14001 certification and by 2002, the certification process had been completed for all Sony manufacturing sites worldwide. In 2004, ISO 14001 certification had been obtained for the headquarters functions of the Sony Group's environmental management and by 2006, the Group had completed a shift to a globally integrated environmental management system based on ISO 14001.

Once the company had developed its overall strategy and objectives, it then became possible, helped by its environmental management system, to set individual targets for priority areas. Table 16.1

sets out some of the key targets in *Green Management 2010* and the generally good progress made in achieving these targets.

Sony has also introduced several other initiatives to support its objectives, including.

Packaging

Since 1989, Sony has regarded environmentally conscious packaging as one of its key design objectives. This involves not only minimizing the amount of packaging involved but also using materials that are easily recyclable, materials for which there are well-developed recycling systems worldwide and recycled materials themselves. To facilitate recycling, Sony attempts to utilize packaging that is easily identified and separable. Moreover, Sony endeavours to ensure that hazardous substances are not incorporated into packaging materials. This is in line with EU directives on packaging and waste.

Chemical Substances

The nature of Sony's products means that many of them contain chemical substances that are classified as hazardous and which may damage the environment if their disposal is not properly controlled. Several countries have developed their own regulations to prevent such harm. Given the global nature of its business and supply chains, Sony incorporates certain standards on a global basis such as the EU's Restriction on the use of certain hazardous substances in electrical and electronic equipment (RoHS) directive and Management Methods on the Pollution Control of Electronic Information Products introduced in China. Sony has also developed its own global standards for the management of chemical standards which incorporate local and regional laws and the views of key stakeholders, and which requires the compliance of its suppliers. The company also complies with the EU's REACH (Registration, evaluation, authorization and restriction of chemicals). Through observance of these standards, Sony hopes to ensure consistent management of chemical substances globally.

TABLE 16.1 Selected Targets and Progress in Sony's *Green Management 2010*

Target	Progress by fiscal 2006 (base year = fiscal 2000)
Prevention of global warming	
Reduce GHG emissions from business sites by at least 7%	Fall of 9%
Reduce annual energy consumption of products	Achieved for 90% of product categories
Measures to reduce CO_2 emissions during transportation of products and materials	A variety of measures adopted
Resource conservation	
Waste reduction from sites of at least 40%	Increase of 31%
Waste reuse/recycle ratio of at least 99% in Japan	99%
Waste reuse/recycle ratio of at least 99% outside Japan	87%
Reduction in volume of water bought or drawn from groundwater of at least 20%	16%
Increased reused/recycled materials utilisation ratio to at least 12%	10%
Continuous increase of resource recovery from end-of-life products and reuse/recycling ratio	Resource recovery: approx 36,300 tons; reuse/recycling ratio 3%
Life cycle assessments for all major products	75% of product categories
Chemical substance management	
Reduction in release of volatile organic compounds of at least 40%	41% decrease
Reduce emissions of nitrogen oxides (NOx) and sulphur oxides (SOx)	NOx: 111 tons SOx: 47 tons
Prohibit, reduce or control use of controlled chemical substances in products	PVCs: ■ eliminated from most packaging materials; ■ switch to polyolefin materials for some power cables; AC adapter cords and electrical cords. Brominated flame retardants: ■ not used in cabinets of VAIO PCs launched in 2006; ■ printed wiring boards in 72% of A4-sized PCs contain no brominated flame retardant.

Source: www.sony.net.

Product Recycling

Sony promotes the collection and recycling of end-of-life products and strives to design products in a way that facilitates recycling. As such it ensures that it complies with appropriate regional and national laws such as the Home Appliance Recycling Law in Japan, the EU directive on Waste Electrical and Electronic Equipment (the WEEE directive) and state recycling laws in the US. *Green Management 2010* also contains two recycling targets – to continuously increase the volume of resource recovered from end-of-life products and to continuously improve the reused/recycled materials utilization ration (that is, the percentage of reused/recycled materials in terms of weight of total resource input).

CASE STUDY QUESTIONS

1. Compare and contrast Sony's environmental strategy with that of another MNE involved in the consumer electronics sector.

2. Sony has adopted a globally integrated environmental management system based on ISO 14001 (see Case Study 16.1). Consider the advantages that such a strategy may bring to Sony.

3. As a multinational firm, Sony is producing and marketing its products throughout the world. What advantages do you envisage from the adoption of an integrated environmental strategy and what obstacles could an MNE encounter in attempting to adopt such a strategy? Use Sony as your starting point, but consider the challenges facing MNEs in general.

Furthermore, the limited evidence that is available suggests that firms which take sustainability more seriously also tend to perform well in terms of profitability. This may simply be because better-managed companies also take environmental issues more seriously. It is also sometimes claimed that attention paid to environmental matters conveys first mover advantages on a firm: that is, firms adopting an aggressively environmental approach ahead of regulation will have significant advantages once regulation is introduced.

CONCLUSION

Environmental issues have a strong international dimension with significant implications for business, both domestic and international. Pollution is no respecter of borders: many anthropogenic environmental problems such as stratospheric ozone depletion and the movement of hazardous waste and chemicals are just some of the cross-border environmental issues demanding the attention of policy makers at local, national, regional and international levels. Even apparently purely domestic environmental concerns that spawn domestic regulations have international implications if the regulations operate as trade barriers. Business must respond to and take into account in its planning the host of environmental regulations to which it is now subject and is increasingly voluntarily undertaking environmental initiatives.

Summary of Key Concepts

1. Many environmental issues have a cross-border or even global dimension. However, a differentiated response may be the best way of dealing with them.
2. Although companies still resist environmental regulations on the grounds that they increase costs, good environmental practice is increasingly seen as boosting competitiveness.
3. Trade–environmental disputes and the potential clash between multilateral environmental agreements (MEAs) and multilateral trade rules have thrust the WTO under the environmental spotlight.
4. Businesses are increasingly responding to the environmental incentive through voluntary measures such as ISO 14001 certification and corporate codes of conduct.

Activity

1. Research the approach to environmental matters in an emerging economy of your choice. Do your findings support or undermine the assumptions of the Environmental Kuznets Curve?

Discussion Questions

1. According to the principles of ecological modernization, attention to environmental issues by business has a positive impact on the bottom line and on competitiveness. Investigate this claim and discuss the extent to which it is justified.

2. 'The criticism of the WTO on environmental matters is totally unjustified.' What are the arguments for and against this statement?

3. Do voluntary measures represent real progress in corporate social responsibility or are they merely a way of businesses avoiding stricter compulsory measures? Try to find examples to support your argument.

4. Choose a multinational company and research its environmental claims and record. Does the evidence indicate that the company's claims are genuine or are they merely a public relations exercise? Justify your conclusions.

5. 'Concerns for the environment and globalization are incompatible.' Discuss this statement.

References and Suggestions for Further Reading

Bhagwati, J. (1997) 'Free trade and the environment', in *Writings on International Economics*, Oxford: Oxford University Press.

Daschle, T. (2007) 'Food for fuel?: debating the tradeoffs of corn-based ethanol', *Foreign Affairs*, Vol. 86, No. 5, 157–162.

Goudie, A. (2006) *The Human Impact on the Natural Environment: Past, Present and Future*, Malden, MA: Blackwell Publishers.

Harvard Business Review (2007) *On Green Business Strategy*, Harvard Business Review, November, Cambridge, MA: Harvard Business Press.

Hussein, A. (2008) *Principles of Environmental Economics*, Rev. edn, London: Routledge.

Kolk, A. and Pinkse, J. (2008) *International Business and Global Climate Change*, London: Routledge.

Lomborg, B. (2001) *The Skeptical Environmentalist: Measuring the Real State of the World*, Cambridge: Cambridge University Press.

OECD (2007) *Biofuels: Is the Cure Worse Than the Disease?* Report for the Roundtable on Sustainable Development held on 11 September 2007, SG/SD/RT(2007)4.

Porter, M. and Van der Linde, C. (1995) 'Green and competitive: ending the stalemate', *Harvard Business Review*, Vol. 73, No. 5, 120–134.

Renner, M. (2000) *Working for the Environment: A Growing Source of Jobs*, Washington, DC: Worldwatch Institute.

Runge, C.F. and Senauer, B. (2007) 'How biofuels could starve the poor', *Foreign Affairs*, Vol. 86, No. 3, 41–53.

Trebilcock, M. and Howse, R. (2005) *The Regulation of International Trade*, 3rd edn, London: Routledge.

Vaughan, S. and Nordström, H. (1999) *Trade and Environment*, WTO Special Studies 4, Geneva: WTO.

Weale, A. (1992) 'The politics of ecological modernisation', in *The New Politics of Pollution*, Manchester: Manchester University Press, Chapter 3.

World Commission on Environment and Development (1987) *Our Common Future* (commonly known as the Brundtland Report), Oxford: Oxford University Press.

Young, S. (ed.) (2000) *The Emergence of Ecological Modernisation: Integrating the Environment and the Economy*, London: Routledge.

Chapter 17

The International Monetary System and Global Financial Integration

Finance is the art of passing currency from hand to hand until it finally disappears.

Robert W. Sarnoff (1919–1997), ex-chairman of RCA

LEARNING OBJECTIVES

This chapter will help you to:

- identify the form, nature and evolution of the international monetary system (IMS)

- appreciate the role of the IMS in international trade

- understand how the IMS impacts upon global business

- understand the emergence of global financial capitalism

- identify causes of instability and uncertainty within the IMS

The integration of financial markets is an important landmark on the road to globalization. In the move towards a global resource base, no other market has exhibited the same degree of maturity in terms of globality. The advocates of financial globalization claim that moves towards integrated capital markets are essential pre-requisites if the global economy is to generate increased trade, economic growth and development. Despite these positive aspects, global financial markets can be a destabilizing force within the global economy. This chapter is based around these two contrasting themes. The chapter first explores the strategic importance of the international monetary system (IMS), tracking its evolution and how it is managed, before leading to an examination of the emergence of global financial capitalism. Thereafter, market failure, notably the recurrent financial crises that have become a feature of the IMS, is addressed. In the light of these issues, it concludes with a discussion of the major issues on the agenda for reform of the IMS in the aftermath of the global financial crisis of 2008 to 2009.

THE FORM AND NATURE OF THE INTERNATIONAL MONETARY SYSTEM AND THE EMERGING GLOBAL FINANCIAL INTEGRATION

The process of globalization is linked intimately with the development of a global capital market. An integrated global capital market exhibits the following features:

- efficiency of transactions, that is, borrowers and lenders can make deals with ease wherever they are;
- mobility of savings, thereby improving efficiency in inter-temporal resource allocation;
- the facilitation of risk sharing, whereby lenders spread risks by distributing loans through holding a diverse range of assets across space;
- capital flows balance out differentials between savings and investment so that balance of payments problems do not lead to friction;
- greater uniformity in terms of the cost of capital (as expressed through real interest rates);
- greater risk transfer, a process that smoothes consumption through risk diversification.

The pervasive adoption of free market ideology; the economic expansion of developing states; advances in ICTs and the removal of barriers to the mobility of goods, services, capital and knowledge have all been fuelled by the simultaneous expansion and globalization of financial markets (see Chapter 2). In addition to the growing importance of ICTs in the global integration of capital markets, the process has been driven by two other factors. First, there has been an increasing concentration of market power in the hands of institutions such as pension funds and insurance companies. Second, financial innovation, notably the securitization of funds (allowing firms to borrow direct from the market rather than through banks), has increased the supply of financial assets that are tradable and priced in global markets.

Overall, 80 per cent of global capital flows are between three regions: the US, the UK and the eurozone. The US operates as the world's financial intermediary, receiving mainly debt but sending out equity and FDI. By 2005, the inflows and outflows of the US totalled $1.5 trillion. The UK's importance is also based on financial intermediation especially in terms of cross-border lending, and its outflows and inflows amounted to $1.4 trillion in 2005. By contrast, due to its isolated position, Japan's capital flows are lower than those of China, even though the latter's financial stock is only a quarter the size of the former. Despite the dominance of these financial hubs of international capital flows, money is also flowing into other parts of the global economy. Indeed, capital inflows into emerging economies have grown twice as fast as those into developed economies since 1990.

The benefits from greater financial liberalization arise from widening the pool of funds available to enterprises and states to promote growth, development and trade. Investors are also able to diversify portfolios and spread risks. Thus, capital mobility implies the following:

- Households, firms or states smooth consumption by borrowing money from abroad when incomes are low, thereby dampening the effects of business cycles.
- Economic actors can reduce exposure to developments in the domestic economy by diversifying investments.

The capability of markets to deliver such benefits depends upon the quality of information available and the ability and willingness of enterprises to act upon it. The poorer the available information, the less financial integration will work to the benefit of the global economy. Financial integration can also be impeded by asymmetric information that causes crises within the system and hinders the willingness of investors to offer funds (see below).

Figure 17.1 highlights the set of interrelationships that expanded the role of international finance in the global economy. It shows that the deregulation of capital flows is merely one stage in the expansion of international capital flows and implies a virtuous cycle of expanding international finance. What is also important in the seemingly inevitable drive towards deregulation of financial markets is the pressure from trade and intense foreign competition that forces a re-examination of the rules.

Over time, there have been notable changes in the form and nature of international capital flows. The first important trend is that finance for trade now constitutes only a small proportion of the total financial flows between states. The vast majority of these flows are driven by portfolio investment. A second trend is the relative rise in private capital flows compared to flows stemming from official bodies. Private capital flows represented over 80 per cent of all flows in 2006. A third trend is the increasing integration of developing states into global financial markets. These states have become an important destination for global capital. The rise in investment in these states has been driven by:

FIGURE 17.1

The Links between Trade and International Finance

Source: Adapted from the *Economist* (1992).

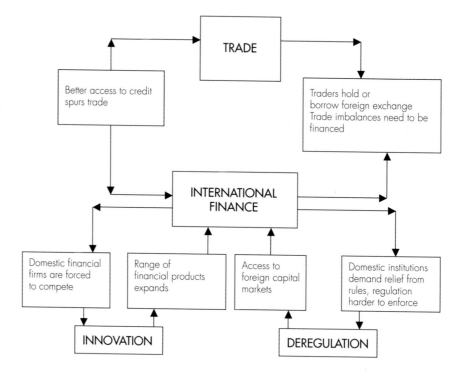

- low international interest rates;
- economic reform in developing states;
- financial liberalization in developed states.

However, the link between financial integration and economic growth has not been firmly established. In addition, there is little evidence that financial markets have created stability and imposed constraints on the actions of policy makers. Indeed, where integration is new, the process has tended to increase instability. This may be because financial integration has occurred in an uneven manner across the global economy. As the market is imperfect with capital moving in directions that would not be expected by liberal theory, financial integration may actually harm some states.

Despite the trend towards increased international capital flows, there is still evidence of a home bias (the so-called home-bias puzzle) in investment decisions as portfolios tend towards domestic assets and as indigenous savings tend to be absorbed domestically (the Feldstein-Horika paradox). These features are not anticipated in a move towards financial integration and create what Okina *et al.* (1999) call a 'globalisation puzzle'. This suggests that national borders create a barrier to the globalisation of financial markets. In order to overcome such problems, new financial instruments such as derivatives have emerged. These have led to new and increasing financial flows, notably in terms of increased interest rate arbitrage (moving assets to exploit rate differentials between states) and the diversification of interest rate and foreign exchange risks.

Home bias and the Feldstein-Horika paradox indicate that, despite the increased flow of capital across borders, there has been no substantial long-term transfer of resources. Indeed, the evidence seems to suggest that much of the capital mobility is driven by short-term capital flows. The notion that low transactions costs and technological advances promote greater capital markets has not really been borne out by experience. Capital seems to be less mobile than some other resources owing to the aforementioned existence of imperfect information. Significantly, while transaction costs have decreased, key enforcement costs (the costs of enforcing contracts) have not. While these costs remain, parties will be reluctant to engage in long-term lending.

Also undermining the true global nature of the financial integration is the so-called Lucas paradox. This suggests that the flow of capital from rich to poor states which would be expected within free markets has not occurred. The causes of this lie in one or more of the following factors. The first arises from differences in fundamentals (such as factors of production, government policy and institutions) that affect the production structure of the economy. The second reflects international capital market imperfections based mainly on sovereign risk (likelihood of default on loans – see Chapter 8) and information asymmetries. Research suggests that institutional quality is the most important factor explaining this paradox. This relates to human capital, government stability, bureaucratic quality, non-corruption and law and order.

GLOBAL BUSINESS AND THE INTERNATIONAL MONETARY SYSTEM

The commercial salience of the international monetary system has grown with the shift towards global financial integration in both developed and developing states. The resulting global capital market is a core asset, enabling businesses to achieve their strategic ambitions (see below). In a true global capital market, the market for savings and wealth is driven by the highest bidder or the outlet that offers the highest returns, irrespective of the location of the investment. A global capital market also means that a wide range of assets carry the same risk-adjusted return. The development of a genuine global capital market is still some way off owing to factors such as currency risk, the threat of government intermediation and the resistance of actors to utilize foreign facilities.

The importance of the IMS to the global business environment derives from the rules established to enable states to value and exchange currencies. The system also provides a mechanism for correcting imbalances between a state's international payments and its receipts. A further aspect of the IMS is the determination of the cost of converting currency. Importantly, the framework provides a system for managing the internal and external aspects of economic policy. Within this framework, governments should seek to rationalize domestic policy objectives and stabilize the external value of their currencies. These policy objectives have increasingly been shaped by the globalization process, notably the moves towards free capital mobility and global financial market integration. Domestic economic policies have often been guided by the need to manage these flows through the sustenance of a stable exchange rate. This underlines the importance of commitment and credibility to the rules of economic policy.

Inevitably, the business environment is shaped by access to and the availability of capital. The point of the system is to ensure that the emerging global capital market can allocate resources to maximize returns for the pool of available investment funds. To enable businesses to access this pool of funds, the system needs a degree of stability to overcome market impediments to their efficient allocation.

There have been concerted efforts by policy bodies to secure an enhanced degree of stability within the system through measures to offer effective and coordinated management of economic policy – whether through intergovernmental bodies such as the IMF and the World Bank or through measures via organizations such as the G-8 (see below).

The most evident impact of the IMS upon business and its performance is through the exchange rate. Exporting businesses need to operate in foreign currencies and the rate of conversion directly influences pricing strategies and feeds through into non-price competition. The rate of conversion has a direct bearing upon the ability of businesses to compete effectively within both domestic and international markets. Issues related to the costs of converting currencies compound the question of overvalued and undervalued currencies. For multinational businesses and for SMEs alike, these costs can be substantial. Thus minimizing such impacts can be an important factor shaping the form and location of an enterprise's activities. The exchange rate can affect the business environment, inducing uncertainty and increasing the risks associated with globalization and trade. Exchange rate effects can also transmit themselves into the broader economic environment, causing further uncertainty and risk within businesses by stimulating inflation, altering the nature of growth and creating unemployment with consequent effects upon fiscal and monetary policy.

Issues surrounding the exchange rate also highlight another key issue for business: economic stability. Economic stability is measured in broad macro-economic terms by low and stable inflation; a sustainable balance of payments position; low and mildly positive real interest rates, and a sustainable fiscal position. These conditions are key factors influencing investment decisions by enterprises. These broadly defined macro criteria are increasingly related to the state of micro-economic reform, especially in terms of the regulation of factor and commodity markets. They are further related to another powerful factor – namely, the degree of political stability within a state or within the IMS as a whole. Political commitment and the credibility of political systems to deliver a favourable set of economic circumstances is a powerful factor promoting the stability of the economic system.

These issues in combination influence the behaviour of investors and their effects have their most evident short-term expression via changes in the value of the exchange rate. These issues also hint at the nature of the interface between businesses and the IMS, which stems from the need for foreign currencies to:

- underpin trade, including export credit;
- realize foreign direct investment (e.g. investment in physical capital);
- support portfolio investment (for the purchase of financial assets for long-term holding);
- financial speculation (a demand based on attempts by speculators to exploit differentials in asset prices and so on purely for short-term gain);
- underpin arbitrage (that is, the exploitation of price or rate of return differentials between states).

These cross-border flows highlight differences between investments made for short-term gain and those made for the long term. Each form of capital movement has a different motive and desired outcome, and can expose the enterprise to risks from instability in local political and financial systems that can either reduce the value of the investment or render the funds irrecoverable. These are financial risks faced by any business involved in the process of globalizing. Changes in financial conditions also have the capability to undermine the profitability of investments. Avoiding this risk has been a primary motive behind the development of the single currency within the EU where it was felt that the elimination of the exchange rate risk would stimulate trade among member states.

While there is an absence of any clear evidence to suggest that exchange rate risk deters globalization, most internationalizing businesses develop strategies to counter such risks. Companies can deal with exchange rate risk because:

- the hedging of risk on specific transactions is easy: the advent of advanced ICTs allows businesses to manage multi-currency cash flows to minimize the effects of currency fluctuations;
- a global financing policy provides a natural hedge as funding foreign assets in local currency will offset currency movements and protect the value of the company;
- not all currencies collapse at once, allowing companies to offset changes in one currency;
- currency movements also affect competitors, meaning that a company may not be adversely affected vis-à-vis its competitors.

THE EVOLUTION OF THE INTERNATIONAL MONETARY SYSTEM

The evolution of the IMS has been shaped by market forces and by changes in policy design as priorities alter. These changes are most evident in terms of how policy makers have sought to reconcile exchange rate stability and domestic policy objectives in an environment marked by increased capital mobility.

The Gold Standard (where a unit of currency was convertible into a pre-set quantity of gold) that prevailed at the beginning of the twentieth century appeared to manage free capital mobility with exchange stability much better than the current system. The persistence of the Gold Standard was underpinned by the commitment of the participants to the maintenance of gold convertibility and domestic policy actions were subordinate to this objective. This was coupled with a lack of political pressure to reorientate policy towards other, more politically expedient objectives. The stability of the system was also assisted by the smooth interaction of the Gold Standard with private markets. Adherence to the Gold Standard was treated by investors as a seal of approval and allowed states greater access to foreign capital. This was aided by other stability-promoting factors such as freer, more flexible markets that facilitated internal adjustments to shocks without the need to resort to a change in the exchange rate.

This period of stability ended with the outbreak of the First World War. The legacy of the war in terms of its massive political and economic upheavals meant that the Gold Standard could not be restored as it had been following previous conflicts. It was resurrected in the mid-1920s but had lost its robustness and was unable to cope with the 1930s depression and the reversal of globalization that accompanied it. This fragility was driven by the emergence of competing policy objectives that undermined the credibility of the system. Further strains were created by the legacy of war reparation and debt, increased market inflexibility and less frequent central bank cooperation. In 1931, the international system collapsed – capital flows diminished rapidly, states developed beggar-thy-neighbour policies and there was a general shift away from the view that internationalization was beneficial. The result was that protectionism increased and the global economy disintegrated.

No firm rules emerged for the IMS until towards the end of the Second World War when the Bretton Woods agreements were signed (see Chapters 2 and 4). The new system allowed for fixed yet adjustable exchange rates and the use of exchange controls to avoid destabilizing speculation. It also created the IMF as a means of facilitating monetary cooperation. Because of this flexibility, realignments were rare within the Bretton Woods system. Policy makers were unconvinced of the desirability of floating exchange rates and thus tried to keep rates as stable as possible. For many states, the exchange rate became the cornerstone of an economic policy in which the stability of the real economy and the exchange rate reinforced each other. With robust growth within the global economy, there was generally an absence of pressure to devalue or to revert to the beggar-thy-neighbour policies of previous eras. This was aided by the fact that states kept a tight rein on any potentially destabilizing capital flows. This was not to last: business attempts to circumvent capital controls, diverging domestic policy objectives and the inadequacy of international reserves helped bring the system to an end. The inflation of the 1970s was a primary cause of the collapse as states sought to delink themselves from the dollar as a means of preventing the spread of inflation to other developed states from the US.

The move to flexible exchange rates was a seemingly spontaneous reaction to changing economic circumstances. States could no longer offer the same policy solutions to solve their problems. Over time, this created a policy shift towards open markets, economic reform and policy priorities shaped by a low inflation goal. This was the era when the removal of global capital controls began. The increased flow of capital across borders, combined with domestic policy imbalances and volatile exchange rates, created a number of crises within the IMS (see below), leading to calls for further reform of the system.

It is clear that a pegged exchange rate, free capital movements and an independent monetary policy cannot be achieved concurrently. Much of the development within the IMS has revolved around shifting priorities among these criteria. For example, pre-1914, domestic policy was subordinate to the exchange rate. Bretton Woods used capital controls to give a greater degree of discretion in domestic economic policy. Policy priorities have been slow to evolve, possibly due to the strong grip of the ideologies that have shaped these arrangements; vested interests in favour of the status quo; a desire not to break ranks with other states for fear of upsetting markets, and the failure of policy makers to promote a coherent strategy for change.

By the turn of the millennium, over 100 states had declared a policy of allowing their currency to float against others. This was a marked increase – around 37 per cent – over the previous decade. Despite this move towards flexibility, other states were trying to induce greater stability by the development of currency boards, dollarization or other semi-fixed exchange rates. This supports the view that the choice of exchange rate objective is perhaps the most important macro-economic policy issue to be addressed by states.

In its current phase of its evolution, the IMS is characterized by a set of 'non-rules'. That is, there are no hard and fast rules regarding the exchange rate regime states must adopt and consequently most states have an independent monetary policy. However, the notion of freedom implied by such a framework is severely limited and states are constrained by market-generated rules over the form and nature of economic policy. These stress the growing interdependence and integration to which domestic economic policies have to adjust. Thus there is a culture of best practice to which states hold as a means of ensuring stability within the context of the IMS. There is, however, a growing dissatisfaction with this framework as it has failed to solve instability within the system (see below). Such instability has the potential to undermine the benefits of the shift towards globalization.

MANAGING THE INTERNATIONAL MONETARY SYSTEM

In the absence of fixed global rules, management of the IMS occurs through a system of coordination and cooperation operating through a number of organizations that seek to promote stability and continuity within the system. The key organizations (which are examined in more detail in Chapter 4) are:

- *G-8*: this group of leading industrialized states meets regularly to address issues of common concern and to make progress on policy coordination.
- *IMF*: the IMF aims to foster stability within the IMS and, towards this end, offers support for short-term financial imbalances.
- *World Bank*: this organization is concerned with long-term economic development.

The emergence of these and other organizations is borne out of a recognition that there are evident constraints upon the functioning of domestic economic policy as well as spill-overs between the respective policy domains of the larger industrial states. Thus changes in the actions of one large state can have economic ramifications for other states. These organizations seek to generate greater certainty and predictability of policy actions as well as to generate information regarding the thinking of key policy actors (through, for example, the publishing of the minutes of central bank meetings on interest rate decisions).

Typical of this framework is the role played by the IMF in developing increased transparency in monetary and financial policies. The organization has developed a best practice guide to ensure that, not only does the public know of the objectives and instruments of policy, but also that there is a degree of accountability. This process is supported by ongoing surveillance by the IMF of these policies. The rationale for this is to promote stability within the system by highlighting sources of potential turmoil and instability before they spill over into financial markets and destabilize the commercial system.

These processes highlight the fundamental and pivotal role of the IMF as a focus of international cooperation within the monetary system. The need for this cooperation is strengthened by the fact that many of the leading currencies (notably the dollar, the yen and the euro) are used for international transactions. This implies that national and supranational monetary policies have a direct policy spill-over in other states. This underlines the IMF view that the IMS is a 'global public good' – that is, a good that is universally consumed, applies equally to all and will benefit all if it works effectively. Likewise, all will suffer should it work poorly.

The mutual influence of economic policies provides the rationale for economic cooperation. Cooperation between states has been a feature of the economic landscape for some time and globalization has strengthened the rationale to engage in cooperation. Policy co-operation does vary with some states – notably within the context of regional integration agreements – going for all-out harmonization and even common policies, as demonstrated by the EU's introduction of the euro. There are four forms of cooperation:

1.   information exchange;
2.   coordination;
3.   harmonization;
4.   unification.

While concerns exist over loss of national autonomy, cooperation is difficult to implement. For example, disagreement between European states on whether interest rates should rise or fall was one of the major factors causing the instability within the European monetary arena in the early 1990s.

The conventional view is that globalization has rendered domestic policy levers less effective than before with national governments finding their room for manoeuvre increasingly limited. In terms of monetary policy, financial innovation has made controlling the money supply increasingly difficult: its definition has been muddied and the link between the growth of money and growth of the economy has proven to be not as direct as previously believed. In short, policy makers found that as they tried to control the money supply, they changed the nature of what they were trying to control. In a world of free-flowing capital, monetary policy has to be dedicated either to an exchange rate target or to meeting domestic objectives. Floating exchange rates give states a degree of autonomy but they still need to consider the implications of autonomous actions that induce instability.

Problems of external debt pinpoint the constraints upon fiscal policy. Excessive borrowing by governments – partly fuelled by increased global capital resources – clearly has the capability to induce uncertainty when states default on borrowings and put financial institutions at risk. Financial markets also do not like reckless spending, as it puts pressure on interest rates and could mean higher taxes. Financial markets can be strong disciplinarians, cutting off the supply of capital quickly. Freer capital flows also allow markets to 'vote' on policies to move money abroad to avoid the risk, inflation or higher taxes that could result from reckless accumulation of government debt. Global markets can constrain tax rises; most evidently those that fall upon businesses as multinationals can easily shift production to those areas where tax obligations are less burdensome.

These issues underline the constraints upon policy makers in developing a domestic policy framework if they wish to avoid denting investor confidence. These constraints upon finance can cause a decline in the exchange rate and result in economic malaise. Governments can seek to generate greater confidence through economic reform and greater independence for key bodies such as central banks. In short, keeping the political cycle out of the development of economic policy can allow for the evolution of a credible set of policies that gives the government greater discretion. This underlines the requirement that in the context of global capital, policy makers need to create strong institutional structures, policy credibility and public sector discipline.

Evidence on the effectiveness of macro-policy coordination is mixed. Some see it as an excuse for political inaction; others see it as overwhelmingly positive and more see it as inevitable. Many argue that although coordination is flawed, it does offer the possibility of developing better policies and is useful for the implementation of unpopular but necessary policies, therefore producing better policies than would exist were it not present.

THE RISE OF GLOBAL FINANCIAL CAPITALISM

Wolf (2007) argues that the degree of financial integration within the global economy is causing capitalism to mutate, giving rise to what he terms 'global financial capitalism'. This process has been driven by deregulation which has led to many new developments within the sector (emerging mainly from the US) to have a true global reach. The core drivers of this mutation are:

1. The explosion of finance: the ratio of global financial assets to annual world output has risen from 109 per cent in 1980 to 316 per cent in 2005 with the stock of financial assets reaching $315 billion (2005). This trend has been especially marked within the eurozone where the ratio of financial assets to GDP has increased from 180 per cent in 1995 to 303 per cent in 2005.
2. Finance has become more transactions orientated: bank deposits have declined. Capital markets are performing the intermediation functions of the banking system which in turn has shifted from short-term commercial lending to longer term investment banking based on durable and sustained relations with customers.
3. A complex set of innovative financial products have emerged (such as derivatives) which have transformed the management of risk within the financial system.
4. New players have emerged (such as hedge funds and private equity funds) which have provided new sources of finance to industry and sources of value within the global network.
5. Financial capitalism has become ever more global as the international financial assets owned by residents of high-income states have risen to 330 per cent of GDP in 2005 from 50 per cent in the mid-1970s.

The combination of global players and assets has given rise to a new financial system. The global reach of the financial system does not merely include the big banks but also extends to smaller hedge funds and private equity investors (see below). These have been driven by technology and liberalization issues (see Chapter 2). Increased freedom of where and how to invest combined with the ability of technology to generate and price increasingly complex transactions has allowed 24-hour trading. These have been aided by two other factors: the revolution in financial economics and the ability of central banks to generate price stability. These longer-term issues have been assisted by more short-term considerations such as the global savings and liquidity gluts. As of 2005, the global reach of the market was visible in a number of segments, notably:

- the international banking market was worth $25 billion of cross-border claims;
- the foreign exchange market with a daily turnover of $2 trillion;
- the $18 billion-worth of international debt securities outstanding;
- a derivatives market worth $415 trillion.

Perhaps the major impact of these trends is that they have democratized global capital markets. Households can hold a more diverse array of assets and borrow more easily, thereby allowing them to smooth out consumption over their lifetime. At the corporate level it has become increasingly easier for companies to merge or be acquired by other companies. This has caused controversy, especially with regard to the activities of private equity funds. However, the global market for corporate control has greatly increased the power of owners over management. Furthermore, the power of national capital has become secondary to global capital. According to Wolf, another consequence has been the emergence of London and New York as the two dominant financial centres based on the legacy of Anglo-Saxon ideas inherent in this new form of capitalism. The move to this global financial capitalism has arguments in its favour:

- active financial investors can identify and attack inefficiency;
- it improves the global efficiency of capital;
- it imposes disciplines upon management;
- it facilitates the finance of new activities;
- it can put old activities into the hands of people who will run them better;
- It is better able to cope with global risk;
- investors can put capital where it will work best;
- it enables ordinary people to manage their finances more successfully.

However, many pessimists feel that the emergence of global financial capitalism is fraught with risks and problems that could erode any advantages from the system. The main concerns revolve around the following issues:

- the system creates new divides in socioeconomic structures;
- the system is based on a series of contingencies, most notably on benign monetary conditions that are unlikely to be sustainable;
- many institutions have taken huge risks that are simply not sustainable and risk undermining the credibility of the system (as was borne out by later events – see below);
- the new capitalism was untested by financial crises and other pressures exerted upon it;
- by allowing legal tax avoidance, the system can undermine its popular support;
- there is little movement of this capital into developing states, creating the risk of further divisions with more developed economies.

There is also increasing concern as to the end-point of this system. There is a danger that the need for ever higher returns makes financiers take greater and greater risks that could undermine confidence and premeditate a crisis in the financial system. This was borne out by the events of 2007 to 2008 (see below). There is concern that many financial funds are too leveraged, taking on too much debt when the likelihood of lower returns is high. Of course, these arguments are similar to those of Strange (1998), who argued that the global system was becoming one big casino which would result in global volatility and erosion of the political power of states. According to Strange (1998), there was a need to see beyond the liberal paradigm and examine the structuralist elements in the international system. Thus the international financial system would merely reinforce existing power structures and not democratize the system.

A further concern is that there is limited scope for developing states to gain by opening their markets to global capital. The growth benefits from global financial integration occur almost solely in the richest states with little direct relationship between financial openness and economic growth being evident. This reflects the Lucas paradox (see above). Research from the IMF suggests that those developing states that grow fastest are those that invest more and rely less on foreign capital. Thus the reliance on global finance may actually reduce growth.

The emergence of the global financial system has created two problems. First, the pace of product innovation has outstripped the capacity of users and regulators to understand these products. The complexity understates not only the nature of the risks involved but also disguises who is responsible for such risks. Second, there is insufficient means or understanding to regulate the global nature of these emergent financial products and organizations. Regulation largely takes place at the national level while the industry is global. The industry has been developed by clever mathematicians whose job it is to make the products complex and difficult to understand. These represent a major barrier to effective regulation.

George Soros (1998) has also been critical of this emergent financial system. He suggests that its ability to create winners and losers will lead to the latter seeking to reimpose capital controls. Soros argues that unconstrained capitalism is an enemy of open society as market values will penetrate all aspects of life, eroding social values and loosening moral constraints. Capitalism and free markets are not natural bedfellows as plural markets do not always need plural societies to flourish. Indeed, if plurality means instability then markets could well do without free speech. In fact, international banks and MNCs can often work with autocratic regimes.

In effect, the rise of global financial capitalism reflects the high point (as highlighted below) of the long process of deregulation that began in the 1970s. The incremental deregulation unleashed high rates of innovation within financial markets. This rate of innovation made global financial markets considerably more difficult to regulate. Devices such as futures, options and swaps are all based on the firm making a small initial exposure but these can lead to much larger risks if conditions turn against the investor. Another innovation was securitization – at the core of the 2008 crisis – which involved bundling loans into packages which were then sold to outside investors. This was popular in the US mortgage market. Thus, when homeowners made their payments to the service agents, these funds were passed on to investors as payment on their bonds. These products were seen as beneficial as they spread risk. Such was their popularity that they grew ever more complex and it was the increased complexity of such products that was at the root of the 2007 to 2008 global financial crisis.

Box 17.1 Key Players in the Emerging Global Financial System

A key feature of global financial capitalism is the rise to prominence of a number of key institutional investors who make large portfolio investments across the global economy. These institutional investors were traditionally dominated by large investment banks, insurance companies and pension funds. These institutions have been joined in the fluid capital markets of the global financial system by more innovative businesses such as:

■ *Private equity funds*: these fluid funds invest in companies or business units with the intention of gaining a controlling interest in the operation. Such funds target a business that is less than the sum of its parts or that is underperforming or undervalued. Upon acquiring the company (often through a leveraged buy-out – a purchase that involves taking on a large debt), the fund will restructure the business to increase efficiency with the intention of selling the business on for a price that is higher than its purchase price. Often these businesses are owned for between three to seven years. Private equity funds are controversial as they often involve job losses and are accompanied by handsome returns for the fund managers. On the positive side, some argue that these funds have a positive net effect on employment and place their businesses in an excellent position for long-term growth. Major private equity funds include KKR and the Texas Pacific Group.

■ *Hedge funds*: these are investment funds that charge a performance fee; are often open to a very few investors, and configure themselves to hedge against adverse market moves. Hedge funds use debt to invest and use these investments to stimulate shareholder activism to generate a takeover or to insist upon management changes. Their assets are very liquid and enable the fund to leave when it sees fit. However, hedge funds have proved controversial, as many have exposed themselves to excessive risk. The collapse of Long Term Capital Fund (a high-profile US hedge fund) highlighted how a lack of scrutiny of these bodies may generate excessive risk taking by these bodies. According to many bankers their collapse has the ability to cause a broader crisis within the financial system.

FINANCIAL STABILITY AND CRISES IN THE GLOBAL ECONOMY

The history of twentieth/twenty-first-century international finance is characterized by bouts of stability and instability. Investors of all shapes and sizes crave stability within the IMS to facilitate the making of investment plans but involvement within the international financial system inevitably sees investors undertaking some degree of risk. While some investors seek out riskier investments in the hope that they generate an above-average return, others seek to avoid risk at all costs (the main forms and types of risk are highlighted in Table 17.1). However, when investors take excessive risks and returns from that risky investment are threatened, the system tends to lurch towards a crisis: investment capital moves quickly out of specific economies or types of investment, causing instability within the financial system if the flows are of sufficient magnitude. Since the mid-1990s, the IMS has witnessed periods of stability and instability as the system continues to adjust to the legacy of a more open global financial system.

In general, the following types of crises may be identified:

■ *Currency crises*: these are generated by a sustained speculative attack on the exchange value of a currency with the result that, to avoid rapid depreciation, the authorities are forced to act by using foreign exchange to defend the currency or by devaluing sharply (see, for example, the Argentinean Crisis of the early twenty-first century).

- *Banking crises*: runs on banks or banking failures induce banks to suspend the internal convertibility of their liabilities. This compels the authorities to act to prevent the failure from causing a damaging loss of confidence in the banking system as highlighted below; this was the type of crisis that was pervasive in 2007 to 2008.
- *Systemic financial crises*: these are severe disruptions to financial markets that curtail their ability to act effectively with consequent damaging effects on the real economy. Again, this type of crisis was evident in the events of 2007 to 2008.
- *Foreign debt crises*: situations where a state cannot meet or service its foreign debt (see, for example, Mexico in the mid-1980s).

TABLE 17.1 The Risks of Neo-liberal Financial Integration

Risk	Definition	Drivers
Currency risk	Risk of a sharp decline in the value of the currency	■ absence of foreign reserves ■ inability to orchestrate multilateral currency rescues
Flight risk	Risk that holders of liquid financial assets will sell their holdings *en masse* in the face of perceived difficulty	■ investor herding ■ interaction with currency risk ■ rise in political uncertainty ■ absence of mechanisms to manage capital flows
Fragility risk	Vulnerability of an economy's internal and external borrowers to internal or external shocks that inhibit their ability to meet obligations	■ borrowers finance long-term obligations with short-term credit, creating vulnerability to changes in credit conditions ■ borrowers finance debt in overseas currency, making them vulnerable to currency shifts ■ finance of debt with capital that is subject to flight risk
Contagion risk	Risk that a state will fall victim to financial and macro-economic instability that is sourced elsewhere	■ financial openness ■ extent of capital flight and fragility risk
Sovereignty risk	Risk that a government will face constraints on its ability to pursue independent socioeconomic policies	■ pursuit of contractionary policies to limit capital flight ■ contractionary policy to attract capital to the state ■ consequence of external assistance

Source: Grabel (2000).

These different forms of crisis often have common origins (all of which can exist simultaneously), notably the accumulation of unsustainable economic imbalances and misalignments in asset prices or exchange rates. A crisis is triggered by a sudden loss of confidence that exposes fundamental weaknesses in the economy in terms of a sudden correction in overvalued assets or through the failure of key institutions. The vulnerability of states to such crises depends upon the credibility of economic policy, the robustness of the financial system and, of course, the size of the imbalance itself.

Financial Instability in the 1990s: The rise of Contagion

The 1990s saw a resurgence of capital flows to developing states. However, the composition of the flows was different to those of the past as portfolio investment replaced bank lending as the primary source of foreign financing for these countries. The other sea change was that the majority of this funding went to the private sector. This shift was stimulated by:

■ higher interest rates in developing economies;
■ increasing investor confidence in the economic reforms underway in developing economies;
■ the legacy of international action that resulted in more successful management of developing country debt;
■ removal of the restrictions imposed by developing states on many forms of foreign investment;
■ the privatization of state-owned enterprises which provided attractive opportunities to foreign investors.

The focus of this foreign investment was Latin America and East Asia. However, the short-term nature of this funding implied that its impact on the long-term economic development of these areas could be negligible. In addition, as these funds tend to be liquid, they could be withdrawn quickly and, indeed, have contributed to the financial crises that have dogged the IMS.

The factors that underlie the emergence of the imbalances which render an economy vulnerable to financial crisis include:

■ unsustainable macro-economic policies (such as a growing budget deficit);
■ large foreign debt;
■ large amount of short-term borrowing (which can result in a liquidity crisis);
■ the size of the current account deficit;
■ weakness in financial structures;
■ global financial conditions;
■ exchange rate misalignment;
■ political instability.

These trends can also be accentuated by shifts in the trade cycle. These underlying causes of crisis need to be differentiated from 'proximate' causes such as news and events. Assessing the vulnerability of states to such crises is difficult. However, indicators such as sharp changes in interest rates and the indebtedness of the banking system may be used as broad indicators.

A core feature of the 1990s crises was contagion – or a clustering of economic crises in temporal terms. Contagion is caused by the following:

- The fact that these crises have a common cause across states (for example, major economic shifts in developing states).
- Growing economic interdependence between states which means that a crisis in one state can have serious economic consequences in another. This was evident in Latin America in the late 1990s where Brazil's problems were transmitted to its neighbours due to the sheer dominance of Brazil over Latin American economies.
- A crisis in one state causing investors to evaluate their position in other states.
- Common shocks.
- Apparent trade spill-overs.
- Strong financial linkages.
- Uniform changes in investor sentiment.

The presence of key features that render a state vulnerable to contagion (such as slow growth, an appreciating real exchange rate and domestic macro-economic imbalances) compound these issues. The herd-like behaviour of contagion is difficult to explain in any other terms than that the cost of collecting information is increasingly at a premium in global markets.

The phenomenon of contagion challenges the conventional wisdom that currency crises are caused by undisciplined fiscal and monetary policy. Currencies are increasingly coming under attack despite underlying policy consistency. Currencies are increasingly attacked simply as a result of a shift in market expectations about the viability of a fixed exchange rate – a position that can become self-fulfilling as authorities raise interest rates to defend the currency's value. These changes in expectations are not formed in a vacuum but are usually the result of weakness in some aspect of an economy's fundamentals. Moreover, it is not evident that globalization is to blame for these developments since, as the IMF has pointed out,

- capital mobility was greater between 1870 and 1914;
- foreign financing was more important during the period of the Gold Standard;
- portfolio investment was more important during the Gold Standard.

In terms of the prevention of contagion, several approaches are possible. A first option is to make certain that banking regulation is adequate to ensure that the financial system is sufficiently constrained to limit the potential for the onset of a crisis, especially in terms of ensuring that banks do not overexpose themselves to risky investments. Second, it is important that a credible exchange rate policy is backed by complementary domestic policies. The third option is for the economy to exhibit sound fundamentals in areas such as public finance and macro-economic performance.

Ensuring stability through market discipline is the solution chosen by many states. Indeed, support from the IMF is dependent upon such measures. Some states have looked at the possibility of returning to capital controls or taxes to limit the flows of 'hot money' across borders. Such measures are unlikely to be promoted as they are seen as a backward step in the globalization process. In this context, pressure falls upon the relevant authorities to ensure the proper regulation of the banking sector and macro-economic stability.

In responding to the crisis, the IMF established Contingent Credit Lines (CCL) to offer financial support for states undergoing turbulence. Yet these actions have opened the IMF to the criticism that it is exposing itself to 'moral hazard'. That is, because states know support will be forthcoming from the IMF, there is no incentive for them not to behave in a reckless manner. This applies to both states and investors. If states know they are to be supported what is the point of undergoing the pain associated with reform? Clearly the threat is overblown, since assistance from the IMF is not given unconditionally. The issue of moral hazard is more problematic for investors as the support offered does little to stall bad investment. Furthermore, offering these supports commits the IMF politically to the states supported and it would be difficult to walk away from them without triggering a crisis.

According to Mishkin (2006), the major lessons for policy makers to learn from financial crises are:

- to establish a sufficiently strong banking regulatory/supervisory system to ensure that banks do not take excessive risks;
- while it is beneficial in the longer term, there are dangers in financial liberalization without sufficient regulation;
- if the banking system of a state is fragile, a pegged or fixed exchange rate becomes increasingly risky;
- that there is an argument for the state to act as a lender of last resort to ensure financial stability;
- price stability is important in solving financial problems, as inflation is a key economic risk.

Stabilty in the IMS: The Formative Years of the Twenty-first Century

If the late twentieth century was characterized by financial instability, the formative years of the twenty-first were characterized by relative harmony. Since the collapse of Argentina in 2001, the IMS entered a period of stability. Some suggested that this is merely serendipity, but Rose (2007) disputes this. According to him, the common cause of most previous financial crises was monetary policy geared towards sustaining a fixed exchange rate. The problem with these exchange rate systems is that they require the subordination of domestic interests. Ultimately, history has shown that when domestic needs conflict with the fixed link, the latter would be broken.

However, the traditional policy of going for at best a managed float has been gradually replaced with monetary strategy based on inflation targeting. Under this regime, the central bank has a transparent pre-set inflation goal for which it is accountable. While less than half of the 30 OECD states follow such a policy, it is influential, as many states (including the US) operate implicit targets. In addition, some developing states follow such a policy.

The attractiveness of inflation targeting is based on the belief that it delivers financial stability. The objective of low inflation reduces risk and adds transparency to the financial system. Financial stability depends on reducing inflation as a means of restoring macro-economic stability. It also limits the ability of governments to use monetary policy to support the political cycle (that is, to engineer mini-economic booms in the run-up to elections). The policy means letting the exchange rate float relatively freely based on liberalized capital movements. Rose (2007) claims that the system would spread through Darwinian principles and that inflation targeting would reduce the role of the IMF and the US in the global economy.

This argument that financial crises were a thing of the past was also advocated by arch-globalists who argue that, in this 'golden era of globalization', past instability was a mere growing pain and states will generate real economic growth and high financial returns. Others argue that the world has a global savings glut which will generate low real interest rates for the foreseeable future.

However, others offered a more pessimistic analysis, suggesting that the world was merely pausing for breath and that new imbalances were emerging within the global economy throughout this period. These were driven by ongoing concerns over the size of the US trade deficit but greater concerns were expressed over levels of Chinese investment (much of which – especially within the least developed economies – will never pay off) and its possession of a financial system that is unfamiliar with risk assessment and which may leave it overexposed to risky investments. However, given China's political system, there is doubt as to whether it would be able to undertake the necessary harsh measures to restore stability. For example, the Chinese government is reluctant to close failing businesses or banks reflecting a low tolerance of high unemployment for reasons of political stability. There is of course the danger that the political response to these crises will be to reimpose central control economically.

Such actions are likely to cause a ripple effect in other states and risk creating contagion throughout the IMS. Those states that were in the immediate proximity of China suffered the last great crisis in 1997. In hindsight, the crisis for these economies was more of a temporary setback. These states began growing again by 2000, a process supported by an increasing reservoir of global reserves. A combination of enhanced flexibility, stronger macro-economic fundamentals and financial and corporate reform/restructuring has all assisted recovery. However, these states are vulnerable to the US-Asia trade issue (i.e. the US's large trade deficit is with this continent). The legacy of the1997 East Asian crisis for these states has been lower investment and has based economic policies around reducing excessive macro-imbalances. However, there was an emerging fear that the Asian states were becoming too dependent on the US for trade while the US was vulnerable to its non-tradable services such as real estate.

This view was supported by the Bank of International Settlements (BIS) which suggested that this period of stability was driven by a combination of macro-economic and firm-specific factors. The former implies that much instability is cyclical: that is, the sustained expansion of the global economy and low inflation contributed to the lack of volatility over this period. To some, this stability was generated by the 'great moderation' according to which output growth has become much less volatile since the mid-1980s. However, this is unlikely according to the BIS. At the firm level, volatility is negatively related to firm performance and positively related to debt and uncertainty over profitability. These have moved in opposite directions to limit the potential for volatility. A final factor relates to the evolution of financial markets. As with liquidity, the market for risk transfer instruments and portfolio diversification has increased as volatility has decreased. Shifts in the conduct and performance of monetary policy have also played their part: as inflation has remained low, interest rates have also moved downward. This is supported by greater predictability and transparency in policy. The BIS believes that all these factors have changed the structure of the market, leading to the supposition that the reduction in volatility is permanent. However, the BIS notes that 'conjunctural factors' are also important, implying that volatility may return as the world economy slows and corporate profitability declines. This view was broadly supported by financial markets.

Renewed instability: The Crisis in Global Financial Management

Tranquillity in the international financial system came to an abrupt end in 2007 when a renewed bout of financial instability emerged. The cause of the crisis lay in a credit crunch (i.e. a sharp reduction in the availability of loans) in which the bursting of the US house price bubble led to a sharp increase in risk and an abrupt reduction in credit throughout the global system. This problem originated in the large number of loans extended to higher risk borrowers (that is, those with lower incomes or chequered credit histories) as a means of sustaining the growth of borrowing – essential to many of the business models within the financial system. These 'sub-prime' borrowers rose from 6 per cent of the market in 1996 to 20 per cent ten years later. Eventually, problems of repayment combined with declining house prices led to rising defaults and foreclosures.

The immediate impact of increasing defaults was felt by the main mortgage lenders (notably, the banks and other financial institutions) who experienced rapidly increasing losses. By the beginning of 2008, collective losses had risen to $130 billion. Due to a device of financial engineering called 'securitization', many of these lenders had passed the rights to the mortgage payments on to third party investors. This spread the risk associated with the sub-prime crisis to financial institutions throughout the global economy. The holders of these assets faced significant losses as revenues and the assets upon which they were based both declined (that is, the assets became 'toxic'). In turn, this limited the ability of banks to lend to each other or to increase interest rates. These problems were compounded by the sheer opacity of these instruments, causing many investors to be unaware of the banks' liabilities.

At the heart of the problem was the rapid rate of innovation within Western financial markets as financiers found new ways to 'slice and dice' up loans which they then sold on to other parties in the form of securities. While precise figures are difficult to come by, it has been suggested that these products increased 12-fold in value in the six years after 2000. For policy makers, many of these diverse instruments were opaque and the risk elements were not fully understood. There was also a concern that, as a result of this innovation, interest rates did not reflect risk and borrowing costs were simply too low. However, most policy makers did not see the credit crisis coming, believing (paradoxically) that rapid financial innovation made the financial system more comprehensible and stable. There was even a view that the effects of any shock would be mitigated as the impact would be dissipated amongst a large number of parties.

However, what was initially a liquidity crisis quickly became a banking crisis as many large financial institutions became exposed due the high value of 'toxic' assets on their balance sheets. The risks associated with these toxic assets were transmitted throughout the banking system by new inter-bank channels which exposed many more banks to the problem of toxic debt. The result was that confidence in the credibility of the system was undermined to the extent that the financial crisis quickly transformed into a banking crisis which was considerably more serious for the global economy. The spread of toxic assets and uncertainty about which institutions were affected caused contagion throughout the global financial system. The credit crunch started to spread: low levels of lending limited borrowing elsewhere which restricted growth potential. This had a negative impact on global stock markets as concerns over credit fed fears that the US economy would slow and that this slowdown would affect corporate earnings globally.

The response of governments was essential to limiting contagion and central banks sought to increase the liquidity within the system. For example, the European Central Bank lent $500 billion to the market to support the banking system. Initially, the US government sought to limit foreclosures via a direct economic stimulus supported by aggressive cuts in interest rates. A significant development was the bailing out of Bear Stearns (a US investment bank) by the US government, demonstrating the belief that events could only be allowed to get so far out of control before intervention became necessary for the sake of the stability of the entire financial system. This was also evident in 2008 when the US government nationalized the major mortgage providers (Fannie Mae and Freddie Mac) and the insurance giant AIG but allowed Lehmann Brothers (an investment bank) to go under.

By the third quarter of 2008, the effects of these events began to spread to other countries. The most immediate victims were Iceland and the emerging economies of Eastern Europe. The problems for these states were driven by their dependence upon external finance, especially bank credit. Heavy overseas borrowing by both public and private sectors combined with weakening economic growth, and commodity prices made it increasingly difficult for these economies to refinance. The most obvious symptoms of these trends were rising current account deficits and an inability to muster sufficient funds to mitigate such problems. Consequently, many of these states turned to the IMF to support their economies. The IMF has $255 billion to assist states (2008) and the ability to elicit funds from other sources. Initially, states proved reluctant to go to the IMF, preferring to appeal to other states for support (see below). This reluctance was driven by the stigma attached to IMF bail-outs and by the damaging domestic political fall-out from having to fulfil the onerous conditions set by the IMF as a prerequisite of its loan.

Iceland found itself especially exposed. Although Iceland had undergone rapid growth in the years prior to the crisis, this had been achieved on the back of heavy borrowing by its banks. Icelandic banks had expanded rapidly, amassing assets valued at over €180 billion by the end of 2007. These dwarfed Iceland's GDP, which was only €14.5 billion. Iceland's banking assets were funded by the notoriously fickle investors in wholesale markets. Problems were compounded by the sharp rise in debt of Icelandic households to 213 per cent of disposable income. In addition, only 30 cents per euro of every loan issued were backed by deposits. Iceland attempted to rebalance its position by attracting foreign deposits into its banks. However, Iceland's position eventually became unsustainable as banks were unable to roll over their debts as credit markets froze. As panic spread, the government had to step in. The government was handed $6 billion by the IMF with further support coming from other states.

MANAGING THE EMERGING GLOBAL FINANCIAL SYSTEM

The emergence of this fluid and complex global financial system poses a problem for the formal and informal regulation of the system. Maintaining stability within the system relies on self-regulated prudence while also ensuring that formal regulation allows capital markets to function without tipping over into risky irrational exuberance. Despite the global market for finance, regulation still largely takes place at the national level but international cooperation has improved via IMF meetings and through initiatives such as the Financial Stability Forum. As highlighted above, the rise of global financial capitalism has been driven by the gradual withdrawal of national governments from the everyday regulation of finance markets. However, under the Basel Regulation there was agreement in 1988 between states to establish minimum capital standards for banks to ensure that large borrowers did not default. As such rules were expensive, banks tried to get around them by removing assets from their balance sheets though innovative financial devices. Moreover, regulation not only lagged behind innovations in financial markets but certain measures encouraged banks to take on ever riskier loans. For example, the US Reinvestment Act of 1977 encouraged banks to lend to higher risk communities and, in the process, highlighted how the interface between social policy and financial regulation led to ever riskier investments.

The 2008 crisis led many states to re-examine their regulations and to update and review constraints in the light of events. Indeed, the severity of the crisis led many states to seek direct control via nationalization of or (at the very least) increased state intervention in key financial institutions. The return of direct state intervention has led many to claim that this vindicates criticisms of a lightly regulated financial system. In addition, some states have taken unilateral actions to outlaw (albeit often temporarily) those products (such as derivatives) and practices (such as short selling) that contributed to the crisis and to limit or even ban investment by Sovereign Wealth Funds (see Case Study 17.1).

CASE STUDY 17.1

Sovereign Wealth Funds

Sovereign Wealth Funds (SWF) have become an increasingly important feature of the IMS. These funds developed out of the surplus savings of developing countries arising from higher commodity prices and increasing exports. The number of SWFs has expanded rapidly over recent years and they have become a powerful balancing force in a global economy hit by the credit crunch that has plagued many developed economies since 2007. Table 17.2 highlights the leading SWFs in 2007.

Normally, many states would welcome investment by SWFs who have an estimated $29 trillion available to invest. However, SWF investment has been a source of controversy given that it represents investment by foreign governments in the assets of host economies. However, these funds represent only 2 per cent of the $165 trillion-worth of traded securities. Indeed, even though the IMF estimates that the size of SWFs will more than treble by 2012, they will still only account for less than 3 per cent of total assets under management.

Part of the controversy surrounding SWFs stems from their objectives. Some (such as Norway's) invest purely on the basis of expected financial return. Others have broader 'strategic' goals such as aiding local development, securing access to key

TABLE 17.2 The World's Leading SWFs (2007)

State of origin	Fund name	Assets ($bn)
UAE	Abu Dhabi Investment Authority	875
Norway	Government Pension Fund	380
Singapore	GIC	330
Saudi Arabia	Various	300
Kuwait	Reserve Fund for Future Generations	250
China	China Investment Corporation	200
Singapore	Temasek Holdings	159.2
Libya	Oil Reserve Fund	50
Qatar	Qatar Investment Authority	50
Algeria	Fond de Regulation Des Recettes	42.6
US	Alaska Permanent Fund Corporation	38
Brunei	Brunei Investment Authority	30
Other		171.4
Total (of which oil and gas related)		2876.4 (2103.4)

resources and/or stabilizing their economies against fluctuation in commodity prices. As these funds are government owned, there is a suspicion that they are more interested in power than in financial return and some fear that these states may utilize these assets purely to forward their own development and political objectives. However, such suspicions remain speculative: the funds themselves are guarded as to their objectives and motives, and the amount of funding under their control. In addition, these funds are able to hide where and how much they are investing, since they can invest through other financial vehicles such as hedge and private equity funds.

Many commodity-driven economies have developed SWFs as a defence mechanism to insure against the day when their main resource runs out or is no longer so lucrative. In this sense, SWFs are a sound mechanism for securing long-term benefits from the short-term boost of high commodity prices. Similarly, many Asian emerging markets have accumulated foreign reserves on the back of rising trade surpluses. However, these reserves now extend beyond the levels needed for defence against commodity price and/or supply shocks.

Historically, even the most liberal states have been hostile to SWFs (see, for example, the US's hostility to the acquisition of its ports by Dubai – see Case Study 8.1). In 1985, the UK's liberal Conservative government resisted attempts by the Kuwait Investment Office to own BP. More recently, states such as Australia and, more especially, the US have grown wary of investment by SWFs. A notable example was Dubai Ports where there was resistance by the US government to ownership of national infrastructure by a foreign government. Such incidents pose the risk that resistance to SWFs could result in financial protectionism. This would be counter-productive, particularly if such protection spread to other areas of trade and investment. It would also undermine any benefits derived by host and home economies from the investment process. In addition, SWFs represent a flow of funds from these resource-rich states back into developed economies. The IMF and several governments are seeking to move towards greater clarity over the role of SWFs, a task that has been aided by the ring fencing of specific sectors by some states as exempt from any degree of foreign control. Greater transparency over the objectives of SWFs would also help and the publication of annual reports by these funds would be a useful starting point.

CASE STUDY QUESTIONS

1. Why has the rise of Sovereign Wealth Funds proved so controversial and are such concerns justified?

2. How do you account for the geographical spread of Sovereign Wealth Funds?

3. Research one of the Sovereign Wealth Funds identified in Table 17.2. Identify its main activities and highlight any areas that have been or may become controversial.

However, the crisis within the global financial system – despite these nationalistic rules – reinforced the mutual dependence between national systems. This was reflected in a common global agreement amongst the leading industrial nations to coordinate efforts to address the problems. To some degree, this action superseded initiatives of multilateral institutions which had not been involved in the formative stages of the crisis. These bodies only began to get involved when the crisis spread from banks to states (see above). As it evolved, the 2007 to 2008 crisis witnessed a sea change: as countries entered more difficult phases, they did not turn first to the IMF for support but to other states, most notably the high-performing emerging economies. These states not only had the necessary resources but did not insist on the onerous conditions linked to the IMF. For example, Iceland turned initially to Russia for help. Ultimately, however, the slow pace of these talks led Iceland to approach the IMF. It is possible that this new approach could lead to the pragmatic emergence of a successor to the IMF. However, aid from these states may come with political rather than economic conditions attached.

The above reflects the credibility gap facing the IMF. The conditions attached to its loans proved unpopular with many recipients, although many states often ignored the requests of the fund to pursue their own interests. In some cases, states bypassed the fund as highlighted by the creation of the Financial Stability Forum (an association of developed state policy makers and regulators) formed in the aftermath of the 1997 to 1998 financial crisis which allowed many states to bypass the IMF.

CASE STUDY 17.2

Islamic Finance

Historically, Islamic finance has been a backwater of the global financial system, limited to customized services to devout Muslims. In international terms, this form of finance was limited to commercial banking and to specific regions such as Malaysia and the Middle East. More recently, there has seen a massive expansion of Islamic finance driven by the hydrocarbon surpluses of the Middle East and by the increasing number of Muslims seeking more religiously sanctioned products.

Islamic finance is based on a strict interpretation of the Koran and Islamic law which prohibits practices that are central to the Western banking system. The most notable prohibited practices are the payment of interest (riba) and financial speculation (gharar). These prohibitions made it impossible for many devout Muslims to use the Western banking system and Islamic investors steer clear of companies that operate in industries considered immoral or that have too much debt (defined as where debt is equivalent to one-third of stock market value). Over the past four decades there has been substantial innovation in Islamic finance, which has allowed for the creation of financial structures that offer many of the benefits of the Westernized banking products without the prohibited elements. Sukuk are Islamic bonds which make regular payments to investors that echo interest payments. These returns are generated by a business activity owned by the issuer and not by interest earned on cash. However, it is estimated that only 5 per cent of Islamic finance adheres strictly to such rules. A board of scholars operates as a 'spiritual rating agency', judging what forms of investment are compatible with sharia law.

For the vast majority of their activities, Islamic banks use a structure called murabaha which involves a cost plus pre-determined profit for the majority of finance deals and which has strong parallels to the interest offered by conventional banking products. To some scholars, such products are conventional products hidden in an Islamic garb. These murabaha look very similar to Western-style venture capital systems. Similarly, 'ijara' resembles Western-style leasing. Indeed, the simplistic notion that Islamic finance outlaws all interest has been widely disputed.

By mid-2008, an estimated $700 billion of assets were managed according to Islamic principles with more than 280 institutions offering Islamic products. According to some estimates, however, total assets under the control of Islamic rules could be as high as $4 trillion. In total, it is estimated that – although Muslims account for 20 per cent of the world's population – less than 1 per cent of global financial instruments are compatible with the principles of Islamic finance. However, assets governed by Islamic principles are growing by 10 to 15 per cent per annum. Along with this growth, there has been a desire to regulate this sector more closely. The main beneficiaries of this emerging Islamic finance have been:

TABLE 17.3 Sharia-compliant Financial Assets, 2007 ($bn)

Iran	154.6
Saudi Arábia	69.4
Malaysia	65.1
Kuwait	37.7
UAE	35.4
Brunei	31.5
Bahrain	26.3
Pakistan	15.9
Lebanon	14.3
Britain	10.4

Source: The Banker.

* international law firms that exploit the legal ambiguities generated by compliance with this exotic legal system;
* multinational banks that have driven innovation in investment and retail banking;
* Islamic scholars who advise on the compliance of products with Islamic law.

The problems of developing Islamic products are also compounded by a lack of standardization and homogeneity. Perhaps the major concern is the lack of consensus on the interpretation of the Koran among scholars. As these religious academics determine which products comply with the Koran and which do not, confusion may often result. The example of Malaysia, where a single Sharia board is overseen by the government rather than by individual banks, presents one potential resolution to this dilemma, a dilemma that is compounded by the fact that – by 2007 – only Bahrain and Kuwait had established separate regulatory regimes for the sector.

A major problem for Islamic finance is that despite its long history, it has failed to add any real value in terms of employment and inventions/ innovations or made Islamic communities any more equitable or just. The Islamic finance industry has been more preoccupied with meeting the letter of Koranic law rather than its spirit. Thus, many claim that this form of finance needs to be extended to new businesses that will aid progress of the Islamic community. Another major problem is that, as a result of ensuring compliance with sharia, Islamic finance tends to incur extra transaction costs. However, expected efficiencies within the system could mitigate extra costs. Development is also hindered by a lack of recognized scholars able to determine compatibility between the demands of finance and Islamic law.

CASE STUDY QUESTIONS

1. Why has Islamic finance become increasingly important within the global financial system?

2. What are the major differences between mainstream and Islamic finance?

3. Are Islamic principles of finance compatible with a modern financial system?

Others accused the US of undermining the IMF by bullying it into forcing exchange rate realignments as part of its strategy to coerce China into a revaluation. The increased reluctance of states to go to the IMF reflects its obsession – so claim its critics – with conditionality. This suggests that the IMF needs to be more flexible in terms of funding (something it is already doing, as over recent times it has gradually loosened its terms and conditions for funding). Indeed, the IMF has moved towards offering policy prescriptions only when absolutely necessary. This suggests that the Washington Consensus (see Chapter 5) is being reined in by stealth. However, there are also concerns as to whether the IMF's instruments offered are quick and flexible enough for the full range of crises.

The impact of the financial crisis of the early twenty-first century was so pervasive that the IMF started to regain some of its lost popularity. Massive extensions in its lending capacity were offered to enable developing states to gain access to the finance that dried up in the credit crunch. Between 2007 and 2009, financial flows into developing economies fell by almost 80 per cent. The fear that developing states could be excluded from an increasingly nationalistic financial system has led many to return to the IMF for finance. However, the extra funding from the IMF is unlikely to be enough. It is estimated that up to $1 trillion is needed, more than double what is currently on offer.

Over the longer term, many believe re-regulation of the banking and finance sectors is needed to avoid future crises. However, it is naive to assume that re-regulation will solve the problems within global financial capitalism: many of the innovations that created the problems in the first place emerged as a direct consequence of the desire of the financial industry to get around regulation. Thus new regulation may only create new products to circumvent such rules. The problem was also created by the actions of politicians keen to spread access to cheap finance in support of their visions of homeowning democracies. To blame the financial crash solely on markets (see above) is simplistic: governments themselves had a key role in feeding the crash, notably through keeping interest rates too low for too long and in placing too much confidence in the ability of markets to regulate themselves. Past experience suggests that re-regulation needs to proceed slowly to control for unintended consequences.

CONCLUSION

The integration of capital markets is only half complete and full integration will only be achieved, if at all, within several decades. Restrictions persist on the ownership of international financial resources, especially by pension funds. Thus international portfolio diversification is very much in its infancy. Despite these limitations, this chapter has indicated that the IMS is a powerful force shaping the global economy. The power of international finance is an increasingly dominant issue on the domestic policy agenda as highlighted by persistent crises within the system. Despite the crises, any large-scale overhaul of the system seems distant.

Summary of Key Concepts

- The development of the IMS is pivotal to maximizing the benefits of globalization.
- Throughout its evolution, the system has veered between rules and non-rules for participants.
- The emergence of debt and financial instability are posing problems for the management of the IMS.
- Further reform will be needed as the system adjusts to these problems.

Activities

1. Using the example of a financial institution with which you are familiar, assess how it coped with the 2008 to 2009 financial crisis.

2. Organize the class into two groups and assess the pros and cons of global financial capitalism in the light of the 2008 to 2009 crisis.

Discussion Questions

1. Do you agree with the contention that economic stability has undermined the need for the IMF?

2. How do you account for the current financial instability within the global financial system?

3. Outline the key ways in which stability in the IMS is important to international business.

4. How can states counteract the challenges of instability?

5. Discuss how the problems of debt can be solved.

6. Assess the merits of private equity funds.

References and Suggestions for Further Reading

Economist (1992) 'Fear of finance: a survey of the world economy', 11 September, London.

Economist (1999) 'Time for a redesign: survey of the global financial system', 28 January, London.

Eichengreen, B. (2008) *Globalizing Capital: A History of the International Monetary System*, 2nd edn, Princeton, NJ: Princeton University Press.

Grabel, I. (2000) 'Identifying risks, preventing crisis: lessons from the Asian crisis', *Journal of Economic Issues*, Vol. 34, No. 2, 377–383.

Griesgraber, J. and Gunter, B. (1996) *The World's Monetary System*, London: Pluto Press.

Kenen, P., Papadia, F. and Saccomanni, F. (1995) *The International Monetary System*, Cambridge: Cambridge University Press.

Lane, P. and Milesi-Ferretti, G. (2003) 'International financial integration', *IMF Staff Papers*, 50, Special issue, 82–113.

Little, J. and Olivei, G. (1999) 'Rethinking the international monetary system: an overview', *New England Economic Review*, Nov–Dec, 3–24.

Michie, J. and Grieve-Smith, J. (1999) *Global Instability*, London: Routledge.

Mishkin, F. (2006) 'Monetary policy strategy: how did we get here?' *NBER Working Papers*, 12515, Cambridge, MA: National Bureau of Economic Research.

O'Brien, R. (1991) *Global Financial Integration*, London: Pinter/RIIA.

Okina, K., Shirakawa, M. and Shimtsuka, S. (1999) 'Financial market globalisation: present and future', *Monetary and Economic Studies*, Vol. 17, No. 3, 1–40.

Pilbeam, K. (2005) *Finance and Financial Markets*, 2nd edn, Basingstoke: Palgrave Macmillan.

Rose, A. (2007). 'A stable monetary system emerges: inflation targeting is Bretton Woods reversed', *Journal of International Money and Finance*, Vol. 26, No. 5, 663–681.

Singh, R. (1999) *The Globalization of Finance*, London: IPSR.

Soros, G. (1998) *The Crisis of Global Capitalism: Open Society Endangered*, New York: Little Brown.

Soros, G. (2008) *The New Paradigm for Financial Markets: The Credit Crisis of 2008 and What it Means*, New York: Public Affairs.

Strange, S. (1998) *States and Markets*, London: Pinter.

Valdez, S. (2006) *An Introduction to Global Financial Markets*, 5th edn, Basingstoke: Palgrave Macmillan.

Wolf, M. (2007) 'Unfettered finance is fast reshaping the global economy', *Financial Times*, 18 June, www.ft.com.

Wolf, M. (2009) *Fixing Global Finance*, London: Yale University Press.

Websites

Bank of International Settlements – www. Bis.org/.
International Monetary Fund – www.imf.org/.

Chapter 18

The Global Information Economy

I'm a great believer in new technology and I think new technology is very scary.

James Packer (1967–), Australian entrepreneur

LEARNING OBJECTIVES

This chapter will help you to:

- understand the form and nature of the information economy

- comprehend the impact of the information economy upon the international business environment

- appreciate the importance of electronic commerce to international business

- understand the policy challenges posed by the emergence of the information economy

- comprehend the implications of the emergence of the information economy for developing states

Conventional economic theory states that firms are based on combining the factors of production (namely land, labour and capital) to produce goods and services. In the modern economy, these traditional factors have been supplemented by a new and increasingly important factor of production, namely knowledge. As Chapters 9 and 10 have highlighted, knowledge has become increasingly important to the functioning of the MNE. This trend has enhanced the ability of the firm to handle and utilize information for its own competitive advantage. Increasingly, the utilization of information and the ability of a company to garner, process and distribute information into enterprise-wide knowledge is a core factor in the competitiveness of the modern enterprise. Information may be reused, shared, distributed or exchanged without any diminution of value. Indeed, sometimes this value is multiplied. This results from the process of technological change, the emergence of ICTs as strategic assets, the rise of the real-time economy and the increased ability of the firm to turn raw data into valuable enterprise-wide knowledge. After examining the nature of the information economy, this chapter draws attention to the increasingly pivotal role of this core resource in international business. In the process, it explores the growing interface between the information economy and international trade and highlights the international policy concerns that need to be addressed if the information economy is to reach its potential. Finally, the implications of the information economy for developing states are explored.

THE NATURE OF THE INFORMATION ECONOMY

The most important development associated with the rise of the information economy is the pervasive use of knowledge and information as both an input and an output throughout the economy. Knowledge workers (that is, those workers for whom embedded knowledge rather than physical capability is the source of their value) account for over 80 per cent of jobs within modern developed economies, according to the OECD. This process has been aided by the shift towards the 'weightless economy' as production becomes increasingly dependent upon intangibles (notably, the exploitation of ideas) rather than physical inputs. This has made it harder to measure economic activity and the size of economies, especially as knowledge and information can be codified into digital bits that can be endlessly replicated, adding value every time it is duplicated.

Increasingly, every business is an information business, especially in activities (such as software and media) where content is a core source of value. In addition, more traditional companies are becoming increasingly information and knowledge intensive. A good example of this trend is the automobile industry where an increasing percentage of the value associated with these companies is directly related to the value of information and knowledge embedded within their products. In short, the salience of information and knowledge across industries is becoming increasingly evident. There are, however, differences between industries where information is the product and those where it is a core component of the final product or service. For example within the automobile industry, a high percentage of the value of the output is reflected in the knowledge of engineering and technology.

Reflecting the above trends, the information economy has given rise to the creation of virtual value chains where the emergence of important information at all stages of physical value chains needs to be captured and utilized to sustain competitive advantage. This information not only improves processes and operations within a business but also enhances the performance of an enterprise by creating greater coordination across it. This increasingly applies not only within enterprises but also between them as witnessed by the growing use of extranets which provide communications links between enterprises and trusted buyers/suppliers.

There are both internal and external challenges for business from the emergence of the information economy. Employees and customers need to be able to deal with increasing quantities of information and to decide what information is most valuable. Information overload has the potential to undermine many of the benefits of the information economy by making decision making more difficult and reducing the efficiency of the business. Enterprises therefore face a challenge, not only to make themselves 'heard' over the vast quantity of information available but also to ensure that internal processes are able to handle the large quantities of information generated in the modern economy.

The more extensive deployment of ICTs is having a major effect upon the nature of the global economy by creating the potential for cost–space and time–space convergence. High-capacity fibre optic cables are a symptom of the latest logistical revolution and constitute an infrastructure that creates instantaneous communication and (in the case of digital goods) trade. Such developments are closely linked to the development of the internet as a global phenomenon. The wider deployment and usage of this core technology has fundamentally altered the costs of conducting business where these capabilities are more developed. In addition, through expansion of human processing power and the collection and dissemination of information, some of the most pervasive effects of the advent of electronic commerce are felt through the provision of services

However, the impact of the internet upon commerce, trade and society depends on the take-up of the technology by all aspects of the socioeconomic spectrum. This is influenced by the following factors:

- *culture*: notably, the openness of society to new ideas and processes;
- *convenience*: the extent to which these technologies meet a defined need;
- *cost*.

If these factors can be reconciled, these technologies will have a profound effect upon consumers, commerce, the structure of companies, politics, government and the nature of the economy as a whole.

The changes in the business environment wrought by ICTs are different to the logistical and commercial revolutions that preceded them. An important facet of the development of the information economy is its sheer pervasiveness. Not only does the information economy apply to all sectors of the economy but it also affects every function within an enterprise. As such, the information economy changes the functioning and structure of industries and also leads to the development of new products in its own right. This process has been aided by the sharp decline in the price of processing power – indeed, an unprecedented fall in the price of a key input. These factors have facilitated the realization of the following commercial advantages:

- cheaper transaction costs;
- the rapid codification and diffusion of the increased range of knowledge;
- fewer claims made on resources by IT than preceding technologies.

Figure 18.1 highlights the three main channels through which the extension of ICT usage can deliver advantages and competitive benefits for businesses. The first channel is through capital productivity growth where rising ICT usage improves the efficiency with which capital contributes to output. The second channel is labour productivity growth where rising ICT usage leads to capital deepening in which the amount of ICT capital per employee increases to assist production across all sectors. Finally, ICT usage improves total factor productivity growth by enhancing managerial and organizational effectiveness through cost savings and improved communication.

The information economy also has an impact on the economy as a whole. As with other 'revolutions', the information economy both destroys and creates jobs, in this case by reducing the demand for manual workers and increasing demand for information/knowledge workers. Thus, the demand for teachers, computer programmers and so on increases as a result of the emergence of the information economy. This places greater pressure upon enterprises to engage in effective training and upon education systems to produce individuals capable of becoming value-adding knowledge and information workers. However, there is a fear that such developments could create a new underclass relying on low-skilled service sector employment, resulting in widening income differentials between low- and high-skilled workers.

Within the information economy, not only is knowledge a key resource but it is also a scarce one. Effectively, knowledge workers own the means of production. The largest group of knowledge workers are what Drucker (1969) terms 'knowledge technologists' who work with their hands but whose pay is determined by their embedded knowledge. This includes computer programmers and dentists. These workers require two things if they are to succeed. The first is formal education to accumulate knowledge and the second is continuing education throughout their working lives to sustain their 'valuable' knowledge. This latter point acknowledges the rapid obsolescence of knowledge and that lifelong learning is a key feature of the information economy.

Development of the information economy has raised fears of a net loss of jobs from developed states as large companies no longer need to sacrifice contact with head office in return for locating production in the more remote states of the global economy. With low wages and a rudimentary IT infrastructure, developing economies could become super-competitive. However, such arguments are simplistic: they ignore productivity differences and misunderstand the difference between absolute and comparative advantage (see Chapter 7). There is however fear that ICTs allow

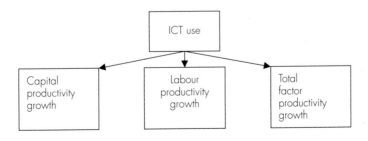

FIGURE 18.1 Channels through which ICT Contributes to Productivity Growth

previously untradable services to be traded globally and that any service undertaken online can be transferred anywhere. There has been a trend, for example, for firms to outsource an array of commercial services from ticketing to computer programming to developing states.

What is more likely is that ICTs will allow firms to decentralize production and specialize by country. ICTs enable enterprises to exploit national comparative advantages more widely and efficiently. Comparative advantage between states will depend upon how well workers apply knowledge and information resources. This means that the better-educated states should be able to sustain their competitive advantage within the information economy.

INTERNATIONAL BUSINESS AND THE INFORMATION ECONOMY

The previous section has highlighted how the development of the information economy is shaping the competitive environment in which international businesses will operate in the coming decades. These changes have a further and more direct effect upon the international business environment through their influence upon international trade and investment. This will be most noticeable, over the short term at least, in trade in ICTs and in the development of electronic commerce.

It is logical that as the information economy matures, trade in its raw materials increases. The late twentieth/early twenty-first century has seen a sharp increase in trade in ICTs. However, the effect of ICTs upon trade amounts to more than the sum of ICT trade. The all-pervasiveness of ICTs across the economy has had a broader impact on the trade of goods and services. The application and dissemination of these technologies enables traditional businesses to expand into new markets, both nationally and internationally. This is especially evident in the domain of electronic commerce (see below). ICT effects are also substantial in the generation of further investment in areas such as training and research and technological development. By helping to disseminate the latest technologies, trade in ICTs also plays a role in the innovation process. ICTs are also important in terms of trade facilitation (that is, the use of ICTs to aid the process of communication and the simplification of the transaction process). However, capturing and measuring these effects is difficult.

In the aftermath of the WTO's (signed in 1996) Information Technology Agreement (ITA), trade in ICTS grew strongly. A key by-product has been the emergence of Eastern European and non-OECD developing states as key producers and growth markets of ICT products. Thus, the information economy is not merely about users but about producers of supporting products. As ICT-related technologies have undergone commoditization, their production has shifted towards low-cost locations. The trade and spread of ICTs have been central to facilitating trade in specific types of services that do not require face-to-face contact.

In 2007, trade in ICTs represented less than 20 per cent of total flows of merchandise across borders. Between 1996 and 2006, the trade in IT products increased from $600 billion to over $1500 billion. The biggest importers and exporters lie in the triad, comprising 98.9 per cent of exports and 95.6 per cent of imports. The dominance of the triad has been challenged by the rise of China as a trading power in IT products with Chinese exports increasing from around 2 per cent of global exports in 1996 to 18 per cent in 2005. Furthermore, by 2006, 93 per cent of the trade in ICTs was tariff-free. Alongside trade in the physical aspect of the information economy, ICT-related exports of services have also grown quickly. Between 2000 and 2005, ICT-enabled services grew faster than total services and totalled $1.1 trillion at the end of the period. This represents around 50 per cent of total services exports – up from 37 per cent in 1995.

Anecdotally, there is an assumption that higher spend on ICTs is linked closely to increased growth and trade. However, this effect has not been universal: some states with high ICT spend do not exhibit such growth (e.g. Greece) while others exhibit the opposite characteristics (e.g. Spain and Mexico). However, given all the other factors that can influence trade, isolating ICT effects can be difficult. Indeed, it is possible that it may take a decade or more for the effects of investment in ICTs to be reflected in trade figures. The impact of ICTs takes a long time to feed through into the broader economy: for example, a prolonged period is needed for workforce training and for labour markets to reflect the structural changes stimulated by the increased investment in ICTs. Thus there is expected to be a prolonged lag before investments in ICTs are reflected in improved competitiveness.

The link between trade and ICTs is further reinforced by evidence provided by the OECD (2006) that there is a direct correlation between investment in ICTs and the openness of economies. Improvements in training should reduce the lag between investment in ICTs and trade growth. However, these factors are directly influenced by the salience of ICTs to the business model of particular sectors and the relevance of their usage to support trade. Clarke and Wallsten (2004) found that a 1 per cent increase in the number of internet users boosts total exports by over 4 per cent. This is supported by evidence from the World Bank (2006) which suggests that exporters and foreign firms are more likely to use ICTs.

As the information economy matures, the effect on trade will increase: as transaction costs decline further, telecommunication costs will fall and the cost of adopting these technologies will also decline. As costs fall, most sectors will utilize these technologies and more sectors will become exposed to international competition. Trade will thus become an option for an increased array of businesses. These changes will also create a demand for a new set of goods and services, notably those that can easily be digitized. For such products, the above issues are especially pertinent given that the marginal production cost is minimal or even zero. Consequently, it will become immediately profitable to export these products, therefore bypassing the need for economies of scale or market testing. The same will also be true of those services that can be easily adapted for delivery online, such as financial services. A more indirect impact of electronic commerce upon international trade will come through trade facilitation, enabling firms to fulfil customs requirements more quickly and easily – a potentially significant impact given that trading costs can represent around 10 per cent of the value of international trade. The submission of documents through electronic media, for example, has the potential to cut the time and costs associated with undertaking international trade.

The expansion of trade related to the development of the information economy is also related to network effects. Improved access to ICTs will spread the benefits but, as more people access these technologies, there is an increased incentive for others to use these technologies. Thus, as new economy trade expands, it creates (eventually) its own virtuous cycle of development. This trend depends upon the improved spread of ICTs throughout the global economy. In turn, the process of dissemination also depends on the progressive liberalization of the telecommunications and IT sectors. These processes are essential to the price effects that stimulate access to these technologies. As it is accessed by more people, the information economy will mature and its relevance spread throughout the socioeconomic spectrum.

CASE STUDY 18.1

Web 2.0 and International Business

The internet has had a vast impact upon the conduct and nature of international business. As with any technology, its impact will evolve over the coming decades as the capabilities of this technology expand and new business opportunities emerge. Web 2.0 is based on shifts in internet technology and competences grounded in an increased use of web-based communities and hosted services (such as social networking sites, wiki, blogs) to facilitate the development of creativity to foster the emergence of new products. Thus, new services will be based on using the collective intelligence of a dispersed population of participants to foster creativity and innovation.

Core to using Web 2.0 as a platform of international business is the recognition that business needs to use the strengths of the internet (notably its global reach) as a platform for development. This will find expression through the ability of firms to utilize the long tail (see Box 18.1). By using dispersed knowledge, businesses can use this technology for innovation. The benefits of this approach are derived from network effects (i.e. where the value of the network is derived from the number of users). Within Web 2.0, users have the ability to use the internet not merely to retrieve information but to interact with that information and participate in the development of websites. Thus, these websites aim to create an environment that offers a rich user experience, encourages user participation and promotes dynamic content.

According to Tapscott and Williams (2006), Web 2.0 has given birth to 'wikinomics', according to which the economy of the internet depends upon mass collaboration and is based on openness, peer-to-peer interaction sharing and 'blogability'. They regard it as important for content-based businesses to harness this global network of collaborative users to help product development. In these cases, the internet may be used to enable users to collaborate to assemble and develop products with their customers and, in some cases, the latter will do most of the value creation. Thus, the customer – instead of being passive – will become an active participant in the value-creation process.

For businesses, the implications of adding value by collaboration imply increasingly porous borders. Firms need to extend their reach extensively in search of the knowledge needed to innovate and create value. It has become evident that value will be created via cooperation: for example, IBM has embraced open source software instead of proprietary technology. Likewise, other technology companies, such as Fujitsu, Hitachi, HP, Intel, NEC to name but a few, are using Linux software. Their funding is enabling a network of collaborators to build new products to aid software development.

As suggested, the most immediate impact of Web 2.0 has been upon information goods. However, the impact is spreading to physical goods. For example, companies can post their product development needs on to websites that link problems with problem solvers to aid innovation from diverse sources. This implies that solutions to business problems often lie outside the confines of the business. It is evident that the emergence of Web 2.0 can open up opportunities for business in a number of new ways, not only by bringing customers into the value-creating process but by tapping into a global network of knowledge to feed innovation. This disperses product development across space and alters the economics of outsourcing.

CASE STUDY ACTIVITY

Using the example of a Web 2.0 business with which you are familiar, identify how the business is shaping and being shaped by internationalization.

Aside from the increased trade in information communication technologies, the more generic impact of the emergence of information economy upon international trade has been through the rise of electronic commerce. Very broadly, electronic commerce involves the use of electronic channels (most notably telecommunications) for the purpose of stimulating or undertaking transactions. With improved customer information and better knowledge of marketplaces, the internet has the potential to create a virtual global marketplace for goods and services by overcoming the problems of distance and costs that inhibit trade for many agents. Analysed through the framework of the five forces, electronic commerce can alter industry dynamics by:

- eroding the power of suppliers;
- increasing competitive rivalry;
- increasing the power of buyers;
- increasing the range of substitutes;
- increasing the threat of new entrants.

Through these pressures, the emergence of this new channel will impact upon international strategy in the following ways (Yip and Dempster, 2005):

- *The internet increases global commonality in customer needs and tastes*: this is especially true if brands are global and products offered are common among states.
- *The internet creates global customers:* MNEs acts as global customers by coordinating or centralising their purchases.
- *The internet facilitates global channels:* channels of distribution that have emerged on a global or regional basis.
- *The internet makes global marketing more possible:* the internet potentially has global reach, enabling global marketing to occur. In addition, the internet increasingly demands globally standard brand names.
- *The internet highlights lead countries:* the internet offers greater openness in identifying industry leaders and monitors their offerings.

The internet has also contributed to globalization through assorted cost factors. First, the internet has enabled global economies of scale and scope by allowing smaller firms to benefit from such efficiencies. Second, it enhances global sourcing efficiency and speeds up global logistics as well as exploiting differences in costs between states. Third, the internet can reduce product development costs. Furthermore, the Internet also reduces barriers to globalization by sidestepping trade policies; spurs the development of global technical standards, and confronts diverse marketing regulations. In terms of the competitive environment, the internet accelerates the necessary speed of competitive action and reaction, makes competitor comparison easier, aids transferability of competitive advantages and creates global rivalry.

Petersen *et al.* (2002) claim that the impact of the internet upon the pace and form of internationalization varies from limited to rapid. Ultimately, its impact is a derivative of the form and nature of the firm as well as use of the internet. The most immediate impact of rising internet usage upon the internationalization process is felt through lower levels of uncertainty as the channel allows better access to host market information and knowledge. Furthermore, the internet enables the firm to access, absorb and utilize host market information more readily and therefore assist experiential learning. Overall, the internet speeds up internationalization if its aids transaction efficiency, facilitates experiential learning and lowers sunk costs linked to market entry. On a more negative note, rising internet usage can also create information overload and spread misinformation within the firm. Consequently, Petersen *et al.* argue that the firm may place false trust in the ability of the internet to solve its problems and overcommit to markets.

Box 18.1 The Long Tail

The emergence of the 'long tail' has been central to the emergence of the internet as a key factor in the development of international business. The long tail is based on the ability of businesses to move into niche segments of the market and to earn a profit from selling low volumes. This business model is built upon selling a small volume of hard-to-find items to a large number of users and represents a shift away from the conventional model based on selling large volumes of a reduced number of items.

This model has been directly facilitated by the globalization of the customer base created by the advent of the internet. Combined with low distribution and stocking costs, these models are viable on a low level of sales. Conventional business models operated on a rule of thumb that 20 per cent of customers generated 80 per cent of revenue and vice versa. Anderson (2006) argues that products that are in low demand or have low sales volumes can collectively make up a market share that rivals or exceeds that of the market leader.

One of the major benefits of the emergence of the internet, therefore, is not low prices but better access to a greater variety of products. It is in the long tail where people will buy hard-to-find, obscure products that value is released. What is more, the fact that the market has been globalized increases the fruitfulness of the search for these products. On the supply side, the long tail has been created by expanded and centralized warehousing, allowing firms to cater to more varied tastes. On the demand side, search engines allow customers to find more obscure products. The long tail has been used by enterprises such as eBay and Amazon to build sustainable business models.

Alongside learning aspects, the spread of the internet can impact upon internationalization in the following ways:

- *Pace*: some firms have experienced demand-driven effects where high profiles have pulled them into overseas markets. In other words, the pace of the process has been speeded up by the internet. However, these effects depend on the interface between culture and the increased interactions that result. These effects could just as well be negative as positive where the ability to enter a market runs ahead of the firm's knowledge about international operations.
- *Product/value chain activity*: the internet should lessen the need for localization of marketing and other sales activities, although elements of the firm's value-adding activities (such as R&D) are often less amenable to the digitization process that allows this to occur.

- *Foreign operation mode effects*: it is accepted that the internet offers the opportunity for externalization as contracts and partners are easier to monitor and transactions costs reduced. This favours the use of the market mechanism rather than internalization of functions. However, these effects may be offset by the need for global coordination. In addition, this effect may also be felt through disintermediation which allows firms to drop their role as intermediaries and sell directly to customers.
- *Geographic spread*: global exposure can increase the reach of the business. This demand-driven process increases the number of markets available to the business, although this will be limited by the spread of usage of the internet and the ability of the website (the basic unit of business on the internet) and the customer to deal with many languages. This could be a problem for smaller businesses. Thus, despite the espoused benefits of uniformity generated by the internet, the issue of languages means that localization remains an important factor for these businesses.

On the demand side, the impact of ICTs on international business is self-evident as firms seek new markets. On the supply side, the effects are less unidirectional. Producers of digital products seek to serve as many customers as possible to mitigate the high up-front costs involved in their production. This encourages the firm to go for global scale. In contrast, producers of physical products have less incentive to internationalize if they are able to use ICTs to create more flexible production.

If we look at economies of scope (instead of scale), the internet allows for the possibility of finding a partner or partners for the firm. This can be especially important for smaller firms and improves the internationalization capacity of firms as better information and knowledge allows them to understand markets better than incremental approaches to internationalization suggest (see Chapter 10). However, the symmetry of such effects may limit the ability to use these technologies to their advantage. As Carr (2004) suggests, it is not the technology that differentiates but how it is used.

In its formative period, the internet was regarded as providing strategies for low-cost leaders whereby customers could find what they want at a cheaper price. Indeed, initial actions involving the disintermediation of retailers allowed customers to buy wholesale and benefit from lower costs. However, strategies in global cyberspace have matured, as there were only so many low-cost leaders that the internet could support. Indeed, the dot.com crash of the late 1990s highlighted the limits of intense cost competition. More recent phases of business model development within electronic commerce have been characterized by a higher degree of commercial maturity as many smaller businesses in particular move into more differentiated strategies and away from low-cost positions. This has been evident in strategies linked to the emergence of the long tail (see Box 18.1).

Overall, electronic commerce affects international trade at many levels. Electronic commerce increases the intensity of competition between states as consumers have access to more information, requiring businesses to be more responsive. Thus, consumers are empowered at the expense of the producer. However, this can be curtailed by too much information clouding market signals. Competition can also benefit companies themselves, especially where business-to-business transactions deliver cost and efficiency benefits. Furthermore, electronic commerce can enhance price flexibility and increase the efficiency of markets. This is especially evident in auction sites. Further benefits to business may be derived from new media for advertising, commercial transactions, after-sales service and from the dematerialization of goods and services with accompanying savings in distribution. While these effects are difficult to measure, the rise in electronic commerce does not always mean that international trade will increase. There can be a substitution effect as existing offline trade goes online and as a result the rapid growth in electronic commerce may not necessarily be reflected in increased trade flows.

THE SPREAD OF THE INFORMATION ECONOMY

Examination of the economic geography of the information economy underlines its uneven development (see Figure 18.2). This new paradigm of economic development and growth remains focused on the leading developed states in the OECD. A key benchmark of the development of the information economy is the expansion in broadband subscribers to 197 million in OECD states in 2006, increasing broadband penetration rates to nearly 20 per cent. As a continent, Europe exhibits the highest broadband penetration rates and in the Nordic states over a quarter of all users have broadband access. Indeed, the Danes and the Dutch were the first states to surpass 30 per cent penetration rates. Outside Europe, this figure is matched only by South Korea. Unsurprisingly, the US has the largest number of subscribers at 58.1 million. This is underlined

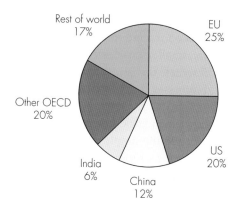

FIGURE 18.2 Geographical Spread of Internet Hosts, 2006

Source: CIA *Factbook.*

by the geography of internet hosts: the US has over 195 million hosts and the EU over 50 million, whereas some African states number their internet hosts in single figures (for example, Chad – nine; Liberia – eight: CIA *World Factbook* (2008)).

For enterprises, internet access is nearly universal with penetration rates as high as 100 per cent for larger enterprises in the major OECD economies. Within developing states, internet access tends to be via dial-up rather than through broadband which is increasingly the norm in developed states. The absence of economies of scale means that broadband in developing states extends little beyond the densely populated urban areas. However, internet use in developing states quadrupled in the five years to 2007. Within emerging and developing economies, internet usage is highest among Eastern European and Central Asian states with six to eight times as many users as South Asia and sub-Saharan Africa; though the latter is again showing very high growth rates, albeit from a low base.

In 2005, developing states accounted for over 60 per cent of all telephone lines (both fixed and mobile) up from less than 20 per cent in 1980. Over this period, while population increased by 50 per cent, the number of telephone subscribers increased 28-fold. This growth has been especially marked over recent years: between 2000 and 2005, the proportion of subscribers tripled to almost 400 per 1,000 people. Most of this growth was in mobile telephony where scarce fixed connections, the increasing mobility of the population, lower transaction costs, deeper trade networks and the search for employment all stimulated growth. Given the maturity of the developed economies, the fastest rates of penetration of communications are currently highest within Central Europe and

TABLE 18.1 Internet Penetration by Level of Development

	2002	2006
World	10	17.3
Developed economies	42	58.2
Developing economies	4.2	9.7
Transition economies	4.1	16.3

Source: UNCTAD.

Central Asia, though the fastest growth has been in sub-Saharan Africa. In terms of absolute number of subscribers, developing states are ahead of developed states, though in terms of rates of penetration they still lag behind (see Table 18.1). In some developed states the penetration rate for mobile phones is over 100 per cent, while in some developing states the level is under 10 per cent.

Much of the growth of mobile telephony in developing states has been driven by affordability schemes. Indeed, in Africa by 2004, nearly 88 per cent of users were on prepaid services tailored to low-income markets. With markets in developed economies looking increasingly mature, the developing economies are the major source of growth for mobile firms. Mobile telephony has proved an especially useful platform for developing economies, as it offers connectivity advantages in locations where fixed line infrastructure is sparse. However, greater spread remains limited given the persistence of low education levels and extreme poverty, and the absence of commercial distribution channels. However, the spread of mobiles brings advantages in terms of business efficiencies and has been aided by prepayment plans that overcome issues of non-payment among population segments regarded as 'unbankable'. This is especially salient for Africa.

In terms of ICTs usage, the mobile phone is the most widespread. Mobile phone usage almost tripled in the five years to 2007 with developing country subscribers accounting for 58 per cent of users globally. This trend is important: these devices act as a digital bridge, allowing these states to close the divide between themselves and more developed economies. These ambitions are especially pronounced in Africa where the increase in penetration has been greatest. Mobile phones have proved especially salient for SMEs in developing states as they hold out the promise of acting as a platform for the spread of m-commerce (mobile electronic commerce) in these economies. This process has been aided by the spread of banking and payments through mobile devices.

As a platform for development, the production of ICT-related products and services has had its most tangible impact in China and India. For the former, this is based on the export of hardware and for the latter on the establishment of ICT-enabled services. Indeed, in 2004 China became the world's leading supplier of ICT goods. India has become the main exporter of ICT services and enabled services such as business process outsourcing.

Unsurprisingly, e-commerce is concentrated within developed economies. By 2005, the number of enterprises engaged in e-commerce for procurement varied between 20 and 60 per cent. While anecdotal evidence suggests that electronic commerce is increasing in developing states (albeit from a low base), the absence of firm statistics prevents the drawing of any definite conclusions. The share of OECD enterprises using the internet for sales is between 10 and 20 per cent. These rates are highest within the retail and wholesale sectors for procurement and retail and tourism for selling. Looking at the spread of electronic commerce, it is apparent that there is differentiation between the developed and developing economies. In 2006, nearly 70 per cent of Swedish businesses and 60 per cent of Canadian businesses placed orders over the internet. However, it is interesting to note that over a half of all Brazilian enterprises receive and make orders over the internet – a figure that is higher than in many developed states. Across many states, e-commerce is used widely for banking services and transactions with public services.

These IT environments have been transformed by emerging competition within developing states. By 2005, nearly three-quarters of developing states had at least three competing mobile services. There appears to be a direct correlation between competition and the state of the supporting infrastructure and the density of usage across developing states. However, increased usage tends to be concentrated in a limited number of states, namely Brazil, China and India. This masks differences within states (especially between urban and rural network development) and slower development elsewhere.

For developing states, the emergence of electronic commerce and the internet offers considerable opportunities to enhance economic growth and welfare. Some states are already proving that they can benefit from the new export opportunities provided by the new technologies through increased exports of data entry, software development and so on. This, in turn, is likely to attract further foreign investment, thereby stimulating economic growth. These states can also expect to benefit from the increased availability of ICTs, notably in important areas such as education and medical services. Furthermore, the advent of the internet should allow enterprises within developing states to integrate themselves into the global economy. Part of the attraction for many developing states of the advent of the information economy is that it offers potential for them to engage in technological 'leapfrogging', thereby enabling them to modernize more rapidly. This will rely on the existence of an open system of innovation and knowledge sharing and creation. Benefits accruing to developing states from the advent of the information economy include:

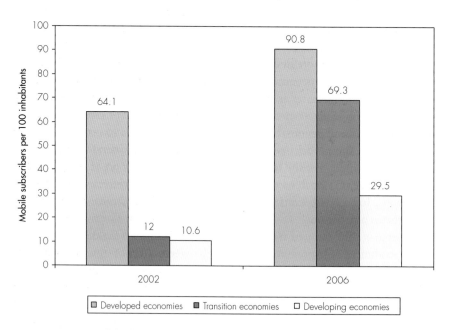

FIGURE 18.3 Mobile Phone Penetration, 2002 and 2006

Source: UNCTAD.

- reduction of the physical distance between buyers and sellers;
- reduction of the need to maintain establishments abroad;
- reduction of the need for an intermediary;
- increased efficiency in public procurement.

This links into the broader competitive benefits generated by the spread of ICTs allowing new forms of employment, enhanced productivity and increased efficiency.

Some sectors that are especially important to developing states in the generation of foreign exchange could be directly assisted by the utilization of electronic commerce. Tourism is an information-intensive industry and IT is used in many aspects of the industry's value chain. Effective and reliable information for customers about the destination is seen as a key factor in influencing choice. The advent of electronic commerce could allow local operators in developing states to reach tourists directly rather than relying on travel agents based in developed states. Other benefits could be derived from increasing the speed of technology transfer, thereby enabling developing states to foster an indigenous IT sector.

There are a number of challenges and dangers that have to be met by developing states in their desire to push electronic commerce. For example, developed states could use the technological change associated with the information economy to reinforce existing differentials. Developing states may find that the adoption of electronic commerce destroys existing supply chains and increases dependence upon MNEs.

Access to the internet is still limited to a small minority in developing states. Incomes in many states are so low that many people do not have access to basic telephony. These problems are compounded by underdeveloped and outdated infrastructure; high prices; low service quality; lack of qualified personnel, and low levels of literacy. In an attempt to overcome these problems, a number of initiatives from a diverse array of sources have emerged.

Trade simulated by ICTs has so far been dominated by developed economies, especially in the service sector. In 2005, developed economies had a market share of over 70 per cent in this sector. In short, despite the much-vaunted potential, there has been little inroad into the dominance of developed economies in the global information economy, despite a rapid growth in the value of exports from developing markets. Exports of ICT-enabled services from emerging and developing countries came mostly from Asia, notably India and China, which specialized in computer and information services. Progress has been impeded across the sector as not all states are committed to liberalization of this sector while others have excluded specific (but important) sub-segments from liberalization. This has been compounded by restrictions on movements of people to support trade in services and by limited mutual liberalization between developing states.

TABLE 18.2 Broadband Penetration by Level of Development (%)

	2002	2006
World		
Developed economies	5	18.4
Developing economies	0	1.3
Transition economies	0.4	1.9

Source: UNCTAD.

Attempts to measure the impact of the spread of ICTs upon growth have focused on developed economies and offer little guidance as to how developing states can also enjoy such benefits. Clearly, if some states follow the principle of competitive advantage, they will be prevented from investing in ICT production. This implies the creation of a link between economic growth and the information economy, and relies on achieving an appropriate policy framework. Of course, the ability of developing states to integrate into the information economy is not uniform. The higher income developing states have a higher propensity to absorb and utilize these technologies.

CASE STUDY 18.2

Voice Over the Internet Protocol (VOIP)

VOIP is proving to be a key technology underpinning the process of globalization. At its core, VOIP is about the switch of voice traffic towards data networks such as the internet. Many businesses of all sizes that engage in international transactions are adopting this technology which has reduced the cost of making international calls to zero. VOIP has been driven by a number of factors:

* *lower costs*: the technology allows users to have a single network to carry voice and data;
* *the growth of global communications*: the technology allows users to streamline these increased traffic flows;
* *increased functionality*: the technology can work in any location with a good internet connection;
* *flexibility*: the service can be adapted to suit user needs;
* *a mobile workforce*: a single handset with a single number aids contactability;
* *globalization*: the technology provides opportunities to connect businesses through an existing network.

VOIP will disrupt global telecommunications in two ways. First, within traditional telecommunications distance, time and geography matter. VOIP undermines all three as it takes no account of where and how long the user talks. Second, the technology decouples network access and service, traditionally provided together. The biggest challenge for voice-based businesses is that they face a choice of cannibalizing existing business models or of being made redundant by the new technology.

As suggested, the main advantage for users of the spread of VOIP is the sharp reduction in the cost of communication systems. For all businesses, benefits are derived from a number of sources. First is portability: with VOIP users can plug into a broadband connector anywhere in the world and seamlessly receive calls at their office number. Second is scalability and network space: it is easy to add new users to the network. Third is flexibility: VOIP allows firms to respond flexibly to demands placed upon the network. For example, in call centres where traffic flow is uneven, VOIP allows users to work from home with all call centre features available and brings call centre operations within the reach of enterprises of all sizes. Thus, the competitive advantage from the use of VOIP has to extend beyond the desire for cost savings and be integrated into the underpinning value proposition.

CASE STUDY QUESTIONS

1. What has been the impact of the advent of VOIP upon the internationalization of value chains?

2. How can the wider adoption of VOIP aid competitive positions in international markets?

STIMULATING THE GLOBAL INFORMATION ECONOMY

From the start, it was agreed by policy makers that the development of the information economy would be market led. In policy terms, this required the removal of barriers to demand led development. Initially, this focused on making the internet a tariff-free environment, including no new taxes on goods delivered via this medium and establishing a uniform commercial code for trade on the internet to provide certainty for enterprises. Thus, in order for the information economy to have a tangible impact upon the development of international business, the following areas need to be addressed by policy makers:

- *Access*: the physical infrastructure needs investment and should be encouraged by creating a more open environment for investors.
- *Human resources*: support and resources are needed from both national and international bodies to support education and training in the use of ICTs.
- *Content*: local content needs to be developed to support SME access and usage. SME-based forums need to be established to share experiences in the use of electronic commerce.
- *Legal and regulatory framework*: legislation that supports e-commerce and the internet and reform of the telecommunications sector to allow increased private sector involvement in the sector are needed.
- *Security, power and governance issues*: international frameworks need to be created to generate the necessary confidence in the utilization of electronic commerce.

Given the accordance on these broad principles, the major developed states aimed for an agreement on the development of the information economy within the context of the WTO. This resulted in three overlapping initiatives: first, the liberalization of trade in ICTs (via the ITA); second, the progressive liberalization of communications services (via the Agreement on Basic Telecommunications), and third, agreement on the underpinning principles of electronic commerce. This confirms that the development of the information economy has been treated in a fragmented manner within the WTO. However, this partly reflects the reactive nature of the WTO as the information economy was not a relevant policy concern at its inception. Thus, many see the need for a coherent Agreement on Electronic Commerce. However, provisions within the WTO framework via GATS and the ITA do provide a basis for action. The WTO work programme divides e-commerce into three stages: the advertising and searching stage; the ordering and payment stage; and the delivery stage. Any or all of these stages may be undertaken online.

The work programme for e-commerce under the WTO has centred on the following issues:

- Characterization: that is, how should electronic transactions be characterized? Are they purely intangible or can other means be included?
- Market access related to e-commerce: are binding tariff obligations altered by electronic trade?
- Classification: how should digitized products be classified?
- Rules of origin: how would these rules apply when digitization of data makes it difficult for source of transmission to be identified?

- Standardization relating to e-commerce: should the WTO develop general standards to cover trade in e-commerce?
- Copyright and related topics: how should the WTO ensure that these rights are protected throughout the multilateral trading system?
- The role of GATS with respect to the electronic delivery of service: does this fall within the scope of GATS and, if so, what are the implications for other services sectors?
- The development dimension of e-commerce: understanding the fiscal implications for developing states of the emergence of e-commerce.
- Zero duty on electronic transmission: it is proposed that this be extended for an indefinite period.
- Is the WTO the right place to deal with e-commerce?

However, little progress has been made, with the issue of characterization proving especially difficult. Efforts need to be more ambitious regarding the extension of agreements, both in terms of geographic reach and products. The lack of ambition of the current initiatives raises the possibility that the e-potential of the global economy could be severely limited. Policy initiatives must have a greater degree of political commitment by the leading industrial states. The first time the WTO addressed internet trade was in the restriction on cross-border internet gambling services (see Case Study 7.2).

The OECD has exercised a more indirect influence over the policy environment shaping the development of electronic commerce. It has developed a framework – essentially private sector led – within which these policy actions can be developed. The OECD guidelines on consumer protection in the context of electronic commerce form the basis of a consensus between states and its principles on privacy are widely accepted as the norm across the global economy. Perhaps the most important contribution of the OECD has been in shaping and developing a policy agenda which seeks to ensure that the global economy (or the leading industrialized states in the short term) is able to maximize the benefits of electronic commerce. In achieving this, the following issues and themes need to be addressed.

- *Privacy*: as increasing quantities of personal (and often confidential) information are offered over the internet and as users engage in extensive navigation around the Web, there is concern about the privacy of users regarding their Web habits and the need for assurances that any information regarding a user is not used in a manner that contravenes the rights of the individual. If users feel they are being unknowingly scrutinized, their confidence in electronic commerce will be directly undermined.
- *Security*: when users pay for goods over the internet, they want to be assured that the information they are volunteering (such as credit card details) is secure and free from unwanted intrusion. Security concerns the totality of safeguards over the internet and protects the system from unwanted access, abuse and damage.
- *Consumer protection*: once a consumer engages in a cross-border transaction, there is a lack of clarity over which state's law of contract applies and the protection afforded to the consumer. The issue of jurisdiction in relation to consumer protection needs to be addressed.
- *Taxation issues*: the impact of the internet upon taxation is manifold. It opens up tax havens to an increasing number of people and increases tax competition between states. There are also issues about how to tax goods that are normally taxable but are delivered via the internet.

- *Content issues*: there is a desire to ensure that the development of the internet does not challenge or hinder cultural and linguistic diversity and that the markets do not result in unfair competition between cultures resulting in harmonization/domination by a single culture. This is a concern for non-English-speaking cultures as the prevalent language on the internet is English (80 per cent of websites are in the English language). A second concern is that there should be control of the content offered over the internet in relation to what is either illegal or potentially harmful. States differ about what constitutes harmful content: in some states there is a broader range of material that is deemed unacceptable and therefore regarded as necessary to control.
- *Standards*: all aspects of the support infrastructure should be both interoperable and inter-connected. Without this, the seamless communication to aid the development of international trade over the internet will be severely curtailed.

Perhaps the most important move towards the successful development of access to the internet has been the increased competition in the provision of internet access, both in terms of services and infrastructure. Evidence suggests that as competition intensifies, the cost of accessing the technology declines. Such developments are linked to mounting evidence of rapidly growing demand as an increasing number of users see direct and tangible benefit from internet access. However, it is evident that sustaining this demand and meeting it with supply depends on developing an adequate balance between the pricing of internet services and content.

Creating markets to stimulate the development of the information economy relies upon stimulating usage in underdeveloped segments. Strategies for the development of the information economy at the national level focus on nine major themes. The first four cover 85 per cent of all actions involved in most developed and developing countries' e-strategies (World Bank, 2006).

- E-government: that is, providing public services to business and consumers via the internet.
- Provision of infrastructure to support more advanced services and with sufficient flexibility to support innovation.
- Education: to improve internet use in schools and to improve ICT literacy throughout the socioeconomic spectrum.
- Legal and regulatory mechanisms to aid adoption, both directly and indirectly.
- ICT industry supply-side measures to aid the hardware, software and content industries.
- IT HR development: developing human resources with ICT skills to support domestic ICT and to attract FDI.
- E-business: the use of ICTs to increase efficiency in existing business.
- Content: the creation of locally relevant multimedia content to stimulate ICT usage.
- E-health: the use of ICTs to improve the efficiency and effectiveness of health care delivery.

These measures need to ensure that the information economy encourages usage in everyday, routine transactions and does not reinforce existing social divides. To this end it is important to include SMEs within the emergent information economy and to ensure that the broad skills base should be as territorially dispersed as possible. These issues need to be coupled with adequate global frameworks to secure consistency of application as well as the integration and interoperability of networks in recognition of the high degree of mutual interest in securing development of the information economy. For this reason, policy actions to develop the information economy resonate across many international organizations, including the G-8 states that have launched their own set of programmes; the International Telecommunication Union (ITU) and the UN. Many NGOs have been active in developing platforms for the emergence of the information economy in remote areas. The World Bank instigated the InfoDev programme to foster diffusion of ICTs in developing states and the ITU implemented WorldTel which sought to raise capital for investment in telecommunications infrastructure aimed at integrating rural communities into the global economy. Support also extends to aiding these states to create the necessary legal and regulatory framework as well as awareness of the potential of the information economy. Policy seeks to balance the needs of economic development with those that provide as broad access as possible. Policy measures to stimulate the development of the information economy within the less developed states include competitive bidding, and subsidies for ICT providers to stimulate private sector investment in those segments of the populace most likely to be excluded and who demand aggregation policies in public sector contracts.

UNCTAD, despite its pro-market stance, underlines the importance of government in creating the momentum behind the process through pushing for the creation of a demand-led virtuous cycle to promote the development of these networks. This may mean that access has to be developed through technologies such as mobile telephony which has a higher penetration rate in developing economies. However, this also means freeing up the ICT sector, aiding trade and investment in local infrastructure and the government acting as a source of demand stimulation in the formative stages of development.

As of late 2006, 44 per cent of developing states had developed a national ICT plan with a further one-fifth in the process of preparing one. Businesses in developing states face a number of problems in the adoption of ICTs, notably:

■ Slow, unreliable and expensive communications that are often undermined by a corrupt system that links market access to bribes.
■ Limited incentives to change business models when the costs of adopting ICTs are high and the returns uncertain. This scenario is created by an inability to perceive or ignorance of the benefits of adopting ICTs.
■ Lack of trust in online activities.
■ Shortages of skilled ICT workers.

Policy must seek to remove these barriers and include direct intervention to create an awareness of the benefits of ICTs, an essentially demand-creating activity. The role of the state is to overcome market failures in the development of the information economy. The World Bank maintains, however, that the impact of any attempt to integrate an economy into the emerging information economy will be a function of its overall development strategy. This often includes targets for access to schools and other public sector organizations. However, effective policy making relies upon the extent of reliable data on the usage and spread of ICTs within states.

Moreover, a general policy environment that is conducive to the development of electronic commerce is needed. Policy needs to create an environment that is open to FDI and to competition. Such measures facilitate access to ICTs. The acceptance by developing states of WTO rules on telecommunications and IT would further support these measures.

One of the more severe restrictions for developing states is lack of access to international bandwidth. This is proving to be a significant bottleneck which inhibits the transmission of large quantities of digitized information. It is feasible that developing states can leapfrog existing technologies and solve this problem by moving straight to wireless technologies. Indeed, this has been the experience in various places, particularly in Latin America. In other areas, telecentres may provide the most sensible solutions for securing remote access. This process has been aided by tourism to more remote areas which has stimulated the spread of internet cafés in developing states.

CASE STUDY 18.3

Free Speech and the Internet

It has been claimed that the internet poses a threat to authoritarian regimes. The open forum of the internet would, it was believed, expose anti-democratic practices and suppression. By making the actions of repressive states transparent, it was believed that the internet would open up these states and advance democracy. This effect would emerge through four domains:

1. *The mass public*: the internet can mobilize the public by exposing them to new ideas and practices.
2. *Civil society organizations*: these bodies can use this technology to aid flows of information or to mobilize support.
3. *The economy*: the internet, via entrepreneurship, can create economic freedom which, in turn, can stimulate demand for political freedom.
4. *The international community*: the internet can expose authoritarian practices to outside and influential bodies such as aid agencies and foreign governments who may try to exert influence over the regime.

In practice, this idealistic perspective has been found to be misplaced. The internet has neither stopped nor curtailed despotic actions as authoritarian regimes are finding ways to control access to the internet or to sites where dissident voices may be accessed. In many cases, these regimes are using the internet to enhance their control and secure their power. Their strategies may be reactive or proactive.

* *Reactive strategies* are the most visible and involve the government clamping down on internet usage. This includes limiting access to internet usage via control of networked computers; filtering content or blocking websites with software tools; by monitoring on-line behaviour or even by prohibiting internet usage entirely.
* *Proactive strategies* are based on the state guiding usage and internet development to promote their own interests. This strategy is based on developing a domestic online environment free from any political challenges but which can consolidate and even extend state power. Thus, the regime may use the technology to distribute propaganda; to build state-controlled intranets that can replace the global internet; to implement e-government services that increase citizen satisfaction, or even engage in information warfare such as hacking or the spreading of viruses. In addition, governments may use the internet to support economic development goals.

Consequently, the internet can, in the hands of an aggressive state, actually work to enhance the power of authoritarian regimes. Cuba and China have followed contrasting strategies to challenges posed by the internet: the former has been reactive while the latter has been more proactive. Their choices reflect differences between the states over the degree of economic development and reform. China realized that economic reform needed the internet and decided to pursue a policy of managing content rather than access. Cuba has only undertaken limited economic reform and thus does not view the internet as an important development tool. However, China is not averse to reactive and draconian measures when it feels its authority is challenged: this has extended to information warfare with sites outside its jurisdiction where it has engaged in hacker attacks. Thus, authoritarian control may be exercised through the internet, despite its democratizing potential.

CASE STUDY ACTIVITY

As a class-based activity, discuss the potential commercial implications of attempts by certain governments to control use of the internet.

CONCLUSION

The emergence of the information economy has great potential to radically alter the nature of international business. However, the path to a truly global impact is still severely blocked. Despite increased awareness, developed states still need to agree on core policy issues that will allow it to emerge as a truly global commercial phenomenon. For developing states, the needs are more basic. While the information economy does provide the potential for economic growth, poor education systems and the absence of basic infrastructures means that the internet is likely to be on the periphery of concerns of policy makers in these states.

Summary of Key Concepts

- Information has proved to be an increasingly core resource for businesses.
- Information is assisting the improved performance of business in terms of its international operations.
- Electronic commerce opens up new international channels for sales.
- A global framework for electronic commerce has to be agreed to aid the maturity of the information economy.

Activity

Using the example of an industry with which you are familiar, identify how the advent of the global information economy has changed structure, strategy and operations.

Discussion Questions

1. What are the key features of the information economy?

2. Discuss the implications for international business of the emergence of the information economy.

3. What are the major impediments to the emergence of the information economy?

4. Do you support the idea that the emergence of the information economy will allow developing states to 'skip' stages of economic development? If not, why not?

References and Suggestions for Further Reading

Anderson, C. (2006) *The Long Tail: Why the Future of Business Is Selling Less of More*, New York: Hyperion.

Carr, N. (2004) *Does IT Matter? Information Technology and the Corrosion of Competitive Advantage*, Boston, MA: Harvard Business School Press.

CIA (2008) *The World Factbook*, www.cia.gov/.

Clarke, G. and Wallsten, S. (2004) 'Has the internet increased trade? Developed and developing country evidence', *Economic Inquiry*, Vol. 44, No. 3, 465–484.

Drucker, P. (1969) *The Age of Discontinuity*, New York: Heinemann.

Goldstein, A. and O'Connor, D. (2000) *E-commerce for Development*, OECD Development Centre, Technical Papers No. 164, Paris: OECD.

Hauser, H. and Wunsch, S. (2001) *E-commerce: A Call for a WTO Initiative*, Swiss Institute for International Economics and Applied Economic Research.

Information Infrastructure Task Force (1997) *A Framework for Global E-commerce*, www.iitf.nist.gov/eleccomm/.

OECD (1998) *Trade Policy Aspects of Electronic Commerce*, Working Paper TD/TC/WP (98)65, Paris: OECD.

OECD (2000) *E-commerce: Impacts and Policy Challenges*, Working Paper ECO/WKP (2000) 25, Paris: OECD.

OECD (2001) 'Electronic commerce: policy brief', *OECD Observer*, Paris: OECD.

OECD (2006) *Information Technology Outlook*, Paris: OECD.

Panagariya, A. (1999) *E-commerce, WTO and Developing Countries*, www.unctad.org/, Geneva: UNCTAD.

Petersen, B., Welch, L. and Liesch, P. (2002) 'The internet and foreign market expansion by firms', *Management International Review*, Vol. 42, No. 2, 207–221.

Tapscott, D. and Williams, A.D. (2006) *Wikinomics: How Mass Collaboration Changes Everything*, New York: Portfolio.

Turner, C. (2000) *The Information E-conomy*, London: Kogan Page.

UNCTAD (2007) *Information Economy Report*, www.unctad.org.

World Bank (2006) *Development Report*, www.worldbank.org.

WTO (1998) *Electronic Commerce and the WTO*, Discussion Paper, www.wto.org/, Geneva: WTO.

Yip, G. (2001) *Global Strategy in the Internet Era*, London Business School, Working Paper CNE WP01/2001.

Yip, G. and Dempster, A. (2005) 'Using the internet to enhance global strategy', *European Management Journal*, Vol. 23, No. 1, 1–13.

Website

Organisation for Economic Cooperation and Development – www.oecd.org.

Chapter 19

Natural Resources

Are We Heading for a New Energy Crisis?

When the well's dry, we know the worth of water.

Benjamin Franklin (1706–1790) in *Poor Richard's Almanac,* 1746

LEARNING OBJECTIVES

This chapter will help you to:

- understand the ongoing importance of natural resources, and energy in particular, to business

- identify key drivers in the international energy industry

- identify and assess sources of potential energy supply shocks

- identify changes in energy demand that could transform the world's energy markets

- assess arguments for and against the proposition that an energy crisis is just around the corner

Natural resources in the form of energy, water and raw materials are essential to the functioning of all businesses in various ways. Energy alone accounts for 10 to 40 per cent of the total production costs of primary metals and construction materials in Europe; 7 to 20 per cent of chemical production costs; 20 to 30 per cent of air transport costs and 2 per cent of engineering and 1 per cent of financial services costs. Indeed, even where the share of energy in total costs is relatively low, as in some service sectors and in aspects of the information society, energy remains a crucial input. High-technology companies with their web servers and process technology are wholly dependent on reliable, non-interruptible sources of electric power. For developing countries, the first stage of development is usually industrialization which is an energy-intensive process. In both developed and developing countries, the use of energy for transportation purposes continues to grow rapidly.

The struggle to acquire secure energy resources is thus seen as an essential element in the continuing flourishing of business, international or otherwise. In recent years, it has become more and more commonplace to hear the assertion that in the twenty-first century increasingly scarce water resources will play their part in international conflicts and that the water demands of multinational corporations could potentially place them in conflict with local communities (see Case Study 19.1). Moreover, as the demand for raw materials surges ahead in emerging economies, particularly in China, the markets for raw materials tighten, creating shortages and pushing up prices. This has occurred in the iron, steel, concrete and other commodity markets. Although the initial impact on this was positive for non-Chinese steel producers, as China develops its own steel-producing and exporting capacity, the international market for steel will become more volatile as marginal prices fluctuate around slight movements in Chinese steel supply and demand.

In short, the markets for many natural resources are international and as these markets are stretched, so the potential for new business challenges and opportunities and for international conflict increases. The purpose of this chapter is therefore twofold:

1. To demonstrate the centrality of international resource issues to business.
2. To develop an understanding of how one industry, energy, is engaging with the globalization process. The oil sector, for example, has always been one of the most global industries as a result of the clear separation between production and consumption, whereas electricity has only latterly taken on a more international perspective as a result of domestic reforms.

The energy sector typifies the challenges facing business in an international context, and from the specific perspective of growing resource scarcity. In order to explore these issues, the chapter first identifies some of the key drivers of the energy sector worldwide. It then examines national policy initiatives and their role in the internationalization of various energy sectors. The chapter then explains previous energy crises and considers whether the world is on the threshold of a new energy crisis. In the process, the role of various political, economic and technological factors in shaping energy sectors becomes apparent.

CASE STUDY 19.1

Water – Conflict or Cooperation?

Although no war has yet been fought over water in modern times, numerous warnings have been issued by senior officials and commentators, including former UN Secretary-General Kofi Annan, about the likelihood that wars in the twenty-first century will increasingly be about access to water. It is not difficult to see how this conclusion has been reached. About one-sixth of the world's population have no access to safe drinking water and over two and a half billion people lack adequate sanitation. Tensions are increasing over water owing to a rising population; increasing agricultural production, especially of water-intensive crops; growing prosperity which itself boosts water demand; climate change which is drying up some regions while resulting in flooding in others; greater pollution, particularly in rapidly growing developing countries, which undermines the amount of fresh water available, and overconsumption in many regions because consumers are not charged the full economic cost of water. Consequently, the UN has estimated that during the first quarter of the twenty-first century, the average supply of water per capita will shrink by one-third.

Overall, the above water problems are bad for human health and undermine the development process in many parts of the world. However, attempts to draw parallels between oil and water are misplaced. Oil resources are concentrated in geographically remote regions far from the main consuming areas, whereas water is distributed across the planet, albeit with varying degrees of plentifulness. Moreover, unlike oil, water can be endlessly reused and recycled, and desalination can increase the total amount of resources. Oil is essential to all aspects of the modern industrial and post-industrial economy, including production itself, consumption and mobility. Although water has a role to play in many industrial processes, its main importance is as a biological and ecological necessity which is equally important for non-industrial processes. The oil

industry is dominated by huge multinationals that have traditionally been able to earn high profits, whereas water provision has frequently been the responsibility of the state and has not generated large profits. Water privatization, which has been pushed in some parts of the world, is gradually changing this. Most importantly of all, however, from the point of potential conflict, oil is an internationally rather than a domestically traded commodity, whereas the supply of water largely comes from domestic sources. In other words, the world's most economically powerful nations and increasingly large emerging economies are competing in international markets for oil, whereas competition for water is more localized.[1]

The above demonstrates why water is unlikely to join oil as a major source of geopolitical conflict. However, that is not to say that there are no potential water flashpoints. Many of these flashpoints are contained within states and concern access to adequate supplies, competition for water and conflict arising from the management of supplies. Such conflicts set various stakeholders against each other, including farmers, industry, rural populations, urban populations, dams, environmentalists and those with a recreational interest. The following are examples of water-driven conflicts that have taken place since 2000.

* *2000*: China – Chinese farmers clashed with police over plans to divert irrigation water to industry and to cities, resulting in a number of fatalities.
* *2002*: India – violence occurred over the allocation of the Cauvery River between Karnataka and Tamil Nadu, resulting in the destruction of properties and dozens of injuries.
* *2005*: Somalia – following an extensive drought, over 250 people were killed in conflicts over water wells.
* *2005*: Kenya – major violence erupted between Kikuyu and Masai groups over water. Over 20 people were killed and over 2,000 were displaced.

* *2006*: Yemen – a struggle over the control of a water well led to armed clashes and forced many families out of their homes.

Although most water-related violence has so far occurred at a local level, tension can occur between states and there are a number of potential flashpoints throughout the world, including India and Pakistan, Israel and Palestine, the Niger and Volta rivers, parts of Southern Europe and the Nile, Mekong and Euphrates. In short, wherever water resources cross boundaries, there is potential for interstate tension. The above flashpoints include areas of high tension regardless of water issues – such as India and Pakistan and the Middle East. Remarkably, however, even the bitterest of enemies have so far put their differences aside when it comes to the issue of water. The River Jordan, for example, is a joint resource for Israel, Jordan and Palestine, and all three states have utilized a model of collaboration in administering the waters, thereby keeping the issue of water availability separate from their political differences. This is a pattern that has so far been repeated in several areas of high tension.

Water conflict need not take a violent form and occurs not only within areas of high tension but between neighbours who normally get on reasonably well. The recent dispute between Texas and Mexico is a case in point. In 1944, the US and Mexico signed a treaty according to which the US was to receive one-third of the flow from six Mexican tributaries to the Rio Grande – approximately 350,000 acre feet of water. The US was obliged to deliver 1.5 million acre feet of water from the Colorado River to Mexico. The US fulfilled its commitments but from 1992 Mexico fell behind with its water deliveries, claiming drought had made the transfers unfeasible. This failure to deliver gave rise to a major dispute between Mexico and Texas, many of whose farmers and ranchers incurred severe losses arising from the resulting water shortages. Diplomacy and threats of legal action finally bore fruit, and in 2005, Mexico announced that it would pay off its entire water debt, thereby bringing to an end a dispute which could have escalated, further damaging local farming interests and the wider US–Mexico relationship in general.

What does all this attention to water mean for business?

On the negative side, incoming businesses need to be aware that their impact on local water supplies can create tension and even conflict with local communities. Coca-Cola's experience is a case in point: the company has been heavily criticized for the impact of its activities in both Latin America and India. For example, the company has been accused of exhausting water supplies and causing pollution from untreated water over a sustained period at a subsidiary in El Salvador. However, the company's problems go even further in India.

In 2000, Coca-Cola opened a plant at Plachimada in Kerala. In March 2004, the Kerala High Court forced the company to suspend production following allegations that it had overused local water supplies to the detriment of farmers and the local community. Subsequently, campaigners, including local villagers and national and international NGOs, claimed that not only was the company drying up local groundwater but it had also contaminated local drinking water and released harmful substances in waste products. Coca-Cola strenuously denied all allegations. However, its water troubles extend beyond Kerala and campaigns against the company's impact upon local water supplies are being waged across several Indian states.

In August 2006, all Coca-Cola's products, along with those of Pepsi, faced a total ban in Kerala on the grounds that they contained unacceptably high levels of pesticides. Several other Indian states either introduced or considered introducing a ban on these products in state schools, colleges and hospitals. The Kerala ban was quickly overturned in the courts on the grounds that the state government had exceeded its role by taking action which only the national government was authorized to take.

Despite the lifting of the ban, Coca-Cola has not seen the end of the campaign against it in India which brings together a range of local interests, environmentalists and anti-capitalist NGOs. The company has responded to the allegations by launching global initiatives to reduce the amount of water consumed in its production processes. These include:

* a pledge to improve the efficiency of its water consumption;
* a commitment to recycle all the water used in manufacturing processes;
* support for a wide range of local initiatives to replenish water supplies.

Moreover, in an astute political move, in June 2007 Coca-Cola announced a partnership with the respected NGO, the World Wildlife Fund (WWF), to help conserve and protect fresh water throughout the world. The partnership includes efforts to conserve seven of the world's most critical fresh water regions; to improve water efficiency both by Coca-Cola and its agricultural suppliers, particularly sugar producers; to reduce carbon emissions throughout the company's operations, and to bring together industries and conservation organizations to conserve fresh water resources worldwide. Indeed, as part of its partnership with the WWF, Coca-Cola has set itself a global target to improve its water-use efficiency by 20 per cent in 2012.

More positively, water creates opportunities for business. These may be divided into water utilities and infrastructure (including water supply, waste water treatment, the construction of sewage and water pipelines, the drilling of water wells and water testing) on the one hand and the provision of equipment and materials on the other. Although water supply remains primarily the preserve of the public sector, water privatization has gathered pace in both the developed and developing world since 1990. These investment opportunities have resulted in the emergence of multinational water utilities such as Veolia and Suez. This business has not always been straightforward, as Bechtel discovered in Bolivia when its attempts to raise water prices were met with serious resistance. Suez has also found it difficult to make profits and in 2002 pulled out of its investments in Manila and Buenos Aires. In 2003 Suez sold the UK's Northumbrian Water and lost its 20-year contract to supply water to the US city of Atlanta amidst claims that it had failed to deliver on promises of improvements to water quality. In short, although water privatization has failed to live up to its early promise, causing countries like South Africa and Brazil to question

earlier commitments to water privatization, international water utilities are likely to focus their activities on more promising investments in the developed world.

The global market for water equipment and materials was valued at $400 billion in 2003 and includes water treatment chemicals, desalination equipment, water treatment appliances, pumps and related equipment and water recycling equipment. The market encompasses all geographical regions and, given the emerging water supply problems alluded to above, this market is anticipated to grow steadily. Consequently, multinational companies like General Electric, Dow Chemicals, Siemens and ABB have set up water-processing technology divisions and smaller, more specialist equipment companies are seizing opportunities in this area.

In conclusion, even if the forecasts of water-related conflicts prove to be misplaced, the supply of water will remain a major preoccupation for policy makers for health, environmental and economic reasons, and provide major opportunities for business throughout the world in the coming decades.

Note:
[1] The points in this paragraph are elaborated in much greater detail in Jan Selby's excellent article in *Government and Opposition* (2005).

CASE STUDY QUESTIONS

1. 'The wars of the twenty-first century will be about water.' What are the arguments for and against this statement?

2. Identify the main issues of corporate social responsibility of specific concern to water utilities.

3. Water has brought Coca-Cola into conflict with local communities in India. Investigate this case further and discuss whether and how such conflict could be avoided. Activists have described Coca-Cola's attempts to address the claims made against it as 'greenwashing' (that is, the company's efforts have been a public relations exercise with little substance). Do you agree?

4. Identify and assess the international business opportunities for the water industry.

KEY DRIVERS IN THE INTERNATIONAL ENERGY INDUSTRY

Like other industries, the energy industry is subject to a number of key influences (see Figure 19.1). These drivers affect many industries, although their precise weighting, manifestation and interaction varies from industry to industry. For the energy industry, these drivers include the following:

- *Globalization*: the energy industry is composed of sectors (oil, gas, coal electricity, nuclear) that demonstrate varying degrees of internationalization and international integration. The oil industry encompasses some of the world's biggest companies and, more than most, is a truly international industry. In 2008, boosted by several years of high oil prices, oil and gas companies comprised six (ExxonMobil, Royal Dutch Shell, BP, Chevron, Total and ConocoPhillips) out of ten of the biggest companies by revenue in *Fortune* magazine's Global 500 companies, and seven (ExxonMobil, Royal Dutch Shell, BP, Gazprom, Chevron, Petronas and Total) out of the top ten companies in terms of profitability. Indeed, the larger publicly owned oil companies determine their strategy from a global perspective, exploring for and producing crude oil on a worldwide basis and serving global markets.

  This contrasts sharply with the electricity supply industry (ESI), a sector that has traditionally operated along regional or national monopoly lines. However, as a result of the deregulation and privatization that has taken hold in many countries and regions, several previously predominantly national power companies are embarking on cross-border electricity trade and developing strategies with a more international perspective, including investment in privatized utilities outside the home country. Although far from reaching the internationalized situation of the oil and gas industry, electricity utilities are becoming increasingly internationalized.

- *Technology*: technology plays a key role in the world's energy industry. In the oil sector, new technology has made the exploitation of previously unprofitable fields profitable, made previously inaccessible fields accessible and increased the amount of oil recoverable from established fields. Technical developments have increased the economic viability of liquefied natural gas (LNG). As the percentage of natural gas transported by LNG carriers increases in relation to pipeline gas which is locationally inflexible, so gas markets will become more

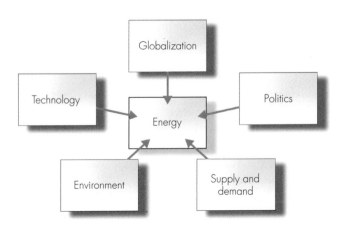

FIGURE 19.1 Major Influences on International Energy Industries

international. The inclusion of more energy-efficient features in many appliances and equipment after the oil prices crises helped break the link between economic growth and energy consumption. Distributed power has reduced the importance of scale economies in electricity production, and fuel cell technology, if it achieves commercial viability, has the potential to relieve the world of its dependence on crude oil.

■ *The environment*: in recent decades, the link between energy and the environment has come under intense scrutiny and is shaping government policies and corporate strategies. The most discussed link has become the alleged link between carbon dioxide emissions (which stem from the burning of fossil fuels like oil, coal and gas) and climate change. This has led to the Kyoto agreement and commitments by some governments to limit their carbon dioxide emissions. The energy–environment link does not stop there: most energy sources involve some environmental concerns, ranging from the disposal of nuclear waste to the impact of hydroelectric dams on the ecology of their region. In turn, the environmental issue has caused oil, gas and other energy-related companies to focus their research and development efforts on initiatives that both increase their environmental credentials and enable them to retain their long-term profitability. These initiatives range from the development of fuel cells to solar power and improvements in fuel efficiency.

■ *Supply and demand*: the energy sector, like all others, is subject to the vagaries of supply and demand. The world's energy crises so far have essentially been temporary crises of supply arising from political disturbances. In the future, there is potential for more fundamental, long-term crises arising from mismatches between the two economic fundamentals of supply and demand. Controversy persists about the size of the world's remaining stock of non-renewable energy resources and when they will run out. Demand growth is also increasingly playing a major role: in the long term, the growth of developing countries, particularly in Asia and Latin America, has the potential to place unsustainable demands on world energy supplies.

■ *Politics*: government–energy industry links can be particularly strong. Many of President George W. Bush's senior appointments were drawn from the ranks of the oil industry. This, plus significant donations to Bush election campaigns from the energy industry, encouraged the perception that energy and environmental policy were determined by the energy industry in its interests rather than by broader national interests. These strong energy links to government are not unique to the US: similar closeness has existed in the Russian oil and gas industry. Viktor Chernomyrdin, Russian prime minister from 1992 to 1998, was a former head of the world's largest gas company Gazprom, an organization that continues to maintain close links with the government. Other senior officials have migrated between Gazprom and the government. Towards the end of the 2000s, some commentators increasingly see Gazprom as a key tool of Russian foreign policy.

However, given the essential nature of energy and the concentration of key energy resources in more politically volatile areas of the world, the energy–politics interface is about much more than lobbying and close government–business links. Indeed, energy has a clear geopolitical dimension: conflict unsettles markets and pushes up prices, and foreign policy is influenced by the need to secure energy supplies. Conflicts in the Middle East, for example, are made much more complex by the concentration of energy resources in the region.

Energy companies cannot remain isolated from these geopolitical concerns. For example, as a result of the 1996 Iran Libya Sanctions Act (ILSA), US companies were excluded from development of Iran and Libya's extensive hydrocarbon resources. Moreover, the ILSA had an extraterritorial dimension that empowered the US government to fine non-US companies conducting business in these countries. In practice, the US refrained from exercising these powers. From 2004, the majority of the sanctions against Libya were lifted, including the possibility of imposing penalties on foreign companies. However, the ILSA (now renamed the Iran Sanctions Act) continues to apply to Iran and energy investments there. Iran is in the process of developing nuclear power and of securing pipeline export routes for its gas. The debate about nuclear power is well documented and the pipeline issue is part of a broader debate about the export of natural gas from Central Asia which brings in many countries and has become a major point of tension involving the US, Russia and Iran, among others.

NATIONAL ENERGY POLICY REFORMS

For many years, energy was regarded as too important to be left to the markets and was subject to extensive government intervention. For example, in 1960, several of the developing world's oil-exporting countries formed the oil cartel, the Organization of Petroleum Exporting Countries (OPEC). During the following decade, OPEC members nationalized their oil resources to regain control over a vital national resource from foreign multinationals.

Elsewhere, coal production, crucial to industrial production and power generation and an important source of regional employment, was heavily subsidized. Indeed, in the UK until well into the 1980s, the ESI was obliged to purchase its coal from the state-owned National Coal Board at prices significantly higher than those of imports. Similar arrangements existed in Germany through the 'jahrhundertvertrag' and the coal sector was also assisted through the existence of the 'kohlpfenning', a levy placed on power users to help fund the use of more expensive domestically produced coal. Such practices have long since ceased and coal has become an internationally traded commodity.

In the electricity sector, state-owned, vertically integrated monopolies were commonplace, although in some countries, particularly those with federal structures like the US and Germany, electricity production was organized at a subnational level. Even in countries where private sector ownership was dominant, as in Germany, a monopolistic situation was the norm.

In the early twenty-first century, most energy sector policy innovation in both the developed and the developing world involved a reduction of state involvement and the introduction of greater competition. The current round of energy sector reform is both a response to the technical and financial needs of the energy industry and is also part of the move towards a neo-liberal economic agenda (see Chapter 2). Although reform takes different forms in different countries in different sectors, and is far more advanced in some countries than in others, the common theme is the move away from intervention and planning towards a more market-oriented approach with greater private sector participation.

Reform of networked gas and electricity industries has been widespread and manifests itself in many ways but its ultimate aim is to reduce costs and increase efficiency through increased competition and greater involvement of the private sector. Power sector reform only became possible when the traditional view of line-bound sectors was overturned. According to the conventional view, high entry costs prevented the development of effective competition within these industries, giving rise to potential abuse of market power in the form of artificially high prices and 'monopoly profits'. Consequently, natural monopoly considerations plus the central and sensitive role of these industries meant that in most countries, they were controlled and/or owned by public institutions at central, regional or local government level. This also ensured that attention was paid to social obligations (often expressed as an obligation to supply) and wide energy-planning objectives (for example, priority for the use of domestically produced fuels).

The growing acceptance of neo-liberalism, with its emphasis on the benefits of competition, facilitated a marked change in the perception of line-bound industries. This change was driven by the disaggregation of the stages of power supply into its component parts, some of which are amenable to the introduction of competition. The key ESI functions are as follows.

- *Generation*: that is, the actual production of electricity. Provided that generators have access to the electricity transmission system, competition between generators can be intense.
- *Transmission*: that is, the long-distance transportation of electricity through high-voltage grids – the one function still considered to be a natural monopoly. A major concern of reformers is to ensure that both generators and customers have fair and equal access to the transmission system. This may be achieved in a variety of ways. Privatization and industrial restructuring, for example, often includes unbundling the vertically operated state-owned company. This prevents the owner of the grid system from extending preferential access to the system for electricity generated by its own stations.
- *Distribution*: the physical transportation of energy from the grid to the end-user through low-voltage grids and which can be subject to competition.
- *Supply*: a trading rather than a physical function which includes activities such as sales, metering, invoicing and collection, and which is suitable for the introduction of competition.

This novel view of the competitive potential of line-bound energy industries provided the theoretical and practical justification for restructuring and deregulation and was given further impetus by the UK's 1989 Electricity Act and reform in the Nordic power markets in the early 1990s. Market opening was gradual in the UK and full competition only occurred in 1998 to 1999 when domestic consumers gained the right to choose their electricity suppliers. Since then UK utility companies have changed hands several times. In the early stages of liberalization, US companies bought up several UK regional electricity companies but they subsequently withdrew when profitability was lower than expected. The main beneficiaries have been large utilities from France and Germany, namely EdF, E.ON and RWE, who own a significant share of the UK ESI. Moreover, the initial post-liberalization distinctions between generating, transmission and distribution and supply have become blurred.

The UK was one of the first countries to embrace power sector reform but this trend has subsequently spread throughout Europe. Pan-European electricity liberalization began with the 1996 Electricity Directive which required one-third of the EU's electricity markets to be open to competition by 2003. A 2003 directive required complete opening of the EU's power market by 2007. The reform process has not proceeded without problems, leading the European Commission to launch investigations into the compliance of EU member states with their liberalization obligations and to propose a third electricity directive in 2007 to correct some of the failures and omissions of the first two directives.

Reform has also caught on in varying degrees elsewhere in the industrialized world and in Latin America, Asia and parts of the Middle East and North Africa. Many US states have also reformed their power sectors, mostly successfully, but the Californian energy crisis, which reached its peak in 2001, demonstrated the problems that may occur when reform is not properly thought through.

The details of reform vary: in some cases it involves privatization, whereas in others it may include investment from independent power producers who co-exist alongside publicly owned utilities. Despite this variation in methods, the common theme is greater openness, private sector involvement and competition with a view to attracting more investment, increased efficiency through the effect of competition and lower electricity prices which improves the competitiveness of other economic sectors.

The consequence of these domestic reforms is that they promote greater internationalization of the power sector. Indeed, the implications of liberalization are quite profound for line-bound power and gas utilities that have traditionally been organized almost entirely along national or even subnational lines. The opening up of markets through liberalization and privatization creates opportunities in foreign markets. Indeed, the opening up of power markets should ensure that they develop in the most economically efficient way rather than being constrained by national boundaries. Cross-border electricity trade has long taken place to smooth out temporary supply shortages but its full potential is yet to be reached. The opening up of markets should also stimulate development of the necessary infrastructure and interconnections to support much higher levels of power trade.

IS THE WORLD HEADING FOR A NEW ENERGY CRISIS?

The oil price volatility of the 2000s has, after years of relative neglect, once more increased the profile of the energy sector. Although energy concerns have not reached the critical levels of 1973 and 1979, they are at least sufficiently acute to warrant greater attention to issues of energy supply and demand and to raise the question of whether the world could be heading for another energy crisis. The precise nature and extent of future crises are contestable but previous experience has demonstrated that the effects of elevated energy prices and/or supply shortages can have profound consequences for economies and business.

The world's first energy crisis occurred in 1973 to 1974 when oil prices increased four- to fivefold. This came after a long period in which OPEC members had taken measures to increase their power against the oil multinationals, including the gradual nationalization of foreign oil concessions. The catalyst for the crisis was the outbreak of the Yom Kippur War in October 1973. Shortly after fighting began, OPEC oil ministers agreed to cut crude oil exports and declared an embargo on oil exports to states deemed unfriendly to the Arab cause. This resulted in a ban on OPEC oil exports to the US, the Netherlands, Portugal, Rhodesia and South Africa. This ban remained in place for almost eight months in relation to the US and longer for other countries. A second oil price crisis occurred after the 1979 Iranian Revolution (see Figure 19.2) when nominal oil prices peaked at three times the pre-revolution level.

FIGURE 19.2
Crude Oil Prices (Saudi Light), 1970–2008, US$ per barrel (%)

Source: Energy Information Administration, US Department of Energy.

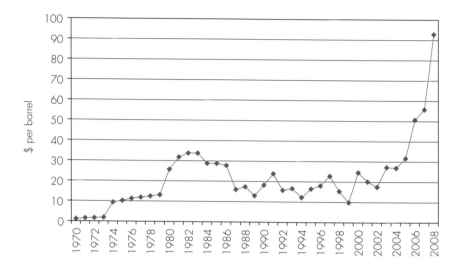

The 1970s and 1980s were decades of unprecedented post-war economic turmoil. Although not wholly responsible for this turmoil, the oil price increases were major contributors to worldwide recession and were instrumental in the rising indebtedness of many developing countries. The oil price shock had the following effects on industrialized countries:

- rising inflation and interest rates;
- a negative effect on domestic demand following the diversion of a greater proportion of spending to energy;
- an increasing import bill and a negative effect on balance of payments.

Developing countries were also hit by higher inflation and negative trade effects. However, trade effects were even more severe in developing countries because oil imports tended to (and still do) form a higher proportion of imports in developing than in developed countries. Developing countries were also indirectly affected because their developed country markets had been plunged into recession by the oil crisis.

In view of the profound and prolonged nature of the oil price shocks, major shifts occurred in key demand-and-supply relationships. Traditionally, there was a direct link between economic growth and growth in energy demand in the industrialized countries. However, as a result of the oil price shocks, this link was broken as manufacturers sought to make their production processes less energy intensive, as consumers looked for more energy-efficient solutions and as governments gave incentives to both to achieve these ends. Although the incentives to greater efficiency lessened somewhat after the mid-1980s when oil markets returned to surplus and real oil prices fell, the former direct link between economic and energy demand growth has not returned. In part, this is because more energy-efficient technology has become embedded in the economic infrastructure and partly owing to the continuing shift away from manufacturing towards service-dominated (and therefore less energy-intensive) economies in the OECD region.

On the supply side, the oil price crises encouraged a shift towards other fuels. This period marked the beginning of the enhanced role for natural gas and the peak construction of nuclear power plants. The trend towards greater exploitation of natural gas was driven by cost and environmental factors. After the 1986 Chernobyl disaster, the prospects for nuclear power declined significantly in Europe and the US as a result of concerns about safety and the disposal of waste. Indeed, by the late 1990s, all EU countries, bar Finland, had a moratorium on the construction of new nuclear plants and/or plans to decommission nuclear plants early. However, the nuclear industry continued to grow in parts of Asia where countries regarded it as a means to satisfy the rapidly growing energy demand accompanying their strong economic development.

By the mid- to late 2000s, however, prospects for nuclear power had improved once more in Europe as a result of the perceived need to replace fossil fuels in power generation. Finland is building a new nuclear power station; a feasibility study for such a plant has been carried out in the Baltic states; a new nuclear installation has been approved in France; Sweden has abandoned its plans to close plants; Switzerland has ended its moratorium on the construction of new nuclear power plants, and the possibility of returning to the nuclear option is under serious consideration in Italy and the UK. New nuclear power plants are once more under consideration in the US and construction of new plants continues across Asia, particularly in India and China.

In the oil sector, the price signals emerging from the crises had a profound effect upon exploration and development. During periods of high prices, oil companies have an incentive to explore for and produce oil in high-cost regions where production was unprofitable at lower prices. This was good for US oil production and it is no coincidence that it was during the 1970s that the major push for development of North Sea resources took place and in other countries outside OPEC, traditionally the world's low-cost oil producers. By the mid-1980s, therefore, oil production had increased in a number of new or previously marginal producers, including, inter alia, Mexico, Columbia, Norway, the UK, Angola, Egypt and Malaysia. Consequently, OPEC's crude oil production fell by almost half between 1979 and 1985, from 31.3 million barrels per day (b/d) to 16.7 million b/d. Non-OPEC production increased from 23 million b/d to almost 29 million b/d to take up some of the slack. Crude oil consumption also fell during this period.

The combined effect of an altered demand function and diversification and expansion of supplies was a return to real oil prices in the mid-1980s to pre-1973 levels and to surpluses rather than shortages of oil. The overwhelming sense of urgency attached to security of supply issues therefore diminished considerably during this period. With the short-lived exception of the first Gulf War, following Iraq's invasion of Kuwait in 1990, the issue of energy supplies and security barely registered in political debate anywhere in the world. Through most of the 1990s, energy debates tended to focus on environmental matters.

This period of relative stability appeared to be coming to an end by the close of the 1990s with prices swinging from their lowest level for many years to their highest within the space of a few months. By 2008, nominal oil prices averaged $93 per barrel (see Figure 19.2), although they peaked at over $130 mid-year. By spring 2009, crude oil prices had plummeted to around $40 per barrel in response to the recession. In the longer term, however, oil price fluctuations are likely to be around a much higher oil price trend which reflects changing supply and demand fundamentals. The remainder of this section examines some of the arguments for and implications of the view that the world could be entering a new period of tight energy markets.

Supply-side Factors

Global energy supply crises have to date been primarily about oil. Oil remains the world's most important source of energy, accounting for 35 per cent of global primary energy consumption (see Figure 19.3) but, as discussed below, serious supply concerns about other energy sources will occur in the future.

At present, there is limited scope for further shifts away from crude oil consumption: most of the easy substitutions for crude oil consumption have already been made and there is a lack of commercially viable substitutes for petroleum in transportation where it remains the dominant fuel. Even if the present optimism about fuel cells proves to be justified, it will be many years before there will be a significant shift away from petroleum in this sector.

Concerns about oil supply fall into two categories. The first stems from the over-concentration of oil reserves in volatile areas like the Middle East where political instability has, in the past, created supply shortages for the rest of the world. Second, there is concern that the world has a finite supply of crude oil and that, at present rates of consumption growth, the depletion of these resources is rapidly approaching. This concern raises fundamental concerns about the long-term sustainability of the currently oil-dominated world economy.

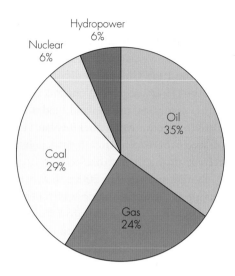

FIGURE 19.3 World Primary Energy Consumption by Tradable Fuel, 2008 (%)

Note: Includes only commercially traded fuels and therefore excludes wood, peat and animal waste – important in many developing countries. It also excludes wind, geothermal and solar power generation.

Source: BP Statistical Review of World Energy (2009).

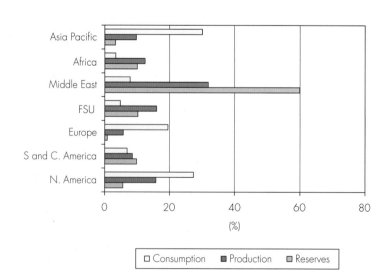

FIGURE 19.4 Oil Reserves, Production and Consumption by Region, 2008

Source: Derived from *BP Statistical Review of World Energy* (2009).

Forecasts about future oil supplies and prices have always proved problematic but there are certain characteristics of the oil markets which suggest possible problems ahead. First, as Figure 19.4 shows, the location of oil reserves and, to a lesser extent oil production, is geographically distant from the main consumption locations. For example, North America, Europe and Asia Pacific consume a far greater proportion of oil than they possess in reserves. Conversely, the Middle East owns a much bigger share of the world's oil reserves and produces more of the world's oil than it consumes. This demand–supply mismatch is increasing as production declines in the North Sea and as the continuing decline in US production is more than matched by growing US consumption, resulting in a large increase in imports needed to meet US demand (see Figure 19.4). In short, over time, even if overall oil reserves continue to grow, either as a result of new discoveries or as a result of reassessment of existing reserves, the location of these reserves is once more becoming increasingly concentrated in fewer suppliers, particularly in the Middle East.

Calculation of total world oil reserves is a complex process and depends upon many assumptions, leading to a range of estimates among experts regarding when oil production will peak, ranging from the mid-2000s in some cases to 2025 or later in others. However, what is incontrovertible is that for some years, the world has been consuming more oil than it has been replacing by new discoveries: in non-OPEC countries, production has consistently exceeded new discoveries since 1988 and in OPEC this has been the case every year since 1978, bar one. Moreover, the more recent oil discoveries have been from smaller fields, which are quicker to deplete and more costly to exploit. Technological developments will undoubtedly extend the life of some fields and exploitation of unconventional resources such as oil shale and sands from Canada and Venezuela will stabilize the situation a little, albeit at an environmental cost.

The world clearly has finite oil supplies but some addition to reserves and increased production is anticipated, particularly in the Middle East, the Caspian Basin, Western Siberia and parts of Africa. The prospects for production in several OPEC countries, especially in the Middle East, are relatively bright, although geopolitical factors in several countries, including Iraq, Iran, Nigeria and Venezuela (and potentially also Saudi Arabia and other Gulf countries), could undermine it. Production in Angola, an OPEC member since 2007, doubled between 2000 and 2006 with even greater increases forecast for the coming decades. This turnaround in Angola's fortunes follows the resolution of the civil war which had dogged the country for two decades and demonstrates the benefits of political stability for foreign investment.

The outlook for non-OPEC producers is more mixed: substantial exploration has taken place in West Africa, where several smaller countries are expected to benefit in future years. North African production is relatively mature and is forecast to decline, but some production increases are possible in East and Southern Africa. Vietnam is regarded as the most promising location in the Asia Pacific; any production increases in India and China will be dwarfed by their increasing demand and Malaysia's output has peaked and started to decline. In the Americas, Mexico's output is in decline while the downward production trend in the US is unlikely to be arrested. Canadian prospects are boosted by the exploitation of tar sands and the possibility of significant output expansion exists in Brazil. Columbia and Ecuador have the potential to boost crude oil production if their political situation allows it. In Europe, the decline in North Sea output will continue but prospects are brighter in the former Soviet Union (FSU) with optimism remaining about Russia and about production in the Caspian basin, despite some downward revisions of reserves. However, the extent to which any newly found reserves will ease the growing reliance on Middle Eastern suppliers will be limited, since many of the potential new resources themselves are located in politically volatile regions and/or have to pass through politically volatile regions to reach the market. Consequently, the balance of production in the first quarter of the twenty-first century will swing much more in OPEC's favour.

A future supply crisis therefore could come from one of two sources or, indeed, from a combination of both: that is, from the long-term decline in the availability of oil supplies (combined with growing demand) and/or geopolitical disturbances ranging from ongoing problems in the Middle East to economic nationalism in Venezuela and to the new version of the 'Great Game' currently being played out in Central Asia in relation to pipeline export routes from the region.

The exploitation of oil and gas reserves from the Middle East, the FSU and other potentially prolific regions requires access to capital and technology, much of which needs to come from foreign investment. This relies to a large extent on the political, social and economic environment as well as on the geology of these regions. At the beginning of Russia's transition to a market economy, many Western oil companies rushed to establish a presence in its oil and gas sector. However, frustration with the government and business practices and the scale of the rehabilitation required by the sector caused many companies to withdraw from investments or to maintain only a minimum profile in Russia. Elf Aquitaine, Amoco, Texaco, Exxon and Norsk Hydro, among others, have abandoned joint ventures. Particularly notorious was the experience of Kenneth Dart who, through his Cyprus-based company Navaramco, had become a minority shareholder in two Russian oil companies. The majority shareholders in these companies, in both cases other Russian companies with major Russian interests, were able to set aside the legal rights of Dart's company, resulting in significant losses for it. The increase in oil prices in the 2000s once more encouraged foreign investors to become involved in Russia's oil and gas industry. Rising oil prices have also encouraged Russia to become more assertive about retaining control over its natural resources (see Case Study 19.2).

Natural gas is more difficult to transport than crude oil which is easily transported by pipeline, rail, sea or road. Therefore, if one export route is blocked, alternatives are usually available. Gas, however, is a different story. The majority of natural gas has always been transported by pipeline. Until recently, gas transported by sea in the form of LNG has been limited: it required technically advanced and expensive ships plus a gas liquefaction plant at the departure point and a gasification plant at the destination. However, technical advances have redressed the economics of gas transport more towards LNG, which is expected to perform a much greater role in gas transportation in the future. In other words, gas transport is becoming less inflexible but it still has some way to go before it equals oil in this regard.

As with oil, the world's gas resources are also located away from the main consuming regions. In 2008, for example, over 70 per cent of proved gas reserves were located in the FSU and the Middle East, whereas these areas accounted for only 31 per cent of world gas consumption (see Figure 19.5). Taken together, these factors make the issue of export routes crucial to the future consumption of gas. In the case of gas, the biggest concentration of reserves is in the FSU, namely in Russia, Kazakhstan, Azerbaijan and Turkmenistan, and, as such, the new 'Great Game' referred to above has an even greater resonance in relation to gas. The Middle East contains about 40 per cent of the world's gas supplies. In short, the relative inflexibility of gas transport combined with the concentration of reserves in more remote and politically sensitive areas and its increased consumption makes the issue of gas security potentially even more serious than that of crude oil. In addition, the foreign investment concerns that apply to oil apply equally to gas (see Case Study 19.2).

Russia Reasserts Control over Its Natural Resources

For many years, oil and gas have been key sectors for the Russia economy in terms of generating budget revenues and hard currency. In the early post-Soviet years, following decades of neglect and mismanagement, the Russia hydrocarbon industry was in a parlous state with damaged wells, inadequate and badly maintained infrastructure and pipeline leakages being the norm. At that time, the overwhelming need of Russia's oil and gas industry was to attract foreign capital to upgrade the industry and to gain access to the advanced technology and know-how. Initially, foreign investors showed intense interest in Russia's oil and gas but interest often did not turn into investment and, when it did, bad experiences often led to a withdrawal from the country or a significant reduction of involvement in Russia.

Despite the potential high rewards from investing in Russia, the lack of an appropriate legal framework to protect foreign investors, frustrations with bureaucracy and dubious business practices combined to increase the perceived risk of investing in Russia and also deterred investors. Russia's continuing reluctance to sign the Energy Charter Treaty, drawn up in the early 1990s to provide certainty and protection for energy trade, transit and investment between the energy-poor but technology/capital-rich countries of Western Europe and the energy-rich but technology/capital-constrained economies of Russia and former Soviet Republics, highlighted the problem. Russian critics of the ECT claim it runs contrary to Russia's economic interests, allowing other countries easier access to Russia's natural resources and perpetuating the country's reliance on its raw materials.

The likelihood of Russia reversing its position on the ECT has diminished even further following the big and sustained oil price increases since the mid-2000s (see Figure 19.2). The massive revenue increases have made it possible for Russia to contemplate development of its oil and gas resources by itself and has bolstered the arguments of those, including former President and current Prime Minister Vladimir Putin, who believe the state should play a major role in the energy sector and that Russia should claw back control of its natural resources. The earliest signs of the assertion of this vision of Russia's energy future occurred with the quashing of the power of the 'oligarchs', those individuals, such as Mikhail Khordokovsky and Boris Bezerovsky, who had become incredibly rich and powerful as a result of their purchases of stakes in Russia's energy sectors. The jailing of the former and the exile of the latter served both to discourage a political challenge from the ranks of the oligarchs to the current regime and to help restore control over significant swathes of Russia's oil and gas industries to the Russian state.

Latterly, the Kremlin's attempts to return its oil and gas deposits to majority state ownership have focused on the Russian investments of three of the world's biggest multinational companies – Royal Dutch Shell, BP and ExxonMobil.

In the mid-1990s, consortia led by ExxonMobil and by Royal Dutch Shell signed contracts (known as Sakhalin 1 and Sakhalin 2 respectively) to develop the significant oil and gas reserves of Sakhalin Island in the North Pacific off the east coast of Russia. By 2006, Sakhalin 2 came in for intense pressure on environmental grounds and was accused by the Ministry of Natural Resources and various environmental NGOs of further endangering the already scarce Western grey whale species, of damaging salmon-spawning streams on the islands and of dumping waste. Although vigorously disputing the accusations, by the end of 2006, Shell and its Japanese partners Mitsui and Mitsubishi were forced to concede a majority stake in Sakhalin 2 to Gazprom, the Russian gas company with a majority state holding, in return for $7.45 billion. The deal was made under duress and generated incredulity regarding the Kremlin's sudden and uncharacteristic commitment to environmentalism. Indeed, another cause for concern for the Russian government was the cost overruns on Sakhalin 2 which occurred, in part, because Shell's attempts to meet environmental concerns but which also reduced the revenues flowing to the Russian state budget from the project. Whatever the reasons behind the dispute, the outcome resulted in a return of important natural resources to Russian control, a major policy objective all along.

In 2003, TNK–BP, a joint venture of BP's Russian oil and gas assets and the gas assets of Alfa Group and Access Renova Group (also known as AAR), was established and became Russia's third largest oil and gas company. TNK–BP is a vertically integrated oil company with upstream and downstream interests in Russia and the Ukraine. BP's involvement came following its disastrous involvement with Sidanko in the 1990s when it lost several hundred million dollars, and demonstrates the risks multinational companies are prepared to take in the Russian oil and gas industry given the potentially huge rewards. However, it was not long before the joint venture ran into problems. In 2007, a row blew up regarding TNK–BP's failure to produce nine billion cubic metres (bcm) of gas by 2006 from the massive Siberian Kovytka gas field in line with its operating licence. TNK–BP had intended to export Kovytka gas to China but Gazprom, which has a monopoly on gas exports and export routes, had refused to allow this. Without Gazprom's co-operation, the only market for Kovytka gas was the Russian domestic market but this did not warrant annual output of nine bcm. The Russian authorities began moves to deprive the joint venture of its licence, disregarding the argument that there was no point in producing any more as it could not be sold locally, since the company had acquired the licence in full knowledge of the situation. In the end, in June 2007, TNK–BP sold its controlling stake in Kovytka gas field to Gazprom for $700–900 million. BP, TNK–BP and Gazprom also signed a deal to establish a $3 billion joint venture for investments in Russia and overseas.

In 2008, all-out war broke out between BP and the four Russian billionaires at the heart of AAR.

Between March and August, BP and TNK–BP were subject to investigations by the Russian authorities, including raids by the FSB, the successor to the KGB. The joint venture was also the focus of an inquiry by the Labour Ministry and a former employee was arrested on a charge of industrial espionage. Key employees were denied visas and the chief executive of the joint venture finally left Russia after the task of running the company became impossible. The roots of the problems are blurred: the four Russian partners in AAR express dissatisfaction with BP's approach to the joint venture which they claim has hampered the company's international growth. In 2009, at the time of writing, the intensity of the conflict has declined but there has been no formal agreement on the appointment of a new chief executive of the joint venture, giving rise to speculation that effective control of the joint venture is now in the hands of AAR.

Some commentators claim, given the Russian authorities' apparent strategy of regaining control over key sectors like oil and gas, that the dispute is a prelude to the sale of the joint venture to the state-owned companies Gazprom or Rosneft. As such, AAR's real objectives could be to obtain BP's share of BP–TNK cheaply and then to sell it at a profit to Gazprom. Whatever the real reasons for the dispute, suspicions are strong that involvement of various arms of the Russian state in the pressure placed on BP in 2008 demonstrates, at the very least, an example of government interference in foreign investment. As such, the case has undermined Russia's credibility, already badly stretched, as a home for foreign investment.

While BP was experiencing problems in Russia, ExxonMobil's Sakhalin 1 project came under pressure. In late June 2007, Gazprom asserted that gas from Sakhalin 1 should be blocked from selling gas to China. Gazprom claimed that the Sakhalin 1 gas was needed to supply the Russian Far East. Another interpretation of Gazprom's intervention, which has received verbal support from Russia's Industry and Energy Ministry, is that ExxonMobil's plans could undermine Gazprom's gas supply talks with China. In other words, as in Gazprom's engagement with BP, Gazprom does not want competition in its gas exports to Asia and to China in particular.

In the case of Sakhalin 1 however, Gazprom does not have the same leverage it had over Shell and TNK–BP: the ExxonMobil-led consortium has not encountered the same intensity of opposition to its activities as has Shell, and it has adhered to the terms of its licence agreement. Nevertheless, the consortium is likely to come under serious pressure not to export gas to China and to perhaps sell all its gas to Gazprom. However, following months of negotiations, no agreement has been reached on the terms of the sale of gas from Sakhalin 1 to Gazprom.

CASE STUDY QUESTIONS

1. What signals do the above cases send out about investing in Russia in general and in the oil and gas industries in particular?

2. Despite the experiences of BP, Shell and Exxon, these three companies and other oil and gas companies continue to invest in and show an interest in investing in Russia. Why?

3. To what extent do the actions of the Russian government and Gazprom raise concerns about energy security in oil and gas-consuming nations?

4. What does the above case tell us about the interaction of business and politics?

5. Assess the Russian position that it should exercise control over its natural resources.

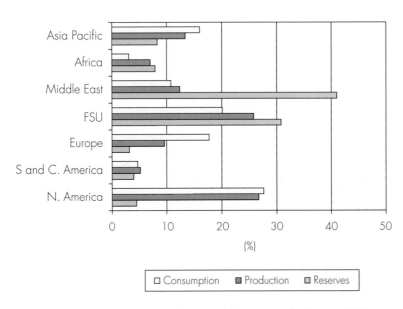

FIGURE 19.5 Gas Reserves, Production and Consumption by Region, 2008

Source: Derived from *BP Statistical Review of World Energy* (2009).

FIGURE 19.6 Coal Reserves, Production and Consumption by Region, 2008

Source: Derived from *BP Statistical Review of World Energy* (2009).

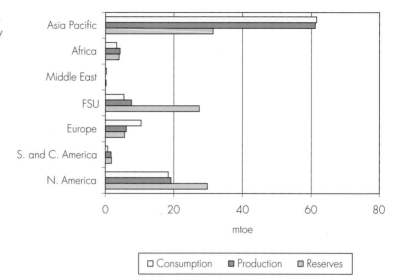

mtoe

□ Consumption   ■ Production   ▣ Reserves

Coal production and consumption are more evenly spread than those of oil and gas (see Figure 19.6), as are reserves. In 2008, North America contained 29.8 per cent of proved reserves, the FSU 27.4 per cent, Asia Pacific 31.4 per cent and the rest of the world 11.4 per cent. Furthermore, the world's coal reserves are plentiful and, according to BP figures, will last 122 years at current rates of production. In short, for coal at least, there is neither a problem regarding the overall level of supply nor about access to existing supplies.

However, coal's fortunes have varied from region to region. Both the production and consumption of coal have fallen within the European Union as European power producers have moved away from coal-fired to gas generation in response to environmental pressures. Indeed, coal production and consumption has been subdued in the OECD area generally since the mid-1990s. However, the big growth area for both coal production and consumption during this period has been in Asia Pacific where emerging economies like China and India have seen major increases in both production and consumption in support of their dynamic economic growth, and more established economies like Japan, Taiwan and South Korea have also seen a bigger role for coal, a fuel with which the region is better endowed than other fuels.

In relation to other forms of energy supply, potential for further hydroelectric capacity expansion is limited, although major construction programmes are underway in a number of countries, including China and Turkey. The problems of overreliance on hydropower were demonstrated in the 2001 Brazilian energy crisis and contributed to the Californian energy crisis during the same year. As seen above, in some countries at least, reconsideration of the role of nuclear power is underway as they seek ways to reduce greenhouse gas emissions. Nuclear energy continues to expand in the Far East given that region's high level of demand growth. Renewable energy has the potential to contribute to resolving the world's energy supply problems but it remains costly and, as yet, its contribution is limited, albeit growing in the areas of wind and solar power. In the longer term, hopes are being pinned on the commercialization of fuel cell technology.

Demand-side Factors

The extent to which the above supply pressures translate into ongoing long-term supply shortages, as opposed to short-lived interruptions brought about by political crises, depends to a significant degree on the evolution of energy demand, the composition of that growth, both regionally and sectorally, and on patterns of energy intensity. The interplay of all these forces is complex but certain trends and forces may be identified that will play an important role.

Demographic trends alone will have a major impact upon future demand. As Figure 19.7 demonstrates, strong world population growth is forecast to continue: in 2005, according to the UN, the world population was 6.5 billion and by 2050 it is expected to reach 9.2 billion. Growth is forecast in all world regions bar Europe where population is roughly expected to remain constant and the FSU where some population decline has been occurring. The largest absolute increase in numbers is forecast for Asia but significant increases are also anticipated for Africa and Latin America. Even if no economic growth-induced increase in energy consumption occurs (which is unlikely in these regions where economic development is the overriding priority), the 42 per cent increase in population would indicate a similar increase in world energy consumption.

Figures for energy consumption per head and energy intensity also need to be taken into account (see Figures 19.8 and 19.9). Energy consumption per head is many times greater in developed than in developing countries. US energy consumption per head, for example, is almost nine times greater than that of Asia and more than 21 times per capita consumption in Africa. Asia has been growing particularly quickly and is expected to continue to do so: as its living standards improve, so its per capita energy consumption may also be expected to increase – even a small increase will lead to a big increase in energy demand given that Asia currently accounts for about 60 per cent of the world's population.

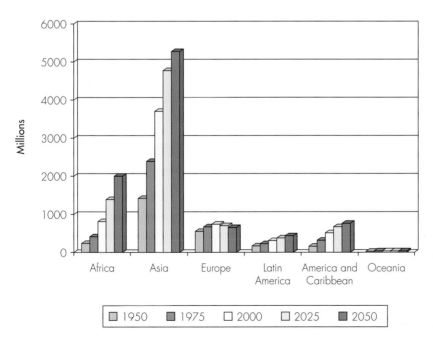

FIGURE 19.7 World Population by Region

Source: Population Division, UN Secretariat.

Legend: 1950 1975 2000 2025 2050

The implications of economic growth for energy consumption become apparent when developments in the car market, for example, are assessed. In the US, there are almost 800 vehicles per 1,000 inhabitants. The equivalent figure for China is about 24 vehicles per 1,000 inhabitants. However, the Chinese car market is increasing rapidly as a result of economic growth, and a doubling of car ownership levels (which is perfectly feasible by 2012) would still leave China way below US levels of car ownerships but would represent a major increase in terms of the absolute numbers of cars to around 65 million. This is exciting news for the motor industry but also places more pressure on world oil supplies and will have severe implications for the environment. This process is also likely to be repeated in India and, to a lesser extent, in other emerging economies.

The increasing energy demand in the transportation sector will be repeated in other economic sectors in China. Economic growth has been responsible, and will continue to be so, for massive increase in electricity-generating capacity. Figures from the China Institute of Atomic Energy suggest that during the first decade of the twenty-first century, generating capacity in China will increase by over 80 per cent and during the first half of the century generating capacity will increase fivefold. This rapid expansion will involve increased consumption of all major fuels but the largest absolute increase will be of coal. Again, such increases in demand will increase competition for primary fuels in the world market and also have a significant negative environmental impact.

Energy intensity (that is, the amount of energy required to produce a given unit of GDP) is another key energy demand indicator. Although energy consumption per capita is higher in developed than in developing countries, energy intensity tends to be higher in developing countries (see Figure 19.9). This is partly a function of changing industrial structures: after the initial industrialization stage, the growth of less energy-intensive, more value-added service sectors tends to accompany economic development. Moreover, the more advanced economies have access to the most technologically advanced equipment and appliances, many of which have been developed with a view to greater energy efficiency. One way, therefore, to offset the potential increased energy demand of emerging countries, at least in part, is through declining levels of energy intensity. There is already limited evidence to support this in Asia, especially in parts of that region where FDI is high. Therefore, it is possible, although not inevitable, that energy intensities in developing countries, especially the most

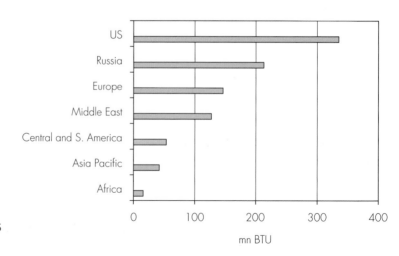

FIGURE 19.8 Energy Consumption per Head, by Region 2006 (MN BTU)

Source: Derived from Energy Information Administration, US Department of Energy.

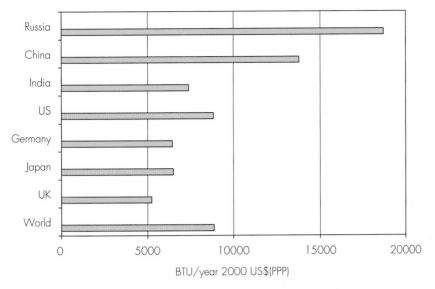

FIGURE 19.9
Energy Intensity by Major Consuming Countries, 2006 (BTU per year 2000 US$ – purchasing power parity)

Note: Energy intensity – the amount of energy required to produce one unit of GDP.

Source: Derived from Energy Information Administration, US Department of Energy.

rapidly growing developing countries, may decline more quickly than was the case for advanced industrialized countries as the former benefit from the experience of the latter.

CONCLUSION

The energy industry is a global industry in all senses of the word. The oil industry has long been one of the most international of all industries and the vicissitudes and sensitivities of the world oil market only serve to confirm this. The globalization of oil markets has intensified the sense of inter-dependence between consumers and producers, and has created a growing sense of long-term common interest.

Other energy sectors are also becoming more international. This is particularly true of the electricity sector. Markets are being opened across the globe, creating investment opportunities for equipment suppliers and increasingly for generators and suppliers. In some areas markets remain nationally constrained, but in others markets are increasingly integrated across borders. Although not without its problems, more electricity trade and the development of cross-border electricity networks with all that entails may be anticipated throughout the world. The experience of California and Brazil in 2001 acts as a warning of how the opening up of markets can go awry if it is ill-thought through and how serious the impact of interrupted flows of energy can be upon business and the wider economy in general.

Particularly concerning are trends in long-term energy supply and demand. On the supply side, the rate of oil consumption continues to outpace the rate of new discoveries and, given that the resources discovered in the early 1980s when oil prices were at historically high levels have passed their peak, production is once more becoming concentrated in the Middle East. Gas supply is also concentrated, but in this case in the FSU as well as in the Middle East. Although improvements are occurring, transportation of gas from the point of production to the point of consumption remains more problematic than for oil. Some supply (and environmental) problems could be overcome by greater utilization of nuclear power and renewables. The former has to overcome the challenge of public acceptability – a process that will require the continuing absence of nuclear incidents like those of Three Mile Island and Chernobyl; a realization that carbon emission targets are unlikely to be met by demand management measures and the substitution of carbon-rich energy sources by renewables alone; and better management of the waste disposal issue.

On the demand side, the usual increase in demand in industrialized countries will be dwarfed in the first decades of the twenty-first century by population increases and, in particular, by the rapid increase in demand from the emerging economies of China and India. This will, in turn, increase competition in international energy markets at a time when supply will tighten. Moreover, a worsening of the supply-and-demand fundamentals could coincide with a worsening geopolitical situation: towards the end of the first decade of the twenty-first century, Russia is reasserting itself in a way which potentially isolates itself from many trading partners, and political problems in the Middle East remain far from resolved. In short, business and the world's economy could encounter a rough ride as a result of movement in energy market fundamentals and the delicate geopolitical situation in the coming years.

Summary of Key Concepts

■ The energy industry demonstrates the power of interdependence in terms of geography and markets, and is of crucial import to the manufacturing and service sectors.
■ Key globalization drivers are at work in the energy industry.
■ The oil sector has always been strongly international and liberalization is rapidly imparting an international dimension to the electricity sector.
■ A combination of changing supply trends and new demand trends makes the world vulnerable to future energy crises.

Activities

1. Investigate the extent to which deregulation of the electricity sector has spread throughout the world. What opportunities has this created for international business? Use examples to demonstrate your case.

2. Politics and energy have shown themselves to be inextricably mixed throughout the world. Choose one of the following countries where this has been the case. Research the link between politics and energy and determine how it has affected foreign investment and the strategy of state and/or international energy companies:

- Nigeria
- Venezuela
- Algeria

3. Research renewable energy sources. To what extent can they make a contribution to plugging the potential gap between supply and demand?

4. Choose one of the major international oil and gas companies (for example, ExxonMobil, Royal Dutch Shell, BP, Chevron, ConocoPhillips) and assess how they have adapted their strategy in light of the expanding environmental agenda and the changing supply-and-demand picture outlined in this chapter.

Discussion Questions

1. Is the world heading for a new energy crisis? What arguments support this view? What factors might intervene to delay or even prevent a crisis?

2. 'A resurgence of nuclear power is inevitable if the world is to overcome emerging environmental and energy supply problems' Do you agree with this statement?

3. Is energy too important to be left to the market?

4. Discuss how the major influences on the energy industry in Figure 19.1 interact. Can you make a case for any one them being more important than the others?

References and Suggestions for Further Reading

Belyi, A. (2003) 'New dimensions of energy security of the enlarging EU and their impact on relations with Russia', *Journal of European Integration*, Vol. 25, No. 4, 351–369.

Leggett, J. (2006) *Half Gone: Oil, Gas, Hot Air and the Global Energy Crisis*, London: Portobello Books.

Makansi, J. (2007) *Lights Out: The Electricity Crisis, the Global Economy and What It Means for You*, Hoboken, NJ: John Wiley.

Marquina, A. (2008) *Energy Security: Visions from Asia and Europe*, Basingstoke: Palgrave Macmillan.

Paul, B. (2007) *Future Energy: How the New Oil Industry will Change People, Politics and Portfolios*, Chichester: John Wiley.

Roberts, P. (2004) *The End of Oil: The Decline of the Petroleum Economy and the Rise of a New Energy Order*, London: Bloomsbury.

Selby, J. (2005) 'Oil and water: the contrasting anatomies of resource conflicts', *Government and Opposition*, Vol. 4, No. 2, 200–224.

Simmons, M. (2005) *Twilight in the Desert: The Coming Saudi Oil Shock and the World Economy*, Chichester: John Wiley.

Stern, J. (2006) *The New Security Environment for European Gas: Worsening Geopolitics and Increasing Global Competition for LNG*, Oxford: Oxford Institute for Energy Studies.

Symon, A. (2004) 'Fuelling Southeast Asia's growth: the energy challenge', *ASEAN Economic Bulletin*, Vol. 21, No. 2, 239–248.

Tertzakian, P. (2007) *A Thousand Barrels a Second: The Coming Oil Break Point and the Challenges Facing an Energy Dependent World*, New York: McGraw Hill.

United Nations Economic Commission for Europe (2008) *Emerging Global Energy Security Risks*, Geneva: UNECE.

Woolf, A.T. (2006) *Conflict and Cooperation over Transboundary Waters*, Human Development Report Office Occasional Paper 2006/19.

Yergin, D. and Stoppard, M. (2003) 'The next prize', *Foreign Affairs*, Vol. 82, No. 6, 103–114.

Youngs, R. (2009) *Energy Security*, London: Routledge.

Website

http://www.pacinst.org/resources/ – this is an excellent source of good-quality material on water resources. It contains reports on current water issues, including business involvement, and has a chronology of water-related conflicts.

Chapter 20

The Evolving International Environment

Everything you know is wrong.

Steven Pinker (1954–), cognitive scientist

During the writing of this book we have – as both authors and observers of international business – witnessed the seemingly 'inevitable' and irreversible process of globalization not only lose momentum but (in some cases) go into decline. Naturally such developments do not erode the value of the preceding analysis but should encourage students to develop a critical approach to the process and to understand the historical forces that have shaped the ebb and flow of globalization throughout the history of humanity's commercial activities. Thus, the fact that globalization appears to have reached a high point should – in historical terms – come as little surprise.

Despite these trends, it is far from evident that globalization will be unwound. Our confidence in this assertion again relates to the historical context of the process. It is apparent that, at times in the twentieth century, conflict and economic turmoil did turn states away from moves towards a global economy. It is too soon to tell whether the economic and financial turmoil that began in 2007 means that globalization is merely pausing for breath or whether there is a genuine and long-term shift away from the global consensus. However, the current disruption of globalization appears different to previous interruptions in the sense that globalization has penetrated deeper into political, social and economic structures than previously. Indeed, it is fair to argue that this phase has permeated directly down to the individual and has not been restricted to political and economic elites.

The themes within this text typify the deep roots that globalization and its associated process have established within the modern business system. While this process has been uneven over time and space, it has made a tangible impact upon the nation state – the conventional building block of the economic system. Indeed, it is noticeable how attempts by nation states to regain some control over key aspects of their economies have either been frustrated or have met with limited success. Thus in spite of the prevailing turmoil, one must not expect the environment analysed within this text to alter radically in its aftermath.

GLOBALIZATION AND THE CONTEXT OF INTERNATIONAL BUSINESS

The nature of international strategy is of an adaptive response by businesses to their evolving commercial environment. Conventionally, the response of firms to this environment has been defined by the integration/responsiveness framework and the consequent typology it has generated. While such a typology is useful, the student of international business should treat its conclusions with caution, as it risks chronically understating the degree of complexity of strategies deployed by the modern MNE. As the complexity of the modern MNE grows, so does the nature of the strategies it follows. As such, the firm can employ multiple strategies across multiple locations. This process is reinforced by the increased complexity of the modern business environment.

While the core drivers behind this increased complexity have been widely acknowledged, what they mean for environmental change is less certain. The very term 'globalization' is suggestive of a process which has a recognizable beginning and end. However, history has shown that environmental conditions can alter markedly over time and that, as a consequence, so does globalization. Thus, globalization is a matter of degree and the conditions and drivers that shape it evolve unevenly over time. What is perhaps more accurate is that globalization historically has both low and high watermarks. Such cycles are driven by the state of the drivers and national sentiment towards them underlining that globalization is anything but a historical certainty.

A more controversial suggestion is that the logical end-point of the 'globalization' process is a global economy. That is an economy in which the mobility of goods, services, labour and capital is entirely without hindrance. Political sentiment suggests that this is unlikely, further underlining that globalization is a process without a recognizable beginning or end and which waxes and wanes over time. This underlines a paradox within the modern international economy, namely that while there is appetite for globalization, the desire to see this process through to its seemingly logical conclusion is notable by its absence.

In the absence of any appetite for the creation of a true global economy, the push for regional integration seems a logical compromise. In a globalizing international economy, overcoming the disadvantages of fragmentation through regionalism makes sense. However, to use the emergence of such agreements as a barometer of the appetite for liberalism would be wholly inaccurate, as the underlying motives behind group formation are not uniform across either space or time. Indeed, sentiment in some groups suggests using these agreements as a deterrent and not as a compromise to globalization. The ability to accentuate the positive and mitigate the negative effects of such processes depends in no small part on measures deployed at the meta level of the global economy. In other words, the emergence of an effective system of global governance will mitigate these pressures.

The role of the main international economic institutions has evolved over the years in parallel with the changing business environment. The World Bank, for example, slipped into a development role as the original reconstruction part of its portfolio, which related to post-war reconstruction in Europe, was fulfilled and superseded by the challenge of development in the rest of the world. As import tariffs fell in successive rounds of trade negotiations and barriers between states generally disappeared, the agenda of GATT and its successor organization the WTO expanded. Indeed, a strong case could be made that issues that had long been considered matters for domestic policy (for example, aspects of competition policy, standards, labour regulation) should increasingly be determined at a higher level by regional groupings or the international economic institutions. Some issues have been increasingly accepted as a matter for supranational governance of some sort, whereas states hold on tightly to others. In general, international institutions have developed slowly and are not noted for their rapid and appropriate response to a swiftly changing business environment.

The major institutions are also the subject of much criticism, both by those opposing and those supporting globalization. For the former, international institutions have too much power and undermine national sovereignty. For the latter, global governance does not go far enough and further development of these institutions is urged to help nations regain some of the control and sovereignty they have lost in the globalization process. Despite the controversies surrounding global governance, nation states have been lining up to join key institutions and the membership of the WTO in particular has expanded significantly in latter years.

The institutions are particularly challenged by the global financial and economic crisis. Questions of blame and of how they should respond to the new situation have dogged the institutions since the crisis began. Given the problems in the banking sector, for example, should there be greater regulation of banking and the financial sector generally? It remains unclear at the time of writing whether the institutions will emerge from the crisis with their powers or roles enhanced or diminished. However, it is certainly true that major changes only tend to occur in such institutions in response to crisis. Moreover, although there are signs of growing protection and of states wishing to take matters into their own hands, there are also strong countervailing indicators of countries searching for a way out of the crisis through greater cooperation and policy coordination. What is clear in the current situation is that, unlike previous crises, the way out of the problem is not overwhelmingly seen as pulling back to national boundaries. As stated above, this is almost certainly a function of the deeper penetration into aspects of contemporary economic, business and social life of the most recent wave of globalization.

A major criticism levelled at globalization and international institutions stems from the alleged exclusion of large parts of the world – particularly the developing countries – from the global economy. In a real sense, this criticism of globalization is an argument in favour of it: that is, if developing countries are marginalized by globalization and are unable to escape their grinding poverty, then the way out of this mess should, logically, be to make it easier for these countries to engage in the globalization process. It is certainly true that large parts of the developing world appear to be trapped in a vicious cycle of underdevelopment but some countries have escaped. The Asian NICs were the first to do so but increasingly, large, emerging economies like China and India are transforming their fortunes.

What unites the success stories is a willingness to embrace both the domestic and international markets by moving away from protected markets and isolation. It is too simplistic to attribute all their success to their embrace of the market and globalization: each country has its own unique history; social context; culture; specific advantages and so on that has helped shaped its fortunes. Parts of sub-Saharan Africa, the world's most problematic region in terms of development, have seen some improvements in the past decade as a result of more open, market-driven policies and have benefited to some extent from higher commodity export prices (although many suffered as a result of higher oil and food import prices). Steering their way through the financial and economic crisis is a major challenge for these countries for whom their integration into the world economy remains limited and vulnerable.

ENTERPRISE ISSUES IN THE GLOBAL ECONOMY

The above issues establish the terms of engagement for enterprises in the international economy. Inevitably the meta-level concerns engendered by these themes have a limited direct impact upon business strategy but trickle down into changes into opportunities and threats in the enterprise's commercial environment. Consequently translating these issues into a set of adaptive strategies relies upon supporting or intermediate conditions. These are the conditions for trade, internationalization and other forms of policy and commercial measures that facilitate a managerial response.

International trade is perhaps global business's greatest success and its greatest failure. Since the Second World War there have undoubtedly been a great number of successes in this domain of the evolving international economy. Sharp reductions in tariffs, the agreement on services and the commitment of states to non-discrimination all stand as testament to progress in promoting international trade. However, the failure of states to agree on agriculture, the emergence of non-tariff barriers and the penchant of states to resort to protectionism when expedient have to some degree mitigated many of the benefits delivered by global agreements on trade. Agriculture is an especially salient issue given the asymmetry between its economic importance and its political influence, and demonstrates the delicate political economy that drives the trade debate.

How such issues will be affected by the global credit crisis is – at the time of writing – a moot point. There are immediate short-term effects on trade in terms of the shortage of credit (as trade finance grows scarce) and of the downturn of demand (as global trade inevitably follows). Indeed, a reduction in the volume of global trade followed hard on the heels of the credit crunch. While this was a market-responsive phenomenon, there have been other changes as states have begun to introduce measures at the national (and sometimes transnational) level to mitigate the effects of the global downturn in nation states. While these are far from the 'beggar thy neighbour' policies of the 1930s, the desire of national policy makers to ensure that the macro-economic stimuli to mitigate the global downturn do not 'leak' into other states and maximize the domestic impact are worrying. Others are more optimistic, suggesting that the international complexity of value chains means that any attempt to discriminate would be self-defeating.

A sea change may also be expected in international investment over the forthcoming period. During the past few decades, international investment has increased many times as markets have opened up, funds increased and the associated risk fell. This was driven in no small part by the aforementioned freeing up of international trade. This phase of globalization was characterized by an increased dispersal of investments as many 'emerging economies' not only attracted funds from developed economies but began to act as overseas investors in their own right. Throughout this text, it is noticeable how the BRIC economies have become increasingly aggressive in international markets as they emerge as economic powerhouses in the global economy. However, it is likely that the major sources of FDI for the forthcoming period will remain the larger developed states.

One would expect that international investment would be substantially affected by the current slowdown in globalization. Shortages of funds combined with increased political-economic risks as well as emerging sentiment stressing economic nationalism are working against the maintenance of high investment flows in the short term. However, while the flow of funds has taken a temporary downturn, it is unlikely that this will persist in the long term. The stock of investments has not been heavily divested, nor have governments started to puruse economic nationalism over this period, suggesting that flows will continue once conditions improve.

At the core of these trade and investment trends have been the MNEs. MNEs are perhaps the most controversial feature of the current globalization phase. In an era of US-led global capitalism, many of these controversies are driven by the legacy of shareholder capitalism and its implications for the management of MNEs. However, for every MNE that acts in a fashion that is detrimental to host economies, there are many more that engage positively with their host for mutual benefit. Furthermore, the majority of MNEs are not the leviathans they are commonly characterized to be but are often relatively small concerns. No matter their size, MNEs are bound by the fact that they are profit-seeking entities.

The process of becoming multinational has been formalized within models of internationalization. In the past decade or so, the main explanations of internationalization have converged around the network-based perspective. The growing hegemony of the network-based perspective reflects the growing complexity of the modern economy in which the decision to internationalize and the process of market penetration and reach cannot be divorced from the broader context of the internationalizing firm.

The emergence of these contextual-based perspectives as the dominant view of the process of internationalization has impacted upon modal choice. Conventionally, internationalization has been conceptualized as sequential as issues of risk are mitigated through experience. However, with the maturity of globalization, firms are moving to relatively high-commitment market entry modes. Again, this reflects the complexity of the modern economy and the relationships that contextualize the decision and which mitigate the risks involved. Thus as internationalization matures, its complexity increases. With maturity, it becomes increasingly inappropriate to talk of a single trajectory or modal choice. Across all locations in which an MNE has a presence, modal choice and the internationalization path will vary according to the set of environmental conditions encountered by the firm.

As mentioned, the major differentiating factor between this phase of globalization and those that have preceded it is its sheer pervasiveness. One of the more demonstrable symptoms of this is the emergence of globalization involving small and medium-sized business, businesses normally expected to be exempt from such developments. The impact of this trend has been both passive and active. The focus in this text is on the latter and highlights how the growing complexity of the international economy has allowed small entrepreneurial concerns to inhabit small, identifiable niches. This process has been supported by business networks which have shaped the context, pace and path of the process. Given such trends and complementary technological developments, this process is likely to continue over the coming decades.

Supporting the rise of the 'Born Global' has been the globalization of the value chain. The trend towards globalization has allowed more firms to disperse both primary and supporting activities across the global economy in order to maximize the value derived from each of these functions. In some cases, this has resulted in the outsourcing and/or offshoring of specific functions as the firm focuses on core competences. In addition, the potential for the dispersion of activities has been supported by the globalization of existing operations as they seek to cope and adjust to the shifting environmental conditions. Thus, as the firm enters new international markets, issues of international human resources management and the diversity of marketing strategies become ever more salient.

Matters of culture, corporate social responsibility and business ethics also add to the complexity of managing international businesses, both large and small. Internationalization poses cross-cultural challenges for MNEs across their major functions. The most successful are able to adapt to new ways of doing business and treat cultural differences as part of their competitive advantage. Closely tied in with culture are business ethics. Although some practices are regarded as ethically wrong throughout the world, many more are subject to different interpretations that are shaped by culture, frequently creating dilemmas for expatriate managers. This is on top of the additional attention paid to corporate social responsibility in recent years and the external scrutiny to which the international activities of firms are increasingly subject.

CHALLENGES FOR THE GLOBAL RESOURCE BASE

Corporate social responsibility is at the heart of many international labour and environmental issues facing the MNE. However, international labour and environmental issues are not merely about CSR, important though that is. Labour, together with finance, knowledge and information, energy and raw materials are crucial inputs and resources for the firm. The environmental challenge for international business is also about managing the use of resources.

Globalization has created challenges for the use of resources. As part of the globalization process, barriers to the free movement of the factors of production have been lifted, a process which has transformed finance and the role of knowledge and information. However, labour mobility is more limited, partly for cultural reasons and partly because nation states continue to exercise control over the movement of people across their borders. Moreover, the continuing fragmentation of labour markets means that significant differences in labour standards and practices persist. This leads to accusations of social dumping. In the current crisis-ridden climate, it would not take much, in an effort to protect local jobs, for countries to use differences in standards and costs to raise trade barriers or to restrict the labour mobility that does exist. In 2008 to 2009, demonstrations took place in parts of Europe, for example, to encourage limits on the use of foreign workers.

In contrast to labour, there is perhaps no other market that represents the high watermark of globalization than finance. By the end of the twentieth century, it was fair to say that global market finance had been created. This generated many benefits and ushered in an era of global financial capitalism. However, it became clear in the early years of the twenty-first century that the business models created by this new form of capitalism could only be sustained by taking ever greater risks within the context of increasingly complicated products. The result was to dry up the global pool of funds that was meant to be a major resource of the emerging global financial system. As has been reiterated throughout this text, this deprivation of finance has had a far-reaching impact across the commercial landscape.

These events demonstrated how far globalization had progressed within this sector. Global products had emerged that undermined the credibility of global businesses by understating the degree of risk and where such risk was sourced. The response of states was a mixture of coordination and unilateral actions. However, governments have attempted to mitigate their relative powerlessness by aiming to ensure that national measures benefit the national economy. Thus should not be read as a lack of appetite for globalization; merely that the form of globalization based on the hegemony of

Anglo-Saxon capitalism is no longer seen as the best or the only way to manage the global economy. As such a more regulated global system may emerge.

The emergence and establishment of the global economy as an information economy gives confidence that the attitude to globalization is not a matter of 'if' but 'how'. The emergence of new technologies has created a time–space and cost–space convergence that has played no small part in the process. Save for the prospect of the disinvention or outlawing of these technologies, we may assume that these are permanent features of the global commercial landscape. This implies that the information and knowledge resources that drive the economy will be sourced from interaction between economic agents over a dispersed spatial domain. This underlines the sheer pervasiveness of the globalization process and how such interactions are now considered the norm for a large majority of the economically active population.

Natural resources, notably energy, water and raw materials, are more tangible inputs of MNEs. Access to supplies of these products is essential for the smooth running of the international economy. Given that the markets for most natural resources (with the exception of water) are international, the impact of any disruptions to the normal supply–demand balance for these heavily commoditized products spreads rapidly throughout the world. In 1973 and 1979, the oil price hikes disrupted economies everywhere and, although not the only cause of the international recessions that followed, were certainly major contributors to them. It did not take long for the oil and commodity price increases of the mid- to late 2000s to take their toll in many areas of business. However, the financial and economic crisis quickly reversed price movements on these products, which was good news for consumers but not so good for developing country producers who, for the first time in many years, had seen the terms of trade move in their favour.

CONCLUSION

As the first decade of the twenty-first century nears its close, globalization is (if not at a crossroads, as that could imply a change of direction) facing a change in the nature of its journey. Throughout history, the balance between the local and the international has shifted, depending on a host of historical and environmental factors. The current international and financial crisis provides potential for another such shift. It is too early to say what form that shift might take: it is possible to conceive of scenarios in which some reversal of globalization might occur. Equally, the process could either decelerate or accelerate. That is, the process of globalization would continue but the pace of the process would change.

It is our contention, supported by evidence throughout this volume, that one of the two latter scenarios will prevail and globalization will not be reversed. This view is based on the argument that many facets of globalization have become so entrenched and embedded in so many aspects of business, economic and social life that it will be both difficult and undesirable to reverse them. This is not to say that there will not be instances in which deglobalization appears to be happening but the overall momentum of globalization will continue, perhaps at a slower pace, perhaps not. We may of course be wrong, but in our view it is the dynamic, rapidly changing rich international business environment that makes international business such an exciting subject.

Index